Lecture Notes in Computer Science 7269

Commenced Publication in 1973
Founding and Former Series Editors:
Gerhard Goos, Juris Hartmanis, and Jan van Leeuwen

Leszek Rutkowski   Marcin Korytkowski
Rafał Scherer   Ryszard Tadeusiewicz
Lotfi A. Zadeh   Jacek M. Zurada (Eds.)

Swarm and Evolutionary Computation

International Symposia, SIDE 2012 and EC 2012
Held in Conjunction with ICAISC 2012
Zakopane, Poland, April 29-May 3, 2012
Proceedings

 Springer

Volume Editors

Leszek Rutkowski
Marcin Korytkowski
Rafał Scherer
Częstochowa University of Technology, Poland
E-mail: lrutko@kik.pcz.czest.pl,
{marcin.korytkowski, rafal.scherer}@kik.pcz.pl

Ryszard Tadeusiewicz
AGH University of Science and Technology, Kraków, Poland
E-mail: rtad@agh.edu.pl

Lotfi A. Zadeh
University of California, Berkeley, CA, USA
E-mail: zadeh@cs.berkeley.edu

Jacek M. Zurada
University of Louisville, Louisville, KY, USA
E-mail: jacek.zurada@louisville.edu

ISSN 0302-9743   e-ISSN 1611-3349
ISBN 978-3-642-29352-8   e-ISBN 978-3-642-29353-5
DOI 10.1007/978-3-642-29353-5
Springer Heidelberg Dordrecht London New York

Library of Congress Control Number: 2012934673

CR Subject Classification (1998): I.2, H.3, F.1, I.4, H.4, I.5

LNCS Sublibrary: SL 1 – Theoretical Computer Science and General Issues

Typesetting: Camera-ready by author, data conversion by Scientific Publishing Services, Chennai, India

Printed on acid-free paper

Springer is part of Springer Science+Business Media (www.springer.com)

Preface

This volume constitutes the proceedings of the International Symposium on Swarm and Evolutionary Computation organized as part of the 11th International Conference on Artificial Intelligence and Soft Computing, ICAISC 2012, held in Zakopane, Poland from April 29 to May 3, 2012. The symposium consisted of the Symposium on Swarm Intelligence and Differential Evolution (SIDE 2012) and the Symposium on Evolutionary Computation. Swarm intelligence (SI) is a computational intelligence technique which mimics and makes use of collective behavior (e.g., fish, birds, bees, ants, bacteria etc.) for solving search and optimization problems. The resulting algorithms are thus population-based systems of simple individuals interacting with one another and with their environment. Differential evolution (DE) is a special example of an optimizer since it shares some features with SI, mainly in the interaction amongst particles and selection scheme, but can also be considered as an evolutionary algorithm (EA). This symposium gathered new theoretical and implementation results, applications, reviews, and comparative studies. Special emphasis was placed on those studies which attempt to explain the working principles of the algorithms. I would like to thank the SIDE Committees, especially Ponnuthurai N. Suganthan, for organizing this successful event. The volume is divided into two parts: proceedings of the 2012 Symposium on Swarm Intelligence and Differential Evolution and the Symposium on Evolutionary Computation. This edition of the ICAISC also hosted the 4th International Workshop on Engineering Knowledge and Semantic Systems (IWEKSS 2012). The whole conference (ICAISC, SIDE and IWEKSS) attracted a total of 483 submissions from 48 countries and after the review process 212 papers were accepted for publication. I would like to thank our participants, invited speakers and reviewers of the papers for their scientific and personal contribution to the conference. Several reviewers were very helpful in reviewing the papers and are listed herein.

Finally, I thank my co-workers Łukasz Bartczuk, Agnieszka Cpałka, Piotr Dziwiński, Marcin Gabryel, Marcin Korytkowski and the conference secretary Rafał Scherer, for their enormous efforts to make the conference a very successful event. Moreover, I would like to acknowledge the work of Marcin Korytkowski, who designed the Internet submission system.

April 2012   Leszek Rutkowski

Organization

ICAISC 2012 was organized by the Polish Neural Network Society in cooperation with the SWSPiZ Academy of Management in Łódź, the Department of Computer Engineering at Częstochowa University of Technology, and the IEEE Computational Intelligence Society, Poland Chapter.

ICAISC Chairs

Honorary Chairmen	Lotfi Zadeh (USA)
	Jacek Żurada (USA)
General Chairman	Leszek Rutkowski (Poland)
Co-chairmen	Włodzisław Duch (Poland)
	Janusz Kacprzyk (Poland)
	Józef Korbicz (Poland)
	Ryszard Tadeusiewicz (Poland)

ICAISC Program Committee

Rafał Adamczak - Poland
Cesare Alippi - Italy
Shun-ichi Amari - Japan
Rafal A. Angryk - USA
Jarosław Arabas - Poland
Robert Babuska - The Netherlands
Ildar Z. Batyrshin - Russia
James C. Bezdek - USA
Marco Block-Berlitz - Germany
Leon Bobrowski - Poland
Leonard Bolc - Poland
Piero P. Bonissone - USA
Bernadette Bouchon-Meunier - France
James Buckley - Poland
Tadeusz Burczynski - Poland
Andrzej Cader - Poland
Juan Luis Castro - Spain
Yen-Wei CHEN - Japan
Wojciech Cholewa - Poland
Fahmida N. Chowdhury - USA
Andrzej Cichocki - Japan
Paweł Cichosz - Poland
Krzysztof Cios - USA

Ian Cloete - Germany
Oscar Cordón - Spain
Bernard De Baets - Belgium
Nabil Derbel - Tunisia
Ewa Dudek-Dyduch - Poland
Ludmiła Dymowa - Poland
Andrzej Dzieliński - Poland
David Elizondo - UK
Meng Joo Er - Singapore
Pablo Estevez - Chile
János Fodor - Hungary
David B. Fogel - USA
Roman Galar - Poland
Alexander I. Galushkin - Russia
Adam Gaweda - USA
Joydeep Ghosh - USA
Juan Jose Gonzalez de la Rosa - Spain
Marian Bolesław Gorzałczany - Poland
Krzysztof Grąbczewski - Poland
Garrison Greenwood - USA
Jerzy W. Grzymala-Busse - USA
Hani Hagras - UK
Saman Halgamuge - Australia

Enrique H. Ruspini - USA
Khalid Saeed - Poland
Dominik Sankowski - Poland
Norihide Sano - Japan
Robert Schaefer - Poland
Rudy Setiono - Singapore
Paweł Sewastianow - Poland
Jennie Si - USA
Peter Sincak - Slovakia
Andrzej Skowron - Poland
Ewa Skubalska-Rafajłowicz - Poland
Roman Słowiński - Poland
Tomasz G. Smolinski - USA
Czesław Smutnicki - Poland
Pilar Sobrevilla - Spain
Janusz Starzyk - USA
Jerzy Stefanowski - Poland
Pawel Strumillo - Poland
Ron Sun - USA
Johan Suykens Suykens - Belgium
Piotr Szczepaniak - Poland
Eulalia J. Szmidt - Poland
Przemysław Śliwiński - Poland
Adam Słowik - Poland
Jerzy Świątek - Poland
Hideyuki Takagi - Japan

Yury Tiumentsev - Russia
Vicenç Torra - Spain
Burhan Turksen - Canada
Shiro Usui - Japan
Michael Wagenknecht - Germany
Tomasz Walkowiak - Poland
Deliang Wang - USA
Jun Wang - Hong Kong
Lipo Wang - Singapore
Zenon Waszczyszyn - Poland
Paul Werbos - USA
Slawo Wesolkowski - Canada
Sławomir Wiak - Poland
Bernard Widrow - USA
Kay C. Wiese - Canada
Bogdan M. Wilamowski - USA
Donald C. Wunsch - USA
Maciej Wygralak - Poland
Roman Wyrzykowski - Poland
Ronald R. Yager - USA
Xin-She Yang - UK
Gary Yen - USA
John Yen - USA
Sławomir Zadrożny - Poland
Ali M.S. Zalzala - United Arab Emirates

SIDE Chairs

Janez Brest, University of Maribor, Slovenia
Maurice Clerc, Independent Consultant
Ferrante Neri, University of Jyväskylä, Finland

SIDE Program Chairs

Tim Blackwell, Goldsmiths College, UK
Swagatam Das, Indian Statistical Institute, India
Nicolas Monmarché, University of Tours, France
Ponnuthurai N. Suganthan, Nanyang Technological University, Singapore

SIDE Program Committee

Ashish Anand, India
Borko Boskovic, Slovenia
Jagdish Chand Bansal, India
Carlos Coello Coello, Mexico
Iztok Fister, Slovenia
Bogdan Filipic, Slovenia
Sheldon Hui, Singapore
Peter D. Justesen, Denmark
Nicolas Labroche, France
Jane Liang, China
Hongbo Liu, China
Efren Mezura Montes, Mexico
A. Nakib, France
Rammohan Mallipeddi, Korea
Slawomir Nasuto, UK
Jouni Lampinen, Finland

Mirjam Sepesy Maucec, Slovenia
Marjan Mernik, Slovenia
Godfrey Onwubolu, Canada
Jérôme Emeka Onwunalu, Canada
Quanke Pan, China
Gregor Papa, Slovenia
Boyang Qu, China
Shahryar Rahnamayan, Canada
Jurij Silc, Slovenia
Josef Tvrdik, Czech Republic
M. N. Vrahatis, Greece
Daniela Zaharie, Romania
Ales Zamuda, Slovenia
Qingfu Zhang, UK
Shizheng Zhao, Singapore

IWEKSS Program Committee

Jason J. Jung, Korea
Dariusz Krol, Poland
Ngoc Thanh Nguyen, Poland
Gonzalo A. Aranda-Corral, Spain
Myung-Gwon Hwang, Korea
Costin Badica, Romania
Grzegorz J. Nalepa, Krakow, Poland

ICAISC Organizing Committee

Rafał Scherer, Secretary
Łukasz Bartczuk, Organizing Committee Member
Piotr Dziwiński, Organizing Committee Member
Marcin Gabryel, Finance Chair
Marcin Korytkowski, Databases and Internet Submissions

Reviewers

R. Adamczak
M. Amasyal
A. Anand
R. Angryk
J. Arabas

T. Babczyński
M. Baczyński
C. Badica
L. Bartczuk
M. Białko

A. Bielecki
T. Blackwell
L. Bobrowski
A. Borkowski
L. Borzemski

B. Boskovic
J. Brest
T. Burczyński
R. Burduk
K. Cetnarowicz
M. Chang
W. Cholewa
M. Choraś
R. Choraś
K. Choros
P. Cichosz
R. Cierniak
P. Ciskowski
M. Clerc
O. Cordon
B. Cyganek
R. Czabański
I. Czarnowski
B. De Baets
J. de la Rosa
L. Diosan
G. Dobrowolski
W. Duch
E. Dudek-Dyduch
L. Dymowa
A. Dzieliński
P. Dziwiński
S. Ehteram
J. Emeka Onwunalu
N. Evans
A. Fanea
I. Fister
M. Flasiński
D. Fogel
M. Fraś
M. Gabryel
A. Gawęda
M. Giergiel
P. Głomb
F. Gomide
M. Gorzałczany
E. Grabska
K. Grąbczewski
W. Greblicki
K. Grudziński

J. Grzymala-Busse
R. Hampel
C. Han
Z. Hasiewicz
O. Henniger
F. Herrera
Z. Hippe
A. Horzyk
E. Hrynkiewicz
S. Hui
M. Hwang
A. Janczak
N. Jankowski
S. Jaroszewicz
J. Jung
W. Kacalak
W. Kamiński
A. Kasperski
W. Kazimierski
V. Kecman
E. Kerre
H. Kim
F. Klawonn
P. Klęsk
J. Kluska
A. Kołakowska
L. Kompanets
J. Konopacki
J. Korbicz
P. Korohoda
J. Koronacki
M. Korytkowski
M. Korzeń
W. Kosiński
J. Kościelny
L. Kotulski
Z. Kowalczuk
J. Kozlak
M. Kraft
D. Krol
R. Kruse
B. Kryzhanovsky
A. Krzyzak
J. Kulikowski
O. Kurasova

V. Kurkova
M. Kurzyński
J. Kusiak
H. Kwaśnicka
N. Labroche
S. Lee
Y. Lei
J. Liang
A. Ligęza
H. Liu
B. Macukow
K. Madani
K. Malinowski
R. Mallipeddi
J. Mańdziuk
U. Markowska-Kaczmar
A. Martin
J. Martyna
A. Materka
T. Matsumoto
V. Medvedev
J. Mendel
E. MezuraMontes
Z. Michalewicz
J. Michalkiewicz
Z. Mikrut
W. Mitkowski
W. Moczulski
W. Mokrzycki
N. Monmarche
T. Munakata
A. Nakib
G. Nalepa
S. Nasuto
E. Nawarecki
A. Nawrat
F. Neri
M. Nieniewski
A. Niewiadomski
R. Nowicki
A. Obuchowicz
M. Ogiela
G. Onwubolu
S. Osowski
M. Pacholczyk

G. Papa
K. Patan
A. Pieczyński
A. Piegat
Z. Pietrzykowski
V. Piuri
R. Ptak
B. Qu
A. Radzikowska
E. Rafajłowicz
S. Rahnamayan
E. Rakus-Andersson
F. Rastegar
Š. Raudys
R. Rojas
L. Rolka
F. Rudziński
A. Rusiecki
L. Rutkowski
S. Sakurai
N. Sano
A. Scherer
R. Scherer
E. Segura
R. Setiono

P. Sevastjanov
J. Silc
W. Skarbek
A. Skowron
K. Skrzypczyk
E. Skubalska-
   Rafajłowicz
K. Slot
A. Słowik
R. Słowiński
J. Smoląg
C. Smutnicki
A. Sokołowski
T. Sołtysiński
E. Straszecka
B. Strug
P. Strumiłło
P. Suganthan
J. Swacha
P. Szczepaniak
E. Szmidt
P. Śliwiński
J. Świątek
R. Tadeusiewicz
H. Takagi

Y. Tiumentsev
K. Tokarz
A. Tomczyk
V. Torra
B. Trawinski
J. Tvrdik
M. Urbański
M. Vrahatis
M. Wagenknecht
T. Walkowiak
H. Wang
L. Wang
J. Wąs
B. Wilamowski
A. Wilbik
M. Witczak
P. Wojewnik
M. Wozniak
J. Zabrodzki
S. Zadrożny
D. Zaharie
A. Zamuda
S. Zhao

Table of Contents

Part II: Evolutionary Algorithms and Their Applications

Part I

Symposium on Swarm Intelligence and Differential Evolution

The *Pachycondyla Apicalis* Ants Search Strategy for Data Clustering Problems

Djibrilla Amadou Kountché, Nicolas Monmarché, and Mohamed Slimane

Université François Rabelais, Laboratoire d'Informatique,
64 Av. Jean Portalis, 37200 Tours, France
djibrilla.amadoukountche@etu.univ-tours.fr,
{nicolas.monmarche,mohamed.slimane}@univ-tours.fr

Abstract. This paper presents a work inspired by the *Pachycondyla apicalis* ants behavior for the clustering problem. These ants have a simple but efficient prey search strategy: when they capture their prey, they return straight to their nest, drop off the prey and systematically return back to their original position. This behavior has already been applied to optimization, as the API meta-heuristic. API is a shortage of *api-calis*. Here, we combine API with the ability of ants to sort and cluster. We provide a comparison against Ant clustering Algorithm and K-Means using Machine Learning repository datasets. API introduces new concepts to ant-based models and gives us promising results.

Keywords: Data mining, Clustering, Ant-Based Clustering, Swarm Intelligence.

1 Introduction

Clustering is an unsupervised classification task which builds clusters from a set of objects or patterns based on similarity or dissimilarity measures between objects. The unknown number of clusters to obtain, the difficulty of defining a cluster for the given data (thereby choosing the appropriate dissimilarity measure) and the challenge of high-dimensionality of the data results in the important number of clustering algorithms that is continually published [9]. These algorithms can be categorized into partitioning or hierarchical. The clustering problem considered here is partitioning clustering in the case of exploratory data analysis. A comprehensive study of clustering can be found in [10,9].

Given a clustering problem, many challenges have to be faced in order to choose the appropriate algorithm. Among them is how to assess the output of a given algorithm. Statistical indexes (Ward, inter/intra class, F-Measure, Rand, Dunn) are the most widely used criteria to answer this question [10].

The API algorithm, based on the foraging behavior of *Pachycondyla apicalis* ants, has initially been proposed for continuous optimization [13]. However, as a meta-heuristic, API can be applied to various search spaces, such as discrete or mixed ones. An example is the training of the Hidden Markov Models [2]. The

L. Rutkowski et al. (Eds.): SIDE 2012 and EC 2012, LNCS 7269, pp. 3–11, 2012.

main motivation of this paper is to study how API algorithm can be transposed to tackle a clustering problem. The difference between the HMM optimization case is that for HMM, each hunting site corresponds to a solution of the problem (i.e. one HMM) but for the clustering problem, a hunting site only corresponds to one object on the grid, the solution built by ants is represented by the whole set of nests each containing objects.

The remainder of this paper is organized as follows: the next section gives a quick presentation of the basic ideas behind ant-based clustering methods since we have used the same kind of ideas to provide clustering skills to API . In section 3, we explain the API algorithm and how we can adapt it to clustering. In section 4, we present the experiments we have done to evaluate the API algorithm as a clustering tool and the last section gives conclusions and perspectives about this work.

2   Bio-inspired and Ant Based Clustering Algorithms

Bio-inspired methods are based on the behavior of self-organized, decentralized systems. In Nature, many ant species have the ability to sort and cluster their dead ants or their brood (eggs, larvae,...) into several piles and have foraging mechanisms [3]. Several attempts have been provided to transpose various behaviors of ants to tackle clustering problems (see recent reviews in [8,6,12]), but, to the best of our knowledge, API algorithm for clustering has been studied once before [1] but in a different manner than what is presented in this study.

Deneubourg et al. [5] proposed a simple model, called DM in the following, aiming at simulating the behavior of ants to gather objects. In this model, robots representing ants are randomly moving on a grid where objects of the same type are scattered. A robot which does not carry an item, will more likely pick up the most isolated object with the probability P_{pickup} and will drop it near a heap with the probability P_{drop}. The DM represents the root model of ant-based clustering methods that directly mimics natural ants.

Lumer and Faieta [11] proposed the first adaptation of DM for data clustering problems. The key idea of their model, called LF, is the definition of a similarity function f based on Euclidean distance d in the space of object attributes. Initially, ants and objects are randomly placed on a 2D grid. The decision of an ant to pick up or drop an object o_i is based on the density $f(o_i)$. Which measures the average similarity of object o_i with the other objects o_j present in the neighborhood of o_i. The main drawbacks of LF algorithm are the large number of clusters found and the slow convergence [11].

The DM and LF algorithms are the basis of many algorithms that have been proposed. The complete description of these ideas is beyond the scope of this paper. However, a constant difficulty over the proposed methods is the way we need to choose the parameter values. A first idea is to divide parameters into two groups: those which are linked to the data (size, type, internal properties...) and those which are independent. For details see the ACA [4] algorithm against which we will compare our results.

Before introducing the API algorithm and its clustering version, it is interesting to quickly describe the work presented in [1] as it is an adaptation of API algorithm to the clustering problem. At the beginning of the algorithm, called AntPart, all the objects are in the nest, and ants are getting out of the nest with one object and tries to find a valuable class for this object. The search for a good class to introduce the object is done according to ant's own memory and, if necessary, to a common memory of the whole colony. Thus, clusters are being built in the opposite way ants usually work: usually ants are looking for food on hunting sites and are bringing some when they are coming back to their nest. In AntPart, ants are spreading the "food" outside of their nest, using hunting sites as clusters they feed with objects. There is also a repairing of mechanisms with specialized ants which are capable of moving objects from one hunting site/cluster towards another one. As we will explain in the next section, our adaptation of API does not operate in this direction.

3 API for Data Clustering

3.1 API Principles

API algorithm is based on the foraging behavior of *Pachycondyla apicalis* ants. These ants have the ability to search for and exploit some distributed food sources without any complicated and centralized behavior such as mass recruitment often encountered in several more populous ant species. Instead of that, *P. apicalis* ants display a simple behavior to bring back enough prey for the survival of their colony. We can describe this behavior with a few rules that can be easily transformed into algorithms: (i) *P. apicalis* are looking for food around their nest (notion of central point and random exploration). (ii) A *P. apicalis* ant memorizes the place where it catches its prey (mainly another insect, dead or alive) and goes back straight to its nest (there is no pheromone trails). (iii) At its next nest exit, a *P. apicalis* ant systematically goes back to its last successful hunting site and starts to look for a new prey from this position (notion of local exploration), (iv) *P. apicalis* ants can not build their own nest and are consequently obliged to move their colony when living conditions are not perennial (restart operator), (v) When the colony decides to move, workers are using a simple form of recruitment, called tandem running: one ant leads another one to the new nest location and again until the whole colony is aware of the new nest.

The model we can deduce from these rules embeds ant agents in a search space in which points correspond to solutions of the corresponding problem. For instance, for a continuous optimization problem, the search space can be a subspace S of $\mathbf{R}^n$ in which we are looking for a minimum value reached by an unknown function f defined on this subspace. The API algorithm in this case, consists in starting at a random position of S for the nest. Then ants are generating random points around the nest which correspond to their initial hunting sites. At each iteration, every ant goes back to its hunting site, operates a local random search. If this attempt is a success, then the ant is considered to have found its prey. If not, several unsuccessful visits at the same hunting site can discourage the ant which consequently starts with a new random point generated around the nest. The general outline of API algorithm shows that it is a population based stochastic optimization algorithm: hunting sites memorized by ants correspond to the population and the nest (and other details not explained here) is playing a role in information exchange between elements of the population.

In the following, we are focusing on API for clustering data.

3.2   Notations and Initial Conditions

We define four sets:

$\mathcal{O} = \{\mathcal{O}_1, \ldots, \mathcal{O}_O\}$ is the set of O objects (i.e. the input dataset), $\mathcal{A} = \{\mathcal{A}_1, \ldots, \mathcal{A}_A\}$ is the set of A ants, $\mathcal{N} = \{\mathcal{N}_1, \ldots, \mathcal{N}_N\}$ is the set of N nests and $\mathcal{G}$ is a two dimensions grid (which can be toroidal or not, often squared) composed of cells. Each cell has 4 neighbor cells (in the toroidal case). All elements of sets $\mathcal{O}$, $\mathcal{A}$ and $\mathcal{N}$ are located on the grid $\mathcal{G}$.

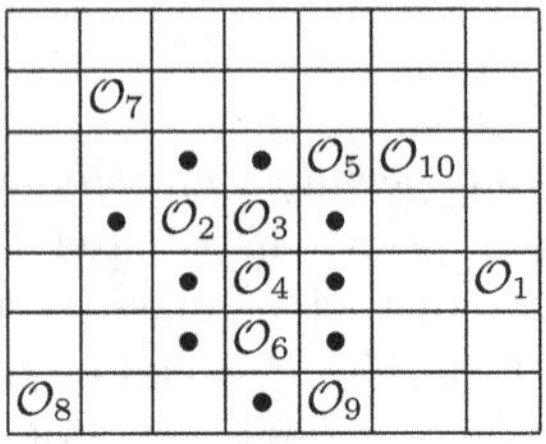

The set of neighboring empty cells of object $\mathcal{O}_3$, denoted by $\mathcal{E}(\mathcal{O}_3)$, is represented by the set of • in the figure. The set $v(\mathcal{O}_3) = \{\mathcal{O}_2, \mathcal{O}_4\}$ denotes the set of objects that are direct neighbors of $\mathcal{O}_3$.

Fig. 1. A 7×7 grid example

We also define the two following notations:

$d(\mathcal{O}_i, \mathcal{O}_j)$ is the distance between objects $\mathcal{O}_i$ and $\mathcal{O}_j$ (we use euclidean distance in the parameters space). Last, the set $\mathcal{E}(X)$ corresponds to the extended empty neighboring cells of object X ($X \in \mathcal{O} \cup \mathcal{A} \cup \mathcal{N} \cup \mathcal{G}$). $\mathcal{E}(X) = \{cells = \phi \in \mathcal{V}(Y), Y \in \mathcal{V}(X)\}$ (see figure 1).

First, the toroidal grid is built with at least $4 \times O$ cells (side length of the grid: $\lceil \sqrt{4 \times O} \rceil$) and nests are regularly scattered on the grid so that there are at least several empty cells between each couple of nests (in order to have an initial separation of nests). Then objects of $\mathcal{O}$ are randomly scattered on the grid $\mathcal{G}$ (with a maximum of one object per cell).

A ants are equally assigned to the N nests and are randomly located on the grid. Each nest correspond to a cluster so N is the initial number of cluster.

3.3   Description of Ant-Agent Behavior

Once the objects, nests and ants are initialized, the algorithm simulates the ants behavior: at each time step, ants can move or perform an action (pick-up and deposit an object). An ant can move from its cell to one of the four neighboring cells and its decisions are governed by probabilities explained in the following.

Ant Behavior for Picking-Up Objects. If one ant finds an object (i.e. the object is on the same cell as the ant), then its behavior depends on the object:

- If the object is free (i.e. it does not belong to any nest) or its similarity with its nest is worse than with the nest of the ant, then the ant picks-up the object $\mathcal{O}_i$ with the probability:

$$P_{\text{pickup}}(\mathcal{O}_i, \mathcal{N}_j) = \left(\frac{f^{\text{pickup}}(\mathcal{O}_i, \mathcal{N}_j)}{k_p + f^{\text{pickup}}(\mathcal{O}_i, \mathcal{N}_j)} \right)^2 \tag{1}$$

where $\mathcal{N}_j$ is the nest from which the ant belongs to, k_p is a constant parameter of the algorithm, and f^{pickup} is a density function calculated according to distances between object $\mathcal{O}_i$ and objects already in nest $\mathcal{N}_j$:

$$f^{\text{pickup}}(\mathcal{O}_i, \mathcal{N}_j) = \max \left\{ \frac{1}{|\mathcal{N}_j|} \sum_{\mathcal{O}_k \in \mathcal{N}_j} 1 - \frac{d(\mathcal{O}_i, \mathcal{O}_k)}{\alpha} ; 0 \right\} \tag{2}$$

where $|\mathcal{N}_j|$ denotes the number of objects belonging to $\mathcal{N}_j$, α is a constant and a given parameter to the algorithm. Note that if the nest $\mathcal{N}_j$ is empty (i.e. $|\mathcal{N}_j| = 0$) the probability $P_{\text{pickup}}(\mathcal{O}_i, \mathcal{N}_j)$ is set to 1. Thus the first free object found by an ant of an empty nest is systematically picked up.
- If $\mathcal{O}_i$ already belongs to a nest $\mathcal{N}_j$, the similarity between $\mathcal{O}_i$ and the nest $\mathcal{N}_k$ of the ant is calculated by:

$$g(\mathcal{O}_i, \mathcal{N}_k) = \frac{f^{\text{pickup}}(\mathcal{O}_i, \mathcal{N}_j)}{f^{\text{pickup}}(\mathcal{O}_i, \mathcal{N}_k) + \varepsilon} \tag{3}$$

where ε is an arbitrary small value. If $g(\mathcal{O}_i, \mathcal{N}_k) < 1$ then object $\mathcal{O}_i$ is considered to be more similar to nest $\mathcal{N}_k$ than to its own nest ($\mathcal{N}_j$) then the ant picks up the object $\mathcal{O}_i$.

Ant Behavior for Dropping Objects. When an ant has just picked up an object $\mathcal{O}_i$, it goes straight back to its nest $\mathcal{N}_j$ and lays down the object in a free cell of the neighborhood $\mathcal{E}(\mathcal{N}_j)$ of its nest. For each empty cell c of $\mathcal{E}(\mathcal{N}_j)$ the probability of dropping the object $\mathcal{O}_i$ is given by:

$$P_{\text{drop}}(\mathcal{O}_i, c) = \left(\frac{f^{\text{drop}}(\mathcal{O}_i, c)}{k_d + f^{\text{drop}}(\mathcal{O}_i, c)} \right)^2 \tag{4}$$

Similarly to equation 1, k_d is a constant value given as a parameter of the algorithm. Function f^{drop} is a kind of density function (also similar to the function given in formula 2) calculated as follows:

$$f^{\text{drop}}(\mathcal{O}_i, c) = \max \left\{ \frac{1}{|v(c)|} \sum_{\mathcal{O}_k \in v(c)} 1 - \frac{d(\mathcal{O}_i, \mathcal{O}_k)}{\alpha} ; 0 \right\} \tag{5}$$

Recall that α is the same parameter than in formula 2 and $v(c)$ is the set of objects that are in the direct neighborhood of cell c. Moreover, if $v(c) = \emptyset$ then $f^{\mathrm{drop}}(\mathcal{O}_i, c) = 1$ (the probability to drop an object to a cell without any object in its neighborhood is 1).

To summarize the dropping and picking-up behavior of one ant we can say that each time an ant takes an object, it brings it back straight to its nest, drops it in the neighborhood of the nest and goes back to the cell where the object has been found. This is exactly what an ant of *Pachycondyla apicalis* species does when it captures a prey: the prey is brought back straight to the nest and at its next nest exit, the ant goes straight to the position, the so called hunting site, of its last catch.

4   Experiments

As a first step we need to evaluate if API is able to produce valid results on classical datasets and secondly we provide a comparison of our results against K-means and ACA [4] algorithms. We will consider the two well known Iris and Wine datasets. Iris dataset is made of 150 objects, each one described with 4 numerical values and there are 3 initial clusters. Wine dataset is made of 178 objects, each one described with 13 numerical values and there are also 3 initial clusters. The data attributes are normalized before using API. For a considered datum $x = [x_i, \cdots, x_n]$ is normalized as:

$$z_i = \frac{x_i - \bar{x}}{\sigma} \tag{6}$$

Where $\bar{x}$ is the mean value and σ the standard deviation. Distances are scaled between $[0, \cdots, 1]$. To study the clustering ability of API, we first focus on two classical indexes: F-Measure, the Classification Error (see [7] for a precise description of these indexes) which will measure the behavior of API during the clustering process. However, clustering quality evaluation is a difficult question and using several points of view can be very informative when we study a new clustering process such as API. In the second step, we provide two more indexes, the Intra cluster variance and the Dunn Index.

Experiments are conducted with the following parameter values: $\alpha = 0.5, k_p = 0.1, k_d = 0.15, \epsilon = 0.03$, the number of ants is chosen to be 10. These values are the commonly used values in ant-based clustering methods based on LF model. However we project to carry a more deeper study of their impacts on API. The current implementation of our method is done in Java and runs on a standard laptop using a Pentium(R) Dual-Core 2.10 GHz CPU.

The Figure 2 gives the evolution of 3 runs of API (10,000 iterations) in order to show the global trend of the performance measures over the time. The F-Measure, computed as the weighted average of the precision and recall, shows that in both datasets, API is reaching good values of F-Measure (i.e. 1 which represents a good equilibrium between precision and recall). Also along the clustering process, the Classification Error is continually decreasing.

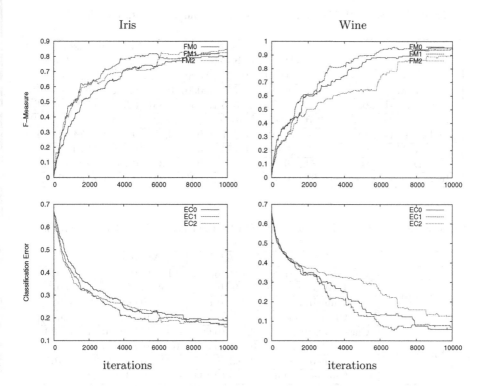

Fig. 2. Evolution of F-Measure (FM) and Classification Error (EC) along the first 10,000 iterations of 3 independent runs for Iris (left) and Wine (right) datasets

Table 1 presents the mean and standard deviation values (obtained from 10 independent runs) of the evaluation functions for API (10,000 iterations) and K-Means when the number of clusters is set to $k = 2$ (*resp.* $k = 4$). The IRIS dataset can be seen as two linear separable classes. Therefore, API should determine these two classes. In the case of kmeans, some methods are used to separate the class containing two sub-classes into two classes. As we go further into our work, the ants should always determine a better number of classes without using an optimization method. k is set to four to study the behaviour of API when k is greater than the real number of classes. The expected behavior of API is the reduction of the number of classes to be found to a number closer to the real number. In this case, the size of some groups found should be zero.

Table 2 presents the comparison of the results of API, K-means and ACA [4]. API and ACA [4] are run (10 independent runs) during 1,000,000 iterations with 10 ants. Mean values and standard deviations obtained with Iris and Wine datasets for the 4 indexes are given. According to the results obtained with these 3 measures, API results are closed to K-means, and they slightly improve ACA results. While K-means performs better than API and ACA [4] on wine dataset.

Table 1. Results of API and K-means for Iris and Wine datasets when $k = 4$

		Iris dataset		Wine dataset	
		API	K-Means	API	K-Means
$k = 2$	Classification Error	0.223(0.000)	0.223 (0.000)	0.31 (0.004)	0.315 (0.009)
	F-Measure	0.777 (0.000)	0.777 (0.000)	0.652 (0.012)	0.677 (0.016)
	Dunn-Index	11.473 (0.040)	0.575 (0.000)	2.851 (0.303)	0.309 (0.004)
	Intra Cluster Variance	2.76 (0.007)	0.0181 (0.000)	0.666 (0.008)	0.106 (0.0004)
$k = 4$	Classification Error	0.166 (0.008)	0.211 (0.019)	0.108 (0.006)	0.114 (0.019)
	F-Measure	0.800 (0.008)	0.753 (0.029)	0.889 (0.008)	0.870 (0.037)
	Dunn-Index	2.342 (0.517)	0.396 (0.089)	1.328 (0.162)	0.194 (0.023)
	Intra Cluster Variance	1.915 (0.374)	0.019 (0.001)	0.345 (0.007)	0.162 (0.008)

Table 2. Results of API, K-means and ACA for the Iris and Wine datasets with $k = 3$

		API	K-Means	ACA
Iris dataset	Classification Error	0.123 (0.004)	0.165 (0.009)	0.230 (0.053)
	F-Measure	0.89 (0.006)	0.838 (0.015)	0.773 (0.022)
	Dunn-Index	5.04 (0.106)	0.411 (0.068)	2.120 (0.628)
	Intra Cluster Variance	2.37 (0.089)	0.018 (0.0004)	4.213 (1.609)
Wine dataset	Classification Error	0.072 (0.007)	0.053 (0.006)	0.142 (0.030)
	F-Measure	0.943 (0.006)	0.96 (0.004)	0.855 (0.023)
	Dunn-Index	2.233 (0.177)	0.293 (0.005)	1.384 (0.101)
	Intra Cluster Variance	0.460 (0.133)	0.123 (0.035)	8.521 (0.991)

We conclude this experimental section saying that the first results obtained by API are very promising, both in terms of quality and time, even if several points (parameters tunning, recruitment) would need deeper experiments.

5   Conclusions

In this article, we have presented an adaptation of the API meta-heuristic to the clustering problem. Our results are very promising compared to ACA [4] and K-means algorithms. The next study is to add a recruitment behavior to the ants in order to introduce a mean to vary the initial given number of clusters. Also, parameters tuning as well as a comparative study with other ant-based clustering algorithms are mandatory steps to improve the use of API for clustering. Finally, we will also investigate real applications of our method on images and clustering in a wireless sensor network.

Acknowledgements. The authors would like to thank Malika Hafidi and Amy Sandoval for their reviews of this paper.

References

1. Admane, L., Benatchba, K., Koudil, M., Siad, L., Maziz, S.: Antpart: an algorithm for the unsupervised classification problem using ants. Applied Mathematics and Computation 180(1), 16–28 (2006)
2. Aupetit, S., Monmarché, N., Slimane, M.: Training of hidden markov models using api ant algorithm. In: Monmarché, N., Guinand, F., Siarry, P. (eds.) Artificial Ants: from Collective Intelligence to Real Life Optimization and Beyond, ch. 12. ISTE - Wiley (2010)
3. Bonabeau, E., Dorigo, M., Theraulaz, G.: From Natural to Artificial Swarm Intelligence. Oxford University Press (1999)
4. Boryczka, U.: Ant Clustering Algorithm. In: Intelligent Information Systems, vol. (1998), pp. 455–458. IEEE (2008)
5. Deneubourg, J.L., Goss, S., Franks, N., Sendova-Franks, A., Detrain, C., Chrétien, L.: The Dynamics of Collective Sorting: Robot-Like Ants and Ant-Like Robots. In: Meyer, J.A., Wilson, S.W. (eds.) Proc. 1st Int. Conf. on Simulation of Adaptive Behaviour, pp. 356–363. MIT Press (1991)
6. Hamdi, A., Antoine, V., Monmarché, N., Alimi, A., Slimane, M.: Artificial ants for automatic classification. In: Monmarché, N., Guinand, F., Siarry, P. (eds.) Artificial Ants: From Collective Intelligence to Real Life Optimization and Beyond, ch. 13, ISTE - Wiley (2010)
7. Handl, J., Knowles, J., Dorigo, M.: Ant-based clustering and topographic mapping. Artificial Life 12(1), 35–61 (2006)
8. Handl, J., Meyer, B.: Ant-based and swarm-based clustering. Swarm Intelligence 1(2), 95–113 (2007)
9. Jain, A.K.: Data clustering: 50 years beyond K-means. Pattern Recognition Letters 31(8), 651–666 (2010)
10. Jain, A.K., Murty, M.N., Flynn, P.J.: Data clustering: a review. ACM Comput. Surv. 31, 264–323 (1999)
11. Lumer, E., Faieta, B.: Diversity and adaptation in populations of clustering ants. In: Meyer, J.A., Wilson, S.W. (eds.) Proc. of the Third Int. Conf. on Simulation of Adaptive Behavior From Animals to Animats, vol. 3, pp. 501–508 (1994)
12. Martens, D., Baesens, B., Fawcett, T.: Editorial survey: swarm intelligence for data mining. Machine Learning 82(1), 1–42 (2010)
13. Monmarché, N., Venturini, G., Slimane, M.: On how *Pachycondyla apicalis* ants suggest a new search algorithm. Future Generation Computer Systems 16(8), 937–946 (2000)

PARADE: A Massively Parallel Differential Evolution Template for EASEA

Jarosław Arabas[1], Ogier Maitre[2], and Pierre Collet[2]

[1] Institute of Electronic Systems, Warsaw University of Technology, Poland
jarabas@elka.pw.edu.pl
[2] LSIIT, University of Strasbourg, 67412 Illkirch, France
{ogier.maitre,pierre.collet}@unistra.fr

Abstract. This paper presents an efficient PARAllelization of Differential Evolution on GPU hardware written as an EASEA (EAsy Specification of Evolutionary Algorithms) template for easy reproducibility and re-use. We provide results of experiments to illustrate the relationship between population size and efficiency of the parallel version based on GPU related to the sequential version on the CPU. We also discuss how the population size influences the number of generations to obtain a certain level of result quality.

1 Introduction

Real-world problems are often continuous problems represented by a vector of real numbers that must be optimized. Because of their continuous nature, such problems can be approached with success by black-box algorithms, such as CMA-ES for instance [4]. However, the context in computer science is changing: CPU clock speed kept increasing ever since the first computers were manufactured in the 1950s until about 2005, when it reached a plateau with 3.8GHz for Intel CPUs. Fortunately Moores law (which states that transistor density on silicon doubles every two years) still applies, so CPU power still increases thanks to parallelism: a quad core 3GHz CPU is more powerful than a single core 3.8GHz CPU. Recently, General Purpose Graphic Processing Units (GPGPUs, or GPUs briefly) have appeared, that contain hundreds of slower cores (the latest nVidia GF110 architecture contains 512 cores running at 772MHz). Current machines often contain such graphic cards, e.g., the Sandy Bridge INTEL CPUs already integrate GPU cores. If the development of the computer hardware follows this line then, in a short future, using only one core of one's machine to solve a problem will mean using only 1/100th of the power of the machine.

This great technical ability raises a fundamental question of benefits that the Differential Evolution (DE) can gain from processing large and huge populations. We concentrated on DE since it appears to be a very simple though quite effective optimization method, according to the results of benchmarking based on the quality of solutions obtained after evaluating a predefined number of individuals [5].

L. Rutkowski et al. (Eds.): SIDE 2012 and EC 2012, LNCS 7269, pp. 12–20, 2012.

This paper therefore presents a parallel implementation of DE using GPU cards and reports on tests which used the CEC2005 benchmark set [9]. We show that increasing the population size can reduce the number of generations to obtain solution at certain accuracy level and improve quality of results obtained at the end of simulation.

The paper is composed in the following way. In section 2 we briefly describe the EASEA platform which can be used to implement EA on GPU. Section 3 provides an overview of earlier works on implementation of DE on GPU. Then we show our approach that is implemented under the EASEA platform . Section 4 reports on experiments we made using the CEC2005 benchmark set, and section 5 concludes the paper.

2   EASEA — Platform for Implementing EA on GPU

GPU cards can contain up to several hundreds of processing cores, their own memory, which can be up to 6GB, and have a high bandwidth. Yet the same constraints that are observed for CPU apply for GPU and increasing the number of cores on the same chip is achieved at the expense of the programming simplicity. The first limitation relates to the cache memory. In modern GPU cards it is accessible in a very limited quantity (16KB per core)[1] and of course is shared by a large number of threads (as for an efficient spatio-temporal parallelization, at least 32 threads are required per core), which increases the pressure on that memory. Another is that cores are grouped by 32 in SIMD bundles (Single Instruction Multiple Data) that must perform the same instruction at the same time.

The scarcity of cache makes very important the average latency time of memory accesses which can be compensated by using three mechanisms:

- On-chip fast (but small) shared memory between cores of a same bundle.
- A thread scheduler, a SMT mechanism (Simultaneous MultiThreading) as implemented on Intel processors under the name of Hyper-Threading. However, if in a classic processor, SMT allows the scheduling between two threads for a single unit, on GPU scheduling is done between 32 threads, which can cover larger latencies.
- A large bus width, which allows a high bandwidth (up to 177GB/s) if neighboring threads access data in adjacent memory.

Taking into account these programming constraints can help to obtain a very interesting speedup with a widely available and cheap hardware. In particular, Evolutionary Algorithms (EAs) seem to be almost perfectly fit to the specificity of the SIMD organization of computation since they proceed populations of chromosomes which are mutually independently evaluated. EASEA (EAsy Specification of Evolutionary Algorithms) is a platform dedicated for scientists with only basic skills in EAs to apply various evolutionary approaches to perform optimization on single GPU cards as well as on clusters of computers [1,6].

---

[1] In first-generation GPU cards the cache memory was not provided at all.

EASEA generates an evolutionary algorithm using a source file (.ez) written in an extended C++. The software analyzes a template and puts the elements defined by the user, applying a treatment if necessary. The resulting source uses an internal library (libeasea) which defines the invariant elements between algorithms (selection operators, migration tools for island model, etc.). By compiling this output code, the user easily obtains an EA set for his problem.

There are several level of customization. Obviously the first is the customization of the .ez file that allows the user to implement his problem using an EASEA internal optimization algorithm. However, implementing a new algorithm in EASEA requires to alter the produced code. It is also possible to implement one's own algorithm using the internal mechanism of EASEA, by redefining a template that is used to generate the sources. These files describe how EASEA uses the user's source file (.ez) and what it must do when filling code files in pure C++ using ibeasea. They use a set of keywords and a pseudo C++ code. These keywords specify the insertion location of codes directly from the source file or modified by internal processing.

3   Massively Parallel Differential Evolution

In August 2010 Zhu [11] claimed that "to the best of our knowledge, the DE implementation presented in this paper is the first one on a GPU platform." He provided a parallel DE implementation which was coupled with Pattern Search to improve precision of the results. He also studied speedup in terms of time needed to run DE on the GeForce GTX 280 card and he showed that at the peak performance the parallel implementation runs about 8 times faster on GPU than on CPU. In parallel, few other DE implementations on GPUs have been reported. Cabido *et al.* [2] presented a preliminary study using the GTX 260 card and a parabola fitness function. They have observed that the speedup, in terms of time needed to complete simulation of a predefined number of generations, varies from 2.85 (100 individuals in population) to 14.80 (1000 individuals) when compared to the CPU time. Veronese and Krohling [10] presented yet another GPU based implementation of DE. They used the GTX 285 card to test the speedup based on time comparison between CPU and GPU to simulate a predefined number of generations for several test problems and they observed that for 100 and 1,000 individuals the maximum speedup was 19.04 and 35.48, respectively. Gonzales and Barriga [3] shortly described their approach which was tested on the Tesla C2050 card. Unfortunately we were unable to find results of their tests.

We have developed an EASEA template that implements a simple DE based on the DE/rand/1/bin pattern [8] to asses ability of speeding up computations by using GPU to parallelize the population evaluation, whereas the rest of the algorithm is implemented on the CPU side. Outline of the method is provided in Fig. 1. The method processes populations P^t and O^t, where t stands for the generation index. Each population contains N_p individuals. With P_i^t and O_i^t we denote the i-th individual from P^t and O^t, respectively. The user defines the fitness function $q : R^n \to R$ and lower and upper limits $l, u \in R^n$.

```
algorithm DE/rand/1/bin
t ← 0
P⁰ ← initialize(l, u)
evaluate P⁰ in parallel
repeat until stop condition met
    for i ∈ 1...Nₚ
        j, k, l ← sample w/o replacement {1, ..., Nₚ}
        v ← Pⱼᵗ + F(Pₖᵗ − Pₗᵗ) + e(l, u)
        w ← crossover(Pᵢᵗ, v)
        Oᵢᵗ ← repair(w, Pᵗ)
    end for
    evaluate Oᵗ in parallel
    for i ∈ 1...Nₚ
        if q(Oᵢᵗ) ≤ q(Pᵢᵗ) then Pᵢᵗ⁺¹ ← Oᵢᵗ
        else Pᵢᵗ⁺¹ ← Pᵢᵗ
    end for
    t ← t + 1
end repeat
```

Fig. 1. Outline of the DE/rand/1/bin algorithm implemented in PARADE

In our implementation we initialize the population P^0 with points picked up at random with uniform distribution from the hyperrectangle $[l, u]$. To avoid stagnation, in the mutation method we add to the scaled difference of two points a zero mean uniformly distributed noise e from the range $[-(u-l)/100, (u-l)/100]$. A binary crossover is used which consists in randomly choosing several coordinate values from P_i^t and inserting them into proper positions into v; probability of selecting a coordinate for the exchange is given by the user. The resulting new point w is checked for feasibility. If it is infeasible then the repairing procedure is performed for each coordinate separately by substituting the i-th coordinate value by $w_i' = 2u_i - w_i$ when $w_i > u_i$ or by $w_i' = 2l_i - w_i$ when $w_i < l_i$. In our implementation we additionally compute the population middlepoint and report its fitness value.

4 Experiments and Results

4.1 Used Benchmark

Since the year 2000 there have been developed two families of widely accepted state-of-the-art sets of numerical optimization benchmark sets that are used by the EC community. The first one is the CEC series, which has been continuously used at the Congress of Evolutionary Computation since 2005, and the second is BBOB that has been used at Genetic and Evolutionary Computation Congress since 2009. Every year, benchmark sets are focused on different aspects of optimization tasks, including unconstrained optimization, highly dimensional tasks, constraint handling techniques, fitness function varying in time and multiple objectives.

In this study we refer to benchmark functions defined in the CEC2005 set [9] which comprises 25 functions which include unimodal functions (f1-f5), basic multimodal functions (f6-f12) and their combinations (f13-f25). Some of these functions include noise (f4, f17). For all functions, except f7 and f25, boundary constraints are defined. Coordinate systems have been shifted, rotated an non-uniformly scaled so that the global minimum is not located in the middle of the coordinate system and one cannot decompose the optimization problem coordinate-wise into a superposition of one-dimensional problems. All optimization problems are defined in 2,10, 30 and 50 dimensional real space. Value of the global optimum is known for each optimization problem, therefore instead of the fitness function of a solution, we speak of the solution error which is defined as a difference in the fitness between the current solution and the global optimum. Conditions of the competition that was held at the CEC2005 conference defined the test methodology which was based on reporting intermediate results from each run of the optimization method achieved after a certain number of the fitness function evaluations. Here we concentrate on the number of generations instead.

The benchmark set is defined in the source code in Matlab, C and Java. We have adopted the C code to implement a CUDA version of CEC2005 benchmark problems and used this version to obtain reported results. We concentrated on 50-dimensional test problems. We have performed experiments for the CEC2005 benchmark set using the DE implementation provided in PARADE. We assumed the same settings as in [7], i.e., both the scaling factor F and the crossover parameter CR were equal to 0.9. In the experiments, the population size was varying in the range $N_p \in \{10^2 - 10^5\}$. For each function in the benchmark set and each population size, we performed 25 independent runs and we reported the best solution error in consecutive generations. In addition we observed the execution time of each generation.

4.2   Execution Time

In EASEA, one or several GPU cards are used to parallelize the fitness function evaluation process. Therefore the execution time t_{gen} to simulate one generation of N_p individual equals $t_{gen}(N_p) = t_{DE}(N_p) + t_{eval}(N_p)$ where $t_{eval}(N_p)$ is the time needed to evaluate the whole population (either on the GPU card or on the CPU) and $t_{DE}(N_p)$ stands for the overhead time, $i.e.$ the time spent on CPU to generate the offspring population, to communicate with the evaluation process and to define the next generation. Since the amount of time needed to generate a single individual to pass its coordinates to the evaluation process is independent of the population size, we conclude that the t_{DE} time depends linearly on the population size $t_{DE}(N_p) = a \cdot N_p + b$. Relation between the t_{eval} time and the population size is more complicated. When using CPU to evaluate, the dependence is linear. For the GPU card, t_{eval} will depend on how effectively

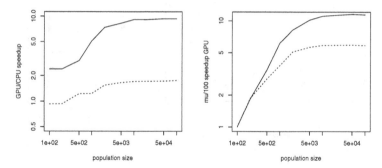

Fig. 2. GPU/CPU speedup (a) and the relative increase of the computing time per single individual related to $N_p = 100$ (b) vs. population size N_p for functions f01 (dotted line) and f11 (solid line)

the cores are used which in turn will relate to the number of cores and the number of threads that can be effectively run in parallel on each core[2].

In Fig. 2 a) we provide comparison of time needed to complete simulation of 100 generations of PARADE which was run with and without the GPU card. We define the GPU/CPU time speedup as a proportion of the average runtime for the CPU version and the GPU version and we investigate how the speedup behaves for various population size from the range $N_p = 10^2 - 10^5$. For the clarity of the picture we present the results for two functions only: f01 (which is evaluated in the shortest time) and f11 (which is evaluated 14 times longer).

In Fig. 2 b) we compare how the runtime of the GPU version depends on the population size from the same range, for benchmark functions f01 and f11. We report the value $\Delta(N_p) = N_p \cdot t_{gen}(100)/(100 \cdot t_{gen}(N_p))$ which indicates how much the computation time per one individual will decrease when the population size will expand from 100 to N_p. Both curves from Fig. 2 have been obtained as an average of 25 independent PARADE runs. Experiments were performed using a computer running under Ubuntu 11.04 x86_64, using a 2.6.38-8 linux kernel. The CPU was an Intel(R) Core(TM) i7 920 at 2.67GHz with 6GB of memory. The computer was equipped with three GPU cards nVidia GTX480 and the CUDA 4.0 platform was used.

For the used hardware we observed that the speedup in terms of the computing time increased with the population size and saturated when the population size was about $N_p = 10,000$. The speedup value was also increasing with the average time to compute one individual's fitness. When looking at values of $\Delta(N_p)$ we observed that the GPU execution time per one individual is reduced with the population size and saturates also at about $N_p = 10,000$. The saturation value

---

[2] If the GPU card were a perfect SIMD machine with an infinite number cores then the evaluation time would be a constant.

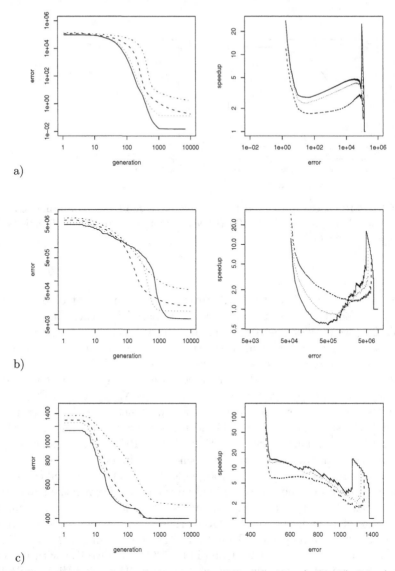

a)

b)

c)

Fig. 3. Convergence and speedup curves for DE, function a) f01, b) f12, c) f15 for population size equal to 100 (dashdot line), 1,000 (dashed line), 10,000 (dotted line) and 100,000 (solid line)

seems to be hardware dependent[3]. Therefore in the next section we investigate if PARADE can benefit from large populations assuming the computing time to be independent of the population size.

---

[3] For example, in earlier experiments with PARADE, for CEC2005 benchmark functions in 10 dimensions optimized using a single GeForce 8400 GS card, the optimum population size was about 3000.

4.3   Quality of Solutions

To illustrate how the population size influences the effectiveness we present convergence curves of the best individual's fitness and "speedup" curves which have been generated in the following way. For each population size N_p we observed the number of generations $g(N_p, L)$ needed for a convergence curve to hit a certain level L of the fitness. We treated the results obtained for $N_p = 100$ as a reference and plotted curves of the proportion $g(N_p, L)/g(100, L)$ vs. the value of L. In Fig. 3 the results of experiments are depicted for functions f01, f12 and f15.

All speedup curves reveal similar pattern of change. For large error values a high speedup was observed (up to 20 when $N_p = 10000$) which we interpret as a consequence of a wide dispersion of populations in the initial exploration phase. Then comes a range of error values with rather small speedup (2–5 times for $N_p = 10000$) that relates to the process of convergence. In all cases we observed premature convergence and for this phase the speedup grew up significantly (up to more than 100 for $N_p = 10000$ and function f15). It should be noted that, in addition to the speedup, usage of a big population may allow to obtain the results of a quality that is inaccessible for small populations.

5   Concluding Remarks

We presented an EASEA template that implements the DE algorithm on GPU cards. In comparison to other implementations which are dedicated to DE only, the presented solution is highly general. The user needs only to define the fitness function. Moreover, if the user needs to check how other EA schemes would manage the optimization problem, he can do it easily just by changing the template declaration. The template allows for faster simulation of DE and the actual speedup in comparison to the CPU grows with time needed to evaluate a single chromosome.

Introduction of the template gave a technical ability to efficiently perform experiments aimed at checking possible advantages of having very large populations in massively parallel DE implementations when time is measured with the number of generations rather than the number on fitness evaluations. Results of experiments performed for the CEC2005 benchmark indicate that the use of very large populations allows to obtain higher quality results. Moreover in early phases of evolution, when the population explores the search space, large populations allow to obtain results of a required quality after executing much smaller number of generations. Finally, very large populations allow to fully utilize the computing power offered by GPU cards.

Acknowledgment. J. Arabas acknowledges kind support in a form of a travel grant funded by the Warsaw University of Technology, Center for Advanced Studies.

References

1. EASEA, https://lsiit.u-strasbg.fr/easea/index.php/EASEA_platform
2. Cabido, R., Duarte, A., Montemayor, A., Pantrigo, J.: Differential evolution for global optimization on gpu. In: Int. Conf. on Metaheuritic and Nature Inspired Computing (2010)
3. Gonzalez, S., Barriga, N.: Fully parallel differential evolution. In: GECCO Competition: GPUs for Genetc and Evolutionary Computation (2011)
4. Hansen, N.: The CMA evolution strategy: a comparing review. In: Lozano, J., Larrañaga, P., Inza, I., Bengoetxea, E. (eds.) Towards a New Evolutionary Computation. Advances on Estimation of Distribution Algorithms, pp. 75–102. Springer (2006)
5. Hansen, N.: Compilation of results on the 2005 cec benchmark function set. Tech. rep., Institute of Computational Science ETH Zurich (2006)
6. Maitre, O., Krüger, F., Querry, S., Lachiche, N., Collet, P.: Easea: Specification and execution of evolutionary algorithms on gpgpu. Soft Computing - A Fusion of Foundations, Methodologies and Applications, pp. 1–19 (May 2011); special issue on Evolutionary Computation on General Purpose Graphics Processing Units
7. Ronkkonen, J., Kukkonen, S., Price, K.: Real-parameter optimization with differential evolution. In: Proc. CEC (2005)
8. Storn, R.: Differential evolution research – trends and open questions. In: Chakraborty, U.K. (ed.) Advances in Differential Evolution, pp. 1–32. Springer, Heidelberg (2008)
9. Suganthan, P.N., Hansen, N., Liang, J.J., Deb, K., Chen, Y.P., Auger, A., Tiwari, S.: Problem definitions and evaluation criteria for the CEC 2005 Special Session on Real Parameter Optimization. Tech. rep., Nanyang Tech. Univ. (2005)
10. Veronese, L., Krohling, R.: Differential evolution algorithm on the GPU with C-CUDA. In: Congr. on Evol. Comp., pp. 1–7 (2010)
11. Zhu, W.: Massively parallel differential evolution — pattern search optimization with graphics hardware acceleration: an investigation on bound constrained optimization problems. J. Glob. Optim. 50, 417–437 (2011)

A 3D Discrete-Continuum Swarm Intelligence Simulation on GPU for Swarm Robotics and Biomedical Applications

Li Bai and David Feltell

School of Computer Science, University of Nottingham, UK
bai@cs.nott.ac.uk

Abstract. In this paper we present a new 3D simulation environment, combining features of both discrete swarm agents and continuous environment defined implicitly as a locally updatable zero-level set surface. The advantage of the proposed framework is the natural support for swarm coordination, as well as for adding other continuum based processes, such as the Eulerian numerical simulation of fluid dynamics equations. In most biomedical applications the influence of gaseous/liquid flows and concentrations becomes a key aspect in any viable model. The level set equations are solved using the finite element method (FEM), which is routinely used for analysing physical properties such as aseous/liquid flows, heat transfer, diffusion and reaction etc.

1 Introduction

Existing swarm agent based models for swarm robotics reiterate the belief that simple probabilistic stimulus-response functions can account for the complexity found in nature. However, the problem with designing agent based models is the inherent dependencies between the various parameters. When compared to continuum PDE models, the agent paradigm suffers from a distinctly poor representation of spatio-temporal scale, e.g., objects are of the same size, agent movements are restricted to discrete 'jumps' from cell to cell.

In this paper we present a new swarm agent modelling environment, combining features of both continuous and discrete methods. Swarm agents are represented as discrete entities with a $\mathbb{R}^3$ location, whereas the environment is a regularly sampled continuum, defined implicitly as a locally updatable zero-level set surface. The level set method [6] allows a substrate to be represented to arbitrary scale and deformed by arbitrary mechanical forces at arbitrary points. The numerical nature of the method allows for a wide variety of metrics to be calculated and the method is routinely used for analysing physical properties such as gaseous/liquid flows, heat transfer, diffusion and reaction etc.

The rest of this paper is organised as follows. Sect. 2 describes a fast, locally deformable level set method, which is used to model a deformable surface. Sect. 3 explains how to agents are embedded on this surface, and Sect. 4 uses inhomogeneous diffusion equations to represent simple fluid embedded on the surface.

L. Rutkowski et al. (Eds.): SIDE 2012 and EC 2012, LNCS 7269, pp. 21–29, 2012.

Finally, Sect. 5 shows an example application of the simulation framework, and Sect. 6 provides a summary of the work.

2   A Localised Level Set

The 0th level set of a scalar field ϕ is surface defined as $\partial\Omega = \{\mathbf{x} \mid \phi_{(\mathbf{x})} = 0\}$. Solving the level set equation $\frac{d\phi}{dt} + \nabla\phi \bullet \frac{\partial\mathbf{x}}{\partial t} = 0$ involves updating the values of a scalar field ϕ at each point in space requires a numerical technique to evolve the zero-level set from an initial specification. Algorithms have been developed to only perform updates on regions near the surface and reinitialising the area near the zero-curve to a signed distance field, to prevent instability. The most well-known is the *narrow band* approach [6], where numerical integration is performed within a band of points initialised either side of the surface. When the zero-level set reaches the edge of the narrow band, the band is reinitialised about the zero-curve using the *fast marching method* [6]. The *sparse field* method improves this by computing the narrow band using a very simple ± 1 scheme, rather than a more complex distance transform. The sparse field method however still assumes that the entire surface must be updated at every iteration. In order to optimize the sparse field method for local modification by agents, we propose some alterations to the method, as shown in Algo. 1, which takes as input a tuple of $\{\phi, \mathcal{A}, \mathcal{X}\}$, where ϕ is the lattice containing elements to be updated, $\mathcal{A}$ is a lattice containing the updates to make to ϕ, and $\mathcal{X}$ gives the specific location of the points in $\mathcal{A}$ and ϕ to be processed.

The layers of the narrow band are stored in an array of linked lists of $\mathbb{Z}^3$ location vectors, $\mathcal{L}$. The locations in the signed distance level set lattice ϕ that lie along the zero-level set (within ± 0.5 of) are stored in the zero-layer linked list $\mathcal{L}_{(0)}$. The layers surrounding the zero-layer are numbered by increasing or decreasing indices for layers outside or inside the surface volume, respectively. Two temporary arrays of linked lists of pointers into elements of $\mathcal{L}$ are first created, $\mathcal{Y}$ and $\mathcal{S}$. $\mathcal{Y}$ stores pointers into outer layer $\mathcal{L}$ elements that must have their distance transform updated as a result of changes to the zero-layer. $\mathcal{S}$ is a 'status change' array of linked lists, which stores those elements flagged to be moved to a different layer, or removed entirely from the narrow band. The maximum area of effect of a zero-layer point using the simplified ± 1 distance transform is $N_{\mathcal{L}} + 1$, where $N_{\mathcal{L}}$ is the number of layers either side of the zero-layer, so there are $2N_{\mathcal{L}} + 1$ layers in total. To reduce the need for searching through linked lists we utilize a secondary regular lattice grid $\mathcal{R}$ of pointers into individual elements within $\mathcal{L}$.

The first major step is to update the zero-layer $\mathcal{L}_{(0)}$ at the points in $\mathcal{X}$ using the values stored in $\mathcal{A}$:

$$\phi_{(\mathbf{x})} = \phi_{(\mathbf{x})} + |\nabla\phi_{(\mathbf{x})}|\mathcal{A}_{(\mathbf{x})} \tag{1}$$

Here, Eq. (1) is derived directly from the level set equation $\frac{d\phi}{dt} = F|\nabla\phi|$. The next step is to test that point to see if it has moved out of the zero-layer range

Algorithm 1. `UpdateSparseField`: main localised sparse field update algorithm

---

Input:
  ◊ $\mathcal{X}$: array of locations to update.
  ◊ $\mathcal{A}$: a lattice of quantities to update by.
  ◊ ϕ : the signed distance level set lattice.
Output:
  ◊ ϕ : an updated signed distance level set lattice.
Data:
  ◊ $\mathcal{L}$: an array of linked lists, one list for each layer of the narrow band, denoted by $\mathcal{L}_{(i)}$, such that i is the narrrow band layer. Each element of a $\mathcal{L}_{(i)}$ linked list stores a $\mathbb{Z}^3$ vector corresponding to the location of an element in the ϕ lattice.
  ◊ $\mathcal{R}$: a lattice equal in size to the ϕ lattice. Each element of $\mathcal{R}$ contains a pointer to an element within $\mathcal{L}$ or is *NULL*.

1 $\mathcal{Y}$ ←array of linked lists, each list reflecting a layer in $\mathcal{L}$;
2 $\mathcal{S}$ ←array of linked lists, each list reflecting a layer in $\mathcal{L}$;
3 $\mathcal{B}$ ←lattice of booleans with same size as ϕ, initially all *false*;
4 $\mathbf{r} = (N_{\mathcal{L}} + 1, N_{\mathcal{L}} + 1, N_{\mathcal{L}} + 1)^T$;
5 **foreach** $\mathbf{x} \in \mathcal{X}$ **do**
    // Update value and add to status change list if moved out of range
6     $\phi_{(\mathbf{x})} = \phi_{(\mathbf{x})} + \mathcal{A}_{(\mathbf{x})}|\nabla\phi_{(\mathbf{x})}|$;
7   **if** $\lfloor\phi_{(\mathbf{x})}\rceil \neq 0$ **then** $\mathcal{S}_{(0)} \to$ append $\mathbf{x}$;
      // Find all outer-layer points within $N_{\mathcal{L}} + 1$ range of x
8   **for** $\mathbf{p} = (\mathbf{x} - \mathbf{r})$ to $(\mathbf{x} + \mathbf{r})$ **do**
9        $\ell = \lfloor\phi_{(\mathbf{p})}\rceil$;
10   **if** $\ell \neq 0$ *AND* $|\ell| \leq N_{\mathcal{L}}$ *AND* $\mathcal{B}_{(\mathbf{p})} = false$ **then**
11          $\mathcal{B}_{(\mathbf{p})} = true$;
12          $\mathcal{Y}_{(\ell)} \to$ append $\mathcal{R}_{(\mathbf{p})}$;
13   **end**
14   **end**
15 **end**
16 $(\mathcal{S}, \phi) = $ `UpdateDistanceTransform`$(\mathcal{Y}, \mathcal{S}, \phi)$;
17 $(\mathcal{L}, \mathcal{R}, \phi) = $ `UpdateLayerMembership`$(\mathcal{L}, \mathcal{S}, \mathcal{R}, \phi)$;
18 **return** ϕ

$[-0.5, 0.5]$ and if so add to the status change list $\mathcal{S}_{(0)}$. Next we must search through all points $\mathbf{p}$ within a range $\mathbf{r}$ from $\mathbf{x}$ and store the found outer layer points according to thier layer. The current layer ℓ is $\lfloor\phi_{(\mathbf{p})}\rceil$. Next we update the distance transform of those outer layer points referenced in $\mathcal{Y}$, giving an updated ϕ lattice along with that need to have their layer membership updated, $\mathcal{S}$. The final step, then, is to update the layer membership of the points referenced in $\mathcal{S}$, giving an updated layer array $\mathcal{L}$, pointer lattice $\mathcal{R}$, and possibly an updated ϕ lattice (if the surface expands).

3 Agents Interacting with Continuum

We embed the agents in a fairly coarse lattice grid on the level set surface. In continuum, agents occupy real-valued locations and interact with the level set surface at these locations. Interpolation is used to weight surface modification contributions to the nearby level set lattice nodes. This results in a much smoother, natural looking surface, rather than sharp discontinuities as with the cellular agent model. The weighting of elements nearer the source point can be easily controlled by varying the standard deviation of the Gaussian function:

$$G(\mathbf{x}_0, \mathbf{x})_\sigma = \frac{1}{\pi^{\frac{3}{2}} \sigma^2} \exp\left(\frac{-|\mathbf{x}_0 - \mathbf{x}|^2}{2\sigma}\right) \tag{2}$$

where $\mathbf{x}_0$ and $\mathbf{x}$ are the start and end points, respectively; and σ is the standard deviation of the distribution.

We must normalise this function when considering a finite set of points if we are to preserve mass. Given a set of points, P, and a quantity to distribute, a, out from location $\mathbf{x}_0$, we use Eq. (2) to calculate the quantity to add at each $\mathbf{x} \in P$ as

$$G^*(\mathbf{x}_0, \mathbf{x}, a)_\sigma = \frac{a G(\mathbf{x}_0, \mathbf{x})_\sigma}{\sum_{\mathbf{p} \in P} G(\mathbf{x}_0, \mathbf{p})_\sigma} \tag{3}$$

Agents may be attracted toward any direction, dependent on factors that are problem-specific to the application or simulation model being constructed (for example, pheromone gradient fields in social insect simulations). However, for agents moving across a surface the ideal velocity (or *movement potential*) from the agent's perspective may not be valid, that is, it is not guaranteed that the direction of this movement potential points along a tangent to the surface. Therefore this potential must be resolved to a valid movement velocity. We calculate a normal pointing away from the surface, $\nabla|\phi|$ and use this to resolve the movement potential vector into a valid direction pointing along the surface. We do this by using the surface normal $\nabla|\phi|$ to remove the component of $\mathbf{u}$ that is perpendicular to the surface. This gives

$$\mathbf{v} = \mathbf{u} - \nabla|\phi| \left(\nabla|\phi| \bullet \mathbf{u}\right) \tag{4}$$

which has the effect of resolving the direction to be tangential to the surface at that location. However, due to the relatively abrupt changes in surface normals as the agent moves between sampling one set of level set lattice nodes to the next, the agent's position may drift away from the zero-curve. This drift must be compensated for by pulling the agent back toward the surface (in an analogue to adhesion), so that the final step to updating the agent's position is

$$\mathbf{x} = (\mathbf{x} + \mathbf{v}) - \varepsilon \nabla|\phi| \tag{5}$$

where $0 < \varepsilon \leq 1$ controls the strength of the pull back onto the zero-curve. Too high a value may pull the agent back to its previous location. Too low a value will allow the agent to drift away from the zero-curve, and away from the narrow band, making spatial derivatives invalid. Although best determined through experimentation to balance movement freedom with accuracy, a general guideline is $\varepsilon \approx \frac{1}{2} |\mathbf{v}_{max}|$, where $\mathbf{v}_{max}$ is the maximum possible agent velocity.

Briefly, the routine for calculating localised surface modifications is as follows: we search within a range r_S from an agent's real-valued location $\mathbf{x}$ for level set lattice ϕ nodes that lie along the zero-layer of the narrow band. The zero-layer points found are appended to the β array and the contributions of their Gaussian weightings are summed to give Σ_G using Eq. (2). With these zero-layer points identified we can cycle through them and compute their contribution to the update lattice $\mathcal{A}$ using Eq. (3). We also append each of these zero-layer locations to the array $\mathcal{X}$, for use outside this routine when cycling through the updated points. The output from agent surface modification then feeds into the algorithm for sparse field updating in order to perform the actual zero-layer and narrow band update.

4   Agent Responding to Diffusion

The most basic numerical fluid dynamics implementation involves the diffusion or heat equation $\frac{\partial \rho}{\partial t} = d\frac{\partial^2 \rho}{\partial x^2}$, where ρ is the quantity of some substance and d is the *diffusion coefficient* controlling the rate of flow. In order to account for different rates of diffusion through varying materials we must solve the *inhomogeneous* diffusion equation, which can be stated as

$$\frac{\partial \rho}{\partial t} = \frac{\partial}{\partial x}\left(d_x \frac{\partial \rho}{\partial x}\right) \tag{6}$$

That is, d is point dependent. Discretisation of this in 3D yields:

$$\begin{aligned}
\frac{\partial \rho}{\partial t} \approx &\frac{d_{i+1,j,k}(\rho_{i+1,j,k} - \rho_{i,j,k}) - d_{i-1,j,k}(\rho_{i,j,k} - \rho_{i-1,j,k})}{\Delta x^2} \\
&+ \frac{d_{i,j+1,k}(\rho_{i,j+1,k} - \rho_{i,j,k}) - d_{i,j-1,k}(\rho_{i,j,k} - \rho_{i,j-1,k})}{\Delta y^2} \\
&+ \frac{d_{i,j,k+1}(\rho_{i,j,k+1} - \rho_{i,j,k}) - d_{i,j,k-1}(\rho_{i,j,k} - \rho_{i,j,k-1})}{\Delta z^2}
\end{aligned} \tag{7}$$

For stability we use a backward Euler formulation for integrating over time:

$$\rho(t + \Delta t) - \Delta t \frac{\partial \rho(t + \Delta t)}{\partial t} = \rho(t) \tag{8}$$

As $\rho(t + \Delta t)$ is unknown, so Eq. (8) requires the solution of a linear system. We can rephrase Eq. (8) in matrix terms as

$$\mathbf{Ax} = \mathbf{b} \tag{9}$$

where $\mathbf{b}$ represents the vector of known initial values of $\rho(t)$ in the system; $\mathbf{A}$ represents the matrix formulation of the transform; and $\mathbf{x}$ represents the vector of $\rho(t + \Delta t)$ values we are trying to find. We could compute the inverse of $\mathbf{A}$ and multiply both sides to find $\mathbf{x}$, but for a sparse matrix such as a diffusion transform this is overkill. Instead we use the Gauss-Seidel iterative relaxation method to solve Eq. (9). This method has the advantage of straightforward implementation on massively parallel SIMD hardware, as well as faster convergence and lower memory requirements than its predecessor, the *Jacobi* method.

Let $\rho_i = \rho_i(t)$, and $\rho_i^* = \rho_i(t + \Delta t)$, the discretisation of Eq. (8) for the inhomogeneous diffusion equation in 1D then yields

$$\rho_i^* - \frac{\Delta t}{\Delta x^2}(d_{i+1}\,\rho_{i+1}^* - (d_{i+1} + d_{i-1})\,\rho_i^* + d_{i-1}\,\rho_{i-1}^*) = \rho_i \qquad (10)$$

From this we can derive the base update equation for use in a relaxation method

$$\rho_i^*\left(1 + \frac{\Delta t}{\Delta x^2}(d_{i+1} + d_{i-1})\right) = \rho_i + \frac{\Delta t}{\Delta x^2}(d_{i+1}\,\rho_{i+1}^* + d_{i-1}\,\rho_{i-1}^*)$$

$$\rho_i^* = \frac{\rho_i + \frac{\Delta t}{\Delta x^2}(d_{i+1}\,\rho_{i+1}^* + d_{i-1}\,\rho_{i-1}^*)}{1 + \frac{\Delta t}{\Delta x^2}(d_{i+1} + d_{i-1})}$$

$$\rho_i^* = \frac{\Delta x^2\,\rho_i + \Delta t\,(d_{i+1}\,\rho_{i+1}^* + d_{i-1}\,\rho_{i-1}^*)}{\Delta x^2 - \Delta t\,(d_{i+1} + d_{i-1})} \qquad (11)$$

Setting an initial guess for ρ^* (for example, $\rho^* = 0$) and applying Eq. (11) over several iterations causes ρ^* to *relax* over time, converging on a stable solution (though not necessarily an accurate solution). For the Jacobi method we would replace ρ^* on the left hand side with $\rho^{(n+1)}$ and the right hand side with $\rho^{(n)}$, where n is the iteration number. That is, we would store the values of $\rho^{(n+1)}$ separately from $\rho^{(n)}$ ready to use on the next iteration. It turns out that this is not necessary, and in fact faster convergence is achieved when the results of the current iteration are used immediately for computing the next node(s) along in the lattice. This in-line approach finally gives us the Gauss-Seidel method. In 3D the iterative update equation becomes

let

$$a = \Delta t\,(d_{i+1,j,k}\,\rho_{i+1,j,k}^* + d_{i-1,j,k}\,\rho_{i-1,j,k}^* + d_{i,j+1,k}\,\rho_{i,j+1,k}^*$$
$$+ d_{i,j-1,k}\,\rho_{i,j-1,k}^* + d_{i,j,k+1}\,\rho_{i,j,k+1}^* + d_{i,j,k-1}\,\rho_{i,j,k-1}^*)$$
$$b = \Delta t\,(d_{i+1,j,k} + d_{i-1,j,k} + d_{i,j+1,k} + d_{i,j-1,k} + d_{i,j,k+1} + d_{i,j,k-1})$$

then

$$\rho_{i,j,k}^* = \frac{\Delta x^2\,\rho_{i,j,k} + a}{\Delta x^2 + b} \qquad (12)$$

where $\rho_{i,j,k}$ is the known value $\rho_{i,j,k}(t)$; $\rho_{i,j,k}^*$ is the iteratively computed solution to $\rho_{i,j,k}(t + \Delta t)$; and $d_{i,j,k}$ is the location-dependent diffusion coefficient.

The inhomogeneous diffusion model is implemented on the GPU (Graphics Processing Unit) device. The implementation detail is omitted here. The addition of inhomogeneous diffusion allows us to add volatile fluids to a solid volume that then diffuse from the volume into the air. This is accomplished simply by adding a quantity g of fluid distributed over those points in the fluid lattice ρ that correspond to the modified points of the level set lattice ϕ. The quantity of fluid g to add/remove depends on whether the surface is being raised or lowered. Raising the surface adds a fixed amount of fluid determined by the agent, whereas lowering the surface removes a portion of the existing fluid. The quantity is further controlled by a normalised Gaussian distribution using exactly the same calculated ratio as the surface modification.

5 Example Application

This section demonstrates the simulation framework using a simple biological model of the termites. Termites of the genus *Macrotermes* provide a unique springboard for investigating self-organising systems. They are a collection of agents, which modify and communicate through their environment toward some goal. Individual termites are tiny and blind but together they build and maintain a vast mound structure, with a royal chamber at its heart and a large chimney-like structure featuring ramifying air passages to provide wind driven respiration for the colony [7]. The termite is an ideal model for swarm robotics, demonstrating coordination through self-organisation. This work evolved from our previous work on simulating multiple agents building a 3D structure and level set segmentation [2,3,5,4].

The simulation environment is configured as follows:

- The environment size (and thus ϕ level set grid size) is set to 128x40x128.
- The level set surface is initialised with $N_{\mathcal{L}} = 3$, giving a total number of layers $2\,N_{\mathcal{L}} + 1 = 7$. The surface represents a layer of deformable soil, initialised to a 120x15x120 surface at the bottom of the ϕ grid.
- Cement pheromone diffusion constant in air, $d^{out} = 0.000625$. This is the same value as the diffusion constant used in [1].
- Cement pheromone diffusion constant in soil (that is, underneath the zero-level set surface), $d^{in} = 0.00000625$.
- Agent movement potential $\mathbf{u}$ is calculated as

$$\mathbf{u} = s \left\| v\,\mathbf{u}_0 + \mu\,\nabla\rho \right\| \tag{13}$$

where $\mathbf{u}_0$ is the resolved movement direction from the previous time step; $\nabla\rho$ is the gradient of the pheromone field; s is the speed of the agents; v and μ are weights controlling the strength of attraction of the pheromone field. The speed parameter is set to $s = 1$. The weights are set to $v = 0.01$ and $\mu = 0.004629$, based on Bonabeau et al.'s PDE model [1].
- The amount of pheromone infused into the soil upon an agent depositing, $g = 0.8888$. This value is taken from the constants k_1, k_2 and k_4 in [1], representing the deposition rate of soil from termites, the emission rate of pheromone from soil and the decay rate of pheromone, respectively.

(a) t=30000   (b) t=70000   (c) t=100000

Fig. 1. The emergence of fairly regularly spaced pillars in the model using curvature based deposition probabilities coupled with gradient based chemotactic movement

(a) t=40000   (b) t=60000, with cement   (c) t=100000
                pheromone.

Fig. 2. The emergence of a royal chamber-like structure in the model when the agents are restricted in their deposits to a zone defined by the edge of a sphere

- The probability of an agent picking up soil (lowering the surface) at any given time step is set to a constant, $P(pick) = 0.1$.
- The probability of an agent dropping soil (raising the surface) at any given time step is given by a response-threshold type function

$$P(drop) = \frac{|\kappa|^n}{|\kappa|^n + \theta^n} \tag{14}$$

where $|\kappa| = |\nabla \bullet \frac{\nabla \phi}{|\nabla \phi|}|$ is the absolute value of the mean curvature; $n = 3$ controls the steepness of the probability distribution; θ controls the magnitude of curvature required before the function returns 0.5. The threshold value is set to $\theta = 2$.

The results of this model as described above is shown in Fig. 1. The model is run for 100 000 time steps. Pillars begin to emerge from an initially homogeneous (but noisy) surface. The cement pheromone gradient following behaviour provides long range coordination controlling the distribution of the pillars, whilst the curvature controlled deposition probability controls the overall shape of the pillars. One further simple extension to this model is then given, where a dome-shaped imposed template is placed at the bottom-centre of the environment. Outside this zone $P(drop) = 0$, whereas inside the zone the probability remains as in Eq. (14). This simplification of queen pheromone diffusion is required because the GPU diffusion implementation/hardware only supports a single gas at present, which in this case is the cement pheromone. The results of this model are shown in Fig. 2. A few sites are reinforced more than others are as a result of the greater curvature and cement pheromone concentrations. As the sites grow they begin to arch toward each other, forming walls and a roof, and giving a completed royal chamber-like structure within 100 000 time steps.

6   Conclusion

We have introduced a novel simulation environment combining descrete agent and continuum environment models. The level set method is extended to provide localised modifications at arbitrary surface points. Agents are allowed to inhabit and modify the environment based on their internal reasoning. An implicit Gauss-Seidel solution to the inhomogeneous diffusion equation is performed on a GPU device. The coupling of a fluid solver and a level set terrain is demonstrated with a simple model of termite mound construction. The underlying physical model can be varied as necessary, making this approach highly extensible for other projects, particularly in biomedical applications involving interactions between discrete and continuum, e.g., cells and tissues.

References

1. Bonabeau, E., Theraulaz, G., Deneubourg, J.-L., Franks, N., Rafelsberger, O., Joly, J.-L., Blanco, S.: A model for the emergence of pillars, walls and royal chambers in termite nests. Philosophical Transactions of the Royal Society of London 353(B), 1561–1576 (1998)
2. Feltell, D., Bai, L.: 3D level set image segmentation refined by intelligent agent swarms. In: IEEE World Congress on Computational Intelligence (WCCI 2010) (2010)
3. Feltell, D., Bai, L., Jensen, H.J.: An individual approach to modelling emergent structure in termite swarm systems. International Journal of Modelling, Identification and Control 3(1), 29–40 (2008)
4. Feltell, D., Bai, L., Soar, R.: Bio-inspired emergent construction. In: IEEE 2nd International Swarm Intelligence Symposium, Pasadena, CA, USA (2005)
5. Feltell, D., Bai, L., Soar, R.: Level set brain segmentation with agent clustering for initialisation. In: International Conference on Bio-inspired Systems and Signal Processing (BIOSIGNALS), Funchal, Madeira, Portugal (2008)
6. Sethian, J.: Level Set Methods and Fast Marching Methods. Cambridge University Press (1999)
7. Turner, J.S.: On the mound of *Macrotermes michaelseni* as an organ of respiratory gas exchange. Physiological and Biochemical Zoology 74(6), 798–822 (2001)

Gathering of Fat Robots with Limited Visibility and without Global Navigation

Kálmán Bolla, Tamás Kovacs, and Gábor Fazekas

Kecskemet College, Department of Informatics,
Izsaki 10, 6000 Kecskemet, Hungary
{bolla.kalman,kovacs.tamas}@gamf.kefo.hu,
fazekas.gabor@inf.unideb.hu
http://www.kefo.hu

Abstract. In the present paper, we introduce two different algorithms for the two dimensional gathering problem for synchronous, fat (disk-like) robots with no global navigation or communication, and with limited visibility. One of the algorithms is a slightly modified version of the local smallest enclosing circle (local SEC) algorithm. The other algorithm uses a new method of the gathering: the robots moves towards the furthest visible robot, and the robots on the perimeter of the visibility graph applies a bigger extent of move than the others. With the help of computer simulations, the two proposed algorithms are shown to be applicable for the gathering problem above and they perform better than the earlier simple SEC algorithm developed for point like robots.

Keywords: mobile robot swarm, gathering problem, fat robots.

1 Introduction

Since the idea of applying robotic swarm as an autonomous system is aroused, the algorithms solving typical swarm intelligence problems have attracted wide attention in the area of robotics.

In the present state of the art, the algorithms of even the basic swarm intelligence tasks are not solved sufficiently or too theoretical to use them in practice. The most studied basic tasks are: gathering of the robots in one point (or into a small area) [1]–[10], discovering of an area starting from a point (base station) ([11]), collecting particles distributed in various ways ([12], [13]).

In this paper we are focusing on the gathering problem on an obstacle-free plane. This means, that the robots have to gather in one point starting from an arbitrary initial condition under a finite. A weaker version of the problem is the convergence task when we require that the diameter of the area enclosing all of the robots tends to zero with the increasing time. It was necessary to introduce the convergence task, because the gathering problem is not solvable in numerous cases [1]. The solution, i.e. the algorithm of the individual robots, depends highly on the properties of the robots. In order to classify the problem we have to decide if the robots:

L. Rutkowski et al. (Eds.): SIDE 2012 and EC 2012, LNCS 7269, pp. 30–38, 2012.

- have memory or not;
- synchronize their acts to each other or not (synchronous or asynchronous case);
- have global navigation tool with common coordination system or not;
- have limited or unlimited radius of visibility;
- can communicate with each other or not;
- are point-like or have an extent (fat robots).

According to the thought of using as simple individuals as possible, most of the gathering algorithms are based on memory-less (oblivious) robots without global navigation. This means that the robots cannot use backtracking steps and common coordinate system. In a typical gathering algorithm each robot repeats the steps of:

- "look" (determining the positions of all visible robots),
- "calculate"(the position in the next time-step for itself),
- "move" (to the calculated position),

in this order. In a synchronous model the robots execute these steps at the same time providing some synchronizing signal. In an asynchronous model, however, the starting times and the durations of the steps above can be different for the individual robots, and, in addition to this, a "wait" phase can be added between the "move" and the next "look" phase.

One straightforward solution is to calculate and move toward the center of gravity (COG) of the robots in each moving step, since it is the same in each local coordinate system. Cohen and Peleg [2] proved the correctness of the COG algorithm for point-like, oblivious robots with unlimited visibility for arbitrary number of robots in the semi-synchronous (and the synchronous) case. The same correctness could be proven only for two such robots in the asynchronous case.

Cieliebak et al. [3] used the center of the smallest enclosing circle (SEC) of all robots instead of the COG, and with this SEC algorithm solved the asynchronous gathering problem for arbitrary number of point-like, oblivious robots with unlimited visibility.

With these algorithms, the gathering problem is solved for point-like robots with unlimited visibility; however, it is necessary to step towards more realistic models. Ando et al. [4] examined the synchronous gathering problem with limited visibility and point-like oblivious robots. Here the concept of the visibility graph arises. This graph contains all robots as vertices, and there is an edge between two vertices (robots), if and only if the two robots see each other. Ando et al. gave solution to the gathering problem with the condition, that the visibility graph is connected. They, too, applied the SEC algorithm, but in this case, the robots calculated and moved towards the center of SEC of the group robots visible by the robot at hand, so each robot had a different center of SEC as purpose at each step cycle. In addition to this the calculated movement of each robot was limited by the condition, that any edge of the visibility graph must not be broken by the step of the robot, so the vector of the planned move was shortened according to this condition. They proved the correctness of their local SEC algorithm in the synchronous case.

Later Flocchini et al. [5] and Souissi et al. [6] introduced algorithms to solve the asynchronous limited visibility problem. However, here the robots could determine the directional angle of a common and global polar coordinate system (with a compass, for example), so, partly, they provided a global navigational tool.

Recently Degener et al. [7] proposed an algorithm for the synchronous limited visibility problem that is based on the local convex hull of the visible robots instead of the GOC or the SEC. In this algorithm no global navigation but communication abilities were supposed, since the robots could share coordinates local the moving strategy with each other.

Another step towards the realistic models is to work with no point-like but "fat" robots, where all of the robots are supposed to be solid discs on a plane with radius R_s. This modification of the problem has serious consequences: it is impossible to gather in a single point, so the original purpose should be modified. Another problem is that the robots now can hinder or totally block the movement of each other; moreover, this is true for the visibility too, since the robots are not transparent in a realistic case.

How should we define the gathering in the case of the fat robots? Czyzowicz et al. [8] defined the gathering so that

- the contact graph of the disks are connected, and
- each robot sees all of the others.

(The contact graph contains the center of the disks as vertices, and two vertices are connected if and only if the two disks are in contact.) Starting out from this definition, they solved the gathering problem for at most four robots. It is obvious, however, that the condition of seeing the other robots at the gathered position cannot be satisfied if there are a numerous robots. Therefore, we define the minimum requirement of gathering as the connectivity of the contact graph.

Cord-Landwehr et al. [9] and later Chaudhuri et al. [10] invented algorithms to gather arbitrary number of disk-like robots around a given point so that the contact graph, and, beyond this, in the gathered state the robot-disks should be as closely packed as possible. In these models, the robots had global navigation tools and total visibility, which meant, in this case, that the robot disks were transparent.

In the present paper, we deal with problem of oblivious, fat robots with limited visibility, but with no global navigation and no communication capabilities at all. We test the local SEC based algorithm, introduced by Ando et al. [4], applied for fat robots without modification, and then, with a slight improvement according to the problems caused by the fat property of the robots. In addition to these, we introduce a new gathering algorithm, which performs better for the problem above. In the next section, we give the details of the algorithms at hand. In Section 3, the results of the computer simulation tests are introduced, and in the last section we conclude.

2   The Proposed Gathering Algorithm

In this work we study the gathering problem with synchronous setting, where the robots are represented as fat robots and they are not transparent (closed disc). For more realistic setting, the robots has limited visibility and there are no a global navigation system. Moreover each robot are oblivious (memory-less) and cannot be identified. Our aim is to present an algorithm which solves the gathering problem in finite time with these minimal conditions. Of course we assume that the visibility graph is connected. In our interpretation the swarm is gathered when the contact graph is connected.

Let $R = \{r_1, \ldots, r_n\}$ be the set of robots and we represent the position of a robot by the vector $\bar{r}_i(t)$ at time t. Each robot is represented as a closed disc with radius R_s, and V be the size of the radius of visibility.

A considerable problem in the fat robot algorithms is that the robots hinders the movements of each other. Typically, the robots on the perimeter are blocked by inner robots. This problem cannot be solved effectively by the SEC based algorithms (as it is demonstrated in Section 3 in this paper). The basic idea of our proposed solution is that the robots try to move away towards the furthest visible robot, which is completely different from the algorithms discussed so far. We will show that this type of algorithm solves the problem of blocking more effectively than the SEC algorithm. In order to make our algorithm more optimal we introduce the concept of the "perimeter robots" that are on the border of the swarm, and give different size of steps for these robots in the algorithm. We call a robot as perimeter robot if all of the visible robots are in a sector centered at the robot at hand with sector angle at most 120 degrees (see figure 1.). We denote the set of perimeter robots by RP. The robots in the set of R/RP (i.e. the complementary set) are considered to be "inside robots", and their set will be denoted by RI. In each step, R is separated into sets of perimeter and inside robots.

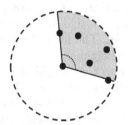

Fig. 1. Perimeter robot

The idea of our algorithm is to make the perimeter robots move towards inside robots. However, this algorithmic element alone can lead to flocking of the discs at the boundary of the visibility graph. Therefore, the movement of the inside robots should solve this problem. The mathematical details of the algorithm are given in the followings.

In the presented algorithm all of the robots execute the *Look*, *Compute* and *Move* phases synchronously. At the *Look* phase each robot collects the visible robots at the time t (denoted by $RV_i(t)$ set) and determines their positions in its own local coordinate system. We call this procedure $GetVisibleRobots(R)$, which takes the set of robots as input. At the *Compute* phase a robot determines if it is a perimeter of inside robot. After that the $GetFurthestVisibleRobot(RV_i(t))$ procedure returns with the position of the furthest visible robot (denoted by $\bar{r}_{di}(t)$). Based on this information the perimeter and the inside robot calculates its local vector of planned move ($\bar{g}$) with a following formula:

$$\bar{g} = c \frac{\bar{r}_{di}(t) - \bar{r}_i(t)}{V} (\bar{r}_{di}(t) - \bar{r}_i(t)). \tag{1}$$

where c is chosen to be 1 or $c = 1/2$ for the cases of perimeter and inside robots, respectively. Regarding the value of c the difference between the two cases is reasonable because in the perimeter there are lower density of robots than in the inner region of the swarm.

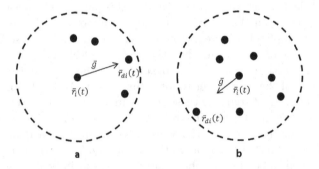

Fig. 2. Perimeter (a) and inside (b) robot step

By the means of this formula each robot move towards its furthest visible neighbor, but with different distance. This distance depends on the current robot position in the local environment. The further is this neighbor the longer is the planned move $\bar{g}$. If the furthest neighbor is at the border of the visibility then a perimeter robot plans to move to that neighbor (i.e. $\bar{g}(t) = \bar{r}_{di}(t) - \bar{r}_i(t)$), in case of an inside robot, the move vector is only the half of that. This is because the perimeter robots are located at the graph border of the visibility graph, hence they have to get closer to the swarm and execute a superior movement.

However, the movement of the robots along the vector $\bar{g}$ should be limited in the SEC algorithm, because the visibility relationships between the robots must not be broken meanwhile a step-cycle. To satisfy this condition the Ando's distance limitation algorithm is used here [4].

2.1 Solution to the Blocking Problem

Because of the fat robot representation, a robot could block the movement of another robot. This can be deadlock situation. However, this deadlock can be solved by a simple technique. The blocked robot should modify its original goal vector so that the new direction is tangential to the blocker robot (see figure 3.). The length of the new vector is calculated as the projection of the original vector to the tangential direction. So, the robot can get closer to its originally planned position. This trick helps only when there is only one blocking robot. We apply a $GetBlockers(r_i, RV_i, r_{di})$ procedure to get all of the blocking robots. If the number of blockers is zero, then nothing is to be done with the original goal vector; if the number of blockers is one, then the goal vector is altered; if the number of blockers more than one, then the robot won't move in this step cycle. Due to this method, in more steps the robots get around each other and the blocking problem is solved. We call this method as slip of the robot.

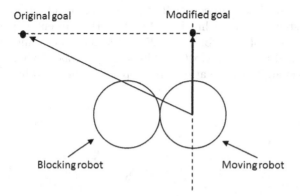

Fig. 3. Solution to the blocking problem

2.2   Gathering Algorithm

As a summary, we give a concise outline of one step-cycle (i.e. *Look*, *Compute* and *Move*), which works on each robots in a synchronous way. In the algorithm the *ComputeMovementLimitation* function computes Ando's movement limitation and *TangentialDirection* is responsible for computing the movement vector resulting from the slip effect discussed before. The final altered movement vector is given by $\overline{m}$.

- $RV_i(t) = GetVisibleRobots(\overline{r}_i, R)$
- $\overline{r}_{di}(t) = GetFurthestRobot(RV_i(t))$
- if $\overline{r}_i(t) \in RP(t)$ then $c = 1$ else $c = \frac{1}{2}$
- $\overline{g} = c \frac{\overline{r}_{di}(t) - \overline{r}_i(t)}{V}(\overline{r}_{di}(t) - \overline{r}_i(t))$
- $\overline{m} = ComputeMovementLimitation(\overline{r}_i, RV_i(t), \overline{g})$
- $B_i(t) = GetBlockers(\overline{r}_i, RV_i(t))$
- if $B_i(t)$ contains more than 1 member then $\overline{m} = r_i$

- else if $B_i(t)$ contains one member then $\overline{m} = TangentialDirection(\overline{r}_i(t),$ $B_i(t), \overline{g})$
- else ith robot moves with $\overline{m}$

3   Computer Tests and Results

To demonstrate the correctness of our algorithm we performed computer simulations in MATLAB. We tested the three mentioned gathering methods (simple SEC, SEC with slip and the present algorithm) with different starting states and different number of robots up to 200 units.

First, we tested the SEC algorithm proposed by Ando for point-like robots, but we applied it for fat robots. Then we upgraded Ando's algorithm with the slip method detailed in Subsection 2.1, so that to avoid the blocking effect. Finally, we tested the algorithm introduced in the present paper. We tested all three gathering solution for N=12,25,50,100,200 robots and at each value of N we generated 5 random start positions for the robots where the visibility graph is connected. The simulation was stopped when the robots did no more

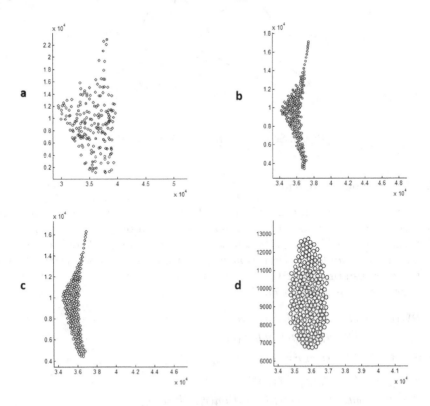

Fig. 4. The gathering results in case N=200. (a) shows the initial state of 200 robots, (b) shows the results of original Ando gathering algorithm, (c) is Ando with slip. Finally (d) demonstrates the results of the presented gathering algorithm.

movement. In figure 4. we can see snapshots of experiments for N=200 robots, which demonstrate the final results of the three gathering algorithms. It can be see that in the final stage the contact graph is connected in the case of our presented algorithm. This is also true for the other values of N. Moreover structure of the swarm is similar to a closely packed one. Nevertheless, we did not examine the question if the structure of the robots is more or less closely packed in every case of the parameters.

Finally, figure 5. represents the cumulative results of our simulations of the gathering methods. We measured the total gathering times (figure 5/a.) (from the starting position to the final state), and the biggest diameters of the contact graphs in the final state (figure 5/b.) It can be seen that there is no significant difference between the gathering times of the different algorithms. However, the diameter of contact graph is always considerably smaller in the case of the presented new method than that of the others. It is also seen that the extension of the original SEC algorithm with the slip method improves the performance of the gathering with respect to the diameter of the contact graph. It is important to remark, that the final contact graph was not connected in a few cases when the simple SEC algorithm was applied, while this failure was not occurred in the case of the other two algorithm.

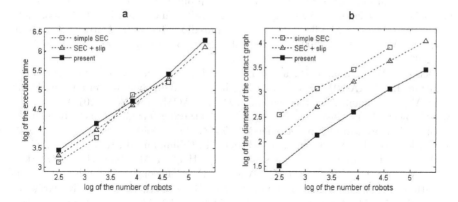

Fig. 5. The average values of the total gathering times (a) and the biggest diameters of the contact graphs (b) as a function of the number of the robots in a log-log scale in the case of the three examined algorithm

4   Conclusions

In this paper, we introduced a new and effective gathering algorithm for fat robots without global navigation and with limited visibility. The computer simulations in MATLAB has shown that

- the SEC algorithm with the "slip" modification and the proposed new gathering algorithm can reach a gathered state with connected contact graph.
- Among the three examined algorithm (simple SEC, SEC with slip and the proposed new) the proposed algorithm can produce the best results with respect to the diameter of the contact graph (considering a smaller diameter as better result).

References

1. Prencipe, G.: Impossibility of gathering by a set of autonomous mobile robots. Theoretical Computer Science 384, 222–231 (2007)
2. Cohen, R., Peleg, D.: Robot Convergence via Center-of-Gravity Algorithms. In: Kralovic, R., Sýkora, O. (eds.) SIROCCO 2004. LNCS, vol. 3104, pp. 79–88. Springer, Heidelberg (2004)
3. Cieliebak, M., Flocchini, P., Prencipe, G., Santoro, N.: Solving the Robots Gathering Problem. In: Baeten, J.C.M., Lenstra, J.K., Parrow, J., Woeginger, G.J. (eds.) ICALP 2003. LNCS, vol. 2719, pp. 1181–1196. Springer, Heidelberg (2003)
4. Ando, H., Suzuki, I., Yamashita, M.: Formation and agreement problems for synchronous mobile robots with limited visibility. In: 1995 IEEE International Symposium on Intelligent Control, pp. 453–460. IEEE Press, New York (1995)
5. Flocchini, P., Prencipe, G., Santoro, N., Widmayer, P.: Gathering of asynchronous robots with limited visibility. Theoretical Computer Science 337, 147–168 (2005)
6. Souissi, S., Défago, X., Yamashita, M.: Using Eventually Consistent Compasses to Gather Oblivious Mobile Robots with Limited Visibility. In: Datta, A.K., Gradinariu, M. (eds.) SSS 2006. LNCS, vol. 4280, pp. 484–500. Springer, Heidelberg (2006)
7. Degener, B., Kempkes, B., auf der Heide, F.M.: A local $O(n^2)$ gathering algorithm. In: SPAA 2010: Proceedings of the 22nd ACM Symposium on Parallelism in Algorithms and Architectures, pp. 224–232. ACM, New York (2010)
8. Czyzowicz, G.J., Gasieniec, L., Pelc, A.: I Gathering few fat mobile robots in the plane. Theoretical Computer Science 410, 481–499 (2009)
9. Cord-Landwehr, A., Degener, B., Fischer, M., Hüllmann, M., Kempkes, B., Klaas, A., Kling, P., Kurras, S., Märtens, M., auf der Heide, F.M., Raupach, C., Swierkot, K., Warner, D., Weddemann, C., Wonisch, D.: Collisionless Gathering of Robots with an Extent. In: Černá, I., Gyimóthy, T., Hromkovič, J., Jefferey, K., Králović, R., Vukolić, M., Wolf, S. (eds.) SOFSEM 2011. LNCS, vol. 6543, pp. 178–189. Springer, Heidelberg (2011)
10. Gan Chaudhuri, S., Mukhopadhyaya, K.: Gathering Asynchronous Transparent Fat Robots. In: Janowski, T., Mohanty, H. (eds.) ICDCIT 2010. LNCS, vol. 5966, pp. 170–175. Springer, Heidelberg (2010)
11. Cohen, R., Peleg, D.: Local Spread Algorithms for Autonomous Robot Systems. Theoretical Computer Science 399, 71–82 (2008)
12. Valdastri, P., Corradi, P., Menciassi, A., Schmickl, T., Crailsheim, K., Seyfried, J., Dario, P.: Micromanipulation, Communication and Swarm Intelligence Issues in a Swarm Microrobotic Platform. Robotics and Autonomous Systems 54, 789–804 (2006)
13. Nouyan, S., Alexandre Campo, A., Dorigo, M.: Gathering Path formation in a robot swarm Self-organized strategies to find your way home. Swarm Intelligence 2(1), 1–23 (2008)

Parallel Migration Model Employing Various Adaptive Variants of Differential Evolution

Petr Bujok[1] and Josef Tvrdík[2]

[1] University of Ostrava, Department of Computer Science
[2] Centre of Excellence IT4Innovations, Division of University of Ostrava,
Institute for Research and Applications of Fuzzy Modeling,
30. dubna 22, 70103 Ostrava, Czech Republic
{petr.bujok,josef.tvrdik}@osu.cz
http://prf.osu.eu/kip/

Abstract. The influence of migration on the performance of differential evolution algorithm is studied. Six adaptive variants of differential evolution are applied to a parallel migration model with a star topology. The parallel algorithm with several different settings of parameters controlling the migration was experimentally compared with the adaptive serial algorithms in six benchmark problems of dimension $D = 30$. The parallel algorithm was more efficient than the best serial adaptive DE variant in a half of the problems.

Keywords: global optimization, differential evolution, self-adaptation, parallel model, experimental comparison.

1 Introduction

When solving a global optimization problem, our natural requirement is to find reliably an acceptable approximation of the global minimum point as quickly as possible. The Differential Evolution (DE) introduced by Storn and Price [13] has appeared to be an efficient heuristic algorithm to solve optimization problems. DE has been intensively studied in the last years, for an overview see [4,9,10].

DE uses a population of N points in the search domain that are candidates of the solutions. The population is developed during the whole search process using evolutionary operators, i.e. selection, mutation and crossover. Mutation is controlled by F parameter, $F > 0$, and crossover is controlled by CR parameter, $0 \leq CR \leq 1$. The combination of mutation and crossover is called DE *strategy* and it is denoted by the abbreviation of DE/m/n/c. A symbol m specifies the kind of mutation, n is used for the number of differences in mutation, and c indicates the type of crossover. Various values of F and CR can be used in each strategy. DE has only a few control parameters. Besides setting the population size N and defining the stopping condition necessary for all evolutionary algorithms, the selection of DE strategy and setting the values of F and CR is all what must be done. However the DE performance is sensitive to the values of these parameters and their appropriate setting is problem-dependent.

L. Rutkowski et al. (Eds.): SIDE 2012 and EC 2012, LNCS 7269, pp. 39–47, 2012.

The goal of this paper is to study how migration applied to DE via a parallel model affects the performance of the algorithm and to compare the efficiency of parallel DE with the serial DE variants.

2   Adaptive Variants Used in Parallel Model

Implementation of an adaptive or self-adaptive mechanism into the DE algorithm is a way how to select a suitable strategy and an appropriate control-parameter setting for a specific problem. Many various self-adaptive DE algorithms have been recently proposed. Four state-of-the-art adaptive DE algorithms [1,7,11,20] have been compared experimentally with DE algorithm using composite trial vector generation strategies and control parameters (CoDE) [17] and with a variant of competitive DE [16][1]. These six adaptive or self-adaptive DE variants employed in the parallel migration model experimentally tested in this study are shortly presented bellow.

Self-adaptive jDE algorithm proposed by Brest et al. [1] uses the DE/rand-/1/bin strategy with an evolutionary self-adaptation of F and CR. A pair of (F, CR) is encoded with each individual of the population. The pair survives with a trial vector which is inserted into next generation. The values of F and CR are initialized randomly from uniform distribution for each point of the population and survive with the individuals in the population but they can be randomly mutated in each generation with given probabilities. Control parameters are set up to the values used in [1].

Differential Evolution with Strategy adaptation (SaDE) [11] uses four strategies. The probability of strategy selection to generate a new trial vector is based on its success rate in the previous LP generations. The values of the parameters F are generated randomly for each trial vector from a normal distribution $N(0.5, 0.3)$, the second parameter of normal distribution is the standard deviation. No adaptation of F is used in this algorithm. The values of the parameter CR are generated from the normal distribution $N(CRm_k, 0.1)$, where the parameter CRm_k, $k = 1, 2, 3, 4$, is adapted during the evolution.

JADE variant of adaptive differential evolution [20] extends the original DE concept with three different improvements – current-to-pbest mutation, a new adaptive control of parameters F and CR, and archive. The mutant vector v is generated in the following manner:

$$v = x_i + F(x_{\text{pbest}} - x_i) + F(x_{r1} - x_{r2}),\qquad(1)$$

where x_{pbest} is randomly chosen from $100\,p\,\%$ best individuals with input parameter $p = 0.05$ recommended in [20]. The vector x_{r1} is randomly selected from $P\,(r1 \neq i)$, x_{r2} is randomly selected from the union $P \bigcup A\ (r2 \neq i \neq r1)$ of the

---

[1] Tvrdík, J., Poláková, R., Veselský, J., Bujok, P.: Adaptive Variants of Differential Evolution: Towards Control-Parameter-Free Optimizers, submitted to Handbook of Optimization, I. Zelinka, V. Snasel, and A. Abraham (eds.), Springer, to appear in 2012.

current population P and the archive A. In every generation, parent individuals replaced by better offspring individuals are put into the archive and the archive size is reduced to N individuals by randomly dropping surplus individuals. The trial vector is generated from v and x_i using the binomial crossover. CR and F are independently generated for each individual x_i, CR is generated from the normal distribution of mean μ_{CR} and standard deviation 0.1, truncated to $[0, 1]$. F is generated from Cauchy distribution with location parameter μ_F and scale parameter 0.1, truncated to 1 if $F > 1$ or regenerated if $F < 0$, see [20] for details of μ_{CR} and μ_F adaptation.

This adaptive DE variant using Ensemble of Parameter values and mutation Strategies (EPSDE) was proposed in [7]. The mutation strategies and the values of control parameters F and CR are stored in pools. Combinations of the strategies and the parameters in the pools have diverse characteristics so that they can exhibit distinct performance during different stages of evolution. A triplet of (*strategy*, F, CR) is stored together with each point of population. The triplets are set randomly for initial generation and they develop during evolution. If the triplet stored with the target vector x_i produces a successful trial vector, the triplet survives adhered to the vector entering into next generation instead of x_i. Each successful triplet of parameters is also stored in auxiliary memory of length of L, usually $L = N$. If the stored triplet of (*strategy*, F, CR) is not successful, it is re-initialized by a triplet whose items are randomly chosen from respective pools or by randomly chosen one from the auxiliary memory of successful triplets. The pool of strategies and the pools of F and CR values are given in [7].

Competitive DE uses H strategies with their control-parameter values held in the pool [15]. Any of H strategies can be chosen to create a new trial point y. A strategy is selected randomly with probability q_h, $h = 1, 2, \ldots, H$. The values of probability are initialized uniformly, $q_h = 1/H$, and they are modified according to the success rate in the preceding steps. The hth strategy is considered successful if it produces a trial vector entering into next generation. Probability q_h is evaluated as the relative frequency of success. A variant of this algorithm (denoted *b6e6rl*), well-performing in benchmark tests [16], is employed in the parallel migration model. In this variant, twelve strategies are in competition, six of them use the binomial crossover, the others the exponential crossover. The randrl/1/ mutation [6] is applied to all the strategies, two different values of control parameter F are used, $\{0.5, 0.8\}$. The binomial crossover uses three different values of CR, $CR \in \{0, 0.5, 1\}$. Three different values of CR are also used in the exponential crossover, their setting is based on the relationship between mutation probability and CR derived in [19]. Three values of the mutation probability are set up equidistantly in the interval $(1/D, 1)$, where D is the dimension of the problem.

DE algorithm with composite trial vector generation strategies and control parameters (labeled CoDE hereafter) has been recently presented [17]. The CoDE combines three well-studied trial vector strategies with three control parameter settings in a random way to generate trial vectors. The strategies are rand/1/bin, rand/2/bin, and current-to-rand/1 and all the three strategies are applied when generating a new trial vector. It results in having three offspring vectors and among them the vector with the least function value is used as the trial vector. The values of control parameters F and CR are chosen randomly from the parameter pool containing $[F = 1, CR = 0.1]$, $[F = 1, CR = 0.9]$, and $[F = 0.8, CR = 0.2]$. A variant of CoDE using the binomial crossover after the current-to-rand/1 mutation appeared to be more efficient compared to the CoDE algorithm without the binomial crossover described in [17] in the preliminary experiments. This modified CoDE variant is applied to the parallel model.

3   Parallel Migration Model

Three types of parallel model are used in parallel EAs: *master-slave*, *diffusion* and *migration* model [3,8]. When the migration model is considered, the interconnection among islands called *topology* [2,12] is an important feature influencing the performance of the algorithm. The migration models with various topologies were also applied in parallel DE [14,18]. The *star* topology shown in Fig. 1 was implemented in the parallel DE algorithm in our experimental tests. There are k islands with the sub-populations P_j, $j = 1, 2, \ldots, k$. Each island is linked only to a special island called *mainland* and individuals can migrate only between the linked islands. A similar version of cooperative star topology was also used in the context of compact DE, see Iacca et al. [5].

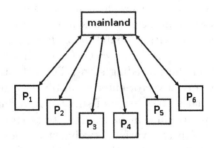

Fig. 1. Star migration model and distribution of sub-populations

The parallel migration model implemented in this study is shown in Algorithm 1. Sub-populations are of the same size, the size NI is an input parameter. Each island sub-population evolves independently by one of the six adaptive DE algorithm described above until the moment to migrate is reached. The migration from the islands to the mainland occurs after performing a given number of generations nde (input parameter of the algorithm). In the migration model used here, the individual with the least function value of the ith sub-population $(x_{best,i})$ replaces the ith individual (x_i^m) of the mainland population and mig other randomly chosen points of the sub-population (except $x_{best,i}$) overwrite *mig* individuals of mainland population on places corresponding to kth sub-population, *mig* is also an input parameter. Thus, $mig + 1$ individuals from each island are copied to mainland. It is obvious that the size of the mainland population NM should be set up to $NM \geq k \times (mig + 1)$. If $NM = k \times (mig + 1)$, the mainland population is renewed completely in each epoch and the elitism of the parallel algorithm is ensured. In order to satisfy this condition, the input parameter *mig* was set up to $mig = 4$ and $NM = 30$ in all the experiments.

After finishing the migration from the islands to the mainland, the search process continues applying a DE variant on the mainland until the stopping condition for the current epoch (2) is reached. In this parallel DE algorithm, competitive *b6e6rl* DE variant as the most reliable in preliminary experiments was chosen for the mainland population. The stopping condition for the mainland and the current epoch was formed as follows:

$$f_{\max} - f_{\min} < 1 \times 10^{-6} \quad \text{OR} \quad nfe_{\mathrm{m}} > 10^{(epoch-1)} \times 2 \times nde \times NM, \qquad (2)$$

where $f_{\max}$ and $f_{\min}$ are the worst and the best function values of the mainland population, respectively, and nfe_{m} is the number of function evaluations in the mainland population during this epoch. Notice that in early epochs the evolution on the mainland tends to stop due to the given limit of allowed function evaluations (after $2 \times nde$ generations in the first epoch) while in late epochs due to the small difference of the function values in the mainland population.

Algorithm 1. Parallel Model Using Adaptive DE Algorithms

> initialize mainland population and sub-populations P_i, $i = 1, 2, \ldots, k$
> $epoch = 1$
> **while** stopping condition (3) not reached **do**
>   **for** $i = 1, 2, \ldots, k$ **do**
>   perform *nde* generations of ith island by ith adaptive DE
>   migrate the best point and *mig* points randomly chosen from P_i to mainland
>   **end for**
>   **while** stopping condition (2) not reached **do**
>   develop mainland sub-population by a DE variant
>   **end while**
>   **for** $i = 1, 2, \ldots, k$ **do**
>   migrate $1 + mig$ points from the mainland to ith island
>   **end for**
> $epoch = epoch + 1$
> **end while**

When development of mainland population is done, the migration from the mainland to islands happens. The point from the ith position in mainland moves to the ith island on the position of the former best point and *mig* points of mainland from positions corresponding to ith island rewrite the points on random positions (except the position of the former best point) in the island sub-population.

This migration accomplishes the epoch. The search continues until the stopping condition (3) on the mainland is satisfied:

$$f_{\max} - f_{\min} < 1 \times 10^{-6} \quad \text{AND} \quad f_{\text{old}} - f_{\text{new}} < 1 \times 10^{-6}, \tag{3}$$

where f_{old} and f_{new} are the minimum function values found in two last subsequent epochs.

4   Experiments and Results

The parallel DE algorithm (hereafter PADE) is experimentally compared with the most efficient and the most reliable serial variants from the former comparison, i.e. with JADE [20] as the most efficient algorithm and the second most reliable and with the *b6e6rl* variant of competitive DE [16] as the most reliable and the second most efficient one. Several different values of input parameters *nde* and *NI* are tested, their setting is based on the previous results [2]. The size of population of serial DE variants was set up to $N = 60$ and the search was stopped if $f_{\max} - f_{\min} < 1 \times 10^{-6}$, where $f_{\max}$ and $f_{\min}$ are the worst and the best function values of the population. Six well-known test functions [7,13] are used as benchmark. Rosenbrock and Schwefel functions were used in their standard form, Ackley, Dejong1, Griewank, and Rastrigin functions were used in their shifted version. The shifted version of function was evaluated at the point $z = x - o$, $o \in S$, $o \neq (0,0,\ldots,0)$, where $S = \prod_{j=1}^{D}[b_j - a_j]$, $a_j < b_j$ is the search domain. The shift o was generated randomly from uniform distribution before each run. The problem dimension is $D = 30$.

One hundred of independent runs were carried out for this algorithm and each test problem, in each run the number of the function evaluations (*nfe*) and the minimum function value in the final generation (f_{min}) were recorded. The reliability rate (R) was evaluated as the number of runs when ($f_{min} - f(x^*)$) < 1×10^{-4}.

The results of experimental comparison of the algorithms are presented in Table 1. The values of *nfe* for PADE that are significantly better than *nfe* for the

Table 1. Basic characteristics of the algorithms' performance

Alg	NI	nde	Ackley nfe	R	DeJong nfe	R	Griewank nfe	R	Rastrigin nfe	R	Rosenbrock nfe	R	Schwefel nfe	R
b6e6rl			71278	100	37781	100	51934	100	73402	100	148185	100	64245	100
JADE			75248	100	13470	100	22759	93	67801	100	76440	93	57994	77
PADE	10	5	**31916**	94	17869	100	24673	85	**41994**	98	163269	95	**33043**	88
PADE	10	10	**32992**	96	18659	100	25096	82	**42705**	98	165302	100	**34390**	91
PADE	10	20	**34502**	99	19757	100	25948	79	**44677**	100	167270	91	**36654**	97
PADE	10	30	**34809**	96	20155	100	27306	86	**46601**	99	162716	97	**37234**	97
PADE	30	10	**44268**	97	28431	100	37283	74	**60452**	100	180133	94	**46746**	98

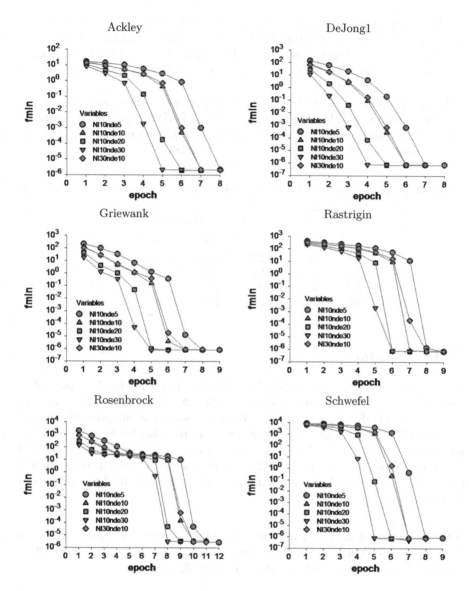

Fig. 2. Minimum function values in the mainland population in epochs

best serial DE variant (by more than 10%) are printed in bold. The parallel DE is more efficient in three out of six benchmark problems, mostly without significant decreasing the reliability. The performance of PADE is not very sensitive to the change of *nde*. Increasing the size of the island population to $NI = 30$ decreases the efficiency without improving the reliability.

The development of the minimum function values (median of 100 runs) in the mainland population during the search is depicted in Fig. 2, logarithmic scale is used for the vertical axis. The PADE variants with $NI = 10$ and longer development on the islands ($nde = 30$ and $nde = 20$) need a smaller number of epochs to find an acceptable solution.

The proportion of the function evaluations performed on the mainland to the total nfe is shown in Table 2. Bad performance of PADE in Rosenbrock problem could be explained by a very high proportion of function evaluations spent on the mainland indicating that the parallelism was not helpful in this problem.

Table 2. Proportion of the function evaluations on the mainland to the total count

NI	nde	Ackley	DeJong	Griewank	Rastrigin	Rosenbrock	Schwefel
10	5	91%	86%	89%	93%	98%	92%
10	10	85%	77%	82%	88%	89%	86%
10	20	76%	63%	71%	81%	93%	77%
10	30	69%	55%	60%	73%	90%	71%
30	10	67%	55%	61%	73%	89%	69%

5   Conclusion

Six adaptive DE variants cooperated in a simple parallel model. The parallelism provided the algorithm with migration, which is an additional evolutionary operator. Parallel DE was more efficient than the best serial adaptive DE variant in a half of benchmark problems. This result is promising for future research in parallel DE and it gives a chance to propose a more robust and efficient parallel DE model applicable in solving optimization problems where the evaluation of the objective function is time-consuming and the reduction of the number of function evolutions is crucial.

Acknowledgments. This paper has been elaborated in the framework of the IT4Innovations Centre of Excellence project, reg. no. CZ.1.05/1.1.00/02.0070. This work was also supported by the SGS 22/2011 project .

References

1. Brest, J., Greiner, S., Boškovič, B., Mernik, M., Žumer, V.: Self-adapting control parameters in differential evolution: A comparative study on numerical benchmark problems. IEEE Transactions on Evolutionary Computation 10, 646–657 (2006)
2. Bujok, P.: Parallel models of adaptive differential evolution based on migration process. In: Aplimat, 10th International Conference on Applied Mathematics, Bratislava, pp. 357–364 (2011)
3. Cantu-Paz, E.: A survey of parallel genetic algorithms (1997),
http://neo.lcc.uma.es/cEA-web/documents/cant98.pdf

4. Das, S., Suganthan, P.N.: Differential evolution: A survey of the state-of-the-art. IEEE Transactions on Evolutionary Computation 15, 27–54 (2011)
5. Iacca, G., Mallipeddi, R., Mininno, E., Neri, F., Suganthan, P.N.: Global supervision for compact differential evolution. In: Proceeding IEEE Symposium on Differential Evolution, Paris, France, pp. 25–32 (2011)
6. Kaelo, P., Ali, M.M.: A numerical study of some modified differential evolution algorithms. European J. Operational Research 169, 1176–1184 (2006)
7. Mallipeddi, R., Suganthan, P.N., Pan, Q.K., Tasgetiren, M.F.: Differential evolution algorithm with ensemble of parameters and mutation strategies. Applied Soft Computing 11, 1679–1696 (2011)
8. Nedjah, N., Alba, E., de Macedo Mourelle, L.: Parallel Evolutionary Computations. SCI. Springer-Verlag New York Inc., Secaucus (2006)
9. Neri, F., Tirronen, V.: Recent advances in differential evolution: a review and experimental analysis. Artificial Intelligence Review 33, 61–106 (2010)
10. Price, K.V., Storn, R., Lampinen, J.: Differential Evolution: A Practical Approach to Global Optimization. Springer, Heidelberg (2005)
11. Qin, A.K., Huang, V.L., Suganthan, P.N.: Differential evolution algorithm with strategy adaptation for global numerical optimization. IEEE Transactions on Evolutionary Computation 13(2), 398–417 (2009)
12. Ruciński, M., Izzo, D., Biscani, F.: On the impact of the migration topology on the island model. Parallel Comput. 36, 555–571 (2010)
13. Storn, R., Price, K.V.: Differential evolution - a simple and efficient heuristic for global optimization over continuous spaces. J. Global Optimization 11, 341–359 (1997)
14. Tasoulis, D.K., Pavlidis, N., Plagianakos, V.P., Vrahatis, M.N.: Parallel differential evolution. In: IEEE Congress on Evolutionary Computation (CEC), pp. 2023–2029 (2004)
15. Tvrdík, J.: Competitive differential evolution. In: Matoušek, R., Ošmera, P. (eds.) MENDEL 2006: 12th International Conference on Soft Computing, pp. 7–12. University of Technology, Brno (2006)
16. Tvrdík, J.: Self-adaptive variants of differential evolution with exponential crossover. Series Mathematics-Informatics, vol. 47, pp. 151–168. Analele of West University Timisoara (2009), http://www1.osu.cz/~tvrdik/ (reprint available [ONLINE])
17. Wang, Y., Cai, Z., Zhang, Q.: Differential evolution with composite trial vector generation strategies and control parameters. IEEE Transactions on Evolutionary Computation 15, 55–66 (2011)
18. Weber, M., Tirronen, V., Neri, F.: Scale factor inheritance mechanism in distributed differential evolution. Soft Computing. A Fusion of Foundations Methodologies and Applications 14(11), 1187–1207 (2010)
19. Zaharie, D.: Influence of crossover on the behavior of differential evolution algorithms. Applied Soft Computing 9, 1126–1138 (2009)
20. Zhang, J., Sanderson, A.C.: JADE: Adaptive Differential Evolution With Optional External Archive. IEEE Transactions on Evolutionary Computation 13 (2009)

A Differential Evolution Algorithm
Assisted by ANFIS for Music Fingering

Roberto De Prisco, Gianluca Zaccagnino, and Rocco Zaccagnino

Musimathics Laboratory Dipartimento di Informatica
Università di Salerno 84084 Fisciano (SA) - Italy
http://music.dia.unisa.it

Abstract. Music fingering is a cognitive process whose goal is to map each note of a music score to a *fingering* on some instrument. A *fingering* specifies the fingers of the hands that the player should use to play the notes. This problem arises for many instruments and it can be quite different from instrument to instrument; guitar fingering, for example, is different from piano fingering. Previous work focuses on specific instruments, in particular the guitar, and evolutionary algorithms have been used.

In this paper, we propose a differential evolution (DE) algorithm designed for general music fingering (any kind of music instruments). The algorithm uses an Adaptive Neuro-Fuzzy Inference System (ANFIS) engine that learns the fingering from music already fingered.

The algorithm follows the basic DE strategy but exploits also some customizations specific to the fingering problem. We have implemented the DE algorithm in Java and we have used the ANFIS network in Matlab. The two systems communicate by using the MatlabControl library. Several tests have been performed to evaluate its efficacy.

1 Introduction

Given a music score for some instrument, a *fingering* is a mapping of each note of the input score to a specific "position" of the hands that should be used to play the notes. The position of the hands in most cases just specifies a finger for each note (like for example for piano scores). In some other case it specifies also other information (like a string on the guitar). In some cases also the two foots are used (like for the church organ). A *fingered* music score is a music score with a fingering.

Fingering involves several aspects: musical analysis, physical constraints, biomechanical constraints (possible figures of the hand). In addition, each musician has different preferences about the positioning of the fingers, as suggested by experience, physical possibilities and so on. Fingered music can be of great help to music students or any one that wishes to play and does not have enough competence to find a good fingering by himself. The process of fingering a music score, however, can be laborious and time consuming, especially if one has plenty of music to be fingered. A publishing house might want to print a book of music

L. Rutkowski et al. (Eds.): SIDE 2012 and EC 2012, LNCS 7269, pp. 48–56, 2012.
© Springer-Verlag Berlin Heidelberg 2012

with the fingering rather than without it. Having computer programs that can automatically find music fingerings can be of great help. A music score can have many possible fingerings. Although each instrument has specific constraint that might reduce the number of possible fingerings, in theory, there is a huge number of possible fingerings for a music score. This makes the evolutionary approach to this problem interesting.

The fingering problem has been given considerable attention in the last few years, although most of the work focuses on the guitar. Each instruments has specific physical and structural features which make the fingering problem instrument-dependant.

In this paper we explore the use of the Differential Evolution (DE) approach for the fingering problem. Although our algorithm follows the general DE strategy, there are several customization specific to the fingering problem. In our approach, the DE algorithm is used to explore good fingered configurations among the solution space. Once the algorithm generates a new solution, an adaptive neuro-fuzzy inference system (ANFIS) [5] is used to determine its fitness value for the evolutionary algorithm to continue its search process. ANFIS is a class of adaptive networks which are functionally equivalent to fuzzy inference systems. In our case, the ANFIS network is trained to learn fingered positions starting from music already fingered. Such fingered music might represent either the particular preferences of a specific user (musician) or standard fingering practice for the instrument for which the music is written.

This paper. In this paper, we propose a general model of fingering, not restricted to one specific instrument but usable for any type of musical instrument, although the algorithm uses a different representation of the fingering which is instrument-dependant. This is transparent to the user. In order to abstract from one specific instrument, the model does not use information on the physical characteristics of the musical instruments, but gets the needed information from already fingered music. To the best of our knowledge this is the first algorithm applicable to any type of musical instrument. We have implemented the DE algorithm in Java and the ANFIS network in Matlab. The two systems communicate by using the MatlabControl library. We have run several tests and finally, the output of the system is validated against the performance of a human expert. In the final section of the paper we report the results of the tests.

Related work. Most of previous works are concerned with the fingering of stringed instruments (in particular the guitar). Expert systems for the guitar fingering problem have been published by Sayegh [10], Miura and Yanagida (MY) [6] and Emura et al [3]. Radisavljevic and Driessen [9] implement and build on Sayegh's idea of dynamic programming. Their interest is in tuning their algorithm to particular styles of music fingering through training over selected scores for guitar. Tuohy and Potter [13] approach the guitar fingering problem with a genetic algorithm. In this algorithm the population is a collection of tablatures that are valid for a given piece of music. A tablature "chromosome" is defined as a sequence of chords. A chord is a "gene" and consists of fretboard positions for all the notes in that chord. The fitness function is based on two separate classes of tablature complexity: difficulty of hand/finger movement and difficulty of hand/finger manipulation. In a later work [14] they introduce a neural network to assign fingers to their tablature.

2   Background

2.1   Music Notation

We assume that the reader is familiar with basic music notions. The twelve notes of an *octave* are denoted with the letters A, A♯ or B♭, B, C, C♯ or D♭, D, D♯ or E♭, E, F, F♯ or G♭, G and G♯ or A♭. In the audible range of sounds there are several octaves, usually denoted with the numbers from 0 to 7. The keyboard of a piano contains all the 88 notes used in music (the lowest notes and also the highest ones are used rarely). We will use MIDI codes to specify the notes. Each MIDI code is a number in the range 0-127. Thus we have more MIDI codes than keys in a standard 88-key piano. The lowest note in the piano, the first A, has MIDI code 21, while the highest note, the last C, has MIDI code 108.

Fingering information is instrument-specific, Figure 1 shows an example of fingering for piano and Figure 2 shows an example of fingering for guitar.

Fig. 1. Piano fingering

Fig. 2. Guitar fingering

Given a score S it is possible to have many fingerings $F_i(S)$. Although each instrument has specific constraint that might reduce the number of possible fingerings, in theory, given a score S there is a huge number of fingerings for S. The goal of the algorithm is to find a "good" fingering, one that would be used by an expert musician.

2.2   Differential Evolution

Given the scope of the conference we assume that the reader is familiar with evolutionary algorithms and in particular with the differential evolution (DE) strategy proposed in [11]. In the next section we will describe the modifications needed to adapt the standard (DE) strategy to our problem.

2.3   Adaptive-Network-Based Fuzzy Inference System (ANFIS)

An *Adaptive Network-Based Fuzzy Inference System* or simply *ANFIS* can be used for constructing a set of fuzzy if-then-rules with appropriate membership functions able to generate correct input-output pairs. Due to lack of space we refer the reader, for example, to [4,12] for more information. In the next section we will explain how we use an ANFIS network for our algorithm.

3   The DE Algorithm

In this section we present the fingering algorithm that we call DE. The DE algorithm adopts the differential evolution strategy and uses an ANFIS network to evaluate the fitness of the solutions. To describe the algorithm we start by describing how we represent individuals, then we describe how we use the ANFIS network and finally how we adapt the DE strategy to the fingering problem.

3.1   Data Representation

In this section we describe how we represent a fingering. The choice of the data representation is a crucial step in the design of an evolutionary algorithm and also of a fuzzy network. We seek a representation that is enough general to deal with fingerings for all kind of instruments.

Regardless of the specific instrument for which it is written, a music score S can be viewed as a temporal sequence of *score-changes*, where each score-change is the appearance of a new note or group of notes. We denote this sequence as $S = S_1, S_2, \ldots, S_N$, where N is the number of score-change in S. Notes in a score-change are specified using the corresponding MIDI code. Figure 3 provides an example. The score fragment consists of 4 score-changes. Notice that the score-change representation of a score loses the information about timing (which is not needed for fingering) retaining only the information about the notes to be played.

Abstracting from the instruments a fingering configuration will be a 12-element array of *notes-information* and an associated 12-element array of *extra-information*. The notes-information will be MIDI codes that specify the score-change. We use a maximum of 12 notes since we assume that with the

S_1={71, 64, 36}

S_2={71}

S_3={69}

S_4={63, 58, 36}

Fig. 3. A fragment of a score and the sequence of score-changes

fingers we can play at most 10 notes and on some instruments (like the organ) we can use the foots to play other 2 notes[1] For many instruments, in particular the ones having a keyboard, the notes-information is all we need to specify a fingering. For other instruments, like for example a guitar, we need additional information. In such cases we use them *extra-information*.

Figure 4 shows examples of fingering. Gray elements are not used. The fingering for piano and organ simply map each note to a finger, numbered from 1 (thumb) through 5 (little), or a foot (left or right). For the guitar we use the notes-information for the left hand: in the example the 2nd and the 5th finger play E (MIDI code 64) and C (MIDI code 60). Moreover the extra information for the left hand tells on which string the fingers should be placed: the 2nd finger on the 4th string and the 5th finger on the 3rd string. Finally the extra-information for the right hand tells which finger of the right hand should pluck the strings specified in the extra-information of the left hand: the 3rd finger should pluck the 3rd string and the 2nd finger the 4th string. For the accordion the extra-information specifies the row of buttons to be used (some notes can be played in different rows).

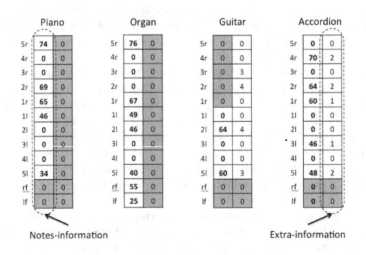

Fig. 4. A fingered score fragment and its matrix representation

Although we have chosen to represent the fingering as a dimensional matrix (just because we have notes-information and associated extra-information), we can store all the fingering information for a score change in one single array of dimension K. The implementation uses $K = 24$ although, depending on the instrument, some entries are always 0.

---

[1] Actually on the organ it is possible to play more than 1 note with each foot. For simplicity we assumed that one can play only one note. In order to accomodate more than one note per foot it is enough to make the array longer.

Given a score S, an entire fingering $F(S)$ is represented as a $K \times N$ matrix, where N is the total number of score-changes in S, and each column represents one fingering-change.

3.2 The ANFIS Model for Learning Fingering

The objective of this network is to learn the preferred fingering, be it that of a single-user musician or that deriving from common practice. The choice of a musician on how to place the fingers for a specific score-change depends on the fingering for the previous score-change and that of the next score-changes. This is because each player tries to move his hands in the most convenient way and as efficiently as possible. Thus the ANFIS network will work with *triples* of consecutive fingering-changes Each instance in the training set is a pair (*triple of fingering-changes, preference*).

To represent each such a pair, we need an array of $3K + 1$ elements, the first $3K$ to represent the three fingering-changes (each one takes K integers), while the last entry of the array will contain the preference that the user gives to this particular fingering.

Let $\{S^1, \ldots, S^M\}$ be a set of scores set and $\{F(S^1), \ldots, F(S^M)\}$ be the corresponding fingerings. We consider all the possible the triples of score-changes $S^i_{j-1} S^i_j S^i_{j+1}$ for all $i = 1, \ldots, M$ and all $j = 2, \ldots, N_i - 1$, where N_i is the number of score changes in S^i (remember that each score-change is a set of notes). Then we count the number of occurrences of a particular fingering for each triple. Such a number (normalized by the total number of appearance of the triple of score-changes to which the fingering is referred) gives the preference for that particular fingering.

3.3 The Differential Evolution Algorithm

The DE algorithm takes as input a score and produces a fingering for the score.

Encoding. The population in our algorithm is made up of individuals that are fingered configurations of the given input score. We represent each individual using the data representation explained in previous sections; that is a chromosome x (individual) is a fingering $x = F(S)$ for the input score S and each fingering-change is a gene of x.

Fitness Measure. The *fitness value* $f(x)$ is defined as follows. Let x be an individual of the population, and $F(S)$ the corresponding fingering. For each $i = 2, \ldots, N - 1$, we consider the triple of consecutive genes $\langle F_{i-1}, F_i, F^{i+1} \rangle$ of $x = F(S)$ and we use the neuro-fuzzy network to evaluate the triple. Let $f(i)$ be the value returned by the neuro-fuzzy network. The overall evaluation of x is

$$f(x) = f(F(S)) = \sum_{i=2}^{N-1} f(i).$$

While evaluating chromosomes our algorithm computes also important information. In particular for each individual we identify points that we call *cut points*.

The cut point is the triple of consecutive genes (score-changes) that contains the worst value. We used a similar approach in [1,2], for a different problem. In the rest of the paper we will identify cut point i with the triple of genes $F_{i-1}F_iF_{i+1}$ that gives the minimum value over all possible i.

Initial Population. We start with a random initial population. We build chromosomes by selecting a random values for entry of the fingering configuration.

Mutation (perturbation) Operator. Now we have to specify how we compute the perturbation. Since the individuals of our problem cannot be described as real numbers over a continuous domain we have to introduce different ways to define the "differential" mutation. To do so we will define specialized '+' (addition) and '×' (multiplication) operations that work with the individuals of our problem.

Let F^1, F^2, F^3 be the three parents chosen at random. We have to compute the mutant vector. To do so, we need to introduce the '+' and '×' operation for the individuals of our problem.

The mutant vector is given by $v = F^1 + Z \times (F^2 - F^3)$, where Z is the scale factor. The "difference" F^2 and F^3 between two fingering is a vector of integers values and is computed as follows. Let $S_i = \{a_1, a_2, \ldots, a_k\}$ be the notes in the ith score-change. For each note $a_j, j = 1, \ldots, k$, the jth component of the difference for the notes-information D_j is given by the change of position of note a_j from F^2 to F^3. For example if note a_j is played by the 4th finger of the right hand in F^2 while in F^3 is played with the 5th finger of the right hand, then $D_j = -1$. For the extra-information, the difference is defined in a similar way (the exact definition depends on the instrument).

To increase the perturbation we use the crossover operator. The crossover operator starts from the mutant and the target vector and produces the trial vector. Let $v = (M_1, \ldots, M_N)$ be the mutant vector. The target vector is x_i. Let $x_i = (G_1, \ldots, G^N)$. Moreover let the trial vector be $u = (T_1, \ldots, T_N)$.

We augment the basic DE algorithm by using two possible crossover:

1. Binomial Crossover. That is, the trial vector is obtained as:

$$T_j = \begin{cases} M_j & if(rand([0,1])) \leq \text{CR} \ \ or \ \ j = i \\ G_j & otherwise \end{cases}$$

   where CR is a user-defined crossover threshold in the range $[0, 1]$ and *rand(j)* is the jth evaluation of a uniform random number generator that returns numbers in the range $[0, 1]$.

2. Cut crossover. In this case we exploit the cut point to perform a crossover operation. Let k be the cut point in the target vector x_i. Then the trial vector u is obtained considering the two individuals $F^1 = (G^1, \ldots, G^k, M^{k+1}, \ldots, M^N)$ and $F^2 = (M^1, \ldots, M^k, G^{k+1}, \ldots, G^N)$. Finally the trial vector u is simply the individual $F_z, z = \{1, 2\}$ with the best fitness value.

To choose which crossover we have to use we exploit a probability distribution $\mathcal{P}_C = (p_n, p_c)$, where the specific choice for the two probabilities can be tuned to improve the results of the tests.

4 Test Results

In order to evaluate the proposed system we have run several tests. As test cases we have used three type of instruments: the piano, the guitar and the chromatic accordion.

4.1 ANFIS Model: Training, Checking and Test Results

Our ANFIS model for fingering preferences is developed using the Matlab Fuzzy Logic Toolbox. For each instrument we selected a set of already fingered scores from which we extracted a data set of triples of fingering changes for each instrument and we used them as shown in Table 1.

Table 1. Number of data instances and performance measures of the ANFIS network

	total instances	training instances	checking instances	testing instances	learning epochs	minimum MSE	coefficient of determination
Piano	1100	770	115	115	110	0.112	0.8722
Guitar	1280	896	192	192	132	0.124	0.8018
Accordion	1030	721	155	154	147	0.132	0.8671

The ANFIS network has been created using generalized bell membership functions with five parameters. To evaluate the errors we used the *MSE* (Mean Square Error) function. We trained the network using the hybrid learning algorithm over a maximum of 200 epochs. For the piano, the total sum of the MES converged to a minimum of 0.112 after 110 training epochs. Therefore for the final learning we used 110 epochs. See Table 1 for the other instruments.

After training we validated the ANFIS network against the testing instances. The coefficient of determination, a number in $[0, 1]$ which specifies the goodness of the network, with 1 being the best possible result, is shown in Table 1.

4.2 Test Results and Conclusions

We have run several tests varying the size of the initial population and the number of generations. The other parameters involved in the tests are the scale factor Z, the crossover threshold CR and the probability distribution $\mathcal{P}_C$ for the crossover operation. We have used $Z = 0.7$ and $CR = 0.8$ as suggested in [7]. For $\mathcal{P}_C$ We have tried several choices and the one that gave best results is $\mathcal{P}_C = \{\frac{1}{3}, \frac{2}{3}\}$.

Finally we have asked an expert musician to evaluate the output of the DE algorithm. We have considered two pieces for piano from the standard jazz repertoire, *Round Midnight* by Thelonious Monk and *All Blues* by Miles Davis, two pieces for guitar from the standard Latin jazz repertoire, *Wave* and *How Insensitive* by Jobim, two pieces for accordion from the tango repertoire, *Libertango* by Astor Piazzolla and *A Evaristo Carriego* by Eduardo Rovira.

For each instrument, we have requested the musician tell which fingerings were correct and which ones were wrong. The percentage of correct fingerings was 89.2% for the piano, 87.3% for the guitar and 85.3% for the accordion.

Finally we have compared the DE algorithm with a standard genetic algorithm (GA) with same features, that is using the same chromosome representation, the same fitness evaluation function, the same ANFIS network. The DE algorithm always outperforms the genetic algorithm. Future work include the investigation of DE variants (see for example [8]).

References

1. De Prisco, R., Zaccagnino, G., Zaccagnino, R.: EvoBassComposer: a multi-objective genetic algorithm for 4-voice compositions. In: Proceedings of the 12th ACM Annual Conference on Genetic and Evolutionary Computation, GECCO 2010, pp. 817–818 (2010)
2. De Prisco, R., Zaccagnino, G., Zaccagnino, R.: A multi-objective differential evolution algorithm for 4-voice compositions. In: Proceedings of IEEE Symposium on Differential Evolution, SDE 2011, pp. 817–818 (2011)
3. Emura, N., Miura, M., Hama, N., Yanagida, M.: A system giving the optimal chord-form sequence for playing a guitar. Acoustical Science and Technology (January 2006)
4. Kandel, A.: Fuzzy expert systems. CRC Press, Boca Raton (1992)
5. Jang, J.R.: ANFIS: An Adaptive-Nework-Based Fuzzy Inference System. IEEE Transactions on Systems, Man, and Cybernetics 23(3) (May/June 1993)
6. Miura, M., Yanagida, M.: Finger-position determination and tablature generation for novice guitar players. In: Proceedings of the 7th International Conference on Music Perception and Cognition (2002)
7. Neri, F., Tirronen, V.: Scale factor local search in differential evolution. Memetic Comp. 1, 153–171 (2009)
8. Neri, F., Tirronen, V.: Recent Advances in Differential Evolution: A Review and Experimental Analysis. Artificial Intelligence Review 33(1), 61–106
9. Radisavljevic, A., Driessen, P.: Path difference learning for guitar fingering problem. In: Proceedings of the International Computer Music Conference (2004)
10. Sayegh, S.: Fingering for string instruments with the optimum path paradigm. Computer Music Journal 6(13), 76–84 (1989)
11. Storn, R., Price, K.: Differential evolution: a simple and efficient adaptive scheme for global optimization over continuous spaces. Technical Report TR-95-012, International Computer Science Institute, Berkeley
12. Takagi, T., Sugeno, M.: Fuzzy identification of systems and its applications to modeling and control. Proceedings of IEEE Transactions on Systems, Man, and Cybernetics 15, 116–132 (1985)
13. Tuohy, D., Potter, W.: A genetic algorithm for the automatic generation of playable guitar tablature. In: Proceedings of the International Computer Music Conference (2004)
14. Tuohy, D., Potter, W.: GA-based music arranging for guitar. In: Procedings of IEEE Congress on Evolutionary Computation, CEC 2006 (2006)

Hybridization of Differential Evolution and Particle Swarm Optimization in a New Algorithm: DEPSO-2S

Abbas El Dor, Maurice Clerc, and Patrick Siarry

Université de Paris-Est Créteil
Laboratoire Images, Signaux et Systémes Intelligents, LiSSi (E.A. 3956)
61 Avenue du Général de Gaulle, 94010 Créteil, France
abbas.eldor@u-pec.fr

Abstract. PSO-2S is a multi-swarm PSO algorithm using charged particles in a partitioned search space for continuous optimization problems. This algorithm uses two kinds of swarms, a main one that gathers the best particles of auxiliary ones. In this paper, we present a new variant of PSO-2S, called DEPSO-2S, which is a hybridization of DE and PSO. DE was used, in this variant, to construct the main swarm. We analyze the performance of the proposed approach on seven real problems. The obtained results show the efficiency of the proposed algorithm.

Keywords: Particle swarm optimization, Differential evolution, Multi-swarm, Global optimization, Partitioned search space.

1 Introduction

Particle swarm optimization (PSO) [3] is an emerging evolutionary computation technique, inspired by social behavior simulations of bird flocking and fish schooling. The system is initialized with a population of random solutions and searches for optima by updating generations. In PSO, the potential solutions, called particles, fly through the problem space by following the current optimum particles until termination criterion is satisfied. The advantage of PSO is that it is easy to implement. It has been successfully applied in many research areas and real problems [7]. As PSO, differential evolution (DE) is an optimization method [8], it works by iteratively trying to improve a candidate solution with regard to a given measure of quality. It is inspired by genetic algorithms and evolutionary strategies. Currently, a large number of industrial and scientific applications rely on DE [10].

Various attempts have been made to improve the performance of standard PSO [10], including such changes as hybrid models, biology-inspired mechanisms, and some basic modifications in the velocity update equations (inertia weight w, topology of informants, ...). PSO-2S [1] is a variant of the standard PSO, which is based on several initializations in different zones of the search space using charged particles. This algorithm uses two kinds of swarms, a main one

L. Rutkowski et al. (Eds.): SIDE 2012 and EC 2012, LNCS 7269, pp. 57–65, 2012.

that gathers the best particles of auxiliary ones initialized several times. PSO-2S has been tested successfully on artificial problems of 10 and 30 dimensions [1], however, in this work we focus only on real lower-dimension problems [6].

In this paper, we present a new variant of PSO-2S, called DEPSO-2S, which consists of the hybridization of PSO and DE. Hence, the particles of the main swarm are created by the algorithm of DE. At first, the particles are randomly initialized in different zones, then DE performs K generations to obtain the best solution found in each zone. Once the main swarm is created, PSO is used to continue the search until the stopping criterion of the algorithm is satisfied.

This paper is organized as follows: in section 2, we present briefly the particle swarm optimization. In section 3, the differential evolution is presented. In section 4, PSO-2S and the new variant DEPSO-2S are described. Experimental analysis and comparisons are done in section 5, followed by a conclusion in section 6.

2   Overview of Particle Swarm Optimization

The particle swarm optimization (PSO) [3] is inspired originally by the social and cognitive behavior existing in the bird flocking. The algorithm is initialized with a population of particles randomly distributed in the search space, and each particle is assigned a randomized velocity. Each particle represents a potential solution to the problem.

In this paper, the swarm size is denoted by s, and the search space is n-dimensional. In general, the particles have three attributes: the current position $X_i = (x_{i,1}, x_{i,2}, ..., x_{i,n})$, the current velocity vector $V_i = (v_{i,1}, v_{i,2}, ..., v_{i,n})$ and the past best position $Pbest_i = (p_{i,1}, p_{i,2}, ..., p_{i,n})$. The best position found in the neighborhood of the particle i is denoted by $Gbest_i = (g_1, g_2, ..., g_n)$. These attributes are used to update iteratively the state of each particle in the swarm. The objective function to be minimized is denoted by f. The velocity vector V_i of each particle is updated using the best position it visited so far and the overall best position visited by its neighbors. Then, the position of each particle is updated using its updated velocity per iteration. At each step, the velocity of each particle and its new position are updated as follows:

$$v_{i,j}(t+1) = wv_{i,j}(t) + c_1 r_{1_{i,j}}(t) [pbest_{i,j}(t) - x_{i,j}(t)] + c_2 r_{2_{i,j}}(t) [gbest_{i,j}(t) - x_{i,j}(t)] \tag{1}$$

$$x_{i,j}(t+1) = x_{i,j}(t) + v_{i,j}(t+1) \tag{2}$$

where w is called inertia weight, c_1, c_2 are the learning factors and r_1, r_2 are two random numbers selected uniformly in the range $[0, 1]$.

3   Overview of Differential Evolution

The Differential Evolution (DE) is inspired by Genetic Algorithms (GA) and Evolutionary Strategies (ES). Hence, GA changes the structure of individuals using the mutation and crossover operators, while ES achieves self-adaptation by a geometric manipulation of individuals. This combination has been implemented through an operation, simple but powerful, of mutation vectors proposed in 1995 by K. Price and R. Storn [8]. Such as PSO, DE is a direct parallel method that uses N vectors of n-dimensions, where:

$$x_{i,t}, i = 1, 2, ..., N \tag{3}$$

is the population at generation t and N is the size of population.

The standard DE uses three techniques (mutation, crossover and selection) for the movement of the agents as well as GA. At first, a vector $x_{i,t}$ is randomly selected, which is the current vector of the agent i at generation t. Then, $x_{i,t}$ moves according to the three following operations:

a - *Mutation:* For each current vector (target vector) $x_{i,t}$, a mutant vector $v_{i,t+1}$ is generated, which will be calculated using the following formula:

$$v_{i,t+1} = x_{r_1,t} + F.(x_{r_2,t} - x_{r_3,t}) \tag{4}$$

where, r_1, r_2 et $r_3 \in \{1, 2, \ldots, N\}$ are randomly selected integers such that r_1, r_2, r_3 and i are all different. F is a real and constant factor $\in [0, 2]$.

b - *Crossover:* The crossover operation is introduced to increase the diversity of the target vectors. This operation generates a new vector (trial vector) $u_{i,t+1} = (u_{1i,t+1}, u_{2i,t+1}, ..., u_{ni,t+1})$, as follows:

$$u_{ji,t+1} = \begin{cases} v_{1i,t+1} & \text{if } (randb(j) \leq CR) \text{ or } j = rnbr(i) \\ x_{ji,t} & \text{if } (randb(j) > CR) \text{ and } j \neq rnbr(i) \end{cases} \quad j \in [1, 2, \ldots, n]. \tag{5}$$

where $rnbr(j)$ is the jth random number $\in [0, 1]$, CR is the crossover factor $\in [0, 1]$ and $rnbr(i)$ is a random index $\in \{1, 2, \ldots, N\}$.

c - *Selection:* To determine which vector, the trial vector $u_{i,t+1}$ or the target vector $x_{i,t}$, should become a member of generation $t + 1$, the fitness function values of these two vectors are compared. Indeed, we keep the vector that has the smallest fitness function value, in the case of minimization.

4   The Proposed Method

4.1   The Original Version of PSO-2S

In this section, we present the first version of PSO-2S [1]. PSO-2S consists of using three main ideas. The first is to use two kinds of swarms: a main swarm, denoted by S1, and s auxiliary ones, denoted by S2$_i$, where $1 \leq i \leq s$. The second idea is to partition the search space into several zones in which the auxiliary swarms are initialized (the number of zones is equal to the number of auxiliary swarms, thus is equal to s). The last idea is to use the concept of the electrostatic repulsion heuristic to diversify the particles for each auxiliary swarm in each zone.

To construct S1, we propose to perform the auxiliary swarms S2$_i$ several times in different areas, and then each best particle for each S2$_i$ is saved and considered as a new particle of S1. To do so, the population of each auxiliary swarm is initialized randomly in different zones (each S2$_i$ is initialized in its corresponding zone i). After each of these initializations, K displacements of particles, of each S2$_i$, are performed in the same way of standard PSO. Then the best solution found by each auxiliary swarm is added to S1. The number of initializations of S2$_i$ is equal to the number of particles in S1.

As we mentioned above the second idea is to partition the search space $[min_d, max_d]^N$ into several zones (max_{zone} zones). Then, we calculate the $center_d$ and the $step_d$ of each dimension separately, according to (6) and (7). The $step_d$ are similar in the case of using a square search space.

$$center_d = (max_d - min_d)/2 \qquad (6)$$

$$step_d = center_d/max_{zone} \qquad (7)$$

where max_{zone} is a fixed value, and d is the current dimension ($1 \leq d \leq N$).

The sizes of the zones of the partitioned search space are different ($Z_1 < Z_2 < \ldots < Z_{max_{zone}}$). Therefore, the number of particles in S2$_i$, denoted by $S2_{isize}$, depends on its corresponding zone size. Indeed, a small zone takes less particles and the number of particles increases when the zone becomes larger. The size of each auxiliary swarm is calculated as follows:

$$S2_{isize} = num_{zone} * nb_{particle} \qquad (8)$$

where $num_{zone} = 1, 2, \ldots, max_{zone}$, is the current zone number and $nb_{particle}$ is a fixed value. After the initializations of the auxiliary swarms in different zones (Z_i, S2$_i$), an electrostatic repulsion heuristic is applied to diversify the particles and to widely cover the search space [2]. This technique is used in an agent-based optimization algorithm for dynamic environments [4]. Therefore, this procedure is applied in each zone separately, hence each particle is considered as an electron. Then a force of $1/r^2$ is applied, on the particles of each zone, until the maximum displacement of a particle during an iteration becomes lower than a given threshold ϵ (where r is the distance between two particles, ϵ is typically equal to 10^{-4}). At each iteration of this procedure, the particles are projected in the middle of the current zone, before reapplying the heuristic repulsion.

4.2   The New Variant of PSO-2S (DEPSO-2S)

DEPSO-2S is a new variant of PSO-2S, which is based on the hybridization of two metaheuristics (DE and PSO). These two metaheuristics have been hybridized [9], and used in a large number of industrial and scientific applications [7]. Hence we propose to hybridize these two algorithms.

This new version consists in using the principle of DE to initialize the particles of the auxiliary swarms, rather than using the standard PSO to construct the main swarm, as it is performed in the old version of PSO-2S. Modifications of DE are proposed to fit the two algorithms together and help to achieve better results.

These modifications are inspired from a variant of DE, denoted by DELG [5]. DELG uses the concept of neighborhood of each vector that is designed to balance the capabilities of exploration and exploitation of the differential evolution, without the need to evaluate the function. This is done through the use of two operators of mutation (the local mutation and global mutation). DELG uses a ring topology, where each particle is connected to k particles in the swarm.

Now for every vector X_i we define a neighborhood of radius k, consisting of vectors $X_{i-k}, \ldots, X_i, \ldots, X_{i+k}$. For each particle i, a local mutation is applied by using the fittest vector in the neighborhood of particle i, and two other vectors chosen from the same neighborhoods. The expression of this mutation is given by:

$$L_{i,t} = X_{i,t} + \lambda.(X_{nbest,t} - X_{i,t}) + F.(X_{p,t} - X_{q,t}) \tag{9}$$

where the subscript *nbest* corresponds to the best vector in the neighborhood of X_i and $p, q \in (i - k, i + k)$. Moreover, for all vectors X_i, a global mutation is applied by using the global best particle with two other randomly selected vectors in the population. The global mutation is expressed as:

$$G_{i,t} = X_{i,t} + \lambda'.(X_{best,t} - X_{i,t}) + F'.(X_{r,t} - X_{r,t}) \tag{10}$$

where the subscript *best* denotes the best vector in the entire population, and $r, s \in (1, n)$. Indeed, the local mutation favors the exploration and the global mutation encourages the exploitation. The two mutations are combined using a scalar weight that changes over the time to provide a good balance between local search and global search. The equation for this combination of mutations is calculated as follows:

$$V_{i,t} = w_{DE}.G_{i,t} + (1 - w_{DE}).L_{i,t} \tag{11}$$

The weight factor varies linearly with time, as follows:

$$w_{DE} = w_{min} + (w_{max} - w_{min}).(\frac{iter}{MAXIT_{DE}}) \tag{12}$$

where *iter* is the current iteration number, $MAXIT_{DE}$ is the maximum number of iterations allowed for DE and w_{max}, w_{min} denote the maximum and minimum values of the weight, respectively, with $w_{max}, w_{min} \in (0, 1)$.

Finally, to improve the performance of the hybridization of PSO-2S with DELG, and to make DELG compatible with the strategy of partitioning of the search space, which was used by PSO-2S, several modifications have been proposed. Equation 11 was changed to make the current zone dynamic: at the beginning of the search, the vector can leave its zone to explore more peripheral regions of the search space, then it returns progressively to the interior of its zone. The new formula for the combination of global and local mutations is:

$$V_{i,t} = (1 - w_{DE}).G_{i,t} + (1 - w_{DE}).L_{i,t} \tag{13}$$

Choosing $w_{min} < 0.5$ and $w_{max} > 0.5$, the vector $\boldsymbol{V}_{i,t}$ is then free to leave its area of search when the values of t are close to 0. $\boldsymbol{V}_{i,t}$ is then progressively reduced, when t increases.

5 Experiments and Discussion

5.1 Real Life Problems

F1: Gas transmission design

$$Min\ f(x) = \begin{cases} 8.61 * 10^5 x_1^{1/2} x_2 x_3^{-2/3} (x_2^2 - 1)^{-1/2} + 3.69 * 10^4 x_3 + \\ 7.72 * 10^8 x_1^{-1} x_2^{0.219} - 765.43 * 10^6 x_1. \end{cases} \tag{14}$$

Bounds:

$$10 \leq x_1 \leq 55, \qquad 1.1 \leq x_2 \leq 2, \qquad 10 \leq x_3 \leq 40$$

F2: Optimal capacity of gas production facilities

$$Min\ f(x) = \begin{cases} 61.8 + 5.72x_1 + 0.2623 \left[(40 - x_1)\, ln\left(\frac{x_2}{200}\right) \right]^{-0.85} + \\ 0.087\, (40 - x_1)\, ln\left(\frac{x_2}{200}\right) + 700.23 x_2^{-0.75}. \end{cases} \tag{15}$$

Bounds:

$$17.5 \leq x_1 \leq 40, \qquad 300 \leq x_2 \leq 600$$

F3: Design of a gear train

$$Min\ f(x) = \left\{ \frac{1}{6.931} - \frac{T_d T_b}{T_a T_f} \right\}^2 = \left\{ \frac{1}{6.931} - \frac{x_1 x_2}{x_3 x_4} \right\}^2. \tag{16}$$

Bounds:

$$12 \leq x_i \leq 60, \quad i = 1, 2, 3, 4 \text{ and } x_i \text{ should be integers.}$$

F4: Optimal thermohydraulic performance of an artificially roughened air heater

$$Max\ L = 2.51\ ln\ e^+ + 5.5 - 0.1 R_M - G_H. \tag{17}$$

where: $R_M = 0.95 x_2^{0.53}$, $G_H = 4.5 (e^+)^{0.28} (0.7)^{0.57}$, $e^+ = x_1 x_3 (\bar{f}/2)^{1/2}$,
$$\bar{f} = (f_s + f_r)/2,$$
$f_s = 0.079 x_3^{-0.25}$, $f_r = 2(0.95 x_3^{0.53} + 2.5 ln(1/2x_1)^2 - 3.75)^{-2}.$

Bounds:

$$0.02 \leq x_1 \leq 0.8,\ 10 \leq x_2 \leq 40,\ 3000 \leq x_3 \leq 20000.$$

F5: Frequency modulation sound parameter identification

$$y(t) = a_1 * sin(w_1 * t * \theta + a_2 * sin(w_2 * t * \theta + a_3 * sin(w_3 * t * \theta))). \quad (18)$$

with $\theta = (2.\pi/100)$. The fitness function is defined as the sum of square error between the evolved data and the model data, as follows: $f(a_1, w_1, a_2, w_2, a_3, w_3) = \sum_{t=0}^{100} (y(t) - y_0(t))^2$. The model data are given by the following equation:

$$y_0(t) = 1.0 * sin(5.0 * t * \theta + 1.5 * sin(4.8 * t * \theta + 2.0 * sin(4.9 * t * \theta))). \quad (19)$$

Bounds:

$$-6.4 \le a_i, w_i \le 6.35, \ i = 1, 2, 3.$$

F6: The spread spectrum radar poly-phase code design problem

$$Min \ f(X) = max \{f_1(X), \ldots, f_{2m}(X)\}. \quad (20)$$

where $X = \{(x_1, \ldots, x_n) \in R^n \mid 0 \le x_j \le 2\pi, j = 1, 2, \ldots, n\}$ and $m = 2n - 1$,
with: $f_{2i-1}(x) = \sum_{j=i}^{n} cos \left(\sum_{k=|2i-j-1|+1}^{j} x_k \right) \quad i = 1, 2, \ldots, n;$
$f_{2i}(x) = 0.5 + \sum_{j=i+1}^{n} cos \left(\sum_{k=|2i-j|+1}^{j} x_k \right) \quad i = 1, 2, \ldots, n - 1;$
$f_{m+i}(X) = -f_i(X), i = 1, 2, \ldots, m.$

5.2 Experimental Settings and Parameter Selection

The experiments compared four algorithms including the proposed DEPSO-2S, DE, SPSO2007 and PSO-2S. Seven real problems with different dimensions are used in this comparison. The four algorithms were implemented in C.

For DE and DEPSO-2S, we chose $Cr = 0.5$ and $F = F' = \lambda = \lambda' = 0.2$. For SPSO2007, PSO-2S and DEPSO-2S, $w = 0.72$ and $c_1 = c_2 = 1.19$ were used. The specific parameters of PSO-2S and DEPSO-2S. $nb_{particle}$ and max_{zone} are set to 2 and 20, respectively, for all problems. Hence, the size of the main swarm S1 is equal to max_{zone} and the number K of generations of swarms S2 is set to 5. The maximum number of function evaluations ($Nb.\ evals$) depends on each problem and problem dimension D is presented in Table 1.

5.3 Experimental Results and Discussion

In experiments, each algorithm was run 30 times and mean best value and standard deviation were calculated. Table 1 presents the dimension of the problem, the number of function evaluations ($Nb.\ evals$), the mean best value and the standard deviation ($mean \pm std.\ dev.$) of 30 runs. The best results among those obtained by the four algorithms are shown in bold.

From the experiments, we can notice that DEPSO-2S obtains the best results on most of the problems used. Thus, this algorithm leads to a remarkable improvement compared to the previous PSO-2S. DEPSO-2S outperforms the other tested algorithms on $F1$, $F3$, $F5$, $F6_{(a)}$ and $F6_{(b)}$. It obtains similar results on $F2$ with SPSO2007 and PSO-2S, and it is outperformed by SPSO2007 on $F4$.

Table 1. Fitness value and standard deviation on seven problems

Function	D	Nb. evals	DE	SPSO − 2007	PSO − 2S	DEPSO − 2S
$F1$	3	24000	2.96438e+006 ± 0.264829	2.96440e+006 ± 4.66e-010	7.43233e+006 ± 2.28e-009	**2.96438e+006 ± 1.40e-009**
$F2$	2	16000	1.69844e+002 ± 0.000021	**1.69844e+002 ± 1.14e-013**	**1.69844e+002 ± 1.14e-013**	1.69844e+002 ± 1.14e-013
$F3$	4	32000	1.76382e-008 ± 3.51577e-008	1.43626e-009 ± 5.05e-009	1.40108e-010 ± 3.35e-010	**1.39732e-010 ± 2.65e-010**
$F4$	3	24000	4.21422 ± 5.08471e-07	**7.26733e-016 ± 5.69e-016**	2.31987e-006 ± 1.25e-005	3.17128e-005 ± 7.54e-005
$F5$	6	144000	3.01253 ± 0.367899	9.75177e+000 ± 6.65e+000	2.58539e+000 ± 3.30e+000	**2.07431e+000 ± 3.07e+000**
$F6_{(a)}$	10	240000	0.626379 ± 0.0821391	5.00750e-001 ± 1.61e-001	3.50806e-001 ± 7.19e-002	**3.00490e-001 ± 7.07e-002**
$F6_{(b)}$	20	480000	1.07813 ± 0.0812955	8.65976e-001 ± 2.52e-001	5.39793e-001 ± 1.25e-001	**5.37990e-001 ± 8.25e-002**

6   Conclusion

A new improved PSO-2S, based on the hybridization of differential evolution and particle swarm optimization was presented. The principle of DE has been used to discover the zones in the search space and create the main swarm of PSO-2S. Experimental results indicate that DEPSO-2S improves the search performance significantly, on most of the real-world problems tested.

References

1. El Dor, A., Clerc, M., Siarry, P.: A multi-swarm PSO using charged particles in a partitioned search space for continuous optimization. In: Computational Optimization and Applications, pp. 1–25 (2011)
2. Conway, J., Sloane, N.: Sphere packings, lattices and groups, 2nd edn. Springer, Heidelberg (1993); 3rd edn. (1999)
3. Kennedy, J.: A new optimizer using particle swarm theory. In: Proceedings of the Sixth International Symposium on Micro Machine and Human Science, pp. 39–43 (1995)
4. Lepagnot, J., Nakib, A., Oulhadj, H., Siarry, P.: A new multiagent algorithm for dynamic continuous optimization. International Journal of Applied Metaheuristic Computing 1(1), 16–38 (2010)
5. Chakraborty, U.K., Konar, A., Das, S.: Differential Evolution with Local Neighborhood. In: Proceedings of the IEEE Congress on Evolutionary Computation, pp. 2042–2049 (2006)
6. Ali, M., Pant, M., Singh, V.P.: Two Modified Differential Evolution Algorithms and their Applications to Engineering Design Problems. World Journal of Modeling and Simulation 6(1), 72–80 (2010)

7. Poli, R.: Analysis of the publications on the applications of particle swarm optimisation. Journal of Artificial Evolution and Applications 2008(10), 1–10 (2008)
8. Storn, R., Price, K.: Differential evolution - A Simple and Efficient Heuristic for Global Optimization over Continuous Spaces. Journal of Global Optimization 11(4), 341–359 (1997)
9. Thangaraj, R., Pant, M., Abraham, A., Bouvry, P.: Particle swarm optimization: Hybridization perspectives and experimental illustrations. Applied Mathematics and Computation 217(12), 5208–5226 (2011)
10. Das, S., Abraham, A., Konar, A.: Particle swarm optimization and differential evolution algorithms: technical analysis, applications and hybridization perspectives. SCI, vol. 116, pp. 1–38 (2008)

A Hybrid Artificial Bee Colony Algorithm
for Graph 3-Coloring

Iztok Fister Jr., Iztok Fister, and Janez Brest

University of Maribor,
Faculty of Electrical Engineering and Computer Science,
Smetanova 17, 2000 Maribor, Slovenia
iztok.fister@guest.arnes.si,
{iztok.fister,janez.brest}@uni-mb.si

Abstract. The Artificial Bee Colony (ABC) is the name of an optimization algorithm that was inspired by the intelligent behavior of a honey
bee swarm. It is widely recognized as a quick, reliable, and efficient methods for solving optimization problems. This paper proposes a hybrid ABC
(HABC) algorithm for graph 3-coloring, which is a well-known discrete
optimization problem. The results of HABC are compared with results
of the well-known graph coloring algorithms of today, i.e., the Tabucol
and Hybrid Evolutionary algorithm (HEA), and results of the traditional
evolutionary algorithm with SAW method (EA-SAW). Extensive exper-
imentations has shown that the HABC matched the competitive results
of the best graph coloring algorithms, and did better than the traditional heuristics EA-SAW when solving equi-partite, flat, and random
generated medium-sized graphs.

Keywords: combinatorial optimization, graph 3-coloring, artificial bee
colony optimization, swarm intelligence, bee's behavior.

1 Introduction

Graph coloring represents a test bed for many newly developed algorithms because of its simple definition, which states: How to color a graph G with the k
colors, so that none of the vertices connected with an edge have the same color.
The coloring c is *proper* if no two connected vertices are assigned to the same
color. A graph is k-*colorable* if it has a proper k-*coloring*. The minimum k for
which a graph G is k-*colorable* is called its *chromatic number* $\chi(G)$.

Many approaches for solving the graph coloring problem (GCP) have been
proposed over the time [12,20]. The most natural way to solve this problem is,
however, in a greedy fashion, where the vertices of the graph are ordered into
a permutation, and colored sequential. Thus, the quality of coloring depends
on the permutation of the vertices. For example, the DSatur algorithm [3], one
of the best traditional heuristics for graph coloring today, orders the vertices
v according to *saturation degrees* $\rho(v)$. The saturation degree represents the
number of distinctly colored vertices adjacent to the vertex v. Furthermore,
DSatur's ordering is calculated dynamically during the coloring process.

L. Rutkowski et al. (Eds.): SIDE 2012 and EC 2012, LNCS 7269, pp. 66–74, 2012.

Many heuristic methods have been developed for larger instances [12] because exact algorithms can only color instances of up to 100 vertices. These methods can be divided into local search methods [1] and hybrid algorithms [19]. The most important representative of the former is Tabucol [15], which utilizes the tabu search, as proposed by Glover [14]. Later were combined local search methods with evolutionary algorithms and improved the results of pure Tabucol, as for example, the hybrid genetic algorithm by Fleurent and Ferland [10], and the hybrid evolutionary algorithm (HEA) by Galinier and Hao [11].

Swarm intelligence is the collective behavior of a self-organized system. Birds, insects, ants, and fish use collective behavior for foraging and defending. These individuals are looking for good food sources and help each other when a lack of food has arisen. This concept was introduced into the computer's world by Kennedy and Eberhart [18]. Moreover, it was successfully applied to several problem domains, for example, particle swarm optimization, which achieves good results during antenna optimization [24]. In addition, ant colony optimization reaches good results by solving the traveling-salesman person [6]. Finally, the artificial bee colony algorithm, proposed by Karaboga and Basturk [17], exhibited excellent results when solving combinatorial optimization problems [21,25].

This paper focuses on the artificial bee colony (ABC) algorithm for graph 3-coloring (3-GCP), which belongs to a class of $NP\text{-}complete$ [13] problems. There, the real-valued weights w are assigned to the vertices v. These weights determine how difficult the vertex is to color. The higher the weight, the earlier the vertex should be colored. Thus, weights define the order in which the vertices should be colored. This ordering is used by the DSatur traditional algorithm for constructing 3-coloring. The ABC algorithm incorporates DSatur as a decoder. In this manner, the ABC algorithm acts as a meta-heuristic concerned for a generation of new solutions (vector of weights), whilst the quality of the solution (its fitness) is evaluated by DSatur. This approach is not new: it was used by the evolutionary algorithm with SAW method (EA-SAW) of Eiben et al. [8], and by the hybrid self-adaptive differential evolution of Fister et al. [9]. In the former case, instead of Dsatur, a greedy heuristic was applied as a decoder. Finally, the proposed ABC algorithm was hybridized with a *random walk with direction exloitation* (RWDE) [23] local search heuristic. This local search heuristic was applied in place of the original sending scouts function and focuses itself on discovering new food sources in the vicinity of the current sources.

The results of the proposed hybrid artificial bee colony algorithm for graph 3-coloring (HABC) was compared with the results obtained with Tabucol, HEA, and EA-SAW for solving an extensive set of random medium-scale graphs generated by the Culberson graph generator [5]. A comparison between these algorithms shows that the results of the proposed HABC algorithm are comparable with results of the other algorithms used in the experiments.

The structure of this paper is as follows: In Section 2, the 3-GCP is discussed, in detail. The HABC is described in Section 3, whilst the experiments and results are presented in Section 4. The paper is concluded with a discussion about the quality of the results, and directions for further work are outlined.

2   Graph 3-Coloring

3-coloring of a graph $G = (V, E)$ is a mapping $c : V \to C$, where $C = \{1, 2, 3\}$ is a set of three colors [2]. Note that V in the graph definition denotes a set of vertices $v \in V$ and E a set of edges that associates each edge $e \in E$ to an unordered pair of vertices (v_i, v_j) for $i = 1 \ldots n \wedge j = 1 \ldots n$.

3-GCP can be formally defined as a constraint satisfaction problem (CSP) that is represented as the pair $\langle S, \phi \rangle$, where $S = C^n$ with $C^n = \{1, 2, 3\}$ denotes the free search space, in which all solutions $c \in C^n$ are feasible and ϕ a Boolean function on S (also a feasibility condition) that divides search space into feasible and unfeasible regions. This function is composed of constraints belonging to edges. In fact, to each $e \in E$ the corresponding constraint b_e is assigned by $b_e(\langle c_1, \ldots, c_n \rangle) = true$ if and only if $e = (v_i, v_j)$ and $c_i \neq c_j$. Assume that $B^i = \{b_e | e = (v_i, v_j) \wedge j = 1 \ldots m\}$ defines the set of constraints belonging to variable v_i. Then, the feasibility condition ϕ is expressed as a conjunction of all the constraints $\phi(c) = \wedge_{v \in V} B^v(c)$.

Typically, constraints are handled indirectly in the sense of the penalty function that transforms the CSP into free optimization problem (FOP) [7] (also unconstrained problem). Thus, those infeasible solutions that are far away from a feasible region are punished by higher penalties. The penalty function that is also used as a fitness function here, is expressed as:

$$f(c) = min \sum_{i=0}^{n} \psi(c, B^i), \tag{1}$$

where the function $\psi(c, B^i)$ is defined as:

$$\psi(c, B^i) = \begin{cases} 1 & \text{if } c \text{ violates at least one } b_e \in B^i, \\ 0 & \text{otherwise.} \end{cases} \tag{2}$$

In fact, Eq. (1) can be used as a feasibility condition in the sense that $\phi(c) = true$ if and only if $f(c) = 0$. Note that this equation evaluates the number of constraint violations and determines the quality of solution $c \in C^n$.

3   HABC for Graph 3-Coloring

In the ABC algorithm, the colony of artificial bees consists of three groups [27]: employed bees, onlookers, and scouts. The employed bees discover each food source, that is, only one employed bee exists for each food source. The employed bees share information about food sources with onlooker bees, in their hive. Then, the onlooker bees can choose a food sources to forage. Interestingly, those employed bees whose food source is exhausted either by employed or onlooker bees, becomes scouts. The ABC algorithm is formally described in Algorithm 1, from which it can be seen that each cycle of the ABC search process (statements within a **while** loop) consists of three functions:

- SendEmployedBees(): sending the employed bees onto the food sources and evaluating their nectar amounts,
- SendOnlookerBees(): sharing the information about food sources with employed bees, selecting the proper food source and evaluating their nectar amounts,
- SendScouts(): determining the scout bees and then sending them onto possibly new food sources.

Algorithm 1. Pseudo code of the ABC algorithm

1: Init();
2: **while** !TerminationConditionMeet() **do**
3:     SendEmployedBees();
4:     SendOnlookerBees();
5:     SendScouts();
6: **end while**

However, before this search process can take place, initialization is performed (function Init()). A termination condition (function TerminationConditionMeet()) is responsible for stoping the search cycle. Typically, the maximum number of function evaluations (MAX_FES) is used as the termination condition.

The ABC algorithm belongs to population-based algorithms, where the solution of an optimization problem is represented by a food source. The solution of 3-GCP is represented as a real-valued vector $Y_i = \{w_{ij}\}$ for $i = 1...NP \wedge j = 1...n$, where w_{ij} denotes the weight associated with the j-th vertex of the i-th solution; NP is the number of solutions within the population, and n the number of vertices. The values of the weights are taken from the interval $w_{ij} \in [lb, ub]$, where lb indicates the lower, and ub the upper bounds. The initial values of the food sources are generated randomly, according to the equation:

$$w_{ij} = \Phi_{ij} \cdot (ub - lb) + lb, \tag{3}$$

where the function Φ_{ij} denotes the random value from the interval $[-1, 1]$.

The employed and onlooker bees change their food positions within the search space, according to the equation:

$$w'_{ij} = w_{ij} + \Phi_{ij}(w_{ij} - w_{kj}), \tag{4}$$

where Φ_{ij} is a random number from interval $[-1, 1]$. The onlooker bee selects a food source with regard to the probability value associated with that food source p_i calculated by the equation:

$$p_i = \frac{f(\Gamma(Y_i))}{\sum_{j=0}^{NP} f(\Gamma(Y_j))}, \tag{5}$$

where Γ indicates a mapping from the real-valued search space to the problem search space, as explained in the next subsection, and f the fitness function according to Eq. (1).

3.1 Fitness Calculation

The ABC for 3-GCP explores continuous real-valued search space, where the solution is represented as $Y_i = \{w_{ij}\}$ for $i = 1...NP \wedge j = 1...n$. Firstly, this solution needs to be transformed into a permutation of vertices $X_i = \{v_{ij}\}$. Such a permutation can be decoded into 3-coloring $C_i = \{c_{ij}\}$ by the DSatur heuristic. The 3-coloring C_i represents the solution of 3-GCP in its original problem space. Whilst a new position regarding a food source is performed within the real-valued search space, its quality is evaluated within the original problem space, according to the equation Eq.(1). This relation can be expressed mathematically as follows:

$$X_i = \Gamma(Y_i), \qquad \text{for } i = 1...NP. \tag{6}$$

Note that the function Γ is not injective, i.e. more than one food source can be mapped into the same value of the fitness function. On the other hand, a weakness of this function is that a small move in the real-valued search space can cause a significant increase or decrease in the fitness function.

3.2 Hybridization with Local Search

In the classical ABC algorithm, scouts act as a random selection process. That is, if the position of a food source cannot be improved further within a predetermined number of cycles called *limit*, then that source is replaced by the randomly generated position. In HABC, instead of randomly generating the new position in the search space (exploration), a deterministic exploitation in the vicinity of the current solution was used [16]. Thus, in place of the original SendScouts() function, the RWDE local search heuristic was implemented, which generates the new food sources according to the following equation [23]:

$$Y_i^{'} = Y_i + \lambda \cdot U_i, \tag{7}$$

where λ is the prescribed scalar step size length and U_i is a unit random vector generated for the i-th solution.

4 Experiments and Results

The goal of the experimental work was to show that HABC can be successfully applied to 3-GCP. In line with this, the proposed HABC was compared with: EA-SAW, Tabucol, and HEA, whose implementations were downloaded from the Internet.

The characteristics of the HABC used during the experiments were as follows: The population size was set at 100 because this value represents a good selection, as was indicated during the experimental work. The value of *limit* was set at 1,000, whilst the (MAX_FES) was limited to 300,000. The former value was obtained through experimental work, whilst the later was selected in order to draw a fair comparison with the other algorithms, i.e. the other algorithms also obey the same limitation. In the end, 25 independent runs were observed, because of the stochastic nature of tested algorithms.

The algorithms were compared according to two measures: *success rate* (SR) and *average number of objective function evaluations to solution* (AES). The first measure expresses the ratio of the number of successful runs from among all runs, whilst the second reflects the efficiency of a particular algorithm.

4.1   Test Suite

All graphs in the test suite were generated using the Culberson random graph generator [5], which allows to generate graphs of different: size n, type t, edge probability p, and seed s. This paper focuses on medium-sized graphs, i.e. graphs with 500 vertices. Three types of graphs were used as follows: uniform (a random graph with variability set at zero), equi-partite, and flat graphs. The edge probability was varied from 0.008 to 0.028 with steps of 0.001. Thus, 21 instances of randomly generated graphs were obtained. Ten different seeds were employed, i.e. from 1 to 10. In summary, each algorithm was solved $3 \times 21 \times 10 \times 25 = 15,750$ different instances of graphs.

An interval of edge probabilities was selected such that the region of *phase transition* was included. Phase transition is a phenomenon that is connected with most combinatorial optimization problems and indicates those regions, where the problem passes over the state of "solvable" to the state of "unsolvable", and vice versa [26]. The 3-GCP determination of this phenomenon is connected with parameter edge probability. Interestingly, this region is identified differently by many authors. For example, Petford and Welsh [22] stated that this phenomenon occurs when $2pn/3 \approx 16/3$, Cheeseman et al. [4] when $2m/n \approx 5.4$, and Eiben et al. [8] when $7/n \leq p \leq 8/n$. In our case, the phase transition needed to be by $p = 0.016$ over Petford and Welsh, by $p \approx 0.016$ over Cheeseman, and between $0.014 \leq p \leq 0.016$ over Eiben et al..

4.2   Influence of Edge Probability

In this experiment, the phenomenon of phase transition was investigated, as illustrated by Fig. 1. The figure is divided into six diagrams according to type, and two different measures SR and AES. The diagrams capture the results of 21 instances that were obtained by varying the edge probability through a region, including phase transition. Due to space limitation of this paper's length, a more detailed analysis of the results is left to the reader.

In summary, the best results on medium-sized graphs were reported by HEA and Tabucol. The results of HABC were slightly worse but comparable to both of the mentioned algorithms, whilst the EA-SAW saw the worst results.

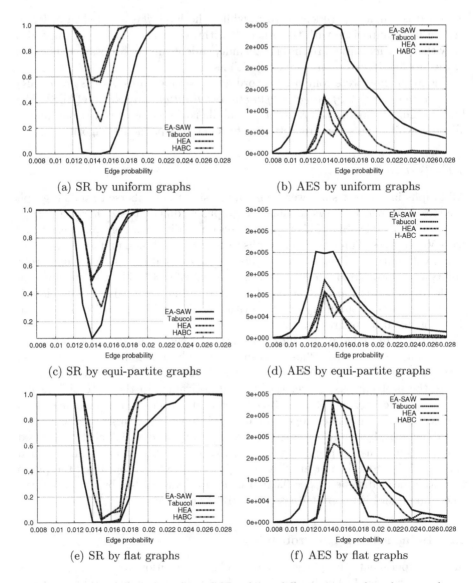

(a) SR by uniform graphs

(b) AES by uniform graphs

(c) SR by equi-partite graphs

(d) AES by equi-partite graphs

(e) SR by flat graphs

(f) AES by flat graphs

Fig. 1. Results of algorithms for 3-GCP solving different types of random graphs

4.3   Influence of the Local Search

During this experiment, the influence of hybridizing the ABC algorithm with a RWDE local search heuristic was observed. Therefore, a especial focus was placed on the instances during phase transition, i.e. $p \in [0.013, 0.017]$. The two versions of ABC were compared: the original and the hybridized version. In the former, the scouts were generated randomly, whilst in the later the RWDE local search heuristic was used.

The results of this experiment are shown in Table 1, where the row *Graphs* indicates different graph types, whilst the columns *Random* and *Hybrid* indicate the original and the hybrid ABC algorithms. Note that the average results of the mentioned instances have a varying seed $s \in [1, 10]$ and are presented in the table.

Table 1. Influence of the local search by HABC on different graph types

Graphs	Uniform		Equi-partite		Flat	
p	Random	Hybrid	Random	Hybrid	Random	Hybrid
0.013	0.816	0.848	0.872	0.912	1.000	1.000
0.014	0.112	0.404	0.200	0.448	0.012	0.256
0.015	0.060	0.248	0.036	0.304	0.000	0.000
0.016	0.180	0.528	0.104	0.524	0.000	0.004
0.017	0.328	0.856	0.340	0.828	0.000	0.028
avg	0.299	0.577	0.310	0.603	0.202	0.258

The results showed that using the RWDE local search, substantially improved the results of the original ABC. For example, this improvement amounted to 92.98% for uniform, 94.52% for equi-partite, and 27.72% for flat graphs. On average, hybridization improved the results of the original ABC for 71.74%.

5 Conclusion

The results of the proposed HABC for 3-GCP convinced us that the original ABC algorithm is a powerful tool for solving combinatorial optimization problems. HABC gained results that are comparable with the results of the best algorithm for k-GCP today (Tabucol and HEA), and improved results obtained with EA-SAW when solving the medium-sized extensive suite of random generated graphs. Note that these graphs are not the hardest to color but are difficult enough that the suitability of the ABC technology for solving the 3-GCP could be successfully proven.

In the future, the HABC for 3-GCP could be additionally improved. In particular, the problem-specific knowledge via local search heuristics could be conducted into the algorithm. The greatest challenge for further work remains the solving of large-scale graph suite (graphs with 1,000 vertices). We are convinced that these graphs could also be successfully solved using the proposed HABC algorithm.

References

1. Aarts, E., Lenstra, J.K.: Local Search in Combinatorial Optimization. Princeton University Press, Princeton (1997)
2. Bondy, J.A., Murty, U.S.R.: Graph Theory. Springer, Berlin (2008)
3. Brelaz, D.: New methods to color vertices of a graph. Communications of the ACM 22(4), 251–256 (1979)

4. Cheeseman, P., Kanefsky, B., Taylor, W.M.: Where the really hard problems are. In: Proceedings of the International Joint Conference on Artificial Intelligence, vol. 1, pp. 331–337. Morgan Kaufmann (1991)

5. Culberson, J.: Graph Coloring Page, http://www.ncbi.nlm.nih.gov

6. Dorigo, M., Stützle, T.: Ant Colony Optimization. MIT Press, Cambridge (2004)

7. Eiben, A.E., Smith, J.E.: Introduction to Evolutionary Computing. Springer, Berlin (2003)

8. Eiben, A.E., Hauw, K., Hemert, J.I.: Graph coloring with adaptive evolutionary algorithms. Journal of Heuristics 4(1), 25–46 (1998)

9. Fister, I., Brest, J.: Using differential evolution for the graph coloring. In: Proceedings of IEEE SSCI 2011 symposium series on computational intelligence, Piscataway, pp. 150–156 (2011)

10. Fleurent, C., Ferland, J.: Genetic and Hybrid Algorithms for Graph Coloring. Annals of Operations Research 63, 437–464 (1996)

11. Galinier, P., Hao, J.: Hybrid evolutionary algorithms for graph coloring. Journal of Combinatorial Optimization 3(4), 379–397 (1999)

12. Galinier, P., Hertz, A.: A survey of local search methods for graph coloring. Computers & Operations Research 33, 2547–2562 (2006)

13. Garey, M.R., Johnson, D.S.: Computers and Intractability: A Guide to the Theory of NP-Completeness. W.H. Freeman & Co., New York (1979)

14. Glover, F.: Future paths for integer programming and links to artificial intelligence. Computers & Operations Research 13(5), 533–549 (1986)

15. Hertz, A., de Werra, D.: Using tabu search techniques for graph coloring. Computing 39(4), 345–351 (1987)

16. Iacca, G., Neri, F., Mininno, E., Ong, Y.-S., Lim, M.-H.: Ockham's Razor in Memetic Computing: Three Stage Optimal Memetic Exploration (2011) (in press)

17. Karaboga, D., Basturk, A.: A survey: algorithms simulating bee swarm intelligence. Artificial Intelligence Review 31(1-4), 61–85 (2009)

18. Kennedy, J., Eberhart, R.C.: Particle swarm optimization. In: Proceedings of the 1995 IEEE International Conference on Neural Networks, vol. 4, pp. 1942–1948. IEEE Service Center, Piscataway (1995)

19. Lü, Z., Hao, J.K.: A memetic algorithm for graph coloring. European Journal of Operational Research 203(1), 241–250 (2010)

20. Malaguti, E., Toth, P.: A survey on vertex coloring problems. International Transactions in Operational Research, 1–34 (2009)

21. Pan, Q.K., Tasgetiren, M.F., Suganthan, P.N., Chua, T.J.: A discrete artificial bee colony algorithm for the lot-streaming flow shop scheduling problem. Information Sciences 181(12), 2455–2468 (2011)

22. Petford, A.D., Welsh, D.J.A.: A randomized 3-coloring algorithms. Discrete Mathematic 74(1-2), 253–261 (1989)

23. Rao, S.S.: Engineering Optimization: Theory and Practice. John Willey & Sons, New Jersey (2009)

24. Robinson, J., Rahmat-Samii, Y.: Particle Swarm Optimization in Electro-Magnetics. IEEE on Antennas and Propagation 52(2), 397–407 (2004)

25. Tasgetiren, M.F., Pan, Q.K., Suganthan, P.N., Chen, A.H.-L.: A discrete artificial bee colony algorithm for the total flowtime minimization and permutation flow shops. Information Sciences 181(16), 3459–3475 (2011)

26. Turner, J.S.: Almost all k-colorable graphs are easy to color. Journal of Algorithms 9(1), 63–82 (1988)

27. Yang, X.-S.: Nature-Inspired Metaheuristic Algorithms. Luniver Press, Cambridge (2008)

Monte-Carlo Swarm Policy Search

Jeremy Fix and Matthieu Geist

Supélec, IMS Research Group
2 rue edouard Belin, 57070 Metz, France
firstname.lastname@supelec.fr

Abstract. Finding optimal controllers of stochastic systems is a particularly challenging problem tackled by the optimal control and reinforcement learning communities. A classic paradigm for handling such problems is provided by Markov Decision Processes. However, the resulting underlying optimization problem is difficult to solve. In this paper, we explore the possible use of Particle Swarm Optimization to learn optimal controllers and show through some non-trivial experiments that it is a particularly promising lead.

Keywords: particle swarm optimization, optimal control, policy search.

1 Introduction

Reinforcement Learning (RL) [12] addresses the optimal control problem. In this paradigm, at each (discrete) time step the system to be controlled is in a given state (or configuration). Based on this information, an agent has to choose an action to be applied. The system reacts by stochastically stepping to a new configuration, and an oracle provides a reward to the agent, depending on the experienced transition. This reward is a local hint of the quality of the control, and the aim of the agent is to choose a sequence of actions in order to maximize some cumulative function of the rewards. A notable advantage of this paradigm is that the oracle quantifies how the agent behaves without specifying what to do (for example, when learning to play chess, a reward would be given for wining the game, not for taking the queen).

The mapping from configurations to actions is called a policy (or a controller); its quality is quantified by the so-called value function which associates to each state an expected measure of cumulative reward from starting in this state and following the policy. The best policy is the one with associated maximal value function. Among other approaches, direct policy search algorithms (*e.g.*, [1]) adopt a parametric representation of the policy and maximize the value function (as a function of the controller's parameters). This approach is sound, but the underlying optimization problem is difficult. Even for simple policies, computing the gradient of the related objective function is far from being straightforward.

In the numerical optimization community, several algorithms requiring only to evaluate the objective function have been devised, among which one finds genetic algorithms, particle swarm optimization and ant algorithms. These approaches

L. Rutkowski et al. (Eds.): SIDE 2012 and EC 2012, LNCS 7269, pp. 75–83, 2012.

involve a set of individuals (each representing a set of parameters related to the objective function of interest) that are combined, trying to reach a global optima. Particle swarm optimization is one of these algorithms, proposed originally by [7]. Variations of this algorithm have been proposed and a thorough review can be found in [3]. It has been shown that PSO (the original or one of its variations) performs well for optimization problems whether uni- or multi-modal, with static or dynamic fitness and even in large search space [4].

In this article, we introduce a simple but new RL policy search algorithm using particle swarm optimization at its core. We show that it is particularly efficient for optimizing the parameters of controllers for three classical benchmark problems in reinforcement learning : the inverted pendulum, the mountain car and the acrobot. The two first problems involve noise in the evolution of the system which introduces random fluctuations in the fitness landscape. In the last problem, we evaluate the performance of PSO in a large search space. The acrobot is known as being a very difficult problem in the RL community, and most approaches fail to solve it.

2   Monte Carlo Swarm Policy Search (MCSPS)

A Markov Decision Process (MDP) is a tuple $\{S, A, P, R\}$ with the state space S, action space A, a set of Markovian transition probabilities P and a reward function R. A policy is a mapping from states to probabilities over actions: $\pi : S \rightarrow \mathcal{P}(A)$. At each time step i, the system to be controlled is in a state s_i, the agent chooses an action a_i according to a policy π, $a_i \sim \pi(.|s_i)$. It is applied to the system which stochastically transits to s_{i+1} according to $p(.|s_i, a_i)$. The agent receives a reward $r_i = R(s_i, a_i, s_{i+1})$. Its goal is to find the policy which maximizes some cumulative function of the rewards, over the long run; this is the so-called value function. There are many ways to define a value function. The more common one is to consider the expected discounted cumulative reward (expectation being according to stochasticity of transitions and of the policy): $V^\pi(s) = E[\sum_{i=0}^\infty \gamma^i r_i | s_0 = s, \pi]$, the term $\gamma \in (0,1)$ being the discount factor and weighting long-term rewards. Another common criterion hold if a finite horizon T is considered: $V^\pi(s) = E[\sum_{i=0}^T r_i | s_0 = s, \pi]$. Another possible criterion, less common because less convenient (from a mathematical point of view) is the mean reward: $V^\pi(s) = \lim_{n \to \infty} \frac{1}{n} E[\sum_{i=0}^n r_i | s_0 = s, \pi]$..

For any definition of the value function, the criterion to be optimized is the expected value over a distribution p_0 of initial states:

$$\rho^\pi = E[V^\pi(s_0)|s_0 \sim p_0]. \tag{1}$$

The optimal policy π^* is the one maximizing this criterion:

$$\pi^* = \underset{\pi:S \to \mathcal{P}(A)}{\operatorname{argmax}} \rho^\pi. \tag{2}$$

In the considered policy search context, we make some assumptions. First, the model (that is transition probabilities and the reward function) is unknown.

However, we assume that a simulator is available, so that we can sample trajectories according to any policy of interest (which can be a well-founded hypothesis, depending on the problem of interest). Second, we assume that a parametric structure is chosen for the controller beforehand: any policy π_θ is parameterized by a parameter vector θ (for example, it can be a Gibbs sampler constructed from a radial basis function networks, and the parameters are the weights of the kernels). The optimization problem to be solved is therefore the following:

$$\theta^* = \operatorname*{argmax}_{\theta \in \mathbb{R}^p} \rho^{\pi_\theta}. \tag{3}$$

Indeed, this is a quite difficult optimization problem. It has been proposed to solve it using a gradient ascent [1] or cross-entropy [9], among other approaches. As the model is unknown, the gradient should be estimated from simulation, which causes a high variance.

In this paper, we introduce a simple idea: using a particle swarm optimizer to solve this difficult optimization problem. Each particle holds a parameter vector, that is a controller, and the fitness function is ρ^{π_θ}. As the model is unknown, it cannot be computed analytically. However, as a simulator is available, it can be estimated using Monte Carlo. For example, consider the finite horizon value function. One generates M trajectories, starting in a random state s_0 sampled according to p_0, and a trajectory of length T is obtained by applying the policy π_θ and following the system's dynamic. From such trajectories $\{(s_0^m, a_0^m, s_1^m, r_0^m \dots s_T^m, r_{T-1}^m)_{1 \le m \le M}\}$, one can compute

$$\hat{\rho}^{\pi_\theta} = \frac{1}{M} \sum_{m=1}^{M} \sum_{i=0}^{T-1} r_i^m, \tag{4}$$

which is an unbiased estimate of the true fitness function ρ^{π_θ}.

More precisely, we consider a swarm with N particles with a von Neumann topology. In all the simulations presented below, we used a swarm of 5×5 particles. Different rules to update the position and velocity of the particles have been proposed in the litterature (see [3] for a review). We used the basic PSO with a constriction factor [7,2]. Namely, we use the following equations to update the velocity $\mathbf{v}_i$ and position $\mathbf{p}_i$ of a particle i:

$$\mathbf{v}_{ij} = w\mathbf{v}_{ij} + c_1 r_1.(\mathbf{b}_{ij} - \mathbf{p}_{ij}) + c_2 r_2.(\mathbf{l}_{ij} - \mathbf{p}_{ij})$$
$$\mathbf{p}_i = \mathbf{p}_i + \mathbf{v}_i \tag{5}$$

with $w = 0.729844, c_1 = c_2 = 1.496180$, r_1, r_2 are random numbers uniformly drawn from $[0, 1]$, $\mathbf{b}_i$ is the best position ever found by the particle i and $\mathbf{l}_i$ the best position ever found by one particle in the neighborhood of particle i. The position of the particles are initialized randomly in the parameter space while the velocities are initialized to zero. The position and velocity of the particles are updated asynchronously. At each iteration, we need to compute the fitness of a particle and update its position given the position and fitness of the particles within their neighborhood. Given our problems are stochastic we evaluate the fitness of a particle each time its position changed and also reevaluate the fitness of its best position each time we want to change it. Each update of a particle's state and fitness is propagated to the neighborhoods to which the particle belongs. The scripts for all the simulations presented in the paper are available online [5].

3   Results

3.1   Inverted Pendulum

Problem
The inverted pendulum is a classic benchmark problem in reinforcement learning and has already been addressed with several methods (see e.g. [8]). We use the same setting as in [8]. It consists of finding the force to apply to a cart, on which a pendulum is anchored, in order to maintain the pendulum still at the vertical position. The state of the system is the angle of the pendulum relative to the upright and its angular speed $(\theta, \dot{\theta})$, which are updated according to the equations : $\ddot{\theta} = \frac{g\sin(\theta) - \alpha ml\sin(2\theta)\dot{\theta}^2/2 - \alpha\cos(\theta)(f+\eta)}{4l/3 - \alpha ml\cos^2(\theta)}$, where g is the gravity constant ($g = 9.8m/s^2$), m and l are the mass and length of the pole ($m = 2.0$ kg, $l = 0.5$ m), M the mass of the cart ($M = 8.0$ kg) and $\alpha = \frac{1}{m+M}$. The time-step τ is set to 0.1s. The pole must be held in $[-\frac{\pi}{2}; \frac{\pi}{2}]$. An episode is constrained to last at most 3000 interactions. At each interaction, a reward of 0 is given until the pole exits this domain which ends the episode and leads to a reward of -1. This reward is actually poorly informative as it is only indicating that the pole should not fall but not that the optimal position is around 0 (which can be induced by a cosine reward for example). The pole is initialized close to equilibrium ($\theta_0 \in [-0.1, 0.1], \dot{\theta}_0 \in [-0.1, 0.1]$). The pole-cart system is controlled by applying a force $f_t \in \{-50, 0, 50\}$ Newtons perturbed by a uniform noise $\eta \in [-5; 5]$ Newtons to the cart.

The controller is defined with a radial basis function network (RBF) with 9 Gaussians and a constant term per action. The means of the basis functions are evenly spread in $[-\pi/4, \pi/4] \times [-1.0, 1.0]$ and the standard deviation is set to $\sigma = 1.0$. Optimizing this controller means finding 30 parameters, i.e. the amplitude of the 27 basis functions and the 3 constant terms. The RBF associated to each action defines the probability to select that action (c_i and $a_{i,j}$ being parameters to be learnt): $\forall i \in [1, 3], P_i = \frac{1}{P}\exp(c_i + \sum_{j=1}^{9} a_{i,j}exp(-\frac{(\theta-\theta_j)^2+(\dot{\theta}-\dot{\theta}_j)^2}{2\sigma^2}))$, where P is a normalizing term so that the probabilities sum to 1.0. An action is selected with a probabilistic toss biased by these probabilities.

Experimental results
The experiment is repeated 1000 times. For each iteration of one swarm, the fitness of a particle is evaluated using a single trajectory which makes an iteration much faster but also much more subject to the stochasticity of the problem due

to the definition of the initial state, to the selection of the action using a random toss and to the uniform noise added to the controller. Random fluctuations of the fitness remains, as it was checked on some trials by evaluating several times the fitness of a set of parameters but this is not shown here. The fitness we report on the illustrations is the fitness of the best particle evaluated on 500 trajectories to get an accurate estimate of it. The swarm is allowed to evolve during 200 iterations.

The average number of balancing steps of the best particle, and its standard deviation, are plotted over the iteration of the swarms on figure 1. As shown on the figure, all the trials converged to a good policy allowing to keep the pendulum balancing for the 3000 time steps, the maximal length of an episode. On average, it took approximately 50 iterations of the swarm to converge to a very good policy.

A standard approach for policy search consists in performing a gradient ascent of the value function respectively to the parameters of the policy [1]. It also requires to simulate trajectories. For this problem, unreported experiments shows that gradient ascent took an order of 200.10^3 trajectories before reaching an optimal policy. The proposed approach took an order of 1250 trajectories to reach the same result (25 particles, 50 iterations and one simulated trajectory per fitness evaluation). Meta parameters (c_1, c_2, w for PSO, learning rates and forgetting factor for the gradient ascent) could certainly be better defined. However this shows that MCPSO easily achieves state of the art policy search performance.

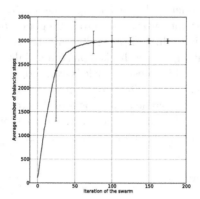

Fig. 1. Average number of balancing steps for the best particle. This average is computed over the 1000 trials, and using 500 trajectories for each trial at each epoch to get an accurate estimate of it. Please note that we plot here the number of balancing steps and not the fitness which is more intuitive. Error bars indicate one standard deviation. The simulation scripts are available at [5].

3.2   Mountain Car

Problem

The second problem we consider is the mountain car as described in [12]. The goal is to control a vehicle in order to escape from a valley. Given the car has a limited power, it must swing forward and backward in the valley to reach the exit. The state is defined as the position $x \in [-1.2, 0.5]$ and velocity $\dot{x} \in [-0.07, 0.07]$ of the car. Three discrete actions are allowed : accelerating to the left, doing nothing or accelerating to the right $a \in \{-1, 0, 1\}$. The system evolves according to discrete time equations provided in [12, Chap 8]. The position is bounded in the domain $[-1.2, 0.5]$. The cart is initialized randomly close to the worst cases, at the bottom of the valley with a speed close to zero ($x_0 \in [-0.75, -0.25]$, $\dot{x}_0 \in [-0.02, 0.02]$). When the cart's position reaches the lower bound, the velocity is set to 0.0. When the cart reaches the upper bound, the episode ends with a reward of 0; the reward is set to -1 otherwise. The length of an episode is limited to 1500 interactions. The goal of the swarm is to find a set of parameters that maximizes the reward which is equivalent to minimizing the number of steps necessary to escape from the valley.

The controller is defined by a set of 9 basis functions (Gaussians) plus a constant term for each action, leading to 30 parameters to optimize. If the state (position and velocity) is scaled in $[0, 1]$, the centers of the basis functions are evenly spread in $[0, 1] \times [0, 1]$ and the standard deviation set to $\sigma = 0.3$. Similar to the inverted pendulum problem, the value of these 3 basis networks is used as probabilities to toss an action.

Experimental results

We repeated 1000 experiments. For each experiment, the swarm is allowed to evolve during 50 epochs (which was enough to get a good policy). At each epoch, the fitness of a particle is evaluated using 30 trajectories (it does not suppress the stochasticity of the fitness as we checked on some trials, but this is not shown here). The reported fitness of the best particle is evaluated using 1000 trajectories to get an accurate estimate of it. The evolution of the average number of steps to reach the goal of the best particles is shown on figure 2a), with its standard deviation. The average number of steps to reach the goal for the initial and final best particles of a typical trial are plotted on figures 2b,c.

3.3   Swing-up Acrobot

Problem

The aim of the acrobot problem is to swing an under-actuated two-arm pendulum, starting from a vertical position pointing down in order to reach the vertical pointing up unstable position. The system's state is defined by four continuous variables (the two joints' angle θ_1, θ_2 and their velocity $\dot{\theta}_1, \dot{\theta}_2$). The system is controlled with a torque $\tau \in \{-1, 0, 1\}$ applied to the second joint. The torque is only applied on the joint between the two segments, the system being

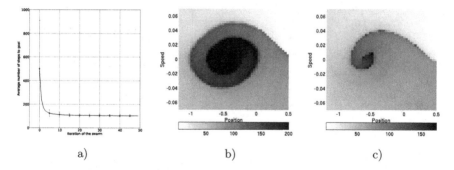

a)   b)   c)

Fig. 2. a) Average number of steps to reach the goal state with its standard deviation. b) Average number of steps to reach the goal state for evenly spread initial conditions $(\theta, \dot{\theta})$ during a typical trial. For the illustration, this average is bounded to 200 but reaches 1500 in the worst case (the length of an episode). c) Average number of steps to reach the goal state for the best particle after 50 iterations.

therefore under-actuated and solving the task requires to swing the pendulum back and forth. The system's state evolves according to the discrete-time equations provided in [11] with the strength $\tau \in \{-1, 0, 1\}$, time-step $\Delta t = 0.01s.$, $\dot{\theta}_{1,t} \in [-9\pi, 9\pi]$, $\dot{\theta}_{2,t} \in [-4\pi, 4\pi]$, $m_1 = m_2 = 1$, $l_1 = l_2 = 1$, $l_{c_1} = l_{c_2} = 0.5$, $I_1 = I_2 = ml^2/12$, $g = 9.8$. The state is initialized at the vertical position pointing down with a null speed $\theta_{1,0} = 3\pi/2, \theta_{2,0} = 0, \dot{\theta}_{1,0} = \dot{\theta}_{2,0} = 0$ (see fig. 3).

Controlling the acrobot is a difficult problem[10]. To ease the problem, we considered a simplified controller which combines a RBF network with an optimal Linear Quadratic Regulator (LQR) [11]. The LQR controller can maintain the pendulum still in the vertical upward position but is unable to swing it. In addition, the LQR controller works perfectly only in a narrow range of the state space; for $\dot{\theta}_1 = \dot{\theta}_2 = 0$, the LQR controller stabilizes the pendulum if the initial state is in $\theta_2 = 0, \theta_1 = \pi/2 \pm \pi/24$. Therefore, the RBF controller has to swing the pendulum in order to bring it at the vertical position with a certain speed to allow the LQR to stabilize it. We used a continuous action defined as the tanh of a RBF involving 4 gaussians per dimension. The RBF controller therefore involves $4^4 = 256$ parameters. When the pendulum is close to the goal state $(\theta_1 = \pi/2 \pm \pi/4, \theta_2 = 0 \pm \pi/4, \dot{\theta}_1 = 0 \pm \pi/2, \dot{\theta}_2 = 0 \pm \pi/2$, denoted $\mathbf{D}_\theta)$, the controller is switched from the RBF to the LQR. It has also to be noted that the LQR controller is not optimized in these experiments but computed beforehand (see [11]). Better controllers could certainly be designed but the point here was to test the ability of PSO to find the parameters in such a large parameter space. Given the simulations are expensive, the problem is here considered deterministic (no noise in the initial state nor in the chosen action).

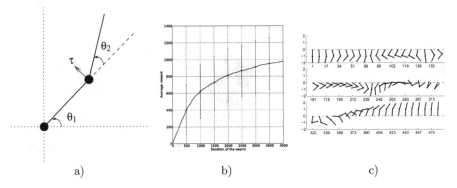

a)   b)   c)

Fig. 3. a) Setup of the acrobot problem. Starting from the vertical pointing-down position, the controller, influencing the pendulum through the torque τ shall bring and keep the pendulum still in a domain close to the vertical pointing-up unstable position b) Average number of steps the pendulum stays in the goal domain. This average is computed over 300 repetitions of the experiment. c) Behavior of one of the best policies.

The controllers are defined as :

$$\tau = \begin{cases} -\mathbf{K}^T.\theta, \theta = (\theta_1 - \pi/2; \theta_2; \dot{\theta}_1; \dot{\theta}_2) & \text{if } \theta \in \mathbf{D}_\theta \\ 2\tanh(\sum_{j=1}^{256} a_j e^{-\frac{\sin^2(\theta_1 - \theta_1^j)}{2\sigma_1^2} - \frac{\sin^2(\theta_2 - \theta_2^j)}{2\sigma_2^2} - \frac{(\dot{\theta}_1 - \dot{\theta}_1^j)^2}{2\sigma_3^2} - \frac{(\dot{\theta}_2 - \dot{\theta}_2^j)^2}{2\sigma_4^2}}) & \text{otherwise} \end{cases}$$
(6)

with $\sigma_1 = \sigma_2 = 0.25, \sigma_3 = \sigma_4 = 4.5$, the centers of the gaussians being evenly spread in $[-\pi/4, 5\pi/4] \times [-\pi/4, 5\pi/4] \times [-9, 9] \times [-9, 9]$.

Experimental results
We repeated the experiments over 300 trials. A simulation is allowed to run for at most $20s$. (2000 interactions). The swarm is evolving during 4000 iterations. A reward of $+1$ is given each time the pendulum is in the goal region (as defined above), and 0 otherwise. The average reward function of the iteration of the swarm is shown on figure 3b. As we can see, the swarm does not always converge to an optimal policy and get stuck in local minima. This is probably due to the architecture of the controller which is certainly not optimal. In addition, during the iteration of the algorithm, the fitness tends to stay on "plateau". There are nevertheless policies that are close to optimal as for example the one depicted on figure 3c. This example illustrates that PSO is able to optimize controllers even in large parameter space but the controller can be improved.

4   Discussion

Particle Swarm Optimization is an efficient algorithm for solving optimization problems. In addition to the different problems on which it has been applied before, we have shown here that it reveals to be very efficient to optimize the parameters of controllers solving challenging optimal control problems. It is also a very convenient algorithm if we compare it to the gradient-based policy search algorithm since we do not have to compute the gradient of the policy nor do we need it to be computable. Moreover, PSO is less prone to local optimum and converges more quickly than gradient-based approaches. A lack of the current approach is that it requires a simulator. However, in some cases, only data sampled according to a fixed behaviorial policy are available. To extend the current approach to this case, we envision to replace the Monte Carlo estimation of the fitness function by value function approximation [6]. Ultimately, on can envision to design an online algorithm, with an agent learning to control optimally the system while interacting with it.

References

1. Baxter, J., Bartlett, P.: Direct gradient-based reinforcement learning. JAIR (1999)
2. Clerc, M., Kennedy, J.: The particle swarm - explosion, stability, and convergence in a multidimensional complex space. IEEE Trans. Evol. Comp. 6(1), 58–73 (2002)
3. Engelbrecht, A.: Fundamentals of Computational Swarm Intelligence. Wiley (2005)
4. Engelbrecht, A.P.: Heterogeneous Particle Swarm Optimization. In: Dorigo, M., Birattari, M., Di Caro, G.A., Doursat, R., Engelbrecht, A.P., Floreano, D., Gambardella, L.M., Groß, R., Şahin, E., Sayama, H., Stützle, T. (eds.) ANTS 2010. LNCS, vol. 6234, pp. 191–202. Springer, Heidelberg (2010)
5. Fix, J., Geist, M.: http://jeremy.fix.free.fr/spip.php?article33
6. Geist, M., Pietquin, O.: Parametric Value Function Approximation: a Unified View. In: ADPRL 2011 (2011)
7. Kennedy, J., Eberhart, R.: Particle swarm optimization. In: Proceedings IEEE International Joint Conference on Neural Networks, pp. 1942–1948 (1995)
8. Lagoudakis, M.G., Parr, R.: Least-squares policy iteration. JMLR 4 (2003)
9. Mannor, S., Rubinstein, R., Gat, Y.: The cross entropy method for fast policy search. In: International Conference on Machine Learning, vol. 20, p. 512 (2003)
10. Munos, R., Moore, A.W.: Variable resolution discretization for high-accuracy solutions of optimal control problems. In: IJCAI, pp. 1348–1355 (1999)
11. Spong, M.W.: The swing up control problem for the acrobot. IEEE Control Systems 15, 49–55 (1995)
12. Sutton, R., Barto, A.: Reinforcement Learning: An Introduction. MIT Press (1998)

Compact Bacterial Foraging Optimization*

Giovanni Iacca, Ferrante Neri, and Ernesto Mininno

Department of Mathematical Information Technology,
P.O. Box 35 (Agora), 40014 University of Jyväskylä, Finland
giovanni.iacca@jyu.fi, ferrante.neri@jyu.fi, ernesto.mininno@jyu.fi

Abstract. Compact algorithms are Estimation of Distribution Algorithms which mimic the behavior of population-based algorithms by means of a probabilistic representation of the population of candidate solutions. Compared to an actual population, a probabilistic model requires a much smaller memory, which allows algorithms with limited memory footprint. This feature is extremely important in some engineering applications, e.g. robotics and real-time control systems. This paper proposes a compact implementation of Bacterial Foraging Optimization (cBFO). cBFO employs the same chemotaxis scheme of population-based BFO, but without storing a swarm of bacteria. Numerical results, carried out on a broad set of test problems with different dimensionalities, show that cBFO, despite its minimal hardware requirements, is competitive with other memory saving algorithms and clearly outperforms its population-based counterpart.

1 Introduction

Bacterial Foraging Optimization (BFO), see [8,18], is a meta-heuristic inspired by the foraging behavior of the E. coli bacteria within some environment with a non-uniform distribution of nutrients. The basic idea is to explore the search space performing tentative moves similar to the swim foraging pattern (called "chemotaxis") observed in motile bacteria. Bacterial chemotaxis is a complex combination of two types of moves, namely tumbling (i.e. changes of direction) and swimming (i.e. moves along a successful direction), which respectively enable the bacteria to search for nutrients in random directions and rapidly approach higher concentrations of nutrients. In other words, the alternation between "swims" and "tumbles" guarantees a balance between exploitation and exploration of the search space, thus making BFO robust and versatile.

Like other Swarm Intelligence algorithms, BFO has been successfully applied to many practical problems. For example, in [10] BFO is applied in image processing. In [13] a hybrid algorithm composed of BFO and a GA is used to tune a PID controller. In [20], BFO is used to design UPFC controllers. In [7], BFO is used to calibrate a volatility option pricing model.

* This research is supported by the Academy of Finland, Akatemiatutkija 130600, Algorithmic Design Issues in Memetic Computing and Tutkijatohtori 140487, Algorithmic Design and Software Implementation: a Novel Optimization Platform.

L. Rutkowski et al. (Eds.): SIDE 2012 and EC 2012, LNCS 7269, pp. 84–92, 2012.

Despite its versatility, however, BFO shows a poor convergence behavior, compared to other meta-heuristics, especially over high dimensional complex optimization problems. To overcome these issues, different strategies have been proposed. In [5,19], cooperative approaches are used to improve the performance of standard BFO. In [3], instead, BFO has been hybridized with Particle Swarm Optimization. Recently, some adaptive and self-adaptive variants of the original BFO have been proposed, see e.g. [4,6] and [9,10]. In [21] the foraging mechanism is combined with an EDA and applied in predictive control.

This paper introduces a compact implementation of BFO, called cBFO. The cBFO algorithm belongs to the class of compact Evolutionary Algorithms (cEA), i.e. optimization algorithms which do not store and process an entire population of individuals, but make use of a probabilistic representation of the population. Thus, a run of these algorithms requires a limited memory compared to their correspondent standard EAs. These algorithms have been developed in order to address industrial optimization problems characterized by limited memory resources, e.g. in mobile robots and control systems, where a powerful computer may be unavailable due to cost and/or space limitations. The remainder of this paper is organized as follows. Section 2 describes the proposed cBFO. Section 3 shows the numerical results of an extensive test on the performance of cBFO compared to a set of algorithms. Section 4 gives the conclusion of this work.

2   Compact Bacterial Foraging Optimization

The classical BFO consists of three phases, namely: 1) chemotaxis, 2) reproduction, and 3) dispersal. During chemotaxis, the movement of the i-th bacterium is modeled as $x_i = x_i + C_i \cdot \Delta_i / \sqrt{\Delta_i^T \Delta}$, where Δ_i is the direction vector of the chemotactic step (being Δ_i^T its transpose), and C_i is a parameter which controls the step size. In tumbles, Δ_i is a random vector whose elements are uniformly distributed in $[-1, 1]$; in swims instead, Δ_i is the same as the last chemotactic step, thus allowing the bacterium to exploit a promising direction. To mimic the asexual reproduction of E. coli, at each iteration BFO sorts all the bacteria according to their fitness and selects the best half of the swarm. Each survivor is then splitted into two replicas, thus keeping the swarm size constant. Finally, in order to prevent premature convergence and keep a high diversity rate, after a fixed number of chemotaxis/reproduction steps a few bacteria are chosen, with some probability, for being replaced with new random individuals.

The original population-based BFO framework can be implemented as a compact algorithm almost straightforwardly. For the sake of clarity, the resulting algorithm, here called cBFO, is shown in Alg. 1. Without loss of generality, let us assume that parameters are normalized so that each search interval is $[-1, 1]$. cBFO consists of the following. A $2 \times n$ matrix, namely perturbation vector $PV = [\mu, \sigma]$, is generated. μ values are set equal to 0 while σ values are set equal to a large number $\lambda = 10$. The value of λ is empirically set in order to simulate a uniform distribution at the beginning of the optimization process. A solution x_e is then sampled from a multivariate Gaussian Probability Distribution Function

(PDF) characterized by a mean value μ and a standard deviation σ. For further details on sampling, see [15]. The solution x_e is called *elite*. Subsequently, at each chemotactic step, a new solution is sampled and a combination of tumble/swim moves is attempted, in the same way as in the population-based BFO. Every time a new offspring is generated, either by sampling or tumble/swim, its fitness is computed and compared with the fitness of the current *elite*. On the basis of their fitness values, a *winner* solution (solution displaying the best fitness) and a *loser* solution (solution displaying the worst fitness) are detected. The winner solution biases the virtual population by affecting the PV values, according to the following update rules:

$$\mu^{t+1} = \mu^t + \frac{1}{N_p}\left(winner - loser\right)$$

$$\sigma^{t+1} = \sqrt{\left(\sigma^t\right)^2 + \left(\mu^t\right)^2 - \left(\mu^{t+1}\right)^2 + \frac{1}{N_p}\left(winner^2 - loser^2\right)} \tag{1}$$

where N_p is a parameter, namely virtual population size. Details for constructing Eq. 1 are given in [14]. In addition to the PV values, also the *elite* is updated, according to a persistent elitism scheme, see [2].

The compact implementation of reproduction and elimination/dispersal deserves an explanation. While BFO keeps the best $S/2$ bacteria and replicate them, cBFO "shifts" the PDF towards the *elite* and "shrinks" over it. In other words, the fitness-based comparison described above is applied to μ and *elite*, and the PV is updated accordingly. In this way, asexual reproduction is crudely approximated by a forced update of the PDF. As for the elimination/dispersal step, the injection of new randomly generated bacteria into the swarm is modeled by means of a perturbation of PV. More specifically, the following perturbation is applied, see [17]:

$$\mu^{t+1} = \mu^{t+1} + 2\tau \cdot rand\left(0, 1\right) - \tau$$

$$\sigma^{t+1} = \sqrt{\left(\sigma^{t+1}\right)^2 + \tau \cdot rand\left(0, 1\right)} \tag{2}$$

where $\tau = 0.1$ is a constant parameter.

3   Numerical Results

The numerical results are divided in three groups, namely results from the testbed in [16] (24 problems) in 10, 20 and 40 dimensions. For each of the three groups, the following algorithms, with the parameter setting suggested in the original paper, have been compared to cBFO:

- Simplified Intelligence Single Particle Optimization: ISPO proposed in [23], with acceleration $A = 1$, acceleration power factor $P = 10$, learning coefficient $B = 2$, learning factor reduction ratio $S = 4$, minimum threshold on learning factor $E = 1e - 5$, and particle learning steps $PartLoop = 30$;

```
{** PV initialization **}
initialize μ = 0̄ and σ = 1̄ · 10
generate elite by means of PV
while budget condition do
    {** chemotaxis **}
    for i = 1 : N_p do
        generate 1 individual x_i by means of PV
        [winner, loser] = compete (x_i, elite)
        update μ, σ and elite
        J_last = f_{x_i}
        {** tumble and move **}
        x_i = x_i + C_i · Δ_i/√(Δ_i^T Δ), with random Δ_i ∈ [-1,1]^n
        {** swim **}
        for i = 1 : N_s do
            [winner, loser] = compete (x_i, elite)
            update μ, σ and elite
            if f_{x_i} < J_last then
                J_last = f_{x_i}
                x_i = x_i + C_i · Δ_i/√(Δ_i^T Δ), with same direction vector Δ_i
            end if
        end for
    end for
    {** reproduction: shift μ towards elite **}
    [winner, loser] = compete (μ, elite)
    update μ and σ
    {** elimination/dispersal: perturb PV **}
    perturb PV according to Eq. 2
end while
```

Algorithm 1: cBFO pseudo-code

- compact Differential Evolution: cDE proposed in [15], employing rand/1/ mutation, binary crossover and persistent elitism, with virtual population size $N_{pop} = 300$, scale factor $F = 0.5$, and crossover rate $Cr = 0.3$;
- Adaptive Bacterial Foraging Optimization: ABFO0 (hereafter simply called ABFO) proposed in [6], with number of bacteria $S = 50$, initial chemotactic step size $C_{initial} = 0.1$, swim steps $N_s = 4$, probability of elimination/ dispersion $P_{ed} = 0.25$, initial epsilon $\varepsilon_{initial} = 100$, adaptation generations $n = 10$, C_i reduction ratio $\alpha = 10$, and ε reduction ratio $\beta = 10$.

As for cBFO, the following parameter setting has been used: number of bacteria $N_p = 300$, chemotactic step size $C_i = 0.1$, swim steps $N_s = 4$. Similarly to the cDE scheme, in this case the number of bacteria represents the virtual population size used in the probabilistic model of the population. The reason for setting the value of N_p much larger than S is that, since it controls the convergence of the compact framework, a lower value would cause premature convergence. On the other hand, a high value of N_p guarantees a fair balance between exploration - in the early stages - and exploitation in the later stages. The value $N_p = 300$ has been chosen empirically after a series of numerical experiments. It should be noticed that the aforementioned set of algorithms has been chosen diverse in terms of search logic. ABFO is a typical population based algorithm which requires a proper population size dependent on the dimensionality of the problem. This fact makes the memory requirement of ABFO heavily dependent on the dimensionality of the problem. On the other hand, ISPO, cDE and cBFO

Table 1. Average final results ± standard deviation and Wilcoxon test in 10 dimensions

Fcn.	ISPO	W	cDE	W	ABFO	W	cBFO
f_1	7.948e+01 ± 1.26e-14	-	7.948e+01 ± 1.07e-14	-	7.950e+01 ± 3.33e-03	+	7.948e+01 ± 5.84e-04
f_2	-2.099e+02 ± 9.65e-14	-	-2.099e+02 ± 1.00e-10	-	3.171e+03 ± 2.72e+03	+	2.289e+02 ± 2.72e+02
f_3	-3.966e+02 ± 7.41e+01	=	-4.507e+02 ± 5.00e+00	-	5.323e+04 ± 7.91e+04	+	-4.191e+02 ± 9.77e+00
f_4	-4.319e+02 ± 1.55e+01	=	-4.339e+02 ± 1.21e+01	-	-1.572e+02 ± 7.42e+01	+	-4.233e+02 ± 1.78e+01
f_5	-9.210e+00 ± 0.00e+00	-	-9.210e+00 ± 3.87e-09	-	-3.895e+00 ± 1.84e+00	+	-9.182e+00 ± 4.95e-03
f_6	1.006e+04 ± 1.34e+04	+	3.052e+02 ± 3.31e+02	+	8.305e+03 ± 3.19e+03	+	3.710e+02 ± 3.41e-01
f_7	1.004e+02 ± 5.59e+00	+	1.075e+02 ± 1.10e+01	+	9.966e+01 ± 3.22e+00	+	9.445e+01 ± 8.16e-01
f_8	1.843e+02 ± 7.71e+01	=	1.587e+02 ± 1.49e+01	=	1.591e+02 ± 3.76e+00	+	1.559e+02 ± 2.13e+00
f_9	1.262e+02 ± 1.12e+00	-	1.756e+02 ± 5.90e+01	+	1.319e+02 ± 9.81e+01	+	1.388e+02 ± 2.50e+01
f_{10}	3.789e+05 ± 4.23e+05	+	5.998e+03 ± 5.88e+03	=	3.413e+03 ± 1.92e+03	=	3.239e+03 ± 2.39e+03
f_{11}	2.673e+04 ± 1.34e+04	+	2.318e+03 ± 9.99e+02	+	8.704e+03 ± 4.03e+03	+	8.985e+01 ± 6.14e+01
f_{12}	-5.732e+02 ± 3.16e+01	-	-5.375e+02 ± 2.85e+02		1.360e+04 ± 6.23e+03	+	1.699e+03 ± 2.20e+03
f_{13}	5.572e+01 ± 1.78e+01	-	4.584e+01 ± 1.46e+01	-	6.169e+01 ± 1.15e+01	=	5.485e+01 ± 1.66e+01
f_{14}	-5.235e+01 ± 9.04e-05	-	-5.235e+01 ± 8.57e-03	-	-1.150e+01 ± 6.83e+00	+	-5.234e+01 ± 1.38e-03
f_{15}	1.580e+03 ± 2.25e+02	+	1.036e+03 ± 1.44e+01	=	1.086e+03 ± 1.97e+01	+	1.043e+03 ± 1.74e+01
f_{16}	8.363e+02 ± 7.75e+02	+	7.670e+01 ± 4.31e+00	=	1.306e+03 ± 3.45e+02	+	7.999e+01 ± 4.30e+00
f_{17}	2.517e+01 ± 2.03e+01	-	-1.537e+01 ± 6.97e-01	+	9.247e+00 ± 1.05e+01	+	-1.598e+01 ± 7.91e-01
f_{18}	1.995e+02 ± 1.38e+01	-	-1.135e+01 ± 3.70e+00	+	7.463e+01 ± 3.25e+01	+	-1.376e+01 ± 1.87e+00
f_{19}	-7.443e+01 ± 1.31e+01	-	-1.006e+02 ± 6.62e-01	-	-3.394e+01 ± 1.95e+01	+	-1.000e+02 ± 7.79e-01
f_{20}	-5.453e+02 ± 2.68e-01	-	-5.455e+02 ± 3.46e-01	-	-5.103e+02 ± 5.80e+01	+	-5.453e+02 ± 2.72e-01
f_{21}	5.317e+01 ± 1.40e+01	+	4.450e+01 ± 5.11e+00	-	5.004e+01 ± 1.18e+01	=	4.728e+01 ± 5.57e+00
f_{22}	-9.889e+02 ± 1.74e+01	=	-9.980e+02 ± 1.40e+00	=	-9.261e+02 ± 1.00e+01	+	-9.963e+02 ± 4.88e+00
f_{23}	1.108e+01 ± 5.90e+00	+	7.601e+00 ± 2.62e-01		9.848e+00 ± 1.18e+00	+	8.126e+00 ± 2.69e-01
f_{24}	5.951e+02 ± 1.12e+02	+	1.515e+02 ± 1.76e+01		1.808e+02 ± 1.45e+01	+	1.467e+02 ± 1.13e+01

Table 2. Average final results ± standard deviation and Wilcoxon test in 20 dimensions

Fcn.	ISPO	W	cDE	W	ABFO	W	cBFO
f_1	7.948e+01 ± 2.96e-15	-	8.005e+01 ± 1.31e+00	-	7.952e+01 ± 8.02e-03	+	7.949e+01 ± 1.21e-03
f_2	-2.099e+02 ± 5.81e-14	-	5.836e+00 ± 4.53e+02	-	1.582e+04 ± 1.10e+04	+	2.847e+03 ± 1.33e+03
f_3	-3.565e+02 ± 8.22e+01	-	3.295e+02 ± 4.77e+02	+	8.079e+05 ± 5.97e+05	+	-3.064e+02 ± 4.05e+01
f_4	-3.919e+02 ± 1.22e+01	-	-3.149e+02 ± 5.65e+01	-		+	-2.871e+02 ± 6.12e+01
f_5	-9.210e+00 ± 0.00e+00	-	-8.718e+00 ± 7.82e-01	-	-2.516e+00 ± 1.16e+00	+	-8.025e+00 ± 1.70e+00
f_6	7.985e+03 ± 6.94e+03	-	4.603e+01 ± 1.71e+03	+	9.264e+06 ± 3.46e+06	+	4.142e+01 ± 3.09e+01
f_7	1.486e+02 ± 6.80e+01	+	1.671e+02 ± 3.18e+01	+	1.113e+02 ± 9.17e+00	+	1.049e+02 ± 4.71e+00
f_8	1.711e+02 ± 3.03e+01	-	4.695e+02 ± 6.53e+02	+	1.900e+02 ± 1.71e+01	+	1.831e+02 ± 3.09e+01
f_9	1.350e+02 ± 2.56e+00	-	4.284e+02 ± 3.52e+02	+	1.457e+02 ± 1.70e+00	-	1.674e+02 ± 4.47e+01
f_{10}	8.883e+05 ± 8.17e+05	+	1.517e+05 ± 1.25e+05	+	1.108e+04 ± 4.28e+03	=	1.675e+04 ± 1.34e+04
f_{11}	8.075e+04 ± 3.37e+04	+	4.852e+03 ± 1.32e+03	+	2.465e+04 ± 6.03e+03	+	1.046e+02 ± 1.06e+01
f_{12}	5.344e+06 ± 2.62e+07	+	2.939e+06 ± 4.56e+06	+	6.616e+04 ± 1.97e+04	+	7.354e+03 ± 3.86e+03
f_{13}	5.491e+01 ± 2.15e+01	-	3.682e+02 ± 1.40e+02	+	7.406e+01 ± 7.61e+00	+	6.921e+01 ± 2.49e+01
f_{14}	-5.235e+01 ± 2.92e-04	-	-4.930e+01 ± 2.37e+00	-	-6.687e+00 ± 3.03e+00	+	-5.233e+01 ± 4.07e-03
f_{15}	2.516e+03 ± 4.52e+02	+	1.178e+03 ± 4.71e+01	+	1.434e+03 ± 7.67e+01	+	1.150e+03 ± 4.11e+01
f_{16}	1.183e+03 ± 6.96e+02	+	1.440e+02 ± 5.22e+01	+	2.394e+03 ± 3.74e+02	+	9.041e+01 ± 7.95e+00
f_{17}	1.638e+01 ± 1.19e+01	-	-1.298e+01 ± 9.02e-01	=	7.463e+00 ± 1.13e+01	+	-1.297e+01 ± 1.53e+00
f_{18}	1.352e+02 ± 5.22e+01	-	-1.782e+00 ± 3.71e+00	=	9.490e+01 ± 3.57e+01	+	-3.647e+00 ± 6.73e+00
f_{19}	-2.505e+01 ± 2.97e+01	-	-9.775e+01 ± 1.73e+00	=	-1.657e+01 ± 1.26e+01	+	-9.747e+01 ± 6.99e-01
f_{20}	-5.452e+02 ± 2.19e-01	=	-5.450e+02 ± 3.89e-01	-	-4.238e+01 ± 9.65e-01	+	-5.449e+02 ± 2.68e-01
f_{21}	5.860e+01 ± 2.02e+01	=	5.076e+01 ± 7.63e+00	+	4.777e+01 ± 7.89e+00	=	4.998e+01 ± 1.22e+01
f_{22}	-9.873e+02 ± 1.12e+01	=	-9.919e+02 ± 9.48e+00	+	-9.001e+02 ± 5.66e+00	+	-9.911e+02 ± 1.25e+01
f_{23}	1.483e+01 ± 5.62e+00	+	8.193e+00 ± 4.61e-01	-	1.495e+01 ± 2.22e+00	+	8.800e+00 ± 2.82e-01
f_{24}	1.495e+03 ± 1.97e+02	+	2.830e+02 ± 3.95e+01	+	2.954e+02 ± 3.30e+01	+	2.542e+02 ± 3.27e+01

can be considered memory saving heuristics, as they require a fixed amount of memory slots which does not depend on the problem dimension. In other words, if one of these algorithms is used to tackle a large scale problem, although the slots are as long as the problem dimensionality, these slots do not increase in number. More specifically, the ISPO scheme is a typical single solution algorithm, requiring only two memory slots, one for the current best solution and the other for a trial candidate solution. The cDE and cBFO structures are memory-wise slightly more expensive than ISPO as they require, on the top of the two slots for single solution algorithms, two extra slots for the virtual population PV. This compromise is made in order to have the advantages of a population-based search and a still low memory usage.

Table 3. Average final results ± standard deviation and Wilcoxon test in 40 dimensions

Fcn.	ISPO	W	cDE	W	ABFO	W	cBFO
f_1	**7.948e+01 ± 1.22e-14**	-	1.120e+02 ± 1.73e+01	+	7.960e+01 ± 9.75e-03	+	7.952e+01 ± 4.83e-03
f_2	**-2.099e+02 ± 1.12e-13**	-	4.907e+04 ± 6.04e+04	+	7.397e+04 ± 2.54e+04	+	9.396e+03 ± 2.90e+03
f_3	**-2.497e+02 ± 1.07e+02**	-	1.322e+04 ± 5.53e+03	+	2.838e+06 ± 1.44e+06	+	-3.848e+00 ± 7.46e+01
f_4	**-1.855e+02 ± 1.27e+02**	-	3.605e+02 ± 1.11e+02	+	4.467e+02 ± 1.16e+02	+	7.343e+01 ± 1.03e+02
f_5	**-9.210e+00 ± 0.00e+00**	-	1.155e+01 ± 7.56e+00	+	-1.921e+00 ± 7.38e-01	-	5.845e+00 ± 5.35e+00
f_6	2.640e+04 ± 2.19e+04	+	1.945e+04 ± 4.09e+03	+	1.983e+07 ± 4.90e+06	+	**1.019e+02 ± 4.10e+01**
f_7	6.123e+02 ± 5.34e+02	+	5.442e+02 ± 1.26e+02	+	3.082e+02 ± 6.89e+01	+	**1.623e+02 ± 2.18e+01**
f_8	**1.848e+02 ± 8.94e+01**	-	2.187e+04 ± 1.36e+04	+	2.305e+02 ± 2.61e+01	=	2.576e+02 ± 7.97e+01
f_9	1.629e+02 ± 2.67e+01	-	1.480e+04 ± 1.24e+04	+	1.828e+02 ± 3.98e+01	+	1.697e+02 ± 2.05e+01
f_{10}	2.349e+06 ± 2.09e+06	+	6.739e+05 ± 2.49e+05	+	6.860e+04 ± 2.07e+04	+	**5.332e+04 ± 3.01e+04**
f_{11}	2.131e+05 ± 1.01e+05	+	1.105e+04 ± 2.10e+03	+	4.285e+04 ± 6.09e+03	+	**1.436e+02 ± 1.76e+01**
f_{12}	**-6.032e+02 ± 1.13e+01**	-	7.085e+07 ± 2.97e+07	+	1.136e+05 ± 1.11e+04	+	7.161e+04 ± 4.75e+04
f_{13}	4.581e+01 ± 2.17e+01	-	1.319e+03 ± 2.46e+02	+	1.048e+02 ± 8.92e+00	+	9.299e+01 ± 3.23e+01
f_{14}	**-5.235e+01 ± 3.05e-04**	-	-3.288e+01 ± 5.51e+00	+	-3.147e+00 ± 1.36e+00	+	-5.231e+01 ± 7.71e-03
f_{15}	4.278e+03 ± 6.81e+02	+	1.693e+03 ± 1.18e+02	+	2.318e+03 ± 1.71e+02	+	**1.493e+03 ± 9.54e+01**
f_{16}	1.895e+03 ± 6.68e+02	+	4.456e+02 ± 1.01e+02	+	3.467e+03 ± 3.72e+02	+	**1.252e+02 ± 1.27e+01**
f_{17}	2.634e+01 ± 1.98e+01	+	-8.793e+00 ± 1.35e+00	=	2.020e+01 ± 2.17e+01	+	**-9.086e+00 ± 1.58e+00**
f_{18}	1.784e+02 ± 6.92e+01	+	**1.037e+01 ± 7.07e+00**	=	1.875e+02 ± 9.10e+01	+	1.050e+01 ± 6.20e+00
f_{19}	-3.630e-01 ± 2.66e+01	-	-8.942e+01 ± 2.43e+00	+	-7.683e+00 ± 2.79e+00	+	**-9.484e+01 ± 8.41e-01**
f_{20}	**-5.453e+02 ± 1.35e-01**	-	2.786e+03 ± 3.42e+03	+	-3.340e+02 ± 1.10e+02	+	-5.446e+02 ± 2.47e-01
f_{21}	7.488e+01 ± 2.37e+01	+	7.935e+01 ± 1.65e+01	+	7.945e+01 ± 2.81e+01	+	**4.975e+01 ± 1.46e+01**
f_{22}	-9.539e+02 ± 1.64e+01	-	-9.613e+02 ± 1.61e+01	+	-8.543e+02 ± 9.64e+00	+	**-9.889e+02 ± 8.18e+00**
f_{23}	1.659e+01 ± 6.73e+00	-	**9.141e+00 ± 4.27e-01**	-	2.298e+01 ± 3.40e+00	+	9.995e+00 ± 2.82e-01
f_{24}	2.861e+03 ± 2.59e+02	+	7.729e+02 ± 8.20e+01	+	8.291e+02 ± 8.52e+01	+	**5.534e+02 ± 3.95e+01**

For each algorithm and each test problem, 30 independent runs have been performed. The budget of each single run has been fixed equal to $5000 \cdot n$ fitness evaluations, where n is the dimensionality of the problem. All the experiments were executed using the optimization platform Kimeme, see [1]. Tables 1-3 show the obtained numerical results. Average final fitness values are computed for each algorithm and each problem over the 30 runs available. In each table, the best results are highlighted in bold face. In order to strengthen the statistical significance of the results, the Wilcoxon Rank-Sum test has also been applied according to the description given in [22], where the confidence level has been fixed to 0.95. In each table, the results of the Wilcoxon test for cBFO against the other algorithms considered in this study are displayed. A "+" indicates the case in which cBFO statistically outperforms, for the corresponding test problem, the algorithm indicated in column; a "=" indicates that a pairwise comparison leads to success of the Wilcoxon Rank-Sum test, i.e., the two algorithms have the same performance; a "−" indicates that cBFO is outperformed.

Numerical results show that cBFO has overall a respectful performance despite its limited memory requirement. In particular, cBFO outperforms, on a regular basis, ABFO (which, in turn, outperforms cBFO only in one case out of 72). This fact is an extremely interesting finding which, according to our interpretation, is related to two different counterbalancing effects. The first one is related to the population modeling of compact algorithms: the sampling mechanism indeed seems to introduce a beneficial randomness, see [15], which endows the original BFO framework with extra search moves that allow the exploration of different regions of the search space. The second effect is related to the inherent exploitative pressure which characterizes a compact algorithm, and which allows, especially in high-dimensional cases, a better exploitation of the most promising search directions.

As for the other memory saving algorithms considered in this study, a clear trend emerges. In 10-dimensional problems, cBFO is outperformed by cDE, especially on separable functions (6 "+" and 13 "−"), while it slightly outperforms ISPO (11 "+" and 6 "−"). In 20-dimensional problems, both ISPO and cBFO display a better performance than in 10 dimensions. In particular, cBFO has a similar performance with respect to ISPO (12 "+" and 10 "−"), while it outperforms cDE (13 "+" and 3 "-"). This trend is confirmed in 40-dimensional problems, where cBFO and ISPO have a similar performance (13 "+" and 11 "−") and cDE is clearly outperformed by cBFO (21 "+" and 1 "−"). In conclusion, cBFO seems to robustly handle various landscapes and offer a good performance in several cases, especially in high-dimensional cases.

3.1   Holm-Bonferroni Procedure

In order to draw some statistically significant conclusions regarding the performance of cBFO, the Holm-Bonferroni procedure, see [11,12], for the four algorithms under study and the 72 problems under consideration has been performed. The Holm-Bonferroni procedure consists of the following. Considering the results in the tables above, the four algorithms under analysis have been ranked on the basis of their average performance calculated over the 72 test problems. More specifically, a score R_i for $i = 1, \cdots, N_A$ (where N_A is the number of algorithms under analysis, $N_A = 4$ in our case) has been assigned in the following way: for each problem, a score of 4 is assigned to the algorithm displaying the best performance, 3 is assigned to the second best, and so on. The algorithm displaying the worst performance scores 1. For each algorithm, a mean score has been calculated averaging the sum of the scores of each problem. On the basis of these scores the algorithms have been sorted. Within the calculated R_i values, cBFO has been taken as a reference algorithm. Indicating with R_0 the rank of cBFO, and with R_j for $j = 1, \cdots, N_A - 1$ the rank of one of the remaining three algorithms, the values z_j, for $j = 1, \cdots, N_A - 1$, have been calculated as $z_j = (R_j - R_0) / \sqrt{\frac{N_A(N_A+1)}{6N_{TP}}}$, where N_{TP} is the number of test problems in consideration ($N_{TP} = 72$ in our case). By means of the z_j values, the corresponding cumulative normal distribution values p_j have been calculated. These p_j values have then been compared with the corresponding $\delta/(N_A - j)$ where δ is the significance level of null-hypothesis rejection, set to 0.05 in our case. Table 4 displays ranks, z_j values, p_j values, and corresponding $\delta/(N_A - j)$. The rank of cBFO is shown in parenthesis. The values of z_j and p_j are expressed in terms of z_{N_A-j} and p_{N_A-j} for $j = 1, \cdots, N_A - 1$. Moreover, it is indicated whether the null-hypothesis (that the two algorithms have indistinguishable performances) is "Rejected" i.e., cBFO statistically outperforms the algorithm under consideration, or "Accepted" if the distribution of values can be considered the same (there is no out-performance). Numerical results in Table 4 show that cBFO has the best rank among the algorithms considered in this study. However, the rank difference is large enough to claim that cBFO "globally" outperforms only ABFO and ISPO, while the null hypothesis is accepted when cBFO is compared to cDE, meaning that the performance of cDE and cBFO is indistinguishable on the selected benchmarks. This result is, in our opinion, remarkable, since it

Table 4. Holm-Bonferroni Procedure

$N_A - j$	Algorithm	$z_{N_A} - j$	$p_{N_A} - j$	$\delta/(N_A - j)$	Hypothesis	Rank
3	ABFO	-6.65e+00	1.48e-11	1.67e-02	Rejected	1.75
2	ISPO	-3.42e+00	3.12e-04	2.50e-02	Rejected	2.4444
1	cDE	-2.39e+00	8.46e-03	5.00e-02	Accepted	2.6667
						(3.1806)

indicates not only that cBFO clearly outperforms its population-based counterpart, but also that it represents a good alternative to a robust and versatile optimizer like cDE. Most importantly, these results confirm our previous finding, see [17], that a properly designed memory saving algorithm can successfully tackle complex problems, with different dimensionality, even better than overwhelmingly complicated population based algorithms. In this light, we think that a proper algorithmic design will allow, in the future, the integration of Computational Intelligence methods within cheap devices notwithstanding the limited hardware.

4 Conclusion

This paper introduces a novel compact optimization algorithm, namely compact Bacterial Foraging Optimization (cBFO). Like its population-based counterpart, this heuristic employs the metaphor of the chemotaxis mechanism which occurs in bacterial foraging. An extensive set of test problems has been considered for algorithmic testing. Numerical results show that, despite an extremely limited memory footprint, cBFO clearly outperforms one of the most recent implementations of population-based BFO which employs adaptation. In addition, cBFO is competitive with another compact algorithm employing a different logic, i.e. the compact Differential Evolution. Further studies will investigate the introduction of adaptive and self-adaptive schemes in the cBFO framework here proposed.

References

1. Cyber Dyne Srl Home Page, http://cyberdynesoft.it/
2. Ahn, C.W., Ramakrishna, R.S.: Elitism based compact genetic algorithms. IEEE Transactions on Evolutionary Computation 7(4), 367–385 (2003)
3. Biswas, A., Dasgupta, S., Das, S., Abraham, A.: Synergy of PSO and Bacterial Foraging Optimization: A Comparative Study on Numerical Benchmarks. In: Corchado, E., et al. (eds.) Innovations in Hybrid Intelligent Systems. ASC, vol. 44, pp. 255–263. Springer, Heidelberg (2007)
4. Chen, H., Zhu, Y., Hu, K.: Self-adaptation in Bacterial Foraging Optimization algorithm. In: Proc. 3rd International Conference on Intelligent System and Knowledge Engineering, ISKE 2008, vol. 1, pp. 1026–1031 (November 2008)
5. Chen, H., Zhu, Y., Hu, K.: Cooperative bacterial foraging optimization. Discrete Dynamics in Nature and Society 2009 (2009)
6. Chen, H., Zhu, Y., Hu, K.: Adaptive bacterial foraging optimization. Abstract and Applied Analysis 2011 (2011)

7. Dang, J., Brabazon, A., O'Neill, M., Edelman, D.: Option Model Calibration Using a Bacterial Foraging Optimization Algorithm. In: Giacobini, M., Brabazon, A., Cagnoni, S., Di Caro, G.A., Drechsler, R., Ekárt, A., Esparcia-Alcázar, A.I., Farooq, M., Fink, A., McCormack, J., O'Neill, M., Romero, J., Rothlauf, F., Squillero, G., Uyar, A.Ş., Yang, S. (eds.) EvoWorkshops 2008. LNCS, vol. 4974, pp. 113–122. Springer, Heidelberg (2008)
8. Das, S., Biswas, A., Dasgupta, S., Abraham, A.: Bacterial foraging optimization algorithm: Theoretical foundations, analysis, and applications. Foundations of Computational Intelligence (3), 23–55 (2009)
9. Dasgupta, S., Das, S., Abraham, A., Biswas, A.: Adaptive computational chemotaxis in bacterial foraging optimization: an analysis. Trans. Evol. Comp. 13(4), 919–941 (2009)
10. Dasgupta, S., Das, S., Biswas, A., Abraham, A.: Automatic circle detection on digital images with an adaptive bacterial foraging algorithm. Soft Comput. 14(11), 1151–1164 (2010)
11. García, S., Fernández, A., Luengo, J., Herrera, F.: A study of statistical techniques and performance measures for genetics-based machine learning: accuracy and interpretability. Soft Computing 13(10), 959–977 (2008)
12. Holm, S.: A simple sequentially rejective multiple test procedure. Scandinavian Journal of Statistics 6(2), 65–70 (1979)
13. Kim, D.H., Abraham, A., Cho, J.H.: A hybrid genetic algorithm and bacterial foraging approach for global optimization. Information Sciences 177(18), 3918–3937 (2007)
14. Mininno, E., Cupertino, F., Naso, D.: Real-valued compact genetic algorithms for embedded microcontroller optimization. IEEE Transactions on Evolutionary Computation 12(2), 203–219 (2008)
15. Mininno, E., Neri, F., Cupertino, F., Naso, D.: Compact differential evolution. IEEE Transactions on Evolutionary Computation 15(1), 32–54 (2011)
16. Hansen, N.: Auger, A., Finck, S., Ros, R., et al.: Real-parameter black-box optimization benchmarking 2010: Noiseless functions definitions. Tech. Rep. RR-6829, INRIA (2010)
17. Neri, F., Iacca, G., Mininno, E.: Disturbed exploitation compact differential evolution for limited memory optimization problems. Information Sciences 181(12), 2469–2487 (2011)
18. Passino, K.M.: Biomimicry of bacterial foraging for distributed optimization and control. IEEE Control Systems Magazine 22(3), 52–67 (2002)
19. Shao, Y., Chen, H.: The optimization of cooperative bacterial foraging. In: World Congress on Software Engineering, vol. 2, pp. 519–523 (2009)
20. Tripathy, M., Mishra, S., Venayagamoorthy, G.: Bacteria foraging: A new tool for simultaneous robust design of upfc controllers. In: IJCNN 2006: International Joint Conference on Neural Networks, pp. 2274–2280 (2006)
21. Wang, X.S., Cheng, Y.H., Hao, M.L.: Estimation of distribution algorithm based on bacterial foraging and its application in predictive control. Dianzi Xuebao (Acta Electronica Sinica) 38(2), 333–339 (2010)
22. Wilcoxon, F.: Individual comparisons by ranking methods. Biometrics Bulletin 1(6), 80–83 (1945)
23. Zhou, J., Ji, Z., Shen, L.: Simplified intelligence single particle optimization based neural network for digit recognition. In: Proceedings of the Chinese Conference on Pattern Recognition (2008)

A Coevolutionary MiniMax Algorithm
for the Detection of Nash Equilibrium

Andrew Koh

Institute for Transport Studies, University of Leeds
34-40 University Road, Leeds LS2 9JT, United Kingdom
a.koh@its.leeds.ac.uk

Abstract. This paper introduces CoMiniMax, a coevolutionary Minimax algorithm, based on Differential Evolution, for the detection of Nash
Equilibrium in games. We discuss the robust theoretical principles of the
proposed algorithm. The algorithm is illustrated on examples in economics, transportation and deregulated electricity markets. Numerical
experience demonstrates that the algorithm is a useful tool for the study
of Nash Equilibrium problems.

Keywords: Coevolution, Nash Equilibrium, Minimax, Equilibrium Problems with Equilibrium Constraints (EPECs).

1 Introduction

This paper introduces a coevolutionary minimax technique specifically designed
for solving Nash Equilibrium (NE) problems. The minimax optimization method
is a mathematical programming technique for identifying solutions that are robust
i.e. provide the best "worst case" performance. Many problems arising in science
and engineering can be formulated as minimax problems [1]. This has resulted
in applications in fields as diverse as game theory [25], control and systems engineering [12] and finance [22]. Hence there has been much research on minimax
optimization using deterministic [1,6], and evolutionary [12,14] methods.

In this paper, we propose a method that is applicable to a broad class of
single shot games. Although we employ evolutionary heuristics, we stress that
the proposed method enjoys robust theoretical backing.

The rest of this paper is organized as follows. Following this introduction,
Section 2 focuses on Nash Equilibrium and the theoretical foundations of the
proposed method. The CoMiniMax Algorithm, outlined in Section 3 is applied to
the examples in economics, transportation systems management and the deregulated electricity market in Section 4. Section 5 concludes.

2 The Nash Equilibrium Problem

We consider single shot normal form games with a set of players indexed by
$v \in \{1, 2, ..., \rho\}$. Each player can play a strategy $x_v \in X_v$ which all players

L. Rutkowski et al. (Eds.): SIDE 2012 and EC 2012, LNCS 7269, pp. 93–101, 2012.

announce simultaneously. $X (\equiv \prod_{v=1}^{\rho} X_v) \subseteq \mathbb{R}^d$ is the collective action space for all players. We assume the absence of any preplay communication or collusion. Our focus is on games with continuous strategy spaces and ignore mixed strategies.

To emphasize the variables chosen by player v, we write (x_v, x_{-v}) where x_{-v} is the combined strategies of all players in the game *excluding* that of player v. Writing (x_v, x_{-v}) *does not* suggest that the components of x are reordered such that x_v becomes the first block. Let $\pi_v(x)$ be the payoff/reward to player v if x is played.

Definition 1. *[20] A combined strategy profile* $x^* = (x_1^*, x_2^*, ..., x_\rho^*) \in X$ *is a Nash Equilibrium (NE) for the game if :*

$$\pi_v(x_v^*, x_{-v}^*) \geq \pi_v(x_v, x_{-v}^*) \ \forall x_v \in X_v \ , v \in \{1, 2, ..., \rho\} \tag{1}$$

At a NE no player can benefit (increase individual payoffs) by unilaterally deviating from the current chosen strategy.

2.1   The Nikaido Isoda Function

The Nikaido Isoda (NI) (or "Ky Fan") function in Eq. 2 is a tool often used in the study of NE problems [2,13]. Each summand of Eq. 2 shows the increase in payoff a player could receive by unilaterally deviating and playing a strategy $y_v \in X_v$ while all others play according to x.

$$\Psi(x, y) = \sum_{v=1}^{\rho} [\pi_v(y_v, x_{-v}) - \pi_v(x_v, x_{-v})] \tag{2}$$

The NI function is always non-negative for any combination of x and y. Eq. 2 is everywhere non-positive when either x or y is a NE [2]. This follows from Definition 1 since at a NE no player can increase their payoffs by unilaterally deviating. The key result is summarized in Definition 2.

Definition 2. *[13] A vector* $x^* \in X$ *is a Nash Equilibrium if* $\Psi(x, y) = 0$.

2.2   Solution Algorithms for NE Problems

The optimal move a player should make is governed by the best response function. If $\pi_v(x)$ is continuously differentiable, then the best response function for player v is given by $d\pi_v(x_v, x_{-v})/dx_v$ [8,11]. The NE is the intersections of these best response functions for all players which leads to solving a system of ρ equations i.e. $d\pi_v(x_v, x_{-v})/dx_v = 0, v \in \{1, 2, ..., \rho\}$ [3,11].

This analytical method is however infeasible for realistic problems. In practice, finding NE amounts to a fixed point iteration [10] or by solving a Complementarity Problem [15]. Convergence of these methods relies on the payoff functions possessing diagonally dominant Jacobians ([8], Theorem 4.1, pp. 280). For a review of such methods see [7]. [18] developed an evolutionary method based on the concept of Nash Dominance which also embodies the NI function as its theoretical foundation (see also [17]).

Ideas from coevolution have been exported into algorithms designed for the detection of NE e.g. [4]. In this paper, we propose a coevolutionary algorithm designed to specifically minimize the maximum of the NI function.

3 A Coevolutionary MiniMax Algorithm - CoMiniMax

CoMiniMax operates on the objective function shown in Eq. 3. The algorithm is designed to terminate when $\Psi(x, y)$ attains the value of 0 (within tolerance) when the NE Solution is found (cf. Definition 2).

$$\min_{x \in X} \max_{y \in X} \Psi(x, y) \tag{3}$$

CoMiniMax utilizes two populations comprising NP chromosomes each, $\mathcal{P}_1$ and $\mathcal{P}_2$ (representing x and y respectively). At each outer iteration loop, we evolve $\mathcal{P}_1$ using Differential Evolution (DE) [21] to minimize $\Psi(x, y)$. Simultaneously $\mathcal{P}_2$ is evolved to maximize $\Psi(x, y)$. The process terminates when either the maximum number of user specified iterations, Max_{it}, is exceeded or when the value of the NI function, $\Psi(x, y)$, reaches the user specified termination tolerance ϵ. Based on Definition 2, the solution thus obtained is a Nash Equilibrium.

Algorithm 1. Coevolutionary MiniMax Algorithm for Nash Equilibrium Problems - CoMiniMax

---

1: Input: NP, Max_{it}, $\epsilon > 0$, Control Parameters of Differential Evolution (DE), players' payoff functions
2: $it \leftarrow 0$
3: Randomly initialize the first population of NP strategy profiles $\mathcal{P}_1^{it}$
4: Randomly initialize the second population of NP strategy profiles $\mathcal{P}_2^{it}$
5: $it = it + 1$
6: **while** $it \leq Max_{it}$ and $\Psi(x, y) > \epsilon$ **do**
7:     Evolve $\mathcal{P}_1^{it}$ using DE for inner iterations in_{it} to minimize $\Psi(x, y^*)$ given $\mathcal{P}_2^{it-1}$
8:     Set x^* as the fittest member of $\mathcal{P}_1^{it}$
9:     Evolve $\mathcal{P}_2^{it}$ using DE for in_{it} to maximize $\Psi(x^*, y)$ given $\mathcal{P}_1^{it}$
10:     Set y^* as the fittest member of $\mathcal{P}_2^{it}$
11:     Compute $\Psi(x^*, y^*)$
12:     $it = it + 1$
13: **end while**

In the numerical examples reported in the following section, we assumed 5 inner iterations, 15 outer iterations and used a population comprising 20 chromosomes each in both $\mathcal{P}_1$ and $\mathcal{P}_2$. DE control parameters are taken from [17].

4   Numerical Examples and Applications

4.1   Example 1: Cournot Duopoly

We consider the standard Cournot Duopoly model from economics [11]. Let the market comprise only two producers maximizing profit through the production and sale of a homogeneous product. Each producer is unaware of the amount produced by his counterpart. The objective is to determine the equilibrium output levels for each producer such that no producer is able to increase its profit by changing production levels (i.e. a NE as given in Definition 1). The payoff/profit for producer $i, i \in \{1, 2\}$, π_i, given by the difference between revenues and production costs, defined as:

$$\pi_i = p(Q)q_i - c_i q_i, i \in \{1, 2\}$$

We assume that the entire market is supplied by these two producers so $Q = q_1 + q_2$. Let $p(Q)$ denote the inverse demand function giving price as a function of quantity and has the functional form:

$$p(Q) = \begin{cases} 24 - Q, \text{if } Q < 24 \\ 0, \text{if } Q \geqslant 24 \end{cases}$$

Assume there are no fixed costs and production cost per unit, $c_i = 9, i \in 1, 2$ for both producers. Following [11], we can analytically solve for the NE output. From the first order conditions for each producer's profit maximum with respect to its own output levels, we obtain the following system of equations:

$$d\pi_1/dq_1 = 15 - 2q_1 - q_2 = 0$$
$$d\pi_2/dq_2 = 15 - 2q_2 - q_1 = 0$$

The solution of this system is $\{q_1^*, q_2^*\} = \{5, 5\}$. CoMiniMax easily converges to this analytical solution as illustrated in Figure 1.

The remaining two examples in this paper focus on a special class of Nash Games with a distinctive hierarchical structure. These are collectively known as Equilibrium Problems with Equilibrium Constraints (EPECs) [19]. In EPECs, players at the upper level, known as "leaders", are assumed to act non cooperatively to maximise individual payoffs. However, each leader's payoff is influenced not only by their competitor's actions but also by the behaviour of the agents or "followers" at the lower level which arise in the form of a constraint specifying equilibrium in a given parametric system [17].

4.2   Example 2: Highway Network with Competing Toll Operators

This example presents a problem that arises in transportation network analysis that fits within the structure of an EPEC. This problem is to find an NE toll (road user charge per vehicle) level for each revenue maximising operator who separately controls a predefined link on a given traffic network in competition

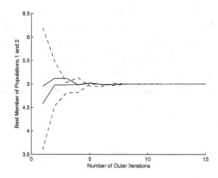

Fig. 1. Cournot Duopoly: Best Member of $\mathcal{P}_1$ (solid lines) and $\mathcal{P}_2$ (dashed lines) at Each Outer Iteration

with others doing the same simultaneously. To facilitate exposition, we introduce the notation as follows:

A: the set of directed links in a traffic network,

B: the set of links which have their tolls optimised, $B \subset A$

K: the set of origin destination (O-D) pairs in the network

f: the vector of link flows $f = [f_a]$, $a \in A$

x: the vector of link tolls $x = [x_a]$, $a \in B$

$c(v)$: the vector of monotonically non decreasing travel costs as a function of link flows $\mathbf{c}(\mathbf{v}) = [c_a(v_a)]$, $a \in A$

d: the continuous and monotonically decreasing demand function for each O-D pair as a function of the generalized travel cost between OD pair k only, $d = [d_k]$, $k \in K$

D^{-1}: the inverse demand function and

Ω: feasible region of flow vectors,defined by a linear system of flow conservation constraints.

Each player wishes to maximize individual revenue from tolls as shown in Eq. 4.

$$\max_{x_v} \pi_v(x) = f_v(x)x_v, v \in 1, 2 \qquad (4)$$

where f is obtained by solving the Variational Inequality (VI) in Eq. 5 (see [5]; [23])

$$c\left(f^*, x\right)^T \cdot \left(f - f^*\right) - D^{-1}\left(d^*, x\right)^T \cdot (d - d^*) \geq 0, \forall (f, d) \in \Omega \qquad (5)$$

This VI represents Wardrop's principle of route choice which states that no road user on the network can unilaterally benefit (reduce travel time) by changing routes at the equilibrium [26]. The equilibrium toll levels can be determined by Definition 1 and it is the very presence of the VI constraint Eq. 5 that transforms our problem into an EPEC because each player at the upper level (individual toll operator) has to take into account the route choices of the users of the network (followers) when setting the toll levels in order to maximize revenue. Once the toll vector is input, solving the VI entails performing a traffic assignment to obtain the link flows and hence allow evaluation of each player's objective.

Assume that links numbered 7 and 10 (shown as dashed lines in Figure 2) are the only two links which are tolled. Table 1 compares the result obtained by the proposed CoMiniMax algorithm against others reported in the literature.

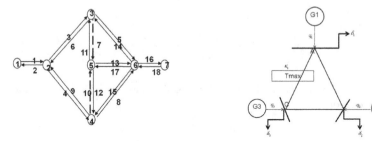

Fig. 2. Example 2: Nine Node 18 Link Highway Network from [16]. Links 7 and 10 (dash lines) are controlled by competing toll operators.

Fig. 3. Example 3: Three bus network model from [24]. Players 1, 2 and 3 are located at G1,G2 and G3 respectively.

Table 1. Example 2: Comparison of results of CoMiniMax with others reported

Source	[16]	[17]	This Paper
Link 7	141.37	141.36	141.36
Link 10	138.29	138.28	138.29

4.3   Example 3: Competition in Deregulated Electricity Markets

In deregulated electricity markets, electricity generating companies ("GENCOs") submit bids of the quantities of electricity they wish to supply to meet the market demand. These bids are then cleared by the Independent System Operator (ISO). However the price (and individual profits) are not only dependent on their individual bids but also that of their competitors and prices are not known until the market clearing is performed by the ISO [3,9,24]. This leads to an EPEC and CoMiniMax can be applied to this "pool based bidding" game.

Consider the three player model from [3] with the 3 bus network used as shown in Figure 3. Three players submit bids of quantities of electricity (in Megawatts per hour) they wish to supply to maximize individual profits according to Eq. 6.

$$\max_{x_v} \ \pi_v(x_v, x_{-v}) = \lambda_v^* x_v - c_v(x_v), v \in \{1, 2, 3\} \tag{6}$$

where λ_v is obtained by the ISO solving the system (Eqs. 7a - 7e) by maximizing the benefits at each bus for a given vector of bid submissions.

$$\max_{\delta_1,\delta_2,\delta_3} \underbrace{B_1(\delta_1) + B_2(\delta_2) + B_3(\delta_3)}_{\text{(Benefits at each bus)}} \tag{7a}$$

subject to

$$2\theta_1 - \theta_2 = x_1 - \delta_1 \tag{7b}$$

$$-\theta_1 + 2\theta_2 = x_2 - \delta_2 \tag{7c}$$

$$-\theta_1 - \theta_2 = x_3 - \delta_3 \tag{7d}$$

$$-T^{Max} \leq \kappa_1 \leq T^{Max} \tag{7e}$$

The system Eq. 7 is analogous to the route choice constraint in the previous example and hence this problem can also be classed as an EPEC. The prices $\lambda_v^*, v \in \{1,2,3\}$ is given by the Lagrange multiplier of the equality constraints 7b, 7c and 7d which model the dc powerflow equations [9]. Note that θ_1 and θ_2 represent the powerflows on lines AC and -AC respectively. The last constraint 7e is the transmission limit.

The individual benefit functions $B_v(\delta_v)$ at each bus and the cost functions $c_v(x_v)$ for each player used are exactly as given as in [3]. T^{Max} is set to 100. Table 2 compares the results from [3] with those obtained by CoMiniMax.

Table 2. Example 3 - 3 Bus Model (Megawatts per Hour)

Player	1	2	3
[3]	1105	1046	995
Results from CoMiniMax:			
Mean	1104.99	1046.47	995.15
Standard Deviation of $\mathcal{P}_1$	0.005	0.000	0.0001
Standard Deviation of $\mathcal{P}_2$	0.001	0.004	0.0003

5   Summary and Conclusions

This paper has presented a coevolutionary algorithm, CoMiniMax, which is based on the minimax framework for evolving solutions to Nash Equilibrium Problems. The algorithm has been demonstrated on a Cournot Nash game as well as on EPECs arising in transportation networks and electricity markets. Although evolutionary heuristics have been employed, the algorithm has robust theoretical backing in the Nikaido Isoda function. On the test problems, we have demonstrated that this algorithm is able to successfully replicate previous results reported in the literature. The limited numerical experience gained thus far supports the view that the algorithm could be a useful aid in the study of Nash Equilibrium problems.

Acknowledgments. The research reported here is funded by the Engineering and Physical Sciences Research Council of the UK under Grant EP/H021345/1.

References

1. Antonio, A., Lu, W.: Practical Optimization Algorithms and Engineering Applications. Springer, New York (2007)
2. Contreras, J., Klusch, M., Krawzyck, J.B.: Numerical solutions to Nash-Cournot equilibrium in electricity markets. IEEE T. Power Syst. 19(1), 195–206 (2004)
3. Cunningham, L.B., Baldick, R., Baughman, M.L.: An Empirical Study of Applied Game Theory: Transmission Constrained Cournot Behavior. IEEE T. Power Syst. 22(1), 166–172 (2002)
4. Curzon Price, T.: Using co-evolutionary programming to simulate strategic behavior in markets. J. Evol. Econ. 7(3), 219–254 (1997)
5. Dafermos, S.C.: Traffic Equilibrium and Variational Inequalities. Transport Sci. 14(1), 42–54 (1980)
6. Dem'yanov, V.F., Malozemov, V.N.: Introduction to Minimax. Dover, New York (1990)
7. Facchinei, F., Pang, J.: Finite Dimensional Variational Inequalities and Complementarity Problems, vol. 1. Springer, New York (2003)
8. Gabay, D., Moulin, H.: On the uniqueness and stability of Nash-equilibria in non cooperative games. In: Bensoussan, A., et al. (eds.) Applied Stochastic Control in Econometrics and Management Science, pp. 271–293. North Holland, Amsterdam (1980)
9. Glover, J., Sarma, M., Overbye, T.: Power Systems Analysis and Design. Thomson, Toronto (2008)
10. Harker, P.T.: A variational inequality approach for the determination of Oligopolistic market equilibrium. Math. Program. 30(1), 105–111 (1984)
11. Henderson, J.M., Quandt, R.E.: Microeconomic Theory. McGraw-Hill, New York (1980)
12. Herrmann, J.W.: A Genetic Algorithm for Minimax Optimization Problems. In: IEEE Congress on Evolutionary Computation, Washington DC, July 6-9, pp. 1099–1103 (1999)
13. von Heusinger, A., Kanzow, C.: Relaxation Methods for Generalized Nash Equilibrium Problems with Inexact Line Search. J. Optimiz. Theory App. 143(1), 159–183 (2009)
14. Jensen, M.: A new look at solving minimax problems with coevolutionary genetic algorithms. In: Resende, M.G.C., de Sousa, J.P., Viana, A. (eds.) Metaheuristics: Computer Decision-Making, pp. 369–384. Kluwer, MA (2004)
15. Karamardian, S.: Generalized complementarity problems. J. Optimiz. Theory App. 8(3), 161–168 (1971)
16. Koh, A., Shepherd, S.: Tolling, collusion and equilibrium problems with equilibrium constraints. Trasporti Europei 43, 3–22 (2010), http://www.istiee.org/te/papers/N44/44NSKAD_KohShepherd.pdf

17. Koh, A.: An evolutionary algorithm based on Nash Dominance for Equilibrium Problems with Equilibrium Constraints. Appl. Soft Comput. 12(1), 161–173 (2012)
18. Lung, R.I., Dumitrescu, D.: Computing Nash equilibria by means of evolutionary computation. Int. J. Comput. Commun. Control III, 364–368 (2008)
19. Mordukhovich, B.S.: Optimization and equilibrium problems with equilibrium constraints. OMEGA-Int. J. Manage. S 33(5), 379–384 (2005)
20. Nash, J.: Equilibrium points in N-person games. P. Natl. Acad. Sci. USA 36(1), 48–49 (1950)
21. Price, K., Storn, R., Lampinen, J.: Differential evolution: a practical approach to global optimization. Springer, Berlin (2005)
22. Rustem, B., Howe, M.: Algorithms for worst case design and applications to risk management. Princeton University Press, Princeton (2002)
23. Smith, M.J.: The existence, uniqueness and stability of traffic equilibria. Transport. Res. B-Meth. 13(4), 295–304 (1979)
24. Son, Y., Baldick, R.: Hybrid coevolutionary programming for Nash equilibrium search in games with local optima. IEEE T. Evolut. Comput. 8(4), 305–315 (2004)
25. Von Neumman, J., Morgenstern, O.: Theory of Games and Economic Behaviour. Princeton University Press, Princeton (1944)
26. Wardrop, J.G.: Some theoretical aspects of road traffic research. P. I. Civil Eng. Pt 2 1(36), 325–378 (1952)

Real-Time Tracking of Full-Body Motion Using Parallel Particle Swarm Optimization with a Pool of Best Particles

Tomasz Krzeszowski[2,1], Bogdan Kwolek[2,1], Boguslaw Rymut[2,1],
Konrad Wojciechowski[1], and Henryk Josinski[1]

[1] Polish-Japanese Institute of Information Technology
Koszykowa 86, 02-008 Warszawa, Poland
bytom@pjwstk.edu.pl
[2] Rzeszów University of Technology
W. Pola 2, 35-959 Rzeszów, Poland
bkwolek@prz.edu.pl

Abstract. In this paper we present a particle swarm optimization (PSO) based approach for marker-less full body motion tracking. The objective function is smoothed in an annealing scheme and then quantized. This allows us to extract a pool of candidate best particles. The algorithm selects a global best from such a pool to force the PSO jump out of stagnation. Experiments on 4-camera datasets demonstrate the robustness and accuracy of our method. The tracking is conducted on 2 PC nodes with multi-core CPUs, connected by 1 GigE. This makes our system capable of accurately recovering full body movements with 14 fps.

1 Introduction

Tracking of 3D articulated body motion in image sequences plays an important role due to wide variety of potential applications. The aim of articulated body tracking is to estimate the joint angles of the human body at any time. The recovery of human body movements from image sequences is a very challenging problem. The difficulties arise mainly due to the high dimensionality and non-linearity of the search space, large variability in human appearance, noisy image observations, self-occlusion, and complex human motions. To cope with such difficulties, much previous work has focused on the use of 3D human body models of various complexity to recover the position, orientation and joint angles from 2D image sequences [3][4][9][10]. An articulated human body can be perceived as a kinematic chain consisting of at least eleven parts, corresponding to the main body parts. Usually such a 3D human model is built on very simple geometric primitives like truncated cones or cylinders. Given the 3D model, a lot of hypothetical body poses are generated and then projected into the image plane in order to find the configuration of the 3D model, whose projection matches best the current image observations. Multiple cameras and simplified backgrounds are commonly used to ameliorate some of practical difficulties arising due to occlusions and depth ambiguities [9][10].

L. Rutkowski et al. (Eds.): SIDE 2012 and EC 2012, LNCS 7269, pp. 102–109, 2012.

2   Searching Schemes for Human Motion Tracking

In tracking of the articulated human motion the particle filtering is utilized in the majority of the trackers. Particle filters [5] are recursive Bayesian filters that are based on Monte Carlo simulations. They approximate a posterior distribution for the human pose on the basis of a series of observations. The high dimensionality of the search space entails vast number of particles to approximate well the posterior probability of the states. Moreover, sample impoverishment may prevent particle filters from maintaining multimodal distribution for longer periods of time. Therefore, many efforts have been devoted to confining the search space to promising regions that contain the true body pose. Deutscher and Reid [3] developed an annealed particle filter, which adopts an annealing scheme together with the stochastic sampling to achieve better concentration of the particle spread close to modes of the probability distribution. To achieve this the fitness function is smoothed using annealing factors $0 = \alpha_1 < \alpha_2, \ldots, < \alpha_n = 1$, and in consequence the particles migrate towards the extremum without getting stuck in local minima. In addition, a crossover operation is employed in order to obtain an improved particle's diversity.

The annealed particle filter greatly improves the tracking performance in comparison to the ordinary particle filtering. However, a considerable number of particles it still required. In contrast, the particle swarm optimization (PSO) [7], which is population-based searching technique, has higher searching capabilities owning to combining the local search and global one. A basic variant of the PSO algorithm is built on particles representing candidate solutions. These particles are moved around in the search-space according to a few very simple rules. The movements of the particles are guided by their own finest known locations in the search-space as well as the entire swarm's best location. Particles move through the solution space, and undergo evaluation according to some fitness function $f()$. While the swarm as a whole gravitates towards the global extremum, the individual particles are capable of ignoring many local optima. In the dynamic optimization the aim is not only to seek the extrema, but also to follow their progression through the space as closely as possible. Since the object tracking is a kind of dynamic optimization, the tracking can be attained through incorporating the temporal continuity information into the ordinary PSO. In consequence, the tracking can be realized by a sequence of static PSO-based optimizations, followed by re-diversification of the particles to cover the possible poses in the next time step. The re-diversification of the particle i can be realized on the basis of normal distribution concentrated around the state estimate $\hat{x}_{t-1}$, $x_t^{(i)} \leftarrow \mathcal{N}(\hat{x}_{t-1}, \Sigma)$.

In the original PSO, convergence of particles towards its attractors is not guaranteed. Clerc and Kennedy [2] studied the mechanisms to improve the convergence speed and proposed constriction methodologies to ensure convergence and to fine-tune the search. They proposed to utilize a constriction factor ω in the following form of the formula expressing the i-th particle's velocity:

$$v^{i,k+1} = \omega[v^{i,k} + c_1 r_1(p^i - x^{i,k}) + c_2 r_2(g - x^{i,k})] \tag{1}$$

where constants c_1 and c_2 are responsible for balancing the influence of the individual's knowledge and that of the group, respectively, r_1 and r_2 stand for uniformly distributed random numbers, x^i denotes position of the i-th particle, p^i is the local best position of particle, whereas g is the global best position.

In our approach the value of ω depends on annealing factor α as follows:

$$\omega = -0.8\alpha + 1.4 \tag{2}$$

where $\alpha = 0.1 + \frac{k}{K+1}$, $k = 0, 1, \ldots, K$, and K is the number of iterations. The annealing factor is also used to smooth the objective function. The larger the iteration number is, the smaller is the smoothing. In consequence, in the last iteration the algorithm utilizes the non-smoothed function. The algorithm termed as annealed PSO (APSO) [8] can be expressed as follows:

1. For each particle i
2.   initialize $v_t^{i,0}$
3. $x_t^{i,0} \sim \mathcal{N}(g_{t-1}, \Sigma_0)$
4. $p_t^i = x_t^{i,0}$, $f_t^i = f(x_t^{i,0})$
5. $u_t^i = f_t^i$, $\tilde{u}_t^i = (u_t^i)^{\alpha_0}$
6. $i^* = \arg\min_i \tilde{u}_t^i$, $g_t = p_t^{i^*}$, $w_t = u_t^{i^*}$
7. For $k = 0, 1, \ldots, K$
8.   update ω_α on the basis of (2)
9. $G = \arg\min_i round(num\_bins \cdot \tilde{u}_t^i)$
10.   For each particle i
11.   Select a particle from $\{G \cup g_t\}$ and assign it to g_t^i
12. $v_t^{i,k+1} = \omega_\alpha[v_t^{i,k} + c_1 r_1(p_t^i - x_t^{i,k}) + c_2 r_2(g_t^i - x_t^{i,k})]$
13. $x_t^{i,k+1} = x_t^{i,k} + v_t^{i,k+1}$
14. $f_t^i = f(x_t^{i,k+1})$
15.   if $f_t^i < u_t^i$ then $p_t^i = x_t^{i,k+1}$, $u_t^i = f_t^i$, $\tilde{u}_t^i = (u_t^i)^{\alpha_k}$
16.   if $f_t^i < w_t$ then $g_t = x_t^{i,k+1}$, $w_t = f_t^i$

The smoothed objective functions are quantized, see 9th line in the pseudo-code. Owing to this the similar function values are clustered into the same segment of values. In each iteration the algorithm determines the set G of the particles, which after the quantization of the smoothed fitness function from the previous iteration, assumed the smallest values (the best fitness scores), see 9th line in the pseudo-code. For each particle i the algorithm selects the global best particle g_t^i from $\{G \cup g_t\}$, where g_t determines the current global best particle of the swarm. By means of this operation the swarm selects the global best location from a pool of candidate best locations to force the PSO jump out of stagnation. We found that this operation contributes considerably toward better tracking, particularly in case of noisy observations. It is worth noting that in the literature devoted to dynamic optimization the problem of optimization of noisy objective functions is considered very rarely.

The fitness score is calculated on the basis of following expression: $f(x) = 1 - (f_1(x)^{w_1} \cdot f_2(x)^{w_2})$, where w denotes weighting coefficients that were determined experimentally. The function $f_1(x)$ reflects the degree of overlap between the segmented body parts and the projected model's parts into 2D image. The function $f_2(x)$ reflects the edge distance-based fitness [8].

3   Parallel APSO for Real-Time Motion Tracking

PSO is parallel in nature. To shorten the optimization time several studies on parallelizing the algorithm were done so far. However, the majority of the algorithms are for the static optimization. In object tracking the calculation of the objective function is the most consuming operation. Moreover, in multi-view tracking the 3D model is projected and then rendered in each camera's view. Therefore, in our approach the objective function is calculated by OpenMP threads [1], which communicate via the shared memory, see Fig. 1. The PSO thread has access to the shared memory with the objective function values, which were determined by the local threads as well as the values of the objective functions that were calculated by the cooperating swarm on another cores or computational nodes. We employ asynchronous exchange of the best particle location and its fitness score. In particular, if a sub-swarm, which as the first one finished object tracking in a given frame, it carries out the re-diversification of the particles using its current global best particle, without waiting for the global best optimum determined by the participating sub-swarms. It is worth mentioning that in such circumstances the estimate of the object state is determined using the available global best locations of cooperating sub-swarms.

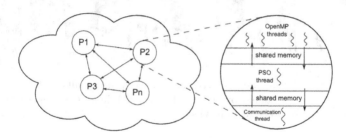

Fig. 1. The communication in parallel PSO for real-time object tracking

4   Experimental Results

The algorithm was evaluated on two image sequences acquired by four synchronized and calibrated cameras. The color images of size 1920×1080 were acquired with rate 25 fps and then subsampled at a factor of 4 both horizontally and vertically. Each pair of the cameras is approximately perpendicular to the other two. A commercial motion capture (moCap) system from Vicon Nexus provides ground truth data at rate of 100 Hz. The system employs reflective markers and sixteen cameras to recover the 3D location of such markers. The synchronization between the moCap and multi-camera system is based on hardware from Vicon.

All computations were conducted on a computer cluster that was composed of 2 identical machines connected with a TCP/IP 1 GigE (Gigabit Ethernet) local area network. Each PC node is equipped with two six-core Intel Xeon 5690 3.46 GHz CPUs. They support Hyper-Threading technology, which enables a single core to act like multiple cores. In this way, a core with Hyper-Threading appears to be more than one core. For example, if the CPU is a dual core processor with Hyper-Threading, the operating system will process as many as four threads through it simultaneously.

The accuracy of human motion tracking was evaluated experimentally in scenarios with a walking person. Although we focused on tracking of torso and legs, we also estimated the head's pose as well as the pose of both arms. The body pose is described by position and orientation of the pelvis in the global coordinate system as well as relative angles between the connected limbs. The overlap of the projected 3D model on the subject undergoing tracking can be utilized to illustrate the quality of tracking, see Fig. 2, which depicts the frontal and side views from two nearly perpendicular cameras. As we can see, the overlap of the projected model on both images is quite good. The estimation of the 3D pose was done in 10 iterations using 300 particles. Given the estimated human pose we calculated the location of virtual markers on the model. The location of such markers on the body corresponds to the location of the real markers on the person undergoing tracking.

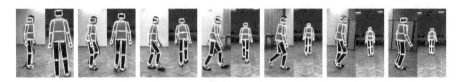

Fig. 2. Articulated 3D human body tracking. Shown are results in frames #20, 40, 60, 80, 100, 120, 140, obtained by APSO. The left sub-images are seen from view 1, whereas the right ones are seen from view 4.

The pose error in each frame was calculated as the average Euclidean distance between corresponding markers. We used 39 markers, where 4 markers were placed on the head, 7 markers on each arm, 12 on the legs, 5 on the torso and 4 markers were attached to the pelvis.

The results obtained on two image sequences were compared by analyses carried out both through qualitative visual evaluations as well as quantitatively by the use of the motion capture data as ground truth. The tracking was done using various number of particle swarms and PC nodes, see Table 1. The pool of the particles was distributed evenly among the sub-swarms. The results shown in Table 1 demonstrate that the motion tracker based on APSO is better than PSO-based one in terms of the tracking accuracy. As we can observe, the tracking error increases slightly with the number of the swarms. The reason for the poorer accuracy of tracking is that we employ the non-blocking parallel PSO. At two PC nodes the processing time of the blocking parallel PSO is a dozen or so milliseconds larger in comparison to the non-blocking version. The discussed results were obtained in ten runs of the algorithm with unlike initializations.

Table 1. Average errors [mm] for M = 39 markers in two image sequences

		#threads		Seq. 1		Seq. 2	
#swarms	#particles	PC1	PC2	PSO	APSO	PSO	APSO
1	300	4	0	59.3 ± 33.4	54.9 ± 30.8	57.7 ± 33.6	52.3 ± 27.3
2	2 × 150	4	4	59.5 ± 33.0	54.2 ± 29.9	61.5 ± 37.0	52.2 ± 28.2
3	3 × 100	8	4	59.9 ± 35.3	55.3 ± 31.2	62.2 ± 38.6	56.9 ± 37.0
4	4 × 75	8	8	59.5 ± 34.0	54.8 ± 30.3	60.6 ± 37.3	54.4 ± 33.7
6	6 × 50	12	12	62.6 ± 36.5	58.2 ± 32.2	62.5 ± 42.1	61.5 ± 43.6
8	8 × 38	16	16	73.0 ± 46.6	57.7 ± 31.1	69.3 ± 47.9	62.3 ± 43.5

Figure 3 depicts the tracking errors versus frame number that were obtained during motion tracking using APSO and PSO-based motion trackers. The experiments were done on an image sequence acquired by the four camera system. As we can observe in the plots shown at Fig. 3, the tracking accuracy obtained by the APSO-based tracker is much better. In particular, in some frames the accuracy of PSO-based tracker considerably drops. This takes place because the PSO is unable to find the global extremum in a given number of iterations.

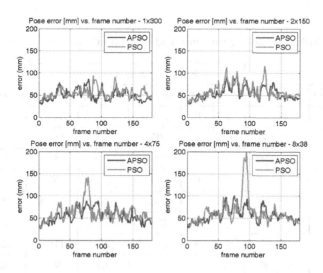

Fig. 3. Tracking errors [mm] versus frame number for PSO and APSO for various number of particles in the sub-swarms

Similar effect has been observed in many runs of the algorithms with unlike initializations. In general, APSO performs better than PSO over the whole image sequences, attaining much better accurateness and robustness.

In Fig. 4 are shown the errors that were obtained using single and eight swarms. In a APSO consisting of eight sub-swarms the optimizations were done using 38 particles in each swarm. As we can see, the tracking errors of both legs are something larger in comparison to tracking errors of the torso.

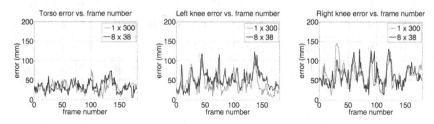

Fig. 4. Tracking errors [mm] versus frame number at 1 and 2 PCs using 1 and 8 particle swarms, respectively

In Table 2 are demonstrated the tracking times that were obtained for various distributions of the sub-swarms into the computational resources. As we can observe, for identical number of the sub-swarms the computation time is larger on single computer in comparison to a configuration consisting of two nodes connected by 1 GigE network. This means that the time necessary for scheduling the threads is larger in comparison to time needed for information exchange in a

Table 2. Tracking time [ms] and speed-up for a single frame

		#threads		Seq. 1		Seq. 2	
#swarms	#particles	PC1	PC2	time [ms]	speed-up	time [ms]	speed-up
1	300	4	0	367.0	-	333.2	-
2	2×150	8	0	195.7	1.9	182.5	1.8
2	2×150	4	4	195.9	1.9	183.1	1.8
3	3×100	12	0	163.8	2.2	153.0	2.2
3	3×100	8	4	136.6	2.7	122.4	2.7
4	4×75	16	0	138.9	2.6	125.7	2.7
4	4×75	8	8	126.2	2.9	116.8	2.9
6	6×50	12	12	86.6	4.2	80.5	4.1
8	8×38	16	16	70.9	5.2	67.6	4.9

distributed system. The image processing and analysis takes about 0.2 sec. and it is not included in the times shown in Table 2. The complete human motion capture system was written in C/C++ and works in real-time. It is worth noting that in [6], the processing time of *Lee walk* sequence from Brown University is larger than one hour.

5 Conclusions

We presented a marker-less motion capture system for real-time tracking of 3D full body motion. The performance of the proposed algorithms was evaluated on two image sequences captured by 4 cameras. In many quantitative comparisons of APSO and the competing PSO algorithm, APSO expressed better tracking accuracy. APSO shows good global search ability making it well suited for unconstrained motion tracking, where no strong prior or dynamic model is available.

Acknowledgment. This paper has been supported by the research project OR00002111: "Application of video surveillance systems to person and behavior identification and threat detection, using biometrics and inference of 3D human model from video."

References

1. Chapman, B., Jost, G., van der Pas, R., Kuck, D.: Using OpenMP: Portable Shared Memory Parallel Programming. The MIT Press (2007)
2. Clerc, M., Kennedy, J.: The particle swarm - explosion, stability, and convergence in a multidimensional complex space. IEEE Tr. Evolut. Comp. 6(1), 58–73 (2002)
3. Deutscher, J., Blake, A., Reid, I.: Articulated body motion capture by annealed particle filtering. In: IEEE Int. Conf. on Pattern Recognition, pp. 126–133 (2000)
4. Deutscher, J., Reid, I.: Articulated body motion capture by stochastic search. Int. J. Comput. Vision 61(2), 185–205 (2005)
5. Doucet, A., Godsill, S., Andrieu, C.: On sequential Monte Carlo sampling methods for bayesian filtering. Statistics and Computing 10(1), 197–208 (2000)
6. John, V., Trucco, E., Ivekovic, S.: Markerless human articulated tracking using hierarchical particle swarm optimisation. Image Vis. Comput. 28, 1530–1547 (2010)
7. Kennedy, J., Eberhart, R.: Particle swarm optimization. In: Proc. of IEEE Int. Conf. on Neural Networks, pp. 1942–1948. IEEE Press, Piscataway (1995)
8. Kwolek, B., Krzeszowski, T., Wojciechowski, K.: Swarm Intelligence Based Searching Schemes for Articulated 3D Body Motion Tracking. In: Blanc-Talon, J., Kleihorst, R., Philips, W., Popescu, D., Scheunders, P. (eds.) ACIVS 2011. LNCS, vol. 6915, pp. 115–126. Springer, Heidelberg (2011)
9. Sigal, L., Balan, A., Black, M.: HumanEva: Synchronized video and motion capture dataset and baseline algorithm for evaluation of articulated human motion. Int. Journal of Computer Vision 87, 4–27 (2010)
10. Zhang, X., Hu, W., Wang, X., Kong, Y., Xie, N., Wang, H., Ling, H., Maybank, S.: A swarm intelligence based searching strategy for articulated 3D human body tracking. In: IEEE Workshop on 3D Information Extraction for Video Analysis and Mining in Conjuction with CVPR, pp. 45–50. IEEE (2010)

Decomposition and Metaoptimization
of Mutation Operator in Differential Evolution

Karol Opara[1] and Jarosław Arabas[2]

[1] Systems Research Institute, Polish Academy of Sciences
[2] Institute of Electronic Systems, Warsaw University of Technology
karol.opara@ibspan.waw.pl, jarabas@elka.pw.edu.pl

Abstract. Metaoptimization is a way of tuning parameters of an optimization algorithm with use of a higher-level optimizer. In this paper it is applied to the problem of choosing among possible mutation range adaptation schemes in Differential Evolution (DE). We consider a new version of DE, called DE/rand/∞. In this algorithm, differential mutation is replaced by a Gaussian one, where the covariance matrix is determined from the contents of the current population. We exploit this property to separate the adaption of search directions from the adaptation of mutation range. The former is characterized by a norm of the covariance matrix while the latter can be expressed as a normed covariance matrix multiplied by the scaling factor. Such separation allows us to introduce a few schemes of direct, explicit control of the mutation range and to compare them with the basic, implicit scheme present in DE/rand/∞. To ensure fair comparisons all versions of DE/rand/∞ are first metaoptimized and then assessed on the CEC'05 benchmark.

Keywords: differential evolution, metaoptimization, adaptation of mutation.

1 Introduction

Tuning an optimization algorithm consists in finding values of its parameters that ensure its maximal performance. This can be seen as an optimization problem in the space of parameters. The process of applying an optimizer to tune parameter values of another optimization method is called metaoptimization and has been used since at least 1980's [2]. In this paper it is applied to the problem of choosing the most effective mutation adaptation scheme in a novel modification of differential evolution algorithm DE/rand/∞ which we introduced in [7]. Each variant of the algorithm is tested on a subset of CEC'05 benchmark functions [11] in order to choose the best-performing one. Reliable comparison of variants of algorithm requires tuning parameters for each of them, which can be achieved by means of metaoptimization. Maximizing performance for a set of test functions can be a noisy multiobjective optimization task with both discrete and continuous variables, which are often subject to constraints. For these reasons, metaoptimization is a non-trivial and very computationally expensive task.

L. Rutkowski et al. (Eds.): SIDE 2012 and EC 2012, LNCS 7269, pp. 110–118, 2012.

This paper aims at summarizing experiences of choosing mutation operator for DE/rand/∞ with use of metaoptimization. In classical DE, both range and direction of mutation are implicitly adopted through the use of difference vectors. Introduction of DE/rand/∞ algorithm (section 2) allows to explicitly control mutation range without hindering the property of adaptation of search directions. In this paper a few explicit methods of controlling mutation range are defined and compared with the original, implicit adaptation scheme. Each of the resulting DE/rand/∞ variants becomes then subject to a metaoptimization procedure discussed in section 3. The paper is concluded with a discussion of the metaoptimized parameter values.

2   From DE/rand/1 to DE/rand/∞

DE/rand/1. Differential evolution (DE) is a simple and effective continuous stochastic optimizer [9], whose outline is presented as Algorithm 1. The fitness function is denoted by f, $\mathbf{P}^t$ is the population in generation t and $\mathbf{P}^t_i$ denotes the i-th individual. The algorithm takes three parameters: population size NP, crossover probability CR and scaling factor F which is used for mutation.

For every individual $\mathbf{P}^t_i$, another individual $\mathbf{P}^t_{i_1}$ is randomly selected. A mutant $\mathbf{u}_i$ is created by adding a scaled difference between two other randomly picked individuals $\mathbf{P}^t_{i_2}$ and $\mathbf{P}^t_{i_3}$ to individual $\mathbf{P}^t_{i_1}$.

$$\mathbf{u}_i \leftarrow \mathbf{P}^t_{i_1} + F \cdot (\mathbf{P}^t_{i_2} - \mathbf{P}^t_{i_3}) \tag{1}$$

The mutant $\mathbf{u}_i$ is then crossed-over with individual $\mathbf{P}^t_i$. Differential mutation is directly dependent on the spread of current population through the use of the difference vectors $F \cdot (\mathbf{P}^t_{i_2} - \mathbf{P}^t_{i_3})$. This leads to an implicit adaptation of range and direction of differential mutation. In our opinion, this adaptation mechanism coupled with the greedy local selection scheme are the main reasons for high performance of DE.

DE method, which uses mutation operator defined in equation (1) is called DE/rand/1, since there is only one difference vector and the index i_1 is chosen randomly with uniform distribution. Observe that scaled difference vector $F \cdot (\mathbf{P}^t_{i_2} - \mathbf{P}^t_{i_3})$ is a random variable, whose distribution depends on the population contents and can be expressed by means of convolution of distributions [7]. Fig. 1 a) shows a population spread in a two-dimensional space, while Fig. 1 b) presents the corresponding difference vector distribution. This distribution is symmetric with respect to origin, has zero mean and its covariance matrix is proportional to the covariance matrix of vectors in the current population.

$$\mathrm{cov}\left(F \cdot (\mathbf{P}^t_{i_2} - \mathbf{P}^t_{i_3})\right) = 2F^2 \mathrm{cov}(\mathbf{P}^t) \tag{2}$$

Equation (2) shows that range and direction of differential mutation is implicitly dependent on contents of the current population $\mathbf{P}^t$.

Algorithm 1. Differential Evolution

Initialize parameters: CR, F, and NP
Initialize population $\mathbf{P}^0$, $t \leftarrow 0$
while stop condition not met **do**
    for all $i \in \{1, 2, ..., NP\}$ **do**
        $\mathbf{u}_i \leftarrow \texttt{mutation}(F; i, \mathbf{P}^t)$
        $\mathbf{o}_i \leftarrow \texttt{crossover}(CR; \mathbf{P}_i^t, \mathbf{u}_i)$
        if $f(\mathbf{o}_i) \leq f(\mathbf{P}_i^t)$ **then**
            $\mathbf{P}_i^{t+1} \leftarrow \mathbf{o}_i$
        else
            $\mathbf{P}_i^{t+1} \leftarrow \mathbf{P}_i^t$
        end if
    end for
    $t \leftarrow t + 1$
end while
return $\arg \min_i f(\mathbf{P}_i^t)$

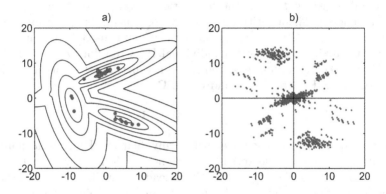

Fig. 1. Population scattered in the search space a), corresponding difference vector distribution b)

DE/rand/∞ [7]. Differential mutation may be generalized by using k difference vectors [9], which is denoted by DE/rand/k ($k = 1$ and $k = 2$ are the most common choices).

$$\mathbf{u}_i \leftarrow \mathbf{P}_{i_1}^t + F \cdot (\mathbf{P}_{i_2}^t - \mathbf{P}_{i_3}^t) + F \cdot (\mathbf{P}_{i_4}^t - \mathbf{P}_{i_5}^t) + ... + F \cdot (\mathbf{P}_{i_{2k}}^t - \mathbf{P}_{i_{2k+1}}^t) \quad (3)$$

Indices i, i_1, i_2, ..., i_{2k+1} are required to be pairwise distinct. If we drop this assumption, then picking each difference vector $F \cdot (\mathbf{P}_{j_1}^t - \mathbf{P}_{j_2}^t)$ would be equivalent to realization of a random variable. Its distribution is determined by the current population $\mathbf{P}^t$ and exemplified in Fig. 1. Hence, summing k difference vectors is equivalent to summing k independent, identically distributed random variables with zero mean and covariance matrix given by (2). The covariance matrix of difference vectors for DE/rand/k equals $2kF^2\text{cov}(\mathbf{P}^t)$ which implies that the range of change introduced by the mutation (3) will increase with k. This effect can be eliminated by dividing the sum by $\sqrt{k}$:

$$\mathbf{u}_i \leftarrow \mathbf{P}_{i_1}^t + \frac{F}{\sqrt{k}} \sum_{j=1}^k \left(\mathbf{P}_{i_{2j}}^t - \mathbf{P}_{i_{2j+1}}^t \right) \qquad (4)$$

On the basis of central limit theorem the distribution of the normed sum of difference vectors 4 weakly converges to the normal distribution with zero mean and the covariance matrix equal to $2F^2\mathrm{cov}(\mathbf{P}^t)$. Consequently, under assumption that $k \to \infty$ one can replace 4 by:

$$\mathbf{u}_i \leftarrow \mathbf{P}_{i_1}^t + \sqrt{2}F \cdot \mathbf{v}_\infty, \text{ where } \mathbf{v}_\infty \sim \mathcal{N}\left(0, \mathrm{cov}(\mathbf{P}^t)\right). \qquad (5)$$

Thus, if we drop the assumption that indices i, i_1, ..., i_{2k+1} must be pairwise distinct, we can replace the differential mutation by the Gaussian mutation with zero mean and covariance matrix proportional to the covariance matrix of the current population. Our earlier analyzes [7] show that performance of DE/rand/∞/bin is comparable to DE/rand/1/bin and may be improved by coupling with an exploitative mutation operator DE/best/1.

Decomposition of mutation. Formula (5) can be reformulated as follows:

$$\mathbf{u}_i \leftarrow \mathbf{P}_{i_1}^t + F \cdot \sqrt{2||\mathrm{cov}(\mathbf{P}^t)||} \cdot \mathbf{v}_i, \text{ where } \mathbf{v}_i \sim \mathcal{N}\left(0, \frac{\mathrm{cov}(\mathbf{P}^t)}{||\mathrm{cov}(\mathbf{P}^t)||}\right) \qquad (6)$$

Observe that mutation range is decomposed to a product of the scalar factor F and a scalar describing the spread of the current population, which we measure as the covariance matrix norm $\sqrt{||\mathrm{cov}(\mathbf{P}^t)||}$. Vector $\mathbf{v}_i$ describes the direction of differential mutation. Decomposition (6) allows us to separately analyze mutation range and direction in DE/rand/∞.

Explicit control of mutation range. In this study we were interested in analysis of the implicit adaptation mechanism in DE. Decomposition (6) shows that mutation range in DE/rand/∞ is proportional to $\sqrt{||\mathrm{cov}(\mathbf{P}^t)||}$. A natural question arises, how does it compare to other possible ways of controlling mutation range? To answer this question we modified the scheme (6) by substituting the product of the scaling factor and the root of covariance matrix norm with a function dependent on the generation index.

$$\mathbf{u}_i \leftarrow \mathbf{P}_{i_1}^t + \sqrt{2}F(t)\bar{s} \cdot \mathbf{v}_i, \text{ where } \mathbf{v}_i \sim \mathcal{N}\left(0, \frac{\mathrm{cov}(\mathbf{P}^t)}{||\mathrm{cov}(\mathbf{P}^t)||}\right) \qquad (7)$$

This provides explicit control over the mutation range while preserving adaptation of search directions. The constant $\bar{s}$ adjusts the scaling factor to the size of a feasible set. In this paper, each fitness function f_i, $i \in \{1, 2, ..., 14\}$ was constrained to a hypercube $[l_i, u_i]^n$ and the value of $\bar{s}$ for i-th problem was defined as $u_i - l_i$. Introduction of the $\bar{s}$ term allows to reinterpret the scaling factor F. Intuitively speaking, $F \approx 1$ means that the mutation range is approximately the same as the size of the feasible set, $F \approx 0.1$ mean that it is 10 times smaller etc. We defined three variants of dynamic control of mutation range (7), namely using a constant value, decreasing it linearly and exponentially—see Table 1. In addition we also considered a noisy version of the const strategy and methods of periodic change along sawtooth saw and sine sin, but they performed consistently worse.

3   Metaoptimization Procedure

Choice of test problems. To our knowledge, there are no theoretical clues about optimal mutation range adaptation. Performance of different methods of mutation adaptation was hence measured on a benchmark of ten-dimensional test problems introduced at the CEC'05 [11] conference. The CEC'05 benchmark contains 5 unimodal functions, 7 basic multimodal ones as well as two multimodal complex functions. Apart from that, there are 11 hybrid functions, each of whom is created as a weighted sum of 10 basic ones. In general, hybrid problems proved to be too complicated to be solved [3]. Therefore, we decided to limit metaoptimization to the first 14 problems only. There are also newer and more elaborated global optimization benchmarks, in particular BBOB [5]. We decided to use CEC'05 mainly because it defines stopping condition based on maximal number of function evaluations, which is convenient in case of dynamic control of mutation range.

In this study an implementation of CMA-ES [4] was used as a metaoptimizer. All investigated mutation range adaptation variants were started with the same seed values of the random number generator.

Metacriterion. Performance for each test problem was assessed on the basis of the final optimization error after 10^5 function evaluations. The results for $N = 14$ investigated problems were aggregated to form a single-objective metaoptimization criterion (metacriterion). Due to a random initialization and stochastic nature of DE, final error values were nondeterministic. Therefore, each algorithm was independently restarted k times. The median value of final optimization errors for i-th test problem is denoted by ϵ^i. The metacriterion f_m is defined as

$$f_m = \frac{1}{N} \sum_{i=1}^{N} \left(m + \log_{10} \left(10^{-m} + \epsilon^i \right) \right), \tag{8}$$

Table 1. Mutation range adaptation schemes

	Parameters	Adaptation scheme
implicit	$NP \in \mathbb{N}, F_0 \in \mathbb{R}$	$F = F_0$, no norming; mutation according to (5)
const	$NP \in \mathbb{N}, F_0 \in \mathbb{R}$	$F(t) = F_0$
lin	$NP \in \mathbb{N}, F_0 \in \mathbb{R}$	$F(t) = F_0 \frac{t_{max}-t}{t_{max}}$
exp	$NP \in \mathbb{N}, F_0, F_1 \in \mathbb{R}$	$F(t) = F_0 \left(\frac{F_1}{F_0} \right)^{t/t_{max}}$

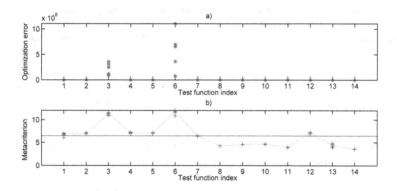

Fig. 2. Derivation of metacriterion, a) raw error values plotted for 5 runs for each of 14 test problems; b) logarithms of the errors (8), medians connected with a dotted line, metacriterion shown by the horizontal line

where $m = 3$ is a parameter ensuring that the metacriterion takes nonnegative values. It also provides a lower bound on the required error level 10^{-m}. We used the logarithmic transformation to reduce a risk that a single problem with the highest error would dominate all other problems within the benchmark set. For instance, in Fig. 2 a), error values for problems number 3 and 6 are of several orders of magnitude greater than all others. Without the logarithmic transformation, metaoptimizer would fit parameters to increase performance for these two problems only.

Choosing the "best" mutation range adaptation scheme basing on benchmark results is justified when the same criterion is used in the metaoptimization and in the evaluation of the final (metaoptimized) benchmark results. There is however a possibility that parameters would be overfitted to the benchmark. Yet, currently available benchmarks are still quite difficult to solve, even for the state-of-the-art optimizers [3,5], so overfitting is arguably not a real threat.

Metalandscapes. A metalandscape graph is the plot of the metacriterion values versus its parameters. Fig. 3 a) shows the metalandscape of DE/rand/∞/none (when $CR = 1$) with the implicit mutation (5). The scaling factor takes values $F_0 \in \{0.4, 0.5, ..., 1.2\}$ while the quotient (NP/n) of population size NP and search space dimension $n = 10$ takes values $(NP/n) \in \{2, 3, 5, 10, 20, 50, 100\}$. Fig. 3 b) presents analogous results published in [8] which were obtained for DE/rand/1/bin for other set of test problems in $n = 30$ dimensions and for a metacriterion defined as the weighted sum of final error values. Nevertheless, the bent shapes of metalandscape are similar in both cases. This may suggest that the metaoptimization method presented here yields robust results and that both algorithms DE/rand/1 and DE/rand/∞ reveal a similar pattern of parameters' influence on the performance on benchmarks. Additionally, conversion of the linear scale to the logarithmic one, as in figures 3 b) and c), seems to improve the conditioning of the metacriterion making it "easier to solve" and "more

Table 2. Parameter values obtained through metaoptimization

Mutation	Metaoptimized paremeter values
implicit	$NP = 11.5 \cdot n,\ F_0 = 0.54$
const	$NP = 4.5 \cdot n,\ F_0 = 0.064$
lin	$NP = 5.2 \cdot n,\ F_0 = 0.14$
exp	$NP = 9.2 \cdot n,\ F_0 = 350,\ F_1 = 8.3 \cdot 10^{-9}$

convex". Consequently, the metaoptimization procedure was applied to logarithms of parameters rather than their raw values.

Interpretation of results. Table 2 contains parameter values obtained during the metaoptimization. Their analysis may give some clues to further the DE/rand/∞ algorithm. First of all, only the implicit and exponential schemes yielded significantly better performance than any other method. Results of the Dunn's and Holm's tests adjusted for multiple comparisons are summarized in Table 3, where significance larger than $1 - \alpha = 0.95$ is denoted by $+$ and lack of it by $\cdot$.

In is noteworthy that for both winning methods population size was of the order $10 \cdot n$ which agrees well with the suggestions for tuning DE given e.g. by Price and Storn [9]. Closer look at the exponential method reveals that the initial mutation range value is huge ($F_0 = 350$) and that it decreases to a very low level ($F_1 = 8.3 \cdot 10^{-9}$). Consequently, for one third of the optimization time, applying differential mutation results in random sampling, since it is nearly entirely guided by a constraint handling method. High performance of the exponential scheme suggests that extending the initialization phase by a period of random sampling compiled with the greedy parent-offspring selection may improve the overall performance of DE/rand/∞.

4   Discussion

Analysis of mutation in DE. Parameter setting in DE has been subject of considerable study [9], [8], as well as various modifications of mutation operators, some of which are surveyed in [6]. Mutation range adaptation in DE was also enhanced by introducing self-adaptation of parameters in jDE [1] and self-adaptation of both parameters and the mutation strategy in SADE [10]. In general, research on differential mutation concentrates on choosing the value of a scale factor F or appropriate variants of mutation operators. The implicit dependence of mutation range and direction on the spread of current population is usually kept as

Table 3. Statistical superiority tests: Dunn's—left hand side, Holm's—right hand side

	implicit	exp	lin	saw	sin	rand	const
implicit		$\cdot\ \cdot$	$\cdot\ \cdot$	$+\ +$	$+\ +$	$+\ +$	$+\ +$
exp	$\cdot\ \cdot$		$\cdot\ \cdot$	$+\ \cdot$	$+\ \cdot$	$+\ \cdot$	$+\ +$

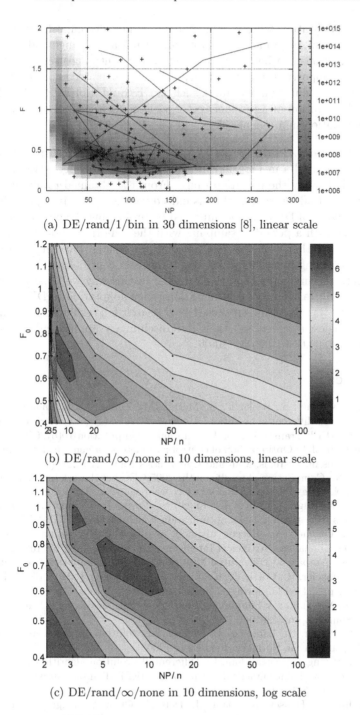

(a) DE/rand/1/bin in 30 dimensions [8], linear scale

(b) DE/rand/∞/none in 10 dimensions, linear scale

(c) DE/rand/∞/none in 10 dimensions, log scale

Fig. 3. Metalandscapes for DE/rand/1/bin in linear scale (a) and DE/rand/∞ in linear (b) and logarithmic (c) scales

an effective adaptation scheme. This paper provides decomposition (6) of mutation operator in DE/rand/∞. Adaptation of mutation range and adaptation of search directions can be therefore analyzed (or controlled) separately, which provides new opportunities for improving DE. Similar decompositions can be derived for other mutation operators, such as DE/rand/1 or DE/best/1. In such cases the distribution of a random vector $\mathbf{v}_i$ is not normal but depends on the current population in a manner shown in Fig. 1.

Concluding remarks. In this paper we reported an ongoing research on adaptation in DE. We used a metaoptimization approach to consider possible alternative methods to vary the mutation range. From the obtained results it appears that the implicit adaptation method is indeed very effective. It appears however that performance of DE could be improved by prolonging the population initialization phase with a period of sampling with the uniform distribution from the feasible area together with the local selection of results. Further research concentrates on finding functions which simultaneously control mutation range and approximate the implicit adaptation scheme. In this way we hope to explicitly model and analyze the process of mutation range adaptation in DE.

This study was partially supported by research fellowship within "Information technologies: research and their interdisciplinary applications" agreement number POKL.04.01.01-00-051/10-00.

References

1. Brest, J., Greiner, S., Boskovic, B., Mernik, M., Zumer, V.: Self-adapting control parameters in differential evolution: A comparative study on numerical benchmark problems. IEEE Transactions on Evolutionary Computation 10(6), 646–657 (2006)
2. Grefenstette, J.J.: Optimization of control parameters for genetic algorithms. IEEE Transactions on Systems, Man and Cybernetics 16(1), 122–128 (1986)
3. Hansen, N.: Compilation of results on the 2005 CEC benchmark function set (2006)
4. Hansen, N.: The CMA evolution strategy webpage (November 2009)
5. Hansen, N., Auger, A., Ros, R., Finck, S., Posik, P.: Comparing results of 31 algorithms from the black-box optimization benchmarking BBOB-2009 (2010)
6. Neri, F., Tirronen, V.: Recent advances in differential evolution: a survey and experimental analysis. Artificical Intelligence Reviews 33(1-2), 61–106 (2010)
7. Opara, K., Arabas, J.: Differential Mutation Based on Population Covariance Matrix. In: Schaefer, R., Cotta, C., Kołodziej, J., Rudolph, G. (eds.) PPSN XI. LNCS, vol. 6238, pp. 114–123. Springer, Heidelberg (2010)
8. Pedersen, M.: Tuning & Simplifying Heuristical Optimization. PhD thesis, University of Southampton (2010)
9. Price, K., Storn, R., Lampien, J.: Differential evolution. A practical approach to global optimization. Springer, Heidelberg (2005)
10. Qin, A., Huang, V., Suganthan, P.: Differential evolution algorithm with strategy adaptation for global numerical optimization. IEEE Transaction on Evolutionary Computation 13(2), 398–417 (2009)
11. Suganthan, P., Hansen, N., Liang, J., Deb, K., Chen, Y., Auger, A., Tiwari, S.: Problem definitions and evaluation criteria for the CEC 2005 special session on real-parameter optimization. Technical report (2005)

Continuous Ant Colony Optimization for Identification of Time Delays in the Linear Plant

Janusz Papliński

Department of Control and Measurement, West Pomeranian University
of Technology, 26 Kwietnia 10, 71-126 Szczecin, Poland
janusz.paplinski@zut.edu.pl

Abstract. Interpolated Ant Colony Optimization (IACO) for a continuous domain was proposed in the paper. The IACO uses the same mechanisms as the classical ACO applied to discrete optimization. The continuous search space is sampled by individuals on the basis of the linear interpolated trace of the pheromone. It allows to obtain a simple and efficient optimization algorithm. The proposed algorithm is then used to identify delays in linear dynamic systems. The examination results show that it is an effective tool for global optimization problems.

Keywords: Continuous optimization, Ant colony algorithm, Time delay, Identification.

1 Introduction

Optimization problems can be found in many areas of industry and engineering problems. One example might be the problem of identifying plant parameters in control systems. Especially the identification of time delay in the linear system is important and should be treated as the first task during system analysis and control design. If the time delay used for controller design does not coincide with the real process time delay, then the close-loop system can be unstable or may cause the efficiency loss, [1,2]. The time delay identification can become more complicated for the multi-input single-output system (MISO), where the solution space is multi-modal.

Most of the conventional system identification techniques, such as those based on the non-linear estimation method, for example the separable nonlinear least squares method (SEPNLS), are in essence the gradient-guided local search methods, [3]. They require a smooth search space or a differentiable performance index. The conventional approaches in the multi-modal optimization can easily fail in obtaining the global optimum and may stop at a local optimum, [4,5].

Ant algorithms are one of the most recent approximate optimization methods to be developed. These algorithms are inspired by the behavior of real ants in the wild [6], and more specifically, by the indirect communication between ants within the colony via the secretion of chemical pheromones. The macro-scale complex behavior emerges as a result of the cooperation in the micro-scale [7].

L. Rutkowski et al. (Eds.): SIDE 2012 and EC 2012, LNCS 7269, pp. 119–127, 2012.

The first ACO algorithm has been applied to many combinatorial problems. Until now, there are few adaptations of such algorithms to continuous optimization problems. In the paper we propose an Interpolated Ant Colony Optimization (IACO) for a continuous domain. The continuous search space is sampled by the individuals on the basis of the interpolated trace of the pheromone. The proposed algorithm is then used to identify delays in linear dynamic systems.

2   Basic Concept of Continuous Ant Colony Optimization

ACO is a metaheuristic algorithm inspired by the foraging behavior of real ants. At the start, when ants are looking for food, they explore the area in a random way. Ants deposit a pheromone trail on the ground on the way back to the nest. They reach food faster via shorter routes and since they leave their marks they are reinforcing the pheromone trail during this path. The pheromone trail guides other ants to the food source. Ants have tendency to follow a trail that contains higher concentration of pheromone [8]. Indirect communication between ants, known as stigmergy, enables them to find shortest paths between their nest and food sources.

The first ACO algorithm was developed by Dorigo et al. [6,9] and used for solving a combinatorial optimization problem. Many ant based optimization algorithms have been developed and applied to discrete optimization problems, like traveling salesman problem (TSP) [10], scheduling [11,12], vehicle routing problem [13]. A direct application of the stigmergy mechanism to solving continuous optimization problem is difficult and only a few methods have been proposed in the literature. The Continuous ACO (CACO) was the first of these methods [14]. It includes two levels: global and local. ACO performs local searches, whereas the global search is handled by a genetic algorithm. The API algorithm [15] was inspired by primitive ants behavior. It uses a 'tandem-running' which involves two ants and leads to gathering the individuals on the same hunting site. This method selects the best point among those evaluated by the ants in order to make the population proceed towards the optimum. A heterarchical algorithm called 'Continuous Interacting Ant Colony' (CIAC) [16] is designed for the optimization of multiminima continuous functions. CIAC uses two communication channels showing the properties of trail and direct communication. However, all these approaches are conceptually quite different from ACO for discrete problems.

The ACO algorithm for continuous optimization proposed by Socha [17], known as $ACO_{\mathbb{R}}$, is the closest to the spirit of ACO for discrete problems. The main idea of this algorithm is shifting from using a discrete probability distribution to using a continuous probability density function (PDF). This density function is produced, for each solution construction, from a population of solutions which the algorithm keeps at all times. The construction of a solution is done by components like in the original ACO algorithm. For a single dimension an ant chooses only one value. For constructing a solution an ant uses a Gaussian kernel which is a weighted superposition of several Gaussian functions, as PDF.

Another algorithm for contiuous optimisiation problem, so-called Differential Ant-Stigmergy Algorithm (DASA) was proposed by Korosec [18]. It transforms a real-parameter optimization problem into a graph-search problem. The parameters' differences assigned to the graph vertices are used to navigate through the search space.

3 Ant Colony Optimization with Interpolated Search Space

ACO is mainly applicable to discrete problems. The usage of pheromones space interpolation allows for the extension of ACO applications to continuous spaces. The IACO carries the same mechanisms as the classical ACO. Ants leave their mark on the road which they pass and it is proportional to the quality of the resulting solution. Pheromones aggregate and evaporate during iteration and a specific map of pheromones is created in the search space. This map is not unalterable and can bring into line with ambient. Each ant looks for food independently of the others and moves from nest to the source of food. There are plenty of ways in which ants can go. Ants choose a way by using three sources of information: own experience, local information, pheromone trail. Ant own experience permits to recognize place already visited and to avoid looping the way. For the artificial ant it permits to allocate a particular value to appropriate seeking parameters. The local information determines a permissible way. Ants can recognize and sidestep hindrances. In the artificial ant colony this is responsible for the search space constraints. The pheromone trail permits to come back to the nest and to find the source of food found earlier by another individual from colony. Ants prefer those directions in which the pheromone intensity is growing.

The process of constructing a solution by an ant is divided into stages in which the ant chooses a value for only one decision variable x_i. When an ant is choosing the value of the i-th decision variable x_i it uses the cumulative distribution function $D(x_i)$ obtained from an interpolation of the pheromone trace. The pheromone trace is treated as a discrete probability distribution function (DPDF) $P_d(x_i)$, where each k-th component of this function is defined by single trace:

$$p_d(x_{ik}) = \frac{\tau(x_{ik})}{\sum_{j=0}^{n} \tau_{ij}} \tag{1}$$

On the base of the (DPDF) the R-probability density function (R-PDF) P_{cR} and similarly the L-probability density function (L-PDF) P_{cL} are created::

$$P_{cR}(x_{ik} < x \leqslant x_{ik+1}) = p_d x_{ik+1} \qquad P_{cL}(x_{ik} < x \leqslant x_{ik+1}) = p_d x_{ik} \tag{2}$$

Next we can use the R-cumulative distribution function (R-CDF) $D_R(x)$ and the L-cumulative distribution function (L-CDF) $D_L(x)$ defined as follows:

$$D_R(x) = \int_{-\infty}^{x} P_{cR}(t) dt \qquad D_L(x) = \int_{-\infty}^{x} P_{cL}(t) dt \tag{3}$$

If we sample the inverse of CDF $D_R(x_i)^{-1}$ or $D_L(x_i)^{-1}$ and use an interpolation procedure we can obtain a new value of the decision variable x_{ik} taken by the k-th ant. The functions R-PDF and L-PDF prefer probabilities obtained from DPDF with its right or left side respectively (Fig. 1 shows an example). This can lead to search on only one side of the best previously known solutions. In order to search the entire space solution one half of the population of ants uses the functions $D_R(x_i)^{-1}$ and the other half uses the function $D_L(x_i)^{-1}$. This solution is simple to implement and does not require complex calculations. The pseudo code of the IACO is presented below.

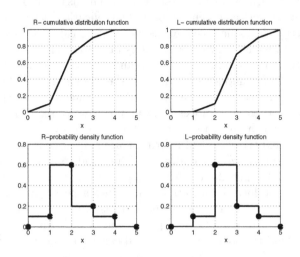

Fig. 1. The example of R-PDF P_{cR} and L-PDF P_{cL} with marked value of the likelihood p_d, and CDF:D_R, and D_L. This illustrates the unilateral preferences, left or right sided, of the above functions.

Pseudo-code of IACO

```
Set_parameters
Initialize_pheromone_trials
While (termination conditions are not met) do
    Calculate_the_L_and_R_cumulative_sum_of_the_pheromone_traces
    Normalize_the_L_and_R_cumulative_sum_to_1
    For (i=all new ants) do
        For (k=all parmeters) do
            Generate_uniformly_distributed_real_number_and_use_it_to:
            Construct_solution_by_inerpolation_of_inverse_of...
                                    _L_or_R_cumulative_sum
            Add_calculated_solution_to_i-th_ant_as_k-th_component
        end
    Compute_quality_of_i-th_ant
```

```
    end
    Update_pheromone_trials
end.
```

The choice made by an ant is determined by the pheromone trace and the cumulative distribution function. It can lead to a local minimum. In order to improve exploration one half of individuals have also disturbed the chosen direction by adding a random component. For the i-th parameter of the k-th ant it can be describe as:

$$x_{ik} = x_{ik}\beta + \xi(1 - \beta), \tag{4}$$

where: x_{ik} - the value obtained on the basis of the cumulative distribution function, ξ - the random value with normal distribution, β - random coefficient of ratio of averaging.

The ants use a pheromone trail which aim is to indicate a promising direction. For this reason the intensity of a trace left by the k-th ants is proportional to the quality of the obtained solution J_k:

$$\tau(x_{ik}) = \frac{n}{m} \frac{J_k^\alpha}{\sum_{j=0}^n J_j^\alpha}, \tag{5}$$

where: n is an amount of ants in the nest, m is an amount of the pheromone trace, α is a parameter that controls the exploration/exploitation mechanism by influencing the ratio of the pheromone trace leaved by the best and the worst ant. The quality function J_k is divided by the sum of all quality functions in order to uniform it to one. The ratio of the number of ants n to the number of rows in the matrix of pheromones m scales the intensity of leaving new pheromones to the already existing traces. In order to avoid a too rapid convergence of the algorithm the pheromone trace evaporates. It introduces a process of forgetting and permits favoring the exploration of new areas in the search space. All the pheromone values are decreasing during time t:

$$\tau(x_{ik}, t + 1) = \rho\tau(x_{ik}, t), \tag{6}$$

where $\rho \in (0, 1]$ is the evaporation rate. The amount of pheromone traces is limited to a specified number by removing the worst traces in each iteration. The ants are looking only for the time delays of a model. The residual parameters of the model are obtained by SEPNLS during the calculation of the quality function of individuals. It can be done because these parameters are linear and SEPNLS works efficiently with them. The SEPNLS algorithm is described bellow.

4   The Optimization Problem

4.1   The Time Delay Identification

Dynamics of continuous-time (MISO) system with unknown time delays can be described as:

$$\sum_{i=0}^n a_i p^{n-1} x(t) = \sum_{j=1}^r \sum_{k=1}^{m_j} b_{jk} p^{m_j - k} u_j(t - \tau_j) \tag{7}$$

where: a and b are parameters describe dynamics of the system, where $a_0 = 1$, $b_{i1} \neq 0$, p - differential operator, $u_j(t)$ - j-th input, τ_j - time delay of j-th input, x - non-disturbed output of the system.

We assume that parameters n and m_j are known. The measured output is disturbed by a stochastic noise. The problem studied here is as follows: how to estimate the time delays and the system parameters from sampled data representation of the inputs and the noisy output.

4.2   SEPNLS and GSNLS Estimation Methods

The linear parameters of the model can be estimated as the minimizing arguments of the LS criterion $V_N(\theta, \tau)$, [19]

$$V_N(\theta, \tau) = \frac{1}{N - k_s} \sum_{k=k_s+1}^{N} \frac{1}{2} \varepsilon^2(k\theta, \tau) = \frac{1}{N - k_s} \sum_{k=k_s+1}^{N} \frac{1}{2} \left(y(t) - \varphi^T(k, \tau)\theta \right)^2 \quad (8)$$

where: $\varepsilon(k\theta, \tau)$ is an error of the model, θ - unknown linear parameters, τ - time delay, φ - observed vector regression, $y(t)$ - observed output of the plant.

The vectors of the time delays τ and linear parameters θ are estimated in a separate manner. The linear parameters, when the time delays are known, can be obtained from linear LS method:

$$\theta = arg \min_{\theta} V_N(\theta, \tau), \quad (9)$$

and the time delays $\hat{\tau}$ can be estimated as the nonlinear LS minimization method:

$$\hat{\tau} = arg \min_{\tau} \check{V}_N(\tau) \quad (10)$$

The SEPNLS method can converge to the local optimum. It is possible to apply a stochastic approximation [20] with convolution smoothing to the SEPNLS method in order to reach the global optimum [21]. The estimate of the time delay in GSNLS can be obtained by disturbing the time delay using a random value β:

$$\hat{\tau}^{(k+1)} = \hat{\tau}^{(k)} + \Delta\hat{\tau}^{(k)} + \beta, \quad (11)$$

where: $\hat{\tau}^{(k)}$ is an astimate of time delay in k-th step of LS procedure, $\Delta\hat{\tau}^{(k)}$ is an incbrenet of the value of $\hat{\tau}^{(k)}$ calculate in k-th step of LS procedure, β is a random disturbans.

5   Simulation Example

The proposed algorithms were used to identify time delay for a set of 14 MISO systems:

$$\ddot{y}(t) + a_1\dot{y}(t) + a_2y(t) = b_{11}u_1(t - \tau_1) + b_{21}u_2(t - \tau_2), \quad (12)$$

where all parameters a_1, a_2, b_{11}, b_{21}, τ_1, τ_2, have been chosen in a random way. The input and output signals are converted by Zero-Order-Hold operation with sampling period $T = 0.05$. As input signals we use an independent sequence of uniform distribution between 0 and 1. The signal to measurement noise ratio SNR is 5%. A data set of 1000 samples was generated for the identification process. The algorithms are implemented for 250 iterations. The initial values of time delays $\tau^{(0)}$ are randomly chosen between 0 and 25. The algorithms presented in the paper were running 100 times for each systems.

The IACO was used to identify time delays and the other parameters of the model (12) have been identified by using SEPNLS method [22]. The fitness function J_k of each individuals was obtained directly from the linear LS method $V_N(\theta, \tau)$ given by the equation (9):

$$J_k = V_N(\theta, \tau) \tag{13}$$

The solution space of time delays is multimodal and the global optimum is not reached every time. Therefore the percentage of identified time delays, with error less than 10%, can be treated as the main quality function and it is presented in Fig. 2. GSNLS identifies time delays correctly in average of 29%, IACO in 86%. Although, IACO does not always cope with the correct identification it is definitely better than GSNLS.

The performance of identification algorithm is determined also by the time of computing. The number of functional evaluations required to reach the true time delay with 10% accuracy is smaller for GSNLS and on average is equal to 650 calls. The corresponding value for IACO is almost twice as much as the length and is equal to 1050 calls.

Based on these results we can conclude that the IACO algorithm is more accurate but requires a longer computation time than the GSNLS.

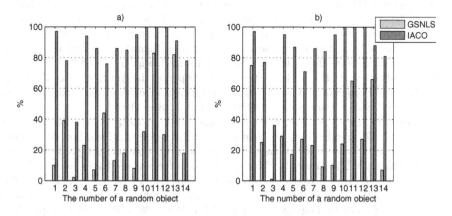

Fig. 2. The percentage of identified time delays with error less than 10%, for respectively a) τ_1 and b) τ_2. The average number of corect identification τ_1 and τ_2 is equal 29% for GSNLS and 86% for IACO.

6   Conclusion

The paper presents a continuous optimization algorithm IACO which uses the same mechanisms as the ACO applied to discrete optimization. The linear interpolation allows to obtain a simple and efficient optimization algorithm. Presented example shows that it is an effective tool for global optimization.

Further research is required to compare the proposed algorithm with other Ant Colony Optimization for continuous domain using for this purpose some classical benchmarks. It will allow a better assessment of the algorithm.

References

1. Bjorklund, S., Ljung, L.: A Review of Time-Delay Estimation Techniques. In: IEEE Conference on Decision and Control 2003, Maui, USA, vol. 3, pp. 2502–2507 (2003)
2. Boukas, E.K.: Stochastic output feedback of uncertain time-delay system with saturing actuators. J. of Optimization Theory and Applications 118(2), 255–273 (2003)
3. Chen, X., Wang, M.: Global optimization methods for time delay estimation. In: Proceedings of the World Congress on Intelligent Control and Automation (WCICA), vol. 1, pp. 212–215 (2004)
4. Chen, B.-S., Hung, J.-C.: A global estimation for multichannel time-delay and signal parameters via genetic algorithm. Signal Processing 81(5), 1061–1067 (2001)
5. Harada, K., Kobayashi, Y., Okita, T.: Identification of Linear Systems With Time Delay and Unknown Order Electrical. Engineering in Japan (English translation of Denki Gakkai Ronbunshi) 145(3), 61–68 (2003)
6. Dorigo, M., Maniezzo, V., Colorni, A.: Ant System: Optimization by a colony of cooperating agents. IEEE Trans. on SMC-Part B 26(1), 29–41 (1996)
7. Bonabeau, E., Dorigo, M., Theraulaz, G.: Swarm Intelligence: From Natural to Artificial Systems. Oxford University Press, New York (1999)
8. Grassé, P.P.: La reconstruction du nid et les coordinations inter-individuelles chez bellicositermes natalensis et cubitermes sp. La thorie de la stigmergie: Essai dinterprtation des termites constructeurs. Insectes Sociaux 6, 41–81 (1959)
9. Dorigo, M.: Optimization, Learning and Natural Algorithms (in Italian). PhD thesis, Dipartimento di Elettronica, Politecnico di Milano, Italy (1992)
10. Bullnheimer, B., Hartl, R.F., Strauss, C.: Applying the Ant System to the Vehicle Routing Problem. In: Voss, S., et al. (eds.) Meta-heuristics: Advances and Trends in Local Search Paradigms for Optimization. Kluwer (1999)
11. Costa, D., Hertz, A.: Ants can color graphs. J. Oper. Res. Soc. 48, 295–305 (1997)
12. Merkle, D., Middendorf, M., Schmeck, H.: Ant colony optimization for resource-constrained project scheduling. IEEE Trans. Evol. Comput. 6(4), 333–346 (2002)
13. Reimann, M., Doerner, K., Hartl, R.F.: D-ants: Savings based ants divide and conquer the vehicle routing problems. Comput. Oper. Res. 31(4), 563–591 (2004)
14. Bilchev, B., Parmee, I.C.: The Ant Colony Metaphor for Searching Continuous Design Spaces. In: Fogarty, T.C. (ed.) AISB-WS 1995. LNCS, vol. 993, pp. 25–39. Springer, Heidelberg (1995)
15. Monmarché, N., Venturini, G., Slimane, M.: On how pachycondyla apicalis ants suggest a new search algorithm. Future Generation Comput. Syst. 16, 937–946 (2000)

16. Dréo, J., Siarry, P.: A New Ant Colony Algorithm Using the Heterarchical Concept Aimed at Optimization of Multiminima Continuous Functions. In: Dorigo, M., Di Caro, G.A., Sampels, M. (eds.) Ant Algorithms 2002. LNCS, vol. 2463, pp. 216–221. Springer, Heidelberg (2002)
17. Socha, K., Dorigo, M.: Ant colony optimization for continuous domains. European J. of Operat.Research 185, 1155–1173 (2006)
18. Koroec, P.: Stigmergy as an approach to metaheuristic optimization, Ph.D.Thesis, Joef Stefan International Postgraduate School, Ljubljana, Slovenia
19. Olinsky, A.D., Quinn, J.T., Mangiameli, P.M., Chen, S.K.: A genetic algorithm approach to nonlinear least squares estimation. Int. J. Math. Educ. SCI. Tehnol. 35(2), 207–217 (2004)
20. Bharth, B., Borkar, V.S.: Stochastic approximation algorithms: overview and resent trends. Sadhana India 24(Parts 4 & 5), 425–452 (1999)
21. Iemura, H., Yang, Z., Kanae, S., Wada, K.: Identification of continous-time systems with unknow time delays by global nonlinear least-squares method. In: IFAC Workshop on Adaptation and Lerning in Control and Signal Processing, Yokohama, Japan (2004)
22. Papliński, J.P.: Hybrid genetic and Nelder-Mead algorithms for identification of time delay. In: 14th IEEE IFAC International Conference Methods and Models in Automation and Robotics, Midzyzdroje, Poland (2009)

A Variable Iterated Greedy Algorithm with Differential Evolution for Solving No-Idle Flowshops

M. Fatih Tasgetiren[1], Quan-Ke Pan[2], P.N. Suganthan[3], and Ozge Buyukdagli[4]

[1] Industrial Engineering Department, Yasar University, Izmir, Turkey
[2] School of Computer Science, Liaocheng University, China
[3] School of Electrical and Electronics Engineering,
Nanyang Technological University 639798, Singapore
[4] Industrial Engineering Department, Yasar University, Izmir, Turkey
fatih.tasgetiren@yasar.edu.tr, panquanke@gmail.com,
epnsugan@ntu.edu.sg, ozge.buyukdagli@stu.yasar.edu.tr

Abstract. In this paper, we present a variable iterated greedy algorithm where its parameters (basically destruction size and probability of whether or not to apply the iterated greedy algorithm to an individual) are optimized by the differential evolution algorithm. A unique multi-chromosome solution representation is presented in such a way that the first chromosome represents the destruction size and the probability whereas the second chromosome is simply a job permutation assigned to each individual in the population randomly. The proposed algorithm is applied to the no-idle permutation flowshop scheduling problem with the makespan criterion. The performance of the proposed algorithm is tested on the Ruben Ruiz's benchmark suite and compared to their best known solutions available in *http://soa.iti.es/rruiz* as well as to a very recent discrete differential evolution algorithm from the literature. The computational results show its highly competitive performance and ultimately, 183 out of 250 instances are further improved. In comparison to the very recent hybrid discrete differential evolution algorithm, 114 out of 150 new best known solutions they provided are also further improved.

Keywords: Differential evolution algorithm, iterated greedy algorithm, no-idle permutation flowshop scheduling problem, heuristic optimization.

1 Introduction

In a no-idle permutation flowshop scheduling (NIPFS) problem, each machine has to process jobs without any interruption from the start of processing the first job to the completion of the last job. For this reason, whenever needed, the start of processing the first job on a given machine must be delayed so as to satisfy the no-idle requirement. The relevant literature about the NIPFS problem can be found in [1-15]. As to the meta-heuristics applications, Pan and Wang proposed a discrete differential evolution and a discrete particle swarm optimization algorithms in [16, 17]. Recently, in [18] an iterated greedy (IG) algorithm for the NIPFS problem with the makespan

L. Rutkowski et al. (Eds.): SIDE 2012 and EC 2012, LNCS 7269, pp. 128–135, 2012.

criterion was presented. In addition, they employed their own benchmark suite and tested the performance of IG against the existing heuristic algorithms from the literature whereas a differential evolution algorithm is presented in [19]. In this paper, a variable iterated greedy algorithm with a differential evolution (vIG_DE) is presented to be compared to the best known solutions in [18] as well as to a very recent hybrid discrete differential evolution algorithm (HDDE) in [24]. The remaining paper is organized as follows. Section 2 introduces the no-idle permutation flowshop scheduling problem. Section 3 presents the vIG_DE algorithm in detail. Section 4 discusses the computational results over benchmark problems. Finally, Section 5 summarizes the concluding remarks.

2   No-Idle Permutation Flowshop Scheduling Problem

The NIPFS problem with n $(j = 1,..,n)$ jobs and m $(k = 1,..,m)$ machines can be defined as follows. Each job will be sequenced through m machines. $p(j,k)$ denotes the processing time in which the setup time is included. At any time, each machine can process at most one job and each job can be processed on at most one machine. The sequence in which the jobs are to be processed is the same for each machine. To follow the no-idle restriction, each machine must process jobs without any interruption from the start of processing the first job to the completion of processing the last job. The aim is then to find the same permutation on each machine and its makespan is minimized. The formulation of makespan criterion is given below:

Let a job permutation $\pi = \{\pi_1,..,\pi_n\}$ represent the schedule of jobs to be processed and $\pi_j^E = \{\pi_1,..,\pi_j\}$ be a partial schedule of π such that j must be between 1 and n ($1 < j < n$). In addition, $F(\pi_j^E, k, k+1)$ refers to the minimum difference between the completion of processing the last job of π_j^E on machines $k+1$ and k, which is restricted by the no-idle constraint. Then, $F(\pi_j^E, k, k+1)$ can be computed as follows:

$$F(\pi_1^E, k, k+1) = p(\pi_1, k+1) \qquad\qquad k = 1,..,m-1 \qquad (1)$$

$$F(\pi_j^E, k, k+1) = max\left\{\left(F(\pi_{j-1}^E, k, k+1) - p(\pi_j, k)\right), 0\right\} + p(\pi_j, k+1)$$

$$j = 2,..,n \text{ and } k = 1,..,m-1 \qquad (2)$$

Then, the makespan of job π_n on machine m can be given by

$$C(\pi_n, m) = C_{max}(\pi_n^E) = \sum_{k=1}^{m-1} F(\pi_n^E, k, k+1) + \sum_{j=1}^{n} p(\pi_j, 1) \qquad (3)$$

We refer to Tasgetiren et al. [19] for the details with examples. Therefore, the objective of the NIPFS with the makespan criterion is to find a permutation π^* in the set of all permutations Π such that

$$C_{max}(\pi^*) \leq C_{max}(\pi_n^E) \quad \forall \pi \in \Pi . \qquad (4)$$

3   IG with Differential Evolution

Differential evolution (DE) is an evolutionary optimization method proposed by Storn and Price [20]. An excellent review of DE algorithms can be found in Das and Suganthan [21]. On the other hand, an IG algorithm in general is either started with a random solution or a problem specific heuristic, which is usually the NEH heuristic [22]. Then a local search based on the best insertion heuristic is applied to the initial solution generated by the NEH heuristic. The solution is destructed and reconstructed by using the NEH heuristic again. This process is repeated until a termination criterion is satisfied. For details regarding the IG algorithm, we refer to Ruiz and Stützle [23] where it is well illustrated with an example.

In this paper, the standard differential evolution algorithm is modified such that the IG algorithm will be able to use a variable destruction size and a probability whether or not to apply the IG algorithm to the associated individual in the population, thus ending up with a variable iterated greedy algorithm guided by a DE algorithm (vIG_DE). For this purpose, we propose a unique multi-chromosome solution representation given in Fig. 1.

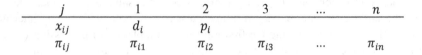

j	1	2	3	...	n
x_{ij}	d_i	p_i			
π_{ij}	π_{i1}	π_{i2}	π_{i3}	...	π_{in}

Fig. 1. Solution representation

In the solution representation, each individual represents the destruction size (d_i) and the probability (p_i) whether or not to apply the IG algorithm, respectively. In addition, a permutation is randomly assigned to each individual in the target population. The basic idea behind the proposed algorithm is that while DE optimizes the d_i and p_i, respectively, these optimized values guide the search for the IG algorithm in order for offspring generation. In other words, a uniform random number r is generated. If r is less than the probability (p_i), offspring is directly generated by applying the IG algorithm with the destruction size d_i to the permutation π_{ij} of the corresponding individual. In the initial population, the d_i and p_i parameters for each individual are established as follows: the destruction size is randomly and uniformly determined as $d_i \in [1, n-1]$. Then, the permutation for the first individual is constructed by the NEH heuristic. The remaining permutations for individuals in the population are randomly constructed and the NEH heuristic is applied to each of them. Once the destruction size and permutation for each individual are constructed, the IG algorithm is applied to each individual at first glance. Then the probability and p_i whether or not to apply the IG algorithm to each permutation is determined as $p_i = 1 - \frac{f(\pi_i)}{\sum_{i=1}^{NP} f(\pi_i)}$. By doing so, the higher the probability is, the higher the chance that the IG algorithm will be applied to corresponding individual i. In the proposed vIG_DE algorithm, mutant individuals are generated as follows:

$$v_{ij}^t = x_{aj}^{t-1} + F\left(x_{aj}^{t-1} - x_{cj}^{t-1}\right) \tag{5}$$

Where a, b and c are three randomly chosen individuals by tournament selection with size of 2 from the target population such that $\left(a \neq b \neq c \neq i \in (1,.., NP)\right)$ and $(j = 1,2)$. $F > 0$ is a mutation scale factor which affects the differential variation between two individuals. Then, an arithmetic crossover operator is applied to obtain the trial individual instead of the traditional uniform crossover such that:

$$u_{ij}^t = Cr \times v_{ij}^t + (1 - Cr) \times x_{ij}^{t-1} \tag{6}$$

where Cr is a user-defined crossover constant in the range $[0,1]$. During the reproduction of the trial population, parameter values violating the search range are restricted to:

$$u_{ij}^t = x_{ij}^{min} + \left(x_{ij}^{max} - x_{ij}^{min}\right) \times r \quad for\ j = 1,2 \tag{7}$$

where $x_{i1}^{min} = 1$ and $x_{i1}^{max} = n - 1$; $x_{i2}^{min} = 0$ and $x_{i2}^{max} = 1$; and r is a uniform random number between 0 and 1. Finally, the selection is based on the survival of the fittest among the trial and target individuals such that:

$$x_i^t = \begin{cases} u_i^t & if\ f(u_i^t) \leq f(x_i^{t-1}) \\ x_i^{t-1} & otherwise \end{cases} \tag{8}$$

The pseudo code of the vIG_DE algorithm is given in Figure 2.

Procedure vIG_DE
Initialize population
Evaluate population and determine d_i and p_i
While (NotTermination) do
       Get mutant individual v_i
       Get trial individual u_i
       if $r(0,1) < p_i = u_{i2}$
       Apply IG algorithm with $d_i = u_{i1}$ to π_i
       Update individual x_i and π_i
Endwhile
Return best solution π_{best}

Fig. 2. vIG_DE algorithm

4 Computational Results

The proposed vIG_DE algorithm was coded in C++ and run on an Intel Core 2 Quad 2.66 GHz PC with 3.5GB memory. Crossover probability and mutation scale factor are taken as $Cr = 0.9$ and $F = 0.9$, respectively. We test the performance of our algorithm on a benchmark suite available in *http://soa.iti.es/rruiz*. The benchmark set is specifically designed for the no-idle permutation flowshop scheduling problem with makespan criterion. It has complete combinations of

$n = \{50,100,150,200,250,300,350,400,450,500\};$ and $m = \{10,20,30,40,50\}$.
There are five instances per combination; hence there are 250 instances in total.

Five runs were carried out for each problem instance as the same as in other competing algorithms. Each run was compared to the best known solution presented in *http://soa.iti.es/rruiz* . The average relative percent deviation from the best known solution is given as follows:

$$\Delta_{avg} = \sum_{i=1}^{R} \left(\frac{(H_i - Best) \times 100}{Best} \right) / R \tag{9}$$

Where H_i, $Best$ and R are the objective function values generated by vIG_DE algorithm in each run; the best known solution value; and the number of runs; respectively. As a termination criterion, the vIG_DE algorithm was run for $T_{max} = n(m/2) \times t$ milliseconds where $t = 30$, which is the same as in Ruiz et al. [18]. The population size is fixed at $NP = 30$.

The computational results are given in Table 1. As seen in Table 1, the vIG_DE algorithm was significantly better than the IG_LS algorithm of Ruiz et al. [18] since the overall Δ_{avg} was improved from 0.34% to −0.12%. In terms of the overall minimum deviation, the whole benchmark suite was further improved by −0.25% whereas the overall maximum deviation was only 0.02%. The vIG_DE algorithm was also robust since the overall standard deviation of the relative percent deviation was 0.11%. Ultimately, 183 out of 250 instances were further improved, 49 being equal and only 18 being worse.

Table 1. Computational result of algorithms

		IG_LS	vIG_DE					HDDE	
n	**m**	Δ_{avg}	Δ_{avg}	Δ_{min}	Δ_{max}	Δ_{std}	Tmax	Δ_{avg}	Tmax
50	10	0.25	0.03	-0.02	0.10	0.05	7.5	0.20	15.0
	20	0.33	-0.04	-0.13	0.04	0.07	15.0	0.29	30.0
	30	0.64	-0.17	-0.33	-0.04	0.11	22.5	0.25	45.0
	40	0.78	-0.41	-0.64	-0.18	0.18	30.0	0.36	60.0
	50	1.52	-0.16	-0.43	0.11	0.22	37.5	1.15	75.0
100	10	0.17	0.04	0.00	0.10	0.05	15.0	0.10	30.0
	20	0.33	-0.09	-0.18	0.01	0.08	30.0	0.09	60.0
	30	0.46	-0.19	-0.34	0.00	0.13	45.0	0.50	90.0
	40	0.87	-0.65	-0.98	-0.40	0.24	60.0	0.07	120.0
	50	0.73	-0.12	-0.40	0.17	0.22	75.0	0.45	150.0
150	10	0.01	0.00	0.00	0.00	0.00	22.5	0.01	45.0
	20	0.34	0.05	-0.03	0.12	0.06	45.0	0.43	90.0
	30	0.42	-0.18	-0.29	-0.11	0.08	67.5	0.14	135.0
	40	0.73	-0.07	-0.31	0.17	0.20	90.0	0.25	180.0
	50	0.68	-0.85	-1.14	-0.62	0.20	112.5	-0.17	225.0
200	10	0.06	0.00	0.00	0.00	0.00	30.0	0.03	60.0
	20	0.12	-0.07	-0.12	-0.01	0.05	60.0	0.04	120.0
	30	0.21	-0.31	-0.44	-0.18	0.11	90.0	0.01	180.0
	40	0.44	-0.26	-0.50	-0.04	0.18	120.0	0.10	240.0
	50	0.42	-0.40	-0.55	-0.24	0.13	150.0	0.45	300.0
250	10	0.01	-0.01	-0.01	-0.01	0.00	37.5	0.00	75.0
	20	0.17	-0.03	-0.08	0.02	0.04	75.0	0.13	150.0
	30	0.31	-0.14	-0.26	-0.02	0.10	112.5	0.00	225.0
	40	0.54	0.02	-0.11	0.16	0.10	150.0	0.31	300.0
	50	0.56	-0.60	-0.85	-0.31	0.22	187.5	0.06	375.0

Table 1. (*continued*)

300	10	0.01	0.00	0.00	0.00	0.00	45.0	0.00	90.0
	20	0.23	0.00	-0.08	0.09	0.06	90.0	0.12	180.0
	30	0.23	0.02	-0.09	0.12	0.08	135.0	0.30	270.0
	40	0.26	-0.34	-0.53	-0.16	0.15	180.0	0.15	360.0
	50	0.42	-0.23	-0.59	0.24	0.34	225.0	0.10	450.0
350	10	0.03	0.00	0.00	0.00	0.00	52.5	0.02	105.0
	20	0.23	-0.01	-0.06	0.05	0.04	105.0	0.05	210.0
	30	0.33	-0.05	-0.15	0.05	0.08	157.5	0.11	315.0
	40	0.39	0.08	-0.09	0.26	0.13	210.0	0.31	420.0
	50	0.40	-0.44	-0.64	-0.21	0.17	262.5	-0.18	525.0
400	10	0.01	0.00	0.00	0.00	0.00	60.0	0.01	120.0
	20	0.14	0.04	-0.04	0.12	0.06	120.0	0.14	240.0
	30	0.25	0.11	0.02	0.23	0.09	180.0	0.23	360.0
	40	0.33	-0.04	-0.20	0.09	0.11	240.0	0.20	480.0
	50	0.37	-0.25	-0.43	0.01	0.18	300.0	0.08	600.0
450	10	0.02	0.00	0.00	0.00	0.00	67.5	0.02	135.0
	20	0.12	0.00	-0.07	0.05	0.05	135.0	0.12	270.0
	30	0.20	-0.03	-0.15	0.10	0.10	202.5	0.08	405.0
	40	0.36	-0.09	-0.24	0.05	0.12	270.0	0.01	540.0
	50	0.58	-0.07	-0.35	0.32	0.26	337.5	0.21	675.0
500	10	0.03	0.00	0.00	0.00	0.00	75.0	0.01	150.0
	20	0.10	-0.04	-0.06	-0.03	0.01	150.0	0.04	300.0
	30	0.20	0.08	-0.01	0.19	0.09	225.0	0.13	450.0
	40	0.35	0.10	-0.06	0.27	0.13	300.0	0.13	600.0
	50	0.45	-0.03	-0.33	0.18	0.20	375.0	0.17	750.0
Avg		0.34	-0.12	-0.25	0.02	0.11	123.8	0.16	247.5

In addition to above, we also compare our algorithm to a very recent HDDE algorithm in [24]. To avoid the CPU time questions, we directly take their results for $(n * m/2) * 60$ milliseconds, which is twice when compared to our termination criterion $((n * m/2) * 30)$. First of all, Table 1 confirms that the vIG_DE algorithm was superior to the HDDE algorithm since Δ_{avg} was improved from 0.16% to -0.12%. In [24], it is reported that 150 out of 250 instances are improved for the benchmark suite. In Table 2, we show that 114 out of 150 best known solutions provided by HDDE in [24] were further improved by the vIG_DE algorithm with the half of the CPU time allocation.

Table 2. New best known solutions by improvement over the HDDE algorithm

Instance	HDDE	vIG_DE	Instance	HDDE	vIG_DE	Instance	HDDE	vIG_DE
I_7_50_30_1	7225	**7223**	I_7_200_40_1	20019	**19965**	I_7_350_50_1	32375	**32144**
I_7_50_30_5	7338	**7333**	I_7_200_40_2	21743	**21724**	I_7_350_50_2	33167	**32911**
I_7_50_40_1	9169	**9168**	I_7_200_40_4	17624	**17507**	I_7_350_50_3	34903	**34718**
I_7_50_40_3	9791	**9782**	I_7_200_50_1	22865	**22729**	I_7_350_50_4	37081	**37009**
I_7_50_50_2	10942	**10893**	I_7_200_50_2	23600	**23488**	I_7_350_50_5	35588	**35390**
I_7_50_50_4	9970	**9967**	I_7_200_50_3	22561	**22431**	I_7_400_20_1	27696	**27686**
I_7_50_50_5	11349	**11316**	I_7_200_50_5	24334	**24275**	I_7_400_20_5	24711	**24688**
I_7_100_10_1	6570	**6570**	I_7_250_20_2	17684	**17683**	I_7_400_30_1	29468	**29405**
I_7_100_20_4	9029	**8972**	I_7_250_20_4	17646	**17645**	I_7_400_40_1	37540	**37440**
I_7_100_20_5	9117	**9109**	I_7_250_30_2	21876	**21853**	I_7_400_40_2	33889	**33805**
I_7_100_30_1	11228	**11210**	I_7_250_30_4	19807	**19794**	I_7_400_40_3	34498	**34482**
I_7_100_30_2	10943	**10938**	I_7_250_30_5	20910	**20906**	I_7_400_40_4	35374	**35306**
I_7_100_30_3	10587	**10571**	I_7_250_40_1	22870	**22820**	I_7_400_50_1	37938	**37825**

Table 2. (*continued*)

L_7_100_30_4	11137	**11103**	L_7_250_40_4	24858	**24748**	L_7_400_50_2	38336	**38237**
L_7_100_40_1	12721	**12606**	L_7_250_50_2	24864	**24577**	L_7_400_50_3	38122	**37880**
L_7_100_40_2	13291	**13117**	L_7_250_50_3	26678	**26512**	L_7_400_50_4	40521	**40465**
L_7_100_40_3	12574	**12488**	L_7_250_50_5	27511	**27389**	L_7_400_50_5	35761	**35516**
L_7_100_40_4	11853	**11781**	L_7_300_30_1	26529	**26501**	L_7_450_20_1	27521	**27514**
L_7_100_50_1	16035	**16019**	L_7_300_30_3	24381	**24370**	L_7_450_20_3	28808	**28770**
L_7_100_50_2	14800	**14787**	L_7_300_30_5	22630	**22568**	L_7_450_20_4	28461	**28446**
L_7_150_20_3	12058	**12046**	L_7_300_40_1	26731	**26599**	L_7_450_30_2	32544	**32517**
L_7_150_20_4	10960	**10936**	L_7_300_40_2	29316	**29158**	L_7_450_30_4	33734	**33700**
L_7_150_30_1	15540	**15505**	L_7_300_40_3	25382	**25362**	L_7_450_40_1	39641	**39562**
L_7_150_30_2	13719	**13667**	L_7_300_40_4	27546	**27479**	L_7_450_40_2	36137	**36020**
L_7_150_30_3	14664	**14651**	L_7_300_40_5	28812	**28760**	L_7_450_40_4	37770	**37606**
L_7_150_30_4	14555	**14549**	L_7_300_50_1	31755	**31667**	L_7_450_40_5	35773	**35712**
L_7_150_40_1	16114	**16025**	L_7_300_50_2	29515	**29490**	L_7_450_50_1	37847	**37563**
L_7_150_40_2	18204	**18122**	L_7_300_50_3	30851	**30731**	L_7_450_50_3	44157	**44087**
L_7_150_40_3	16391	**16356**	L_7_300_50_5	29205	**29051**	L_7_450_50_5	41180	**40923**
L_7_150_50_1	20388	**20364**	L_7_350_20_3	22899	**22880**	L_7_500_20_3	31102	**31066**
L_7_150_50_2	19374	**19121**	L_7_350_20_4	22975	**22968**	L_7_500_20_4	30905	**30900**
L_7_150_50_3	19655	**19447**	L_7_350_20_5	22750	**22746**	L_7_500_30_2	39365	**39357**
L_7_150_50_4	20166	**20139**	L_7_350_30_2	27765	**27744**	L_7_500_30_4	33972	**33918**
L_7_150_50_5	19342	**19308**	L_7_350_30_3	27673	**27653**	L_7_500_40_1	40768	**40708**
L_7_200_20_5	14181	**14175**	L_7_350_30_4	29305	**29295**	L_7_500_40_3	40485	**40366**
L_7_200_30_1	17116	**17053**	L_7_350_40_1	29282	**29182**	L_7_500_40_5	36343	**36312**
L_7_200_30_3	17501	**17428**	L_7_350_40_2	29154	**29043**	L_7_500_50_1	46331	**46238**
L_7_200_30_4	20005	**19991**	L_7_350_40_4	34744	**34644**	L_7_500_50_3	45394	**45206**

5   Conclusions

In this paper, we present a DE based variable iterated greedy algorithm to solve the the no-idle permutation flowshop scheduling problem with makespan criterion. A unique multi-chromosome solution representation is presented in such a way that first chromosome represents the destruction size and the probability of applying the IG algorithm to the permutation of each individual whereas second chromosome is simply a permutation assigned to each individual in the population randomly. The performance of the vIG_DE algorithm is tested on the Ruben's benchmark suite and compared to the best known solutions presented in [18]. Ultimately, 183 out of 250 instances were further improved, 49 being equal and only 18 being worse. When compared to the HDDE algorithm, 114 out of 150 best known solutions provided by HDDE in [24] were further improved by the vIG_DE algorithm with the half of the CPU time allocation.

Acknowledgments. M. Fatih Tasgetiren acknowledges the support provided by the TUBITAK (The Scientific and Technological Research Council of Turkey) under the grant # 110M622.

References

1. Saadani, N.E.H., Guinet, A., Moalla, M.: Three stage no-idle flow-shops. Computers & Industrial Engineering 44(3), 425–434 (2003)
2. Tanaev, V.S., Sotskov, Y.N., Strusevich, V.A.: Scheduling Theory. Multi-Stage Systems. Kluwer Academic Publishers, Dordrecht (1994)

3. Baptiste, P., Hguny, L.K.: A branch and bound algorithm for the F/no–idle/Cmax. In: Proceedings of the International Conference on Industrial Engineering and Production Management, IEPM 1997, Lyon, France, pp. 429–438 (1997)
4. Saadani, N.E.H., Guinet, A., Moalla, M.: Three stage no-idle flow-shops. Computers & Industrial Engineering 44(3), 425–434 (2003)
5. Baraz, D., Mosheiov, G.: A note on a greedy heuristic for the flow-shop makespan minimization with no machine idle-time. European Journal of Operational Research 184(2), 810–813 (2008)
6. Adiri, I., Pohoryles, D.: Flow-shop/no-idle or no-wait scheduling to minimize the sum of completion times. Naval Research Logistics Quarterly 29(3), 495–504 (1982)
7. Vachajitpan, P.: Job sequencing with continuous machine operation. Computers and Industrial Engineering 6(3), 255–259 (1982)
8. Woollam, C.R.: Flowshop with no idle machine time allowed. Computers and Industrial Engineering 10(1), 69–76 (1986)
9. Cepek, O., Okada, M., Vlach, M.: Note: On the two-machine no-idle flowshop problem. Naval Research Logistics 47(4), 353–358 (2000)
10. Narain, L., Bagga, P.C.: Flowshop/no-idle scheduling to minimise the mean flowtime. Anziam Journal 47, 265–275 (2005)
11. Saadani, N.E.H., Guinet, A., Moalla, M.: A traveling salesman approach to solve the F/no – idle/Cmax problem. In: Proceedings of the International Conference on Industrial Engineering and Production Management (IEPM 2001), Quebec, Canada, pp. 880–888 (2001)
12. Saadani, N.E.H., Guinet, A., Moalla, M.: A travelling salesman approach to solve the F/no–idle/Cmax problem. European Journal of Operational Research 161(1), 11–20 (2005)
13. Kamburowski, J.: More on three-machine no-idle flow shops. Computers and Industrial Engineering 46(3), 461–466 (2004)
14. Narain, L., Bagga, P.C.: Flowshop/no-idle scheduling to minimize total elapsed time. Journal of Global Optimization 33(3), 349–367 (2005)
15. Kalczynski, P.J., Kamburowski, J.: On no-wait and no-idle flow shops with makespan criterion. European Journal of Operational Research 178(3), 677–685 (2007)
16. Pan, Q.-K., Wang, L.: A novel differential evolution algorithm for no-idle permutation flowshop scheduling problems. European Journal of Industrial Engineering 2(3), 279–297 (2008)
17. Pan, Q.-K., Wang, L.: No-idle permutation flow shop scheduling based on a hybrid discrete particle swarm optimization algorithm. International Journal of Advanced Manufacturing Technology 39(7-8), 796–807 (2008)
18. Ruiz, R., Vallada, E., Fernández-Martínez, C.: Scheduling in Flowshops with No-Idle Machines. In: Chakraborty, U.K. (ed.) Computational Intelligence in Flow Shop and Job Shop Scheduling. SCI, vol. 230, pp. 21–51. Springer, Heidelberg (2009)
19. Tasgetiren, M.F., Pan, Q.-K., Suganthan, P.N., Chua, T.-J.: A differential evolution algorithm for the no-idle flowshop scheduling problem with total tardiness criterion. International Journal of Production Research, 1–18 (2010); iFirst
20. Storn, R., Price, K.: Differential Evolution - A Simple and Efficient Heuristic for Global Optimization over Continuous Space. Journal of Global Optimization 11, 341–359 (1997)
21. Das, S., Suganthan, P.N.: Differential Evolution: A survey of the State-of-the-Art. IEEE Transaction on Evolutionary Computation (2011) (in press)
22. Nawaz, M., Enscore Jr., E.E., Ham, I.: A heuristic algorithm for the m-machine, n-job flow shop sequencing problem. Omega 11(1), 91–95 (1983)
23. Ruiz, R., Stützle, T.: A simple and effective iterated greedy algorithm for the permutation flowshop scheduling problem. European Journal of Operational Research 177(3), 2033–2049 (2007)
24. Deng, G., Gu, X.: A hybrid discrete differential evolution algorithm for the no-idle permutation flowshop scheduling problem with makespan criterion. Computers & Operations Research (2011), doi:10.1016/j.cor.2011.10.024

Differential Evolution with Competing Strategies Applied to Partitional Clustering

Josef Tvrdík and Ivan Křivý

Centre of Excellence IT4Innovations, Division of University of Ostrava,
Institute for Research and Applications of Fuzzy Modeling,
30. dubna Street 22, 701 03 Ostrava, Czech Republic
{josef.tvrdik,ivan.krivy}@osu.cz
http://www.osu.cz/

Abstract. We consider the problem of optimal partitional clustering of real data sets by optimizing three basic criteria (trace of within scatter matrix, variance ratio criterion, and Marriottt's criterion). Four variants of the algorithm based on differential evolution with competing strategies are compared on eight real-world data sets. The experimental results showed that hybrid variants with k-means algorithm for a local search are essentially more efficient than the others. However, the use of Marriottt's criterion resulted in stopping hybrid variants at a local minimum.

Keywords: optimal partitional clustering, adaptive differential evolution, k-means algorithm, hybrid search, numerical comparison.

1 Introduction

Cluster analysis is an important exploratory technique used for grouping objects into relatively homogeneous clusters on the basis of object similarities or distances.

Clustering problem can be defined as follows. Let O be a set of n objects, each of which is characterized by p real-valued attributes. Furthermore, let Z be a data matrix of size $n \times p$. Therefore, the matrix can be considered as composed of n data vectors z_i, where each element z_{ij} represents the jth real-valued attribute of the ith object. Given the matrix Z, the aim of the partitional clustering algorithm is to find such a partition $G = \{C_1, C_2, \ldots, C_g\}$, $C_k \neq \emptyset$ for all k, $C_k \cap C_l = \emptyset$ for all $k \neq l$, $\cup_{k=1}^{g} C_k = O$ that the objects belonging to the same cluster are as similar to each other as possible, while the objects belonging to different clusters are as dissimilar as possible.

The partitional clustering algorithms try to decompose the data sets directly into a set of disjoint clusters using available optimizing criteria. Among evolutionary algorithms, the differential evolution (DE) appeared to be the most efficient in partitional clustering [2,3,10,11,13]. We have recently studied a few improved adaptive DE variants: variants based on an exponential crossover with a high probability of mutation [18], hybrid variants including k-means algorithm for local search [19], and variants with a special rearrangement of the rank of

L. Rutkowski et al. (Eds.): SIDE 2012 and EC 2012, LNCS 7269, pp. 136–144, 2012.

cluster centers after completing each generation [19]. Our experimental results obtained on four real data sets using only one optimizing criterion indicated that hybrid variants are substantially more efficient when compared with other DE variants.

In this paper, we are searching for an optimal partitional clustering of real data sets by using improved DE algorithms with competing strategies and three basic optimizing criteria.

2 Criteria of Optimal Partitioning

There are several optimizing criteria convenient for comparing the degree of optimality over all possible partitions (see [8]). We use the following three criteria in experimental comparison.

Trace within criterion (hereafter TRW), proposed by Friedman and Rubin [7], is based on minimizing the trace of pooled-within groups scatter matrix (W) defined as

$$W = \sum_{k=1}^{g} W_k,\tag{1}$$

W_k being the variance matrix of attributes for the objects belonging to cluster C_k,

$$W_k = \sum_{j=1}^{n_k} (z_j^{(k)} - \bar{z}^{(k)})(z_j^{(k)} - \bar{z}^{(k)})^T,\tag{2}$$

where $z_j^{(k)}$ is the vector of attributes for the jth object of cluster C_k, $\bar{z}^{(k)} = \left(\sum_{j=1}^{n_k} z_j^{(k)}\right)/n_k$ the vector of means (centroids) for cluster C_k, and $n_k = |C_k|$. The between groups scatter matrix can be expressed analogously in the form

$$B = \sum_{k=1}^{g} n_k (\bar{z}^{(k)} - \bar{z})(\bar{z}^{(k)} - \bar{z})^T,\tag{3}$$

$\bar{z} = \left(\sum_{i=1}^{n} z_i\right)/n$ being the vector of means for all objects. It can be easily proved that the total scatter matrix T, defined as $T = \sum_{i=1}^{n}(z_i - \bar{z})(z_i - \bar{z})^T$, meets the equality $T = W + B$.

Variance ratio criterion (VRC) based on maximizing the ratio of between and within variance and Marriott's criterion (MC) to be minimized have the form:

$$\text{VRC} = \frac{\text{tr}(B)/(g-1)}{\text{tr}(W)/(n-g)}, \qquad \text{MC} = g^2 \frac{\det(W)}{\det(T)}.\tag{4}$$

3 Differential Evolution Algorithm

The differential evolution (DE), introduced by Storn and Price [15], has become one of the most frequently evolutionary algorithms used for solving the continuous global optimization problems [14]. When considering the minimization problem, for a real function $f(x) \to \mathbb{R}$, where x is a continuous variable (vector of length d) with the domain $D \subset \mathbb{R}^d$, the global minimum point x^* satisfying condition $f(x^*) \le f(x)$ for $\forall x \in D$ is to be found. The domain D is defined by specifying boundary constraints, $D = \prod_{j=1}^{d} [a_j, b_j]$, $a_j < b_j$, $j = 1, 2, \ldots, d$.

The initial population of N points is generated at random uniformly distributed in D, each point in D is considered as a candidate of the solution and then the population is evolving generation by generation until the stopping condition is met. Next generation is created by application of evolutionary operators to the current generation.

A new trial point y is generated by using mutation and crossover. There are various strategies of mutation and crossover [4,5,12,14,15]. The most popular mutation strategy rand/1 generates the mutant point u by adding the weighted difference of two points

$$u = r_1 + F(r_2 - r_3), \quad F > 0, \tag{5}$$

where r_1, r_2, and r_3 are three mutually distinct points randomly taken from population P, not coinciding with the current x_i, and F is an input parameter. Kaelo and Ali [9] proposed an amendment of this mutation denoted as randrl/1. The point r_1 in (5) is the best among r_1, r_2, and r_3, $r_1 = \arg\min_{i \in \{1,2,3\}} f(r_i)$. Such mutation improves the efficiency of the search with preserving the reliability of the search.

The elements y_j, $j = 1, 2, \ldots, d$, of the trial point y are built up by the crossover of the current point x_i and the mutant point u. The number of mutant vector elements used in the trial point is controlled by parameter CR, $0 \le CR \le 1$. Two kinds of crossover (binomial and exponential) were proposed in [15]. Let p_m be the probability of mutation defined as the mean relative length of overwritten elements of x_i, i.e. $p_m = E(L)/d$. The relation between the p_m and control parameter CR was studied by Zaharie [21]. For binomial crossover, the relation between p_m and control parameter CR is linear, while for exponential crossover the relationship is strongly non-linear,

$$CR^d - d\, p_m\, CR + d\, p_m. - 1 = 0. \tag{6}$$

The equation (6) has only one real solution in the open interval of $(0,1)$ for $p_m \in (1/d, 1)$. The crossover parameter CR satisfies the conditions $CR = 0$ for $p_m = 1/d$ and $CR = 1$ for $p_m = 1$. Thus, for given p_m we can find a unique corresponding value of CR.

A combination of the mutation and the crossover gives the DE strategy, mostly abbreviated by DE/m/n/c, where m stands for the type of mutation, n for the number of differences used in mutation, and c for the crossover type. The strategy with the setting of F and CR defines a DE variant. Efficiency of the DE variants varies very substantially and is problem-depending. That is why many adaptive or self-adaptive DE algorithms were proposed.

Adaptive DE with competition of different DE strategies and control parameter settings was introduced in [16]. Any of H strategies in the pool can be chosen for the generation of a new trial point y. The strategy is selected randomly with probability q_h, $h = 1, 2, \ldots, H$. At the start the values of probability are set uniformly, $q_h = 1/H$, and they are modified according to the success rate in the preceding steps of the search process. The hth setting is considered successful if it generates such a trial vector y satisfying $f(y) \leq f(x_i)$. Probability q_h is evaluated as the relative frequency according to

$$q_h = \frac{n_h + n_0}{\sum_{j=1}^{H}(n_j + n_0)}, \tag{7}$$

where n_h is the current count of the hth setting successes, and $n_0 > 0$ is an input parameter. The setting of $n_0 > 1$ prevents from a dramatic change in q_h by one random successful use of the hth strategy. To avoid degeneration of the search process, the current values of q_h are reset to their starting values if any probability q_h decreases bellow some given limit $\delta > 0$. The input parameters controlling competition are recommended to set up to $n_0 = 2$ and $\delta = 1/(5 \times H)$.

For optimal partitioning we use a variant of this algorithm that appeared well-performing in several benchmark tests [17]. In this variant, denoted cde hereafter. 12 strategies are in competition $(H = 12)$, six of them use a binomial crossover, the others an exponential crossover. The randrl/1/ mutation is applied in all the strategies, two different values of control parameter F are used, $F = 0.5$ and $F = 0.8$. Binomial crossover uses three different values of CR, $CR \in \{0, 0.5, 1\}$. Values of CR for exponential crossover are evaluated from (6), three values of probability p_m are set up equidistantly in the interval $(1/d, 1)$. This cde algorithm was applied to partitioning [19] and outperformed the other algorithms [1,20].

4 Encoding in Clustering Problems

During a search process, it is desirable to solve the problem how to encode a feasible partition of objects. Data matrix Z is size of $n \times p$ with real-valued elements and it should be partitioned into g clusters. Each center of the cluster of a partition could be considered to be just one vector of length p so that each partition could be represented by g-tuple of such vectors. Therefore, any partition of g clusters can be encoded using a floating point array of length $g \times p$. Each object is classified into a cluster with the least Euclidean distance to the center of the cluster. If it happens that a cluster or even more clusters are empty within the search process and make the current classification unfeasible, such a classification can be repaired for example by assignment of a randomly chosen element from the cluster of the highest cardinality to each empty cluster. This attempt is used in the implemented algorithms.

Another question arises when we consider how to encode an object-to-cluster association. In this paper, a direct encoding of the object-to-cluster association was used. The encoding is based on the idea to represent any feasible partition by a vector (of length n) whose ith component gives the number of the corresponding cluster. However, this scheme is ambiguous, e.g. the vectors $(2, 2, 3, 1, 1)$ and $(3, 3, 1, 2, 2)$ represent the same partitions. The unambiguity could be solved by using a convenient rearrangement of the rank of cluster centers making the object-to-cluster association as similar as possible for all individuals in the current population. To find such rearrangement of one individual representation making the object-to-cluster association equivalent to object-to-cluster association of another individual is easy when the both individuals produces the same classifications as in the example given above. However, the rearrangement is a hard problem when the classifications differ. We proposed a new heuristic search for the most similar object-to-cluster association based on the comparing of the g the most promising rearrangements and the selection of the best of them.

The rearrangement was applied at random after completing a generation with the probability increasing in the course of the optimizing process. The DE variants, where this recoding is used, are denoted by suffix "G" at the end of their labels.

5 Hybrid DE with k-Means Algorithm

In order to improve the search of minimum value of the clustering criterion, a modified hybrid DE algorithm was proposed. After finding a trial vector y satisfying the condition $f(y) \leq f(x_i)$, the k-means algorithm with y as input is used to get the locally best solution. This solution is then used as a trial vector. Similar approach has been recently applied in [11]. Advantages of k-means algorithm are fast convergence to a local minimum and low complexity $O(n)$. The DE variants, where this hybrid local search is used, are denoted by suffix "H" at the end of their labels.

6 Data Used in Benchmark Tests

All DE algorithms under consideration were tested using eight real-world data sets. The data labeled as bcw, iris, glass, and vowel were received directly from [10], while the remaining data were taken from the Machine learning repository [6]. When labeling the data from the repository, we use hereafter abbreviations wine, iono, thyroid, and liver. The data sets are briefly described in Table 1. All the objects attributes are numeric. No missing attribute values occur.

Table 1. Description of data

Data name	bcw	iris	glass	vowel	wine	ionosphere	thyroid disease	liver disorders
No. of classes	2	3	6	6	3	2	3	2
No. of objects	683	150	214	871	178	371	215	345
No. of attributes	9	4	9	3	13	34	5	6

7 Experiments and Results

The search space D for all the DE variants was chosen to give the Z matrix domain $[z_{min}, z_{max}]$, where z_{min} and z_{max} are vectors of minimum and maximum values of each variable in data set Z. The population size was set up to

$N = 30$ in all experiments. Individuals in initial population were generated as g randomly taken rows of matrix $\boldsymbol{Z}$. The stopping condition of the search was in the form $(f_{max} - f_{min})/|f_{min}| < 1 \times 10^{-3}$, where f_{max}, f_{min} are maximum and minimum function values in the current generation, respectively. The control parameter of k-means algorithm is the relative difference of objective function values in two subsequent steps and it was set up to 1×10^{-5}. For each algorithm and each test problem, 50 independent runs were performed. Computational cost of a run was measured by the number of objective-function evaluations denoted by *nfe*. The average values of the optimizing criterion are presented in Table 2 with their standard deviations in % of the mean. The best values are printed in bold, where the average values obtained by the algorithms are not the same for the given problem. Values of MC for iono data are missing because the values of the second attribute are constant and then $\det(\boldsymbol{Z}) = 0$.

Table 2. Means of the best criterion values and their standard deviations in % of the mean (vc)

	cde		cdeG		cdeH		cdeGH	
TRW	mean	vc	mean	vc	mean	vc	mean	vc
bcw	19323.18	6e-5	19323.18	5e-5	**19323.17**	0	**19323.17**	0
liver	**423980.9**	0	**423980.9**	0	**423980.9**	0	423985.6	4e-3
glass	341.1419	3.09	336.8895	1.22	**336.0605**	0	**336.0605**	0
iono	2419.377	1e-3	2419.366	3e-4	**2419.365**	0	**2419.365**	0
iris	**7885.144**	0	**7885.144**	0	**7885.144**	0	**7885.144**	0
thyroid	**28560.15**	0	**28560.15**	0	**28560.15**	0	**28560.15**	0
vowel	30876830	1.37	30742870	0.73	**30686240**	0	**30686240**	0
wine	**2370690**	0	**2370690**	0	**2370690**	0	**2370690**	0
VRC	mean	vc	mean	vc	mean	vc	mean	vc
bcw	**1026.262**	4e-5	**1026.262**	5e-5	**1026.262**	0	**1026.262**	0
liver	**322.2691**	0	**322.2691**	0	322.2667	5e-3	322.2667	5e-3
glass	124.1408	1.54	123.6517	2.35	**124.6162**	0	**124.6162**	0
iono	**118.8265**	0	**118.8265**	0	**118.8265**	0	**118.8265**	0
iris	**561.6277**	0	**561.6277**	0	**561.6277**	0	**561.6277**	0
thyroid	**131.8364**	0	**131.8364**	0	**131.8364**	0	**131.8364**	0
vowel	1450.04	1.79	1463.036	0.79	**1465.88**	0	**1465.88**	0
wine	**561.8157**	0	**561.8157**	0	**561.8157**	0	**561.8157**	0
MC	mean	vc	mean	vc	mean	vc	mean	vc
bcw	0.356116	3.92	**0.352645**	0.03	0.432092	0	0.432092	0
liver	1.207571	0.49	**1.201166**	0.49	1.257056	0	1.257056	0
glass	0.025077	22.60	**0.023289**	21.13	0.034508	0	0.034508	0
iris	**0.198357**	0	**0.198357**	0	0.29001	0	0.29001	0
thyroid	**0.496504**	2.05	0.497565	1.92	0.805791	0	0.805791	0
vowel	0.306145	6.99	**0.297856**	5.38	0.344496	0.39	0.34468	0.32
wine	**0.550134**	36.91	0.574409	30.98	0.82154	0	0.82154	0

All four algorithms are able to find the optimal value of TRW and VRC criteria very reliably with a standard deviation near or equal zero, while for the MC criterion the hybrid algorithms are trapped in the local minimum area and the non-hybrid algorithms are able to find better solution but the variability is greater.

The average values of nfe are shown in Table 3 with their standard deviations in % of the mean, the least values of nfe for each data set are printed in bold. From the results it is apparent that the hybrid algorithms using k-means are much more efficient than their non-hybrid counterparts. One function evaluation takes about 0.001 sec on a standard PC with Intel Pentium 4CPU, 3.00 GHz, 992 MB RAM, which means that a solution can be found in 1 sec for the majority of the problem in tests.

The influence of the centers rearrangement on the efficiency of algorithms was evaluated by two-sample Wilcoxon test, the results are presented in Table 4. The comparison of cde and $cdeG$ algorithms is in the lines denoted "plain", the comparison of $cdeH$ and $cdeGH$ in line "hybrid", symbol "+" means significant

Table 3. Means of nfe values and their standard deviations in % of the mean (vc)

		cde		cdeG		cdeH		cdeGH	
		mean	vc	mean	vc	mean	vc	mean	vc
TRW	bcw	2100	24	2639	32	**321**	21	327	27
	liver	1453	26	1937	42	469	26	**450**	23
	glass	23869	51	33706	106	6760	23	**3931**	16
	iono	9365	30	19797	108	**713**	3	723	3
	iris	2132	32	2977	43	782	34	**749**	29
	thyroid	2966	32	3195	39	1405	33	**1289**	21
	vowel	12628	40	40988	130	7126	31	**4392**	20
	wine	1873	32	3346	36	**552**	36	589	38
VRC	bcw	2867	29	3545	58	328	24	**317**	24
	liver	1498	23	1933	35	494	30	**435**	20
	glass	25738	45	41140	112	6798	25	**4038**	16
	iono	14379	39	31337	72	**716**	3	717	3
	iris	2194	37	2749	43	**829**	31	878	34
	thyroid	3559	28	4635	55	**1292**	24	1327	28
	vowel	13480	43	39324	92	7408	22	**4746**	22
	wine	2020	31	3563	48	**525**	22	577	33
MC	bcw	4895	28	6092	38	2257	51	**1346**	33
	liver	4591	28	5823	42	607	32	**582**	33
	glass	56678	114	81032	147	7386	24	**4615**	15
	iris	4436	35	8455	71	5458	130	**2243**	50
	thyroid	13764	64	15092	70	2837	70	**1847**	29
	vowel	26276	41	55072	65	11132	29	**6911**	18
	wine	22290	51	99756	154	526	27	**509**	20

Table 4. Influence of centers rearrangement on nfe value using Wilcoxon test

Criterion	alg	bcw	liver	glass	iono	iris	thyroid	vowel	wine
TRW	plain	–	–	–	–	–		–	–
	hybrid	+	–					+	
VRC	plain	–	–	–	–	–		–	–
	hybrid	+	+					+	
MC	plain	–	–		–			–	–
	hybrid	+	+				+	+	

decrease in nfe by rearrangement, symbol "–" significant increase of nfe, and the empty field denotes no significant influence on nfe. The two-tailed tests at 0.05 significance level is applied. A significant benefit of rearrangement is surprisingly rare. It was found in glass and vowel data for the hybrid algorithms and three other problems but negative influence on nfe (increase) is more frequent.

8   Conclusion

Adaptive DE with competing strategies and control parameter settings was applied to solve optimal partitioning. Four variants of the algorithm were tested in eight real-world data sets. The hybrid variants using k-means algorithm for local search were found much more efficient compared with non-hybrid DE algorithms. The group centers rearrangement was beneficial only in some hard problems, while in other problems no influence or even negative influence on the efficiency of the algorithms was detected. The hybrid algorithms performed well with TRW and VRC criteria but they were not effective in partitioning with MC criterion, where their search systematically stopped at a local minimum. It is the theme for future research as well as some other questions connected with optimal partitioning by evolutionary algorithms.

Acknowledgments. This paper has been elaborated in the framework of the IT4Innovations Centre of Excellence project, reg. no. CZ.1.05/1.1.00/02.0070. This work was also supported by the SGS 22/2011 project.

References

1. Brest, J., Greiner, S., Boškovič, B., Mernik, M., Žumer, V.: Self-adapting control parameters in differential evolution: A comparative study on numerical benchmark problems. IEEE Transactions on Evolutionary Computation 10, 646–657 (2006)
2. Das, S., Abraham, A., Konar, A.: Automatic clustering using an improved differential evolution algorithm. IEEE Transactions on Systems Man and Cybernetics Part A-Systems and Humans 38(1), 218–237 (2008)
3. Das, S., Sil, S.: Kernel-induced fuzzy clustering of image pixels with an improved differential evolution algorithm. Information Sciences 180(8), 1237–1256 (2010)

4. Das, S., Suganthan, P.N.: Differential evolution: A survey of the state-of-the-art. IEEE Transactions on Evolutionary Computation 15, 27–54 (2011)
5. Feoktistov, V.: Differential Evolution in Search of Sotution. Springer, Heidelberg (2006)
6. Frank, A., Asuncion, A.: UCI machine learning repository (2010), http://archive.ics.uci.edu/ml
7. Friedman, H.P., Rubin, J.: On some invariant criteria for grouping data. Journal of the American Statistical Association 62(320), 1159–1178 (1967)
8. Jain, A., Murty, M., Flynn, P.: Data clustering: A review. ACM Computing Surveys 31(3), 264–323 (1999)
9. Kaelo, P., Ali, M.M.: A numerical study of some modified differential evolution algorithms. European J. Operational Research 169, 1176–1184 (2006)
10. Krink, T., Paterlini, S., Resti, A.: Using differential evolution to improve the accuracy of bank rating systems. Computational Statistics & Data Analysis 52(1), 68–87 (2007)
11. Kwedlo, W.: A clustering method combining differential evolution with the K-means algorithm. Pattern Recognition Letters 32(12), 1613–1621 (2011)
12. Neri, F., Tirronen, V.: Recent advances in differential evolution: a survey and experimental analysis. Artificial Intelligence Review 33, 61–106 (2010)
13. Paterlini, S., Krink, T.: Differential evolution and particle swarm optimisation in partitional clustering. Computational Statistics & Data Analysis 50(5), 1220–1247 (2006)
14. Price, K.V., Storn, R., Lampinen, J.: Differential Evolution: A Practical Approach to Global Optimization. Springer, Heidelberg (2005)
15. Storn, R., Price, K.V.: Differential evolution - a simple and efficient heuristic for global optimization over continuous spaces. J. Global Optimization 11, 341–359 (1997)
16. Tvrdík, J.: Competitive differential evolution. In: Matoušek, R., Ošmera, P. (eds.) MENDEL 2006: 12th International Conference on Soft Computing, pp. 7–12. University of Technology, Brno (2006)
17. Tvrdík, J.: Self-adaptive variants of differential evolution with exponential crossover. Analele of West University Timisoara, Series Mathematics-Informatics 47, 151–168 (2009), http://www1.osu.cz/~tvrdik/ (reprint available [ONLINE])
18. Tvrdík, J., Křivý, I.: Differential evolution in partitional clustering. In: Matoušek, R. (ed.) 16th International Conference on Soft Computing, MENDEL 2010, pp. 7–14 (2010)
19. Tvrdík, J., Křivý, I.: Hybrid adaptive differential evolution in partitional clustering. In: Matoušek, R. (ed.) 17th International Conference on Soft Computing, MENDEL 2011, pp. 1–8 (2011)
20. Wang, Y., Cai, Z., Zhang, Q.: Differential evolution with composite trial vector generation strategies and control parameters. IEEE Transactions on Evolutionary Computation 15, 55–66 (2011)
21. Zaharie, D.: Influence of crossover on the behavior of differential evolution algorithms. Applied Soft Computing 9, 1126–1138 (2009)

Contiguous Binomial Crossover
in Differential Evolution

Matthieu Weber and Ferrante Neri[*]

Department of Mathematical Information Technology,
University of Jyväskylä, P.O. Box 35 (Agora), FI-40014, Finland
{matthieu.weber,ferrante.neri}@jyu.fi

Abstract. This paper compares the binomial crossover used in the Differential Evolution with a variant named the contiguous binomial crossover. In the latter, a contiguous block of variables is used for selecting which variables are exchanged, in a fashion similar to that of the exponential crossover, allowing to using a single, normally-distributed random number to decide the number of exchanged variables. Experimental results show that this variant of the binomial crossover exhibits in general similar or better performance than the original one, and allows to increase significantly the execution speed of the Differential Evolution, especially in higher dimension problems.

1 Introduction

Differential Evolution (DE), see [1,2], is an optimization algorithm for continuous problems that has shown high performance in various types of applications e.g., [3]. As a stochastic algorithm, DE makes use of an important quantity of pseudo-random numbers (for simplicity, the term random will be used instead of pseudo-random in the remainder of this paper), especially for the algorithmic component known as the crossover. To clarify the notation used in this article we refer to the minimization problem of an objective function $f(x)$, where x is a vector of n design variables in a decision space D.

In this study, we present a new variant of the crossover, named the contiguous binomial crossover, that uses only one, normally distributed random number to decide of the length of the crossover, instead of using n, uniformly distributed random numbers. Since this new variant exchanges a contiguous block of variables during the crossover, instead of a set of variables scattered along the whole length of x, it is necessary to verify that it does not lead to a loss of performance and that it indeed increases the execution speed of DE. It must be noted that with regard to the quality of the solutions produced by the algorithms, this study is, in first intention, non-regression test rather than a performance test: its aim is to find out whether the new crossover scheme has adverse effects on the performance of DE, rather than to present a new, better-performing algorithm. For

---

[*] This work is supported by Academy of Finland, Akatemiatutkija 130600, Algorithmic Design Issues in Memetic Computing.

L. Rutkowski et al. (Eds.): SIDE 2012 and EC 2012, LNCS 7269, pp. 145–153, 2012.

this reason, DE with the contiguous binomial crossover will be compared solely to DE with the original binomial crossover, and not to any other, state-of-the-art algorithm.

1.1 Differential Evolution with Binomial Crossover

This section gives the description of DE according to its original definition given in [4]. A schematic description of DE highlighting the working principles of the algorithms is given in Fig. 1.

An initial sampling of S_{pop} individuals is performed randomly with a uniform distribution function within the decision space D. At each generation, for each individual x_i of the S_{pop}, three individuals x_r, x_s and x_t are randomly extracted from the population. According to the DE logic, a provisional offspring x'_{off} is generated by mutation:

$$x'_{off} = x_t + F(x_r - x_s) \tag{1}$$

where $F \in [0, 1 + \epsilon[$ is a scale factor which controls the length of the exploration vector $(x_r - x_s)$ and thus determines how far from point x_i the offspring should be generated. With $F \in [0, 1 + \epsilon[$, it is meant here that the scale factor should be a positive value which cannot be much greater than 1 (i.e. ϵ is a small positive value), see [1]. While there is no theoretical upper limit for F, effective values are rarely greater than 1.0. The mutation scheme given in Equation (1) is also known as DE/rand/1. Other variants of the mutation rule have been subsequently proposed in literature, see [5].

When the provisional offspring has been generated by mutation, each gene of the individual x'_{off} is exchanged with the corresponding gene of x_i with a uniform probability and the final offspring x_{off} is generated, as shown in equation 2:

$$x_{off,j} = \begin{cases} x'_{off,j} & \text{if} \quad rand\,(0,1) < CR \\ x_{i,j} & \text{otherwise} \end{cases} \tag{2}$$

where $rand\,(0,1)$ is a uniformly distributed random number between 0 and 1; j is the index of the gene under examination.

The resulting offspring x_{off} is evaluated and, according to a one-to-one spawning strategy, it replaces x_i if and only if $f(x_{off}) \leq f(x_i)$; otherwise no replacement occurs. It must be remarked that although the replacement indexes are saved one by one during generation, actual replacements occur all at once at the end of the generation.

The crossover used in the above description (see Equation 2) is referred to as *binomial crossover*, due to the fact that the number of variables x_i that are exchanged during one crossover (the *length* of the crossover) is following a binomial distribution (the discrete counterpart of the normal distribution) characterized by a mean value of nCR and a standard deviation of $\sqrt{nCR(1 - CR)}$. When associated to the DE/rand/1 mutation, the algorithm is referred to as DE/rand/1/bin.

```
generate S_pop individuals of the initial population randomly
while budget condition do
   evaluate the fitness values of the population
   for i = 1 : S_pop do
      {** Mutation **}
      randomly select three individuals x_r, x_s, and x_t
      compute x'_off = x_t + F(x_r - x_s)
      {** Crossover **}
      x_off = x_i
      generate j_0 ← 1 + round(n × rand(0, 1))
      for j = 1 : n do
         if rand(0, 1) ≤ CR OR j = j_0 then
            x_off,j = x'_off,j
         end if
      end for
      {** Selection **}
      if f(x_off) ≤ f(x_i) then
         save index for replacement x_i = x_off
      end if
   end for
   perform replacements
end while
```

Fig. 1. Pseudo code of DE with binomial crossover

1.2   The Exponential Crossover

Another commonly used crossover function is the *exponential crossover*, where the number of variables x_i that are exchanged during one crossover is following a geometric distribution (the discrete counterpart of the exponential distribution). In the exponential crossover, a design variable of the provisional offspring $x'_{off}(j)$ is randomly selected and copied into the jth design variable of the solution x_i. This guarantees that parent and offspring have different genotypes. Subsequently, a set of random numbers between 0 and 1 are generated. As long as $\text{rand}(0, 1) \leq CR$, where the crossover rate CR is a predetermined parameter, the design variables from the provisional offspring (mutant) are copied into the corresponding positions of the parent x_i. The first time that $\text{rand}(0, 1) > CR$ the copy process is interrupted. Thus, all the remaining design variables of the offspring are copied from the parent. When this crossover is combined with the DE/rand/1 mutation, the algorithm is referred to as DE/rand/1/exp. For the sake of clarity the pseudo-code of the exponential crossover is shown in Fig. 2.

For illustration purposes, Fig. 3 graphically represents the distribution of the exchanged variables for both a scattered crossover (such as the original binomial crossover) and a contiguous crossover (such as the exponential crossover).

```
x_off ← x_i
generate j ← 1 + round(n × rand(0, 1))
x_off(j) ← x'_off(j)
p ← 0
while rand(0, 1) ≤ CR AND p < n − 1 do
    x_off(1 + (j + p) mod n) ← x'_off(1 + (j + p) mod n)
    p ← p + 1
end while
```

Fig. 2. Pseudo code of the exponential crossover

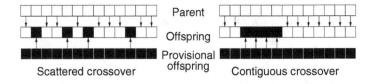

Fig. 3. Illustration of scattered and contiguous crossovers

2   Considerations on the Crossover

In [6], the author remarks that since the variables exchanged during the crossover are contiguous (possibly wrapping around the end of the vector x to its beginning), it is possible to mathematically transform a single, uniformly distributed random number into a geometrically distributed one and use that number as the length of the crossover. Evolutionary algorithms are consuming a large number of random numbers, and [7] shows that replacing one algorithm for pseudo-random number generation by another, faster one can significantly reduce the execution speed of DE (crossover alone in DE/rand/1/bin consumes something in the order of magnitude of $D \times budget$ random numbers, where $budget$ is the number of fitness evaluations allocated for running the algorithm). It follows that by reducing the usage of random numbers, one should increase the speed of execution of the algorithm by a significant amount (see Section 3 for experimental results).

The binomial distribution can be approximated by a normal distribution. Several methods have been published to generate normally distributed random numbers: e.g., [8] uses at least two uniformly distributed random numbers to produce one normally distributed number, while [9] (presented in Equations 3 and 4) uses exactly two uniformly distributed random numbers from the $[0, 1)$ interval (thereafter U_1 and U_2) to produce two normally distributed numbers, with a mean of 0 and a standard deviation of 1 (thereafter N_1 and N_2), at the cost of using trigonometric functions. The method in [9] has been selected for this work, since it makes a lower usage of the random number generator.

$$N_1 = \cos(2\pi U_1)\sqrt{-2\log(1 - U_2)} \tag{3}$$

$$N_2 = \sin(2\pi U_1)\sqrt{-2\log(1 - U_2)} \tag{4}$$

The crossover in DE is then modified into a contiguous binomial crossover, as described in Fig. 4, where $N(0,1)$ is a normally distributed random number with a mean of 0 and a standard deviation of 1, generated according to either of Equations 3 or 4.

```
generate L ← nCR + N(0,1)√(nCR(1 − CR))
clamp L to [0, n − 1] and round it to the nearest integer
x_off ← x_i
generate j ← 1 + round(n × rand(0,1))
x_off(j) ← x'_off(j)
for p = 1 : L − 1 do
    x_off((j + p) mod n) ← x'_off((j + p) mod n)
end for
```

Fig. 4. Contiguous binomial crossover pseudo-code

The new variant of DE using the contiguous binomial crossover is thus named DE/rand/1/binC, and its performance is compared to that of DE/rand/1/bin in the next Section.

3   Experimental Results

The comparison of DE/rand/1/bin and DE/rand/1/binC has been made on a subset of the benchmark used in [10], using functions F1 to F8, composed of a blend of unimodal (F1, F2, F7, F8) or multimodal (F3–F6) functions, additively separable (F1, F4, F6, F7) or not (F2, F3, F5, F8), easily optimized dimension by dimension (F1, F3, F4, F6, F7) or not (F2, F5, F8).

To compare the algorithms in as many configurations as possible, those functions have been considered in $n = 50, 100, 200, 500$ and 1000 dimensions, as suggested by the benchmark used in [10]. Moreover, populations sizes of $S_{pop} = 30$, 60, 90 and 120 have been considered: although values equal to at lease $2n$ have been advocated, a study in [11] shows that a population size lower than the dimensionality of the problem can be optimal in many cases and [12] indicates that for large-scale problems (500–1000 dimensions), the population size must be limited, values of 60 and 100 having given satisfactory results. Regarding the crossover rate, values of $CR = 0.1, 0.3, 0.5, 0.7$ and 0.9 have been used, while the value of F has been set in every case to 0.7, in accordance with suggestions given in [13] and [14]. The number of fitness evaluations alloted to each experiment was set to $n_{fe} = 5000n$, following the suggestions of [10]. Finally, each experiment has been run 30 times, and the average of these 30 runs has been considered.

It must be noted that the combination of all test functions, numbers of dimensions, values of S_{pop} and CR, and number of runs produce 48,000 runs altogether (which translates into 2.64×10^9 fitness evaluations). Due to the very large amount of computation time required by this study, a tradeoff had to be found between the number of different values of n, S_{pop} and CR on one hand, and the number of test functions on the other hand. A smaller benchmark of only eight test function presenting a variety of characteristics and difficulties has thus been selected.

Moreover, this large number of experiments makes it is impossible to publish the usual average and standard deviation values for every combination of algorithm, function, dimension, population size and crossover rate. A more synthetic approach has thus been adopted by using statistical significance tests, such as Wilcoxon's signed-rank test [15] and the Holm procedure [16].

Wilcoxon's signed-rank test produces a probability (the p-value) that two samples have been extracted from the same statistical distribution (which constitutes the test's null-hypothesis). Table 1 presents the results of this test where the two samples are made of the average fitness, at the end of the optimization process, of DE/rand/1/bin and DE/rand/1/binC, using the same CR and S_{pop} values, over functions F1 to F8, in a given number of dimensions. Note that in Table 1(f), the samples are made of the average fitness for all functions F1 to F8 in all the number of dimensions considered, thus giving an even more synthetic view of the performance of the two algorithms. A threshold for the p-value was set to 0.05, and symbols are used for indicating the outcome of the test: the symbol "=" indicates that the null-hypothesis holds, meaning that the performance of the two algorithms cannot be distinguished, while a "+" indicates that DE/rand/1/binC performs significantly better than DE/rand/1/bin; a "−" symbol indicates the opposite case where DE/rand/1/binC is outperformed by DE/rand/1/bin.

Table 1. Results of the Wilcoxon signed-rank test for DE/rand/1/bin compared to DE/rand/1/binC over functions F1 to F8 in different numbers of dimensions

(a) 50 dimensions

CR \ S_{pop}	30	60	90	120
0.1	=	=	=	=
0.3	=	=	=	=
0.5	+	=	=	=
0.7	=	=	=	=
0.9	=	=	−	−

(b) 100 dimensions

CR \ S_{pop}	30	60	90	120
0.1	=	=	=	=
0.3	=	=	=	=
0.5	=	=	=	=
0.7	=	=	=	=
0.9	=	=	=	−

(c) 200 dimensions

CR \ S_{pop}	30	60	90	120
0.1	=	=	=	=
0.3	+	=	=	=
0.5	+	=	=	=
0.7	=	+	=	=
0.9	=	=	=	=

(d) 500 dimensions

CR \ S_{pop}	30	60	90	120
0.1	=	=	=	=
0.3	+	+	=	=
0.5	+	+	+	=
0.7	=	=	=	=
0.9	=	=	=	=

(e) 1000 dimensions

CR \ S_{pop}	30	60	90	120
0.1	+	=	=	=
0.3	+	+	+	+
0.5	+	+	+	+
0.7	=	=	=	=
0.9	=	=	=	=

(f) All dimensions

CR \ S_{pop}	30	60	90	120
0.1	+	=	−	−
0.3	+	+	=	=
0.5	+	+	=	=
0.7	=	=	=	=
0.9	=	=	−	−

Those results show that with a few exceptions, DE/rand/1/binC performs at least as well as DE/rand/1/bin, and in several cases it is even outperforming the original DE algorithm. Tables 1(d) and 1(e) especially indicate that DE/rand/1/binC seems more promising on high-dimension problems, when $CR = 0.3$ or 0.5. Moreover, Table 1(f) shows that the contiguous binomial crossover is generally detrimental to the performance with larger populations (90 or 120 individuals) combined with extreme values of CR (0.1 and 0.9), but smaller populations sizes (30 or 60 individuals) combined with lower values of CR (0.1 to 0.5) lead to an improved performance compared to the original DE.

Wilcoxon's signed-rank test has also been applied to the results produced by DE/rand/1/bin and DE/rand/1/binC on a given function over numbers of dimensions ranging from 50 to 1000. The corresponding tables are not presented in this paper, but it is worth mentioning that they were all, with no exception, filled with "=" symbols, meaning that the performance of the two crossovers were not significantly different.

To further compare the performance of the binomial and contiguous binomial crossovers, the Holm procedure was applied to the results produced by every possible combination of crossover algorithm, crossover rate and population size. Each of those algorithm combinations was applied to every possible combination of test function and number of dimensions, and retaining the average over 30 runs, as described in the beginning of that section. Similarly to Wilcoxon's rank-sum test, the Holm procedure allows to decide whether two samples are extracted from the same statistical distribution (constituting the test's null-hypothesis), but takes into account the cumulative error that arises from multiple comparisons (see [17,18] for a detailed explanation). The procedure thus ranks the algorithms by their performance over the set of test functions (here F1 to F8 in dimensions

Table 2. Results of the Holm procedure (the reference algorithm is DE/rand/1/binC with $S_{pop} = 30$ and $CR = 0.1$)

i	Cros.	S_{pop}	CR	p-value	α/i	Hypoth.	i	Cros.	S_{pop}	CR	p-value	α/i	Hypoth.
39	bin	120	0.5	1.68e-34	1.28e-03	Rejected	19	binC	60	0.5	8.38e-11	2.63e-03	Rejected
38	binC	120	0.7	1.37e-33	1.32e-03	Rejected	18	bin	30	0.3	2.12e-10	2.78e-03	Rejected
37	binC	120	0.5	1.94e-33	1.35e-03	Rejected	17	binC	90	0.1	2.37e-08	2.94e-03	Rejected
36	bin	120	0.7	1.51e-30	1.39e-03	Rejected	16	bin	30	0.5	5.55e-08	3.13e-03	Rejected
35	bin	90	0.5	1.34e-29	1.43e-03	Rejected	15	bin	90	0.9	1.15e-07	3.33e-03	Rejected
34	binC	120	0.3	5.04e-28	1.47e-03	Rejected	14	bin	120	0.1	1.21e-07	3.57e-03	Rejected
33	binC	90	0.7	1.71e-24	1.52e-03	Rejected	13	binC	60	0.3	2.57e-07	3.85e-03	Rejected
32	binC	90	0.5	3.07e-24	1.56e-03	Rejected	12	bin	90	0.1	1.18e-05	4.17e-03	Rejected
31	bin	120	0.3	4.12e-23	1.61e-03	Rejected	11	binC	60	0.9	1.59e-05	4.55e-03	Rejected
30	bin	90	0.7	6.62e-23	1.67e-03	Rejected	10	bin	30	0.7	1.88e-05	5.00e-03	Rejected
29	bin	60	0.5	2.97e-22	1.72e-03	Rejected	9	binC	30	0.9	2.83e-05	5.56e-03	Rejected
28	binC	120	0.9	1.05e-20	1.79e-03	Rejected	8	bin	30	0.9	4.24e-05	6.25e-03	Rejected
27	bin	90	0.3	4.33e-20	1.85e-03	Rejected	7	bin	60	0.9	9.58e-05	7.14e-03	Rejected
26	binC	90	0.3	2.94e-19	1.92e-03	Rejected	6	bin	60	0.1	8.54e-04	8.33e-03	Rejected
25	bin	60	0.3	1.85e-16	2.00e-03	Rejected	5	binC	30	0.7	3.92e-03	1.00e-02	Rejected
24	bin	60	0.7	2.10e-13	2.08e-03	Rejected	4	bin	30	0.1	4.15e-03	1.25e-02	Rejected
23	bin	120	0.9	2.59e-13	2.17e-03	Rejected	3	binC	60	0.1	1.23e-02	1.67e-02	Rejected
22	binC	120	0.1	4.86e-13	2.27e-03	Rejected	2	binC	30	0.5	5.20e-02	2.50e-02	Accepted
21	binC	90	0.9	2.87e-12	2.38e-03	Rejected	1	binC	30	0.3	2.80e-01	5.00e-02	Accepted
20	binC	60	0.7	4.75e-11	2.50e-03	Rejected							

50 to 1000) and compares the best-ranking algorithm with every other algorithm. For each comparison, a p-value is computed, compared to a threshold (α/i where i is the rank of the algorithm), and the null hypothesis is then either accepted or rejected. Table 2 presents the results of the Holm procedure over the forty variants of DE analyzed in this paper and shows that DE/rand/1/binC variants with $S_{pop} = 30$ and $CR \leq 0.5$ are significantly better than the other variants (but none of these three variants performs significantly better than the two others).

Finally, Table 3 shows the benefits of using the binomial contiguous crossover in terms of execution speed of the algorithm, by computing the ratio of the running times of DE/rand/1/binC over DE/rand/1/bin applied to function F1 in dimensions 50, 100, 200, 500 and 1000. The decrease in runtime ranges from 20% in 50 dimensions to 74% in 1000 dimensions, which translates into an increase in speed ranging from 25% to 270%.

Table 3. Ratio of the running time of DE/rand/1/binC over DE/rand/1/bin for F1 in different dimensions

Dimension	50	100	200	500	1000
Time ratio	0.80	0.64	0.49	0.33	0.27

4   Conclusion

The contiguous binomial crossover presented in this paper is a variant of the canonical binomial crossover in DE. In a fashion inspired by the exponential crossover, it replaces variables in one block, the length of which is chosen by the means of a normally distributed random number. This approach considerably reduces the number of times the random number generator is used, thus significantly increasing the execution speed of the algorithm. Moreover, an experimental study shows that the contiguous binomial crossover is, with most parameter settings, exhibiting similar or better performance compared to the original DE.

Due to the very large number of different sets of parameters, the benchmark was voluntarily limited to only eight functions. To make a better comparison, future work should consider a much broader benchmark.

References

1. Price, K.V., Storn, R., Lampinen, J.: Differential Evolution: A Practical Approach to Global Optimization. Springer, Heidelberg (2005)
2. Das, S., Suganthan, P.: Differential evolution: A survey of the state-of-the-art. IEEE Transactions on Evolutionary Computation 15, 4–31 (2011)
3. Tirronen, V., Neri, F., Kärkkäinen, T., Majava, K., Rossi, T.: An enhanced memetic differential evolution in filter design for defect detection in paper production. Evolutionary Computation 16, 529–555 (2008)

4. Storn, R., Price, K.: Differential evolution - a simple and efficient adaptive scheme for global optimization over continuous spaces. Technical Report TR-95-012, ICSI (1995)

5. Qin, A.K., Suganthan, P.N.: Self-adaptive differential evolution algorithm for numerical optimization. In: Proceedings of the IEEE Congress on Evolutionary Computation, vol. 2, pp. 1785–1791 (2005)

6. Zaharie, D.: Influence of crossover on the behavior of differential evolution algorithms. Applied Soft Computing 9, 1126–1138 (2009)

7. Tirronen, V., Äyrämö, S., Weber, M.: Study on the Effects of Pseudorandom Generation Quality on the Performance of Differential Evolution. In: Dobnikar, A., Lotrič, U., Šter, B. (eds.) ICANNGA 2011, Part I. LNCS, vol. 6593, pp. 361–370. Springer, Heidelberg (2011)

8. Kinderman, A., Monahan, J.: Computer generation of random variables using the ratio of uniform deviates. ACM Transactions on Mathematical Software 3, 257–260 (1977)

9. Box, G.E.P., Muller, M.E.: A note on the generation of random normal deviates. The Annals of Mathematical Statistics 29, 610–611 (1958)

10. Weber, M., Neri, F., Tirronen, V.: Shuffle or update parallel differential evolution for large-scale optimization. Soft Computing - A Fusion of Foundations, Methodologies and Applications (2011) (to appear)

11. Neri, F., Tirronen, V.: On memetic differential evolution frameworks: a study of advantages and limitations in hybridization. In: Proceedings of the IEEE World Congress on Computational Intelligence, pp. 2135–2142 (2008)

12. Herrera, F., Lozano, M., Molina, D.: Components and parameters of de, real-coded chc, and g-cmaes. Web document (2010)

13. Zielinski, K., Weitkemper, P., Laur, R., Kammeyer, K.D.: Parameter study for differential evolution using a power allocation problem including interference cancellation. In: Proceedings of the IEEE Congress on Evolutionary Computation, pp. 1857–1864 (2006)

14. Zielinski, K., Laur, R.: Stopping Criteria for Differential Evolution in Constrained Single-Objective Optimization. In: Chakraborty, U.K. (ed.) Advances in Differential Evolution. SCI, vol. 143, pp. 111–138. Springer, Heidelberg (2008)

15. Wilcoxon, F.: Individual comparisons by ranking methods. Biometrics Bulletin 1, 80–83 (1945)

16. Holm, S.: A simple sequentially rejective multiple test procedure. Scandinavian Journal of Statistics 6, 65–70 (1979)

17. García, S., Molina, D., Lozano, M., Herrera, F.: A study on the use of non-parametric tests for analyzing the evolutionary algorithms' behaviour: a case study on the cec'2005 special session on real parameter optimization. Journal of Heuristics 15, 617–644 (2008)

18. García, S., Fernández, A., Luengo, J., Herrera, F.: A study of statistical techniques and performance measures for genetics-based machine learning: accuracy and interpretability. Soft Computing 13, 959–977 (2008)

Population Reduction Differential Evolution with Multiple Mutation Strategies in Real World Industry Challenges

Aleš Zamuda and Janez Brest

Faculty of Electrical Engineering and Computer Science, University of Maribor,
Smetanova ul. 17, 2000 Maribor, Slovenia, EU
ales.zamuda@uni-mb.si
http://labraj.uni-mb.si/zamuda

Abstract. This paper presents a novel differential evolution algorithm for optimization of state-of-the-art real world industry challenges. The algorithm includes the self-adaptive jDE algorithm with one of its strongest extensions, population reduction, and is now combined with multiple mutation strategies. The two mutation strategies used are run dependent on the population size, which is reduced with growing function evaluation number. The problems optimized reflect several of the challenges in current industry problems tackled by optimization algorithms nowadays. We present results on all of the 22 problems included in the Problem Definitions for a competition on Congress on Evolutionary Computation (CEC) 2011. Performance of the proposed algorithm is compared to two algorithms from the competition, where the average final best results obtained for each test problem on three different number of total function evaluations allowed are compared.

Keywords: self-adaptive differential evolution, population reduction, multiple mutation strategies, real world industry challenges.

1 Introduction

In this paper we present multiple mutation strategies into a variant of jDE differential evolution algorithm [1], by extending its population reduction variant as published in [3]. We assess our new algorithm performance on real world optimization problems, consisting of recent industry challenges. The optimization of models for these challenges is lately being addressed using evolutionary algorithms and published in journals on optimization. The models of these challenges are now gathered in a suite as 22 functions [6]. We report our results for all functions, for three different termination criteria based on total number of function evaluations allowed. Also, results of our algorithm are compared to two related algorithms which were presented at the competition at Congress on Evolutionary Computation 2011 [9,10].

In the following section we present related work. In the third section, we propose our multi-strategy extension for population reduction differential evolution.

L. Rutkowski et al. (Eds.): SIDE 2012 and EC 2012, LNCS 7269, pp. 154–161, 2012.

Then, the enhancement is assessed in the fourth section using functions modelling real world industry challenges (RWIC). In the fifth section, conclusions are drawn and guidelines for further work are given.

2 Related Work

Differential Evolution (DE) [17] is a floating-point encoding evolutionary algorithm for global optimization over continuous spaces, which can also work with discrete variables. Its main performance advantages over other evolutionary algorithms lie in floating-point encoding and a good combination of evolutionary operators, the mutation step size adaptation, and elitist selection [1,12]. DE was proposed by Storn and Price [17] and since then, it has been modified and extended several times with new versions proposed [4,5,7,11,13–16,19,20,22,23,25] and its derivations have won evolutionary algorithm competitions. DE was also introduced for multi-objective optimization [18,23]. Among real world problems tackled using jDE, is also our reconstruction of procedural tree models with differential evolution [24].

The DE algorithm has a main evolution loop in which a population of vectors is computed for each generation of the evolution loop. During one generation G, for each vector $\mathbf{x}_i$, $\forall i \in \{0, NP\}$ in the current population, DE employs evolutionary operators, namely mutation, crossover, and selection, to produce a trial vector (offspring) and to select one of the vectors with the best fitness value. NP denotes population size and G the current generation number.

Mutation creates a mutant vector $\mathbf{v}_{i,G+1}$ for each corresponding population vector. Among many proposed, one of the most popular DE mutation strategies are 'rand/1' [15,17]:

$$\mathbf{v}_{i,G+1} = \mathbf{x}_{r_1,G} + F(\mathbf{x}_{r_2,G} - \mathbf{x}_{r_3,G}) \tag{1}$$

and 'best/1':

$$\mathbf{v}_{i,G+1} = \mathbf{x}_{best,G} + F(\mathbf{x}_{r_1,G} - \mathbf{x}_{r_2,G}), \tag{2}$$

where the indexes r_1, r_2, and r_3 represent the random and mutually different integers generated within the range $\{1, NP\}$ and also different from index i. $\mathbf{x}_{best,G}$ denotes the currently best vector. F is an amplification factor of the difference vector within the interval $[0, 2]$, but usually less than 1. Vector at index r_1 is a base vector. The term $\mathbf{x}_{r_2,G} - \mathbf{x}_{r_3,G}$ denotes a difference vector which after multiplication with F, is named amplified difference vector.

After mutation the mutant vector $\mathbf{v}_{i,G+1}$ is taken into recombination process with the target vector $\mathbf{x}_{i,G}$ to create a trial vector $u_{i,j,G+1}$. The binary crossover operates as follows:

$$u_{i,j,G+1} = \begin{cases} v_{i,j,G+1} & \text{if } rand(0,1) \le CR \text{ or } j = j_{rand} \\ x_{i,j,G} & \text{otherwise} \end{cases},$$

where $j \in \{1, D\}$ denotes the j-th search parameter of D-dimensional search space, $rand(0,1) \in [0,1]$ denotes a uniformly distributed random number, and

j_{rand} denotes a uniform randomly chosen index of the search parameter, which is always exchanged to prevent cloning of target vectors. CR denotes the crossover rate for which the influence has been thoroughly studied in [21].

Finally, the selection operator propagates the fittest individual in the new generation (for minimization problem):

$$\mathbf{x}_{i,G+1} = \begin{cases} \mathbf{u}_{i,G+1} & \text{if } f(\mathbf{u}_{i,G+1}) < f(\mathbf{x}_{i,G}) \\ \mathbf{x}_{i,G} & \text{otherwise} \end{cases}.$$

The jDE algorithm [1] extends the original DE algorithm with self-adaptive control mechanism to change the control parameters F and CR during the evolutionary process. The third control parameter NP is kept unchanged in [1]. Each individual in the jDE population is extended using the values of these two control parameters. The better values for these (encoded) control parameters lead to better individuals which, in turn, are more likely to survive and produce offspring and, hence, propagate these better parameter values [1]. New control parameters $F_{i,G+1}$ and $CR_{i,G+1}$ are calculated as [1]:

$$F_{i,G+1} = \begin{cases} F_l + rand_1 \times F_u & \text{if } rand_2 < \tau_1 \\ F_{i,G} & \text{otherwise} \end{cases} \quad CR_{i,G+1} = \begin{cases} rand_3 & \text{if } rand_4 < \tau_2 \\ CR_{i,G} & \text{otherwise}. \end{cases}$$

They produce control parameters F and CR in a new vector. The $rand_j \in [0,1]$, $j \in \{1,2,3,4\}$ are uniform random values. τ_1 and τ_2 represent the probabilities of adjusting control parameters F and CR, respectively. τ_1, τ_2, F_l, F_u are taken fixed values as proposed in [1]. The new F takes a value from $[0.1, 1.0]$ in a random manner. The new CR takes a value from $[0, 1]$. $F_{i,G+1}$ and $CR_{i,G+1}$ are obtained before the mutation is performed. So they influence the mutation, crossover, and selection operations of the new vector $\mathbf{x}_{i,G+1}$.

As later reported in [14] to be one of best extensions for jDE, in [3] an extension of the jDE algorithm was presented which reduces population size to half in certain generations when the generation number exceeds the ratio between maximum number of function evaluations allowed and population size:

$$G_p > \frac{N_{max\_Feval}}{p_{max} NP_p},$$

where N_{max_Feval} is total number of function evaluations and NP_p is population size reduced as of current generation. Vectors are discarded index neighbour pairwise, as drawn in [3].

3   Population Reduction Differential Evolution with Multiple Mutation Strategies

We introduce a new version of differential evolution algorithm, jDE$_{NP,MM}$. To the algorithm dynNP-DE [3], we include besides the population reduction enhancement of jDE [1], to select one among two mutation strategies to mutate one individual vector.

We select to execute the first mutation strategy, rand/1, always when population size is $NP \geq 100$, or in three out of four cases uniform randomly otherwise. When population size is $NP < 100$, in one out of four cases uniform randomly we select to execute the best/1 strategy. Therefore, the two mutation strategies used are selected dependent on the population size, which is reduced with growing function evaluation number. We set initial population size (NP) to 200 and number of reductions to $pmax = 4$. The described strategy selection mechanism in mutation operator for our algorithm can be implemented as:

```
int s = int(random() * 4); // s = {0, 1, 2, 3}
if (s <= 2 || NP >= 100) use mutation as in Eq. (1)
else use mutation as in Eq. (2)
```

Therefore, our proposed DE variant adds very few to the computational cost of the dynNP-DE, and also dynNP-DE follows the inspiration of the original DE and does not require many additional operations to original DE, as noted in [3].

4   Results

We assess the proposed algorithm using a toolkit from competition at Congress on Evolutionary Computation (CEC) 2011 [6] which comprises of several real world industry challenges. We have used the Linux toolkit variant which includes C++ function call stubs encapsulating a Matlab environment implementing the functions to model these problems. The toolkit includes various functions, which after weighting the penalties sum are exposed as merely unconstrained functions to an optimizer. Namely, the sum is added to a fitness evaluation. Since the constraint valuation is partly handled by fitness evaluation increase, by comparing two vectors in selection mechanism, we penalize infeasible vectors by always discarding vectors which have infeasible non-assessed evaluation (i.e. not a number), otherwise we simply compare the obtained fitness values of two vectors.

Results of 25 independent runs for our algorithm on these functions are gathered. For each function, three different stopping conditions are used, i.e. for three different number of total function evaluations allowed, 50000, 100000, and 150000, respectively. In Table 1, best, worst, median, average values and their standard deviation for our $jDE_{NP,MM}$ algorithm are reported.

Comparison of these results to results from some other most similar algorithms are seen in Table 2, where in the third column, average final values of our algorithm are presented; in the fourth column, results of the algorithm of Korošec and Šilc [2,8] denoted as C-0036 [9] are listed; and in the fifth column, results of the algorithm of Mallipeddi and Suganthan [11] denoted as C-0362 [10] are listed. In the sixth and seventh column, differences between results are listed for our algorithm and other algorithms. The results in bold text are the results where our algorithm outperforms other algorithms on average for these 25 independent runs. The results in italic text denote the opposite, when our algorithm is outperformed by a certain algorithm.

As seen from the comparison, our algorithm outperforms algorithm C-0036 on 47 instances, performs worse on 13 instances and performs with no difference on 6

Table 1. Best, worst, median, average values and their standard deviation for 25 independent run results of our jDE$_{NP,MM}$ algorithm

Fun.	FES	Best	Worst	Median	Average	Std. dev.
F1	50000	3.5067e-27	1.7616e+01	1.0167e+01	7.9306e+00	6.9176e+00
F1	100000	0.0000e+00	1.7325e+01	0.0000e+00	1.5262e+00	4.3884e+00
F1	150000	0.0000e+00	1.6460e+01	0.0000e+00	1.1067e+00	3.9046e+00
F2	50000	-2.4458e+01	-1.4863e+01	-2.0507e+01	-2.0288e+01	2.1585e+00
F2	100000	-2.5423e+01	-1.9449e+01	-2.3028e+01	-2.2839e+01	1.5306e+00
F2	150000	-2.6033e+01	-2.1875e+01	-2.4207e+01	-2.4284e+01	1.0418e+00
F3	50000	1.1515e-05	1.1515e-05	1.1515e-05	1.1515e-05	1.6120e-19
F3	100000	1.1515e-05	1.1515e-05	1.1515e-05	1.1515e-05	1.7033e-19
F3	150000	1.1515e-05	1.1515e-05	1.1515e-05	1.1515e-05	1.3730e-19
F4	50000	1.3771e+01	2.0820e+01	1.4329e+01	1.5316e+01	2.4938e+00
F4	100000	1.3771e+01	2.0820e+01	1.4329e+01	1.5158e+01	2.3877e+00
F4	150000	1.3771e+01	2.0820e+01	1.4329e+01	1.5158e+01	2.3877e+00
F5	50000	-3.6291e+01	-3.1447e+01	-3.3875e+01	-3.3386e+01	1.2044e+00
F5	100000	-3.6124e+01	-3.3942e+01	-3.4106e+01	-3.4374e+01	6.6266e-01
F5	150000	-3.6450e+01	-3.4086e+01	-3.4441e+01	-3.4779e+01	7.7855e-01
F6	50000	-2.9131e+01	-2.1268e+01	-2.7427e+01	-2.7050e+01	2.1680e+00
F6	100000	-2.9166e+01	-2.3006e+01	-2.8734e+01	-2.8021e+01	1.6751e+00
F6	150000	-2.9166e+01	-2.7429e+01	-2.9147e+01	-2.8651e+01	7.8281e-01
F7	50000	8.9644e-01	1.6204e+00	1.3414e+00	1.3231e+00	1.6425e-01
F7	100000	8.5265e-01	1.4976e+00	1.1417e+00	1.1477e+00	1.7377e-01
F7	150000	8.0404e-01	1.4326e+00	1.1421e+00	1.1677e+00	1.5041e-01
F8	50000	2.2000e+02	2.2000e+02	2.2000e+02	2.2000e+02	2.2000e+00
F8	100000	2.2000e+02	2.2000e+02	2.2000e+02	2.2000e+02	0.0000e+00
F8	150000	2.2000e+02	2.2000e+02	2.2000e+02	2.2000e+02	0.0000e+00
F9	50000	1.4667e+03	7.6387e+03	2.8741e+03	3.2413e+03	1.6096e+03
F9	100000	1.7671e+03	4.0275e+03	2.3870e+03	2.5200e+03	5.3784e+02
F9	150000	1.2819e+03	3.4166e+03	2.1349e+03	2.2419e+03	5.2331e+02
F10	50000	-2.1217e+01	-1.7052e+01	-2.0392e+01	-1.9870e+01	1.3676e+00
F10	100000	-2.1361e+01	-1.7881e+01	-2.1217e+01	-2.0743e+01	1.1578e+00
F10	150000	-2.1421e+01	-2.0780e+01	-2.1321e+01	-2.1300e+01	1.2491e-01
F11	50000	7.4678e+04	5.2735e+05	2.0435e+05	2.2755e+05	1.1962e+05
F11	100000	5.1197e+04	2.4823e+05	5.9560e+04	8.3780e+04	5.6018e+04
F11	150000	5.1030e+04	6.8184e+04	5.2497e+04	5.3040e+04	3.2412e+03
F12	50000	1.0757e+06	1.2337e+06	1.1354e+06	1.1424e+06	4.4843e+04
F12	100000	1.0725e+06	1.1323e+06	1.0749e+06	1.0803e+06	1.3601e+04
F12	150000	1.0713e+06	1.0780e+06	1.0743e+06	1.0745e+06	1.6768e+03
F13	50000	1.5444e+04	1.5479e+04	1.5448e+04	1.5452e+04	9.4020e+00
F13	100000	1.5444e+04	1.5459e+04	1.5445e+04	1.5446e+04	3.4605e+00
F13	150000	1.5444e+04	1.5445e+04	1.5444e+04	1.5444e+04	4.4370e-01
F14	50000	1.8427e+04	1.9139e+04	1.8653e+04	1.8666e+04	1.3434e+02
F14	100000	1.8339e+04	1.8744e+04	1.8532e+04	1.8560e+04	1.2390e+02
F14	150000	1.8338e+04	1.8783e+04	1.8508e+04	1.8529e+04	8.7554e+01
F15	50000	3.2769e+04	3.3033e+04	3.2889e+04	3.2882e+04	5.5334e+01
F15	100000	3.2757e+04	3.2929e+04	3.2842e+04	3.2843e+04	4.4323e+01
F15	150000	3.2719e+04	3.2898e+04	3.2812e+04	3.2815e+04	4.2736e+01
F16	50000	1.3214e+05	1.4639e+05	1.3529e+05	1.3652e+05	3.5227e+03
F16	100000	1.3101e+05	1.4055e+05	1.3309e+05	1.3359e+05	2.3260e+03
F16	150000	1.2958e+05	1.3529e+05	1.3260e+05	1.3266e+05	1.5770e+03
F17	50000	1.9246e+06	2.2007e+06	1.9499e+06	1.9650e+06	5.5502e+04
F17	100000	1.9211e+06	2.1883e+06	1.9474e+06	1.9629e+06	5.7849e+04
F17	150000	1.9028e+06	1.9876e+06	1.9421e+06	1.9462e+06	2.1343e+04
F18	50000	9.3784e+05	1.1032e+06	9.4637e+05	9.5964e+05	4.0189e+04
F18	100000	9.3942e+05	9.4961e+05	9.4396e+05	9.4397e+05	2.6203e+03
F18	150000	9.3899e+05	9.4986e+05	9.4419e+05	9.4397e+05	2.7674e+03
F19	50000	1.1204e+06	1.6541e+06	1.2904e+06	1.3137e+06	1.5365e+05
F19	100000	1.0366e+06	1.5295e+06	1.2547e+06	1.2818e+06	1.3172e+05
F19	150000	1.0013e+06	1.4053e+06	1.2602e+06	1.2464e+06	1.2539e+05
F20	50000	9.3784e+05	1.1032e+06	9.4637e+05	9.5964e+05	4.0189e+04
F20	100000	9.3942e+05	9.4961e+05	9.4396e+05	9.4397e+05	2.6203e+03
F20	150000	9.3899e+05	9.4986e+05	9.4419e+05	9.4397e+05	2.7674e+03
F21	50000	1.3416e+01	2.2495e+01	1.7869e+01	1.7961e+01	2.2384e+00
F21	100000	1.4534e+01	2.0373e+01	1.7188e+01	1.6921e+01	1.6142e+00
F21	150000	1.1470e+01	1.9076e+01	1.6734e+01	1.6599e+01	1.7991e+00
F22	50000	1.1162e+01	2.0083e+01	1.4415e+01	1.4754e+01	2.2620e+00
F22	100000	1.0376e+01	1.7406e+01	1.3290e+01	1.3154e+01	1.7894e+00
F22	150000	9.1802e+00	1.5959e+01	1.1707e+01	1.2404e+01	1.7697e+00

Table 2. Comparison of average final best values of 25 independent runs for our and other algorithms

Fun.	FES	jDE$_{NP,MM}$	C-0036 [9]	C-0362 [10]	diff(C-0036)	diff(C-0362)
F1	50000	7.9306e+00	1.3995e+01	7.06E+00	**-6.0644e+00**	*8.7060e-01*
F1	100000	1.5262e+00	1.0872e+01	2.29E+00	**-9.3458e+00**	**-7.6380e-01**
F1	150000	1.1067e+00	1.0128e+01	1.78E+00	**-9.0213e+00**	**-6.7330e-01**
F2	50000	-2.0288e+01	-1.5775e+01	-1.26E+01	**-4.5130e+00**	**-7.6880e+00**
F2	100000	-2.2839e+01	-1.6766e+01	-1.64E+01	**-6.0730e+00**	**-6.4390e+00**
F2	150000	-2.4284e+01	-1.7566e+01	-1.83E+01	**-6.7180e+00**	**-5.9840e+00**
F3	50000	1.1515e-05	1.1515e-05	1.15E-05	0.0000e+00	*1.5000e-08*
F3	100000	1.1515e-05	1.1515e-05	1.15E-05	0.0000e+00	*1.5000e-08*
F3	150000	1.1515e-05	1.1515e-05	1.15E-05	0.0000e+00	*1.5000e-08*
F4	50000	1.5316e+01	1.4173e+01	1.67E+01	*1.1430e+00*	**-1.3840e+00**
F4	100000	1.5158e+01	1.4039e+01	1.67E+01	*1.1190e+00*	**-1.5420e+00**
F4	150000	1.5158e+01	1.3936e+01	1.67E+01	*1.2220e+00*	**-1.5420e+00**
F5	50000	-3.3386e+01	-3.3533e+01	-2.38E+01	*1.4700e-01*	**-9.5860e+00**
F5	100000	-3.4374e+01	-3.3834e+01	-2.75E+01	**-5.4000e-01**	**-6.8740e+00**
F5	150000	-3.4779e+01	-3.3909e+01	-2.90E+01	**-8.7000e-01**	**-5.7790e+00**
F6	50000	-2.7050e+01	-2.3150e+01	-1.28E+01	**-3.9000e+00**	**-1.4250e+01**
F6	100000	-2.8021e+01	-2.5581e+01	-1.55E+01	**-2.4400e+00**	**-1.2521e+01**
F6	150000	-2.8651e+01	-2.6748e+01	-1.70E+01	**-1.9030e+00**	**-1.1651e+01**
F7	50000	1.3231e+00	1.0262e+00	1.61E+00	*2.9690e-01*	**-2.8690e-01**
F7	100000	1.1477e+00	9.6956e-01	1.49E+00	*1.7814e-01*	**-3.4230e-01**
F7	150000	1.1677e+00	9.3895e-01	1.42E+00	*2.2875e-01*	**-2.5230e-01**
F8	50000	2.2000e+02	2.2000e+02	2.20E+02	0.0000e+00	0.0000e+00
F8	100000	2.2000e+02	2.2000e+02	2.20E+02	0.0000e+00	0.0000e+00
F8	150000	2.2000e+02	2.2000e+02	2.20E+02	0.0000e+00	0.0000e+00
F9	50000	3.2413e+03	1.6940e+03	2.875E+03	*1.5473e+03*	*3.6630e+02*
F9	100000	2.5200e+03	1.2338e+03	2.529E+03	*1.2862e+03*	**-9.0000e+00**
F9	150000	2.2419e+03	1.0692e+03	2.529E+03	*1.1727e+03*	**-2.8710e+02**
F10	50000	-1.9870e+01	-1.2655e+01	-1.52E+01	**-7.2150e+00**	**-4.6700e+00**
F10	100000	-2.0743e+01	-1.3213e+01	-1.55E+01	**-7.5300e+00**	**-5.2430e+00**
F10	150000	-2.1300e+01	-1.3540e+01	-1.56E+01	**-7.7600e+00**	**-5.7000e+00**
F11	50000	2.2755e+05	5.2607e+04	5.26E+04	*1.7494e+05*	*1.7495e+05*
F11	100000	8.3780e+04	5.2160e+04	5.24E+04	*3.1620e+04*	*3.1380e+04*
F11	150000	5.3040e+04	5.2017e+04	5.22E+04	*1.0230e+03*	*8.4000e+02*
F12	50000	1.1424e+06	1.2750e+06	1.08E+06	**-1.3260e+05**	*6.2400e+04*
F12	100000	1.0803e+06	1.2733e+06	1.07E+06	**-1.9300e+05**	*1.0300e+04*
F12	150000	1.0745e+06	1.2717e+06	1.07E+06	**-1.9720e+05**	*4.5000e+03*
F13	50000	1.5452e+04	1.5516e+04	1.55E+04	**-6.4000e+01**	**-4.8000e+01**
F13	100000	1.5446e+04	1.5512e+04	1.55E+04	**-6.6000e+01**	**-5.4000e+01**
F13	150000	1.5444e+04	1.5511e+04	1.55E+04	**-6.7000e+01**	**-5.6000e+01**
F14	50000	1.8666e+04	1.9341e+04	1.82E+04	**-6.7500e+02**	*4.6600e+02*
F14	100000	1.8560e+04	1.9332e+04	1.82E+04	**-7.7200e+02**	*3.6000e+02*
F14	150000	1.8529e+04	1.9323e+04	1.81E+04	**-7.9400e+02**	*4.2900e+02*
F15	50000	3.2882e+04	3.3185e+04	3.28E+04	**-3.0300e+02**	*8.2000e+01*
F15	100000	3.2843e+04	3.3183e+04	3.28E+04	**-3.4000e+02**	*4.3000e+01*
F15	150000	3.2815e+04	3.3181e+04	3.27E+04	**-3.6600e+02**	*1.1500e+02*
F16	50000	1.3652e+05	1.4715e+05	1.32E+05	**-1.0630e+04**	*4.5200e+03*
F16	100000	1.3359e+05	1.4669e+05	1.31E+05	**-1.3100e+04**	*2.5900e+03*
F16	150000	1.3266e+05	1.4666e+05	1.31E+05	**-1.4000e+04**	*1.6600e+03*
F17	50000	1.9650e+06	2.4168e+06	1.92E+06	**-4.5180e+05**	*4.5000e+04*
F17	100000	1.9629e+06	2.2476e+06	1.92E+06	**-1.8470e+05**	*4.2900e+04*
F17	150000	1.9462e+06	2.0375e+06	1.92E+06	**-9.1300e+04**	*2.6200e+04*
F18	50000	9.5964e+05	1.0127e+06	9.44E+05	**-5.3060e+04**	*1.5640e+04*
F18	100000	9.4397e+05	9.4803e+05	9.43E+05	**-4.0600e+03**	*9.7000e+02*
F18	150000	9.4397e+05	9.4569e+05	9.43E+05	**-1.7200e+03**	*9.7000e+02*
F19	50000	1.3137e+06	1.5823e+06	9.94E+05	**-2.6860e+05**	*3.1970e+05*
F19	100000	1.2818e+06	1.4433e+06	9.91E+05	**-1.6150e+05**	*2.9080e+05*
F19	150000	1.2464e+06	1.4012e+06	9.90E+05	**-1.5480e+05**	*2.5640e+05*
F20	50000	9.5964e+05	1.0567e+06	9.44E+05	**-9.7060e+04**	*1.5640e+04*
F20	100000	9.4397e+05	9.8217e+05	9.43E+05	**-3.8200e+04**	*9.7000e+02*
F20	150000	9.4397e+05	9.4887e+05	9.43E+05	**-4.9000e+03**	*9.7000e+02*
F21	50000	1.7961e+01	2.8815e+01	2.26E+01	**-1.0854e+01**	**-4.6390e+00**
F21	100000	1.6921e+01	2.7518e+01	1.98E+01	**-1.0597e+01**	**-2.8790e+00**
F21	150000	1.6599e+01	2.6419e+01	1.88E+01	**-9.8200e+00**	**-2.2010e+00**
F22	50000	1.4754e+01	3.3463e+01	1.99E+01	**-1.8709e+01**	**-5.1460e+00**
F22	100000	1.3154e+01	3.0902e+01	1.57E+01	**-1.7748e+01**	**-2.5460e+00**
F22	150000	1.2404e+01	2.9620e+01	1.39E+01	**-1.7216e+01**	**-1.4960e+00**
B/W					47 / 13	31 / 32

problem instances regarding the assessment used. Compared to the algorithm C-0362, these values are 31, 32, and 3, respectively. We have also made a preliminary comparison of our algorithm $jDE_{NP,MM}$ versus the dynNP-DE [3] algorithm and the new algorithm seems to outperform the existing one in most of cases.

5 Conclusion

We presented an algorithm which combines multiple mutation strategies and population reduction in self-adaptive differential evolution $jDE_{NP,MM}$. We have assessed its performance on 22 real world industry challenges from a competition at Congress on Evolutionary Computation (CEC) 2011. We have also reported a performance comparison with two algorithms from the competition. In the future research, additional measurements to compare the proposed extension in the new algorithm could be done with existing algorithms. More strategies inclusion like [20] could be addressed. Population size control and best strategy mutation enhancement are two interesting goals to pursue for our algorithm, too.

References

1. Brest, J., Greiner, S., Bošković, B., Mernik, M., Žumer, V.: Self-Adapting Control Parameters in Differential Evolution: A Comparative Study on Numerical Benchmark Problems. IEEE Transactions on Evolutionary Computation 10(6), 646–657 (2006)
2. Brest, J., Korošec, P., Šilc, J., Zamuda, A., Bošković, B., Maučec, M.S.: Differential evolution and differential ant-stigmergy on dynamic optimisation problems. International Journal of Systems Science (2012), doi:10.1080/00207721.2011.617899
3. Brest, J., Maučec, M.S.: Population Size Reduction for the Differential Evolution Algorithm. Applied Intelligence 29(3), 228–247 (2008)
4. Das, S., Abraham, A., Chakraborty, U., Konar, A.: Differential Evolution Using a Neighborhood-based Mutation Operator. IEEE Transactions on Evolutionary Computation 13(3), 526–553 (2009)
5. Das, S., Suganthan, P.N.: Differential Evolution: A Survey of the State-of-the-art. IEEE Transactions on Evolutionary Computation 15(1), 4–31 (2011)
6. Das, S., Suganthan, P.N.: Problem Definitions and Evaluation Criteria for CEC 2011 Competition on Real World Optimization Problems. Tech. rep. Dept. of Electronics and Telecommunication Engg., Jadavpur University, India and School of Electrical and Electronic Engineering, Nanyang Technological University, Singapore (2011)
7. Feoktistov, V.: Differential Evolution: In Search of Solutions Springer Optimization and Its Applications. Springer-Verlag New York, Inc., Secaucus (2006)
8. Korošec, P., Šilc, J., Filipič, B.: The differential ant-stigmergy algorithm. Information Sciences (2012), doi:10.1016/j.ins.2010.05.002
9. Korošec, P., Šilc, J.: The continuous differential ant-stigmergy algorithm applied to bound constrained real-world optimization problem. In: The 2011 IEEE Congress on Evolutionary Computation (CEC 2011), New Orleans, USA, June 5-8, pp. 1327–1334 (2011)

10. Mallipeddi, R., Suganthan, P.N.: Ensemble Differential Evolution Algorithm for CEC2011 Problems. In: The 2011 IEEE Congress on Evolutionary Computation (CEC 2011), p. 68. IEEE Press (2011)
11. Mallipeddi, R., Suganthan, P.N., Pan, Q.K., Tasgetiren, M.F.: Differential evolution algorithm with ensemble of parameters and mutation strategies. Applied Soft Computing 11(2), 1679–1696 (2011)
12. Mezura-Montes, E., Lopez-Ramirez, B.C.: Comparing bio-inspired algorithms in constrained optimization problems. In: The 2007 IEEE Congress on Evolutionary Computation, September 25-28, pp. 662–669 (2007)
13. Mininno, E., Neri, F., Cupertino, F., Naso, D.: Compact Differential Evolution. IEEE Transactions on Evolutionary Computation 15(1), 32–54 (2011)
14. Neri, F., Tirronen, V.: Recent Advances in Differential Evolution: A Survey and Experimental Analysis. Artificial Intelligence Review 33(1-2), 61–106 (2010)
15. Price, K.V., Storn, R.M., Lampinen, J.A.: Differential Evolution: A Practical Approach to Global Optimization. Natural Computing. Springer, Berlin (2005)
16. Qin, A.K., Huang, V.L., Suganthan, P.N.: Differential evolution algorithm with strategy adaptation for global numerical optimization. IEEE Transactions on Evolutionary Computation 13(2), 398–417 (2009)
17. Storn, R., Price, K.: Differential Evolution – A Simple and Efficient Heuristic for Global Optimization over Continuous Spaces. Journal of Global Optimization 11, 341–359 (1997)
18. Tušar, T., Korošec, P., Papa, G., Filipič, B., Šilc, J.: A comparative study of stochastic optimization methods in electric motor design. Applied Intelligence 2(27), 101–111 (2007)
19. Tvrdík, J.: Adaptation in differential evolution: A numerical comparison. Applied Soft Computing 9(3), 1149–1155 (2009)
20. Wang, Y., Cai, Z., Zhang, Q.: Differential evolution with composite trial vector generation strategies and control parameters. IEEE Transactions on Evolutionary Computation 15(1), 55–66 (2011)
21. Zaharie, D.: Influence of crossover on the behavior of Differential Evolution Algorithms. Applied Soft Computing 9(3), 1126–1138 (2009)
22. Zamuda, A., Brest, J., Bošković, B., Žumer, V.: Large Scale Global Optimization Using Differential Evolution with Self Adaptation and Cooperative Co-evolution. In: 2008 IEEE World Congress on Computational Intelligence, pp. 3719–3726. IEEE Press (2008)
23. Zamuda, A., Brest, J., Bošković, B., Žumer, V.: Differential Evolution with Self-adaptation and Local Search for Constrained Multiobjective Optimization. In: IEEE Congress on Evolutionary Computation 2009, pp. 195–202. IEEE Press (2009)
24. Zamuda, A., Brest, J., Bošković, B., Žumer, V.: Differential Evolution for Parameterized Procedural Woody Plant Models Reconstruction. Applied Soft Computing 11, 4904–4912 (2011)
25. Zhang, J., Sanderson, A.C.: JADE: adaptive differential evolution with optional external archive. Trans. Evol. Comp. 13(5), 945–958 (2009)

Part II

Evolutionary Algorithms
and Their Applications

Genetic Optimization of Fuzzy Rule Based MAS Using Cognitive Analysis

Petr Cermak[1,*] and Michal Mura[2]

[1] Research Institute of the IT4Innovations Centre of Excellence,
Faculty of Philosophy and Science in Opava,
Silesian University in Opava,
Bezruc Sq. 13
746 01 Opava Czech Republic
petr.cermak@fpf.slu.cz
[2] Tieto Czech s.r.o,
Varenská 2723/51, CZ- 702 00 Ostrava
michal.mura@tieto.com

Abstract. The aim of the contribution is to present Cognitive Analysis of fuzzy rule bases used in Genetic optimization of Multiagent system behaviour. This Cognitive analysis allows to analyze behaviour caused by rules and sort them to Social, Group or Individual sets of the rules. Rules, which have same behaviour, can be reduced. This allows to decrease of the rules and number of genes in chromosome and also GA Search Space. The Fuzzy Rule Based Evolution System is presented. This system consists of three main parts the FUZNET, the GA-MPI and the Webots. Simple example based on the Box Pushing problem is presented.

Keywords: Fuzzy rule base, Cognitive analysis, Optimization, Genetic algorithm, Simulation, FUZNET, MPI, Webots.

1 Introduction

Behavior of each agent A^i is given by rule base RB^i, nA is number of Agent in MAS. We use fuzzy rule based system for Agent behavior modeling, namely Mamdani like fuzzy system. This system we select especially for following reasons[1]:

- *Prevent oscillations*
- *Aprox. function are nonlinear*
- *Rules we can express natural language like (small distance, middle distance, long distance)*

    The rule base of Mamdani fuzzy system are given by (1) where x_i are inputs, $A_{n,r}$ is linguistic values of rules an antecedent and C_r are linguistic values of rules in consequent.

---

* This paper has been elaborated in the framework of the IT4Innovations Centre of Excellence project, reg. no. CZ.1.05/1.1.00/02.0070 supported by Operational Programme 'Research and Development for Innovations' funded by Structural Funds of the European Union and state budget of the Czech Republic. Work also partially supported by Czech grant MSM 4781305903.

L. Rutkowski et al. (Eds.): SIDE 2012 and EC 2012, LNCS 7269, pp. 165–173, 2012.

$IF\ (x_1\ is\ A_{1,1})\ AND\ (x_2\ is\ A_{2,1})\ AND\ \dots\ (x\ is\ A_{n,1})\ THEN\ (y_1\ is\ C_1)$

$IF\ (x_1\ is\ A_{1,1})\ AND\ (x_2\ is\ A_{2,1})\ AND\ \dots\ (x\ is\ A_{n,1})\ THEN\ (y_2\ is\ C_2)$

$$\vdots$$

$IF\ (x_1\ is\ A_{1,r})\ AND\ (x_2\ is\ A_{2,r})\ AND\ \dots\ (x\ is\ A_{n,r})\ THEN\ (y_r\ is\ C_r)$

$$(1)$$

2   Cognitive Analysis Rule Bases of Multiple Agents

Offered cognitive analysis is based on Question Answering Mechanism. With this analysis we can determine how the r-th rule from rule base is consistent with another rule base [1]. The consistency analysis process is following, we select one rule from one agent. We separate antecedent part and set them as input to another agent. We get response and check consistence between consequent part rule of first agent and response of the second one. With this we can determine similar partitionaly behaviour of two agents described by concrete rule/s.

2.1   Measuring of Consistency

Let's have as vector that contain all n linguistic values antecedent part r-th rule from rule base of agent A^i[1].

$$\boldsymbol{X}_r^i = \left(A_{1,r}^i, A_{2,r}^i, \dots, A_{n,r}^i\right) \qquad (2)$$

and make question to fuzzy system with response to input:

$$By_{r,j}^{i\,*} = Response\left(R_{B_j}, \boldsymbol{X}_r^i\right) \qquad (3)$$

And check consistency between response $By_{r,j}^{i\,*}$ and consequent part of r-th rule of agent A^i. as follows:

$$Cons_{r,j}^i = \frac{\int\limits_0^1 By_{r,j}^{i\,*} \bigcap C_r^i}{\int\limits_0^1 By_{r,j}^{i\,*}} \qquad (4)$$

Where j is index, that determinine checked agent. Index r determine checked rule selected from i-th agent. Determining rule error is described earlier. We must first define Consistency matrix and matching criterion.

$$CMA^i = \begin{bmatrix} Cons_{1,1}^i & Cons_{1,2}^i & \cdots & Cons_{1,nA}^i \\ Cons_{2,1}^i & Cons_{2,2}^i & \cdots & Cons_{2,nA}^i \\ \vdots & \vdots & \ddots & \vdots \\ Cons_{nR,1}^i & Cons_{nR,2}^i & \cdots & Cons_{nR,nA}^i \end{bmatrix} \qquad (5)$$

where nR is number of rules in the i-th rule base. Rows determine consistency for each rules and columns consistency for all rule basis. Matching criterion must decide if consistency is satisfied or unsatisfied. The satisfy we define as equation

$$DMAS_{r,j}^i = \begin{cases} Cons_{r,j}^i \geqslant \varepsilon_j & 1 \\ \\ Cons_{r,j}^i < \varepsilon_j & 0 \end{cases} \tag{6}$$

The next image show the graphical ilustration of consistency measures for third agent and his r-th rule.

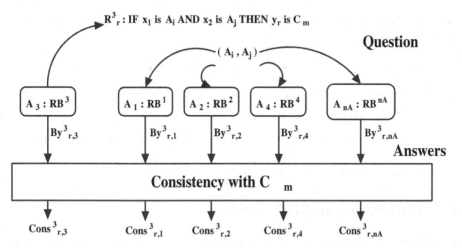

Fig. 1. Cognitive analysis with Q-A mechanism

2.2   Determinimg the Type of Behaviour and Equivalent Rule Set

Basicly we can clasify behaviour rule description into three main types [1]. The first is social behaviour, individual behaviour and number of Group's behaviors. For determining behaviour's types we need dependency matrix of the i-th rule from base to all rule basis of MAS is defined as

$$DMAS^i = \begin{bmatrix} DMAS_{1,1}^i & \cdots & DMAS_{1,nA}^i \\ \vdots & \ddots & \vdots \\ DMAS_{nR_i,1}^i & \cdots & DMAS_{nR_i,nA}^i \end{bmatrix} \tag{7}$$

Dependency Histogram defines numbers of dependencies i-th rule to each rule bases of MAS.

$$DMASN^i = \begin{bmatrix} \sum_{j=1}^{nA} DMAS_{1,j}^i \\ \vdots \\ \sum_{j=1}^{nA} DMAS_{nR_i,j}^i \end{bmatrix} \tag{8}$$

Social Behaviour of i-th Agent is given by the set of rules consistent with all rule basis of MAS as follows

$$M^i_{Social} = \left\{ R^i_r; DMASN\,[r] = nA, r = 1 \ldots nR_i \right\} \tag{9}$$

and rule set of Social Behaviour for all possible Agents is given by

$$M_{Social} = \left\{ M^i_{Social}; i = (1 \ldots nA) \right\} \tag{10}$$

Individual behaviour of i-th Agent is given by the set of rules with consistence only with ourselves

$$M^i_{Individual} = \left\{ R^i_r; DMASN\,[r] = 1 \wedge DMAS_{r,j} = 1, r = (1 \ldots nR_i) \right\} \tag{11}$$

Group behaviour is given by rules:

$$M_{Group} = \left\{ R^i_r; DMAS^i_{r,j} = 1 \forall j \epsilon Group,\ r = (1 \ldots nR_i)\,, ,j = (1 \ldots nA) \right\} \tag{12}$$

where Group is set of indexes off all agents in group.

3   Optimization of MAS Behaviour

As optimization technique we used genetic optimization. Genetic algorithm use standard and advanced operators. As the extension of GA is simultaneity used. Genetic algorithm can divide each generation computation on to the number of Clusters or cores. This allows shorter the time of the simulation.

3.1   Genetic Algorithm

Genetic optimalization of MAS behaviour consist of two tasks. Structure and parametric identification of Agent's rule bases. We must also define Fitness function as best and desired behaviour of the MAS.

For structure and parametric identification, we must code into chromosome information, such as number of rules, number of inputs, relation between Inputs and Outputs and membership function's shapes. The example of configuration will be shown in chapter Experiment. In presented Genetic algorithm we used following operators[2]:

- parent selection
- crossover operator
- mutation operator
- restricted lifetime of gene

Because we have for this simulation 8 core server, we used GA parallelization. This parallelization is implemented in MPI. Each generation is characterized by population of chromosomes. This generation we can separate, in this case, onto 8 parts and compute indepedently. This division allows speedup of computation.

3.2   Reduction of GA Space Search

As we mentioned earlier, we can extract from MAS different types of the behaviours. If we have some Rules, which are belonging to the social behaviour, we need not have those rules in all agents of MAS. These rules will be apear on MAS only once. With this reduction, we can also decrease the size of chromosome structure and also reduce GA Space Search. This main idea is applicable also on to the Group's Behaviours.

4   Implementation

4.1   FuzNet

The Programme tool FUZNET was developed based on fuzzy neural network technology, including the new identifying procedures presented in [3,4]. This fuzzy neural network environment appears to be suitable for fuzzy non-linear model identification as well as introduces the programme FUZNET including its application in real system modeling. This system is an extension of the neural network (NN) development system based on the Back Propagation algorithm. The FUZNET structure is mentioned in [3,4]. We actually need not adaptation procedures, because identification and optimization are business of GA part. We used FuzNet for computation. Actually we need for computation two description files, namely Rule description files *.dsc and Fuzzy neural network description file Net.wri. The Core of Fuznet is Dynamic Link Library FuzNet.dll in the Windows and binary library FuzNet.a in Linux. This part we used for simulations and FRBES system design.

4.2   GA-MPI Implementation

GA-MPI implementation is, infact very simple, first we apply GA operators. Next we distribute the number of chromosomes from actual generation from cluster or core 0 to the other clusters or cores. In separate processes will be computing values of fitness functions as simulation of the given task. After calculating of fitness functions will be fitness values send back to cluster or core 0. As paralelization tool we used well known Message Parsing Interface [5].

4.3   Webots-Robot simulator

This simulator is widely used for experiments in Robotic simulation [6]. Webots contain Virtual world with the possibility of physical modelling. Virtual world is realized by 3D model depicted in VRML. Programming interface could be realized in C/C++ and numerous methods receiving information from sensors and set actuators, like motors, etc. For robot programming is used special entity called "Robot Controller" and "Supervisor" in case of MAS. For future we used robot Koala and program some additional functionality, like pan tilt camera. This 3D virtual model is the same as hw robot Koala in our Laboratory.

4.4   FRBES System Design

Now we get all together. We design Fuzzy Rule Based Evolution System (FRBES) adopted to Box-Pushhing problem [7,8]. This system is based on client - server architecture with parallelization using MPI (Message Parsing Interface).

The Supervisor block realizes Genetic algorithm with MPI paralelization, cognitive analysis of rule bases and calculation of global fitness function. The supervisor sends part of population certain generation to Wserver in separate processes. The Wserver converts chromosome structure to fuzzy rule base. Each fuzzy rule bases is described by descriptions file using by FuzNet.

The Supervisor also acts as role of the virtual agent. Startup of Webots instance is initiated from Wserver. In Webots we can implement agents with physical properties in 3D. Here are implemented Left pusher, Right pusher and Watcher. Each agent in Webots has two functions, Initialization and Main function. In initialization function is the instance FuzNet created and fuzzy rule base builds from description file. In main function is initiated inference of fuzzy rule base as the reaction onto sensors, state and comm. values. Inferenced values makes changes actuators, state and comm. in Enviroment. In main function is also determined value of agent fitness function, which is propagated back to the supervisor. This inference repeats untill the end of an experiment with concrete fuzzy rule base ie. concrete chromosome.

5   Experiment

As the experiment we select Box-Pushing problem. In this experiment we have 3 robots, left pusher, right pusher and watcher [8]. Pushers cooperate to pushing a box and get information from watcher about pushing direction. Watcher has the function of explorer and finder of the target. Following table shows each robot with their role and function with behaviour classification.

The Box Pushing problem consists of two subtasks. The first, search box and prepare to push. The second, explore and track the target by watcher and communicate with Pushers to push the box. We describe the first subtask and results. The second task is actually in the course of simulations.

First we need to define the structure of rule for all agent/robots, the rules have the same structure. The rule on the next table consists from antecedent and consequent parts. Antecedent part of the Rule contains State of simulation, Comunication with watcher, detected marks from camera and information from range finder sensors.

Consequent part consists of actuators - left and right motors, feedback State and Communication. This rule configuration is sufficient for solving Box pushhing Task. The numbers in the second row will describe the number of linguistic values, fuzzy sets and crisp parameters.

The configuration of a genetic algorithm was following, each generation has 218 members. Maximal number of generation was set to 200 and fitness function is defined as normalized distance (13) to the Goal - Box with colored circles. Maximal number of rules was set to 9.

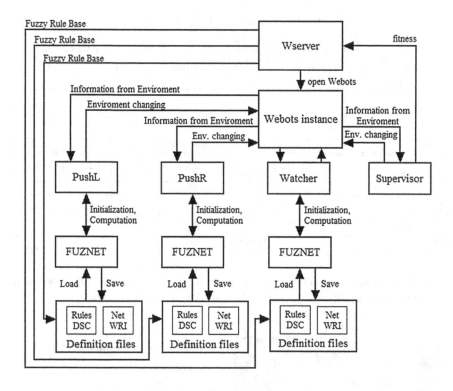

Fig. 2. FRBES System design in case Box-Pushing

Table 1. Classification of rules by type of behaviour/function

PushL	PushR	Watcher
Social behaviour rules / Breitenberg alg.(obstacle avoidance)		
Group behaviour rules / box pushing		Individual behaviour rules /
Individual behaviour rules /	Individual behaviour rules /	searching green circle,
searching blue circle,	searching red circle,	comm to PushL,
communication with watcher	communication with watcher	comm to PushR,
		Explore and tracking target

$$fitness = \left(\frac{ActualDistR1}{MaxDistR1} + \frac{ActualDistR2}{MaxDistR2} + \frac{ActualDistR3}{MaxDistR3} \right) \quad (13)$$

We made one experiment (S0) without cognitive analysis and six experiments (S0x) with cognitive analysis and different random generators. Labels in table are Simulation time in Hours, Average Time of One generation in Minutes, Best Fitness function value, Number of generation to Best Fitness value, Random Generator Type and Best Time to arriving Robots to Box with circles. We tested two random generators, namely classical rand from GCC libraries, The second, MT was Merssene Twister random generator [9].

Table 2. Structure of Agent's rule

Antecedent part of Rule									Consequent part of Rule			
State	Com	CamP	CamT	In01	In02	In03	In04	In05	State	Com	MotR	MotL
1,2	1	0,1,2,3	1,2	0,1,2,3					1,2	1	1,2,3,4	

Table 3. Experiment results

ID	SimTm/Hrs	AvgTmOneGener/Min	BestFit	nGenersToBF	RandGen	BestTimeToGoal/Sec
S0	185.4	55	1.9595	109	MT	None
S01	79.7	24	0.804	84	RAND	29
S02	79.1	24	0.616	93	MT	33
S03	83.8	25	0.7105	179	RAND	60
S04	85.5	26	0.7436	39	RAND	25
S05	90.2	27	0.785	139	MT	35
S06	87.2	26	0.6533	126	MT	52

For illustration two pictures are presented, configuration of an experiment when starting and when finishing with best fitness function value.

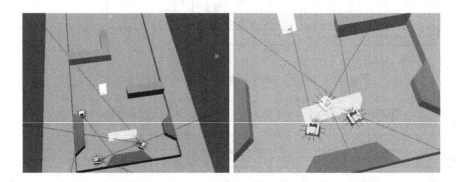

Fig. 3. Start and finish of the experiment with best fitness function

6   Conclusions

The Cognitive analysis could be very useful in the reduction of the rule basis of agents in MAS optimized by the Genetic algorithm. This analysis could be also used for the analyzing of the emergence processes in MAS. In this time, we were continuing with experiments on the second subtask. We are also considering reinplementation of the FuzNet, the Genetic algorithm and the Cognitive analysis onto the mobile automotive platform and move this experiment from the Webots simulator to the Koala hardware robotic platform.

References

1. Cermak, P.: Social, Group and Individual Mind extracted from Rule Bases of Multiple Agents. International Journal of Mathematical and Computer Sciences 3(3), 144–148 (2007)
2. Roupec, J.: Genetic optimization algoritms in fuzzy regulators, Ph.D. thesis in czech, VUT Brno, Brno, CZ (1999)
3. Cermak, P., Pokorny, M.: An Improvement of Non-Linear Neuro-Fuzzy Model Properties. Neural Network World 11(5), 503–523 (2001)
4. Cermak, P., Chmiel, P.: Parameters optimization of fuzzy-neural dynamic model. In: NAFIPS 2004, Banff, Canada, vol. 2, pp. 762–767 (2004)
5. LAM Team.: Message Parsing Interface, Open Systems Lab, Indiana university, Bloomington, IN, USA (2007), http://www.lam-mpi.org/
6. Cyberbotics: Webots Reference Manual, release 6.3.4, Cyberbotics Ltd., Lausanne, Switzerland (2011), www.cyberbotics.com
7. Nemrava, M., Cermak, P.: Solving the Box Pushing Problem by Master-Slave Robots Cooperation. JAMRIS 2(3), 32–37 (2008)
8. Mura, M.: Collective Robot Intelligence Tune up using Genetic Algorithms, MSc. thesis in czech, Silesian university in Opava, Opava, CZ (2011)
9. L'Ecuyer, P., Simard, R.: A C Library for Empirical Testing of Random Number Generators. ACM Transactions on Mathematical Software 33(4), Article 22 (2007)

Does Memetic Approach Improve Global Induction of Regression and Model Trees?

Marcin Czajkowski and Marek Kretowski

Faculty of Computer Science, Bialystok University of Technology,
Wiejska 45a, 15-351 Białystok, Poland
{m.czajkowski,m.kretowski}@pb.edu.pl

Abstract. Memetic algorithms are popular approaches to improve pure evolutionary methods. But were and when in the system the local search should be applied and does it really speed up evolutionary search is a still an open question. In this paper we investigate the influence of the memetic extensions on globally induced regression and model trees. These evolutionary induced trees in contrast to the typical top-down approaches globally search for the best tree structure, tests at internal nodes and models at the leaves. Specialized genetic operators together with local greedy search extensions allow to the efficient tree evolution. Fitness function is based on the Bayesian information criterion and mitigate the over-fitting problem. The proposed method is experimentally validated on synthetical and real-life datasets and preliminary results show that to some extent memetic approach successfully improve evolutionary induction.

Keywords: data mining, evolutionary algorithms, memetic algorithms, regression trees, model trees, global induction.

1 Introduction

The most popular algorithms for decision tree induction are based on top-down greedy search [10]. Top-down induction starts from the root node where locally optimal split (test) is searched according to the given optimality measure. Then, the training data is redirected to newly created nodes and this process is repeated recursively for each node until some stopping-rule is reached. Finally, the post-pruning is applied to improve the generalization power of the predictive model.

Nowadays, many research focus on approaches that evolve decision trees as alternative heuristics to the traditional top-down approach [2]. The main advantage of evolutionary induced trees over greedy search methods is the ability to avoid local optima and search more globally for the best tree structure, tests at internal nodes and models at the leaves. On the other hand the induction of global regression and model trees is much slower. One of the possible solutions to speed up evolutionary approach is a combination of evolutionary algorithms with local search techniques, which is known as Memetic Algorithms [6].

In this paper, we focus on regression and model trees that may be considered as a variant of decision trees, designed to approximate real-valued functions.

L. Rutkowski et al. (Eds.): SIDE 2012 and EC 2012, LNCS 7269, pp. 174–181, 2012.
© Springer-Verlag Berlin Heidelberg 2012

Main difference between regression tree and model tree is that, for the latter, constant value in the terminal node is replaced by a regression plane. In our previous works we investigated the global approach to obtain accurate and compact regression [8] and model trees with simple linear regression [4] and multivariate linear regression [5] at the leaves. We also investigated the influence of memetic extensions on the global induction of classification trees [7]. In this paper we would like to apply a similar approach for globally induced regression and model trees.

The rest of the paper is organized as follows. In the next section a memetic induction of regression and model trees is described. Experimental validation of the proposed approach on artificial and real-life data is presented in section 3. In the last section, the paper is concluded and possible future works are sketched.

2 Memetic Induction of Regression and Model Trees

In this section we present a combination of evolutionary approach with local search techniques in inducing the regression and model trees. The general structure of proposed solution follows a typical framework of evolutionary algorithms [9] with an unstructured population and a generational selection. New memetic extensions are proposed in 2.2 and 2.4.

2.1 Representation

Regression and model trees are represented in their actual form as classical univariate trees (tests in internal nodes are based on a single attribute). Depending on the tree type, each leaf of the tree can contain a mean of dependent variable from training objects (regression trees) or a linear model that is calculated at each terminal node of the model tree using standard regression technique (model trees). Additionally, in every node information about learning vectors associated with the node is stored. This enables the algorithm to perform more efficiently the local structure and tests modifications during applications of genetic operators.

2.2 Memetic Initialization

Initial individuals are created by applying the classical top-down algorithm [10]. At first, we learn standard regression tree that has a mean of dependent variable values from training objects at each leaf. The recursive partitioning is finished when all training objects in the node are characterized by the same predicted value (or it varies only slightly, default: 1%) or the number of objects at node is lower than the predefined value (default value: 5). Additionally, user can set the maximum tree depth (default value: 10) to limit initial tree size. Next, if necessary, a linear model is calculated at each terminal node of the model tree.

Traditionally, the initial population should be generated randomly to cover the entire range of possible solutions. Due to the large solution space the exhaustive search may be infeasible. Therefore, while creating initial population we search for a good trade off between a high degree of heterogeneity and relatively low computation time. To create initial population we propose several memetic strategies which involves employing the locally optimized tests and models on randomly chosen internal nodes and leaves. For all non-terminal nodes one of the four test search strategies is randomly chosen:

- *Least Squares (LS)* function reduces node impurity measured by sum of squares,
- *Least Absolute Deviation (LAD)* function reduces the sum of absolute deviations. It has greater resistance to the influence of outlying values to *LS*,
- *Mean Absolute Error (MAE)* function which is more robust and also less sensitive to outliers to *LS*,
- *dipolar*, where a dipol (a pair of feature vectors) is selected and then a test is constructed which splits this dipole. First instance that constitutes dipol is randomly selected from the node. Rest of the feature vectors are sorted decreasingly according to the difference between dependent variable values to the firstly chosen instance. To find a second instance that constitutes dipol we applied mechanism similar to the ranking linear selection [9].

For the leaves, algorithm finds the locally optimal model that minimizes the sum of squared residuals for each attribute or for randomly chosen one.

2.3   Genetic Operators

To maintain genetic diversity, we have proposed two specialized genetic operators corresponding to the classical mutation and cross-over. At each evolutionary iteration one of the operators is applied with a given probability (default probability of selecting mutation equals 0.8 and cross-over 0.2) to each individual. Both operators have influence on the tree structure, tests in non-terminal nodes and models at the leaves. Cross-over solution starts with selecting positions in two affected individuals. In each of two trees one node is chosen randomly. We have proposed three variants of recombination [4] that involve tests, subtrees and branches exchange. Mutation solution starts with randomly choosing the type of node (equal probability to select leaf or internal node). Next, the ranked list of nodes of the selected type is created and a mechanism analogous to ranking linear selection is applied to decide which node will be affected. Depending on the type of node, ranking take into account the location of the internal node (internal nodes in lower parts of the tree are mutated with higher probability) and the absolute error (worse in terms of prediction accuracy leaves and internal nodes are mutated with higher probability). We have proposed several variants of mutation for internal node [4] and for the leaf [5] that involve tests, models and modifications in the tree structure (pruning the internal nodes and expanding the leaves).

2.4   Memetic Extensions

To improve the performance of evolutionary process, we propose additional local search components that are built into the mutation-like operator. With the user defined probability a new test can be built on a random split or can be locally optimized similarly to 2.2. Due to the computational complexity constraints, we calculate optimal test for single, randomly chosen attribute. Different variant of the test mutation involve shifting the splitting threshold at continuous-valued feature which can be locally optimized in the similar way. In case of model trees, memetic extension can be used to search for the linear models at the leaves. With the user defined probability a new, locally optimized linear regression model is calculated on a new or unchanged set of attributes.

In previous research, after performed mutation in internal nodes the models in corresponding leaves were not recalculated because adequate linear models could be found while performing the mutations at the leaves. In this paper we test the influence of this recursive model recalculations as it can also be treated as local optimization.

2.5 Fitness Function, Selection and Termination Condition

A fitness function is one of the most important and sensitive element in the design of the evolutionary algorithm. It measures how good a single individual is in terms of meeting the problem objective and drives the evolutionary search process. Direct minimization of the prediction error measured on the learning set usually leads to the overfitting problem. In a typical top-down induction of decision trees [10], this problem is partially mitigated by defining a stopping condition and by applying a post-pruning.

In our previous works we used different fitness functions like Akaike's information criterion (AIC) [1] and Bayesian information criterion (BIC) [11]. In this work we continue to use BIC as a fitness function with settings like in [5] but with new assumption. When the sum of squared residuals of the tree equals to zero the original BIC fitness is equal infinity therefore no better individual can be found. In our research we continue the search to find the best individual with the lowest complexity.

Ranking linear selection [9] is applied as a selection mechanism. Additionally, in each iteration, single individual with the highest value of fitness function in current population in copied to the next one *(elitist strategy)*. Evolution terminates when the fitness of the best individual in the population does not improve during the fixed number of generations. In case of a slow convergence, maximum number of generations is also specified, which allows to limit the computation time.

3 Experimental Validation

The proposed memetic approach is evaluated on both artificial and real life datasets. It is compared only to the pure evolutionary versions of our global inducer since in previous work [4] we had a detailed comparison of our solutions with popular counterparts. All results presented in this paper correspond to averages of 10 runs and were obtained by using test sets (when available) or by 10-fold cross-validation. Root mean squared error (*RMSE*) is given as the prediction error measure of the tested systems. The number of nodes is given as a complexity measure (size) of regression and model trees.

3.1   Synthetical Datasets

In the first group of experiments, two simple artificially generated datasets illustrated in figure 1 are analyzed. Both datasets have the same analytically defined decision borders and contain two independent and one dependent feature with 5% noise. Dataset *armchair1* was designed for the regression trees (dependent feature contains only a few distinct values) and *armchair2* for the model trees (dependent variable is modeled as a linear function of single variable). One thousand observations for each dataset were divided into a training set (33.3% of observations) and testing set.

In order to verify the impact of memetic approach on the results, we prepared a series of experiments for global regression trees *GRT* and global model trees *GMT*. Let m denote the percentage use of local optimizations in the mutation of evolutionary induced trees and equals: *0%*, *10%* or *50%*. The influence of these memetic components on the evolutionary process is illustrated in the figure 2 for *GRT* and in figure 3 for *GMT*. On both figures the *RMSE* and the tree size is shown.

Illustrations on the left side, present the algorithms *GRT* and *GMT* in which after each performed mutation in the internal node corresponding leaves were not recalculated since they could be found during the leaves mutation. In the illustrations on the right, for the algorithms denoted as *GRTr* and *GMTr*, all the mean values or models in corresponding leaves were recursively recalculated which can also be treated as local optimization 2.4.

In table 1 we summary the results for the figure 2. All the algorithms managed to find minimum RMSE and the optimal tree size which was equal 7. Stronger impact of the memetic approach results in significantly faster algorithm convergence however it also extends the average iteration time. The pure evolutionary algorithm *GRT* managed to find optimal solution but after 28000

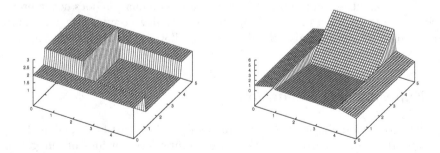

Fig. 1. Three-dimensional visualization of artificial datasets: *armchair1* - left, *armchair2* - right

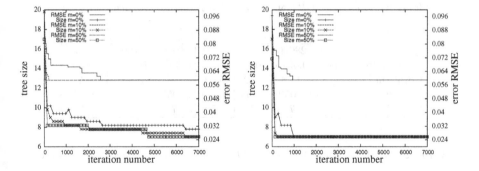

Fig. 2. The influence of memetic parameter m on the performance of the algorithm without (GRT - left) , or with (GRT_r - right) recursive recalculations

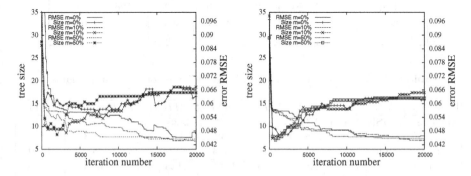

Fig. 3. The influence of memetic parameter m on the performance of the algorithm without (GMT - left), or with (GMT_r - right) recursive recalculations

iterations where for example $GRTr$ with memetic impact $m = 50\%$ need only 100 generations. We can observe that the best performance was achieved for the $GRTr$ algorithms with local optimization m equal *10%*.

Dataset *armchair2* was more difficult to analyse and none of the GMT and $GMTr$ algorithm presented in figure 3 and described in table 2 managed to find the optimal solutions. Similarly to the previous experiment, the algorithms with memetic approach convergence much faster and were able to find good results even after few iterations. The $GMTr$ with m equal *50%* managed to achieve the highest performance in the terms of $RMSE$ and the total time.

3.2   Real-Life Datasets

In the second series of experiments, two datasets from UCI Machine Learning Repository [3] were analyzed to assess the performance of memetic approach on real-life problems. Table 3 presents characteristics of investigated datasets and obtained results after 5000 performed iterations.

We can observe that for the higher memetic impact, the $RMSE$ is the smallest but at the cost of the evolution time. Additional research showed that if we run

Table 1. Results of the GRT and $GRTr$ algorithms for the *armchair1* dataset

Algorithm	GRT_0	GRT_{10}	GRT_{50}	$GRTr_0$	$GRTr_{10}$	$GRTr_{50}$
performed iterations	28000	6400	4650	970	190	100
average loop time	0.0016	0.0044	0.011	0.0017	0.0045	0.012
total time	44.8	28.2	51.2	1.65	0.855	1.2
RMSE	0.059	0.059	0.059	0.059	0.059	0.059
size	7	7	7	7	7	7

Table 2. Results of the GMT and $GMTr$ algorithms for the *armchair2* dataset

Algorithm	GMT_0	GMT_{10}	GMT_{50}	$GMTr_0$	$GMTr_{10}$	$GMTr_{50}$
performed iterations	20000	20000	20000	20000	20000	20000
average loop time	0.0040	0.0060	0.011	0.0041	0.0063	0.011
total time	80	120	220	82	126	220
RMSE	0.047	0.044	0.045	0.046	0.044	0.045
size	16	18	17	16	17	16

Table 3. Results of the GMT and $GMTr$ algorithms for the real-life datasets

Dataset	Alg.	GRT_0	$GRTr_0$	$GRTr_{10}$	$GRTr_{50}$	GMT_0	$GMTr_0$	$GMTr_{10}$	$GMTr_{50}$
Abalone	RMSE	2.37	2.34	2.31	2.30	2.25	2.23	2.23	2.23
inst: 4177	size	39	35	35	39	17	15	13	15
attr: 7/1	time	52	56	207	414	149	336	521	1240
Kinemaics	RMSE	0.195	0.191	0.186	0.185	0.185	0.179	0.176	0.174
inst: 8192	size	77	109	129	109	59	61	59	81
attr: 8	time	96	99	719	1429	285	442	1203	2242

the pure evolutionary algorithm for the same amount of time as $GRTr_{50}$ or $GMTr_{50}$ the results would be similar. Therefore, if we consider the time limit, the global trees with small memetic impact ($m = 10\%$) would achieved the highest performance in the terms of $RMSE$ and size.

4 Conclusion

In the paper the memetic approach for global induction of decision trees was investigated. We have assessed the impact of local optimizations on evolutionary induced regression and model trees. Preliminary experimental results suggest that at some point memetic algorithms successfully improve evolutionary induction. Application of the memetic approach results in significantly faster algorithm convergence however it also extends the average iteration time. Therefore, too much of local optimizations may not really speed up the evolutionary process. Experimental results also suggest that additional recursive model recalculations after performed mutation for corresponding leaves may be a good idea.

Further research to fully understand the influence of the memetic approach for the decision trees is advised. Currently we plan to analyze each local optimization separately to see how it affects three major elements of the tree: structure, test and models at the leaves.

Acknowledgments. This work was supported by the grant S/WI/2/08 from Bialystok University of Technology.

References

1. Akaike, H.: A New Look at Statistical Model Identification. IEEE Transactions on Automatic Control 19, 716–723 (1974)
2. Barros, R.C., Basgalupp, M.P., et al.: A Survey of Evolutionary Algorithms for Decision-Tree Induction. IEEE Transactions on Systems, Man, and Cybernetics, Part C (2011) (in print)
3. Blake, C., Keogh, E., Merz, C.: UCI Repository of Machine Learning Databases (1998), http://www.ics.uci.edu/~mlearn/MLRepository.html
4. Czajkowski, M., Kretowski, M.: Globally Induced Model Trees: An Evolutionary Approach. In: Schaefer, R., Cotta, C., Kołodziej, J., Rudolph, G. (eds.) PPSN XI. LNCS, vol. 6238, pp. 324–333. Springer, Heidelberg (2010)
5. Czajkowski, M., Kretowski, M.: An Evolutionary Algorithm for Global Induction of Regression Trees with Multivariate Linear Models. In: Kryszkiewicz, M., Rybinski, H., Skowron, A., Raś, Z.W. (eds.) ISMIS 2011. LNCS, vol. 6804, pp. 230–239. Springer, Heidelberg (2011)
6. Gendreau, M., Potvin, J.Y.: Handbook of Metaheuristics. International Series in Operations Research & Management Science, vol. 146 (2010)
7. Kretowski, M.: A Memetic Algorithm for Global Induction of Decision Trees. In: Geffert, V., Karhumäki, J., Bertoni, A., Preneel, B., Návrat, P., Bieliková, M. (eds.) SOFSEM 2008. LNCS, vol. 4910, pp. 531–540. Springer, Heidelberg (2008)
8. Kretowski, M., Czajkowski, M.: An Evolutionary Algorithm for Global Induction of Regression Trees. In: Rutkowski, L., Scherer, R., Tadeusiewicz, R., Zadeh, L.A., Zurada, J.M. (eds.) ICAISC 2010. LNCS, vol. 6114, pp. 157–164. Springer, Heidelberg (2010)
9. Michalewicz, Z.: Genetic Algorithms + Data Structures = Evolution Programs, 3rd edn. Springer, Heidelberg (1996)
10. Rokach, L., Maimon, O.: Top-down induction of decision trees classifiers - A survey. IEEE Transactions on Systems, Man, and Cybernetics - Part C 35(4), 476–487 (2005)
11. Schwarz, G.: Estimating the Dimension of a Model. The Annals of Statistics 6, 461–464 (1978)

Evolutionary Optimization of Decomposition Strategies for Logical Functions

Stanisław Deniziak and Karol Wieczorek

Kielce University of Technology, Department of Computer Science
S.Deniziak@computer.org, K.Wieczorek@tu.kielce.pl

Abstract. This paper presents a method of searching for the best decomposition strategy for logical functions. The strategy is represented by a decision tree, where each node corresponds to a single decomposition step. In that way the multistage decomposition of complex logical functions may be specified. The tree evolves using the developmental genetic programming. The goal of the evolution is to find a decomposition strategy for which the cost of FPGA implementation of a given function is minimal. Experimental results show that our approach gives significantly better outcomes than other existing methods.

Keywords: developmental genetic programming, functional decomposition, FPGA devices.

1 Introduction

Decomposition is a process of splitting a complex function into a set of smaller sub-functions. It is used in machine learning, pattern analysis, data mining, knowledge discovery and logic synthesis of digital systems [14]. The goal of the decomposition is to optimise certain system features. In the case of digital circuits, objectives of optimisation are the minimal cost and the minimal latency of target system implementation.

There exist a lot of different decomposition methods dedicated to Boolean functions [14]. As far as LUT-based FPGA (Look-Up Table Based Field Programmable Arrays) implementations are considered, the most effective method is the functional decomposition [3]. It splits a logical function into two smaller functions using a parallel or a serial strategy. This step should be repeated recursively for each result function which is not implementable in one logic cell. There are efficient methods of single-step functional decomposition, giving quite good results [9], but it seems that multilevel decomposition strategies are not studied enough. The only known method is the balanced decomposition [9], but it was not proved that this strategy is optimal.

This paper presents a new approach to the multilevel functional decomposition. For each circuit a dedicated strategy of decomposition is evaluated. The strategy defines the methods of decompositions which are applied during each step. In our approach the strategy of decomposition is optimized using the developmental genetic programming. We observed that our method gives significantly

L. Rutkowski et al. (Eds.): SIDE 2012 and EC 2012, LNCS 7269, pp. 182–189, 2012.
© Springer-Verlag Berlin Heidelberg 2012

better results, than other existing methods, for the most of the evaluated benchmark circuits.

In the next section the functional decomposition is described. Section 3 presents the developmental genetic programming used in our approach. In the section 4 our method is presented. Section 5 contains experimental results. The paper ends with conclusions.

2   Functional Decomposition

Let F be a multiple-input/multiple-output function. The function may be decomposed using a parallel or a serial strategy. The parallel decomposition expresses the function F(X) through functions G and H with disjoint sets of output variables. The serial decomposition expresses the function F(X) through functions G and H, such that F=H(U,G(V)), where U ∪ V=I. If the number of inputs and outputs of the result function does not exceed the number of inputs and outputs in the LUT, then the function is implementable in one LUT cell.

The following problems of defining the decomposition strategy should be resolved: which decomposition method should be used, and which sets of separated inputs (in serial decomposition) or outputs (in parallel decomposition) should be chosen. The only known solution for the first problem is the balanced decomposition [9]. In this strategy the parallel decomposition is chosen if the decomposed function has more outputs than inputs, otherwise the serial decomposition is applied. However, it was not proved that this strategy is the best one for the functional decomposition. Thus alternative approaches should be studied, and the strategy giving the best final results should be found.

For the variable partitioning problem a lot of heuristics were proposed [11]. In [13] the best variable partition is determined using the information relationship measures that express relations between input and output variables. Separated sets of inputs may be also optimised using evolutionary algorithms [12]. An efficient method of finding variable partitions, based on so called r-admissibility was proposed in [11]. A method applying "divide-and-conquer" paradigm was presented in [10].

The goal of all above methods is to find the input partitions providing the best serial decomposition of a given input function. It should be noticed that a decision giving the best results in a single step does not guarantee obtaining the optimal solution. Thus the local as well as the global optimisation methods should be studied, to find the best strategy of the multilevel decomposition.

3   Developmental Genetic Programming

Genetic programming (GP) [7] creates computer programs using genetic algorithm (GA) [5]. The population is a set of individuals representing computer programs which evolve. In the developmental genetic programming (DGP) [6], methods creating solutions evolve instead of computer programs. In this method the genotype and the phenotype are distinguished. The genotype is composed of genes representing elementary functions that constructs the solution of a problem. Phenotype represents the target solution. During evolution only genotypes are evolved, while the genotype-to-phenotype mapping is used to create phenotypes. Next, all genotypes are rated according to the estimated quality of the corresponding phenotypes. The goal of the optimisation is to find the procedure constructing the best solution of a problem.

DGP is especially helpful in optimizing solutions of hard-constrained problems. In these cases most of randomly generated solutions are not valid. Thus in probabilistic methods like GA some restrictions should be applied to enforce genetic operators to produce only legal individuals. But these restrictions may also create infeasible regions in a search space, eliminating sequences of genes which may lead to high quality solutions. This problem does not appear in DPG, because in the DGP genotypes are evolved without any restrictions and legal only phenotypes are guaranteed by appropriate genotype to phenotype mapping. DGP proves to be effective in such problems like synthesis of electronic circuits, synthesis of the control algorithms, co-synthesis of embedded systems, etc. [8].

The only constraint in the functional decomposition is that the original behaviour must be preserved. Since generation of networks of Boolean functions which are equivalent to the given function is a hard problem, there is no efficient GP approach for optimising functional decomposition. However, taking into consideration that DGP evolves a system construction procedure instead of the system itself, such an approach seems to be very promising for optimisation of the decomposition strategy for Boolean functions.

4   Evolution of the Multilevel Decomposition Strategy

In our method genotypes are represented by binary trees specifying the decomposition strategy. Each node (gene) specifies the decomposition of the function created by the parent node into 2 functions passed to offspring nodes for further processing. Thus each level in the tree represents a single stage of the multi-level decomposition process. Functions created by tree leaves constitute the target solution.

4.1   Genotypes and Phenotypes

Each gene specifies a decomposition strategy used in a single step. The strategy is defined by the type of decomposition (parallel or serial) and the rules according to which the sets of separated inputs or outputs are determined. As yet, 16 different genes are defined.

The initial generation consists of individuals generated randomly, where all genes are selected with the same probability. The size of the genotype should be attuned to the complexity of the function, therefore the number of nodes in each genotype is calculated according to the following formula:

$$G = \Theta(\frac{n * m}{I_{LUT}} * A_{0.8}^{1.2}) \tag{1}$$

where: n - is the number of inputs, m - is the number of outputs, I_{LUT} – is the number of LUT's inputs, $A_{0.8}^{1.2}$ is a random value from range $[0.8\ldots1.2]$, Θ – returns the argument rounded upward to the nearest natural odd value.

A sample genotype tree is shown in Fig.1. The genotype corresponds to a function with 8 inputs and 3 outputs. For LUT with 4 inputs and 1 output possible number of nodes is equal to 5, 7 or 9. OS1, OS2, OS8 and IS3, IS4, IS5 mean different strategies for separation of outputs and inputs.

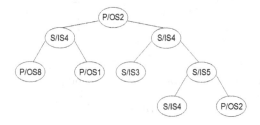

Fig. 1. Sample genotype

Genotype to phenotype mapping is done by traversing the genotype in the depth-first order, for each node the decomposition is performed according to rules defined by the corresponding gene. The methods of the functional decomposition based on the blanket algebra [3] are applied. Two exceptions are possible: first, the node has successors but further decomposition is not necessary, second, the node is a leaf but the function requires further decompositions. In the first case, the decomposition of the given subfunction is not continued and useless nodes are removed from the genotype tree immediately. This process is similar to withering of unused features in live organisms. In the second case, the decomposition result is estimated using the expected cost of implementation:

$$ECI = 2^{n-k} * m \tag{2}$$

Results estimated by this rule are enough pessimistic to be worse than most of the fully decomposed solutions. In that way the probability of reproducing such solutions to the next generations is very low.

The phenotype is a network of result functions which is functionally equivalent to the original function. According to the sample genotype shown in Fig.1, a function F was decomposed into 5 smaller functions(Fig.2). Assuming that the target LUT has 4 inputs and 1 output the genotype to phenotype mapping proceeded as follows: function F was split into functions (g, h) using the parallel decomposition, next function g was decomposed into (gg, gh) and function h was decomposed into (hg, hh), finally function hh was decomposed into (hhg, hhh).

4.2   Genetic Operators

Each generation contains the same number of individuals. To ensure that the examined solution space will be proportional to the function complexity, the size of the generation is calculated according to the following formula:

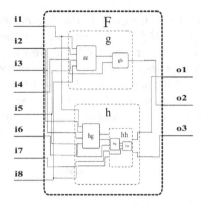

Fig. 2. The phenotype mapped from the genotype presented in Fig.1

$$N = (n + m) * \Omega \tag{3}$$

where Ω is a DGP parameter.

Genotypes are ranked according to the implementation cost of the corresponding phenotypes. Solutions which require less LUT cells for implementation have higher position in the ranking. During evolution the rank selection operator is used. Reproduction copies the selected individuals from the current generation to the next generation. Cross-over selects 2 genotypes, then both trees are pruned by removing randomly selected edge, next, sub-trees are swapped between both parent genotype. In that way 2 new individuals are created and added to the next generation. Mutation selects one genotype, then one of the following modifications is done for the chosen genotype:

- randomly selected gene is changed to another,
- randomly selected edge is pruned and the subtree is removed,
- two random nodes are created and added to the randomly selected leaf.

Each type of modification is selected with the same probability, except that for single-node genotypes the subtree extraction can not be selected. Implementation of genetic operators ensures that the correct genotype-tree structure is always kept. Each node in the genotype has exactly 2 child-nodes or it is a leaf node.

The new generation is created using the above operations in the following way: $r = \alpha * N$ individuals are reproduced, $c = \beta * N$ individuals are created using cross-over, and $m = \gamma * N$ individuals are created using mutation. The following requirement must be fulfilled:

$$\alpha + \beta + \gamma = 1 \tag{4}$$

If the algorithm does not find any bettter solution in λ succeeding generations, the evolution stops. Values of Ω, α, β, γ and λ are experimentally attuned.

5   Experimental Results

The described method has been implemented and evaluated with the help of some MCNC benchmarks [15]. The following values of DGP parameters have been assumed: $\Omega=12$, $\alpha=0.05$, $\beta=0.65$, $\gamma=0.3$, $\lambda=20$. The same experiments were performed using other existing methods of logic synthesis for FPGAs: GUIDek [1], an academic tool which decomposes functions using deterministic approach, it also uses the functional decomposition, the ABC system [2], it is also an academic tool but it performs FPGA mapping based on cofactoring and disjoint-support decomposition, and commercially available tool Quartus II v.10.0 from Altera Corp. Experimental results are shown in Tab. 1. The following columns contain: the name of the benchmark, results obtained using our (DGP) method(the best results obtained in 20 trials), GUIDek, ABC and Quartus. The results represent the cost of the FPGA implementation (number of LUT cells). DGP gives 18% better implementations than GUIDek and 21% better result than Quartus, on average.

Table 1. Decompositon results (number of LUT4x1 cells, Cyclone II devices)

Benchmark	DGP	GUIDek	ABC	Quartus II
5xp1	18	22	34	33
9sym	8	9	92	9
dk17	27	32	34	31
dk27	12	13	11	11
f51m	15	22	39	19
inc	27	35	39	42
m1	20	25	23	20
misex1	16	20	14	22
newcpla2	24	33	26	24
rd53	5	5	14	7
rd73	9	9	43	11
seq	18	23	22	20
sqn	21	24	42	33
sqrt8	11	13	17	14
squar5	13	14	17	16
t4	15	17	14	14
tms	60	73	87	80
$\sum$	321	389	568	406
Avg. improvement	–	18%	44%	21%

In GP approaches it is very important to attune the genetic parameters. Thus we performed some experiments to analyze the influence of certain parameters on the final result. First, we have analyzed the number of individuals in one generation (Ω). Results obtained for the benchmark *dk17* with 300, 800, 1600 individuals in each generation ($\Omega=15$, 40 and 80) are presented in Fig.3. We observed that increasing the generation size improves the final result, but there is no dependence between the generation size and the number of generations required to get the final result. In all cases the best result was found after less than 40 steps.

Another important parameter is the number of mutations applied during each step. Fig.4 presents results obtained for *9sym* benchmark using DGP with 5%,

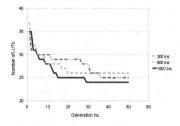

Fig. 3. Evolution for different numbers of individuals in one generation

Fig. 4. Results of the evolution with 5%(a), 15%(b) and 30%(c) of mutations

15% and 30% of mutations. Each evolution was repeated 50 times. The best solution was found in 16%, 36% and 52% of trials, respectively. Results confirmed that in the DGP approach the number of mutations should be relatively high.

6   Conclusions

In this paper the developmental genetic programming was applied to the problem of functional decomposition of Boolean functions. In our approach the multilevel decomposition strategy for given function evolves, instead of the solutions itself. In that way we use strategy optimized for the given system instead of the global decomposition strategy. To our best knowledge this is the first DGP approach targeting the multilevel decomposition problem. DGP approach requires more CPU time compared to other methods. But genetic algorithms can be efficiently parallelized, thus the implementation for multicore processors will significantly reduce this time [4].

Preliminary results show, that the method is efficient; it gives significantly better results than existing methods. We considered only the cost issue, but it is possible to consider, during the fitness computation, the number of logic levels in a system. In this way the performance of the target implementation also may be optimised. Future work will concentrate on analyzing other implementations of genetic operators. We will work also on developing new types of genes using different input variable partitioning methods, some metric measures and other methods of input selection known from the literature.

References

1. http://rawski.zpt.tele.pw.edu.pl/pl/node/161
2. http://www.eecs.berkeley.edu/~alanmi/abc
3. Brzozowski, J., Łuba, T.: Decomposition of Boolean Functions Specified by Cubes. Journal of Multiple-Valued Logic and Soft Computing 9, 377–417 (2003)
4. Deniziak, S., Wieczorek, K.: Parallel Approach to the Functional Decomposition of Logical Functions using Developmental Genetic Programming. In: Proc. of 9th International Conference on Parallel Processing and Applied Mathematics. LNCS, Springer, Heidelberg (2011) (to appear)
5. Goldberg, D.E.: Genetic Algorithms in Search, Optimization and Machine Learning. Addison-Wesley Longman Publishing Co., Inc., Boston (1989)
6. Keller, R., Banzhaf, W.: The Evolution of Genetic Code in Genetic Programming. In: Proc. of the Genetic and Evolutionary Computation Conference, pp. 1077–1082 (1999)
7. Koza, J.: Genetic Programming: On the Programming of Computers by Means of Natural Selection. MIT Press, Cambridge (1992)
8. Koza, J., Keane, M.A., Streeter, M.J., Mydlowec, W., Yu, J., Lanza, G.: Genetic Programming IV: Routine Human-Competitive Machine Intelligence. Kluwer Academic Publisher, Norwell (2003)
9. Łuba, T., Nowicka, M., Rawski, M.: FPGA-based Decomposition of Boolean Functions. Algorithms and Implementation. In: Proc. of the 6th International Conference on Advanced Computer Systems (1999)
10. Morawiecki, P., Rawski, M., Selvaraj, H.: Input Variable Partitioning Method for Functional Decomposition of Functions Specified by Large Truth Tables. In: Proc. of International Conference on Computational Intelligence and Multimedia Applications, pp. 164–168 (2007)
11. Muthukumar, V., Bignall, R.J., Selvaraj, H.: An Efficient Variable Partitioning Approach for Functional Decomposition of Circuits. Journal of Systems Architecture 53, 53–67 (2007)
12. Rawski, M.: Efficient Variable Partitioning Method for Functional Decomposition. Electronics and Telecommunications Quarterly 53(1), 63–81 (2007)
13. Rawski, M., Jóźwiak, L., Łuba, T.: Functional Decomposition with an Efficient Input Support Selection for Sub-functions Based on Information Relationship Measures. Journal of Systems Architecture 47(2), 137–155 (2001)
14. Scholl, C.: Functional Decomposition with Application to FPGA Synthesis. Kluwer Academic Publishers, Norwell (2001)
15. Yang, S.: Logic Synthesis and Optimization Benchmarks. version 3.0. Tech. rep., Microelectronics Center of North Carolina (1991)

Tournament Feature Selection with Directed Mutations

Grzegorz Dudek

Department of Electrical Engineering, Czestochowa University of Technology,
Al. Armii Krajowej 17, 42-200 Czestochowa, Poland
dudek@el.pcz.czest.pl

Abstract. A tournament searching method with new mutation operators for a problem of the feature subset selection is presented. The probability of the bit mutation in a classical approach is fixed. In the proposed methods this probability is dependent on the history of the searching process. Bit position whose mutation from 0 to 1 (from 1 to 0) improved the evaluation of the solution in early iterations, are mutated more frequently from 0 to 1 (from 1 to 0). The roulette wheel method and the tournament method are used to select the bits for the mutation according to the adaptive probability. The algorithms were tested on several tasks of the feature selection in the supervised learning. The experiments showed the faster convergence of the algorithm with directed mutations in relation to the classical mutation.

Keywords: feature selection, tournament feature selection, directed mutation, roulette wheel mutation, tournament mutation, supervised learning, k-nearest neighbour method.

1   Introduction

Feature selection (FS) is an important stage in the design of classification and approximation systems, as well as in modelling the phenomena, processes and physical objects in general. The aim of FS is to reduce the dimension of the input vectors by the feature (variable) subset selection which describes object in the best manner and ensures the best quality of the model. In this process the irrelevant, redundant and unpredictive features are omitted.

The methods of FS can be generally divided into filter and wrapper ones [1]. Filter methods do not require application of learning model to select relevant features. They select features as a preprocessing step, independent on the choice of the predictor. They also use information included in the dataset, e.g. the correlation between variables or discriminatory abilities of the individual features, to create the most promising feature subset before commencement of learning. The main disadvantage of the filter approach is the fact that it totally ignores the effect of the selected feature subset on the performance of the learning model.

The wrapper approach operates in the context of the learning model – it uses feature selection algorithm as a wrapper around the learning algorithm and has usually better predictive accuracy than the filter approach. The wrapper approach using the

L. Rutkowski et al. (Eds.): SIDE 2012 and EC 2012, LNCS 7269, pp. 190–198, 2012.

learning model as a black box is remarkably universal. However, this approach can be very slow because the learning algorithm is called repeatedly. The comparative experiments between the wrapper and filter models confirmed that it is inappropriate to evaluate the usefulness of an input variable without taking into consideration the algorithms that built the classification or regression model [1].

Some learning models have internal build-in mechanisms of FS. For example decision trees (CART, ID3, C4.5) which incorporate FS routine as a subroutine and heuristically search the space of feature subsets along tree structure during the learning process or artificial immune system proposed in [2] which includes the local feature selection mechanism. This approach, inspired by the binding of an antibody to an antigen, which occurs between amino acid residues forming an epitope and a paratope, allows the detection of many relevant feature sets (a separate relevant feature set is created for each learning point and its neighborhood).

In [3] the wrapper method of FS called tournament feature selection (TFS) was proposed. The solution strings processed by TFS are vectors composed of bits representing all m features: $\mathbf{x} = [x_1, x_2, \ldots, x_m]$. Ones and zeros in these vectors indicate whether the feature is selected or not. TFS is a simple stochastic search mechanism which explores the solution space starting from an initial solution and generating new ones by perturbing it using a mutation operator. This operator switches the value of one randomly chosen bit (but different for each candidate solution) of the parent solution. When the set of new l candidate solutions is generated (l represents the tournament size), their evaluations are calculated. The best candidate solution (the tournament winner), with the highest value of the criterion function, is selected and it replaces the parent solution, even if it is worse than the parent solution. This allows us to escape from the local maxima of the criterion function. If l is equal to 1, this procedure comes down to a random search process. On the other hand, when l is equal to the total number of features this method becomes a hill climbing method where there is no escape from the local maxima.

The TFS turned out to be very promising in the feature selection problem, better than a genetic algorithm and simulated annealing, as well as deterministic sequential forward and backward selection algorithms [3]. The TFS method, similarly to the genetic algorithm, has a parallel structure – several candidate solutions can be generated and evaluated at the same time. This results in the runtime decreasing. The main advantage of TFS is only one parameter to adjust – the tournament size l.

This paper presents TFS with specialized binary search operators: roulette wheel and tournament mutations. These operators use information gained during the searching process about the effect of mutations at different bit positions on the solution quality. Bit position whose mutation from 0 to 1 (or 1 to 0) improved the evaluation of the solution in earlier iterations are more frequently mutated from 0 to 1 (or 1 to 0). This mechanism should speed up the convergence of the algorithm.

The biological inspiration for the proposed directed mutations is a hypothesis of directed mutagenesis proposing that organisms can respond to environmental stresses through directing mutations to certain genes or areas of the genome [4].

2   Roulette Wheel Mutation

In the roulette wheel method the mutation intensity is determined individually for each bit position $i = 1, 2, ..., m$. The indexes of mutation intensity from 0 to 1 $w_{0-1}(i)$ and from 1 to 0 $w_{1-0}(i)$ are introduced and initialized with zeros for each position i. The index values are updated after each algorithm iteration according to the following scheme:

- if the solution evaluation after mutation increases, the index values for mutated positions increase, i.e. $w_{0-1}(i)$ or $w_{1-0}(i)$ (respectively to the direction of mutation (from 0 to 1 or from 1 to 0) and the mutated bit position) is incremented by u.
- if the solution evaluation after mutation decreases, the index values for mutated positions decrease, i.e. $w_{0-1}(i)$ or $w_{1-0}(i)$ is decremented by u.
- if the solution evaluation after mutation does not change, the index values remain unchanged.

This can be expressed by formulas:

$$w_{0-1}(i) = \begin{cases} w_{0-1}(i) + u, & \text{if } i \in M \land F(\mathbf{x'}) > F(\mathbf{x}) \land x_i = 0 \\ w_{0-1}(i) - u, & \text{if } i \in M \land F(\mathbf{x'}) < F(\mathbf{x}) \land x_i = 0 \ , \\ w_{0-1}(i), & \text{otherwise} \end{cases} \tag{1}$$

$$w_{1-0}(i) = \begin{cases} w_{1-0}(i) + u, & \text{if } i \in M \land F(\mathbf{x'}) > F(\mathbf{x}) \land x_i = 1 \\ w_{1-0}(i) - u, & \text{if } i \in M \land F(\mathbf{x'}) < F(\mathbf{x}) \land x_i = 1 \ , \\ w_{1-0}(i), & \text{otherwise} \end{cases} \tag{2}$$

where: $u > 0$ – the incrementation/decrementation constant, $\mathbf{x}$, $\mathbf{x'}$ – the solution before and after mutation, M – the set of mutated position in the solution $\mathbf{x}$, $F(\mathbf{x})$, $F(\mathbf{x'})$ – the evaluation values of the solution $\mathbf{x}$ before and after mutation, respectively.

The high value of the index $w_{0-1}(i)$ ($w_{1-0}(i)$) informs that in the current realization of the searching process the change of the i-th bit value from 0 to 1 (from 1 to 0) caused improvement of the evaluation in the most cases. Thus the probability of the mutation of this bit from 0 to 1 (from 1 to 0) in the next iterations should be adequately high, depending on the value of $w_{0-1}(i)$ ($w_{1-0}(i)$) index. The mutation probability is calculated according to the formula:

$$p(i) = \frac{f\left(w_{d(i)}(i)\right)}{\sum_{j \in \Omega_0(i)} f\left(w_{0-1}(j)\right) + \sum_{k \in \Omega_1(i)} f\left(w_{1-0}(k)\right)}, \tag{3}$$

where: $w_{d(i)} = w_{0-1}(i)$ if the i-th bit value in the mutated solution is equal to 0 and $w_{d(i)} = w_{1-0}(i)$ otherwise, $\Omega_0(i)$ is a set of positions of zeros and $\Omega_1(i)$ is a set of positions of ones in the mutated solution, $f(.)$ is a logistic function of the form:

$$f(z) = \frac{1}{1+e^{-z}}.$$ (4)

The task of the logistic function having an "S" shape is to reduce the mutation probability of positions with large values of the mutation indexes and transform the negative values of indexes to the positive ones. This is illustrated in Fig. 1. Index values after transformation using (5) are in the range from 0 to 1. The positive values of indexes are necessary for the proper operation of the roulette wheel method. The reduction of mutation probability for positions with large index values eliminates the premature convergence to the superindividuals. The mutation probability is proportional to the value of $f(w_{d(i)}(i))$ now, and not to the value of $w_{d(i)}(i)$, which may increase/decrease to +/- infinity during the searching process and which may affect the mutation probabilities in an undesirable way. The mutation probability of z_2 in Fig. 1 is only about 11% larger than the mutation probability of z_1, although z_2 is two times larger than z_1.

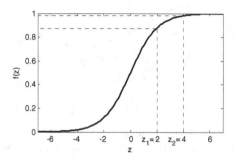

Fig. 1. The logistic function transforming the mutation index values

The mutation positions are chosen according to the probabilities $p(i)$ using the roulette wheel. The roulette wheel is composed of m sectors which sizes depend on $p(i)$, and their boundaries are determined as follows:

$$S(i) = \begin{cases} (0, \ p(1)] & \text{for } i = 1 \\ \left(\sum_{j=1}^{i-1} p(j), \sum_{j=1}^{i} p(j) \right] & \text{for } i = 2,3,...,m \end{cases}.$$ (5)

The circuit of the roulette wheel equals 1.

The scheme of the roulette wheel mutation for TFS is as follows:

1. For each position $i = 1, 2, ..., m$, according to the values of $w_{0\text{-}1}(i)$ and $w_{1\text{-}0}(i)$ indexes, the values of probability $p(i)$ are calculated from equation (3).
2. For each candidate solution the roulette wheel is constructed taking into account sector boundaries (5).

3. For each candidate solution the uniformly distributed random number r from the range $(0, 1]$ is drawn. The sector including number r determines the position and direction of the mutation.

In the original TFS algorithm, each candidate solution is mutated in a different position. If we want to introduce such a requirement in the roulette wheel mutation, before calculating probabilities (3) for the mutated candidate solution, we assume $p(i) = 0$ for all previously mutated positions in the current iteration and remove these positions as forbidden from the sets $\Omega_0(i)$ and $\Omega_1(i)$. For illustration in Fig. 2 the roulette wheels are shown for three 8-bit candidate solutions, where the parent solution is $\mathbf{x} = [0\ 1\ 1\ 0\ 0\ 0\ 1\ 0]$, the mutation indexes are: $\mathbf{w}_{0\text{-}1} = [-0.1, 0.5, 0.8, -0.4, -0.6, -0.2, 0.9, 0.0]$, $\mathbf{w}_{1\text{-}0} = [0.4, -0.3, -0.8, 0.5, 0.9, 0.6, -0.9, 0.1]$, and the random numbers are $r = 0.76, 0.28$ and 0.59.

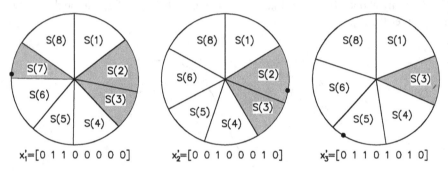

Fig. 2. The roulette wheels for the three successive candidate solutions generated from the parent solution $\mathbf{x} = [0\ 1\ 1\ 0\ 0\ 0\ 1\ 0]$. (Dark sectors correspond to ones in the parent solution, and white sectors correspond to zeros.)

The mutation parameter u allows to control the selection pressure. The higher u value increases the selection pressure. Since the function (4) does not reach zero there is nonzero probability of mutation of each bit in both directions.

3   Tournament Mutation

Analogically to the roulette wheel mutation, in the tournament mutation the mutation intensity indexes $w_{0\text{-}1}(i)$ and $w_{1\text{-}0}(i)$ are defined. For each candidate solution h bit positions are sampled uniformly at random with replacement, where $h = 1, 2, \ldots$ is the tournament mutation size. Among h positions the one with the highest value of $w_{d(i)}(i)$ is chosen, and the value of this position is changed to the opposite one.

Note that here we do not need to calculate the probability of mutation and the sizes of sectors such as in the case of the roulette wheel mutation, because in the tournament selection procedure there is not important what is the difference between the mutation index values $w_{d(i)}(i)$ corresponding to the bit positions competing in the tournament.

The tournament size h controls the selection pressure. If $h = 1$, the tournament mutation is reduced to the classical random mutation.

Restriction used in TFS, that every candidate solution is mutated in a different position, is implemented here in such a way that the positions mutated in the previously considered candidate solutions do not participate in the tournament for the current candidate solution.

The roulette wheel and tournament mutations should bring good results in the tasks where the i-th bit value influences the value of objective function in the same way, independently of the bit context (values of the remaining bits in the solution).

4   Application Examples

The proposed TFS method with roulette wheel and tournament mutations was verified on several test problems of data classification. Benchmark datasets, described in Table 1, were taken from the UCI Machine Learning Repository. The features in the datasets were standardized to zero-mean and unit-variance.

Table 1. Description of data used in experiments

Dataset	Size	Features	Classes	Optimal k value
Ionosphere	351	34	2	3
Cancer	569	30	2	4
Heart Statlog	270	13	2	7
Wine	178	13	3	4
Glass	214	9	6	5
Diabetes	768	8	2	14

where: Cancer – the Wisconsin diagnostic breast cancer dataset.

k-nearest neighbor method (k-NN) was used as a classifier, with k determined a priori for all features (optimal k values are shown in Table 1). The classification accuracy was determined in the leave-one-out procedure. For each dataset the feature space was optimized running algorithms 30-times. The number of solutions generated in the searching process was the same for all mutation variants: $40 \cdot \text{round}(m/2)^2$. The parameter values are listed below:

- tournament size in TFS: $l = \text{round}(m/3)$,
- incrementation/decrementation constant $u = 0.1$,
- tournament mutation size: $h = 2$ or 4.

Experiments were carried out using TFS with standard mutation (SM), roulette wheel mutation with replacement (the same mutations for different candidate solutions are possible, RWM1), roulette wheel mutation without replacement (the same mutations for different candidate solutions are not possible, RWM2), tournament mutation with replacement for $h = 2$ (TM1), tournament mutation without replacement for $h = 2$ (TM2) and tournament mutation with replacement for $h = 4$ (TM3).

The results are presented in Table 2, where Acc_{mean}, Acc_{min}, Acc_{max} are accuracies of the classifier using selected features (mean, minimal and maximal accuracies returned in 30 runs) and σ_{Acc} is the standard deviation of accuracy.

The convergence curves averaged from 30 runs for SM, RWM2 and TM2 are shown in Fig. 3. Characteristically, the convergence curve for SM is the lowest. This indicates the large variance of the searching process (we observe high variability of the process). Directed mutations RWM and TM reduce the variance leading the searching process to the promising regions of the solution space, which have been identified in an earlier stage of searching and stored in the mutation indexes. But from Table 2 it can be seen that TFS with the simple standard mutation usually leads to no worse results than the directed mutations.

Table 2. Results of classification using k-NN and TFS

Dataset		SM	RWM1	RWM2	TM1	TM2	TM3	Without FS
Ionosphere	Acc_{mean}	94.78	94.09	94.12	94.68	94.62	94.23	84.33
	Acc_{min}	94.59	92.88	92.88	94.30	94.02	92.88	
	Acc_{max}	95.44	94.87	94.87	95.44	95.44	94.87	
	σ_{Acc}	0.26	0.45	0.47	0.35	0.26	0.40	
Cancer	Acc_{mean}	98.25	97.87	97.89	98.05	98.01	97.91	96.61
	Acc_{min}	97.89	97.72	97.72	97.72	97.54	97.36	
	Acc_{max}	98.42	98.24	98.42	98.42	98.42	98.42	
	σ_{Acc}	0.18	0.15	0.17	0.20	0.23	0.22	
Heart Statlog	Acc_{mean}	86.16	85.84	85.84	86.06	86.04	85.83	82.22
	Acc_{min}	85.93	84.81	84.81	85.93	85.93	85.19	
	Acc_{max}	86.30	86.30	86.30	86.30	86.30	86.30	
	σ_{Acc}	0.18	0.30	0.32	0.18	0.17	0.27	
Wine	Acc_{mean}	98.88	98.86	98.86	98.88	98.88	98.67	96.07
	Acc_{min}	98.88	98.31	98.31	98.88	98.88	98.31	
	Acc_{max}	98.88	98.88	98.88	98.88	98.88	98.88	
	σ_{Acc}	0.00	0.10	0.10	0.00	0.00	0.28	
Glass	Acc_{mean}	74.77	74.77	74.77	74.77	74.77	74.77	65.89
	Acc_{min}	74.77	74.77	74.77	74.77	74.77	74.77	
	Acc_{max}	74.77	74.77	74.77	74.77	74.77	74.77	
	σ_{Acc}	0.00	0.00	0.00	0.00	0.00	0.00	
Diabetes	Acc_{mean}	77.21	77.21	77.20	77.21	77.21	76.94	73.96
	Acc_{min}	77.21	77.21	76.69	77.21	77.21	76.30	
	Acc_{max}	77.21	77.21	77.21	77.21	77.21	77.21	
	σ_{Acc}	0.00	0.00	0.10	0.00	0.00	0.33	

In order to confirm the faster convergence of TFS with directed mutation, we check whether the difference d between the average evaluation of the parent solutions in all iterations and runs of the algorithm in the case of TFS with standard mutation and TSF with directed mutation is statistically significant. Because we cannot assume a normal distribution of accuracies we use for this purpose two nonparametric tests: the sign test for the null hypothesis that the difference d has zero median and

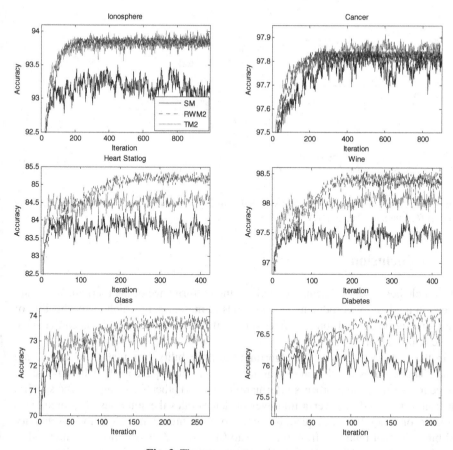

Fig. 3. The mean convergence curves

Wilcoxon rank sum test for equality of medians of two distributions. The 5% significance level is applied in this study. The test results confirmed that in all cases TFS with the directed mutation (RWM1, RWM2, TM1, TM2 and TM3) converges faster than TFS with standard mutation.

Fig. 4 demonstrates how for the Diabetes dataset the transformed values of the mutation indexes changed during the searching process. Decreasing values of w_{0-1} and in the same time increasing values of w_{1-0} for features 1, 3, 4 and 5 inform, that these features are irrelevant, because switching bits corresponding to them from 0 to 1 most frequently resulted in the deterioration of the classifier accuracy, and switching these bits from 1 to 0 resulted in increased accuracy. The $w_{1-0}(2)$ decreases very rapidly which means that the mutation of the second bit from 1 to 0 is unfavourable. As a result, this bit often takes value 1, so the mutation from 0 to 1 does not occur and $w_{0-1}(2)$ cannot adapt its value (straight line for $w_{0-1}(2)$ in Fig. 4(a)). A similar but opposite situation is for the 4-th feature.

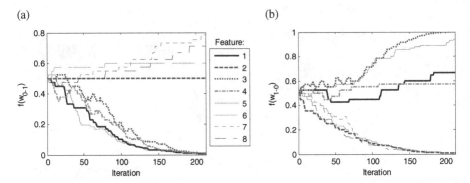

Fig. 4. The mutation index values transformed using logistic function (4) during the searching process for Diabetes data and RWM2

5   Conclusion

The article describes an attempt to improve the performance of the tournament feature selection method by introducing new methods of mutation, in which the probability of the bit mutation depends on the effectiveness of mutation of this bit in an earlier stage of the searching process.

In the early iterations of the algorithm the probability of mutation of all bits are equal. This ensures the thorough search of the solution space in the whole range. In the course of the search process information about whether the change of the specific bit from 0 to 1 and vice versa improves or deteriorates the solutions are stored. This information is used in subsequent iterations to adapt mutation probabilities of individual bits: bits that mutation from 0 to 1 (1 to 0) increased the solutions are mutated in this direction more often. As a result, the algorithm exploitation capabilities are enhanced: the neighborhood of the best solution is searched more intensively. This mechanism is effective when the value of the bit affects the evaluation of solutions in the same way, regardless of the context.

The results of this investigation have shown that the convergence of the algorithm was improved through the use of the roulette wheel and tournament mutations, but better classifier accuracy than using tournament feature selection with the standard mutation operator were not achieved.

References

1. Kohavi, R., John, G.H.: Wrappers for Feature Subset Selection. Artificial Intelligence 1-2, 273–324 (1997)
2. Dudek, G.: Artificial Immune System for Classification with Local Feature Selection. IEEE Transactions on Evolutionary Computation (in print)
3. Dudek, G.: Tournament Searching Method to Feature Selection Problem. In: Rutkowski, L., Scherer, R., Tadeusiewicz, R., Zadeh, L.A., Zurada, J.M. (eds.) ICAISC 2010. LNCS (LNAI), vol. 6114, pp. 437–444. Springer, Heidelberg (2010)
4. Cairns, J., Overbaugh, J., Miller, S.: The Origin of Mutants. Nature 335, 142–145 (1988)

Fully Controllable Ant Colony System
for Text Data Clustering

Piotr Dziwiński, Łukasz Bartczuk, and Janusz T. Starczewski

Department of Computer Engineering, Czestochowa University of Technology,
Al. Armii Krajowej 36, 42-200 Czestochowa, Poland
{piotr.dziwinski,lukasz.bartczuk,janusz.starczewski}@kik.pcz.pl

Abstract. The paper presents a new Fully Controllable Ant Colony
Algorithm (FCACA) for the clustering of the text documents in vector
space. The proposed new FCACA is a modified version of the Lumer and
Faieta Ant Colony Algorithm (LF-ACA). The algorithm introduced new
version of the basic heuristic decision function significantly improves the
convergence and greater control over the process of the grouping data.
The proposed solution was shown in a text example proving efficiency of
the proposed solution in comparison with other grouping algorithms.

1 Introduction

Ant Colony Optimization (ACO) was introduced in 1990 by M. Dorigo [1] as
a novel inspired be nature metaheuristic for solution of the hard Combinatorial Optimization (CO) problem. For many years it was used for different CO
where enough good results were obtained in reasonable time. Ants randomly
search the food exploring the area around their nest. When ants find a food
resource, it deposits pheromone trail on the ground in the return trip. Quantity
of the pheromone deposited depends on the quantity and quality of the found
food. Deposited pheromone guides other individuals of the colony to the food
resource [1]. The form of the indirect communication via pheromone trails between all ants enables them to find the shortest path between the nest and food
resources of the best quality and quantity. This characteristic behavior of the
real ant was exploited in artificial ant colonies in order to solve CO problems
such as travelling salesman problem (TSP) [2, 3, 4, 5], asymmetric TSP, quadric
assignment problem (QAP) [6], task assignment problem [7], time tabling problem [8, 9]. Other interesting behavior is based on cluster dead ants in the nest
in so-called cemeteries to clean up them. Similar sorting behaviour also was observed in the clustering of the larvae. Ants placed smaller larvae near the center,
larger ones towards the edge of the cluster. Similar artificial ants randomly walk
around, pick up and drop information objects based on local information only
in order to group them in the clusters. Lumer and Faieta in [10] proposed LF
algorithm to solve clustering problem, later it was applied to clustering hard
multidimensional text data [11].

Despite of a significant development of methods for natural language processing, the main way to represent textual document remains Vector Space Model

L. Rutkowski et al. (Eds.): SIDE 2012 and EC 2012, LNCS 7269, pp. 199–205, 2012.
© Springer-Verlag Berlin Heidelberg 2012

(VSM). Systems using VSM are called vector space information retrieval system originated by Gerard Salton [12,13], developed by many authors and used today. The documents set it is represented by matrix $\mathbf{V}$ of the real crisp values v_{ij} determining the degree of the connection between each keyword k_i and document d_j. Matrix values are determine using one of the terms weighting methods in documents [14,15,16,17,18]. The main problem of this type of representation is the size of the space despite of the elimination of the irrelevant terms [17,18,19].

Even for small number of documents it takes large sizes. Moreover, the individual vectors representing the text documents contain values different from zero only in a few positions - there are so called sparse vectors. High dimensionality significantly hinders the use of popular classification methods such as Hard C-means (HCM), Fuzzy C-Means (FCM), [20,21] or Classification Systems (CS) building decision rules based on sample data [22,23,24,25].

2   LF Ant Colony Algorithm

First LF Ant Colony Algorithm (LF-ACA) for clustering task was proposed in [10]. LF-ACA is based on behaviour of some ants species - cluster dead ants in the nest or sorting larvae. Artificial ants similarly randomly walk on the grid pick up and drop information objects based on local information only in order to group them in the clusters. First, all information data and ants are placed randomly on the two dimensional grid. Secondly, ants can walk through the grid by moving to the neighbouring cells. If ant moves with the data item and the cell is empty, they drop the data with probability P_{drop}, otherwise, if ant moves empty and the cell contain the data item, they pickup the data with probability P_{pickup}.

$$P_{pickup}(i) = \left(\frac{k_1}{k_1 + f(i)} \right)^2, \quad P_{drop}(i) = \begin{cases} 2 \cdot f(i) & \text{if } f(i) < k_2 \\ 1 & \text{otherwise} \end{cases} \tag{1}$$

$$f(i) = \max \left(0, \frac{1}{s^2} \sum_{j \in N(j)} \left(1 - \frac{d(i,j)}{\alpha} \right) \right) \tag{2}$$

The values of the probability P_{pickup} and P_{drop} are based on the neighbourhood function $f(i)$. Their value depends on the similarity between the data item i and its surrounding data items in neighbourhood $N(i)$ of radius s. The s parameter influences on the quality of the obtained clusters. By changing parameter α, algorithm can be adopted to the input field. Function $d(i,j)$ is specific distance measure between information objects. If k_1 takes small values, the probability P_{pickup} value decreases rapidly with decreasing value of similarity function. The parameter k_2 is threshold value for neighborhood function $f(i)$. Above k_2 value, function $f(i)$ has no effect on P_{drop} probability - sufficient similar objects are not distinguished, which affects the quality of the obtained clusters, especially for hard multidimensional data. Main drawback of the LF-ACA is slow convergence to optimal solution - algorithm requires approximately 10^6 iterations, more clusters are formed that are in the data set, some modifications are necessary.

A first real application consisting of text document clustering is presented in [26]. In the paper [11] authors propose some modification LF-ACA using cosine similarity function normalized by the length of the document vectors.

In the paper [27] authors summarize proposed modification of the ant algorithm. Some ants are able to move over several grid units forming coarse clusters, other ants moves more slowly, they should place the information objects more precisely. Each ant has short term memory, remembering the location of the formed clusters, so the ants do not moves randomly, just chooses the best location on the basis of memory. Adaptive Time-dependent Transporter Ants (ATTA) has been proposed in [28]. In ATTA radius s is modified during the algorithm from small values - perception ability of the ants are smaller - more different objects form clusters, to bigger values - perception ability of the ants are bigger - clusters are more optimal. The base heuristic functions P_{drop}, P_{pickup} (1) and $f(i)$ (2) were modified to (3) and (4) for speed up process respectively, $f(i) \in [0, 1]$.

$$P_{pickup}(i) = \begin{cases} 1 & \text{if } f(i) \leq 1 \\ \frac{1}{f(i)^2} & \text{otherwise} \end{cases}, \quad P_{drop}(i) = \begin{cases} 1 & \text{if } f(i) \geq 1 \\ f(i)^4 & \text{otherwise} \end{cases} \quad (3)$$

$$f(i) = \begin{cases} \max\left(0, \frac{1}{s^2} \sum_{j \in N(j)} \left(1 - \frac{d(i,j)}{\alpha}\right)\right) & \text{if } \forall j \left(1 - \frac{d(i,j)}{\alpha}\right) > 0 \\ 0 & \text{otherwise} \end{cases} \quad (4)$$

The new neighborhood function $f(i)$ (4) prevents objects from remaining in areas, where no clusters are formed - when there is at least a distant object.

Main drawback of the ATTA algorithm has less influence on the distinguishing grouping objects by parameters. Firstly, function domain $f(i)$ is interval $[0, 1]$, thus function $P_{pickup}(i)$ always adopts value 1. Ants move on the grid always pick up random objects from the grid. Only α parameter influences on the ability of the distinguishing different objects. The shape of the function is constant, we can not influence on the ability of each artificial ant to distinguish more similar objects.

3   Fully Controllable Ant Colony Algorithm

In this section we propose new Fully Controllable Ant Colony Algorithm (FCACA) with new version of the function $P_{pickup}(i)$ and $P_{drop}(i)$ (5), which ensures a rapid improvement of convergence of the algorithm and providing the full capabilities of the artificial ants to sensitivity control on the value of the similarity function $f(i)$, for which classify the objects into different groups.

$$P_{pickup} = (1 - f(i))^{\gamma_p}, \quad P_{drop} = f(i)^{1/\gamma_d} \quad (5)$$

A parameter $\gamma_p \in [0, 1)$ in function $P_{pickup}(i)$ influences on the level of the destruction of the created clusters. For $\gamma_p = 0$, ants randomly pick up information objects, large values of γ_p, increases the likelihood of picking up similar objects - following destruction of clusters. In order to reduce the destruction of the clusters, the γ_p value should be reduced to a value close to zero.

A parameter $\gamma_d \in (0, 10)$ in function $P_{drop}(i)$ controls the ability of the artificial ants to distinguish similar objects during the formation of the clusters. For small values of the γ_d artificial ants are more sensitive to small changes in the similarity function $f(i)$ for values closer to one. Parameter γ_d should be reduced in the case of formation too small number of clusters of the information objects.

Similarity function $f(i)$ also requires modification - the parameter δ is introduced modifying function depending on the threshold of the likelihood of the σ - the function $f^*(i)$ is obtained. If $\sigma \leq 0.5$ then, the function $f^*(i)$ is more likely do determine arithmetic mean of the similarities of the information objects, otherwise it is more likely do determine density of the objects in some area s - the number of the objects is more important than the similarity between them. Parameter η is a random value form 0 to 1. Good results are obtained for $\sigma = 0.8$, especially in early stages, rapid speeding up of a grouping process is observed.

$$f^*(i) = \begin{cases} \delta \cdot \sum_{j \in N(i)} \left(1 - \frac{d(i,j)}{\alpha}\right) & \text{if } \forall j \left(\frac{d(i,j)}{\alpha}\right) \leq 1 \\ 0 & \text{otherwise} \end{cases} \tag{6}$$

$$\delta = \begin{cases} \frac{1}{s^2} & \text{if } \eta \leq \sigma \\ \frac{1}{|N(j)|} & \text{otherwise} \end{cases} \tag{7}$$

In addition, each artificial ants are equipped with a short term memory, such as [28], in which recently visited location where the information objects are dropped is remembered. This allows to compare carried objects with those in memory instead of moving in random direction additionally it speeding up the convergence of the algorithm.

In order to obtain better classification results, HCM algorithm used in time work of the artificial ants was adopted. Each ant moving on the grid if puts information object near other objects, create a cluster with center c. Another ant placing an other objects in the neighbourhood, updates this center. Artificial ants move on the grid compare picked up object not with there objects in some area $N(i)$, but with the created center, function $f^{HCM}(i)$ (8). Each ones represents objects in their neighbourhood.

Certain influence in the area $N(i)$ the objects is still required in order to achieve consistency of the clusters. This had been obtained by using weight parameter ρ (9).

$$f^{HCM}(i) = \begin{cases} \delta \cdot \left(1 - \frac{d(i,C(i))}{\alpha}\right) \cdot \min\left(|C(i)|, s^2\right) & \text{if } \frac{d(i,C(i))}{\alpha} \leq 1 \\ 0 & \text{otherwise} \end{cases} \tag{8}$$

where: C(i) - center for placed object, if center does not exist, then it is created, $|C(i)|$ - number of the objects which are added to the center, s^2 - maximal number of the objects visible by the ants.

$$f(i) = f^*(i) \cdot \rho + f^{HCM}(i) \cdot (1 - \rho) \tag{9}$$

$$c^+ = \frac{c \cdot N + i}{N + 1}, \quad c^- = \frac{c \cdot N - i}{N - 1} \tag{10}$$

where: c - old value for the center, N - number of the objects added to the center, i - information object.

Artificial ants placing the object simple update center using c^+, if pick up the object, update the center using c^- (10).

4   Simulation

The FCACA for clustering of the hard multidimensional data firstly, it was tested for a iris dataset [29], secondly in two text data set d2 [30] and d3 [31]. The document set are parsed, stemmed and weighted by using $TFIDF$ weight [14, 17, 18] normalized with cosine normalization. Obtained vectors firstly were clustered in using FCM with a known number of classes, secondly with LF-ACA and FCACA with not known number of them. Obtained results are shown in table 1 and table 2. The experiments are performed 20 times for all data from d1 and d2 dataset. In the case d2 and d3 dataset part of the dataset are used.

Table 1. The results obtained with different algorithms and data sets - part 1

Data set	NP	NI	NC	HCM	Max	F-M	FCM	Max	F-M
d1	150	4	3	0.64	0.73	0.76	0.87	0.88	0.88
d2	568	447	4	0.44	0.85	0.63	0.54	0.8	0.65
d3	300	135	3	0.34	0.45	0.45	0.33	0.39	0.46

NP - number of patterns, NI - number of input, NC - the actual number of classes, HCM - Hard c-means algorithm, Max - the maximum efficiency of the grouping algorithm, F-M - F-Measure uses ideas of precision and recall, FCM - Fuzzy C-means algorithm.

Table 2. The results obtained with different algorithms and data sets - part 2

Data set	LF-ACA	Max	F-M	NOC	NOI	FC-ACA-HCM	Max	F-M	NOC	NOI
d1	0.74	0.86	0.77	3.2	$14.5 \cdot 10^6$	0.75	0.85	0.79	3	$0.7 \cdot 10^6$
d2	0.23	0.33	0.4	4	$71 * 10^6$	0.34	0.476	0.43	3.8	$0.82 * 10^6$
d3	0.34	0.4	0.48	3	$9.8 * 10^6$	0.34	0.41	0.48	3	$0.28 * 10^6$

LF-ACA - Lumer and Faieta Ant Colony Algorithm, NOC - obtained the average number of the classes, NOI - the number of the iterations.

5   Conclusion

The new proposed FC-ACA algorithm for grouping text data was obtain similar results with compare LF-ACA algorithm in very small number of the iterations. Moreover, proposed new algorithm obtain better results than HCM algorithm despite not known number of the clusters. Obtained results are comparable with the FCM algorithm. It is worth nothing that the complexity of the new algorithm grows very slowly depending on the number of the input data. Future research will focus on design neuro-fuzzy system [?, ?, ?] by making use the FC-ACA algorithm to determine fuzzy rules represent local groups created during the algorithm works. We expect much better clustering results overcomes FCM algorithm.

References

1. Deneubourg, J.L., Goss, S., Pasteels, J.M.: The self-organizing exploratory pattern of the argentine ant. Journal of Insect Behavior 3(159) (1990)
2. Colorni, A., Dorigo, M., Maniezzo, V.: Distributed optimization by ant colonies. In: Proceedings of ECAL 1991: European Conference on Artificial Life, pp. 134–142. Elsevier, Paris (1991)
3. Dorigo, M., Gambardella, L.M.: Ant colony system: A cooperative learning approach to the traveling salesman problem. IEEE Transactions on Evolutionary Computation 1(1), 53–66 (1997)
4. Cheng, C.-B., Mao, C.-P.: A modified ant colony system for solving the travelling salesman problem with time windows. Mathematical and Computer Modelling (46), 1225–1235 (2007)
5. Gambardella, L.M.: Ant-Q: A reinforcement learning approach to the traveling salesman problem. In: International Conference on Machine Learning, pp. 252–260 (1995)
6. Dorigo, M., Maniezzo, V., Colorni, A.: Ant system: Optimization by a colony of cooperating agents. IEEE Transactions on Systems, Man, and Cybernetics – Part B 26(1), 29–41 (1996)
7. Salman, A., Ahmad, I., Al-Madani, S.: Particle swarm optimization for task assignment problem. Microprocessors and Microsystems 26, 363–371 (2002)
8. Socha, K., Knowles, J., Sampels, M.: A Max-Min ant system for the university course timetabling problem. IRIDIA, Université Libre de Bruxelles, CP 194/6 (2003)
9. Socha, K.: A Max-Min ant system for international timetabling competition. IRIDIA, Université Libre de Bruxelles, CP 194/6 (March)
10. Lumer, E., Faieta, B.: Diversity and adaptation in populations of clustering ants. In: Proceedings of the 3rd International Conference on Simulation of Adaptive Behavior: From Animals to Animats, vol. 3 (1994)
11. Bin, W., Yi, Z., Shaohui, L., Zhongzhi, S.: CSIM: A document clustering algorithm based on swarm intelligence. In: Evolutionary Computation, CEC 2002, vol. (1), pp. 477–482 (2002)
12. Salton, G.: The smart retrieval system. Prentice-Hall, Englewood Cliffs (1971)
13. Salton, G., McG'ill, J.M.: Introduction to modern information retrieval (1983)
14. Baldi, P., Frasconi, P., Smyth, P.: Modeling the Internet and the Web, Probabilistic Methods and Algorithms. Wiley (2003)

15. Robertson, S.E.: The probability ranking principle in IR. Journal of the American Society for Information Science (33), 294–304 (1997)
16. Robertson, S.E., Maron, M.E., Cooper, W.S.: Probability of relevance: a unification of two competing models for document retrieval. Information Technology: Research and Development (1), 1–21 (1982)
17. Robertson, S.E.: Understanding inverse document frequency: on theoretical arguments for IDF. Journal of Documentation 60(5), 503–520 (2004)
18. Robertson, S.E.: A statistical interpretation of term specificity and its application in retrieval. Journal of Documentation 28(1), 11–21 (1972)
19. Hotho, A., Nurnberger, A., Paab, G.: A brief survey of text mining. LDV Forum - GLDV Journal for Computational Linguistics and Language Technology 20(19-62) (2005)
20. Cheng, T.W., Goldgof, D.B., Hall, L.O.: Fast fuzzy clustering. Fuzzy Sets and Systems (93), 49–56 (1998)
21. Yang, M.-S., Tsai, H.-S.: A gaussian kernel-based fuzzy c-means algorithm with a spatial bias correction. Pattern Recognition Letters (29), 1713–1725 (2008)
22. Cortez, E., Park, S., Kim, S.: The hybrid application of an inductive learning method and a neural network for intelligent information retrieval. Information Processing & Management 31(6), 789–813 (1995)
23. Lam, W., Ho, C.: Using a generalized instance set for automatic text categorization. In: SIGIR 1998: 21st ACM Int. Conf. on Research and Development in Information Retrieval, pp. 81–89 (1998)
24. Sebastiani, F.: Machine learning in automated text categorization. ACM Computing Surveys, 1–47 (2002)
25. Dziwiński, P., Rutkowska, D.: Algorithm for Generating Fuzzy Rules for WWW Document Classification. In: Rutkowski, L., Tadeusiewicz, R., Zadeh, L.A., Żurada, J.M. (eds.) ICAISC 2006. LNCS (LNAI), vol. 4029, pp. 1111–1119. Springer, Heidelberg (2006)
26. Handl, J., Meyer, B.: Improved Ant-Based Clustering and Sorting. In: Guervós, J.J.M., Adamidis, P.A., Beyer, H.-G., Fernández-Villacañas, J.-L., Schwefel, H.-P. (eds.) PPSN VII. LNCS, vol. 2439, pp. 913–923. Springer, Heidelberg (2002)
27. Martens, D., Baesens, B., Fawcett, T.: Editorial survey: swarm intelligence for data mining. 25th Anniversary Machine Learning 85(25), 1–42 (2011)
28. Handl, J., Meyer, B.: Ant-based clustering and topographic mapping. Artificial Life 12(1), 35–61 (2006)
29. Fisher, R.A.: (1936), http://archive.ics.uci.edu/ml/datasets/iris
30. Web-Kb, http://www.cs.cmu.edu/afs/cs.cmu.edu/project/theo-20/www/data/
31. Web-Kb, http://www-2.cs.cmu.edu/afs/cs.cmu.edu/project/theo-11/www/wwkb/

Creating Learning Sets for Control Systems Using an Evolutionary Method

Marcin Gabryel[1], Marcin Woźniak[2], and Robert K. Nowicki[1]

[1] Department of Computer Engineering, Czestochowa University of Technology,
Al. Armii Krajowej 36, 42-200 Czestochowa, Poland
[2] Institute of Mathematics, Silesian University of Technology,
ul. Kaszubska 23, 44-100 Gliwice, Poland
{Marcin.Gabryel,Robert.Nowicki}@kik.pcz.pl, Marcin.Wozniak@polsl.pl

Abstract. The acquisition of the knowledge which is useful for developing of artificial intelligence systems is still a problem. We usually ask experts, apply historical data or reap the results of mensuration from a real simulation of the object. In the paper we propose a new algorithm to generate a representative training set. The algorithm is based on analytical or discrete model of the object with applied the k–nn and genetic algorithms. In this paper it is presented the control case of the issue illustrated by well known truck backer–upper problem. The obtained training set can be used for training many AI systems such as neural networks, fuzzy and neuro–fuzzy architectures and k–nn systems.

Keywords: genetic algorithm, control system, training data acquisition.

1 Introduction

Very important phase in the process of designing solution based on artificial intelligence, e.g. artificial neural networks, fuzzy and neuro-fuzzy architectures [1], [2], [3], type-2 neuro-fuzzy systems [4], [5], as well as its ensambles [6] is the acquisition of knowledge. The expert, fuzzy, neuro-fuzzy, rough systems and it's hybrids [7], [8] can apply the knowledge that come from human experts. In many projects this is a main source which determines the prototypes of rules. However, usually it is insufficient. These systems require also the other type of knowledge - the set of examples of proper operation of the system. This type of knowledge is necessary for tuning and evaluating the solution. In the case of developing neural networks and often even neuro-fuzzy architectures the set of examples, i.e. training set, is the one and only form of knowledge used both for training and evaluating [9], [10]. Moreover, the set of examples can be used to obtain other forms of knowledge including rules [11], [12], [13], [14], [15], [16]. As we see the set of examples is quite versatile knowledge form. The common practice in training and evaluating new AI systems is to use available to the public sets - benchmarks [17]. Such proceedings are obviously unsuitable in a real problem. During the building of medical diagnostic system the source of the case is historical diagnosis of real patients. During the development of the control

L. Rutkowski et al. (Eds.): SIDE 2012 and EC 2012, LNCS 7269, pp. 206–213, 2012.

or diagnostic system the samples come from measurement of the real objects or from model simulation. When we neglect the cost of first method and problem with imperfection of model in a second one, we have still two problems. The first one is poor representativity of obtained set. The second one is more serious. To proceed the work or simulation, in one of structures depicted in Fig. 1 or 2, we have to know how to control the object or detect the threat of damage. We can use the past controller or human operator. The training set of Truck backer–upper control problem [18], [19] (see Section 2) used in many experiments and publications comes from registration the trajectories when the truck was being controlled by the driver.

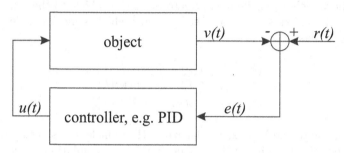

Fig. 1. Classical control system

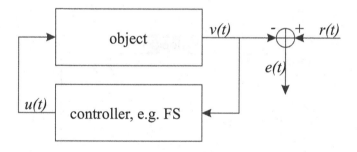

Fig. 2. AI control system

In the next part of the paper we will present the new method to generate a representative training set without the proper knowledge about control procedure. The algorithm is based on an analytical or discrete model of object with applied the k–nn [20] and genetic algorithms.

2 Truck Backer–Upper Control Problem

The problem of truck parking has been proposed and used as an example issue of non-linear control of the object by Nguyen and Widrow [18] and also used by Kong'a, Kosko [19]. It has become quite popular in experiments of control systems.

Truck goes to the back of a constant speed, and its goal is to reach the ramp. The parameter controlling the steering angle θ. State of the vehicle in the parking determine four parameters: coordinates x and y – determine the location of the parking lot, ϕ – angle to the axis Y of the vehicle, θ – turn the wheels of the vehicle. Truck moves backwards in the following steps in order to reach axis of the ramp (point $x = 0$, $\phi = 0$). Distance from the dock is ignored, since goal is assumed that any further driving in a straight line is not a problem. Problem posed in the article is to generate a learning set based on the model describing the motion of the vehicle in the following steps. The individual data within the learning set should be chosen in such a way that for a given position in which the vehicle is, in the next step to bring the vehicle to the ramp turning the wheels. The next steps of the simulation (vehicle's motions) describe the following formulas:

$$
\begin{aligned}
x(k + 1) &= x(k) + \delta t v \cos\left(\phi(k)\right), \\
y(k + 1) &= y(k) + \delta t v \sin\left(\phi(k)\right), \\
\phi(k + 1) &= \phi(k) + \frac{\delta t v \sin(\theta(k))}{L},
\end{aligned} \tag{1}
$$

where ϕ – angle to the Y axis, L – length of the vehicle, θ – steering angle, v – vehicle speed, δt – time interval, k – iteration in the simulation, (x, y) – vehicle position. The range of variation of the variables is as follows: $x \in (-150, 150)$, $y \in (0, 300)$, $\phi \in (-45, 45)$, $\theta \in (-180, 180)$. The problem is shown in Fig. 3.

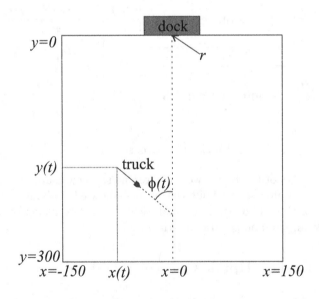

Fig. 3. Model of vehicle parking

3 k Nearest Neighbor Controller

To check the quality of the individual training sets we could build a Controller on each of them. This solution has one serious defect. Constructing the controller is time-consuming. The results can depend on the type of controller and above all it do not allow an individual assessment of the samples. Rating would apply to all drivers and so the entire training set.

In the proposed algorithm, there was proposed a special Controller, based on the algorithm of k–nn [20]. The driver will be the used knowledge contained in a single set of learning samples. The set is composed of M samples, each of them has two parts — the value in the input space $\mathbf{v}_i \in \mathbf{V}$ and the corresponding baseline values in the output space of $u_i \in \mathbf{U}$. The fitness function $f_i = F(X_i)$ is assigned to each sample (see Section 4).

The control system shown in Fig. 2 will be used in this case. State of the controlled object is described by the vector $\mathbf{v}(t) \in \mathbf{V}$, which is passed to the input driver. In the collection of samples used by the driver there is no sample for which $\mathbf{v}_i = \mathbf{v}(t)$ (omitting digitizing measurement and representation of samples, this situation is infinitely improbable). To design the control value $u(t)$ there will be used all samples contained in a set, each depending on the distance

$$d_i(t) = ||\mathbf{v}(t) - \mathbf{v}_i|| \tag{2}$$

and fitness function for each sample f_i according to

$$u(t) = \frac{\sum\limits_{i=1}^{M} g\left(d_i(t)\right) f_i u_i}{\sum\limits_{i=1}^{M} g\left(d_i(t)\right) f_i}, \tag{3}$$

where g is a not increasing function for positive values in the space of variations $d_i(t)$ defined by the formula (2).

We can also consider the inclusion $k < M$ the nearest $\mathbf{v}$ samples, however this requires a sort to the distance d_i. Controll value willbe calculated by the formula

$$u(t) = \frac{\sum\limits_{i:\, d_i \in \Omega_k(t)} f_i u_i}{\sum\limits_{i:\, d_i \in \Omega_k(t)} f_i}, \tag{4}$$

where $\Omega_k(t)$ is a set of k lowest values of $d_i(t)$. Hence the name of the proposed controller.

4   Testing Procedure and Results

Implemented system was tested using truck. Due to discrete nature of the model used in the model integrals were replaced by the sums of the successive steps of the simulation. Described problem will be solved using the evolutionary strategy

(μ, λ) (see [21], [22]). It is well known that evolution strategies are distinguished by self-adaptation of additional strategy parameters, which enable them to adapt the evolutionary optimization process to the structure of the fitness [23]. It is assumed that the chromosome of an individual is formed by a pair of real-valued vectors (X, σ). The strategy vector σ is a subject to a random mutation according to the formula

$$\sigma'_i = \sigma_i \cdot e^{\tau' \cdot N(0,1) + \tau \cdot N(0,1)}, \tag{5}$$

where $\tau' = \frac{1}{\sqrt{2L}}, \tau = \frac{1}{\sqrt{2\sqrt{L}}}, i = 1, \ldots, L$ and L is the length of the chromosome. The mutation in the algorithm is based on the formula

$$X'_i = X_i + \sigma'_i \cdot N_i(0,1), \tag{6}$$

replaces the parent X' with the descendant X. The standard evolution strategy based on mutation is extended by using of a uniform recombination operator [21] . In a single chromosome is encoded $M = 50$ possible samples (triplets of numbers (X, ϕ, θ)). The length of the chromosome is therefore $L = 3M = 150$. The proposed algorithm uses an evolutionary algorithm in addition to the calculation algorithm of the additional k-nearest neighbor algorithm (k–nn) [20]. The algorithm consists of several steps:

1. Initialize the algorithm – Enter the number of steps N.
2. For $k = 1, \ldots, N$, repeat steps 3-6.
3. Random selection of the initial position of truck:
   (a) $x_k = N(0,1) \cdot (x_{max} + x_{min}) + x_{min}$.
   (b) $\phi_k = N(0,1) \cdot (\phi_{max} + \phi_{min}) + \phi_{min}$.
4. Initiation of an evolutionary strategy (μ, λ).
   (a) Determination of parameters of an evolutionary strategy.
   (b) Random the vectors X_j of initial population for $j = 1, \ldots, \mu, i = 1, \ldots, M$.
      i. $X_{j, i \cdot 3} = N(0,1) \cdot (x_{max} + x_{min}) + x_{min}$.
      ii. $X_{j, i \cdot 3+1} = N(0,1) \cdot (\phi_{max} + \phi_{min}) + \phi_{min}$.
      iii. $X_{j, i \cdot 3+2} = N(0,1) \cdot (\theta_{max} + \theta_{min}) + \theta_{min}$.
5. Commissioning strategy (μ, λ) for 100 generations of evolution and the calculation of fitness function according to algorithm:
   (a) $F(X_j) = 0$.
   (b) Perform a full simulation of motion for the point (x_k, ϕ_k):
      i. $t = 0$.
      ii. Find the turning angle θ of wheels for your vehicle from all samples using the algorithm k–nn.
      iii. Move the vehicle to a new position $x(t + 1), y(t + 1)$ according to equations (1), $t = t + 1$.
      iv. $F(X_j) = F(X_j) + x(t) + \phi(t)$ (see Fig. 4).
      v. Finish the simulation of T steps if the vehicle approaches the ramp, otherwise go to step ii.
6. The introduction of all the samples with the winning chromosome which participated in the k–nn algorithm and adding them to the learning set Ω.

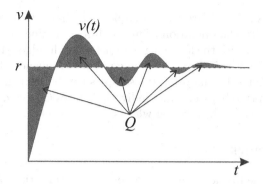

Fig. 4. Method of fitness function calculate

The algorithm uses the following designations: N – the number of subjects of the vehicle states, $x_{max}, x_{min}, \phi_{max}, \phi_{min}, \theta_{max}, \theta_{min}$ – maximum and minimum values are defined in Section 2, $N(0,1)$ – random number generated from the range $(0,1)$, M – number of samples encoded in the chromosome, t – iteration in the simulation, $F(X_j)$ – value of fitness function for the j-th chromosome.

Generated samples are collections of three numbers (x, ϕ, θ), where for input data x and ϕ is adjusted steering angle θ to make the vehicle closer to the ramp in the next move. Algorithm in the steps satisfies the conditions $x = 0$, $y = 0$ and $\theta = 0$. To simplify the operations it is assumed that the y position of the truck will not be taken into account.

The idea behind the algorithm is to generate many of the initial states of the model, and then evolutionary selection of parameters affecting its performance taking into account his current state. After finishing the simulation the

Table 1. The results obtained in the algorithm

No.	x	ϕ	θ	No.	x	ϕ	θ
1	-98.19	-14.16	60.00	16	26.36	66.86	-5.37
2	-76.53	-57.65	-3.38	17	31.28	15.75	19.96
3	-53.56	-15.10	56.88	18	37.56	48.22	0.03
4	-36.71	-34.93	60.00	19	39.83	54.27	2.79
5	-33.48	7.49	60.00	20	40.56	51.23	5.63
6	-30.20	-2.35	36.72	21	45.28	61.24	-20.88
7	-16.42	48.89	0.33	22	49.29	39.68	-38.75
8	-16.35	34.85	29.16	23	50.51	61.57	-41.48
9	-9.61	32.19	-12.92	24	57.68	24.44	-2.31
10	-9.51	81.89	-16.01	25	57.69	30.45	-60.00
11	-6.11	41.96	-5.69	26	73.51	117.22	-1.39
12	-2.96	118.15	-4.17	27	79.76	110.37	-10.74
13	-1.07	33.32	-9.31	28	90.79	31.61	-2.13
14	3.43	95.29	-4.33	29	98.52	57.67	-19.50
15	4.09	7.98	-21.92	30	105.12	-43.77	-60.00

best chromosomes selected are those samples that have been generated by the algorithm k–nn with the operation of fitness function. The algorithm has been implemented in Java with the following parameters of the algorithm: $N = 10, \mu = 10, \lambda = 50, M = 50, k = 5, T = 500$. The generated sequence of learning states can be found in Table 1. Analyzing the samples can be seen that the generated sequence is appropriately diverse and individual states (X, ϕ) corresponds to the appropriate response to the steering wheel θ.

5 Final Remarks

The article proposed a new method to generate a collection of representative samples, which can be used in the preparation of the target driver based on various methods of artificial intelligence, but also other, using the knowledge in the form of examples [24]. This method can be useful when we have a model of controlled object, and we have no knowledge of it's proper control. Conducted experiments confirm it's usefulness. An important restriction only need to carry out a large number of simulation control process to determine the assessment of individual sets of samples and the same samples. It is therefore time-consuming procedure. Further work should therefore be carried out in the direction of reducing time-consuming solution, eg. by using some knowledge prior to generating the initial population.

References

1. Rutkowska, D., Nowicki, R.K.: Implication-based neuro–fuzzy architectures. International Journal of Applied Mathematics and Computer Science 10(4), 675–701 (2000)
2. Rutkowski, L., Cpałka, K.: A general approach to neuro - fuzzy systems. In: Proceedings of the 10th IEEE International Conference on Fuzzy Systems, December 2-5, vol. 3, pp. 1428–1431 (2001)
3. Rutkowski, L., Cpałka, K.: A neuro-fuzzy controller with a compromise fuzzy reasoning. Control and Cybernetics 31(2), 297–308 (2002)
4. Starczewski, J., Rutkowski, L.: Interval type 2 neuro-fuzzy systems based on interval consequents. In: Rutkowski, L., Kacprzyk, J. (eds.) Neural Networks and Soft Computing, pp. 570–577. Physica-Verlag, Springer-Verlag Company, Heidelberg, New York (2003)
5. Starczewski, J.T., Rutkowski, L.: Connectionist Structures of Type 2 Fuzzy Inference Systems. In: Wyrzykowski, R., Dongarra, J., Paprzycki, M., Waśniewski, J. (eds.) PPAM 2001. LNCS, vol. 2328, pp. 634–642. Springer, Heidelberg (2002)
6. Korytkowski, M., Rutkowski, L., Scherer, R.: From Ensemble of Fuzzy Classifiers to Single Fuzzy Rule Base Classifier. In: Rutkowski, L., Tadeusiewicz, R., Zadeh, L.A., Zurada, J.M. (eds.) ICAISC 2008. LNCS (LNAI), vol. 5097, pp. 265–272. Springer, Heidelberg (2008)
7. Nowicki, R.: Rough–neuro–fuzzy structures for classification with missing data. IEEE Trans. on Systems, Man, and Cybernetics—Part B: Cybernetics 39 (2009)
8. Nowicki, R.: On classification with missing data using rough-neuro-fuzzy systems. International Journal of Applied Mathematics and Computer Science 20(1), 55–67 (2010)

9. Scherer, R.: Boosting Ensemble of Relational Neuro-fuzzy Systems. In: Rutkowski, L., Tadeusiewicz, R., Zadeh, L.A., Żurada, J.M. (eds.) ICAISC 2006. LNCS (LNAI), vol. 4029, pp. 306–313. Springer, Heidelberg (2006)
10. Korytkowski, M., Scherer, R., Rutkowski, L.: On combining backpropagation with boosting. In: 2006 International Joint Conference on Neural Networks, Vancouver, BC, Canada, pp. 1274–1277 (2006)
11. Wang, L.X.: Adaptive Fuzzy Systems and Control. PTR Prentice Hall, Englewood Cliffs (1994)
12. Wang, L.X., Mendel, J.M.: Generating fuzzy rules by learning from examples. IEEE Transactions on Systems, Man, and Cybernetics 22(6), 1414–1427 (1992)
13. Grzymala-Busse, J.W.: LERS — a system for learning from examples based on rough sets. In: Sowiski, R. (ed.) Intelligent Decision Support: Handbook of Applications and Advences of the Rough Sets Theory, pp. 3–18. Kluwer, Dordrecht (1992)
14. Grzymala-Busse, J.W.: An overview of the LERS1 learning systems. In: Proceedings of the 2nd International Conference on Industrial and Engineering Applications of Artificial Intelligence and Expert Systems, pp. 838–844 (1989)
15. Nozaki, K., Ishibuchi, H., Tanaka, H.: A simple but powerful heuristic method for generating fuzzy rules from numerical data. Fuzzy Sets and Systems 86, 251–270 (1997)
16. Sugeno, M., Yasukawa, T.: A fuzzy-logic-based approach to qualitative modeling. IEEE Transactions on Fuzzy Systems 1(1), 7–31 (1993)
17. Mertz, C.J., Murphy, P.M.: UCI respository of machine learning databases, http://www.ics.uci.edu/pub/machine-learning-databases
18. Nguyen, D., Widrow, B.: The truck backer-upper: An example of self-learning in neural network. IEEE Control Systems Magazine 10(3), 18–23 (1990)
19. Kong, S.G., Kosko, B.: Comparison of fuzzy and neural truck backer upper control system. In: Proceedings of IJCNN 1990, vol. 3, pp. 349–358 (1990)
20. Cover, T., Hart, P.: Nearest neighbor pattern classification. IEEE Transactions on Information Theory 13(1), 21–27 (1967)
21. Michalewicz, Z.: Genetic Algorithms + Data Structures = Evolution Programs. Springer, Heidelberg (1998)
22. Eiben, A.E.: Introduction to Evolutionary Computing. Springer, Heidelberg (2003)
23. Back, T.: Evolutionary Algorithms in Theory and Practice. Oxford University Press, Oxford (1996)
24. Scherer, R.: Neuro-fuzzy Systems with Relation Matrix. In: Rutkowski, L., Scherer, R., Tadeusiewicz, R., Zadeh, L.A., Zurada, J.M. (eds.) ICAISC 2010. LNCS (LNAI), vol. 6113, pp. 210–215. Springer, Heidelberg (2010)

Random State Genetic Algorithm

Louis Gacôgne[1,2]

[1] LIP6 - Université Paris VI 2 Place Jussieu 75251 Paris 5
Louis.Gacogne@lip6.fr
[2] ENSIIE 1 Square de la Résistance 91025 Evry
gacogne@ensiie.fr

Abstract. Following earlier results, the purpose of this paper is to show a new evolutionary algorithm whose parameters are moving in ranges defined by experiments. That is to say, no parameters must be fixed at the beginning of the course of generations. Comparing the performance of two methods, we arrive to the conclusion that the random often is a better way.

Keywords: Evolutionary algorithms, Optimization.

1   Introduction

In the field of evolutionary computation, one strategy called steady-state genetic algorithm (SSGA) takes some distance with the biological mechanisms which inspired. Since the canonical genetic algorithm (GA) [1, 2, 3], many ways of research intend to accelerate evolution in order to optimization problems with elitist heuristics [4] or small population [5, 6]. It is well known that a too homogeneous population must be avoided. Diversity is thought to be important for evolutionary computation. A lot of different ideas have been proposed (clearing, changing the fitness, parallel evolution…) and in previous studies [7, 8, 9], according to the criteria of the average number of fitness calls to reach a solution, we observed, as always, better results with small populations, according to a methodical way of replacement.

Now, our aim is to avoid fixed parameters for this algorithm. A first idea was to move them with fuzzy rules [10]. But those parameters must be in a range and also must be changed following fuzzy rules. The question is how to find the "best" fuzzy rules ?

If a population is forced to optimize a function f, at each generation, let a be the population amplitude $f(i_\mu) - f(i_1)$ as a measure of the phenotype diversity inside the population. So, a natural way to express what must be done could be :

If the amplitude a is strong or increasing, then we can focus on exploitation with a weak elimination.

Conversely, if amplitude a is weak (a too homogeneous population on the contrary), then exploration must increase, strong elimination (weak π, see further) and a strong replacement threshold τ, means more exploration.

So, we want actually make a comparison between SSGA for small values and a new algorithm RSGA which randomly takes its parameters into the range seen as the best interval for SSGA.

L. Rutkowski et al. (Eds.): SIDE 2012 and EC 2012, LNCS 7269, pp. 214–221, 2012.
© Springer-Verlag Berlin Heidelberg 2012

2   The Steady State Genetic Algorithm SSGA(μ, τ, π)

In evolutionary computation, a very simple way is to go on exploration searching in the same time as exploitation of real-time results of optimum. Thus, each generation, in the population of μ individuals, the τ best children remove the τ worst parents under the condition $0 < \tau < \mu$ and an elimination is performed with a similarity threshold π.

In respect to search global minimum of a positive function f from $[a, b]^m$ to R, a population P is a set of μ individuals which are vectors of m components $x = (x_1, x_2, \dots, x_m)$ evaluated by $f(x)$.

In all the following : m is the dimension of space of research

ε is the threshold we want to reach to stop the run if we get $f(x) < \varepsilon$

$eval_{max}$ is the maximum number of evaluation of f to avoid infinite course

n_v = number of evaluation to reach $f(x) < \varepsilon$ (average of it on 100 runs)

The main criterion for comparison is the mean number n_v of calls of f to reach the goal. So the SSGA(μ, τ, π) will be :.

1) $t \leftarrow 0$, the initial population P_0 of μ random float-vector in $[0, 1]^m$ is built.

Each x of P_0 is evaluated by f (x), v_m is the best value of the μ individuals and $n_v \leftarrow \mu$

2) Loop while $v_m > \varepsilon$ and $n_v < eval_{max}$ do

Offspring: for $i = 1$ to μ do let $C_t(i) = op(P_t(i))$ where op is a genetic operator randomly chosen between mutation, any other unary operator, or a crossover with another random $P_t(j)$ (C_t is called the population offspring and P_t the parents)

Evaluations by f of the μ children and sorting of C_t,

Updating: let P_{t+1} be the sorted union of the best τ children in C_t and the best μ - τ parents of P_t.

Clearing: according to a similarity measure in the space of research, each time a pair of individual i, j with $f(i) < f(j)$ and $prox(i, j) > \pi$, then j is killed and removed by a new individual.

Sort of P_{t+1} according to f and incrementation $n_v \leftarrow n_v + \mu +$ (number of new individuals).

3) Return the number n_v of evaluations and the best individual with the best value v_m

Previous work showed that SSGA(μ, τ, π) is a very good optimization strategy with small population, and clearing with a similarity measure π for the genotypes is an easy method for maintenance of diversity. To obtain an experimental view of it, we tried to find the optimum on various problems according to different values of the parameters. For example, the well known Griewank function

$$F_G(x) = (1/4000)\sum_{1 \le i \le m} x_i^2 - \prod_{1 \le i \le m} cos(x_i/\sqrt{i}) + 1)$$

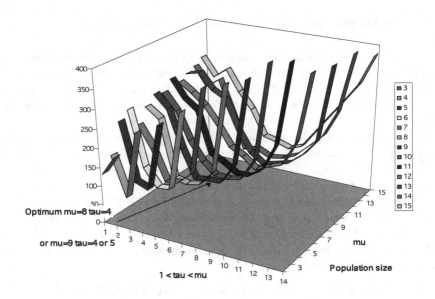

Fig. 1. Curves of the mean number of evaluations for the 30-dimension Griewank function according to μ and τ

The Griewank function in 30-dimension is here solved with (μ, τ) = (8, 4) or (9, 4) or (9, 5) but a lot of problems raise towards similar results, that is to say the shortest time to find the optimum is with a small population μ between 7 and 12 and a threshold τ around the third or half part of population.

Now, we use SSGA(100, 33, 66) which is a quite good experimental strategy, to search the best individuals (μ, τ, π). We shall give a score F to each of them as the total number of averaging calls of functions (f_1, f_2, ... , f_k) on k different functions to minimize, to reach their minima's.

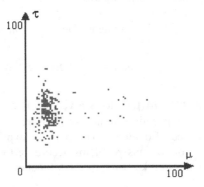

Fig. 2. Projections of an example of population of triples (μ, τ, π) after 50 generations (and 4500 evaluations of F)

For any evolutionary algorithm SSGA, let us define $\Phi\mu$, τ, $\pi(f)$, the random variable equal to the number (bounded for example by the parameter max = 100 000) of evaluations of a positive function f to reach $f < \varepsilon$ defined in a range $[a, b]^m$. Moreover, because of a quite large dispersion, we take $n = 100$ to average each function test f. Let now $(f_1, f_2, \ldots, f_k)$ be a sequence of functions and :

$$F(\mu, \tau, \pi) = (1/nk) \sum_{1 \cdot i \cdot k} \sum_{1 \cdot j \cdot n} \Phi\mu, \tau, \pi (f_i)$$

defined on $[1, 100]^3$ where $\Phi\mu$, τ, π is the number of evaluations given by SSGA(μ, τ, π). We use again $\mu = 100$ to have a sufficient visualization, $\tau = 33$ because one of the best empirical rate and $\pi = 66$ not too low to keep a compact swarm but still enough to get optimization. So, we make runs to minimize $\Phi_{100, 33, 66}$ (F) to get solutions (μ, τ, π).

For test functions we choose (f_1, f_2, f_2, f_4) Jong, Parabola or Rosenbrock, Rastrigin and Griewank functions on [-500, 500]^2 for a benchmark based on easy or difficult functions to optimize the triple (μ, τ, π).

Different combinations F, always provided after long runs of $\Phi_{100, 33, 66}$ (F), a population where μ is very small, between 3 and 12, a rate τ between 33% and 50% and π roughly around 33%. But for this last item we had often two sub-swarms as above with also π around 66% for a worse part of population.

A third observation is that many operators may be imagined according to the problem. The following operators are used to explore the neighborhood :

migration-0 : gives an entirely new individual (Monte-Carlo method, not only used to initialize the population, but also to replace double or similar individuals and moreover as an operator)
migration-1 : everything is replaced except the only first element of each component
migration-2 : a random half of the individual is replaced

mutation-1 : mutation for a randomly chosen digit in a component
mutation-2 : "small" mutation adding ±1 to one digit.

addition : a new digit is added at the end of one component

transposition : two digits are swapped

crossover-0 : uniform crossover with a random other parent [9]
crossover-1 : one site crossover inside the list of components
crossover-2 : two sites crossover
crossover-3 : crossover only with one the 10% best individuals ("coral-fish" idea inspired by the breeder genetic algorithm [10]

3   The Random Genetic Algorithm

As we showed that the averaging number of calls to f is the best for small populations, we tried to leave the parameters randomly picked in some ranges. So, the algorithm is :

1) $t \leftarrow 0$, $\mu \leftarrow$ *random in [2, 12]*

A population P_0 of μ random individuals is built and estimated with f.
The number of calls is $n_v \leftarrow \mu$

2) Loop while $v_m > \varepsilon$ and $n_v < eval_{max}$ do

    $\tau \leftarrow$ random($\mu/3$, $\mu/2$)

    $\pi \leftarrow$ random(10, 90)

    Offspring generation, evaluation and updating are the same as in SSGA(μ, τ, π),v_m is the best value of f

    $\mu \leftarrow$ random(2, 12)

    Clearing with the new size μ and incrementation of n_v.

3) Return the number n_v of evaluations and the best individual with the best value v_m

4   Results

4.1   Test on Rastrigin Function

Our first test is on the well known function :

$$f_R(x) = \Sigma_{i=1..m}[x_i^2 + 10 - 10\, cos(2\pi x_i)] / 100$$

We use for example, in the 3-dimensional Rastrigin's function, individuals could be 3*5 digits and we use a *decode* function to be in the space $[0, 1]^3$ and next in $[-30, 30]^3$ with the dilatation ϕ from $[0, 1]$ to $[a, b]$ defined by :

$$\phi(x) = a + x(b - a).$$

Thus in one dimension *decode* $(3, 4, 5, 6, 7) \rightarrow 0.34567$

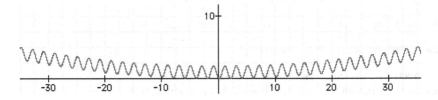

Fig. 3. The Rastrigin's function in one dimension

For this problem with $\varepsilon = 0.001$ we got 192 evaluations of f_R before discovery of minimum 0 by SSGA(9, 4, 75), and 156 evaluations by RSGA.
For $\varepsilon = 0.00001$, we got 702 evaluations by SSGA and 596 by RSGA.

4.2   The Gauss' Queens Problem

We can solve the famous Gauss' queens problem taking the function *gauss* equal to the number of couple of queens in catching positions on a chessboard, for instance : *queens* (4) → (2 4 1 3), *queens* (8) → (6 3 1 8 4 2 7 5), *queens* (9) → (4 1 7 9 2 6 8 3 5) or *queens* (7) → (3 1 6 2 5 7 4) :

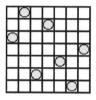

Fig. 4. Example of solution for the Gauss' queens problem in 7 dimension

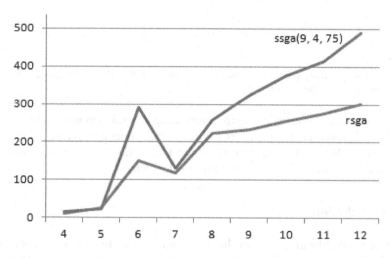

Fig. 5. Results of the average of evaluation number to reach the first solution in the Gauss' queens problem

4.3   The Royal Road Problem

In the royal road problem, for a list of 8*m binary digits, the function we want to minimize is the number of octets different of 0 [15]. This problem is very difficult because most of the genetic operators don't infer on the phenotype, that is to say do not move the fitness function.

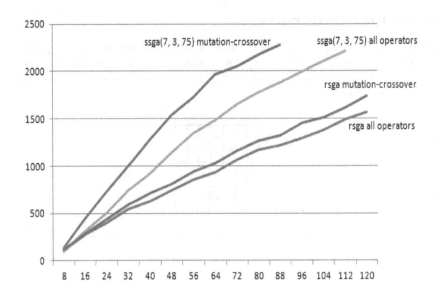

Fig. 6. For lists of binary digits from one to 15 octets, the figure shows the average of number of evaluation to reach the minimum 0

As seen before, we have an improvement using several operators instead of only mutation and crossover. We have better results if those operators are randomly picked in their family [8]. Let us say that if we use fuzzy rules to change the parameters μ, τ, π, results are not so good as it is with a random way.

5   Conclusion

Ideally we would like to have an evolutionary strategy able to optimize every problem especially difficult ones. There is no doubt that a small population, whose quite important part is removed at each generation, is a good way, moreover with a large family of operators.

But the size of the population may have some freedom to change. However, the population size has to be variable in a certain extent as well as the updating rate.

References

1. Goldberg, D.E.: Genetic algorithms in search, optimization and machine learning. Addison-Wesley (1989)
2. Holland, J.H.: Adaptation in natural and artificial system. University of Michigan Press, Ann Arbor (1975)
3. Schwefel, H.P.: Evolution and optimum seeking. Sixth Generation Computer Technology. Wiley (1995)

4. Bäck, T., Fogel, D.B., Schwefel, H.P.: Handbook of evolutionary computation. Oxford University Press (1997)
5. Oscar, M., Oscar, C., et al.: Human Evolutionary Model: A new approach to optimization. Information Science 177(10), 2075–2098 (2007)
6. Coello, C., Pulido, G.: A micro genetic algortihm for multiobjective optimization, Intrenal report Laboratorio National de Informatica Avanzada (2000)
7. Gacôgne, L.: Steady-state evolutionary algorithm with an operators family, EISCI Kosice, pp.173–182 (2002)
8. Gacôgne, L.: Methods to apply operators in a steady-state evolutionary algorithm. In: IPMU Conference, Paris (2006)
9. Gacôgne, L.: A very simple steady-state evolutionary algorithm. In: Mendel Conference, Brno (2008)
10. Gacôgne, L.: Fixed, random or fuzzy adaptive parameters in an evolutionary algorithm. In: SSCI, Paris (2011)
11. Michalewicz, Z.: Genetic algorithms + data structures= evolution programs. Springer, Heidelberg (1992)
12. Schierkamp-Vosen, D., Mühlenbein, H.: Predictive models for breeder genetic algorithm. Evol. Comp. 1, 25–49 (1993)
13. Sugeno, M.: An introductory survey of fuzzy control Information and Science 3, 59 (1985)
14. Whitley, D., Kauth, J.: Genitor: a different genetic algorithm. In: Proc. of Rocky Mountain Conf. on A.I, p. 118 (1988)
15. Mitchell, M., Forrest, S., Holland, J.H.: The royal road for genetic algorithm: fitness landscapes and GA performances. In: Varela, F.J., Bourgine, P., eds. (1992)

Accuracy vs. Interpretability
of Fuzzy Rule-Based Classifiers:
An Evolutionary Approach

Marian B. Gorzałczany and Filip Rudziński

Department of Electrical and Computer Engineering,
Kielce University of Technology,
Al. 1000-lecia P.P. 7, 25-314 Kielce, Poland
{m.b.gorzalczany,f.rudzinski}@tu.kielce.pl

Abstract. The paper presents a generalization of the Pittsburgh approach to learn fuzzy classification rules from data. The proposed approach allows us to obtain a fuzzy rule-based system with a predefined level of compromise between its accuracy and interpretability (transparency). The application of the proposed technique to design the fuzzy rule-based classifier for the well known benchmark data sets (*Dermatology* and *Wine*) available from the http://archive.ics.uci.edu/ml is presented. A comparative analysis with several alternative (fuzzy) rule-based classification techniques has also been carried out.

1 Introduction

Methods and algorithms for discovering "knowledge" from data sets play an important role in the intelligent decision support systems design not only in technical applications but also in medicine, economy, management, marketing and many others, see e.g. [5], [11], [12]. These techniques provide tools for revealing valid, useful and understandable structures, patterns, trends and decision mechanisms in data. One of the most commonly used structures for knowledge representation are fuzzy classification (or, decision) rules characterized by high readability and modularity. Fuzzy systems themselves, however, are neither capable of learning fuzzy rules from available data nor even tuning the parameters of fuzzy sets occurring in the fuzzy rules. In order to address this problem, various hybrid solutions - in particular, neuro-fuzzy systems (implementations of fuzzy rules in neural-network-like structures) - have been proposed (see e.g. [8], [13]). In most of them, however, the learning consists in tuning only the parameters of membership functions occurring in predefined, "initial' fuzzy rule bases by means of backpropagation-like algorithms that lead local optima of the assumed quality indices. Therefore, the optimal or sub-optimal solution of the problem of discovering fuzzy rule-based knowledge in data can be obtained by: a) the formulation of the considered problem as a rule-structure- and rule-parameter-optimization task, and b) the application of global search and optimization methods in complex spaces. In paper [9] by the same authors such a solution - based on modified

L. Rutkowski et al. (Eds.): SIDE 2012 and EC 2012, LNCS 7269, pp. 222–230, 2012.

Pittsburgh approach from the area of evolutionary computations - has been proposed. A broader perspective as far as evolutionary learning of fuzzy rule-based systems is concerned is presented e.g. in [6].

This paper presents a generalization of the solution of [9] allowing us to obtain from data a fuzzy rule-based system with a predefined level of compromise between, on the one hand, its accuracy and, on the other hand, its interpretability and transparency (measured by the number and complexity of fuzzy rules). The considered problem attracts the interest of many researchers, e.g. according to [7] "...Linguistic fuzzy modelling, developed by linguistic fuzzy rule-based systems, allows us to deal with the modelling of systems by building a linguistic model which could become interpretable by human beings. Linguistic fuzzy modelling comes with two contradictory requirements: interpretability and accuracy. In recent years the interest of researchers in obtaining more interpretable linguistic fuzzy models has grown...".

A conceptual illustration of the regulation of the accuracy-interpretability compromise level is shown in Fig. 1. Shifting a "slider" in Fig. 1 to the left, directs the learning process towards more accuracy-oriented fuzzy system, whereas shifting it to the right produces more interpretability-oriented fuzzy rule base. Such solutions may be useful in achieving different goals as far as decision support is concerned. First, some aspects of the fuzzy rule-based classifier design from data are discussed. Then, the mechanisms allowing us to regulate the learning process of fuzzy classification rules from data in order to achieve an assumed level of compromise between system's accuracy and interpretability is presented. In turn, the application of the proposed technique to the well known benchmark data sets (*Dermatology* and *Wine*) available from the http://archive.ics.uci.edu/ml is presented. These data sets have been selected due to their popularity to enable a broad comparative analysis with alternative methods of designing (fuzzy) rule-based classifiers. A comparison with selected alternative techniques has also been included in the paper.

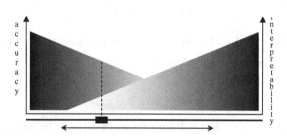

Fig. 1. An illustration of regulating the accuracy-interpretability compromise level

2 Some Aspects of Fuzzy Rule-Based Classifier Design

The proposed classification system has n inputs (attributes) $x_1, x_2, ..., x_n$ and an output in the form of a possibility distribution over the set $Y = \{y_1, y_2, ..., y_c\}$ of class labels. In general, each input attribute x_i (taking values from the set X_i)

may be described either by numerical values (e.g., pulse rate is equal to 80 beats per minute) or by linguistic terms (e.g., blood pressure is "high") represented by appropriate fuzzy sets.

Let $A' = \{A'_1, A'_2, ..., A'_n\}$ and $A'_i \in F(X_i)$, $i = 1, 2, ..., n$, where $F(X_i)$ is a family of all fuzzy sets defined on the universe X_i. Also, let $F_X = \{F(X_1), F(X_2), ..., F(X_n)\}$. $A' \in F_X$ is a general fuzzy-set-representation of the collection of input attributes. Each x_i is represented by a corresponding fuzzy set A'_i. In particular, when we deal with a numerical representation x'_i of x_i, the fuzzy set A'_i is reduced to a fuzzy singleton $A'_{i(sgl)}$ with $\mu_{A'_{i(sgl)}}(x'_i) = 1$ and 0 elsewhere. Moreover, let $B' \in F(Y) = F_Y$ be a fuzzy set representing a possibility distribution defined over the set Y of class labels. The possibility distribution assigns to each class y_j, $j = 1, 2, ..., c$ from the set Y a number from the interval $[0, 1]$, indicating the possibility that the object described by A' belongs to that class. In particular, when we deal with a non-fuzzy possibility distribution over Y, the fuzzy set B' is reduced to a fuzzy singleton $B'_{(sgl)}$ that indicates one class $y' \in Y$ only ($\mu_{B'_{(sgl)}}(y') = 1$ and 0 elsewhere).

The classifier is designed from the learning data that, in general, have the form of K input-output records:

$$L_1 = \{A'_k, B'_k\}_{k=1}^{K}. \tag{1}$$

In particular, when we deal with numerical, non-fuzzy representation $x'_k = (x'_{1k}, x'_{2k}, ..., x'_{nk}) \in X = X_1 \times X_2 \times ... \times X_n$ ($\times$ stands for Cartesian product of ordinary sets) of input attributes, expression (1) reduces to

$$L_2 = \{x'_k, B'_k\}_{k=1}^{K}. \tag{2}$$

Additionally, if we deal with a singleton-type possibility distribution $B'_{k(sgl)}$ in (2), formula (2) becomes equivalent to

$$L_3 = \{x'_k, y'_k\}_{k=1}^{K}. \tag{3}$$

Fuzzy classification rules that will be synthesized from the learning data L_1 (or, their special cases L_2 or L_3) by the proposed later in the paper genetic technique have the following form (for the case when all n input attributes are involved):

$$\text{IF } (x_1 \text{ is } A_{1r}) \text{ AND ... AND } (x_n \text{ is } A_{nr}) \text{ THEN } (B_{r(sgl)}), \tag{4}$$

where $A_{ir} \in F(X_i)$, $i = 1, 2, ..., n$ is one of the S-, M-, or L-type fuzzy sets (see below), and $B_{r(sgl)} \in F(Y)$ is the singleton possibility distribution; all in the r-th fuzzy rule, $r = 1, 2, ..., R$. As already mentioned, the input attributes are described by three types of fuzzy sets corresponding to verbal terms "*Small*" (S-type), "*Medium*" (M-type) and "*Large*" (L-type). Their membership functions are of the form: $\mu_{M_i}(x_i) = \exp[-0.5(x_i - c_{M_i})^2/\sigma_{M_i}^2]$, where $\sigma_{M_i} = \sigma_{ML_i}$ for $x_i \leq c_{M_i}$ and $\sigma_{M_i} = \sigma_{MR_i}$ elsewhere, $\mu_{S_i}(x_i) = \exp[-0.5(x_i - c_{S_i})^2/\sigma_{S_i}^2]$ only for $x_i \geq c_{S_i}$ and 1 elsewhere, and, analogously, $\mu_{L_i}(x_i) = \exp[-0.5(x_i - c_{L_i})^2/\sigma_{L_i}^2]$ for $x_i \leq c_{L_i}$ and 1 elsewhere (see Figs. 3 and 5 later in the paper); $\sigma_{S_i} > 0$, $\sigma_{M_i} > 0$, $\sigma_{L_i} > 0$, $i = 1, 2, ..., n$. In general, one S-type, one L-type and several M-type fuzzy sets can be considered for a given attribute x_i. It is worth stressing that a given verbal term for a given attribute is represented by the same fuzzy set in all rules in which it occurs.

Genetic learning of fuzzy classification rules from data requires an evaluation of particular individuals (fuzzy rule bases in Pittsburgh-based approach) in each generation. For this reason a formal representation of fuzzy rule base (4) as well as fuzzy inference scheme have to be employed. Both prevalent in the literature fuzzy reasoning schemes, that is, compositional rule of inference and similarity based reasoning with various definitions of fuzzy implications, t-norms and t-conorms (see e.g. [2]) can be implemented in our approach. In the case of most widely used Mamdani's model (with min-type t-norm, max-type t-conorm and min operator playing the role of fuzzy implication), one can obtain - for the input numerical data $x^0 = (x_1^0, x_2^0, ..., x_n^0)$ - a fuzzy response (possibility distribution B^0 represented by its membership function $\mu_{B^0}(y_j)$, $j = 1, 2, ..., c$) of the fuzzy classifier (4):

$$\mu_{B^0}(y_j) = \max_{r=1,2,...,R} \mu_{B_r^0}(y_j) = \max_{r=1,2,...,R} \min[\alpha_r, \mu_{B_r}(y_j)], \qquad (5)$$

where $\alpha_r = \min(\alpha_{1r}, \alpha_{2r}, ..., \alpha_{nr}) = \min[\mu_{A_{1r}}(x_1^0), \mu_{A_{2r}}(x_2^0), ..., \mu_{A_{nr}}(x_n^0)]$. α_r is the activation degree of the r-th fuzzy rule by the input numerical data x^0.

3 Genetic Learning of Fuzzy Classification Rules with Regulated Accuracy-Interpretability Compromise Level

The fitness function ff that plays an essential role in the "orientation" of genetic learning has been defined as follows:

$$ff = (1 - \alpha)ff_{ACU} + \alpha ff_{INT}, \qquad (6)$$

where $\alpha \in [0, 1)$ is the accuracy-interpretability coefficient (it regulates the level of the compromise between both aspects of the system design), whereas ff_{ACU} and ff_{INT} are components "responsible" for accuracy and interpretability, respectively, of the fuzzy rule base. In particular, the learning process can be directed to produce exclusively accuracy-oriented fuzzy classifier ($\alpha = 0$), exclusively interpretability-oriented one (α close to 1 but $\alpha \neq 1$), or the fuzzy classifier that fulfills an intermediate level of compromise between its accuracy and interpretability.

The accuracy component ff_{ACU} has the form:

$$\mathit{ff}_{ACU} = 1 - Q_{RMSE} = 1 - \sqrt{\frac{1}{Kc}\sum_{k=1}^{K}\sum_{j=1}^{c}[\mu_{B_k'}(y_j) - \mu_{B_k^o}(y_j)]^2}, \quad (7)$$

where Q_{RMSE} is the root-mean-squared-error cost function ($Q_{RMSE} \in [0,1]$), $\mu_{B_k'}(y_j)$ is the desired response of the fuzzy classifier for the k-th sample of the learning data L_1 (1) (or, L_2 (2)), and $\mu_{B_k^o}(y_j)$ is the actual response of the classifier (calculated according to (5)).

The interpretability component ff_{INT} has been defined as follows:

$$\mathit{ff}_{INT} = 1 - Q_{CPLX} = 1 - \frac{ACAR + NNR}{2}, \quad (8)$$

where Q_{CPLX} is the rule base complexity measure (smaller values of Q_{CPLX} correspond to lesser complexity; $Q_{CPLX} \in [0,1]$), $ACAR$ and NNR are the average complexity of all rules in the rule base and the normalized number of rules in the rule base, respectively. They are defined in the following way:

$$ACAR = \frac{1}{R}\sum_{r=1}^{R}\frac{NA_r}{n}, \qquad NNR = \frac{R - R_{min}}{R_{max} - R_{min}}, \quad (9)$$

where NA_r is the present number of antecedents in the r-th rule, $r = 1, 2, ..., R$, $NA_r \leq n$ (n is the number of all possible antecedents), R_{min} and R_{max} are the minimal and maximal numbers of rules collected in the rule base. R_{min} is equal to the number of classes unless determined differently by the user. R_{max} is equal to the number of all combinations of verbal terms for rule antecedents not exceeding the number K of records in the learning data L_1 (1) or L_2 unless the user assumes a smaller value.

In the course of the operation of the genetic algorithm - in the framework of the modified Pittsburgh approach proposed by the same authors in [9] - two separate entities: a rule base and a data base that represent a given fuzzy rule collection (an individual) are processed. An essential role is played by the proposed in [9] non-binary crossover and mutation operators. Due to a limited space for this publication these issues cannot be discussed here - see [9] for details.

4   Application to Selected Classification Problems

The application of the proposed technique to design the genetic fuzzy rule-based classifiers for various levels of the accuracy-interpretability compromise for two well known benchmark data sets (*Dermatology* and *Wine*) available from the http://archive.ics.uci.edu/ml will now be presented. The original data sets (366 records with 34 input attributes and 6 classes for *Dermatology* and 178 records with 13 input attributes and 3 classes for *Wine*) have been divided into the learning- and test-parts (244 and 122 as well as 119 and 59 records, respectively, randomly selected from the original data sets preserving the proportion of the class occurrence).

In all experiments, the genetic algorithm with population of 200 individuals and tournament selection method (with the number of individuals participating in the competition equal to 2) supported by elitist strategy as well as with crossover and mutation probabilities equal to 0.8 and 0.7, respectively, has been used.

As far as the *Dermatology* data set is concerned, Fig. 2 presents the plots of Q_{RMSE} as in (7) for the learning and test data as well the number R of fuzzy rules in the rule base versus the accuracy-interpretability coefficient α as in (6). Table 1 presents the fuzzy rule base of the interpretability-oriented classifier ($\alpha = 0.9$) whereas Fig. 3 shows examples of the membership functions of fuzzy sets representing selected verbal terms occurring in fuzzy rules of Table 1.

Fig. 4, Table 2 and Fig. 5 provide an analogous information for the *Wine* data set as that in Fig. 2, Table 1 and Fig. 3 for the *Dermatology* data.

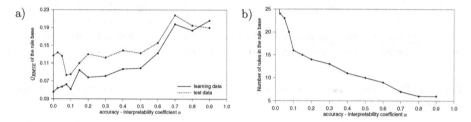

Fig. 2. Q_{RMSE} for the learning and test data as well the number R of fuzzy rules in the rule base versus the accuracy-interpretability coefficient α (*Dermatology* data set)

Table 1. Fuzzy rule base of the interpretability-oriented classifier (with $\alpha = 0.9$) for the *Dermatology* data set

No.	Fuzzy classification rules	Number of records activating the rule	
		learning data	test data
1	**IF** x_{20} *is* Medium3 **THEN** Class 1 (psoriasis)	75	36
2	**IF** x_5 *is* Small **AND** x_{28} *is* Large **THEN** Class 2 (seboreic dermatitis)	41	20
3	**IF** x_{33} *is* Large **THEN** Class 3 (lichen planus)	47	23
4	**IF** x_{26} *is* Medium2 **THEN** Class 4 (pityriasis rosea)	34	20
5	**IF** x_{15} *is* Large **THEN** Class 5 (cronic dermatitis)	36	18
6	**IF** x_{30} *is* Large **THEN** Class 6 (pityriasis rubra pilaris)	11	5
	Q_{RMSE} for the learning and test data:	0.19016	0.20608
	Number (and percentage) of correct decisions:	229 (93.8%)	115 (94.3%)

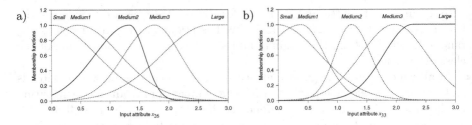

Fig. 3. The final membership functions of fuzzy sets occurring in fuzzy rules of Table 1 for input attributes x_{26} (a) and x_{33} (b) (*Dermatology* data set)

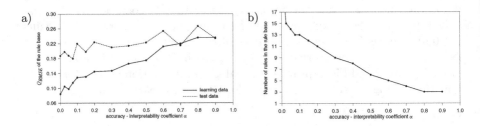

Fig. 4. Q_{RMSE} for the learning and test data as well the number R of fuzzy rules in the rule base versus the accuracy-interpretability coefficient α (*Wine* data set)

Table 2. Fuzzy rule base of the interpretability-oriented classifier (with $\alpha = 0.9$) for the *Wine* data set

No.	Fuzzy classification rules	Number of records activating the rule	
		learning data	test data
1	**IF** x_{13} *is* Large **THEN** Class 1	36	19
2	**IF** x_{10} *is* Small **THEN** Class 2	52	24
3	**IF** x_7 *is* Small **THEN** Class 3	31	16
	Q_{RMSE} for the learning and test data:	0.23646	0.23375
	Number (and percentage) of correct decisions:	110 (92.4%)	59 (100%)

In turn, Table 3 presents the results of comparative analysis with several alternative approaches to design (fuzzy) rule-based classifiers from data. One has to keep in mind that sometimes it is hard to find a "common denominator" for various solutions due to, e.g., different formats of fuzzy rules considered. It is evident, however, that the approach presented in this paper is characterized by high flexibility as far as the accuracy-versus-interpretability design of fuzzy rule-based classifiers is concerned. For this reason as well as taking into account the numerical results presented in Table 3, the proposed approach is a strong option in the area under consideration.

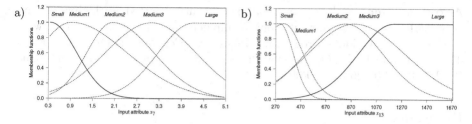

Fig. 5. The final membership functions of fuzzy sets occurring in fuzzy rules of Table 2 for input attributes x_7 (a) and x_{13} (b) (*Wine* data set)

Table 3. Comparative analysis with several alternative approaches - percentages of correct decisions for learning (CD_{learn}) and test (CD_{test}) data sets, for the whole data set (CD), numbers of rules and (if available) the numbers of fuzzy sets used

Dermatology	Our appr.[1]	Alcala[1]	Stavros[14]	ANFIS[15]
data set	CD_{learn} = 93.8%, CD_{test} = 94.3%, 6 rules, 7 fuzzy sets	CD_{learn} = 99.1%, CD_{test} = 95.2%, 9.13 rules[2], 14.93 fuzzy sets[2]	CD = 97.5%, 18 rules	CD = 95.5%, 54 rules
Wine	Our appr.[1]	Ishibuchi[10]	Chen[4]	Chang[3]
data set	CD_{learn} = 92.4%, CD_{test} = 100%, 3 rules, 3 fuzzy sets	CD = 90.4%, 3 rules, 3 fuzzy sets	CD = 98.3%, 4 rules, 10 fuzzy sets	CD = 98.9%, 5 rules, 13 fuzzy sets

[1] Our appr. = Our approach for the interpretability-oriented classifier (with α = 0.9),
[2] average number of rules or fuzzy sets,

5   Conclusions

The generalization of the Pittsburgh-based approach (proposed by the same authors in [9]) to design a fuzzy rule-based classifier from data has been presented in this paper. It allows us to obtain a system with a predefined level of compromise between its accuracy and interpretability (measured by the number and complexity of fuzzy rules). Such solutions may be very useful in achieving different goals in the applications of decision support systems. The mechanism that governs the accuracy-interpretability compromise has been implemented by appropriate definition of the fitness function of the genetic algorithm. The application of the proposed technique to design the fuzzy rule-based classifiers characterized by various accuracy-interpretability relations for the well known benchmark data sets (*Dermatology* and *Wine*) available from the http://archive.ics.uci.edu/ml has been presented. A comparative analysis with several alternative (fuzzy) rule-based classification approaches has also been carried out demonstrating that the proposed technique is a strong option (first of all, in terms of flexibility and effectiveness) in the field of the rule-based classifier design.

Acknowledgments. The numerical experiments reported in this paper have been performed using computational equipment purchased in the framework of the EU Operational Programme Innovative Economy (POIG.02.02.00-26-023/09-00) and the EU Operational Programme Development of Eastern Poland (POPW.01.03.00-26-016/09-00).

References

1. Alcala, R., Nojima, Y., Herrera, F., Ishibuchi, H.: Multiobjective genetic fuzzy rule selection of single granularity-based fuzzy classification rules and its interaction with the lateral tuning of membership functions. Soft Computing - A Fusion of Foundations, Methodologies and Applications, 1–16 (2010)
2. Baczyński, M., Jayaram, B.: Fuzzy Implications. Springer, Heidelberg (2008)
3. Chang, X., Lilly, J.H.: Evolutionary Design of a Fuzzy Classifier from Data. IEEE Transactions on Systems, Man and Cybernetics, Part B 34(4), 1894–1906 (2004)
4. Chen, J., Hou, Y., Xing, Z., Jia, L., Tong, Z.: A Multi-objective Genetic-based Method for Design Fuzzy Classification Systems. IJCSNS International Journal of Computer Science and Network Security 6(8A), 110–117 (2006)
5. Cios, K.J. (ed.): Medical Data Mining and Knowledge Discovery. Physica-Verlag, Springer-Verlag Co., Heidelberg, New York (2001)
6. Cordon, O.: A historical review of evolutionary learning methods for Mamdani-type fuzzy rule-based systems: Designing interpretable genetic fuzzy systems. International Journal of Approximate Reasoning 52, 894–913 (2011)
7. Gacto, M.J., Alcala, R., Herrera, F.: Interpretability of Linguistic Fuzzy Rule-Based Systems: An Overview of Interpretability Measures. Information Sciences 181(20), 4340–4360 (2011)
8. Gorzałczany M.B.: Computational Intelligence Systems and Applications, Neuro-Fuzzy and Fuzzy Neural Synergisms. Physica-Verlag, Springer-Verlag Co., Heidelberg, New York (2002)
9. Gorzałczany, M.B., Rudziński, F.: A Modified Pittsburg Approach to Design a Genetic Fuzzy Rule-Based Classifier from Data. In: Rutkowski, L., Scherer, R., Tadeusiewicz, R., Zadeh, L.A., Zurada, J.M. (eds.) ICAISC 2010. LNCS, vol. 6113, pp. 88–96. Springer, Heidelberg (2010)
10. Ishibuchi, H., Nakashima, T., Murata, T.: Three-objective genetics-based machine learning for linquistic extraction. Information Sciences 136(1-4), 109–133 (2001)
11. Maimon, O., Rokach, L. (eds.): Data Mining and Knowledge Discovery Handbook. Springer, New York (2005)
12. Ponce J., Karahoca A. (eds): Data Mining and Knowledge Discovery in Real Life Applications. IN-TECH, Vienna (2009)
13. Rutkowski, L.: Flexible Neuro-Fuzzy Systems: Structures, Learning and Performance Evaluation. Kluwer Academic Publishers, Boston (2004)
14. Stavros, L., Ludmil, M.: Evolving fuzzy medical diagnosis of Pima Indians diabetes and of dermatological diseases. Artificial Intelligence in Medicine 50, 117–126 (2010)
15. Ubeyli, E.D., Guler, I.: Automatic detection of erythemato squmous diseases using adaptive neuro-fuzzy inference systems. Computer in Biology and Medicine 35, 421–433 (2005)

Genetic Fuzzy Rule-Based Modelling
of Dynamic Systems Using Time Series

Marian B. Gorzałczany and Filip Rudziński

Department of Electrical and Computer Engineering
Kielce University of Technology
Al. 1000-lecia P.P. 7, 25-314 Kielce, Poland
{m.b.gorzalczany,f.rudzinski}@tu.kielce.pl

Abstract. The paper presents a genetic fuzzy rule-based technique for
the modelling of generalized time series (containing both, numerical and
non-numerical, qualitative data) which are a comprehensive source of information concerning the behaviour of many complex systems and processes. The application of the proposed approach to the fuzzy rule-based
modelling of an industrial gas furnace system using measurement data
available from the repository at the http://www.stat.wisc.edu/~reinsel/
bjr-data (the so-called Box-Jenkins' benchmark) is also presented.

1 Introduction

Mathematical models of dynamic systems and processes are necessary in various applications such as model-based control, prediction, simulation, or fault
diagnosis. Modelling based on conventional mathematical tools (e.g. linear or
nonlinear differential or difference equations) is not well suited for dealing with
ill-defined, complex and uncertain systems. It is neither able to effectively process
quantitative and qualitative data describing the system's behaviour nor provides
transparent and understandable "image" of its operation. For this reason, it is
worth considering techniques from the field of data mining and knowledge discovery for the purposes of the dynamic systems modelling from data. These
techniques reveal valid, useful and understandable structures, trends and patterns in data. Among them, fuzzy conditional rules belong to the most commonly
used knowledge-representation structures. Hybrid approaches that combine genetic algorithms and fuzzy logic (referred to as genetic fuzzy systems, cf. [3]) are
particularly effective in fuzzy rule-based modelling since they provide tools for
a global optimization of both the structures of the rules and the parameters of
fuzzy sets occurring in them.

This paper presents a genetic fuzzy rule-based technique for the dynamic
systems modelling from generalized time series. The term a "generalized time
series" means a time series which contains both, quantitative, numerical data
coming from experiments and measurements as well as non-numerical, qualitative data (most conveniently represented with the use of fuzzy sets) usually
provided by human experts. The proposed technique is a generalization (for the

L. Rutkowski et al. (Eds.): SIDE 2012 and EC 2012, LNCS 7269, pp. 231–239, 2012.
© Springer-Verlag Berlin Heidelberg 2012

case of systems with continuous outputs) of the genetic fuzzy classifier introduced by the same authors in [5] (another generalization of the latter - towards
the design fulfilling an assumed accuracy-interpretability compromise level - is
presented in [7]). First, a fuzzy rule-based computational scheme for the generalized time series modelling is presented. Then, a genetic learning of fuzzy
rules from data in the framework of a Pittsburgh approach (cf. [5]) is outlined.
Finally their application to the fuzzy rule-based modelling of an industrial gas
furnace system using measurement data available from the repository at the
http://www.stat.wisc.edu/~reinsel/bjr-data (the so-called Box-Jenkins' benchmark [2]) is also discussed.

2 Fuzzy Rule-Based Computational Scheme for Generalized Time Series Modelling and Forecasting

Consider a dynamic system or process with r physical inputs $u_1, u_2, ..., u_r$ ($u_c \in U_c$, $c = 1, 2, ..., r$) and s outputs $z_1, z_2, ..., z_s$ ($z_d \in Z_d$, $d = 1, 2, ..., s$). Assume
that the behaviour of the system is described by $r + s$ associated generalized
time series (each containing T records):

$$S_1 = \{D'_t, E'_t\}_{t=1}^{T} = \{D'_{1t}, D'_{2t}, ..., D'_{rt}, E'_{1t}, E'_{2t}, ..., E'_{st}\}_{t=1}^{T}, \qquad (1)$$

where $\{D'_{ct}\}_{t=1}^{T}$, $c = 1, 2, ..., r$, and $\{E'_{dt}\}_{t=1}^{T}$, $d = 1, 2, ..., s$ (t stands for a discrete
time instant) are generalized time series describing inputs and outputs of the
system, respectively. $D'_{ct} \in F(U_c)$, $c = 1, 2, ..., r$ and $E'_{dt} \in F(Z_d)$, $d = 1, 2, ..., s$
are fuzzy sets that represent verbal terms or numerical values describing the c-th
input and d-th output of the system, respectively, at time instant t ($F(U_c)$ and
$F(Z_d)$ are families of all fuzzy sets defined on the universes U_c and Z_d). When
we deal with a numerical value u'_{ct} of u_c, the fuzzy set D'_{ct} is reduced to a fuzzy
singleton $D'_{ct(singl)}$ with $\mu_{D'_{ct(sgl)}}(u'_{ct}) = 1$ and 0 elsewhere (analogously, for
an output numerical value z'_{dt}).

In particular, when we deal exclusively with non-fuzzy, numerical data in (1),
it reduces to the collection of fuzzy singletons that is equivalent to

$$S_2 = \{u'_t, z'_t\}_{t=1}^{T} = \{u'_{1t}, u'_{2t}, ..., u'_{rt}, z'_{1t}, z'_{2t}, ..., z'_{st}\}_{t=1}^{T}, \qquad (2)$$

where $u'_t \in U = U_1 \times U_2 \times ... \times U_r$ and $z'_t \in Z = Z_1 \times Z_2 \times ... \times Z_s$ ($\times$ stands for
Cartesian product of ordinary sets).

Due to the dynamics of the system, the particular data records in (1) or (2)
are interrelated. For instance, for a dynamic system with one input u and one
output z its dynamics can be described, in general, by the following formula:

$$z_t = f(u_t, u_{t-1}, ..., u_{t-M}, z_{t-1}, z_{t-2}, ..., z_{t-N}), \qquad M \geq 0, \quad N \geq 1. \qquad (3)$$

Only in the case of a static system, formula (3) reduces to $z_t = f(u_t)$. Expression (3) can be easily generalized for the case of the system with r inputs and s outputs.

Therefore, an important stage of the fuzzy rule-based model design consists in determining the structure of the model in terms of its inputs and outputs (similarly as in (3) for the single-input single-output case). It is an approximation of the system's dynamics. As we demonstrate later in the paper, the (close-to-) optimal structure of the model can be found by repeating the learning process for different structures of the model and selecting the structure that gives the best results of learning. Assume now that such a structure of the model has been determined and the model has n inputs $x_1, x_2, ..., x_n$, $x_i \in X_i$ ($n \geq r$), and m outputs $y_1, y_2, ..., y_m$, $y_j \in Y_j$ (usually $m = s$ and $y_j = z_j$). For instance, for a single input single output system with the dynamics (3), $x_1 = u_t, x_2 = u_{t-1}, ..., x_{M+1} = u_{t-M}, x_{M+2} = z_{t-1}, x_{M+3} = z_{t-2}, ..., x_n = x_{M+N+1} = z_{t-N}$, and $y_1 = y = z_t$. The generalized time series S_1 (1) describing the behaviour of the dynamic system has to be now reedited to the "static" form according to the selected structure of the model:

$$L_1 = \{A'_k, B'_k\}_{k=1}^{K} = \{A'_{1k}, A'_{2k}, ..., A'_{nk}, B'_{1k}, B'_{2k}, ..., B'_{mk}\}_{k=1}^{K}, \qquad (4)$$

where $A'_{ik} \in F(X_i)$, $i = 1, 2, ..., n$ and $B'_{jk} \in F(Y_j)$, $j = 1, 2, ..., m$ ($F(X_i)$ and $F(Y_j)$ are families of all fuzzy sets defined on the universes X_i and Y_j). Fuzzy sets A'_{ik} represent corresponding sets D'_{ct} and E'_{dt} of (1) and fuzzy sets B'_{jk} - corresponding output sets E'_{dt} of (1), k is the number of model's input-output static data pattern and K is the overall number of such patterns.

In particular, when we deal with the numerical time series (2), it has to be reedited (in an analogous way as data (1)) to the "static" form:

$$L_2 = \{x'_k, y'_k\}_{k=1}^{K} = \{x'_{1k}, x'_{2k}, ..., x'_{nk}, y'_{1k}, y'_{2k}, ..., y'_{mk}\}_{k=1}^{K}, \qquad (5)$$

where $x'_k \in X = X_1 \times X_2 \times ... \times X_n$ and $y'_k \in Y = Y_1 \times Y_2 \times ... \times Y_m$. From now on data (4) or their special case (5) will be referred to as the learning data.

Fuzzy rules that will be synthesized from data (4) or (5) (for the case of single output system, that is, for $m = 1$ and $y_1 = y$) by the proposed later in the paper genetic technique have the following form (when all n inputs are involved):

$$\text{IF } (x_1 \text{ is } A_{1r}) \text{ AND ... AND } (x_n \text{ is } A_{nr}) \text{ THEN } (y \text{ is } B_r), \qquad (6)$$

where $A_{ir} \in F(X_i)$, $i = 1, 2, ..., n$ and $B_r \in F(Y)$, $r = 1, 2, ..., R$, are the S-, M-, or L-type fuzzy sets corresponding to verbal terms "Small" (S-type), "Medium" (M-type) and "Large" (L-type). Their membership functions (for rule antecedents) are of the form: $\mu_{M_i}(x_i) = \exp[-0.5(x_i - c_{M_i})^2 / \sigma_{M_i}^2]$, where $\sigma_{M_i} = \sigma_{ML_i}$ for $x_i \leq c_{M_i}$ and $\sigma_{M_i} = \sigma_{MR_i}$ elsewhere, $\mu_{S_i}(x_i) = \exp[-0.5(x_i - c_{S_i})^2 / \sigma_{S_i}^2]$ only for $x_i \geq c_{S_i}$ and 1 elsewhere, and, analogously,

$\mu_{L_i}(x_i) = \exp[-0.5(x_i - c_{L_i})^2/\sigma_{L_i}^2]$ for $x_i \leq c_{L_i}$ and 1 elsewhere (see Fig. 2 later in the paper); $\sigma_{S_i} > 0, \sigma_{M_i} > 0, \sigma_{L_i} > 0, i = 1, 2, ..., n$. Fuzzy sets describing rule consequents are defined in an analogous way. In general, one S-type, one L-type and several M-type fuzzy sets can be considered for a given antecedent or consequent. It is worth stressing that a given verbal term for a given antecedent or consequent is represented by the same fuzzy set in all rules in which it occurs.

3   An Outline of Genetic Learning of Fuzzy Rules from Data

In the course of the genetic learning process, an evaluation of particular individuals (fuzzy rule bases in the considered Pittsburgh-based approach) must be performed in each generation. For this reason, a fuzzy-set-theory representation of fuzzy rule base (6) and fuzzy inference scheme have to be employed. Various definitions of fuzzy implications, t-norms and t-conorms in the framework of two dominating in the literature fuzzy reasoning schemes (compositional rule of inference and similarity based reasoning; see e.g. [1]) can be implemented in our approach. In case of the most widely used Mamdani's model (with min-type t-norm, max-type t-conorm and min operator playing the role of fuzzy implication), one can obtain - for the input numerical data $x^0 = (x_1^0, x_2^0, ..., x_n^0)$ - a fuzzy system's response in the form of fuzzy set $B^0 \in F(Y)$ represented by the following membership function:

$$\mu_{B^0}(y_j) = \max_{r=1,2,...,R} \mu_{B_r^0}(y_j) = \max_{r=1,2,...,R} \min[\alpha_r, \mu_{B_r}(y_j)], \qquad (7)$$

where $\alpha_r = \min(\alpha_{1r}, \alpha_{2r}, ..., \alpha_{nr}) = \min[\mu_{A_{1r}}(x_1^0), \mu_{A_{2r}}(x_2^0), ..., \mu_{A_{nr}}(x_n^0)]$. α_r is the activation degree of the r-th fuzzy rule by the input numerical data x^0. If non-fuzzy system's response $y^0 \in Y$ is required, a defuzzification procedure must be applied to fuzzy set B^0. In this paper, a "half of the field" method (see e.g. [4]) has been used.

The fitness function ff for a multi input single output system has been defined as follows: $ff = const. - Q$, where $const.$ is a constant value selected in such a way that $ff > 0$ and Q is the cost function (a root mean squared error):

$$Q = \sqrt{\frac{1}{K} \sum_{k=1}^{K} (y_k' - y_k^0)^2}, \qquad (8)$$

where K is the number of the learning samples, y_k' is the desired model's response for the k-th learning data sample of (5), and y_k^0 is the actual response of the model for that sample.

In the framework of the considered Pittsburgh-based approach, each individual (a fuzzy rule collection) is represented by two entities: a rule base (representing the rule structures) and a data base (representing the parameters of fuzzy sets that occur in fuzzy rules). An essential role in processing the population of individuals is played by the proposed non-binary crossover and mutation operators (due to a limited space of this publication they cannot be presented here - see [6] for details).

4   Model of an Industrial Gas Furnace System

The application of the proposed approach to design the genetic fuzzy rule-based model of an industrial gas furnace system from the data available from the repository at the http://www.stat.wisc.edu/~reinsel/bjr-data (the so-called Box-Jenkins' benchmark [2]) will now be presented. The data consists of 296 pairs of the gas flow rate (input u_t) measured in ft^3/min and the concentration of CO_2 in the exhaust gas (output z_t) expressed in % (the sampling period is equal to 9 sec.). Therefore, it is a single input single output dynamic process described by data (2) with $r = 1$, $s = 1$ and $T = 296$.

As stated in the previous section of this paper, an essential stage of the fuzzy model design consists in determining the input-output structure of the model. Since the optimal model's structure is not known, one of possible solutions is repeating the learning for several different structures of the model and selecting the structure that gives the best results of learning. For a single input single output dynamic system, the simplest structure of the model is characterized by two inputs and one output:

$$z_t = f(u_{t-t_u}, z_{t-t_z}), \tag{9}$$

where $t_u = 0, 1, ..., t_z = 1, 2, ..., t = max(t_u, t_z) + 1, max(t_u, t_z) + 2, ...$ In such a case, original set (2) of data pairs (u_t, z_t) must be reedited to the set (5) of data triplets $(u'_{t-t_u}, z'_{t-t_z}, z'_t) = (x'_1, x'_2, y')$, $k = t - max(t_u, t_z)$ and $K = T - max(t_u, t_z)$. In the learning experiments, the genetic algorithm with the population of 100 individuals and the tournament selection method (with the number of individuals participating in the competition equal to 2) supported by the elitist strategy as well as with crossover and mutation probabilities equal to 0.8 and 0.7, respectively, has been used. The results of the experiments have been collected in Fig. 1 that presents the minimal value Q_{min} of the cost function (8) for several sets of parameters t_u and t_z of (9). The best results have been obtained for $t_u = 4$ and $t_z = 1$, that is, for the model $z_t = f(u_{t-4}, z_{t-1})$. Table 1 presents its rule base that has been obtained after the completion of the learning process. The last column and the last row in Table 1 represent fuzzy rules with single antecedent, $x_1 = u_{t-4}$ and $x_2 = z_{t-1}$, respectively. Fig. 2 shows final shapes of the membership functions of fuzzy sets describing system's input u_t (*gas flow rate*) - Fig. 2a, and system's output z_t (*CO_2 concentration*) - Fig. 2b. The final stage of the genetic fuzzy rule-based model design (the pruning of the rule base) consists in gradual removing of "weaker", superfluous rules from the model's rule base (in order to increase its transparency), and analyzing how it affects the model's accuracy. This process is illustrated in Fig. 3. Q is the cost function of (8) calculated for the model (after the completion of the learning process) for different numbers of fuzzy rules in model's rule base. After removing nine "weakest" rules (represented by dark cells in Table 1) from the full rule base, the model with reduced rule base - containing four "strongest" fuzzy rules - has been obtained (see Fig. 4).

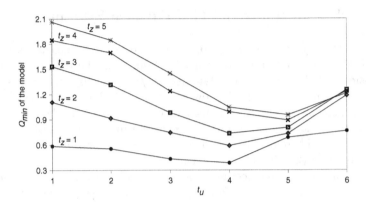

Fig. 1. Minimal value Q_{min} of the cost function (8) for several sets of parameters t_u and t_z of (9)

Table 1. Full fuzzy rule base of the genetic fuzzy model - dark cells represent fuzzy rules removed from the rule base as a result of a pruning (see below)

$x_2 = z_{t-1}$ / $x_1 = u_{t-4}$	S	M1	M2	M3	M4	L	-
S	M2			M3			
M1					L		
M2			M2				M4
M3		M1	M2	M3		M4	
M4							
L	S						
-	S	S				L	

S = Small; M1,..., M4 = Medium1,..., Medium4; L = Large - see Fig. 2 $y = z_t$

a)   b)

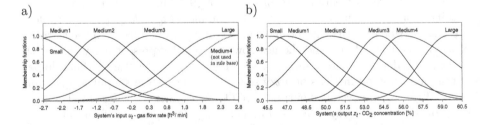

Fig. 2. Final shapes of membership functions of fuzzy sets describing system's input u_t (a) and output z_t (b)

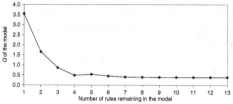

IF (u_{t-4} is MEDIUM2) THEN (z_t is MEDIUM4)

IF (u_{t-4} is MEDIUM3) AND

(z_{t-1} is MEDIUM2) THEN (z_t is MEDIUM2)

IF (z_{t-1} is MEDIUM1) THEN (z_t is SMALL)

IF (z_{t-1} is LARGE) THEN (z_t is LARGE)

Fig. 3. Accuracy vs. transparency criteria for the genetic fuzzy model

Fig. 4. Reduced fuzzy rule base of the genetic fuzzy model

Both fuzzy models (with full and reduced rule bases) will now be tested in "OSA predictions" mode and "AFT predictions" mode. OSA predictions stand for One-Step-Ahead predictions. This means that the model - using $x_1' = u_{t-4}'$ and $x_2' = z_{t-1}'$ from the learning data set - generates a response $y^0 = z_t^0$ (one-step-ahead prediction) which, in turn, can be compared with the desired response $y' = z_t'$. A much more demanding test of model's accuracy is its operation as the AFT ("All-Future-Times") predictor. In such a case, the model using $x_1' = u_{t-4}'$ from the learning data set and $x_2' = z_{t-1}^0$ generated by the model itself in the previous iteration, produces a response $y^0 = z_t^0$. The cumulation of errors associated with generation of $y^0 = z_t^0$ by the model in the consecutive iterations can cause - for models of insufficiently high accuracy - that they become more and more divergent with regard to the data. The operation of the genetic fuzzy model with full and reduced rule bases is illustrated in Fig. 5.

a) OSA predictions   b) AFT predictions

c) OSA predictions   d) AFT predictions

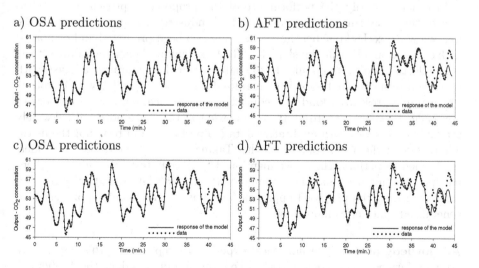

Fig. 5. Genetic fuzzy model with full (a), b)) and reduced (c), d)) rule bases

Table 2 summarizes the accuracy vs. interpretability results of the genetic fuzzy model with full and reduced rule bases. Additionally, the results - regarding exclusively the accuracy - of the conventional Box-Jenkins' approach [2] have been included. The genetic fuzzy model with the reduced rule base containing only four fuzzy rules provides excellent results as far as both, the model's accuracy and transparency are concerned. The fuzzy rules describe precisely and clearly the mechanisms that govern the operation of the system.

Table 2. Accuracy and transparency of genetic fuzzy model with full and reduced rule bases and conventional Box-Jenkins' model

	Full rule base	Reduced rule base	Box-Jenkins' model [2]
Q (OSA predictions)	0.385	0.487	0.251
Q (AFT predictions)	0.936	1.064	0.979
Number of rules in the rule base	13	4	–

5   Final Remarks

The generalization - for the case of systems with continuous outputs - of the genetic fuzzy classifier introduced by the same authors in [5] has been presented in this paper. The proposed technique is a tool for the dynamic systems modelling from generalized time series that describe their behaviour. The generalized time series may contain both, quantitative, numerical data coming from experiments and measurements as well as non-numerical, qualitative data (most conveniently represented with the use of fuzzy sets) usually provided by human experts.

In order to verify the performance of the proposed approach, its application to the fuzzy rule-based modelling of an industrial gas furnace system (the well known Box-Jenkins' benchmark [2]) has also been presented and compared with conventional Box-Jenkins' model. The Box-Jenkins' benchmark data set has been selected due to its popularity to enable a broad comparative analysis with possible alternative methods of (generalized) time series modelling. Obviously, the example presents a kind of "reduced" (to numerical data only) test of our approach. However, according to our knowledge, there are now neither widely available time series with qualitative data (to perform a full test) nor the methods to model them (to compare with). Taking into account these limitations, we decided to perform the above-mentioned "reduced" test (obtaining excellent results), treating it as a kind of "minimal" (numerical-data-based only) requirement regarding the proposed approach (and any other possible approaches) to generalized time-series modelling.

Acknowledgments. The numerical experiments reported in this paper have been performed using computational equipment purchased in the framework of the EU Operational Programme Innovative Economy (POIG.02.02.00-26-023/09-00) and the EU Operational Programme Development of Eastern Poland (POPW.01.03.00-26-016/09-00).

References

1. Baczyński, M., Jayaram, B.: Fuzzy Implications. Springer, Heidelberg (2008)
2. Box, G.E., Jenkins, G.M.: Time Series Analysis: Forecasting and Control. Holden Day, San Francisco (1970)
3. Cordon, O., Herrera, F., Hoffmann, F., Magdalena, L.: Genetic Fuzzy Systems: Evolutionary Tuning and Learning of Fuzzy Knowledge Bases. World Scientific, Singapore (2001)
4. Gorzałczany, M.B.: Computational Intelligence Systems and Applications, Neuro-Fuzzy and Fuzzy Neural Synergisms. Physica-Verlag, Springer-Verlag Co., Heidelberg, New York (2002)
5. Gorzałczany, M.B., Rudziński, F.: A Modified Pittsburg Approach to Design a Genetic Fuzzy Rule-Based Classifier from Data. In: Rutkowski, L., Scherer, R., Tadeusiewicz, R., Zadeh, L.A., Zurada, J.M. (eds.) ICAISC 2010. LNCS, vol. 6113, pp. 88–96. Springer, Heidelberg (2010)
6. Gorzałczany, M.B., Rudziński, F.: Measurement data in genetic fuzzy modelling of dynamic systems. Pomiary, Automatyka, Kontrola 56(12), 1420–1423 (2010)
7. Gorzałczany, M.B., Rudziński, F.: Accuracy vs. Interpretability of Fuzzy Rule-Based Classifiers: An Evolutionary Approach. In: Rutkowski, L., et al. (eds.) ICAISC 2012. LNCS, vol. 7269, pp. 222–230. Springer, Heidelberg (2012)

Application of the Ant Colony Optimization Algorithm for Reconstruction of the Thermal Conductivity Coefficient

Edyta Hetmaniok, Damian Słota, and Adam Zielonka

Institute of Mathematics,
Silesian University of Technology,
Kaszubska 23, 44-100 Gliwice, Poland
{edyta.hetmaniok,damian.slota,adam.zielonka}@polsl.pl

Abstract. In this paper the parametric inverse heat conduction problem with the third kind boundary condition is solved by applying the Ant Colony Optimization algorithm introduced in recent years and belonging to the group of optimization algorithms inspired by the behavior of swarms of individuals living in real word. In this case the applied algorithm is based on the technique of searching for the shortest way connecting the ant-hill with the source of food and is used for minimizing the functional playing a crucial role in the proposed procedure prepared for reconstruction of the thermal conductivity coefficient.

Keywords: Artificial Intelligence, Swarm Intelligence, Ant Colony Optimization Algorithm, Inverse Heat Conduction Problem.

1 Introduction

In recent decades a number of biologically inspired optimization algorithms have been developed. There are, for example, the genetic algorithms and neural networks inspired by the mechanisms of natural evolution, the immune algorithms imitating the rules of functioning of the immunological system in the bodies of vertebrates, swarm intelligence algorithms based on the intelligent behavior of the swarm resulting from the cooperation of many simple individuals building the common solution of the problem by finding independently only a small piece of the solution [1,2].

The Ant Colony Optimization algorithm, introduced in 1992 by Marco Dorigo [3,4,5], imitates the organization of the swarm of ants and method of communication between members of this community. By observing these insects, it was interesting how these almost blind creatures can find the best way from the ant-hill to the source of food, how they are able to communicate and what makes them to follow one after another. Solution of this mystery is given by the pheromone – a chemical substance produced and recognized by the most of ant species. Ants are not endowed with any special instincts, but they leave the pheromone trace in the ground giving the information for the other ants which

L. Rutkowski et al. (Eds.): SIDE 2012 and EC 2012, LNCS 7269, pp. 240–248, 2012.

path to choose and for the ant itself how to return to the ant-hill. The more ants traverse the path, the stronger is the pheromone trace. The shorter is the way, the sooner the ant can reach the source of food and return to the ant-hill, which makes the pheromone trace stronger and forces the other ants to choose this specific way. This natural procedure has been transformed to the language of computer programming which resulted in form of the ACO algorithm – efficient tool used for solving different kinds of optimization problems [3,4,5,6,7].

In this paper we propose to use the ACO algorithm for numerical solution of the inverse parametric heat conduction problem consisting in identification of the thermal conductivity parameter of a material in course of the ingot cooling. Mathematical model of this problem is represented by the heat conduction equation with boundary conditions of the second and third kind, but formulated for the incomplete set of data. Incomplete input data are compensated by the additional information which can be, for example, the measurements of temperature in selected points of the domain [8,9]. On this basis the sought thermal conductivity coefficient is identified and the distribution of temperature in the considered domain is reconstructed. Solving of the inverse heat conduction problem is much more difficult than solving of the direct heat conduction problem and, except the simplest cases, impossible by means of analytical methods. That is why the approximate methods are wanted, among which we can listed, for example, the Monte Carlo method [10], method using the Green function [11], mollification method introduced by Mourio [12], methods based on the wavelets theory [13] and applying the genetic algorithms [14,15], as well as the algorithms of swarm intelligence applied by the Authors to reconstructing the boundary condition of the first and second kind [16,17]. The inverse parametric heat conduction problems consisting in identification of the thermal conductivity [18,19,20] or other parameters [21,22] play an important role in literature devoted to the inverse problems, however the idea of applying the swarm intelligence algorithm for solving this problem, used already by the Authors in [23], is recent.

2 Ant Colony Optimization Algorithm

In ACO algorithm the role of ants is played by vectors $\mathbf{x}^k$, randomly dispersed in the searching region. In each step, one of the ants is selected as the best one $\mathbf{x}^{best}$ – the one, for which the minimized function $F(\mathbf{x})$ takes the lowest value. In the next step, to each vector $\mathbf{x}^k$ is applied a modification based on the pheromone trail. Vector of each ant is updated at the beginning of each iteration by using the following formula: $\mathbf{x}^k = \mathbf{x}^{best} + \mathbf{dx}^k$, where $\mathbf{dx}^k$ is a vector determining the length of jump, elements of which are randomly generated from the interval $[-\beta, \beta]$ (where $\beta = \beta_0$ is the narrowing parameter, defined in the initialization of the algorithm). At the end of each iteration the range of ants dislocations is decreasing, according to the formula $\beta_{t+1} = 0.1\beta_t$, which simulates the evaporation of the pheromone trail in nature. The role of the simulated source of food is played by the point of the lowest value of minimized function, that is why the presence of ants – vectors is condensing around this point. The described procedure is iterated until the assumed maximal number of iterations.

Detailed ACO algorithm is presented below.

Initialization of the algorithm.

1. Initial data:
   $F(\mathbf{x})$ – minimized function, $\mathbf{x} = (x_1, \ldots, x_n) \in D$;
   m – number of ants in one population;
   I – number of iterations;
   β – narrowing parameter.
2. Random selection of the initial ants localization: $\mathbf{x}^k = (x_1^k, \ldots, x_n^k)$, where $\mathbf{x}^k \in D$, $k = 1, 2, \ldots, m$.
3. Determination of the best located ant $\mathbf{x}^{best}$ in the initial ants population.

The main algorithm.

1. Updating of the ants locations:
   – random selection of the vector $\mathbf{dx}^k$ such that

   $$-\beta_i \le dx_j^k \le \beta_i;$$

   – generation of the new ants population:

   $$\mathbf{x}^k = \mathbf{x}^{best} + \mathbf{dx}^k, \quad k = 1, 2, \ldots, m.$$

2. Determination of the best located ant $\mathbf{x}^{best}$ in the current ant population.
3. Points 1 and 2 are repeated I^2 times.
4. Narrowing of the ants dislocations range: $\beta_{i+1} = 0.1\beta_i$.
5. Points 1 – 4 are repeated I times.

There are three basic advantages of such approach – the algorithm is effective, even for the not differentiable functions with many local minimums, time needed for finding the global minimum is respectively short and the algorithm does not require any specific assumptions. If the solution of the optimized problem exists, it will be found with some given precision of course. Moreover, the ACO algorithm belongs to the group of heuristic algorithms which means that solution received by using this algorithm should be treated as the best solution in the given moment. Another running of the algorithm can give different solution, slightly better or worse. Because of this the effective application of the ACO algorithm desires multiple execution and taking the average results as the solution. However, it does not decrease the usefulness of the algorithm.

3   Formulation of the Problem

We consider the problem in which distribution of temperature is described with the aid of the heat conduction equation

$$c\rho\frac{\partial u}{\partial t}(x, t) = \lambda\frac{\partial^2 u}{\partial x^2}(x, t), \quad x \in [0, d], \quad t \in [0, T], \tag{1}$$

with the following initial and boundary conditions

$$u(x,0) = u_0, \qquad x \in [0,d], \qquad\qquad (2)$$

$$\frac{\partial u}{\partial x}(0,t) = 0, \qquad t \in [0,T], \qquad\qquad (3)$$

where c, ρ and λ are, respectively, the specific heat, mass density and thermal conductivity, t and x denote, respectively, the time and spatial location, whereas u defines the temperature. On boundary for $x = 1$ the third kind boundary condition is assumed

$$-\lambda\frac{\partial u}{\partial x}(d,t) = \alpha(t)\,(u(d,t) - u_\infty), \qquad t \in [0,T], \qquad\qquad (4)$$

where u_∞ denotes the ambient temperature and $\alpha(t)$ describes the heat transfer coefficient. Solving of the considered problem consists in identifying the value of thermal conductivity coefficient λ and in reconstructing the distribution of temperature $u(x,t)$ in domain of the problem. By assuming the value of sought parameter λ as given, the problem defined by equations (1)–(4) can be solved by using one of the known method for direct problems, for instance the finite difference method or finite element method. In this way, the values of temperature $\widetilde{u}(x_i,t_j)$ in selected points of the domain can be received.

In considered inverse problem for the known values of temperature $u(x_i,t_j)$, $i = 1,...,k$, $j = 1,...,m$, in selected points of the domain, we will determine the desired thermal conductivity coefficient. By using the calculated temperatures $\widetilde{u}(x_i,t_j)$ and the given temperatures $u(x_i,t_j)$ we can construct the following functional

$$P(\lambda) = \sqrt{\sum_{i=1}^{k}\sum_{j=1}^{m}\left(u(x_i,t_j) - \widetilde{u}(x_i,t_j)\right)^2}, \qquad\qquad (5)$$

representing the error of approximate solution $\widetilde{u}$, which will be minimized. By this means, the value of parameter λ will be determined in such a way that the approximate distribution of temperature will be as close as possible to the known values of temperature in control points. For minimizing the functional (5) will we use the ACO algorithm, paying attention to the fact that each execution of the procedure means the necessity of solving the appropriate heat conduction problem.

4   Numerical Experiment

The proposed approach will be tested for the following values of parameters: $c = 1000\,[J/(kg \cdot K)]$, $\rho = 2679\,[kg/m^3]$, $T = 1000\,[s]$, $d = 1\,[m]$, $u_0 = 980\,[K]$, $u_\infty = 298\,[K]$ and the following values of $\alpha(t)\,[W/(m^2 \cdot K)]$:

$$\alpha(t) = \begin{cases} 250 & \text{for } t \in [0,90], \\ 150 & \text{for } t \in (90,250], \\ 28 & \text{for } t \in (250,1000]. \end{cases}$$

We know the exact value of the sought parameter λ which is equal to $240\,[W/(m \cdot K)]$. For constructing the functional (5) we use the control values of temperature, determined for the known exact value of λ and values noised by the random error of 1, 2, 5 and 10%. The measurement point is located on the boundary for $x = 1$, where the third kind boundary condition is reconstructed, and in the 5% and 10% distance away from this boundary. The measurements of temperature are taken at every 1 s. We will verify how much the shift of measurement point away from the boundary affects the quality of results. The initial population of ants representing the localization of the sought parameter is randomly selected from the range $[0, 1000]$. We evaluate the experiment for number of ants $m = 10$ and number of iterations $I = 10$, because the simulations indicated those values as sufficient for receiving satisfying results. Value of the narrowing parameter is $\beta = 0.1$ and the initial $\beta_0 = 600$. The approximate value of reconstructed coefficient is received by running the algorithm 20 times and by averaging the obtained results. Selected results are presented in figures.

Fig. 1 presents the results of the thermal conductivity parameter reconstruction calculated for the successive iterations of ACO algorithm (from 1 till 10), for input data burdened by the error of 1% and control point located in the 5% distance away from the boundary for $x = 1$. Distribution of the reconstruction error, with respect to the number of iterations, is also displayed. The other sought element in the considered problem is the distribution of temperature. Distribution of temperature $u(x, t)$ on the boundary for $x = 1$ (where the boundary condition is reconstructed) calculated for 10 iterations in ACO algorithm, for input data burdened by the error of 1% and control point located in the 5% distance away from the considered boundary is presented in Fig. 2. Similar collection of results, but for the case of 5% perturbation of input data and location of measurement point in the 10% distance away from the boundary for $x = 1$ is showed in Figures 3 and 4, whereas, for 10% perturbation of input data and measurement point located on the boundary for $x = 1$ – in Figures 5 and 6.

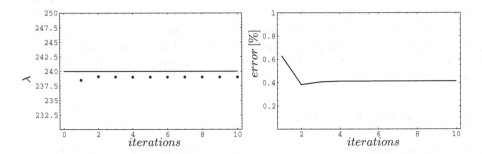

Fig. 1. Reconstruction of parameter λ for the successive iterations, for input data burdened by the error of 1% and control point located in the 5% distance away from the boundary for $x = 1$ (left figure) and error of this reconstruction (right figure)

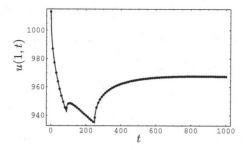

Fig. 2. Distribution of temperature $u(x,1)$ on the boundary for $x = 1$ reconstructed for input data burdened by the error of 1% and control point located in the 5% distance away from the boundary for $x = 1$ (solid line – exact solution, dashed line – approximated values)

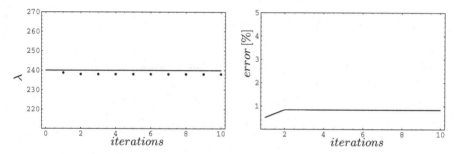

Fig. 3. Reconstruction of parameter λ for the successive iterations, for input data burdened by the error of 5% and control point located in the 10% distance away from the boundary for $x = 1$ (left figure) and error of this reconstruction (right figure)

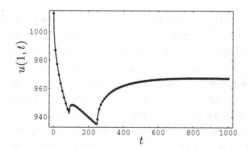

Fig. 4. Distribution of temperature $u(x,1)$ on the boundary for $x = 1$ reconstructed for input data burdened by the error of 5% and control point located in the 10% distance away from the boundary for $x = 1$ (solid line – exact solution, dashed line – approximated values)

Executed numerical experiment indicated that the proposed procedure gives satisfying results for this kind of problem. For the exact input data we received in few iterations the results almost equal to the exact solution. In case of the

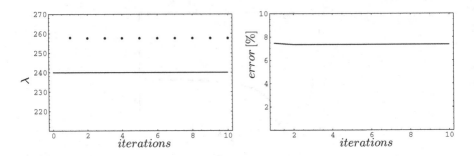

Fig. 5. Reconstruction of parameter λ for the successive iterations, for input data burdened by the error of 10% and control point located on the boundary for $x = 1$ (left figure) and error of this reconstruction (right figure)

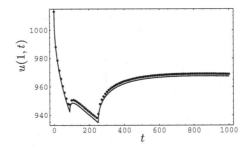

Fig. 6. Distribution of temperature $u(x, 1)$ on the boundary for $x = 1$ reconstructed for input data burdened by the error of 10% and control point located on the boundary for $x = 1$ (solid line – exact solution, dashed line – approximated values)

measurement point located on the boundary for $x = 1$ (where the boundary condition is reconstructed), or in the 5% or 10% distance away from this boundary, the reconstruction errors are smaller than the 1, 2 and 5% errors of input data. For 10% perturbation of input data the results are good for the control point located on the considered boundary and shifted 5% away from this boundary. Moreover, the experiment gave similar results in 20 repetitions made for the same input data which confirms stability of the procedure.

In presented simulation the optimal number of algorithm iterations $I = 10$ and size of ants population $m = 10$ were determined experimentally. Other researches aimed to reconstruct the thermal conductivity coefficient or other coefficients in the inverse heat conduction problem of considered kind, like the heat transfer coefficient, in various conditions and for various numbers of measurements, indicated that proposed procedure based on ACO algorithm gives satisfying results for the number of ants and number of iterations not exceeding 10. However, to conclude more general conclusions some further researches must be made.

5 Conclusions

In this paper the procedure for solving the inverse heat conduction problem with boundary condition of the third kind, using one of the Swarm Intelligence algorithms, is proposed. Solution of this problem consisted in identification of the thermal conductivity parameter and reconstruction of the temperature distribution in considered region. Essential part of the approach concerned minimization of the functional expressing the errors of approximate results, for minimization of which the Ant Colony Optimization algorithm was used. The proposed procedure was investigated with regard to the speed of execution and the precision of obtained results, as well as to the sensitivity to the initial parameters of the algorithm, error of input data and location of the control points.

Presented results indicated that the proposed algorithm constitutes the effective tool for solving such kind of inverse problem, for different cases of the input data error, distance of the control point away from the boundary of the region and selection of parameters in the ACO algorithm (number of individuals and number of iterations). The listed elements exert of course some influence on the quality of solution, however, in each considered case of input data the reconstruction errors are smaller than perturbations of input data and the numbers of individuals and iterations in the algorithm needed for receiving the satisfying results are relatively small which makes the algorithm fast working and the entire procedure useful and efficient.

References

1. Beni, G., Wang, J.: Swarm intelligence in cellular robotic systems. In: Proceed. NATO Advanced Workshop on Robots and Biological Syst., Tuscany (1989)
2. Eberhart, R.C, Shi, Y., Kennedy, J.: Swarm Intelligence. Morgan Kaufmann, San Francisco (2001)
3. Dorigo, M.: Optimization, Learning and Natural Algorithms (in Italian). PhD thesis, Dipartimento di Elettronica e Informazione, Politecnico di Milano, Milan (1992)
4. Dorigo, M., Stützle, T.: Ant Colony Optimization. Massachusetts Institute of Technology Press, Cambridge (2004)
5. Dorigo, M., Maniezzo, V., Colorni, A.: The ant system: Optimization by a colony of cooperatin gagents. IEEE Transactionson Systems, Man and Cybernetics – Part B 26(1), 29–41 (1996)
6. Maniezzo, V., Colorni, A., Dorigo, M.: The ant system applied to the quadratic assignment problem. Technical Report IRIDIA, Universite Libre de Bruxelles, 94–128 (1994)
7. Schoonderwoerd, R., Holland, O., Bruten, J., Rothkrantz, L.: Ant-based load balancing in telecommunications networks. Adaptive Behavior 5(2), 169–207 (1996)
8. Beck, J.V., Blackwell, B., Clair, C.R.: Inverse Heat Conduction: Ill Posed Problems. Wiley Intersc., New York (1985)
9. Beck, J.V., Blackwell, B.: Inverse Problems. In: Handbook of Numerical Heat Transfer. Wiley Intersc., New York (1988)
10. Haji-Sheikh, A., Buckingham, F.P.: Multidimensional inverse heat conduction using the Monte Carlo method. Trans. of ASME. Journal of Heat Transfer 115, 26–33 (1993)

11. Beck, J.V., Cole, K.D., Haji-Sheikh, A., Litkouhi, B.: Heat Conduction Using Green's Functions. Hempisphere, Publishing Corporation, Philadelphia (1992)

12. Mourio, D.A.: The Mollification Method and the Numerical Solution of Ill-posed Problems. John Wiley and Sons Inc., New York (1993)

13. Qiu, C.Y., Fu, C.L., Zhu, Y.B.: Wavelets and regularization of the sideways heat equation. Computers and Mathematics with Applications 46, 821–829 (2003)

14. Słota, D.: Solving the inverse Stefan design problem using genetic algorithm. Inverse Problems in Science and Engineering 16, 829–846 (2008)

15. Słota, D.: Restoring boundary conditions in the solidification of pure metals. Computers and Structures 89, 48–54 (2011)

16. Hetmaniok, E., Zielonka, A.: Solving the inverse heat conduction problem by using the ant colony optimization algorithm. In: Kuczma, M., Wilmański, K., Szajna, W. (eds.) 18th International Conference on Computer Methods in Mechanics, CMM 2009, pp. 205–206. University of Zielona Góra Press (2009)

17. Hetmaniok, E., Słota, D., Zielonka, A.: Solution of the Inverse Heat Conduction Problem by Using the ABC Algorithm. In: Szczuka, M., Kryszkiewicz, M., Ramanna, S., Jensen, R., Hu, Q. (eds.) RSCTC 2010. LNCS, vol. 6086, pp. 659–668. Springer, Heidelberg (2010)

18. Ardakani, M.D., Khodadad, M.: Identification of thermal conductivity and the shape of an inclusion using the boundary elements method and the particle swarm optimization algorithm. Inverse Problems in Science and Engineering 17(7), 855–870 (2009)

19. Majchrzak, E., Dziewoński, M., Jasiński, M.: Identification of Thermal Conductivity by Means of The Gradient Method and The BEM. Scientific Research of the Institute of Methematics and Computer Science 6, 147–158 (2007)

20. Telejko, T., Malinowski, Z.: Application of an inverse solution to the thermal conductivity identification using the finite element method. Journal of Materials Processing Technology 146(2), 145–155 (2004)

21. Grzymkowski, R., Słota, D.: Numerical calculations of the heat-transfer coefficient during solidification of alloys. In: Sarler, B., Brebbia, C.A. (eds.) Moving boundaries VI. Computational Modelling of Free and Moving Boundary Problems, pp. 41–50. WIT Press, Southampton (2001)

22. Ryfa, A., Białecki, A.: The heat transfer coefficient spatial distribution reconstruction by an inverse technique. Inverse Problems in Science and Engineering 19, 117–126 (2011)

23. Zielonka, A., Hetmaniok, E., Słota, D.: Using the Artificial Bee Colony Algorithm for Determining the Heat Transfer Coefficient. In: Czachórski, T., et al. (eds.) Man-Machine Interactions 2. AISC, vol. 103, pp. 369–376. Springer, Heidelberg (2011)

Comparison of ABC and ACO Algorithms Applied for Solving the Inverse Heat Conduction Problem

Edyta Hetmaniok, Damian Słota, Adam Zielonka, and Roman Wituła

Institute of Mathematics,
Silesian University of Technology,
Kaszubska 23, 44-100 Gliwice, Poland
{edyta.hetmaniok,damian.slota,adam.zielonka,roman.witula}@polsl.pl

Abstract. In this paper we present the comparison of numerical methods applied for solving the inverse heat conduction problem in which two algorithms of swarm intelligence are used: Artificial Bee Colony algorithm (ABC) and Ant Colony Optimization algorithm (ACO). Both algorithms belong to the group of algorithms inspired by the behavior of swarms of insects and they are applied for minimizing the proper functional representing the crucial part of the method used for solving the inverse heat conduction problems. Methods applying the respective algorithms are compared with regard to their velocity and precision of the received results.

Keywords: Swarm Intelligence, Artificial Bee Colony algorithm, Ant Colony Optimization algorithm, Inverse Heat Conduction Problem.

1 Introduction

The group of intelligence algorithms, also called the swarm intelligence algorithms, belong to the group of artificial intelligence algorithms and they represent the special way of solving various problems in which the intelligent behavior results from the cooperation of many simple individuals. Single individuals are not aware of the complete problem which should be solved, but big number of them and their specific forms of behavior cause the common success and, in result, lead to find the solution. Such kind of methods is represented by the ants and bees algorithms in which the imaginary individuals – ants or bees – built the common solution of the problem by finding independently only a small part of the solution, about quality of which they inform the other members of the swarm by using the virtual pheromone, in case of ants, or imitation of a special dance taking place in the hive, in case of bees. Effectiveness of those algorithms in solving the optimization problems exceeds the effectiveness of traditional approaches [1,2,3,4].

Ant Colony Optimization algorithm (ACO) and Artificial Bee Colony algorithm (ABC) were used, so far, for solving various optimization problems of

L. Rutkowski et al. (Eds.): SIDE 2012 and EC 2012, LNCS 7269, pp. 249–257, 2012.
© Springer-Verlag Berlin Heidelberg 2012

combinatoric kinds, such as the traveling salesmen problem, determination of the vehicle routes, sequential sorting, graph coloring and flow control in the networks [1]. Moreover, there were developed the procedures, basing on the ants and bees algorithms, serving for finding the solution of more analytical problems, like determining the global minimum of the function [2,3,4]. In regard to application of the considered algorithms in the inverse problems in engineering, there were published so far only few works concerning this subject [5,6,7].

The inverse heat conduction problem is a heat conduction problem formulated for the incomplete set of data and it consists in determining the temperature distribution and one of the boundary conditions [8,9]. Incomplete set of data is compensated by the additional information which can be given, for example, by the measurements of temperature in selected points of the domain. Solving of the inverse problem is much more difficult than solving of the direct heat conduction problem in which the distribution of temperature in the considered domain should be determined for the given initial and boundary conditions. However, the scientists constantly make some efforts for receiving the approximate solutions of inverse problems. The successful methods of solving such kind of problems are, for example, the Monte Carlo method [10], method using the Green function [11], mollification method introduced by Mourio [12], homotopy perturbation method [13,14], methods based on the wavelets theory [15] or applying the genetic algorithms [16,17,18].

Successful trials of using the ants and bees algorithms in solving the inverse heat conduction problems were made by authors of the current work in papers [19,20]. Idea of applying the algorithms of swarm intelligence in solving such kind of problems consists in minimizing the properly constructed functional, expressing the error of approximate solution, with the aid of ACO and ABC algorithms, according to the approach presented in papers [2,3,4]. The current paper is devoted to summarizing the obtained calculations and comparing the effectiveness of ants and bees algorithms in determining the approximate solution of inverse problems.

2   Ant Colony Optimization Algorithm

ACO algorithm was inspired by observation of the real ant community behavior and the technique of looking for the food around the ant-hill by the ants. Those almost blind creatures are able to find the shortest way connecting the ant-hill with the source of food by passing round the obstacles which can appear on the way. Answer to the question what makes the swarm of ants to follow one after another, choosing by this way the best of the possible trails, is the pheromone. Pheromone is a chemical substance which is produced and recognized by most of the ant species. Such kind of substance is leaved in the ground by the moving ant and, afterwards, is smelled by the other ants which makes them to follow its trace. As stronger is the pheromone trace, as greater number of ants will choose the trail covered by it. According to this, as shorter is the way to the source of food, as faster will be traversed by the ant. After that the ant returns to the ant-hill by using the same trail and by intensifying the pheromone trace. Whereas, the pheromone trace leaved on the longer trail evaporates little by little.

Such simple mechanism has been used in elaborating the optimization algorithm in which the role of ants is played by the vectors $\mathbf{x}^k$, randomly dispersed in the considered region. In each step, one of the ants-vectors is selected as the best one $\mathbf{x}^{best}$ – the one for which the minimized function $F(\mathbf{x})$ takes the lowest value. At the beginning of each iteration, vector representing each ant is updated (for the assumed number of times) according to the following formula: $\mathbf{x}^k = \mathbf{x}^{best} + \mathbf{dx}^k$, where $\mathbf{dx}^k$ denotes the vector determining the length of jump, elements of which are randomly selected from the interval $[-\beta, \beta]$. Parameter β is called the narrowing parameter and its initial value β_0 is defined in the initialization of the algorithm. At the end of each iteration value of the narrowing parameter is modified according to the formula $\beta_{i+1} = 0.1\,\beta_i$, thanks to which the range of ants dislocations is decreasing. This procedure simulates the evaporating process of the pheromone trail because it causes that the individuals $\mathbf{x}^k$ are getting together more and more densely around the best solution, whereas the points of the considered region giving worse solutions are visited more and more rarely.

Detailed scheme of the ACO algorithm can be found in [19].

3   Artificial Bee Colony Algorithm

ABC algorithm imitates the technique of searching for the nectar around the hive by the colony of real bees. The way of communication between bees, unique in nature, is the following: after discovering the attractive source of nectar the bee (called as the scout) flies back with the sample of nectar to the hive where it informs the other bees (called as the viewers) with the aid of the special kind of dance. Dance of the bees, called as the waggle dance, happens in the special place in the hive (near the exit) and consists of two parts: moving straight and moving back to the starting point along the semicircle, once to the right side, next to the left side. During the straight movement the bee swings with its whole body, once to the right, once to the left, and it emits the buzzing sounds which can be well heard by the human ears. The sound is produced by the very quick movements of the bee's wings, about 200-300 per one second. Direction of the bee's dance determines the angle between the localized source of food and the sun. By taking into account the fact that position of the sun is changing during the day, the bee modifies the angle of its straight movement about 1 degree at every 4 minutes. Duration of the straight movement determines the distance between the hive and the source of food (each 75 milliseconds of moving straight denotes 100 metres of distance). Magnitude of the bee's body vibration during the dance indicates the quality of nectar.

Population of artificial bees in the algorithm is divided into two equal parts. First part is made by the bees-scouts exploring the environment in search for the nectar. Second part is made by the bees-viewers waiting in the hive for information. In the first part of the algorithm the bees-scouts localize the assumed number of the sources of nectar – points $\mathbf{x}^k$ of the investigated region. By doing this, they make some number of control movements in order to check whether in the neighborhood of the selected point some better localization can be found. The quality measure of the selected point is obviously the value of minimized function $F(\mathbf{x})$ (as smaller is the value, as the source is more attractive). Next, the scouts return to the hive, give the information to the bees-viewers and wait in the hive for the next cycle of algorithm. In the second part of the algorithm the bees-viewers choose the sources of nectar with the given probabilities (as greater as better is the quality of the source) from among the points of the domain selected by the scouts. Of course, one source can be chosen by a group of bees. Next, the bees-viewers explore the selected sources by making also some number of the control movements around, in order to improve the quality of the localized source. Each cycle of the algorithm is ended by choosing the best source of nectar in the current cycle – if the chosen source is better than those one selected in the previous cycles, the chosen source is considered as the best solution so far in the entire algorithm execution.

More detailed description of the ABC algorithm is presented in paper [20].

It is worth to mention in this moment that the ABC algorithm, as well as the ACO algorithm, belong to the group of heuristic algorithms, which means that each running of the algorithm can give slightly different solution. Thus, the reasonable application of those algorithms should consist in averaging the results received in some number of their repeated executions. However, it is not problematic because of the simplicity, easiness of implementation and relative high speed of execution of the presented algorithms. Moreover, their important advantage is ensured by the fact that the ABC and ACO algorithms do not require to satisfy any assumptions about the minimized function or the considered domain which significantly increases the range of their usefulness. If only the solution exists, it will be found with the aid of those algorithms with the bigger or smaller precision.

4   Formulation of the Problem

In the considered problem distribution of temperature is described by means of the heat conduction equation

$$c\rho\frac{\partial u}{\partial t}(x,t) = \lambda\frac{\partial^2 u}{\partial x^2}(x,t), \quad x \in [0,d], \quad t \in [0,T], \tag{1}$$

with the given initial condition

$$u(x,0) = u_0, \qquad x \in [0,d] \tag{2}$$

and boundary condition

$$\frac{\partial u}{\partial x}(0,t) = 0, \qquad t \in [0,T], \tag{3}$$

where c, ρ and λ are, respectively, the specific heat, mass density and thermal conductivity, t and x denote, respectively, the time and spatial location, whereas u defines the distribution of temperature. On boundary for $x = 1$ the third kind boundary condition is assumed

$$-\lambda\frac{\partial u}{\partial x}(d,t) = \alpha(t)\,(u(d,t) - u_\infty), \quad t \in [0,T], \tag{4}$$

where u_∞ denotes the ambient temperature and $\alpha(t)$ describes the heat transfer coefficient. Form of this coefficient is unknown and solving of the problem will consist in its determination. Another unknown element which should be determined is the distribution of temperature $u(x,t)$ in the considered domain.

For the fixed value of heat transfer coefficient the above problem, described by equations (1)–(4), turns into the direct problem, solving of which enables to find the values of temperature $\tilde{u}(x_i, t_j)$ in the selected points of the domain. By using the calculated temperatures $\tilde{u}(x_i, t_j)$ and the given temperatures $u(x_i, t_j)$ we can construct the following functional

$$P(\alpha) = \sqrt{\sum_{i=1}^{k}\sum_{j=1}^{m}\left(u(x_i,t_j) - \tilde{u}(x_i,t_j)\right)^2}, \tag{5}$$

representing the differences between the received approximate results $\tilde{u}$ and the known values of temperature u in the measurement points. By this means, we will calculate the values of parameters such that the approximate distribution of temperature will be as close as possible to its known values. For minimizing the functional (5) will we use the ACO and ABC algorithms, paying attention to the fact that for finding the solution α we need to solve many times the direct problem associated with the considered inverse problem.

5   Numerical Example

The inverse problem, described in the previous section, is considered for the following values of parameters: $c = 1000\,[J/(kg \cdot K)]$, $\rho = 2679\,[kg/m^3]$, $\lambda = 240\,[W/(m \cdot K)]$, $T = 1000\,[s]$, $d = 1\,[m]$, $u_0 = 980\,[K]$ and $u_\infty = 298\,[K]$. We need to determine the values of three parameters $\alpha_i\,[W/(m^2 \cdot K)]$, $i = 1, 2, 3$, denoting the successive values of the heat transfer coefficient. Exact values of the sought parameters are the following:

$$\alpha(t) = \begin{cases} 250 & \text{for } t \in [0,90], \\ 150 & \text{for } t \in (90,250], \\ 28 & \text{for } t \in (250,1000]. \end{cases}$$

Moreover, in calculations we have used the measurements of temperature taken in point located on the boundary for $x = 1$, read in five series: at every 1, 2, 5, 10 and 20 s.

In case of applying the ACO algorithm for minimization of functional (5) we assume that the initial population of ants, which suppose to locate the sought values of parameters, is randomly selected from the range $[0, 500]$ and the initial value of the narrowing parameter β_0 is equal to 300. Approximate values of the desired parameters α_i, $i = 1, 2, 3$ are determined by running the algorithm 30 times and by averaging the received results. In course of the researches, made for various numbers of ants population n^M and various numbers of iterations I in the algorithm execution, it turned out that the satisfying results are obtained for the number of ants $n^M = 5$ and number of iterations $I = 5$.

Similar investigations were made in case of using for minimization of functional (5) the ABC algorithm, also executed 30 times. The initial population of bees, corresponding with the explored sources of nectar, is also randomly selected from the range $[0,500]$. In course of researches it appeared that the satisfying results are received for the number of bees $n^P = 5$, similarly like in case of ACO algorithm, but the maximal number of cycles C in the algorithm execution, necessary for obtaining good results, is equal to 14.

Note that successful results of the temperature distribution reconstruction are received for 5 iterations in ACO algorithm execution, as well as for 5 cycles of ABC algorithm execution. However, the differences appear by comparing the reconstructed values of heat transfer coefficient α. It turned out that in case of ACO algorithm, for the series of control measurements of temperature made at every 1 s, as well as for the measurements made at every 20 s, 5 iterations is enough for receiving the small values of relative errors δ_{α_i} of the reconstructed parameter α_i, which is presented in Fig. 1. Whereas, in case of the ABC algorithm, number of cycles necessary for obtaining the small relative errors δ_{α_i} of the reconstructed parameter α_i is grater and is equal to 14, especially for the series of measurements taken at every 20 s which can be seen in Fig. 2.

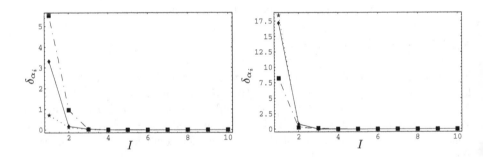

Fig. 1. Relative errors of reconstruction of parameters α_i for the successive iterations of ACO algorithm and for the series of measurements taken at every 20 s (left figure) and at every 1 s (right figure) ($\blacklozenge$ – for α_1, $\bigstar$ – for α_2, $\blacksquare$ – for α_3)

Fig. 3 presents the distribution of temperature on the boundary for $x = 1$, where the boundary condition of the third kind is reconstructed, calculated for the control measurements of temperature taken at every 1 s, by using, respectively, 5 iterations of the ACO algorithm and 14 cycles of the ABC algorithm.

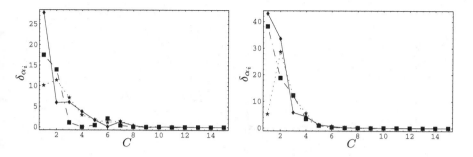

Fig. 2. Relative errors of reconstruction of parameters α_i for the successive cycles of ABC algorithm and for the series of measurements taken at every 20 s (left figure) and at every 1 s (right figure) ($\blacklozenge$ – for α_1, $\bigstar$ – for α_2, $\blacksquare$ – for α_3)

The numbers of iterations and cycles are those for which the satisfying reconstruction of heat transfer coefficient is received. Numbers of ants and bees are equal to 5. One can see that the reconstruction of temperature distribution is very good in both cases, which is additionally confirmed by the relative errors δ_u of the respective approximations, distribution of which are showed in Fig. 4.

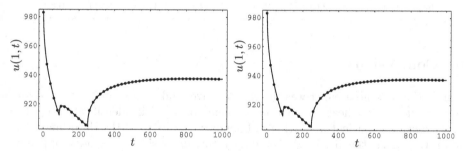

Fig. 3. Distribution of temperature on the boundary for $x = 1$ calculated by using 5 iterations of ACO algorithm (left figure) and 14 cycles of ABC algorithm (right figure) (solid line – exact values of temperature, dashed line – reconstructed values)

Moreover, in Table 1 the statistical comparison between ACO and ABC algorithms in reconstruction of parameters α_i is displayed. The table presents, in turn, the maximal and minimal relative errors of parameters α_i approximations, their mean values and standard deviation values received in 30 runnings of the algorithms, for measurements taken at every 20 s and for 5 iterations and cycles, respectively. Obtained results indicate superiority of ACO algorithm.

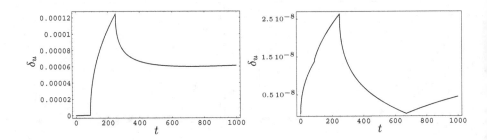

Fig. 4. Relative error of reconstruction of the temperature distribution on the boundary for $x = 1$ calculated by using 5 iterations of ACO algorithm (left figure) and 14 cycles of ABC algorithm (right figure)

Table 1. Statistical comparison between ACO and ABC algorithms in α_i reconstruction (first line presents results obtained by ACO, second line – by ABC)

$\max \Delta_{\alpha_i}$ [%]	$\min \Delta_{\alpha_i}$ [%]	$\overline{\alpha}_1$	σ_1	$\overline{\alpha}_2$	σ_2	$\overline{\alpha}_3$	σ_3
$1.2 \cdot 10^{-11}$	$8 \cdot 10^{-12}$	250.000	$2.3 \cdot 10^{-11}$	150.000	$1.1 \cdot 10^{-11}$	28.000	$3.1 \cdot 10^{-11}$
2.981	0.812	249.612	1.219	150.412	1.376	28.211	0.692

6   Conclusions

Aim of the presented paper was the comparative study of two methods used for solving the inverse heat conduction problem consisted in identification of the heat transfer coefficient appearing in boundary condition of the third kind and reconstruction of the distribution of temperature in considered region. Compared methods differ in the way of minimizing the functional, expressing the differences between the received approximate results and the known values of temperature and representing the crucial element in the process of solving the problem. For minimizing the functional in the first approach the ACO algorithm was used, whereas in the second approach the ABC algorithm was applied. Investigations indicated that both algorithms are very well suitable for solving the considered problem, they give satisfying results for the small numbers of individuals, as well as for the small numbers of iterations or cycles. However, by taking into account the number of calculations needed for receiving good results, which means the velocity of the algorithms working, the ant algorithm appeared to be more efficient in solving the considered problem. Number of iterations in the ACO algorithm execution, implying the number of direct heat conduction problems which should be solved, is half as big in comparison with the ABC algorithm.

References

1. Dorigo, M., Stützle, T.: Ant Colony Optimization. MIT Press (2004)
2. Duran Toksari, M.: Ant Colony Optimization for finding the global minimum. Applied Mathematics and Computation 176, 308–316 (2006)
3. Karaboga, D., Basturk, B.: On the performance of artificial bee colony (ABC) algorithm. Applied Soft Computing 8, 687–697 (2008)
4. Karaboga, D., Akay, B.: A comparative study of Artificial Bee Colony Algorithm. Applied Mathematics and Computation 214, 108–132 (2009)
5. Fainekos, G.E., Giannakoglou, K.C.: Inverse design of airfoils based on a novel formulation of the ant colony optimization method. Inverse Problems in Engineering 11, 21–38 (2003)
6. Souto, R.P., Stephany, S., Becceneri, J.C., Campos Velho, H.F., Silva Neto, A.J.: On the use the ant colony system for radiative properties estimation. In: Proc. of the 5th Int. Conf. on Inverse Problems in Engineering: Theory and Practice, vol. 10, pp. 1–10. University of Leeds, Cambridge (2005)
7. Wang, R.X., Wang, L.G.: Solving inverse heat conduction problems in steady state with ant colony optimization. Journal of Liaoning Technical University (Natural Science Edition) 26, 80–82 (2007)
8. Beck, J.V., Blackwell, B., Clair, C.R.: Inverse Heat Conduction: Ill Posed Problems. Wiley Intersc., New York (1985)
9. Beck, J.V., Blackwell, B.: Inverse Problems. Handbook of Numerical Heat Transfer. Wiley Intersc., New York (1988)
10. Haji-Sheikh, A., Buckingham, F.P.: Multidimensional inverse heat conduction using the Monte Carlo method. Trans. of ASME Journal of Heat Transfer 115, 26–33 (1993)
11. Beck, J.V., Cole, K.D., Haji-Sheikh, A., Litkouhi, B.: Heat Conduction Using Green's Functions. Hempisphere, Publishing Corporation, Philadelphia (1992)
12. Mourio, D.A.: The Mollification Method and the Numerical Solution of Ill-posed Problems. John Wiley and Sons Inc., New York (1993)
13. Słota, D.: Homotopy perturbation method for solving the two-phase inverse Stefan problem. Numerical Heat Transfer Part A: Applications 59, 755–768 (2011)
14. Hetmaniok, E., Nowak, I., Słota, D., Wituła, R.: Application of the homotopy perturbation method for the solution of inverse heat conduction problem. International Communications in Heat and Mass Transfer 39, 30–35 (2012)
15. Qiu, C.Y., Fu, C.L., Zhu, Y.B.: Wavelets and regularization of the sideways heat equation. Computers and Mathematics with Applications 46, 821–829 (2003)
16. Słota, D.: Solving the inverse Stefan design problem using genetic algorithm. Inverse Problems in Science and Engineering 16, 829–846 (2008)
17. Słota, D.: Restoring boundary conditions in the solidification of pure metals. Computers and Structures 89, 48–54 (2011)
18. Słota, D.: Reconstruction of the boundary condition in the problem of the binary alloy solidification. Archives of Metallurgy and Materials 56, 279–285 (2011)
19. Hetmaniok, E., Zielonka, A.: Solving the inverse heat conduction problem by using the ant colony optimization algorithm. In: Kuczma, M., Wilmański, K., Szajna, W. (eds.) 18th International Conference on Computer Methods in Mechanics, CMM 2009, pp. 205–206. University of Zielona Góra Press (2009)
20. Hetmaniok, E., Słota, D., Zielonka, A.: Solution of the Inverse Heat Conduction Problem by Using the ABC Algorithm. In: Szczuka, M., Kryszkiewicz, M., Ramanna, S., Jensen, R., Hu, Q. (eds.) RSCTC 2010. LNCS, vol. 6086, pp. 659–668. Springer, Heidelberg (2010)

Optimising Search Engines
Using Evolutionally Adapted Language Models
in Typed Dependency Parses

Marcin Karwinski

Institute of Computer Science,
University of Silesia,
Katowice, Poland
mkarwin@gmail.com
http://ii.us.edu.pl

Abstract. In this paper, an approach to automatic optimisation of the retrieval quality of search engines using a language model paradigm is presented. The topics of information retrieval (IR) and natural language processing (NLP) have already been investigated. However, most of the approaches were focused on learning retrieval functions from existing examples and pre-set feature lists. Others used surface statistics in the form of n-grams or efficient parse tree utilisations – either performs poorly with a language open to changes. Intuitively, an IR system should present relevant documents high in its ranking, with less relevant following below. To accomplish that, semantics/ontologies, usage of grammatical information and document structure analysis were researched. An evolutionary enrichment of language model for typed dependency analysis acquired from documents and queries can adapt the system to the texts encountered. Futhermore, the results in controlled experiments verify the possibility of outperforming existing approaches in terms of retrieval quality.

Keywords: Natural Language Processing (NLP), Genetic Algorithms (GA), Information Retrieval (IR), Search Systems, Ranking Algorithms.

1 Introduction

The problem of information retrieval (IR) can be expressed as an open-ended research problem for practical language technology: "How can I find documents about this?", thus equivalent to searching for a suitable definition of appropriate semantic relevance. Current IR techniques are based on the recovering of documents that are related to a specified query using implementations of algorithms for indexing of materials, for matching them to the query and for ranking the results (eg. RankBoost, RankingSVM, AdaRank or Google PageRank). Despite the improvements in search effectiveness, failures on filling user information needs and capturing the information request semantics are still not fully adressed [16,17,18]. To improve the quality of the searches, intelligent IR systems tend to

L. Rutkowski et al. (Eds.): SIDE 2012 and EC 2012, LNCS 7269, pp. 258–266, 2012.

utilise linguistic information. Considerable attention dedicated to language modelling methods in IR resulted in various approaches [1], with a classic n-gram model most popular [12,13,14,15,16] and language syntax modeling for IR second [2,3,4], [18]. Signicant contribution of dependency types language structure modeling for IR is still to be presented.

From the linguistics perspective, language model resilience to linguistic impurities and malforms is important for the contemporary language analysis [9]. „Language is an immensely democratising institution. To have learned a language is immediately to have rights in it. You may add to it, modify it, play with it, create in it, ignore bits of it, as you will."[10] As English is often considered global lingua franca (discussed in [5] and [10]), it is influenced by several cultural accretions. Grammar is subject to changes [15] and the dictionary is enriched with eg. opaque fixed expressions like francophone *next tomorrow* (British *day after tomorrow*). These have ramifications for IR systems [11], thus text analysis with language model creation/update may be used. It is usually done with recurrent neural networks, gradient descent, simulated annealing and evolutionary programming (according to [19]).

The following paper discusses typed dependency parses for IR system search effectiveness improvement. As this type of parses offers another level of useful information to a regular syntactical approach, the syntax-driven IR model will first be presented. Due to system's planned adaptability to various languages, author proposed evolutionary approach to the problem of optimisation of language modelling according to encountered texts. Next, the importance and theoretical information increase obtained from typed dependency parse of the syntactical parse results is discussed. Experiments in the area of computer generated and updated language grammar models with their results are described and discussed in the following section. Finally, the last section concludes and gives some directions for future work.

2   Language Modelling and IR

A language grammar G is a four tuple $\{N, T, P, S\}$, where N and T are sets of terminals and nonterminals comprising the alphabet of the grammar, P is a set of appropriate production rules, and S is the start symbol. For every grammar, there exists a set of terminal symbol strings known as a language L, that the grammar can generate or recognise. There are also automata that recognise and generate the grammar from that set. These facts are used in language modelling approaches to many problem solutions, as once there are enough sets of the strings, many linguistic methods may be used to improve on other approaches.

In language modelling based IR, for each query $q_i \in Q$ ($Q = \{q_1, q_2, \ldots, q_n\}$) consisting of query terms $q_i = \{q_{i1}, q_{i2}, \ldots, q_{im}\}$, all of the documents $d_j \in D$ to be ranked by relevance to the query are ranked by the probability $P(d_j|q_i)$ of being generated by the query language model. This is further extended into ranking according to the probability $P(d_j|Q)$ of being generated by the query-set language model. From the Bayes formula and the facts that $P(Q)$ is constant and

$P(d_j)$ is considered uniform across the document collection, the documents can be ranked with the same result by the $P(Q|d_j)$ probability. Instead of estimating probability of documents generated by language model defined by Q, the query probability being generated from the documents' language model is used (as in [1]). The probability of a dependency bigram (with $h(q_{ik})$ depicting head and q_{ik} its modifier) in a language model of documents D is denoted as $P_D(h(q_{ik}), q_{ik})$. P_D is thus considered a simplified notation for documents' probability and P_{dj} its counterpart for a single document. $Fr_{dj}(h(q_{ik}), q_{ik})$ is the frequency of dependency bigram in document d_j. The size of the document, denoted by $\|d_j\|$, is the number of dependency relations defined by dependency syntax tree of the document. There is a bijection between words of the sentence and nodes of the tree and, except for the root usually being the predicate of the sentence, each word has one parent, therefore it is possible to introduce the following estimate:

$$P_{dj}(q_i) = \prod_{q_{ik}:\exists h(q_{ik})} P_{dj}(h(q_{ik}), q_{ik}) \approx \prod_{q_{ik}:\exists h(q_{ik})} \frac{Fr_{dj}(h(q_{ik}), q_{ik})}{\|d_j\|}. \qquad (1)$$

3   Syntax-Based IR System

Classic IR systems use the n-gram model, in which any (text) document is treated as a set of words and only frequencies of the corresponding language phenomena and/or adjacency relationship are considered. The term adjacency is usually measured in a number of characters or words between the terms. It is commonly understood that words within a certain distance from each other are in some relation to each other – the closer the query terms are in a document the higher ranking position it gets. For example, a search for *wide lenses* excludes documents with *wide and fast lenses*, lowering the recall. With the query formulated as *wide* AND *lenses*, the precision decreases since documents with *a wide variety of contact lenses* are also returned and ranked higher than those with *wide and water-resistant quality lenses*. The basic idea of a syntax-based IR system is that the syntactical relationships of the user query and documents are compared. Linguists defined a whole battery of syntactical relations used to build more complex structures with corresponding semantics. For instance, noun

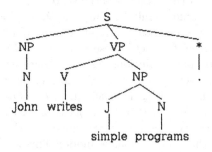

Fig. 1. Example of a sentence syntax analysis

phrases (NP) carry more information than do verb ones (VP) and still can be identified relatively easily, as seen in Fig. 1. In a syntax-based IR system the user is able to search for a structure consisting of a noun *lenses* and an adjective *wide*. The sentences of the documents and the user query are represented by syntactical parse trees. The tree vertices are the words of the text while the edges are the relationships between them. Vertices can also store additional information eg. lexical form (in morphologically rich languages [3]) or negation. Matching is defined in the sense of sub-graph match. Some systems use a simple Boolean match, while others may assign a relevance value to the document. In the case of Boolean matchers, the topological match of the query and the texts is examined and only complete structural match is accepted (no vertex match is considered). In the case of relevance match calculators, the percentage of matching nodes and term inclusion in phrase types is used. If a lexical index (eg. inverse word list) is used for lexical filtering of the documents, the query is matched with both the lexical and the structural index, and the intersection of the results is used. The structural index fastens up searches for complex structures and the lexical index allows the system to work better with non-common terms. For partially unfilled queries the undefined vertices are not looked up in the lexical index. If the queries or documents consist of structures previously unknown or ungrammatical, the parsing process may still fail. The easiest solution is to continually adapt the rule-set to better conform to the texts. If we are trying to identify an intended theme of a text, which is important for IR systems, it seems to be intuitive to further assume that definite nouns are better for theme recognition than indefinite ones. Syntactical analysis with thorough dictionary definition allows for that. Another assumption is that identification of the (surface) subject of a clause is useful and simplified within syntax-based framework.

4   Typed Dependencies for IR

Typed dependencies and phrase structures (as used in syntax-based analysis) are different ways of representing the structure of sentences. While the second approach to parsing represents nesting of multi-word structures, dependency parses represent dependencies between individual words in the texts. A typed dependency parse additionally labels them with existing grammatical relations. There has been much linguistic discussion of the two formalisms and formal isomorphisms between certain linguistic structures since 1980s [7]. Recent years have seen an increased interest in using dependency parses for a range of NLP tasks. IR applications benefit particularly well from having access to typed dependencies between words, since these provide additional information (eg. about predicate-argument structure) not easily available from simple phrase structure parses. This results in several more recent treebanks and parser classes adopting the dependency representation as primary annotation format. However, existing dependency parsers for English such as Minipar or LinkParser are not always as accurate and effective as phrase structure (syntax) parsers trained on very large corpora. Grammatical relations used for typed dependencies approach are

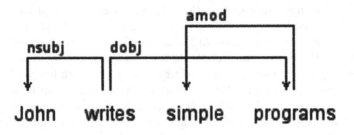

Fig. 2. Example of a sentence typed dependency analysis

arranged in a hierarchy, rooted with the most generic relation of being *dependent (dep)*. When the relation between a phrasal head and its dependent is recognised, relations further down in the hierarchy are analysed and possibly used. For the English language, the *dependent* relation might be further specified as eg. *argument (arg)* or *modier (mod)*. *Arg* can again be divided into several relations eg. a *subject (subj)* relation with its *nominal subject (nsubj)* subtype or a *complement (comp)* relation with *object (obj)* subtype that includes *direct (dobj)*, *indirect (iobj)* and *prepositional (pobj)* objects. *Mod* relations include eg. *adjectival modifier (amod)* relations (as presented on Fig. 2). These dependencies offer not only theoretically but also practically efficient approach, as they offer information useful in the context of textual inference and retrieval applications. Generating typed dependencies requires appropriate rules and dictionary definition for the language, so it is an even better exemplification of how important adapting a pre-defined model to query and document contents language model is. When typed dependencies are used for IR, the process is similar to syntax-based IR. First, a document is parsed with a phrase structure parser. Then, heads of each constituent (structural element) of the document text are identied using specially prepared rules for retrieving the semantic rather than the syntactic heads (as in [2]). Next, the dependents are found and the relations are specified. As there is at least one pattern defined over the phrase structure parse tree for each grammatical relation, each pattern is matched against every corresponding tree node and one with the most specic grammatical relation is taken as the type of the dependency. Dependency trees form the index similarly to syntax-based IR systems. Finally, lexical index is built. When searching, the query is matched with both indices. The intersection of the results is used for further analysis. The relevance calculator that is proposed for typed dependency analysing systems measures distance between two terms $dist(t_i, t_j)$ as:

$$dist(t_i, t_j) = min_{\forall r \in routes}(e(t_i, t_j)) \tag{2}$$

where $min()$ depicts minimum of the set provided as the parameter, $e(x, y)$ depicts the number of edges traversed between the node of x and the node of y. Routes are possible ways for the dependency tree to be traversed between the nodes.

5   Genetic Approach

As described in [6], languages change over time in a fashion similar to evolutionary changes of living organisms. The language model (specimen) defined by the document is encapsulated in the form of syntactic rules, dependency relations and a dictionary. The processes of mutation are defined as dictionary changes (class changes, addition and removal of items) and rule modifications (as in [11]). The crossover is a ,,cut and splice" approach with roulette-based crossover point selection. If in a children model duplicates of elements are detected, only the first occurrence is preserved. Starting specimens are defined by selected documents. Adaptation process is run at start and whenever result-page clickthrough data suggest it (as in [15], [16]). The fitness function for the specimens (language models) is:

$$F_{evo} = \frac{\sum_{\forall t \in tests} \frac{F_f * R_f}{F_r * R_r}}{tests} \tag{3}$$

where F_f represents a vector of returned documents and R_f a corresponding vector of weights. F_r is a vector of possible answers (eg. defined by experts) and R_r depicts a vector with their weights. The * (star symbol) represents dot product of the vectors. The weights correspond to the relevance of a document to the query and are calculated from:

$$w = (c_1 * P) + \frac{c_2 - \frac{\sum_{i=1}^{N_p-1} \sum_{j=i+1}^{N_p} min(dist(i,j),c_2)}{\sum_{k=1}^{N_p-1}(N_p-k)}}{\frac{c_2}{c_1}} + \frac{N_t}{c_3} \tag{4}$$

where $P = P_{dj}(q_i)$ from (1), N_p is the number of unique and N_t of total term occurrences in the document, $dist(i,j)$ is the distance from (2). The variables c_i are parametres set to (97, 1013, 0.0011). The two-parameter $min(x,y)$ function returns the smaller parameter. Due to GP similarities of the approach (as shown in [14]) to text analysis methodology described and used by the author in [11], these elements of the approach to linguistic text analysis in searching are not further described. The stop conditions for the experiments performed during preparations of this article were as follows: evolution reached 1'000'000 generations or at least one specimen returned fitness function result ≥ 0.97 or no changes in fitness function results of the population were observed during last 1'000 generations. Best specimen (from last generation) is used.

6   Experiments

All the experiments were done using sets of documents and query-and-answers by respective experts. The Digital Photography Review (dpreview) website forums offered wide range of real-life linguistic peculiarities. For the second experiment the TREC WebTrack.*gov* collection was used as it is often used in IR evaluation. Each experiment was performed 10 times in a series of 100 repetitions each, average values obtained are presented in the appropriate tables.

6.1 Dpreview

The website forum was used to search for information on possible Pentax K-7 usage during a holiday trip to France. The starting model was built from the K-7 review. After training the system to the language of the comments to the review, experiments consisted of searching on an August 2011 copy of the forum database for: ,,Pentax camera for France", ,,Pentax K7 gear for a trip to France", ,,Pentax camera for a french trip", ,,Pentax camera gear for a french trip", ,,Pentax system" + ,,holiday in France", ,,Pentax k-7" + ,,Pentax camera for France", ,,Pentax k-7" + ,,Pentax camera for a french trip", ,,Pentax k-7" + ,,Pentax system" + ,,holiday in France", ,,Pentax k-7" + ,,Paris trip", ,,k-7 in France". Table 1 presents results obtained for the full query set. R depicts size of the genetic population and was set into either 100 or 1000 specimens (due to platform restrictions). Mutation probability P_m was either 0.001 or 0.01. The Nr column depicts experiment series. F_G shows the evolution quality function results for Google rankings. The data shows that evolutionarily modified language model used in typed dependency approach results in highly increased *relative* correctness of the search system.

Table 1. Dpreview result set

		R = 100		R = 1000	
Nr	F_G	$P_m = 0.001$	$P_m = 0.01$	$P_m = 0.001$	$P_m = 0.01$
1	0.760	0.863	0.927	0.862	0.963
2	0.780	0.954	**0.994**	0.893	0.961
3	0.711	0.856	0.844	0.922	0.943
4	0.603	0.917	0.917	0.998	0.922
5	0.804	0.899	0.878	0.919	**0.999**
6	0.755	0.913	0.976	0.905	0.936
7	**0.827**	0.943	0.993	0.974	0.988
8	0.769	0.890	0.869	0.667	**0.999**
9	0.799	**0.988**	0.983	0.685	0.995
10	0.701	0.962	0.879	**0.999**	0.901

Even for the smaller population of 100 specimens the results obtained by own search engine were usually better than those by Google PageRank. Whatever the mutation probability, the results were clearly better: for 0.001 a value of 0.988 was achieved, and for 0.01 – 0.994. With the population size increase, the language model space was better explored, thus, for both mutation probabilities, the best result was 0.999. For the same query and document set Google PageRank only returned a value of 0.827.

6.2 TREC.gov

For the better comparison to other systems TREC WebTrack.*gov* collection of 225 queries and preferred answers was used. The starting specimens were constructed on the basis of randomly chosen first 10 English language documents of the collection. Table 2 shows the results similarly to the previous experiment.

Table 2. TREC *.GOV* results

Nr	F_G	$R = 100$		$R = 1000$	
		$P_m = 0.001$	$P_m = 0.01$	$P_m = 0.001$	$P_m = 0.01$
1	0.755	0.853	0.909	0.862	0.936
2	0.680	0.914	**0.977**	0.885	0.919
3	0.711	0.756	0.894	0.922	0.873
4	0.603	0.852	0.921	0.998	0.922
5	0.734	0.893	0.898	0.919	0.954
6	0.725	0.913	0.946	0.905	0.899
7	0.679	0.549	0.615	0.845	0.969
8	0.712	0.890	0.860	0.737	**0.999**
9	**0.789**	**0.991**	0.893	0.659	0.795
10	0.601	0.923	0.897	**0.999**	0.801

Again, bigger populations lead to better results. Still, with a population of 100 the best results achieved were 0.991 for the mutation probability $P_m = 0.001$ and 0.977 for $P_m = 0.01$. Both values are better than the one reached by Google PageRank – 0.789. Increasing the population size tenfolds improved the solution space searching, which resulted in achieving 0.999 faster. Allowing for more mutation to take place resulted in faster reaching of those high values with larger group of specimens.

7 Conclusions

The conducted experiments show that appropriate genetic algorithm can create highly efficient language model (the genome of the specimen). This further leads to building forests and indices that represent results of linguistic analysis of the texts. Through the use of efficient forest search algorithms and correct indices, high quality query answer sets are obtained. The results show that the best specimen reaches over 0.9 and often into 0.99 territory. As with other GA-based solutions, experiments that use population of total size approx. 1'000 proved that such approach guarantees better results. These values look better when compared to the results of Google PageRank approach: maximum = 0.79 with an average of 0.721. There are, however, problems still ahead: resources needed to make the correct genome, analyse the text and create indices prevents this solution from being used as an on-the-fly continuous adaptive search tool. Still, once one uses distributed computing solutions, this method may offer even better results, and probably faster.

References

1. Croft, W.B., Ponte, J.M.: A Language Modeling Approach to Information Retrieval. In: Proceedings of the 21st Annual International ACM SIGIR Conference on Research and Development in Information Retrieval, pp. 275–281. SIGIR ACM, Melbourne (1998)
2. Lee, C., Lee, G.G.: Probabilistic Information Retrieval Model for a Dependency Structured Indexing System. In: Information Processing Management, vol. 41, pp. 161–175. Pergamon Press, Tarrytown (2005)
3. Pecina, P., Strakova, J.: Czech Information Retrieval with Syntax-based Language Models. In: Proceedings of the seventh International Conference on Language Resources and Evaluation, pp. 1359–1362. European Language Resources Association, Valletta (2010)
4. Allan, J., Nallapati, R.: Capturing Term Dependencies Using a Language Model Based on Sentence Trees. In: Proceedings of the Eleventh International Conference on Information and Knowledge Management, pp. 383–390. ACM, New York (2002)
5. Ahulu, S.: Grammatical Variation in International English. English Today 56, 19–25 (1998)
6. Millikan, R.G.: Language, a Biological Model. OUP, New York (2005)
7. Ottenheimer, H.J.: The Anthropology of Language. Wadsworth, Belmont (2006)
8. Myers-Scotton, C.: Contact Linguistics: Bilingual Encounters and Grammatical Outcomes. OUP, New York (2002)
9. Yule, G.: The Study of Language. CUP, Cambridge (2006)
10. Crystal, D.: English as a Global Language. CUP, Cambridge (2003)
11. Karwinski, M.: English language grammar models' dynamics and its analysis for information retrieval purposes in written language of the Internet. In: Decision Support Systems, pp. 391–398. Institute of Computer Science, Katowice (2010) (in Polish)
12. Manning, C.D., Schuetze, H.: Foundations of Statistical Natural Language Processing. MIT Press, Cambridge (1999)
13. Potthast, M., Stein, B., Trenkmann, M.: Retrieving Customary Web Language to Assist Writers. In: Gurrin, C., et al. (eds.) Advances in Information Retrieval, pp. 631–635. Springer, Milton Keynes (2010)
14. Konchady, M.: Text Mining Application Programming. Charles River Media, Hingham (2006)
15. Liu, B.: Web Data Mining – Exploring Hyperlinks, Contents, and Usage Data. Springer-Verlag New York, Secaucus (2006)
16. Cormack, G.V.: Information Retrieval – Implementing and Evaluating Search Engines. MIT Press, Cambridge (2010)
17. Manoj, M.: Information Retrieval on Internet Using MSEs. Journal of Scientific and Industrial Research 67, 739–746 (2008)
18. Benko, B.K., Katona, T.: On the Efficient Indexing of Grammatical Parse Trees for Information Retrieval. In: Proceedings of Innovations in Intelligent Systems and Applications, pp. 366–369. Karadeniz Technical University, Trabzon (2005)
19. Fong, S., Giles, C.L., Lawrence, S.: Natural Language Grammatical Inference with Recurrent Neural Networks. IEEE Transactions on Knowledge and Data Engineering 12(1), 126–140 (2000)

The Modified IWO Algorithm
for Optimization of Numerical Functions

Daniel Kostrzewa and Henryk Josiński

Silesian University of Technology, Akademicka 16 PL-44-100 Gliwice, Poland
{Daniel.Kostrzewa,Henryk.Josinski}@polsl.pl

Abstract. The Invasive Weed Optimization algorithm (IWO) is an optimization method inspired by dynamic growth of weeds colony. The authors of the present paper have modified the IWO algorithm introducing a hybrid strategy of the search space exploration. The goal of the project was to evaluate the modified version by testing its usefulness for numerical functions minimization. The optimized multidimensional functions: Griewank, Rastrigin, and Rosenbrock are frequently used as benchmarks which allows to compare the experimental results with outcomes reported in the literature. Both the results produced by the original version of the IWO algorithm and the Adaptive Particle Swarm Optimization (APSO) method served as the reference points.

Keywords: Invasive Weed Optimization algorithm, Griewank function, Rastrigin fuction, Rosenbrock function.

1 Introduction

The Invasive Weed Optimization (IWO) algorithm is an optimization method, in which the exploration strategy of the search space (similarly to the evolutionary algorithm) is based on the transformation of a complete solution into another one. Its idea was inspired by observation of dynamic spreading of weeds and their quick adaptation to environmental conditions [1].

The authors of the method from University of Tehran emphasized its usefulness for continuous optimization tasks. Their research was focused inter alia on minimization of the multimodal functions and tuning of a second order compensator [1], antenna configurations [2], electricity market dynamics [3], and a recommender system [4].

The authors of the present paper have modified the IWO algorithm introducing a hybrid strategy of the search space exploration (described in detail in section 2) and broadened the scope of the IWO algorithm application dealing skillfully with an important discrete optimization task from the databases area – the join ordering problem – for both – centralized and distributed data [5]-[6]. The symmetric TSP was also successfully solved by the modified IWO equipped with the *inver-over* operator [7].

The goal of the present paper is an evaluation of the modified IWO based on the effects of the optimization of the Griewank, Rastrigin and Rosenbrock

L. Rutkowski et al. (Eds.): SIDE 2012 and EC 2012, LNCS 7269, pp. 267–274, 2012.

functions. The results (minima values) produced by the modified IWO were compared with the outcomes generated by the original IWO as well as with the results of the Adaptive Particle Swarm Optimization (APSO) [8], [9].

The organization of this paper is as follows – section 2 contains a brief description of the IWO algorithm taking into serious consideration the proposed hybrid method of the search space penetration. Optimized functions are presented in section 3. Section 4 deals with procedure of the experimental research along with its results. The conclusions are formulated in section 5.

2   Description of the Modified IWO Algorithm

The modified version of the IWO algorithm provides the opportunity to experiment with different search space exploration strategies. The pseudocode mentioned below describes the algorithm by means of terminological convention consistent with the „natural" inspiration of its idea:

```
Create the first population composed of n randomly generated
individuals.
For each individual {
  Compute the value of the fitness function
  as the reciprocal of the minimized function.
}
While the stop criterion is not satisfied {
  For each individual from the population {
    Compute the number of seeds depending on the value
    of the fitness function.
    For each seed {
      Determine a place of fall of the seed choosing
      with the fixed probability one of the following
      methods: dispersing, spreading or rolling down.
      Create a new individual according to the randomly
      chosen method.
      Compute the value of the fitness function
      for the new individual.
    }
  }
  Create a new population composed of n best adapted
  individuals taking into account members of the former
  population as well as new individuals.
}
```

The number of seeds S_{ind} produced by a single individual depends on the value of its fitness function f_{ind} – the greater the degree of individual's adaptation, the greater its reproduction ability according to the following formula:

$$S_{ind} = S_{min} + \left\lfloor (f_{ind} - f_{min}) \frac{S_{max} - S_{min}}{f_{max} - f_{min}} \right\rfloor, \qquad (1)$$

where S_{max}, S_{min} denote maximum and minimum admissible number of seeds generated, respectively, by the best population member (fitness f_{max}) and by the worst one (fitness f_{min}).

The character of the operation described as ,,Determine a place of fall of the seed" differs depending on the method chosen randomly for its realization. Probability values of selection assigned to the particular methods: dispersing, spreading and rolling down form parameters of the algorithm.

In case of dispersing the aforementioned operation computes the distance between the place where the seed falls on the ground and the parent individual (Fig. 1a). The distance is described by normal distribution with a mean equal to 0 and a standard deviation truncated to nonnegative values. The standard deviation is decreased in each algorithm iteration (i.e. for each population) and computed for the iteration $iter$, $iter \in [1, iter_{max}]$ according to the following formula:

$$\sigma_{iter} = \left(\frac{iter_{max} - iter}{iter_{max}} \right)^m (\sigma_{init} - \sigma_{fin}) + \sigma_{fin} . \tag{2}$$

The total number of iterations ($iter_{max}$), equivalent to the total number of populations, can be either used in form of the algorithm parameter with the purpose of determination of the stop criterion or can be estimated based on the stop criterion defined as the execution time limit. The symbols σ_{init}, σ_{fin} represent, respectively, initial and final values of the standard deviation, whereas m is a nonlinear modulation factor.

According to the *dispersing* method construction of a new individual represented by a vector of a length equal to n, where element i, $i \in [1, n]$ contains argument x_i of the optimized n-dimensional function, is based on the random generation of the values for all arguments x_i. Those values determine the direction of the seed's ,,fly". Because the seed has to fall on the ground at the determined distance from the parent individual, the values of function arguments are scaled so that this condition is fulfilled.

The *spreading* is a random disseminating seeds over the whole of the search space. Therefore, this operation is equivalent to the random construction of new individuals (Fig. 1b).

The *rolling down* is based on the examination of the neighbourhood of the parent individual. In case of continuous optimization the term ,,neighbours" stands for individuals located at the same randomly generated distance from the considered one. The best adapted individual is chosen from among the determined number of neighbours, whereupon its neighbourhood is analyzed in search of the next best adapted individual. This procedure is repeated k times (k is a parameter of the method) giving the opportunity to select the best adapted individual found in the k-th iteration as a new one (Fig. 1c).

3   Characterization of the Optimized Functions

According to [10] there are following classes of functions used as benchmarks for numerical optimization problems:

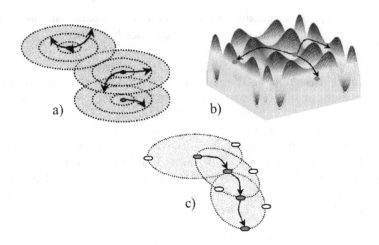

Fig. 1. Idea of: a) dispersing b) spreading c) rolling down ($k = 3$)

1. Unimodal, convex, multidimensional.
2. Multimodal, two-dimensional with a small number of local extremes.
3. Multimodal, two-dimensional with a huge number of local extremes.
4. Multimodal, multidimensional with a huge number of local extremes.

Griewank and Rastrigin functions belong to the 4. class. The classical Rosenbrock function is a two-dimensional unimodal function, whereas the n-dimensional ($n = 4 \sim 30$) Rosenbrock function has 2 minima [11]. The global minimum for all functions is equal to 0.

The formula defining the n-dimensional Griewank function (Fig. 2a) is as follows:

$$f(x) = \frac{1}{4000} \sum_{i=1}^{n} x_i^2 - \prod_{i=1}^{n} \cos\left(\frac{x_i}{\sqrt{i}}\right) + 1 . \tag{3}$$

The n-dimensional Rastrigin function (Fig. 2b) is described by the following formula:

$$f(x) = 10n + \sum_{i=1}^{n} \left[x_i^2 - 10\cos\left(2\pi x_i\right)\right] . \tag{4}$$

The following formula defines the n-dimensional ($n > 1$) Rosenbrock function (Fig. 2c):

$$f(x) = \sum_{i=1}^{n-1} \left[100\left(x_{i+1} - x_i^2\right)^2 + \left(1 - x_i\right)^2\right] . \tag{5}$$

4   Experimental Research

The goal of the experiments was to compare the results (minima values) found by the modified IWO with the outcomes generated by other methods. As reference

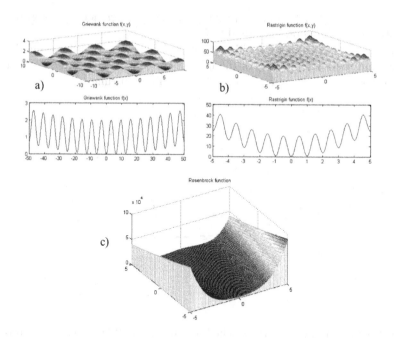

Fig. 2. a) The Griewank function b) the Rastrigin function c) the Rosenbrock function

points served the results achieved from experiments with the original version of the IWO algorithm and those reported in [9] as minima found by the APSO method. For purpose of comparison the initial scope of the search space for particular functions as well as other optimization parameters correspond with values proposed in the literature. The initial scopes given in Figures 5, 6, 7 are asymmetric according to the suggestion expressed in [9]. Values of the modified IWO parameters describing the hybrid strategy of the search space exploration were collected in Table 1. They were found during the research as the most appropriate values for the considered problem.

The workstation used for experiments is described by the following parameters: Intel Core2 Quad Q6600 2.4GHz processor, RAM 2GB 800MHz. The number of

Table 1. Modified IWO parameters describing the search space exploration strategy

Description	Griewank ($n = 10$)	Griewank ($n = 20, 30$)	Rastrigin	Rosenbrock
Number k of neighbourhoods examined during the rolling down	1	1	1	1
Probability of the dispersing	0.7	0.3	0.8	0.1
Probability of the spreading	0.2	0.2	0	0.1
Probability of the rolling down	0.1	0.5	0.2	0.8

trial runs for each function in the presence of a single parameters configuration of the optimization method was equal to 500.

Minima of the 30-dimensional Rastrigin and Griewank functions found by the original and modified versions of the IWO algorithm are presented in Figures 3, 4, respectively. The X values denote the optimization time.

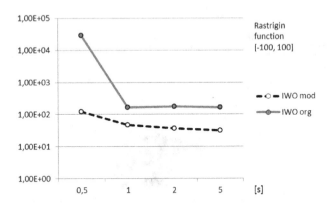

Fig. 3. Comparison between the original and modified IWO based on the Rastrigin function

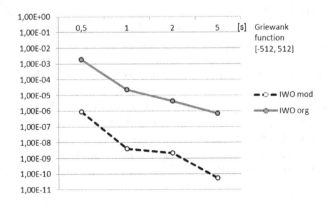

Fig. 4. Comparison between the original and modified IWO based on the Griewank function

Minima of the n-dimensional Rastrigin, Rosenbrock, and Griewank functions ($n = 10, 20, 30$) found by the modified IWO algorithm and the APSO method are presented in Figures 5, 6, 7, respectively. The n value is strictly related to the number of algorithm iterations (respectively: 1000, 1500, 2000) used as a stop criterion. The X values denote the number of individuals.

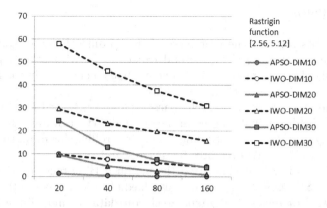

Fig. 5. Comparison between the APSO and IWO algorithms based on the Rastrigin function

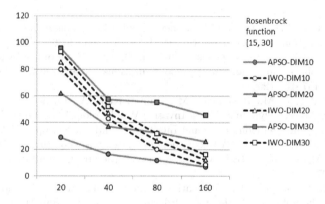

Fig. 6. Comparison between the APSO and IWO algorithms based on the Rosenbrock function

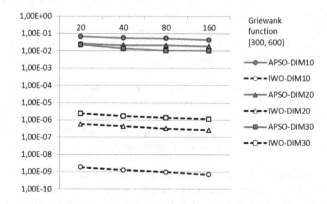

Fig. 7. Comparison between the APSO and IWO algorithms based on the Griewank function

5 Conclusion

The experiments revealed the usefulness of the modified IWO for solving continuous optimization tasks. The method can compete with other algorithms, although it should be compared with some methods mentioned in the literature as successful ones (e.g. Artificial Bee Colony).

The hybrid strategy of the search space exploration turned out to be more efficient than the dissemination used in the original IWO. However, the influence of the strategy components (dispersing, spreading, rolling down) on the solution found by the modified IWO requires further research.

In the area of discrete optimization the modified IWO takes part at present in the *World TSP Challenge* (www.tsp.gatech.edu/world/index.html) and in the *Mona Lisa TSP Challenge* (www.tsp.gatech.edu/data/ml/monalisa.html).

References

1. Mehrabian, R., Lucas, C.: A novel numerical optimization algorithm inspired from weed colonization. Ecological Informatics 1(4), 355–366 (2006)
2. Mallahzadeh, A.R., Oraizi, H., Davoodi-Rad, Z.: Application of the Invasive Weed Optimization Technique for Antenna Configurations. Progress in Electromagnetics Research, 137–150 (2008)
3. Sahraei-Ardakani, M., Roshanaei, M., Rahimi-Kian, A., Lucas, C.: A Study of Electricity Market Dynamics Using Invasive Weed Colonization Optimization. In: IEEE Symposium on Computational Intelligence and Games, pp. 276–282 (2008)
4. Sepehri Rad, H., Lucas, C.: A Recommender System based on Invasive Weed Optimization Algorithm. In: IEEE Congress on Evolutionary Computation, pp. 4297–4304 (2007)
5. Kostrzewa, D., Josiński, H.: Verification of the Search Space Exploration Strategy Based on the Solutions of the Join Ordering Problem. In: Man-Machine Interactions, AISC, pp. 447–455 (2011)
6. Kostrzewa, D., Josiński, H.: The Comparison of an Adapted Evolutionary Algorithm with the Invasive Weed Optimization Algorithm Based on the Problem of Predetermining the Progress of Distributed Data Merging Process. In: Man-Machine Interactions. AISC, pp. 505–514 (2009)
7. Kostrzewa, D., Josiński, H.: Application of the IWO Algorithm for the Travelling Salesman Problem. In: Proceedings of the 3rd KKNTPD, pp. 238–247 (2010) (in Polish)
8. Hossen, S., Rabbi, F., Rahman, M.: Adaptive Particle Swarm Optimization (APSO) for multimodal function optimization. International Journal of Engineering and Technology 1(3), 98–103 (2009)
9. Xie, X.-F., Zhang, W.-J., Yang, Z.-L.: Adaptive Particle Swarm Optimization on Individual Level. In: International Conference on Signal Processing, pp. 1215–1218 (2002)
10. Molga, M., Smutnicki, C.: Test functions for optimization needs (2005), http://www.zsd.ict.pwr.wroc.pl/files/docs/functions.pdf
11. Shang, Y.-W., Huang-Qiu, Y.: A Note on the Extended Rosenbrock Function. Evolutionary Computation 14(1), 119–126 (2006)

Solving Fuzzy Job-Shop Scheduling Problem by a Hybrid PSO Algorithm

Junqing Li[1], Quan-Ke Pan[1], P.N. Suganthan[2], and M. Fatih Tasgetiren[3]

[1] School of Computer Science, Liaocheng University, Liaocheng, 252059
lijunqing.cn@gmail.com
[2] School of Electrical and Electronic Engineering, Nanyang Technological University,
Singapore 639798
epnsugan@ntu.edu.sg
[3] Industrial Engineering Department, Yasar University, Izmir, Turkey

Abstract. This paper proposes a hybrid particle swarm optimization (PSO) algorithm for solving the job-shop scheduling problem with fuzzy processing times. The objective is to minimize the maximum fuzzy completion time, i.e., the fuzzy makespan. In the proposed PSO-based algorithm performs global explorative search, while the tabu search (TS) conducts the local exploitative search. One-point crossover operator is developed for the individual to learn information from the other individuals. Experimental results on three well-known benchmarks and a randomly generated case verify the effectiveness and efficiency of the proposed algorithm.

Keywords: Fuzzy processing time, Job-shop scheduling problem, Particle swarm optimization, Tabu search.

1 Introduction

The job shop scheduling problem (JSP) has received much attention in recent decades [1]. The processing time for each operation is deterministic in the classical JSP. However, in most practical industries, the processing time for each operation is just a fuzzy value, because various factors are involved in the real-world problems.

In 1996, Kuroda and Wang [2] proposed a branch-and-bound algorithm for solving both the static and the dynamic JSP. Sakawa and Mori designed an efficient genetic algorithm (GA) for solving the FJSP with one objective, in reference (1999) [3], and two objectives, in reference (2000) [4]. Song et al. (2006) [5] developed a hybrid algorithm combined GA and ant colony optimization (ACO), a local search approach was also embedded in the hybrid algorithm. Inés et al. (2010) [6] considered a multi-objective JSP with uncertain durations and crisp due dates. A fuzzy goal programming approach embedded in GA was also proposed. Lei (2010) [7] developed a random key GA algorithm. The other swarm intelligent algorithms have also been introduced for solving the fuzzy JSP. Wu et al. (2006) [8] designed an efficient algorithm by combining fuzzy ranking method and shifting bottleneck procedure to

L. Rutkowski et al. (Eds.): SIDE 2012 and EC 2012, LNCS 7269, pp. 275–282, 2012.

solve the FJSP. Lei (2007) [9] proposed a particle swarm optimization (PSO) algorithm to solve the FJSP with three objectives. The Pareto archive structure is conducted in the proposed PSO algorithm. Niu et al. (2008) [10] introduced a hybrid algorithm combined with PSO and GA for the problem.

PSO is introduced in 1995 by Kenney and Eberhart (Kennedy & Eberhart, 1995) [11, 12]. In PSO, each particle records the best experience it has encountered, and denotes as *pbest*. The best particle found so far is also recorded and denoted as *gbest*. Each particle in the current population learns from both *pbest* and *gbest* with a certain probability. However, PSO has limited ability to escape from local optima. Tabu Search (TS) proposed by Glober in 1986 is an effective local search algorithm to solve combinatorial optimization problems [13, 14, and 15]. In this paper, we propose a hybrid algorithm combining PSO with TS (HPSO) for solving the fuzzy JSP. In the proposed algorithm, the exploration task is performed by PSO, while the exploitation task is completed by TS.

The rest of this paper is organized as follows: Section 2 briefly describes the problem. Then, the framework of the proposed algorithm is presented in Section 3. Section 4 illustrates the experimental results and compares against competitive algorithms from the existing literature to demonstrate the superiority of the proposed algorithm. Finally, Section 5 presents the concluding remarks and future research directions.

2   Problem Formulation

The job shop scheduling with fuzzy processing time can be formulated as follows.

There are n jobs and m machines. Each job visits each machine exactly once in a predefined order. Each machine can process only one operation at a time. There are no set-up times, no release dates and no due dates. Let O_{ij} be the jth operation of job J_i; Let $\tilde{p}_{ijk}$ be the fuzzy processing time of O_{ij} on machine M_k. The objective of the problem is to sequence each operation on each machine in order to minimize the maximum completion time. The fuzzy makespan is represented by a triplet (s_1, s_2, s_3).

3   The Proposed Algorithm

3.1   Individual Representation

For FJSP with n jobs and m machines, the individual representation used in [4] is by a $n \times 3m$ matrices of fuzzy completion times. In [7], each individual is denoted by a $n \times 3m$ real string. In this study, we represent each individual by an $n \times m$ integer value. Each value represents the job number which the corresponding operation belongs to. Therefore, in each individual, each job number occurs m times. For example, given a 3-jobs-3-machines FJSP case, one of the possible individual is denoted by {1,2,2,1,3,3,1,3,2}. The first element in the individual represents the first operation of the job J_1. Then, the following element tells the first operation of J_2. The next one shows the second operation of J_2, while the last element is the last operation of J_2. It should be noted that the individual in this study only tells the scheduling sequence among all operations, the individual does not contain the information of the fuzzy processing time. The advantage of the coding is that, when considering the evolving operators, computational time can be reduced.

3.2   Initial Population

In this study, the initial population is generated in a random way. That is, each individual in the population is produced without making use of any prior experience. The advantage of this approach is simplicity and ease of maintaining the population diversity. The disadvantage is ignoring prior knowledge, if such knowledge is available.

3.3   Iterations

In the basic PSO, a particle flies by learning from both the local best and the global best. In this study, the individual is represented by lots of integer numbers. Therefore, it is hard to utilize the classical PSO directly to solve the FJSP. In the proposed algorithm, the crossover operator in the classical GA is introduced into the PSO to help the individuals to learn from others. The detailed implementation of the crossover operator is defined as follows.

Step 1. Given an n-jobs-m-machines problem, two individuals are denoted by p_1 and p_2, respectively.

Step 2. Select a random number r, which is ranged at $[1, m]$.

Step 3. Copy the first r elements in p_1 to the corresponding location in a new particle c_1. Select the first r elements in p_2 to the corresponding location in a new particle c_2.

Step 4. Read each element in p_1 from left to right, if the element has occurred in c_2 m times, then ignore it; otherwise, place the element in the first empty location in c_2. Scan each element in p_2 from left to right, if the element has occurred in c_1 m times, then ignore it; otherwise, place the element in the first empty location in c_1.

Step 5. Evaluate the c_1 and c_2, select the one with better fuzzy makespan as the new particle to replace the old particle in the current population.

3.4   Local Search

In DPSO, each particle learns information from the two best particles. Thus, the whole algorithm converges rapidly. However, the classical PSO may not be able to escape from a locally optimal solution. In this study, TS was conducted to complete the exploitation task. In the proposed algorithm, TS was applied for the global best particle found so far. In each generation, after crossover, the best particle will be improved by TS-based local search. Then, the new improved best particle will direct the swarm of particles to a better location in the search space.

3.5   Framework

The main framework of the proposed algorithm is as follows.

Step 1. Generate P_{size} particle to construct the initial population. Evaluate each particle in the population and record each one as the local best. Select the best particle in the population as the global best.

Step 2. If stop condition is satisfied, then terminate; otherwise perform Steps 3-6.

Step 3. For each particle in the population, apply the one-point crossover with the local best and global best.

Step 4. Evaluate each new generated particle, and select the best particle as the new global best. Record the local best for each particle.

Step 5. Apply TS-based local search to the global best found so far.

Step 6. Go back to Step 2.

4   Numerical Results

This section discusses the computational experiments used to evaluate the performance of the proposed algorithm. The dimensions of the instances range from 6 jobs 6 machines to 16 jobs 16 machines. Our algorithm was implemented in C++ on an Intel Pentium IV 1.7GHz PC with 512MB memory. The best and average results of experiments from 30 independent runs were collected for performance comparison.

4.1   Experimental Parameters

Firstly, we set several fixed parameters for the experiment as follows: the probability for PSO are set: c_1=0.5, c_2=0.5; the population size is set 10; the tabu list size is set $n \times m$; the tabu tenure is set $n \times m/2$; the algorithm stops when the solution is close enough to the lower bound of the objective function value. Otherwise, it stops when the best solution is not improved for $n \times m$ iterations or the time budget is exhausted.

4.2   Experimental Results on Three Benchmarks

Three benchmarks are conducted by the proposed algorithm. Tables 1 to 3 give the fuzzy processing time for the three benchmarks, respectively. The first case in Table 1 is a 6-jobs-6-machines problem; the scale of other two problems is 10-jobs-10-machines.

To make a detailed comparison with the current algorithms, we select two famous algorithms in the present literature. RKGA refers to the algorithm in [7], while SMGA is the algorithm proposed in [4]. Table 4 gives the comparison results for solving the three benchmarks. It can be concluded form Table 4 that: (1) for solving the three fuzzy JSP, the proposed algorithm obtains all optimal solutions; (2) the proposed algorithm obtains the near-optimal solutions in each run, and the average values obtained by our algorithm are also the best.

Table 1. The fuzzy processing time for Case1. (6-jobs-6-machines).

	Processing machines (fuzzy processing time)
Job1	3(9,13,17) 2(6,9,12) 0(10,11,13) 4(5,8,11) 1(10,14,17) 5(9,11,15)
Job 2	3(5,8,9) 1(7,8,10) 4(3,4,5) 2(3,5,6) 0(10,14,17) 5(4,7,10)
Job 3	4(3,5,6) 3(3,4,5) 2(2,4,6) 0(5,8,11) 1(3,5,6) 5(1,3,4)
Job 4	5(8,11,14) 2(5,8,10) 0(9,13,17) 3(8,12,13) 1(10,12,13) 4(3,5,7)
Job 5	2(8,12,13) 4(6,9,11) 5(10,13,17) 1(4,6,8) 0(3,5,7) 3(4,7,9)
Job 6	1(8,10,13) 3(8,9,10) 5(6,9,12) 2(1,3,4) 4(3,4,5) 0(2,4,6)

Table 2. The fuzzy processing time for Case2. (10-jobs-10-machines).

	Processing machines (fuzzy processing time)
Job 1	7(2,3,4) 5(3,5,6) 4(2,4,5) 1(4,5,6) 0(1,2,3) 2(3,5,6) 8(2,3,5) 3(1,2,3) 6(3,4,5) 9(2,3,4)
Job 2	9(2,3,4) 6(2,3,5) 3(2,4,5) 5(1,2,3) 7(4,5,6) 2(2,4,6) 1(2,3,4) 0(1,3,4) 4(2,3,4) 8(3,4,5)
Job 3	5(2,4,5) 8(1,2,3) 9(2,3,5) 7(1,2,4) 0(3,5,6) 6(1,3,4) 3(1,3,5) 1(1,2,4) 4(2,4,5) 2(1,3,5)
Job 4	0(1,2,3) 4(3,4,5) 7(1,3,5) 8(2,4,6) 9(2,4,5) 5(1,2,4) 6(3,4,5) 1(1,3,5) 3(1,3,6) 2(1,3,4)
Job 5	1(2,3,4) 6(1,3,4) 2(1,3,4) 4(1,2,3) 7(1,3,5) 8(2,3,4) 9(3,4,5) 5(1,3,4) 0(3,4,5) 3(1,3,4)
Job 6	3(2,3,4) 1(2,3,4) 2(1,2,3) 4(2,4,5) 5(1,3,4) 7(1,3,4) 6(3,4,5) 8(1,2,3) 9(2,4,5) 0(1,3,4)
Job 7	2(2,3,4) 4(1,4,5) 3(1,3,5) 0(3,4,5) 8(2,3,4) 6(3,4,5) 1(1,2,3) 9(3,5,6) 7(3,5,6) 5(1,2,2)
Job 8	6(3,4,5) 0(1,2,3) 8(3,4,5) 5(2,4,5) 9(1,3,4) 1(2,3,4) 4(1,2,3) 2(2,4,5) 3(3,4,5) 7(2,3,5)
Job 9	8(3,4,5) 3(1,3,4) 9(1,3,5) 1(2,3,4) 2(3,5,6) 5(2,4,5) 7(1,3,4) 0(3,4,5) 4(1,2,3) 6(1,2,4)
Job 10	6(2,4,5) 4(1,2,3) 1(3,4,5) 3(2,3,4) 0(1,2,3) 7(3,4,5) 9(2,4,5) 5(3,4,5) 2(1,2,3) 8(1,2,4)

Table 3. The fuzzy processing time for Case3. (10-jobs-10-machines)

	Processing machines (fuzzy processing time)
Job 1	3(10,13,16) 5(4,7,9) 6(10,12,13) 7(5,6,7) 8(6,8,9) 1(7,8,12) 4(10,12,15) 2(5,6,7) 0(2,3,5) 9(10,14,18)
Job 2	1(3,5,6) 0(9,10,13) 2(5,8,9) 9(9,12,16) 5(5,6,9) 6(7,11,12) 4(9,13,14) 8(8,12,16) 7(2,4,6) 3(4,7,10)
Job 3	6(9,12,14) 9(10,13,14) 8(5,7,8) 3(3,4,6) 4(4,7,8) 1(3,5,7) 7(3,4,6) 2(1,2,4) 0(5,7,9) 5(9,11,13)
Job 4	4(10,12,16) 6(1,2,4) 9(6,8,10) 5(1,3,5) 3(7,8,11) 0(5,8,10) 7(9,10,14) 8(4,7,8) 1(4,7,10) 2(2,3,5)
Job 5	4(9,12,15) 5(8,11,14) 9(10,14,17) 0(5,7,9) 1(2,4,5) 3(1,3,5) 6(7,8,10) 8(3,4,6) 7(9,11,13) 2(1,2,3)
Job 6	7(4,7,9) 1(10,12,15) 2(3,4,5) 3(10,14,18) 0(5,6,9) 4(10,14,16) 8(10,12,15) 5(8,9,12) 9(5,8,9) 6(4,7,10)
Job 7	4(8,12,13) 9(2,4,6) 7(10,14,18) 0(5,7,9) 5(4,5,8) 8(4,5,7) 6(7,10,11) 1(10,11,12) 2(10,13,15) 3(9,12,13)
Job 8	1(10,12,15) 5(5,6,9) 2(1,2,4) 7(6,9,12) 3(4,6,9) 0(7,11,14) 8(7,11,13) 4(6,9,11) 9(8,11,13) 6(7,9,13)
Job 9	8(2,4,6) 5(2,3,5) 1(2,3,4) 3(4,6,7) 9(6,8,9) 2(8,12,14) 0(4,7,9) 6(8,11,14) 7(1,2,3) 4(3,5,6)
Job 10	6(5,8,9) 7(6,8,9) 2(8,12,16) 0(6,9,12) 8(7,11,13) 4(10,11,14) 3(7,10,11) 1(3,5,7) 9(3,4,6) 5(8,11,15)

Table 4. The comparisons with other two algorithms

	RKGA		SMGA		HPSO	
	avg	*opt*	*avg*	*opt*	*avg*	*opt*
1	56, 80, 103	56, 80, 103	56, 80, 103	56, 80, 103	56, 80, 103	56, 80, 103
2	95.1,130.9,162.2	96, 129, 60	96.8, 134.9, 164.7	95, 133, 161	93.8, 130.6, 161.2	96, 129, 60
3	28.4, 48, 64.1	28, 47, 62	29.1, 48.3, 64.5	28, 47, 66	26.8, 47, 64	27, 47, 62

4.3   Experimental Result on a Random Generated Problem

To verify the ability to solve large scale problems, we randomly generated a fuzzy JSP with 16 jobs and 16 machines. The problem is given in Table 5. The fuzzy makespan for the best solution obtained by the proposed algorithm is (162,200,247). The Gantt chart obtained by the proposed algorithm is given in Fig. 1. In the Gantt chart, each machine faces a base line. All operations operated on the machine are placed on the base line one by one in the scheduling order. The two groups of values

Table 5. The fuzzy processing time for the randomly generated case. (16-jobs-16-machines).

	Processing machines (fuzzy processing time)
Job 1	5(4,4,5) 15(10,10,14) 1(3,7,10) 2(2,6,9) 14(3,3,3) 9(6,10,13) 8(3,6,8) 11(5,8,9) 16(5,8,8) 13(6,8,9) 6(9,13,15) 7(10,10,14) 12(5,5,5) 10(6,9,12) 3(1,2,5) 4(3,5,7)
Job 2	3(8,8,11) 14(2,5,8) 7(8,8,12) 6(6,6,9) 13(4,6,9) 16(4,6,10) 8(4,8,9) 10(9,11,14) 2(1,2,5) 5(5,8,9) 15(1,5,8) 9(1,1,4) 4(8,9,12) 1(6,7,7) 12(9,12,16) 11(5,8,11)
Job 3	15(10,12,13) 3(5,5,8) 10(7,8,8) 7(6,7,11) 2(7,11,11) 12(5,7,7) 9(4,6,7) 6(9,11,12) 13(7,10,14) 8(5,5,6) 5(3,3,6) 1(6,7,8) 14(2,6,10) 11(7,9,10) 16(9,11,11) 4(6,7,7)
Job 4	15(2,2,3) 4(8,9,9) 5(1,3,7) 10(4,7,8) 13(3,6,8) 7(4,8,11) 2(5,8,9) 1(9,13,15) 6(4,8,11) 11(1,1,4) 3(9,9,9) 8(2,6,9) 16(7,10,14) 9(3,4,8) 14(9,11,14) 12(5,5,7)
Job 5	14(4,5,9) 16(9,13,16) 1(10,11,14) 3(6,7,11) 4(3,3,6) 11(9,13,15) 12(9,11,11) 13(2,6,9) 5(2,6,9) 6(6,10,12) 2(10,13,13) 15(2,6,8) 7(6,6,6) 8(1,5,7) 10(9,11,15) 9(6,6,10)
Job 6	12(5,5,5) 14(2,3,3) 8(10,10,13) 15(4,7,9) 4(3,4,8) 9(4,7,8) 2(1,4,7) 11(9,13,16) 5(1,2,2) 1(5,6,9) 7(8,11,11) 16(9,9,10) 10(10,10,13) 6(10,13,14) 13(1,2,6) 3(8,11,15)
Job 7	12(5,6,6) 14(7,8,9) 4(7,8,10) 8(2,6,6) 3(7,8,10) 16(2,6,10) 5(6,8,11) 13(5,6,6) 15(3,6,7) 11(7,10,13) 2(3,5,7) 10(2,4,5) 9(1,5,9) 6(5,6,6) 1(4,5,7) 7(5,5,8)
Job 8	12(9,10,12) 15(2,6,10) 16(9,11,15) 11(6,8,12) 7(10,13,16) 10(9,10,14) 6(9,10,11) 5(3,6,9) 1(3,4,6) 4(8,8,10) 2(9,11,13) 13(9,9,11) 3(1,4,8) 9(3,6,8) 14(1,1,1) 8(3,5,6)
Job 9	7(8,11,13) 8(9,10,11) 15(1,5,5) 5(9,13,13) 1(1,1,3) 13(3,3,3) 10(3,4,8) 3(9,10,14) 14(7,10,14) 11(9,12,12) 2(6,7,7) 9(6,9,13) 12(1,1,5) 4(8,10,11) 16(5,9,13) 6(1,4,4)
Job 10	4(4,4,4) 15(8,9,11) 16(9,12,13) 7(5,9,10) 11(10,10,10) 1(8,12,14) 9(4,8,8) 2(9,12,13) 10(6,8,11) 8(3,7,8) 14(7,8,10) 3(10,10,14) 12(10,13,14) 6(2,6,10) 13(6,6,6) 5(7,7,7)
Job 11	13(10,14,15) 11(4,8,12) 15(1,1,4) 2(10,11,13) 3(9,12,13) 10(9,10,10) 9(3,7,11) 5(1,3,5) 16(2,2,6) 14(5,9,11) 7(6,6,10) 4(3,4,6) 12(8,10,14) 8(6,6,10) 1(1,4,8) 6(2,4,6)
Job 12	16(10,13,15) 8(3,5,8) 11(6,9,12) 15(10,14,18) 3(7,11,14) 2(6,7,8) 4(1,3,5) 12(8,10,11) 7(5,7,8) 6(4,6,7) 9(7,10,13) 13(4,6,9) 5(7,7,8) 10(3,4,4) 1(6,10,11) 14(8,12,15)
Job 13	14(5,7,10) 11(9,10,11) 1(4,7,9) 3(7,8,10) 8(3,6,8) 4(9,9,12) 6(6,9,11) 7(4,7,8) 5(1,4,5) 2(1,5,7) 12(5,9,10) 9(6,8,11) 10(4,8,10) 15(3,3,4) 16(3,5,7) 13(1,3,7)
Job 14	13(2,2,5) 15(8,11,15) 16(6,10,12) 14(3,3,5) 12(9,10,12) 3(1,4,5) 10(9,12,12) 11(4,5,7) 2(1,3,6) 5(5,6,9) 6(4,6,6) 4(9,10,12) 9(1,5,8) 8(9,10,13) 7(7,9,12) 1(10,10,10)
Job 15	13(6,7,8) 12(4,4,4) 1(9,12,14) 11(4,4,5) 6(6,6,10) 4(8,10,12) 3(9,11,15) 10(5,9,12) 5(3,5,7) 16(6,9,13) 7(8,11,15) 14(6,7,11) 15(1,3,6) 8(4,5,9) 2(4,5,5) 9(5,5,7)
Job 16	12(10,10,13) 4(2,6,6) 9(8,12,12) 1(4,7,9) 3(4,6,7) 14(1,5,5) 16(8,8,12) 11(1,1,2) 2(3,3,7) 5(9,13,14) 7(8,11,14) 15(1,3,4) 8(7,7,9) 10(9,13,16) 13(10,14,18) 6(5,7,7)

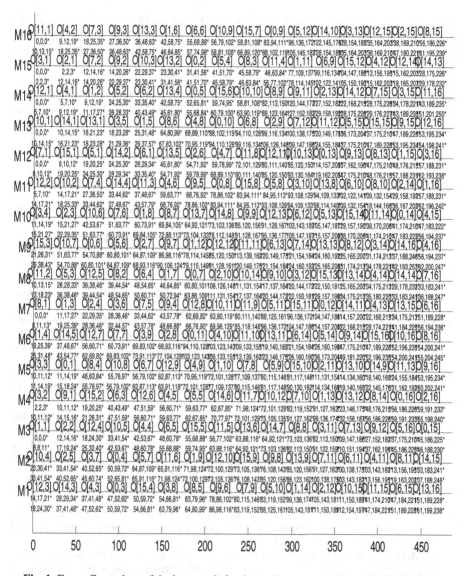

Fig. 1. Fuzzy Gantt chart of the best result for the random-generated case ((162,200,247))

under each operation are the starting and completing fuzzy time, respectively, for the corresponding operation. The random-generated large scale problem also shows the efficiency and effectiveness of the proposed algorithm.

5   Conclusions

This paper proposed a hybrid algorithm combining PSO and TS for solving the fuzzy JSP. A novel crossover operator was introduced into the PSO to make it capable of solving the JSP. TS-based local search was conducted for the global best particle to enable it to escape from locally optimal points. Experimental results show the efficiency and robustness of the proposed algorithm. The future work will apply the proposed hybrid PSO to solve other combinatorial problems.

Acknowledgement. This research is supported by National Science Foundation of China under Grant 61104179, 61174187 and Science Research and Development of Provincial Dept of Public Education of Shandong under Grant (J09LG29, J11LG02 and J10LG25).

References

1. Wang, L., Zheng, D.Z.: A modified genetic algorithm for job shop scheduling. Int. J. Adv. Manuf. Technol. 20, 72–76 (2002)
2. Kuroda, M., Wang, Z.: Fuzzy job shop scheduling. Int. J. Prod. Econ. 44(1), 45–51 (1996)
3. Sakawa, M., Mori, T.: An efficient genetic algorithm for job shop scheduling problems with fuzzy processing time and fuzzy due date. Comput. Ind. Eng. 36(2), 325–341 (1999)
4. Sakawa, M., Kubota, R.: Fuzzy programming for multi-objective job shop scheduling with fuzzy processing time and fuzzy due date through genetic algorithm. Eur. J. Oper. Res. 120(2), 393–407 (2000)
5. Song, X.Y., Zhu, Y.L., Yin, C.W., Li, F.M.: Study on the combination of genetic algorithms and ant colony algorithms for solving fuzzy job shop scheduling. In: Proceedings of the IMACS Multi-Conferences on Computational Engineering in Systems Application, Beijing, pp. 1904–1909 (2006)
6. Inés, G.R., Camino, R.V., Jorge, P.: A genetic solution based on lexicographical goal programming for a multiobjective job shop with uncertainty. J. Intell. Manuf. 21, 65–73 (2010)
7. Lei: Solving fuzzy job shop scheduling problems using random key genetic algorithm. Int. J. Adv. Manuf. Technol. 49, 253–262 (2010)
8. Wu, C.S., Li, D.C., Tsai, T.I.: Applying the fuzzy ranking method to the shifting bottleneck procedure to solve scheduling problems of uncertainty. Int. J. Adv. Manuf. Technol. 31(1-2), 98–106 (2006)
9. Lei, D.M.: Pareto archive particle swarm optimization for multi-objective fuzzy job shop scheduling problems. Int. J. Adv. Manuf. Technol. 37(1-2), 157–165 (2007)
10. Niu, Q., Jiao, B., Gu, X.S.: Particle swarm optimization combined with genetic operators for job shop scheduling problem with fuzzy processing time. Applied Mathematics and Computation 205, 148–158 (2008)
11. Eberhart, R.C., Kennedy, J.: A new optimizer using particle swarm theory. In: Proceedings of the Sixth International Symposium on Micro Machine and Human Science, Nagoya, Japan, pp. 39–43. IEEE Service Center, Piscataway (1995)
12. Sha, D.Y., Hsu, C.Y.: A hybrid particle swarm optimization for job shop scheduling problem. Computers and Industrial Engineering 51(4), 791–808 (2006)
13. Glover, F.: Tabu Search: A Tutorial. Interfaces 20(4), 74–94 (1990)
14. Li, J.Q., Pan, Q.K., Liang, Y.C.: An effective hybrid tabu search algorithm for multi-objective flexible job shop scheduling problems. Computers and Industrial Engineering 59(4), 647–662 (2010)
15. Li, J.Q., Pan, Q.K., Suganthan, P.N., Chua, T.J.: A hybrid tabu search algorithm with an efficient neighborhood structure for the flexible job shop scheduling problem. Int. J. Adv. Manuf. Technol. 52(5-8), 683–697 (2011)

On Designing Genetic Algorithms for Solving Small- and Medium-Scale Traveling Salesman Problems

Chun Liu and Andreas Kroll

Measurement and Control Department, Mechanical Engineering
University of Kassel, Mönchebergstraße 7, 34125, Kassel, Germany
{chun.liu,andreas.kroll}@mrt.uni-kassel.de

Abstract. Genetic operators are used in genetic algorithms (GA) to generate individuals for the new population. Much research focuses on finding most suitable operators for applications or on solving large-scale problems. However, rarely research addresses the performance of different operators in small- or medium-scale problems. This paper studies the impact of genetic operators on solving the traveling salesman problem (TSP). Using permutation coding, a number of different GAs are designed and analyzed with respect to the impact on the global search capability and convergence rate for small- and medium-scale TSPs. In addition, the differences between small- and medium-scale TSPs on suitable GA design are studied. The experiments indicate that the inversion mutation produces better solutions if combined with insertion mutation. Dividing the population into small groups does generate better results in medium-scale TSP; on the contrary, it is better to apply operators to the whole population in case of small-scale TSP.

Keywords: Genetic algorithm, Genetic operators, Convergence, Global search capability, TSP.

1 Introduction

The Genetic Algorithm (GA) proposed by Holland [1] mimics some of the processes of natural evolution to solve global optimization problems. It is a general problems solver and has been used in a variety of real world problems [2,3] due to its advantages such as simplicity, minimal problem restrictions, global search capability, etc. As the new population is generated by selection, crossover and mutation operators in classical genetic algorithms, it is important to select appropriate operator realizations. A lot of enhanced genetic algorithms have been proposed, such as adaptive crossover and mutation probability [4], different crossover operators [5,6], suitable population sizes [7,8], etc. The research particularly addresses large-scale problems [2,9,10], while little work is done on GA design for small- and medium-scale problems.

Different mutation operators were compared in [11] for solving small-scale problems, and inversion mutation was compared with insertion operator based on different crossover in [12] for solving 80-cities TSP. The results in both papers [11,12]

L. Rutkowski et al. (Eds.): SIDE 2012 and EC 2012, LNCS 7269, pp. 283–291, 2012.

are similar to the one presented in this paper: the algorithm with inversion mutation outperforms other mutation operators. However, they do neither study the
results for simultaneous use of different operators (e.g. inversion combined with insertion mutation), nor do they consider the impact of different crossover/mutation
rates and different population sizes on the algorithm performance.

This paper studies GA design with different crossover and mutation operators for small- and medium-scale permutation problems. Assessment criteria are
the global search capability and convergence rate in the benchmark - Traveling
Salesman Problem (TSP). The research is restricted to the symmetrical single-
salesman problem, in which the salesman should visit each city exactly once
and return to the start city. This is a Hamiltonian cycle, which is a cycle in an
undirected graph that visits each vertex exactly once and finally returns to the
starting vertex [13].

The total traveled distance is used as the evaluated cost with d_{ij} (Euclidean distance) as the traveled cost between cities. Given N cities, named $\{c_1, c_2, ..., c_N\}$,
and a traveling sequence $\{s_1, s_2, ..., s_N\}$ of the salesman, the objective is to determine the sequence of cities that minimizes the total cost:

$$\min\left[\left(\sum_{k=s_1}^{s_{(N-1)}} d_{k(k+1)}\right) + d_{s_N s_1}\right]$$

For the symmetric TSP, the number of possible tours is $(N-1)!/2$. Small-,
medium-, and large-scale TSP were defined differently in the literature: [9] and
[10] referred to more than 100 cities as large-scale TSP, [2] referred 40 cities as
medium-scale TSP, [14] considered the number of cities between 100 and 200 as
medium-scale TSP, but [15] referred to 51 cities as a small-scale TSP. In this
paper, a number of cities $N \leq 20$ is considered as small scale, $20 < N < 100$
as medium scale, and $N > 100$ as large scale. Problems with 10, 15, 20 and 50
cities are selected as examples for analyzing the properties of genetic algorithms
in small- and medium-scale TSP, with the number of possible solution candidates
are 1.8×10^5, 4.4×10^{10}, 6.1×10^{16}, and 3.0×10^{62}, respectively. Although the
small-scale problems can be solved by exhaustive search, using GA is much
faster [16].

The content of this paper is organized as follows. Section 2 describes the
process of the general genetic algorithm proposed in this paper. Two strategies
for generating the new population are presented. Section 3 designs a number
of GA variants with different genetic operators based on section 2. Section 4
analyzes the global search capabilities and convergence rates of GAs designed
in section 3 in small- and medium-scale TSP. Finally, conclusions are drawn in
section 5.

2   General Algorithm Design

In this paper, permutation coding is used to represent a tour (i.e. one chromosome codes one tour), which is an integer coding scheme. A consecutive integer
number is assigned to each city, and a possible tour is a sequence of cities.

Although a binary matrix (N by N) can be used to represent a tour [6], permutation coding is more intuitive, easier to visualize, and requires less storage space than matrix coding. Elitism strategy is used for selection, in which at least one best individual (elite) is copied without changes to the new population. Such a strategy prevents losing the best solutions found so far, while GA design avoids dominance of a super-fit individual. In this paper, the new population is generated by four operators: elitism selection, crossover, mutation and random generation. Therefore, the new population with PS individuals is composed of four offsprings groups: EC elite chromosomes, CC children of crossover, MC children of mutation and RC random generated chromosomes. The four operators are:

- **Elite** chromosomes with the best fitness (elites) in current population that are transferred unchanged to the new population, the rate is $r_e := EC/PS$.
- **Crossover** chromosomes generated by crossover operator, the rate is $r_c := CC/PS$. The parents of crossover are chosen randomly from the parental pool composed of the best $r_p \cdot N_g$ chromosomes of the current population. r_p is the rate of chromosomes selected into the parental pool, and N_g is the number of chromosomes in each group for generating offsprings as explained in the following strategies. Note that not all of the chromosomes in parental pool can be chosen for crossover if $r_c < r_p$.
- **Mutation** chromosomes generated by mutation operators, the rate is $r_m := MC/PS$.
- **Random** chromosomes generated randomly, the rate is $r_r := RC/PS$.

The rate of these four types of offsprings satisfies $r_e + r_c + r_m + r_r = 1$, that is, $PS = EC + CC + MC + RC$. Two strategies for generating the new population are proposed:

Strategy 1: ($N_g < PS$) The population is randomly divided into non-overlapping groups (tournament team) with each group having N_g chromosomes in each generation. Then the elite selection, crossover and mutation are performed in each group, respectively. The number of the chromosomes that are chosen into the parental pool is $r_p \cdot N_g$. Mutation operators are applied to the best chromosome in each group in parallel. This strategy is inspired from keeping both global best and local best chromosomes.

Strategy 2: ($N_g = PS$) The population is not divided into groups. The elite selection, crossover and mutation are applied to the entire population. The number of chromosomes which are chosen into the parental pool is $r_p \cdot PS$. Mutation operators are applied to the best chromosome in the population in parallel. This strategy is inspired from keeping the global best and sub-best chromosomes in the population.

A two-point crossover - the partially mapped crossover (PMX) [17] and three mutation operators (swap [18], insertion [18] and inversion [1]) are used for generating the new offsprings in this paper. The next section designs a number of different variants of genetic algorithms for analyzing the impact of different operators and of different operator combinations.

3   Algorithmic Variants

Twelve genetic algorithms were designed (Table 1) to analyze the impact of different crossover and mutation operators. GA1 without PMX crossover is inserted randomly generated chromosomes for keeping the constant population size. GA3-GA5 and GA9-GA11 test impact of different mutation operators with different crossover rates. GA6-GA8 test the impact of different combinational mutation operators. As premature convergence could be emerged if the genetic algorithms without mutation operators, random chromosomes are inserted for increasing the diversity of the population in GA12. The performance of the designed algorithms on both strategies is analyzed in the next section.

Table 1. Genetic algorithms with different operators

GA	Elitist (r_e)	Parents (r_p)	PMX (r_c)	Mutation(r_m) swap	insertion	inversion	Random (r_r)	r_c	r_m
GA1	0.2	0	0	0.2	0.2	0.2	0.2	0	0.6
GA2	0.2	0.4	0.2	0.2	0.2	0.2	0	0.2	0.6
GA3	0.2	0.4	0.2	0.6	0	0	0	0.2	0.6
GA4	0.2	0.4	0.2	0	0.6	0	0	0.2	0.6
GA5	0.2	0.4	0.2	0	0	0.6	0	0.2	0.6
GA6	0.2	0.4	0.4	0.2	0.2	0	0	0.4	0.4
GA7	0.2	0.4	0.4	0	0.2	0.2	0	0.4	0.4
GA8	0.2	0.4	0.4	0.2	0	0.2	0	0.4	0.4
GA9	0.2	0.4	0.6	0.2	0	0	0	0.6	0.2
GA10	0.2	0.4	0.6	0	0.2	0	0	0.6	0.2
GA11	0.2	0.4	0.6	0	0	0.2	0	0.6	0.2
GA12	0.2	0.4	0.6	0	0	0	0.2	0.6	0

4   Experimental Study

The experiments analyze the global search capability (GSC) and convergence rate (CR) of the genetic algorithms with different operators and population sizes for the same predefined computational load. Each algorithm runs independently 200 times, if the global optimal solution is found k times, the global search capability is $GSC := k/200$. The convergence rate is $CR := (\sum_{i=1}^{200}(FG)_i)/200$, FG is the generation in which the global optimal solution appears for the first time (due to the elitist operator it cannot get lost again). The smaller CR is, the better.

For each TSP size, the performance of the designed GA is addressed with different population sizes PS. To analyze the efficiency of the algorithms at the same computing cost, the termination criterion is selected as maximum number of generations G_{max}. In the experiments, $G_{max} \cdot PS =$ constant is chosen for each TSP size. Five population sizes $PS \in \{10, 20, 40, 80, 120\}$ are analyzed in the experiments and compared based on the same computational load ($G_{max} \cdot PS$ = 2000 in TSP with 10 cities, $G_{max} \cdot PS$ = 4000 in TSP with 15 cities, $G_{max} \cdot PS$ = 8000 in TSP with 20 cities, and $G_{max} \cdot PS$ = 2×10^5 in TSP with 50 cities).

4.1 Small-Scale TSP

Based on strategy 1, set N_g = 10, the global search capability and the convergence rate are shown in Fig. 1. Algorithms GA1, GA2, GA5, GA7, GA8 and GA11 obtain much better GSC than the others, and all of them use inversion mutation. Among those, GA1, GA2 and GA7 are similar and better than the others. Although inversion mutation provides for better GSC, the algorithm without insertion mutation yields sub-best GSC (GA5, GA8 and GA11). Therefore, using inversion combined with insertion mutation is suggested.

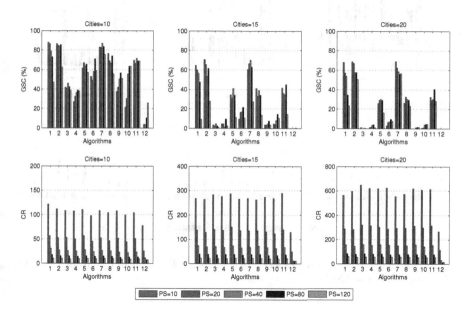

Fig. 1. GSC and CR based on strategy 1 in small-scale TSP (left most bar for PS = 10, right most for PS = 120 for each algorithm)

The results of GA3-GA5 and GA9-GA11 show that the effects of different mutation operators alone on GSC from better to worse are: inversion, insertion, swap. This emphasizes that inversion is the most powerful of these three genetic operators, as the inversion mutation based on the individuals with the best fitness in each group allows small adjustments (for instance, swapping two adjacent genes) and also can generate big adjustments (e.g. inverting the whole chromosome), so that it can evolve with great efficiency while keeping the genetic diversification. Although random chromosomes are inserted for increasing the diversity of the population, GA12 without mutation still leads to premature convergence and has very low global search capability.

For strategy 2, the global search capability and the convergence rate are shown in Fig. 2. The results provide for the same conclusions as strategy 1: inversion combined with insertion mutation produces better solutions, and the effects of these mutation operators on GSC from better to worse are: inversion, insertion, swap. The algorithm with strategy 2 has better GSC and converges significantly faster than strategy 1 in small-scale TSP. Therefore, for small-scale TSP, it is suggested to use GA based on strategy 2 with inversion and insertion mutation operators.

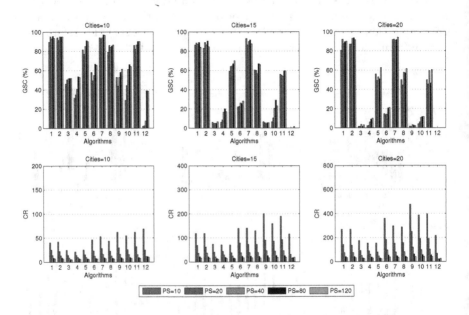

Fig. 2. GSC and CR based on strategy 2 in small-scale TSP (left most bar for $PS = 10$, right most for $PS = 120$ for each algorithm)

4.2   Medium-Scale TSP

The following experiment is an example for the medium-scale problem with 50 cities. The global search capability and the convergence rate of these algorithms based on strategy 1 and strategy 2 are shown in Fig. 3. The results show that GA1, GA2 and GA7 perform much better than the others. Similar to the small-scale TSP, inversion combined with insertion mutation offers good GSC, inversion has better GSC than insertion and swap, and strategy 2 has much faster convergence rate than strategy 1. But the algorithm with strategy 1 has significantly better GSC than strategy 2 in medium-scale TSP. This is contrary to the results for small-scale TSP.

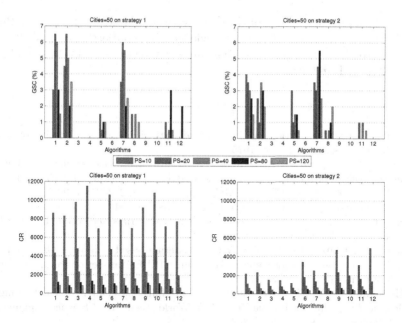

Fig. 3. GSC and CR of 50 cities (left most bar for $PS = 10$, right most for $PS = 120$ for each algorithm)

For medium-scale TSP with a much more complex search space than for small-scale TSP, it is better to use strategy 1 for keeping the local optimal solutions, that better maintains the genetic diversity and avoids premature convergence. Therefore, for designing GA for solving medium-scale TSP, it is suggested to use strategy 1 with inversion and insertion mutation operators.

5   Conclusion

This paper investigates the design of Genetic Algorithms for small- and medium-scale permutation problems on the example of the traveling salesman problem. Based on elitism selection, two strategies are proposed for generating the new population. Several genetic algorithms are designed and tested based on both strategies to analyze the impact of different genetic operators (crossover, inversion, insertion and swap mutation). From the experiments, the following conclusions can be drawn:

(1) For medium-scale TSP, it is better to use a tournament approach (strategy 1), while for small-scale TSP the population should not be divided into groups (strategy 2) for genetic operations.

(2) The genetic algorithm with inversion combined with insertion mutation operator offers better GSC in all test cases and all strategies.

A companion paper [19] presents an application study for task allocation and tour planning for a multi-robot system for plant inspection. Future work will address design issues for multi-TSP with cooperative tasks.

Acknowledgements. Parts of the work were supported by the project Robo-Gas[Inspector] [20], which is greatly acknowledged. The project RoboGas[Inspector] is funded by the Federal Ministry of Economics and Technology due to a resolution of the German Bundestag.

References

1. Holland, J.H.: Adaptation in Natural and Artificial Systems. The University of Michigan Press, Ann Arbor (1975)
2. Onoyama, T., Oyanagi, K., Kubota, S., Tsuruta, S.: GA Applied Method for Interactively Optimizing a Large-Scale Distribution Network. In: Proceedings of TENCON 2000, Kuala Lumpur, Malaysia, vol. 2, pp. 253–258 (2000)
3. Paszkowicz, W.: Genetic Algorithms, a Nature-Inspired Tool: Survey of Applications in Materials Science and Related Fields. Materials and Manufacturing Processes 24(2), 174–197 (2009)
4. Zhang, J., Chung, H.S.H., Lo, W.L.: Clustering-based Adaptive Crossover and Mutation Probabilities for Genetic Algorithms. IEEE Transactions on Evolutionary Computation 11(3), 326–335 (2007)
5. Al-Dulaimi, B.F., Ali, H.A.: Enhanced Traveling Salesman Problem Solving by Genetic Algorithm Technique (TSPGA). World Academy of Science, Engineering and Technology 38, 296–302 (2008)
6. Homaifar, A., Guan, S., Liepins, G.E.: Schema Analysis of the Traveling Salesman Problem Using Genetic Algorithms. Complex Systems 6(2), 183–217 (1992)
7. Smorodkina, E., Tauritz, D.: Greedy Population Sizing for Evolutionary Algorithms. In: Proceedings of IEEE Congress on Evolutionary Computation (CEC 2007), Singapore, pp. 2181–2187 (2007)
8. Zhang, G., Liu, X., Zhang, T.: The Impact of Population Size on the Performance of GA. In: Proceedings of the Eighth International Conference on Machine Learning and Cybernetics, Baoding, China, pp. 1866–1870 (2009)
9. Park, D.C., Figueras, A.L., Chen, C.: A Hierarchical Approach for Solving Large-Scale Traveling Salesman Problem. In: 1994 IEEE World Congress on Computational Intelligence, Neural Networks, Orlando, USA, vol. 7, pp. 4613–4618 (1994)
10. Kobayashi, K.: Introducing a Clustering Technique into Recurrent Neural Networks for Solving Large-Scale Traveling Salesman Problems. In: Proceedings of Internet Corporation for Assigned Names and Numbers, Skövde, Sweden, vol. 2, pp. 935–940 (1998)
11. Ferreira, C.: Combinatorial Optimization by Gene Expression Programming: Inversion Revisited. In: Proceedings of the Argentine Symposium on Artificial Intelligence, Santa Fe, Argentina, pp. 160–174 (2002)
12. Walkenhorst, J., Bertram, T.: Multi-criteria Optimization Techniques for Pickup and Delivery Problems. In: Proceedings of 21 Workshop Computational Intelligence, Dortmund, Germany, pp. 61–75 (2011)
13. DeLeon, M.: A Study of Sufficient Conditions for Hamiltonian Cycles. Department of Mathematics and Computer Science, Seton Hall University (2000)
14. Yang, M., Kang, L., Guan, J.: An Evolutionary Algorithm for Dynamic Multi-Objective TSP. In: Kang, L., Liu, Y., Zeng, S. (eds.) ISICA 2007. LNCS, vol. 4683, pp. 62–71. Springer, Heidelberg (2007)
15. Luo, X., Yang, Y., Li, X.: Solving TSP with Shuffled Frog-Leaping Algorithm. In: Proceedings of Eighth International Conference on Intelligent Systems Design and Applications, Kaohsiung, Taiwan, vol. 3, pp. 228–232 (2008)

16. Ediger, P., Hoffmann, R., Halbach, M.: Evolving 6-State Automata for Optimal Behaviors of Creatures Compared to Exhaustive Search. In: Moreno-Díaz, R., Pichler, F., Quesada-Arencibia, A. (eds.) EUROCAST 2009. LNCS, vol. 5717, pp. 689–696. Springer, Heidelberg (2009)
17. Goldberg, D.E., Lingle, R.: Alleles, Loci, and the Traveling Salesman Problem. In: Proceedings of the First International Conference on Genetic Algorithms and Their Application, Hillsdale, NJ, pp. 154–159 (1985)
18. Larrañaga, P., Kuijpers, C.M.H., Murga, R.H.: Tackling the Travelling Salesman Problem with Evolutionary Algorithms: Representations and Operators. Technical Report (1998)
19. Liu, C., Kroll, A.: A Centralized Multi-Robot Task Allocation for Indutrial Plant Inspection by Using A* and Genetic Algorithms. In: Proceedings of ICAISC, Zakopane, Poland (2012) (accepted)
20. RoboGas^{Inspector}, http://www.robogasinspector.de/

Explore Influence of Differential Operator in DE Mutation with Unrestrained Method to Generate Mutant Vector

Hao Liu[1], Han Huang[1,2], and Shusen Liu[1]

[1] School of Software Engineering South China University of Technology Guangzhou, P.R. China
[2] Department of Management Sciences, College of Business City University of Hong Kong, Hong Kong
liuhaoscut@gmail.com, hhan@scut.edu.com

Abstract. Differential Evolution (DE) is an efficient optimizer in current use. Although many new DE mutant vectors have been proposed by alter the differential operator, there are few works studying the differential operator's effect in DE algorithm. This paper proposes a correlation between the DE performance and the mutant vector. That is, for a particular mutant vector, increase the number of differential operator would influence the performance of the algorithm linearly. These mutant vectors are evaluated by 23 benchmarks selected from Congress on Evolutionary Computation (CEC) competition. Additionally, this paper proposes an unrestrained method to generate mutant vector. Unlike the old method selects mutually exclusive individuals, the new method allows same individuals appear repeatedly to generate mutant vector. This new method could enhance the potential diversity of the population and improve the performance of DE in general. *abstract* environment.

Keywords: Differential Evolution (DE), differential operator, mutant vector generation.

1 Introduction

Since 1995 Storn and Price proposed DE, it is accepted widely as an excellent and reliable function optimizer. DE is a special case of evolutionary algorithm, it distinguished to other EAs because it generates offspring by a scaled difference perturb vector. Ferrante Neri and Ville Tirronen[1] have given an overview of DE, Swagatam Das[2] has given a conclusion of recent years development and future trend of DE. In forestall research, except noise problems [3][4], DE achieved excellent result to most benchmarks. In previous CEC, DE is best as an applicable evolutionary algorithm. Although recent papers show some strong EA like restart covariance matrix adaptation ES (CMA-ES) outperforms classical and adaptive DE at CEC2005 competition, DE is still outstanding to solve real-valued test functions.

L. Rutkowski et al. (Eds.): SIDE 2012 and EC 2012, LNCS 7269, pp. 292–300, 2012.

As DE is simple and effective, various mutate vectors have been proposed to get further optimization. Storn and Price have suggested a mutant vector family and many other scientists have expanded the vector family. It is easy to perceive that some vectors are improved by add one more differential operator, however, few papers have pay attention to the performance tendency of DE with various differential operator. With this consideration, this paper explores the relation between DE performance and the number of differential operator in mutant vector.

In the following part this paper proposes a new method to generate mutant vector. Classical DE select individuals in the population randomly and subtract other randomly selected individuals to gain perturb parameter. This paper proposes an unrestrained method which could enhance potential diversity of the population. The new method improves the performance of DE steadily. In this paper, 2.1 concludes framework of DE, 2.2 presents classical mutate vectors and the author gives new mutate vectors, 2.3 proposes a new method to generate effective mutate vector. Part 3.1 introduces experiment benchmarks and 3.2 presents the result of experiments and analysis. The paper gives a conclusion in part 4.

2 Benchmark Optimization by DE

2.1 Framework of DE

DE optimization means to find the minimum value of objective function f(x). This problem can be encoded as a NP population with D dimension parameters vector $X = [x_1, x_2, \ldots, x_{NP}]$,initial population distributed in search space S randomly. The goal of the algorithm is to find out $x_{min} \in S$, by using pre-prepared benchmarks.

The framework of DE:

a) Initialization

For each individual with D dimension at G generation $x_i = \{x_{i1}^G, x_{i2}^G, \ldots, x_{iD}^G\}$, there have a certain range for each dimensions, the initial population should randomly distributes in a prescribed space.

b) Mutation

DE employs a mutate vector to perturb individuals to get a mutation in the search space. The classical vector could be expressed as

$$V_i^G = x_{r1}^G + F(x_{r2}^G - x_{r3}^G) \tag{1}$$

r1, r2, r3 are integers randomly selected in the range [1, NP].

c) Crossover

After mutation, for each individual xi crossover operation is used to generate a trial vector $U_i^G = [u_{1i}^G, u_{2i}^G, \ldots u_{Di}^G]$,. This paper uses binomial crossover to generate trail vector.

d) Select

In this step the select operation if the trail vector has less or equal benchmark value than the target vector, the trail vector would replace the parent as a member of the offspring, otherwise the target vector would remain in the next generation.

b)c)d)would be repeated until certain criterion is met.

2.2   Construct New Mutation Family

The difference vector (1) has only one scaled difference to perturb the population, which is known as DE/rand/1. Storn and Price suggest other difference vectors known as:

1.$DE/best/1 : V_i^G = x_{best} + F(x_{r2}^G - x_{r3}^G)$

2.$DE/best/2 : V_i^G = x_{best} + F(x_{r2}^G - x_{r3}^G) + F(x_{r4}^G - x_{r5}^G)$

3.$DE/rand/2 : V_i^G = x_{r1}^G + F(x_{r2}^G - x_{r3}^G) + F(x_{r4}^G - x_{r5}^G)$

4.$DE/cur - to - best/1 : V_i^G = x_i^G + F(x_{best}^G - x_{r1}^G) + F(x_{r2}^G - x_{r3}^G)$

5.$DE/rand - to - best/1 : V_i^G = x_{r1}^G + F(x_{best}^G - x_{r2}^G) + F(x_{r3}^G - x_{r4}^G)$

r1, r2, r3, r4, r5 are integers randomly selected in the range [1, NP]. is the best individual in G generation. These vectors could be seen at [6].

It is easy to perceive rand/1, rand/2 and best/1, best/2 all achieve acceptable result and they are in regular pattern. Based on this observation, this paper gives a hypothetical that increase the number of differential operator would have influence on the performance on DE algorithms. These vectors are expanded by adding difference parameters to rand/3 and best/3. Moreover, cur-to-best/1 and cur-to-rand/1 vector could derive new vectors best-to-cur/1, rand-to-cur/1 by changing the parameter positions. In the same theory of expand best/1, cur-to-best/1 and rand-to-best/1 could expand to cur-to-best/2 and rand-to-best/2, etc.

These new vectors are listed below:

6.$DE/best/3 : V_i^G = x_{best} + F(x_{r2}^G - x_{r3}^G) + F(x_{r4}^G - x_{r5}^G) + F(x_{r6}^G - x_{r7}^G)$

7.$DE/rand/3 : V_i^G = x_{r1}^G + F(x_{r2}^G - x_{r3}^G) + F(x_{r4}^G - x_{r5}^G) + F(x_{r6}^G - x_{r7}^G)$

8.$DE/best - to - cur/1 : V_i^G = x_{best} + F(x_i^G - x_{r1}^G) + F(x_{r2}^G - x_{r3}^G)$

9.$DE/cur - to - rand/1 : V_i^G = x_i^G + F(x_{r1}^G - x_{r2}^G) + F(x_{r3}^G - x_{r4}^G)$

10.$DE/rand - to - cur/1 : V_i^G = x_{r1}^G + F(x_i^G - x_{r2}^G) + F(x_{r3}^G - x_{r4}^G)$

11.$DE/cur-to-best/2 : V_i^G = x_i^G + F(x_{best}^G - x_{r1}^G) + F(x_{r2}^G - x_{r3}^G) + F(x_{r4}^G - x_{r5}^G)$

12.$DE/rand - to - best/2 : V_i^G = x_{r1}^G + + F(x_{best}^G - x_{r2}^G) + F(x_{r3}^G - x_{r4}^G) + F(x_{r5}^G - x_{r6}^G)$

To prove this hypothesis, the following new mutant vectors will be tested in part 3.

These vectors perhaps not excellent enough to handle test functions, but they are useful to present performance of vectors with different difference parameter.

As the vector has a simple structure, change the value of control parameter or change the different operator are common methods to optimize the vector.

2.3   Improved Method to Generate Mutant Vector

Since 1950s, with the idea of using Darwinian principles to solve problems, evolutionary computation emerges distant ideas as a competitive discipline. This part we propose a new method to generate mutant vector and try to explain it by

Darwinian principles. In biological, the mutant vector means a sudden change in the gene characteristics of a chromosome [2]. This has proposed for a long time and it is widely accepted. To evolutionary computing, mutation is a perturb factor, a parent vector with a mutation operation generates an offspring, the mutant vector is also called donor vector.

Classical method selects r1,r2,r3,r4,r5,r6,r7, and are mutually exclusive integers from the range [1,NP][6] [8] [9]. For each mutant vector these integers would generate again. However, this method declines performance of DE. As these 7 parameters are mutually exclusive, it decreases the diversity of the perturb vector. The new method ignores the restriction that selects integers mutually exclusive, same integers can appear repeatedly in one mutant vector.

Fig1 illustrates the development of the new method. Use rand/2 as example, if $x_{r1},x_{r2},x_{r3},x_{r4},x_{r5}$, are all different,$x_{r1},F(x_{r2}^G - x_{r3}^G)$,and $F(x_{r4}^G - x_{r5}^G)$, are not zero. But this restriction is unreasonable. Restrict integers mutually exclusive predefined a scope to mutant the population and the new scope is smaller than the search space.

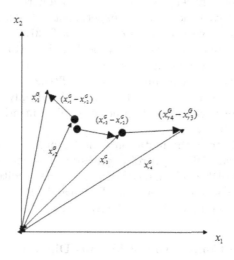

Fig. 1. Illustrating DE mutant vector scheme in 2-D parametric space. The new method increases the potential diversity of the population, $F(x_{r2}^G - x_{r3}^G)$,is the increased choice of the Difference Vector.

In biological evolution, each individual would influence the evolution of the whole group. Bases on this theory, previous DE algorithms select all integers mutually exclusive. However, this approach is one-sided understanding of Darwinian principle. At biosphere, new offspring influenced by other individuals, but the number of other individuals is undecided. As all factors selects from the parent population which means new mutation generates by deformation and combination of parent individual. Some genes are called recessive genes would not certainly show their influence. Fixing the number of differences decreases the diversity of population individuals. So in this paper we select r1, r2, r3, r4, r5, r6, r7 randomly in [1, NP], even all of them are same is acceptable, but remember the distinct individual should different to the base vector , this restrict ensures the mutant vector would not be same to its parent -which is useless in the biological evolution process.

This simplified strategy not only simplifies the mutant vector generate process but also improves the performance of DE because it enriches the potential perturb diversity.

3   Experiment Result

3.1   Extend Benchmark Functions and Parameter Setting

Ferrante Neri and E. Mezura-Montes [1] [7] have explored the performance of some mutate vectors. It suggests that no one vector can achieve best result to all problems [7]. But this result is artless and sketchy, the experiment by using only 13 benchmarks is not sufficient as many new benchmarks are given now. This paper use comprehensive benchmarks to experiment different mutate vectors. 23 benchmarks are used to experiment various vectors. f1-f6 are unimodal functions, f7-f13 are multimodal functions with many local minima, f14-f20 are multimodal functions with a few local minima, especially f18-f20 are multimodal functions with deceiving, above functions are seen in [8]. f21-f23 are rotated functions. These rotated functions are generate by f7,f10,f11 multiply an orthogonal matrix.. As DE does not perform good on noise problem mentioned, in this paper no noise problems is discussed.

In the traditional sense, the mutation scale factor F, the crossover constant CR and population size NP is control parameters. The effects of them are well studied. To ensure all DE performance are in the same conditions, this paper set NP=100, dimension=30 as constant value, F=0.5 and CR=0.9. Iteration number of each function is given in TABLE1and TABLE 2.

3.2   Performance Comparison of Various Difference Vectors

This part we compare the result between DE with various differential operator. As cur-to-best/2 and rand-to-best/2 does not achieve good result and restricted by paper's length, we does not list performance of these two vectors in Table2. With 6 classical vectors and expanded 5 vectors, 11 vectors are listed in Table1 -Table4.

The result of various benchmarks shows that best/2 is best to handle unimodal functions and rand/1 is best to handle multimodal functions with many local minima. To unimodal functions with a few local minima, best/2 is weak in the vector family.

Here we give some details of these vectors to different benchmarks:

To f1-f6 unimodal functions, best/2 achieves best result, following is best-to-cur/1, rand/1, rand-to-best/1. Best/1 is worst.

Table 1. Experiment Result of Rand/1,Rand/2,Rand/3,Best/1,Best/2 and Best/3 over 50 Independent Runs

bench mark	gener ation		rand/1	rand/2	rand/3	best/1	best/2	best/3
f1	1500	Mean	2.71e-19	1.30e-03	6.20e+03	1.89e+03	**5.56e-49**	3.55e-06
		Std.Dev	1.79e-19	5.36e-4	1.05e+03	9.29e+02	**9.11e-49**	2.42e-06
f2	2000	Mean	4.18e-13	2.53e-02	5.69e+01	1.08e+01	**3.53e-34**	8.67e-04
		Std.Dev	2.59e-13	1.16e-02	4.91e+00	2.79e+00	**4.11e-34**	6.26e-04
f3	5000	Mean	1.74e-16	9.78e+00	1.94e+04	5.271e+03	**8.72e-49**	1.58e-01
		Std.Dev	1.25e-016	5.35e+00	3.84e+03	1.80e+003	**1.52e-48**	1.01e-01
f4	5000	Mean	5.74e-001	1.28e-03	4.09e+01	2.91e+001	**1.58e-07**	4.84e-04
		Std.Dev	1.245e+00	4.65e-04	3.82e+00	4.22e+000	**2.69e-07**	2.96e-04
f6	1500	Mean	0	0	6.12e+03	2.02e+003	0	0
		Std.Dev	0	0	9.12e+02	6.29e+002	0	0
f7	3000	Mean	1.55e+002	1.65e+02	2.82e+02	2.00e+002	**3.72e+01**	1.94e+02
		Std.Dev	1.063e+01	1.12e+01	1.16e+01	8.66e+00	1.28e+01	1.65e+01
f10	1500	Mean	**1.24e-010**	1.31e-02	1.41e+01	9.14e+000	6.07e-01	9.61e-04
		Std.Dev	**4.91e-011**	3.36e-03	6.33e-001	1.79e+000	7.59e-01	3.37e-04
f11	2000	Mean	**0**	2.77e-02	3.99e+01	2.05e+001	9.22e-03	5.34e-02
		Std.Dev	**0**	9.53e-02	6.18e+00	1.01e+001	1.13e-02	1.35e-01
f12	1500	Mean	**2.10e-020**	1.56e-03	3.24e+12	6.01e+010	1.35e-01	1.11e-03
		Std.Dev	**2.34e-020**	1.71e-03	2.11e+12	1.29e+011	3.05e-01	3.74e-03
f13	1500	Mean	**1.62e-019**	4.03e-03	1.47e+13	7.27e+011	6.33e-02	4.92e-05
		Std.Dev	**1.32e-019**	3.04e-03	5.69e+12	8.72e+011	2.68e-01	7.10e-05
f21	3000	Mean	1.77e+002	1.76e+02	1.78e+02	**8.32e+001**	**6.49e+01**	1.72e+02
		Std.Dev	1.43e+001	1.65e+01	1.32e+01	**1.55e+001**	**1.49e+01**	2.19e+01
f22	1500	Mean	**1.29e-006**	8.62e-03	2.04e+01	2.01e+001	4.20e-01	2.09e+01
		Std.Dev	**3.94e-006**	2.41e-03	6.60e-001	7.72e-002	6.56e-01	7.64e-02
f23	2000	Mean	**0**	4.95e-02	9.27e+001	1.59e+001	1.13e-02	1.99e-02
		Std.Dev	**0**	1.51e-01	2.32e+01	7.85e+00	1.09e-02	6.69e-02

To f7-f13 multimodal functions with many local minima, rand/1 achieves best result, following is ran-to-best/1, cur-to-best/1, best/3. best/2 is worse and other vectors achieve little optimize. f7 is special as best/2 achieves best and next is best/3.

To f14-f20 multimodal functions with a few local minima, in f14-f17, all vectors achieve similar result, in f18-f20, best/2 and best-to-cur/1 achieve best result, next is rand/1, others perform weak.

To observe rotated benchmarks, the sequence of these vectors does not change, but their convergence ability is weak. Specially, in f23 best/1 does not achieve best result any more, but cur-to-best is outstanding.

Moreover, best-to-cur/1 achieves similar result to best/2 but perform weak on multimodal functions, it is interesting that its brother vector cur-to-best/1 perform in contrary. To rand-to-cur/1, the brother of best/2, perform worse than best2 but still good in the whole family.

Table 2. Experiment Result of Cur-to-best/1,Bets-to-cur/2,Rand-to-best/1,Best-to-rand/1 and Rand-to-cur/1 over 50 Independent Runs

benchmark	generation		Cur-to -best/1	Best-to -cur/1	Rand-to -best/1	Best-to -rand/1	Rand-to -cur/1
f1	1500	Mean	1.17e-08	7.04e-044	3.19e-009	5.89e-003	2.10e-001
		Std.Dev	1.55e-008	7.41e-044	2.96e-009	2.59e-003	1.73e-001
f2	2000	Mean	1.12e-005	3.11e-031	3.79e-006	1.45e-001	1.10e+000
		Std.Dev	6.31e-006	2.58e-031	1.90e-006	1.05e-001	4.07e-001
f3	5000	Mean	6.61e-009	1.45e-048	1.71e-006	5.67e-001	6.91e+001
		Std.Dev	7.1e-009	3.26e-048	1.48e-006	4.74e-001	3.35e+001
f4	5000	Mean	6.02e-004	4.34e-007	1.12e-007	9.59e-002	8.52e-002
		Std.Dev	8.28e-004	4.87e-007	2.29e-007	4.13e-001	2.37e-002
f6	1500	Mean	0	0	0	0	2.50e-001
		Std.Dev	0	0	0	0	4.33e-001
f7	3000	Mean	1.55e+002	2.34e+001	1.75e+002	1.98e+002	2.11e+002
		Std.Dev	7.49e+000	7.31e+000	1.61e+001	1.25e+001	1.05e+001
f10	1500	Mean	3.74e-005	7.95e-001	1.94e-005	3.10e-002	3.21e-001
		Std.Dev	1.05e-005	9.22e-001	6.16e-006	1.01e-002	1.14e-001
f11	2000	Mean	3.57e-003	9.48e-003	1.48e-003	1.41e-002	1.15e-001
		Std.Dev	4.64e-003	7.71e-003	3.60e-003	5.45e-002	2.05e-001
f12	1500	Mean	4.50e-009	1.19e-001	1.65e-009	6.39e-003	1.11e-03
		Std.Dev	6.25e-009	1.95e-001	1.31e-009	8.57e-003	3.29e-001
f13	1500	Mean	5.49e-004	3.75e-001	5.33e-009	1.49e-002	4.46e-001
		Std.Dev	2.39e-003	9.45e-001	7.19e-009	9.52e-003	2.25e-001
f21	3000	Mean	1.79e+002	1.76e+002	1.63e+002	1.75e+002	1.72e+02
		Std.Dev	1.93e+001	2.08e+001	2.32e+001	2.13e+001	1.80e+001
f22	1500	Mean	2.09e+001	1.14e+000	2.09e+001	2.09e+001	3.69e-001
		Std.Dev	5.24e-002	9.41e-001	7.20e-002	4.32e-002	1.52e-001
f23	2000	Mean	4.92e-003	1.17e-002	3.08e-003	2.36e-002	1.06e-001
		Std.Dev	7.69e-003	1.29e-002	5.82e-003	1.02e-001	1.74e-001

Bases on the experiment we could gain some useful concludes:

Increase more than two difference parameter would decrease the performance of the perturb vector. To bets/n, best/2 is best and best/1 is weak, if n is bigger than two, increase difference parameter would decrease the performance of perturb vector. To rand/n, rand/1 performs weak inmultimodal function and rand/2 get best result. Because best/1 with only one difference parameter it is constrained by limited search ability, with more difference parameter, although it is outstanding in search ability but performs weak in convergence ability. In this theory rand/1 is easy to entrap into local minima.

Rand/1 performs best to unimodal functions and best/2 is best to multimodal functions. Specially, vectors with parameter perform excellent in the vector family.

cur-to-best/1 and this series mutant vectors performs not best in mutate family. But these vectors present exceptional features that same parameter in different position lead to vary results. This feature should further study.

3.3   Performance of New Method Generates Mutant Vector

Restricted by the length, this paper presents part of the result comparison between new method and old method in Table 5 and Table 6. According to the experiment result, the new method optimizes the algorithm steadily. The new method optimizes unimodal functions, multimodal functions with many local minima, multimodal functions with deceiving and rotated functions well.

The new method achieves better performance in unimodal functions. To multimodal functions with many local minima, best/2 use the new method does not optimize the performance as obvious as unimodal functions done, but the rand/1 and cur-to-best/1 achieve outstanding optimized results. To multimodal functions with a few local minima, all the mutant vectors achieves same results, the new method achieves same-level result, too. To rotated benchmarks, many DE achieve weak results, but the new method still achieves obvious optimized results.

4   Conclusion

Under the standard DE framework, considerable research has put forward many mutant vectors. This paper proposed the linear relation between the algorithm performance and the differential operator. According to experiment result, increasing the differential operator would not certainly optimize the performance of DE. In contrary, adds more than two difference parameters would decrease the convergence ability. Some of the mutant vector like cur-to-best/1 and rand-to-best did not perform best in the mutate family, but it is exceptional and worth further study because in these mutate vectors parameters at different position lead to different performance.

Moreover, we use rand/1, rand/2 and best/2, three best mutant vectors to test the new method. The new method is more effective and achieves better result than old method. The new method could optimize the performance of DE in general. DE with three different mutant vectors all achieve optimized result.

References

1. Neri, F., Tirronen: Recent Advances in Differential Evolution: A Survey and Experimental Analysis. Artif. Intell. Rev. 33(1), 61–106 (2010)
2. Das, S., Suganthan, P.N.: Differential evolution: A survey of the state-of-the-art. IEEE Trans. on Evolutionary Computation (2011),
   doi:10.1109/TEVC.2010.2059031
3. Caponio, A., Neri, F.: Differential Evolution with Noise Analyzer. In: Giacobini, M., Brabazon, A., Cagnoni, S., Di Caro, G.A., Ekárt, A., Esparcia-Alcázar, A.I., Farooq, M., Fink, A., Machado, P. (eds.) EvoWorkshops 2009. LNCS, vol. 5484, pp. 715–724. Springer, Heidelberg (2009)
4. Liu, B., Zhang, X., Ma, H.: Hybrid differential evolution for noisy optimization. In: Proc. IEEE Congr. Evol. Comput., vol. 2, pp. 1691–1698 (2009)

5. Wang, Y., Cai, Z., Zhang, Q.: Differential evolution with composite trial vector generation strategies and control parameters. IEEE Trans. 15(1), 55–66 (2011)
6. Qin, A.K., Huang, V.L., Suganthan, P.N.: Differential evolution algorithm with strategy adaptation for global numerical optimization. IEEE Trans. Evol. Comput. 13(2), 398–417 (2009)
7. Mezura-Montes, E., Vel azquez-Reyes, J., Coello Coello, C.A.: A comparative study of differential evolution variants for global optimization. In: Proc. Genet. Evol. Comput., pp. 485–492 (2006)
8. Brest, J., Greiner, S., Boskovic, B., Mernik, M., Zumer, V.: Self-adapting control parameters in differential evolution: A comparative study on numerical benchmark problems. IEEE Trans. Evolut. Comput. 10(6), 646–657 (2006)
9. Epitropakis, G., Tasoulis, D.K., Pavlidis, N.G., Plagianakos, V.P., Vrahatis, M.N.: Enhancing differential evolution utilizing proximity-based mutation operators. IEEE Trans. Evol. Comput., 99–119 (2011)

Survey on Particle Swarm Optimization Based Clustering Analysis

Veenu Mangat

University Institute of Engineering and Technology, Panjab University 160014,
Chandigarh, India
veenumangat@yahoo.com

Abstract. Clustering analysis is the task of assigning a set of objects to groups such that objects in one group or cluster are more similar to each other than to those in other clusters. Clustering analysis is the major application area of data mining where Particle Swarm Optimisation (PSO) is being widely implemented due to its simplicity and efficiency. When compared with techniques like K-means, Fuzzy C-means, K-Harmonic means and other traditional clustering approaches, in general, the PSO algorithm produces better results with reference to inter-cluster and intra-cluster distances, while having quantization errors comparable to the other algorithms. In recent times, many hybrid algorithms with PSO as one of the techniques have been developed to harness the strong points of PSO and increase its efficiency and accuracy. This paper provides an extensive review of the variants and hybrids of PSO which are being widely used for the purpose of clustering analysis.

Keywords: Clustering Analysis, Particle Swarm Optimization, Hybrid Methods.

1 Introduction

This section gives a brief introduction on clustering analysis and the application of PSO for clustering analysis. The amount of information available and collected nowadays is beyond the human capability of analysing and extracting relevant information or discovering knowledge from it. Such data is heterogeneous, uncertain, dynamic and massive. It is of great significance to explore how to automatically extract the implicit, unknown and potentially helpful information so that it can help in the commercial decision-making activities. This is precisely the task of data mining and knowledge discovery from databases. A dramatic increase in the amount of information requiring in depth analysis has led to the design of new techniques that can perform knowledge extraction efficiently and automatically.

1.1 Clustering Analysis

Clustering analysis is an important technique used in data mining. It involves grouping together similar multi-dimensional data vectors into a number of clusters.

L. Rutkowski et al. (Eds.): SIDE 2012 and EC 2012, LNCS 7269, pp. 301–309, 2012.

The main objective of clustering is to minimize inter-cluster similarity and to maximize intra-cluster similarity [1]. Clustering techniques are basically divided into two types:

- *Hierarchical*: This approach provides a series of nested partitions of the dataset. It divides the data into a nested tree structure where the levels of the tree show similarity or dissimilarity among the clusters at different levels. It is further divided into 'Agglomerative' and 'Divisive' approaches. The divisive approach splits one large cluster into different sub clusters e.g. CHAMELEON [2], BIRCH [3]. In agglomerative approach, the clustering process starts with every data element in individual clusters which are then merged on the basis of their proximity until all data elements are finally in a single cluster e.g. CURE [4] and ROCK [5]. This approach does not need the number of clusters to be specified in advance. It is deterministic and has lower execution time efficiency than partitioning techniques.

- *Partitioning*: In contrast to hierarchical technique which yields a successive level of clusters by iterative fusions or divisions, this technique assigns a set of objects to clusters with no hierarchical structure. These methods try to minimize certain criteria, like square error function. These methods are further divided into 'supervised' and 'unsupervised' algorithms. The supervised algorithms are provided with both the cases (data points) and the concept to be learnt for each case. Common algorithms include K-means and its variants like Fuzzy c-means, Spherical K-Means etc.

1.2   Particle Swarm Optimization

PSO is a technique based upon Swarm Intelligence (SI); an artificial intelligence paradigm for solving optimization problems that originally took its inspiration from the biological examples such as in swarming, flocking and herding phenomena in vertebrates. Particle Swarm Optimization (PSO) incorporates swarming behaviour observed in flocks of birds, schools of fish, or swarms of bees, and even human social behaviour. It is a population-based optimization tool, which could be implemented and applied easily to solve various function optimization problems, or the problems that can be transformed to the function optimization problem. For applying PSO successfully, one of the key issues is finding how to map the problem solution into the PSO particle, which directly affects its feasibility and performance. Many evolutionary techniques based on Particle Swarm Optimization have also been developed for unsupervised method.

2   Related Work

2.1   Original Version (Early Developments)

PSO was first introduced by J. Kennedy and Eberhart in 1995 [6]. They developed this method for optimization of continuous non-linear functions. A '*swarm*' refers to a collection of a number of potential solutions where each potential solution is known as a *'particle'*. In the standard PSO method, each particle is initialized with random positions X_i and velocities V_i, and a function, f *(fitness function)* is evaluated. The aim of PSO is to find the particle's position that gives the best evaluation of a given fitness function using the particle's positional coordinates as input values. In a k-dimensional search space, $X_i = (x_i1, x_i2, x_i3,...,x_ik)$ and $V_i = (v_i1, v_i2, v_i3,...,v_ik)$. Positions and velocities are adjusted, and the function is evaluated with the new coordinates at each step. In each generation, each particle updates itself continuously by following two extreme values: the best position of the particle in its neighbourhood *(lbest or localbest or personalbest)* and the best position in the *swarm* at that time *(gbest or globalbest)* [7]. After finding the above values, each particle updates its position and velocity as follows:

$$v_{i,k}(t+1) = wv_{i,k}(t) + c_1r_{1,k}(t)(y_{i,k}(t) - x_{i,k}(t)) + c_2r_{2,k}(t)(y`_k(t) - x_{i,k}(t)) \qquad (1)$$

$$x_i(t+1) = x_i(t) + v_i(t+1) \qquad (2)$$

Where: $v_{i,k}$ is the velocity of the *i-th* particle in the *t-th* iteration of the *k-th* dimension; $x_{i,k}$ is the position of the *i-th* particle in the *t-th* iteration of the *k-th* dimension; r_1 and r_2 are random numbers in the interval [0, 1]; c_1 and c_2 are learning factors, in general, $c_1=c_2=2$. An improvement in these parameters and their optimized values have been done in recent papers by the researchers which will be discussed later. *'w'* is the inertia weight factor generally selected in the range (0.1, 0.9). This parameter was introduced in [8] which illustrated its significance in the particle swarm optimizer. Equation (1) is used to calculate the particle's new velocity according to its previous velocity and the distances of its current position from its own best experience and the group's best experience. The velocity is thus calculated based on three contributions:

- A fraction of the previous velocity.
- The cognitive component which is a function of the distance of the particle from its personal best position.
- The social component which is a function of the distance of the particle from the best particle found thus far (i.e. the best of the personal bests).

The personal best position y_i of particle 'i' can be computed as:

$$y_i(t+1) = y_i(t) \quad \text{if} \quad f(x_i(t+1)) >= f(y_i(t))$$

$$\text{or} \quad y_i(t+1) = x_i(t+1) \quad \text{if} \quad f(x_i(t+1)) < f(y_i(t)) \qquad (3)$$

Equation (1) reflects the *gbest* version of PSO whereas in the lbest version the swarm is further divided into overlapping neighbourhoods and the best particle in each neighbourhood is determined. For the *lbest* version the social component of (1) changes to:

$$C_2r_{2,k}(t)(y`_{j,k}(t) - x_{i,k}(t)) \qquad (4)$$

Where: $y`_j$ is the best in the neighbourhood of *i-th* particle. The particle flies towards a new position according to equation (2). The PSO is usually executed with repeated application of equations (1) and (2) until a specified number of iterations have been exceeded or when the velocity updates are close to zero over a number of iterations.

2.2   PSO Clustering

In [7] the authors have used the first kind of hybrid PSO technique for data clustering by hybridizing PSO with the popular K-means algorithm. The k-means algorithm has been used to seed the initial swarm and PSO is then used to refine the clusters formed by K-means. In this algorithm a single particle represents the N_c cluster centroid vectors. That is, each particle x, is constructed as follows:

$$x_i = (m_{i1}... : m_{ij},..,m_{iNc})$$ (5)

Where: m_{ij} is the j-th cluster centroid vector of the i-th particle in cluster C_{ij}. The fitness of particles can be easily measured as the quantization error,

$$J_e = \sum_{j=1}^{Nc} \frac{[\sum_{\forall z_p \in C_{ij}} d(z_p.m_j)/|C_{ij}|]}{N_c}$$ (6)

where d is the distance to the centroid given by equation:

$$d(z_p.m_j) = \sqrt{\sum_{k=1}^{Nd} (z_{pk} - m_{jk})^2}$$ (7)

'k' subscripts the dimension and $|C_i|$ in equation (7) is the number of data vectors belonging to cluster C_{ij} i.e. the frequency of that cluster. The authors also proposed the standard $gbest$ PSO clustering algorithm using this hybrid technique. Results proved that this hybrid technique is more efficient than the standard PSO technique or traditional K-means algorithm alone. In [9] the authors have used PSO to decide the vector of the cluster centre. The following fitness function in equation (4) is evaluated and then compared with the particle's best solution. The updating of position and velocities vectors are carried out according to (1) and (2) till the algorithm meets its stopping criterion.

$$J = \sum_{i=1}^{K}\sum_{i=1}^{N} \| xi\text{-}zj\|^2$$ (8)

In [10] the authors have applied hybrid of K-means and PSO for the purpose of fast and high-quality document clustering to effectively navigate, summarize and organize information. C.M Cohen and Castro [11] used PSO for data clustering by adapting this algorithm to position prototypes (particles) in regions of the space that represent natural clusters of input data set. They proposed the PSC $(particle\ swarm\ clustering)$ which behaves more like a self-organizing neural network that aids the positioning of the particles (prototypes) in the space following the spatial distribution of the input data. Other than the introduction of inertia weight parameter; another improvement in original PSO proposed by Kennedy and Eberhart was the introduction of the constriction factor [12] that too resulted in fast convergence of PSO algorithm. In equation (1) of the original version of PSO, $v_{i,k}$ is limited to the range ($-V_{max}$, $+V_{max}$) where V_{max} parameter was introduced to limit the step size or the velocity to prevent explosion that results due to the random weighting of the control parameters in the algorithm. Constriction Coefficients are used to prevent such an explosion. Specifically, the application of constriction coefficients allows control over the dynamic characteristics of the particle swarm, including its exploration versus exploitation properties. Eberhart and Shi [13] have also concluded that constriction factor does not alone guarantee fast convergence and that the fastest convergence can be achieved by a combined approach of V_{max} parameter clamping strategy and constriction coefficients. Engelbrecht and Bergh proposed a new locally convergent particle swarm optimizer [14] called the *Guaranteed Convergence Particle Swarm Optimizer (GCPSO)*. This new algorithm significantly resulted in faster convergence compared to the original PSO, especially when smaller swarm sizes are used. Yet another paper by Bergh and Engelbrecht [15] employs heuristic approach for initialization of the inertia weight and acceleration of coefficient values of PSO to guarantee convergent trajectories. In [16] an improved PSO method has been proposed in order to solve the problem of easy fall into local optimal solutions, lower convergent precision, slower convergence rates and the poor population diversity. The simulation results of this improved PSO indicated that its performance in terms of optimal precision, efficiency and the stability are much better than that of traditional PSO.

In another version of PSO [17] based on initial population of clustering, the diversity of the population was analyzed according to discrepancy in the solution space and objective function space. The clustering algorithm is used to grab the information of the initial population in order to generate the representative individuals, and then the size of the initial population composed by these representative individuals is reduced. This method provides an effective method to generate initial populations and offers the basis for assessment and regulation of the population diversity in the process of running the algorithm. In a paper [18] by Dai, Lui, and Li, an intelligent method for optimum parameter selection is proposed. Firstly it analyzes the effect of each parameter on algorithm performance in detail. Tests to the benchmark function show that these parameters are better than the experience parameters and results in the optimal fitness and convergence rate. A discrete binary version of the improved PSO has been discussed in [19].On one hand, to improve the convergence rate, the improved algorithm combines the traditional binary particle swarm algorithm with the simulated annealing in order to guide the evolution of the optimal solution, and on the other hand, to simplify the structure of algorithm, the cross-operation of the genetic algorithm is used to replace the update operation of the speed and location.

3   Survey of Hybrid Techniques Based on PSO

Evolutionary algorithms are used nowadays for clustering. Hybridization is a method of combining two or more techniques in a judicious way so that the resulting algorithm contains the positive features of all the combined algorithms. Many hybrids of PSO have been developed so far in order to harness the strong points of the PSO algorithm and further improve its efficiency and accuracy.

3.1   Hybridization Perspective of Clustering of Multi-objective and High-Dimensional Problems

For Multi-objective optimization problems (MOPs), the objectives to be optimized are normally in conflict with respect to each other, which means that there is no single solution for these problems. A research paper [20] published in 2009 proposed a PSO method for MOP using Fuzzy Clustering technique named *Fuzzy Clustering Multi-objective Particle Swarm Optimizer (FC-MOPSO)*. Fuzzy clustering technique provides a better distribution of solutions in decision variable space by dividing the whole swarm into sub-swarms. In FC-MOPSO, the migration concept is used to exchange information between different sub-swarms and to ensure their diversity. The actual data sets used in data mining are high-dimensional and very complex, hence, effective hybrid techniques are required to efficiently cluster them. To reduce dimensionality of datasets PSO along with the *Principal Component Analysis technique (PCA)* [21] is used. PSO has been proved to be effective in clustering data under static environments. In 2010, Serkan, Jenn and Moncef proposed a PSO technique [22] for multidimensional search in dynamic environment by introducing the *Fractional Global Best Formation (FGBF)* technique. This technique exhibits a significant performance for multi-modal and non-stationary environments.

3.2   PSO and Genetic Algorithm (GA) Hybridization

The hybrid of PSO and Genetic Algorithm (GA) is one of the most widely used and efficient technique for clustering data [23]. GA is a randomized global search technique that solves problems by imitating processes observed from natural evolution. Based on the survival and reproduction of the fittest, GA continually exploits new and better solutions. For a specific problem, the GA codes a solution as a binary string called a chromosome (individual). A set of chromosomes is randomly chosen from the search space to form the initial population that represents a part of the solution space of the problem. Next, through computations, the individuals are selected in a competitive manner, based on their fitness measured by a specific objective function. The genetic search operators such as selection, mutation and crossover are then applied one after another to obtain a new generation of chromosomes in which the expected quality over all the chromosomes is better than that of the previous generation. The major problem with the traditional K-means algorithm is that it is sensitive to the selection of the initial partitions and it may converge to local optima. The hybrid of GA and PSO and K-means [23] avoids premature convergence and provides fast data clustering. This hybrid combines the ability of the globalized searching of the evolutionary algorithms and the fast convergence of the k-means algorithm and can avoid the drawbacks of both.

3.3   PSO and DE (Differential Evolution) Hybridization

DE algorithm was proposed by Storn and Price [24] in 1995. DE involves the same operators as GA (selection, mutation and crossover) but differs in the way it operates. PSO-DE hybrids usually combine the evolutionary schemes of both algorithms to propose a new evolutionary position scheme. A modified PSO with differential evolution operator mutations is introduced in [25] to eliminate stagnation and premature convergence of standard PSO. In [26] the authors have used this hybrid technique in an attempt to efficiently guide the evolution and enhance the convergence. They have evolved the personal experience of the swarm with the DE algorithm [27].

3.4   Other Variants of PSO

A novel technique named *Selective Regeneration Particle Swarm Optimization (SRPSO)* [29] suggests parameter setting and the mechanism of selective particle regeneration. The suggested unbalanced setting of *c1* and *c2* in equation (1) accelerates the convergence of the algorithm while the particle regeneration operation enables the search to escape from local optima and explore other areas for better solutions. A comprehensive review of the various hybridization techniques of PSO and K-means has been discussed in [30]. An improved particle swam optimization algorithm with *synthetic update mechanism* is presented. The synthetic update is made up of three parts: the first is disturbance operation, the second is mutation operation and the last is *gbest* value distribution. Multi-objective PSO algorithm [32] has been used for clustering and feature selection. Features are assigned weights automatically by an algorithm and the features with low weights are then omitted which helps in omitting irrelevant features. Experimental results show that the proposed algorithm performs clustering independently for the shape of clusters and it can have good accuracy on dataset of any shape or distribution. In [33], the authors have developed a new PSO technique which can be applied both when the number of clusters is known as well as when this number is unknown. The authors have proposed a fitness function in case where the number of clusters is known:

$$f^t_p = \sigma^t_p = \sum^{Kp}_{k=1} \sum^n_{i=1} w^{pt}_{ik} D(o_i.z^{pt}_k) \tag{9}$$

Where f_p is the fitness value of particle p at iteration t. If the number of clusters is unknown the following fitness function is proposed:

$$f^t_p = \sigma^t_p - \min_{k \neq l} D(z^{pt}_k.z^{pt}_l) \tag{10}$$

When the partitioning is compact and satisfactory, the value of σ^t_p should be low, while $min_{k \neq l} D(z^{pt}_k.z^{pt}_l)$ should be high, thereby yielding lower values from the fitness function. Nowadays meta heuristic optimization algorithms have become popular choice for solving complex and intricate problems which are otherwise difficult to solve by traditional methods [34].

4   Conclusion

One of the major reasons for the wide use of Particle Swarm Optimization is that there are very few parameters to adjust. A single version, with very slight variations works well in a wide variety of applications. PSO has been used for approaches that can be used across a wide range of applications such as clustering of web usage data, image segmentation, system design, multi-objective optimization, classification, pattern recognition, biological system modelling, scheduling, signal processing and robotic applications. The hybridisation of PSO with other evolutionary algorithms like

GA and DE has been very effective in improving its efficiency and accuracy. Due to its simplicity and efficiency, PSO is gaining a lot of attention from the researchers and the recent developments show that hybrid PSO methods will emerge as a successful optimization technique in diverse applications.

References

[1] Han, J., Kamber, M.: Data Mining: Concepts and Techniques. Morgan Kaufmann Publishers (2002)

[2] Karypis, G., Han, E.-H., Kumar, V.: CHAMELEON: A Hierarchical Clustering Algorithm using Dynamic Modelling. Computer 32, 68–75 (1999)

[3] Zhang, T., Ramakrishnan, R., Livny, M.: BIRCH: An Efficient Data Clustering Method for very Large Databases. In: Widom, J. (ed.) Proceedings of the 1996 ACM SIGMOD International Conference on Management of Data, SIGMOD 1996, Montreal, Quebec, Canada, pp. 103–114. ACM Press, New York (1996)

[4] Guha, S., Rastogi, R., Shim, K.: Cure: An efficient clustering algorithm for large databases. In: Proceedings of the 1998 ACM SIGMOD International Conference on Management of Data, Seattle, WA, pp. 73–84 (1998)

[5] Guha, S., Rastogi, R., Shim, K.: ROCK: A robust clustering algorithm for categorical attributes. In: Proceedings of the International Conference on Data Engineering, pp. 512–521 (1999)

[6] Kennedy, J., Eberhart, R.C.: Particle Swarm Optimization. In: Proceedings of the IEEE International Conference on Neural Networks (ICNN), Australia, vol. IV, pp. 1942–1948 (1995)

[7] Van Der Merwe, D.W., Engelbrecht, A.P.: Data clustering using particle swarm optimization. In: Proceedings of the IEEE Congress on Evolutionary Computation, Canberra, Australia (2003)

[8] Shi, Y., Eberhart, R.C.: A modified particle swarm optimizer. In: Proceedings of the IEEE International Conference on Evolutionary Computation, Alaska (1998)

[9] Cheo, C.Y., Ye, F.: Particle Swarm Optimization Algorithm and Its Application to Clustering Analysis. In: Proceedings of the 2004 IEEE International Conference on Networking, Sensing Control, Taiwan (2004)

[10] Cui, Potok, Palathingal: Document clustering using Particle Swarm Optimization. In: IEEE Swarm Intelligence Symposium, SIS (2005)

[11] Cohen, S.C.M., de Castro, L.N.: Data Clustering with Particle Swarms. In: Proceedings of the IEEE Congress on Evolutionary Computation (2006)

[12] Clerc, M., Kennedy, J.: The Particle Swarm- Explosion, Stability and Convergence in a Multidimensional Complex Space. IEEE Transactions on Evolutionary Computation 6(1) (February 2002)

[13] Eberhart, R.C., Shi, Y.: Comparing inertia weights and constriction factors in particle swarm optimization. In: Proceedings of the 2000 Congress on Evolutionary Computation, pp. 84–89 (2000)

[14] van den Bergh, F., Engelbrecht, A.P.: A New locally convergent Particle Swarm optimizer. In: Proceedings of the IEEE Conference on Systems, Man and Cybernetics (2002)

[15] van den Bergh, F., Engelbrecht, A.P.: A study of particle swarm optimization particle trajectories. Information Sciences 176, 937–971 (2006)

[16] Yang, J., Xue, L.: Adaptive Population Differentiation PSO Algorithm. In: Third International Symposium on Intelligent Information Technology Application (2009)

[17]   He, D., Chang, H., Chang, Q., Liu, Y.: Particle Swarm Optimization Based on the Initial Population of Clustering. In: Proceedings of the Sixth International Conference on Natural Computation, ICNC (2010)

[18]   Dai, Y., Liu, L., Li, Y.: An Intelligent Parameter Selection Method for Particle Swarm Optimization Algorithm. In: Proceedings of the Fourth International Joint Conference on Computational Sciences and Optimization (2011)

[19]   Jun, X., Chang, H.: The Discrete Binary Version Of The Improved Particle Swarm Optimization Algorithm. In: Proceedings of the IEEE International Conference on Management and Service Science MASS (2009)

[20]   Benameur, L., Alami, J., El Imrani, A.: A New Hybrid Particle Swarm Optimization Algorithm for Handling Multiobjective Problem Using Fuzzy Clustering Technique. In: Proceedings of the International Conference on Computational Intelligence, Modelling and Simulation (2009)

[21]   Qian, X.-D., Li-Wie.: Date Clustering using Principal Component Analysis and Particle Swarm Optimization. In: Proceedings of the 5th International Conference on Computer Science & Education Hefei, China (2010)

[22]   Kiranyaz, S., Pulkkinen, J., Gabbouj, M.: Multi-dimensional particle swarm optimization in dynamic environments. Expert Systems with Applications 38, 2212–2223 (2011)

[23]   Abdel-Kader, R.F.: Genetically Improved PSO Algorithm for Efficient Data Clustering. In: Proceedings of the IEEE Second International Conference on Machine Learning and Computing (2010)

[24]   Price, K., Storn, R., Lampinen, J.: Differential Evolution: A Practical Approach to Global Optimization. Springer, Berlin (2005)

[25]   Zheng, X.: Modified Particle Swarm Optimization with Differential Evolution Mutation. In: Proceedings of the Sixth International Conference on Natural Computation, ICNC (2010)

[26]   Epitropakis, M.G., Plagianakos, V.P., Vrahatis, M.N.: Evolving cognitive and social experience in Particle Swarm Optimization through Differential Evolution. In: IEEE Congress on Evolutionary Computation, CEC (2010)

[27]   Xu, R., Xu, J., Wunsch: Clustering with Differential Evolution Particle Swarm Optimization. In: IEEE Congress on Evolutionary Computation CEC (2010)

[28]   Kuo, R.J., Lin, L.M.: Application of a hybrid of genetic algorithm and particle swarm optimization algorithm for order clustering. Decision Support Systems 49(4), 451–462 (2010)

[29]   Tsai, C.-Y., Kao, I.-W.: Particle swarm optimization with selective particle regeneration for data clustering. Expert Systems with Applications 38, 6565–6576 (2011)

[30]   Shen, Jin, Zhu, Zhu: Hybridization of Particle Swarm Optimization with the K-Means Algorithm for Clustering Analysis. In: Proceedings of the IEEE 5th International Conference on Bio-Inspired Computing: Theories and Applications BIC-TA (2010)

[31]   Li, F.: An Improved Particle Swarm Optimization Algorithm with Synthetic Update Mechanism. In: IEEE Third International Symposium on Intelligent Information Technology and Security Informatics (2010)

[32]   Javani, M., Faez, K., Aghlmandi, D.: Clustering and feature selection via PSO algorithm. In: IEEE International Symposium on Artificial Intelligence and Signal Processing (2011)

[33]   Cura, T.: A particle swarm optimization approach to clustering. Expert Systems with Applications 39, 1582–1588 (2012)

[34]   Thangaraj, R., Pant, M., Abraham, A., Bouvry, P.: Particle swarm optimization: Hybridization perspectives and experimental illustrations. Applied Mathematics and Computation 217, 5208–5226 (2011)

Glowworm Optimization

Jakub Niwa

Westpomeranian University of Technology in Szczecin,
Department of Computer Science
jniwa@wi.zut.edu.pl

Abstract. Modern optimization algorithms are often metaheuristic, and they are very effective and promising in solving NP-hard optimization problems. Many of them are based on nature, like the particle swarm optimization, which purely outperforms its predecessors. This paper provides an insight into improved metaheuristic of Particle Swarm Optimization extended with stronger social links.

Keywords: PSO, particle swarm optimization, glowworm optimization.

1 Introduction

Most problems faced by engineers are nonlinear with many constraints. Finding optimal solutions in short amount of time requires efficient optimization algorithms. Optimization algorithms can be classified in two groups: deterministic and stochastic. Deterministic methods, like hill climbing, are not reliable and are easily trapped in local optimums. However, they also give us unchanging solutions if the initial parameters are being used. Stochastic algorithms often produce different solutions, but tend to converge to a similar solution with a given accuracy. Many modern metaheuristic algorithms are based on nature. An example of such an algorithm is the particle swarm optimization, which is trying to optimize functions by simulating bird flocks or fish schools behavior.

2 Particle Swarm Optimization and Its Implementation

Particle Swarm Optimization (PSO), introduced by Kennedy and Eberhart in 1995 [1], is an optimization method based on social behaviours of birds and fish. Although, this method does not calculate a gradiet of the objective function, so it does not have to be differentiable. Swarm methods can also be used for very noisy and dynamic functions. It can also be used with dynamically changing domains. The PSO algorithm searches the space of the objective function by adjusting the movement trajectory for each individual agent called particle. The particles adjust their velocity in each dimmension by being attracted to the best global position and their own best known position along with ϕ_S and ϕ_P, which are responsible for gregariousness and individuality of the particles and Ω which is responsible for extinction of the particle movement. When a particle finds a

L. Rutkowski et al. (Eds.): SIDE 2012 and EC 2012, LNCS 7269, pp. 310–316, 2012.

position that is better than the previous one, it will categorize this position as the best for itself. Futhermore, it also checks to see if this new position is better than the global best and will update if so. At the end of the algorithm the global best is the final solution.

3   Glowworm Optimization and Its Implementation

Glowworms are insects which have the ability to light up their abdomen. They use this ability to exchange information between each other with large distances. Females usually attract males with their light and highlight their position. This knowledge was used here to add an information exchange system between particles in the swarm. It was assumed that all of the particles are unisex and are capable of attracting other particles whilst having a better position than the current one. A similar approach was presented by Xen-She Yang [2]. Information exchanging allows particles to find solutions faster than in standard PSO implementation. In the Glowworm Optimization we have four initial parameters:

Ω responsible for movement velocity extinction, which translates into limiting search space with time.

Φ_S responsible for gregariousness of the particles in the swarm, larger than ϕ_P tends global best to attract stronger than local best.

Φ_P responsible for individuality of the particles in the swarm, larger than ϕ_S tends local best to attract stronger than global best.

Ψ parameter which modulates attractiveness, larger value tends particles to attract other particles stronger. Studies show, that it should be lower than Ω.

The main benefit of adding global information exchange is a better exploitation of the search space, whlist randomness given by R_p, R_s makes the exploration of the search space more efficient. Thus the swarm is able to find a more accurate solution in static problems and to find new solutions faster in dynamic problems. The remaining rules are exactly like the PSO and are presented in the pseudocode 3.

4   Comparison of PSO and GWO

Tables 1, 2, 3, 4, 5, and 6 presents results on Particle Swarm Optimization(PSO) , Glowworm Optimization(GWO), Evolutionary Strategy Plus(ES+), Evolutionary Strategy Comma(ES/), and Immune System(IS) testing on multiple benchmark functions with given initial boundaries. The greater the initial boundaries are, the harder it is to find a solution. In tables statistics from 100 simulations for each algorithm to get meaningful statistical analysis are stored. The algorithm stops after reaching the global objective function optimum with a tolerance $\epsilon \leq 10^{-5}$. The results are summarized in the table below. The numbers are in format: '3204.4±123.2 (98 %)' which means mean±std(succes rate). Where mean is mean value of iterations needed to find a solution with given tolerance, std

1: **for** each particle in swarm **do**
2:     particles position as uniformly distributed random vector $U(lo, up)$
3:     particles velocity as uniformly distributed random vector $U(-|up-lo|, |up-lo|)$
4:     set particle best known position as initial position
5:     **if** particle best known position is better than swarm best position **then**
6:         set global best as particles initial position
7:     **end if**
8:
9: **end for**
10: **while** Terminal condition is not met **do**
11:     **for** each particle i in swarm **do**
12:         set R_p, R_s as random numbers $U(0,1)$
13:         update the particle velocity: $v_i = \Omega * v_i * \Phi_p R_p (p_i - x_i) + \Phi_s R_s (g - x_i)$
14:         **for** each particle j in swarm **do**
15:             **if** j has better position than i **then**
16:                 update the particle velocity: $v_i = \Psi * v_i * \Phi_p R_p (p_i - x_j) + \Phi_s R_s (g - x_i)$
17:             **end if**
18:         **end for**
19:         update particles position $x_i = x_i + v_i$
20:         **if** current position is better than best known **then**
21:             update best known position as current position
22:             **if** best known position is better than global best position **then**
23:                 update global best position as best known position
24:             **end if**
25:         **end if**
26:     **end for**
27: **end while**

Fig. 1. Glowworm Optimization Pseudo-code

is standard deviation of same set. Succes rate means % of simulations ended in less than 10×10^3 function evaluations.

Algorithm parameters used for simulations:

PSO : particles :15, Ω: 0.8, Φ_P: 0.9, Φ_S: 0.3

GWO : particles :15, Ψ: 0.7, Ω: 0.9, Φ_P: 0.5, Φ_S: 0.8

ES+ : μ: 6, ρ: 5, λ: 40

ES/ :μ: 6, ρ: 5, λ: 40

IS μ : 20, clones: 5, α: 1.5, β: 0.5

The benchmark functions used in Tables are: (1) Beale (d=2), (2) Quadric (d=2), (3) Booth (d=2), (4) Zakharov(d=2), (5) Bohachevsky (d=2), (6) Hump (d=2), (7) Rosenbrock (d=2), (8) Easom (d=2), (9) Michalewicz (d=2, m=10), (10) Ackley (d=2). Parameters for PSO and GWO have been checked forcefully from range of parameters -2.5 *to* 2.5 with step 0.1. Benchmark has run on set of functions [(1), (2), (8)] on initial boundaries from range [1 → 100). The set of parameters that gave the best mean result with the restriction of 3500 objective function evaluations has been chosen. In the studies good parameter sets were found for:

small ranges (0 *to* **10)** Ψ: 0.8, Ω: 0.6, Φ_P: 0.4, Φ_S: 0.8
medium ranges (10 *to* **100)** Ψ: 0.6, Ω: 0.4, Φ_P: 0.6, Φ_S: 0.7
big ranges (100 *to* **10000)** Ψ: 0.7, Ω: 0.9, Φ_P: 0.5, Φ_S: 0.8

Which statistically performs better on benchmark sets with given initial boundaries.

As we can see in tables with comparison for really big initial boundaries, swarm finds a solution with high success rate and greater accuracy. For lower initial bounds in function with flase attractor like function (9) the swarm does not perform well because it will not exploit the search space. Instead, it tries to explore the flase attractor.

Table 1. Comparison of the algorithms performance for initial bounds [-10000, 10000]

fun.	PSO($\times 10^3$)	GWO($\times 10^3$)	ES+($\times 10^3$)	ES/($\times 10^3$)	IS($\times 10^3$)
(1)	54.0±46.0 (52)	8.0±15.0 (98)	24.0±30.0 (89)	28.0±38.0 (78)	47.0±45.0 (62)
(2)	2.0±0.1 (100)	1.3±0.1 (100)	2.3±2.1 (100)	1.0±0.1 (100)	2.1±1.5 (100)
(3)	2.2±0.2 (100)	1.5±0.1 (100)	3.6±6.3 (100)	1.3±0.2 (100)	2.6±1.5 (100)
(4)	3.0±0.7 (100)	3.9±1.3 (100)	4.1±2.7 (100)	5.9±3.1 (100)	7.7±6.5 (100)
(5)	2.2±0.1 (100)	1.4±0.1 (100)	2.5±1.9 (98)	1.1±0.1 (100)	2.3±1.6 (97)
(6)	2.3±0.2 (100)	1.5±0.1 (100)	5.0±3.3 (75)	1.4±0.2 (100)	2.5±1.7 (96)
(7)	9.4±1.5 (12)	9.1±1.7 (24)	9.9±0.5 (5)	10.0±0.0 (0)	9.9±7.0 (4)

Table 2. Comparison of the algorithms performance for initial bounds [-1000, 1000]

fun.	PSO($\times 10^3$)	GWO($\times 10^3$)	ES+($\times 10^3$)	ES/($\times 10^3$)	IS($\times 10^3$)
(1)	27.0±39.0 (80)	3.0±9.0 (99)	10.0±18.0 (97)	15.0±32.0 (87)	30.0±37.0 (83)
(2)	1.6±0.1 (100)	1.1±0.0 (100)	1.6±0.1 (100)	0.8±0.1 (100)	1.6±0.6 (100)
(3)	1.8±0.1 (100)	1.3±0.1 (100)	2.0±1.5 (100)	1.1±0.1 (100)	2.2±1.4 (100)
(4)	1.9±0.1 (100)	1.8±0.3 (100)	2.2±1.6 (100)	1.7±0.6 (100)	2.7±1.6 (100)
(5)	1.8±0.1 (100)	1.2±0.0 (100)	1.7±1.1 (100)	0.9±0.1 (100)	2.0±1.6 (98)
(6)	1.9±0.1 (100)	1.2±0.1 (100)	4.1±3.2 (83)	1.1±0.3 (100)	2.1±1.9 (96)
(7)	8.8±2.3 (25)	6.9±2.6 (67)	9.1±1.7 (29)	10.0±0.0 (0)	9.6±1.4 (9)

Table 3. Comparison of the algorithms performance for initial bounds [-100, 100]

fun.	PSO($\times 10^3$)	GWO($\times 10^3$)	ES+($\times 10^3$)	ES/($\times 10^3$)	IS($\times 10^3$)
(1)	8.3±21.5 (96)	2.6±9.8 (99)	6.2±16.9 (97)	5.9±19.7 (96)	16.6±30.0 (90)
(2)	1.2±0.1 (100)	0.8±0.0 (100)	1.4±1.6 (100)	0.6±0.1 (100)	1.4±1.0 (100)
(3)	1.5±0.1 (100)	1.0±0.1 (100)	1.5±1.6 (100)	0.8±0.1 (100)	1.5±0.5 (100)
(4)	1.4±0.1 (100)	1.0±0.1 (100)	1.1±0.7 (100)	0.8±0.1 (100)	1.5±0.6 (100)
(5)	1.5±0.1 (100)	0.9±0.0 (100)	1.4±0.8 (100)	0.7±0.1 (100)	1.9±1.7 (97)
(6)	1.5±0.2 (100)	1.0±0.1 (100)	3.3±3.2 (84)	0.9±0.2 (100)	1.8±1.7 (97)
(7)	6.5±3.1 (62)	4.1±1.8 (98)	7.0±2.5 (70)	10.0±0.0 (0)	8.8±2.3 (27)
(8)	5.3±3.4 (72)	5.1±2.1 (93)	7.9±3.7 (26)	9.9±0.9 (1)	5.2±2.8 (88)

Table 4. Comparison of the algorithms performance for initial bounds [-10, 10]

fun.	PSO($\times 10^3$)	GWO($\times 10^3$)	ES+($\times 10^3$)	ES/($\times 10^3$)	IS($\times 10^3$)
(1)	1.2±0.2 (100)	1.0±0.4 (100)	6.3±21.5 (95)	13.9±33.2 (87)	5.2±16.9 (97)
(2)	0.9±0.1 (100)	0.6±0.0 (100)	0.6±0.2 (100)	0.4±0.1 (100)	10.2±0.5 (100)
(3)	1.1±0.1 (100)	0.8±0.1 (100)	0.9±0.5 (100)	0.7±0.1 (100)	1.5±2.5 (100)
(4)	1.0±0.1 (100)	0.7±0.1 (100)	0.8±1.1 (100)	0.5±0.1 (100)	1.0±0.5 (100)
(5)	1.1±0.1 (100)	0.7±0.0 (100)	1.2±1.7 (97)	0.7±0.9 (99)	1.4±1.7 (98)
(6)	1.1±0.1 (100)	0.8±0.1 (100)	1.8±2.1 (97)	0.7±0.2 (100)	1.2±0.7 (100)
(7)	3.5±2.3 (94)	2.8±0.8 (100)	4.3±2.0 (97)	10.0±0.0 (0)	7.9±2.5 (56)
(8)	0.9±0.1 (100)	0.7±0.0 (100)	1.0±1.1 (99)	1.2±2.4 (93)	1.0±0.6 (100)
(9)	5.1±4.0 (64)	8.0±3.2 (38)	6.1±3.9 (55)	7.7±3.7 (33)	5.6±4.3 (54)
(10)	2.0±0.1 (100)	1.3±0.1 (100)	2.0±1.1 (100)	3.0±13.8 (100)	4.6±13.8 (100)

Table 5. Comparison of the algorithms performance for initial bounds [-5, 5]

fun.	PSO($\times 10^3$)	GWO($\times 10^3$)	ES+($\times 10^3$)	ES/($\times 10^3$)	IS($\times 10^3$)
(1)	1.4±2.4 (100)	0.9±0.2 (100)	5.3±19.3 (96)	14.8±34.3 (86)	3.1±10.9 (99)
(2)	0.8±0.1 (100)	0.5±0.0 (100)	0.5±0.3 (100)	0.4±0.1 (100)	0.8±0.5 (100)
(3)	1.0±0.1 (100)	0.7±0.1 (100)	0.9±0.4 (100)	0.4±0.7 (100)	1.2±0.9 (100)
(4)	0.9±0.1 (100)	0.6±0.0 (100)	0.6±0.2 (100)	0.4±0.1 (100)	0.9±0.7 (100)
(5)	1.0±0.1 (100)	0.7±0.0 (100)	0.8±0.9 (100)	0.7±1.3 (98)	1.2±1.4 (98)
(6)	1.0±0.1 (100)	0.7±0.1 (100)	2.1±2.7 (92)	0.8±1.3 (98)	1.0±0.9 (100)
(7)	2.7±1.7 (98)	2.6±0.9 (100)	4.1±2.0 (97)	10.0±0.0 (0)	7.3±2.7 (63)
(8)	0.9±0.1 (100)	0.7±0.1 (100)	0.9±0.6 (100)	0.8±1.3 (98)	0.9±0.6 (100)
(9)	8.8±2.7 (18)	6.0±3.6 (61)	6.6±3.8 (51)	6.6±4.2 (45)	5.2±4.5 (55)
(10)	1.9±0.1 (100)	1.2±0.1 (100)	1.7±1.5 (100)	5.9±21.5 (100)	2.1±2.2 (100)

Table 6. Comparison of the algorithms performance for initial bounds [-2, 2]

fun.	PSO($\times 10^3$)	GWO($\times 10^3$)	ES+($\times 10^3$)	ES/($\times 10^3$)	IS($\times 10^3$)
(1)	0.9±0.2 (100)	0.8±0.3 (100)	2.0±9.8 (99)	8.9±26.8 (92)	4.3±16.8 (97)
(2)	0.7±0.1 (100)	0.4±0.0 (100)	0.4±0.2 (100)	0.3±0.0 (100)	0.7±0.3 (100)
(3)	0.9±0.1 (100)	0.6±0.0 (100)	0.9±0.4 (100)	0.7±0.1 (100)	1.0±0.6 (100)
(4)	0.8±0.1 (100)	0.5±0.0 (100)	0.4±0.2 (100)	0.4±0.1 (100)	8.0±0.5 (100)
(5)	0.8±0.1 (100)	0.5±0.0 (100)	0.7±0.3 (100)	0.7±1.4 (98)	0.9±1.0 (99)
(6)	0.8±0.1 (100)	0.6±0.1 (100)	1.1±1.8 (98)	0.5±0.1 (100)	0.9±0.5 (100)
(7)	2.7±1.6 (100)	2.1±0.6 (100)	4.8±2.2 (100)	10.0±0.0 (0)	7.2±2.9 (65)
(8)	0.8±0.1 (100)	0.6±0.0 (100)	1.2±1.7 (97)	1.4±2.5 (93)	0.9±0.9 (99)
(9)	9.9±0.6 (2)	3.4±3.2 (87)	6.9±3.8 (44)	7.3±3.8 (42)	7.3±4.0 (33)
(10)	1.8±0.1 (100)	1.2±0.0 (100)	2.7±9.8 (100)	1.8±9.8 (100)	1.8±8.2 (100)

c

5   Conclusions

In this paper, a new metaheuristic Glowworm Optimization is performed and analysed similarities and differences with Particle Swarm Optimization. Simulations show that in most cases, Glowworm Optimization outperforms PSO and have higher success rate than PSO and other metaheuristics. Future studies may be able to form automatic parameter selection and dynamically change parameters. This would allow the algorithm to find solutions faster.

References

1. Kennedy, J., Eberhart, R.: Particle swarm optimization. In: Proceedings of IEEE International Conference on Neural Networks, vol. 4, pp. 1942–1948 (August 2002), http://dx.doi.org/10.1109/ICNN.1995.488968
2. Yang, X.-S.: Firefly algorithm, lévy flights and global optimization. In: Bramer, M., Ellis, R., Petridis, M. (eds.) Research and Development in Intelligent Systems XXVI, pp. 209–218. Springer, London (2010)

A Comparison of Two Adaptation Approaches in Differential Evolution

Radka Poláková[1] and Josef Tvrdík[2]

[1] Department of Mathematics, University of Ostrava
[2] Centre of Excellence IT4Innovations, Division of University of Ostrava,
Institute for Research and Applications of Fuzzy Modeling,
30. dubna Street 22, 701 03 Ostrava, Czech Republic
radka.polakova@wo.cz, josef.tvrdik@osu.cz

Abstract. Two adaptive approaches applied in competitive differential evolution and in differential evolution with an ensemble of mutation strategies and parameter values are compared. The approach used in each of these two algorithms can be divided into two parts: adaptive mechanism and pool of strategies. Four variants of adaptation in differential evolution mutually combining these two parts of the two algorithms are experimentally compared in six benchmark functions at two levels of dimension. It was found out that the algorithms with the pool of competitive differential evolution are more reliable, whereas the variants using the pool of the other algorithm need mostly a smaller number of function evaluations to reach the stopping condition.

Keywords: global optimization, differential evolution, adaptation, experimental comparison.

1 Introduction

Differential evolution (DE) is one of the most frequently used evolutionary algorithms solving a continuous optimization problem. Differential evolution has a few parameters but its efficiency is very dependent on setting of parameters to appropriate values, which often requires a lot of time. That is why many adaptive or self-adaptive DE versions have appeared in literature, for an overview see [6,3]. Among the adaptive variants of DE, jDE [2], $SADE$ [7], $JADE$ [13], and $EPSDE$ [5] the state-of-the-art algorithms are considered. The approaches to the implementation of adaptive or self-adaptive mechanism vary but some common features can be found in some pairs of approaches used in the adaptive DE. We focus on $EPSDE$ and a *competitive DE* variant [10]. The aim of our study is to compare the adaptive mechanisms used in these two algorithms.

The remainder of this paper is organized as follows. Section 2 deals with DE algorithm. Two studied approaches of adaptation in DE and their implementation are described in section 3 as well as the algorithms compared in experiments. Benchmark functions used in tests are briefly mentioned in section 4, where the setting of experiments is also described. The results of experiments are presented in section 5. Last section gives brief conclusions.

L. Rutkowski et al. (Eds.): SIDE 2012 and EC 2012, LNCS 7269, pp. 317–324, 2012.

2   Differential Evolution

Differential evolution is simple and powerful population-based algorithm for the global optimization introduced by Storn and Price [8]. DE works with two alternating generations of population, P and Q. The points of population are considered as candidates of solution.

At the beginning, the generation P is initialized randomly in the search domain S, $S = \prod_{j=1}^{D}[a_j, b_j]$, $a_j < b_j$, $j = 1, 2, \ldots, D$. A new point y (trial point) is produced by mutation and crossover operations for each point $x_i \in P$, $i \in \{1, 2, \ldots, NP\}$, where NP is the size of population. The point y is inserted into new generation Q if $f(y) \leq f(x_i)$, otherwise the point x_i enters into Q. After completing the new generation, Q becomes the old generation P and the whole process continues until the stopping condition is satisfied.

The trial vector y is generated by crossover operation of two vectors (points), the target one (x_i) and a mutant one (v). The mutant vector v is obtained by a mutation. F is parameter of mutation. The $rand/1$ [8], $randrl/1$ [4], $best/2$ [8], and $current\text{-}to\text{-}rand/1$ [5] mutations were used in our work. Binomial or exponential crossover can be used in generating a new trial points with all the mutations except $current\text{-}to\text{-}rand/1$ which generates the trial point y directly because it includes so-called arithmetic crossover. Probability of mutation (p_m) determines the number of exchanged elements in crossover and it is controlled by crossover parameter CR, $0 \leq CR \leq 1$. The relation between p_m and CR in the binomial crossover is linear. However, this relation is strongly nonlinear in the exponential crossover [12].

3   Different Approaches to Adaptation in DE

Four state-of-the-art adaptive DE algorithms (jDE [2], $SADE$ [7], $JADE$ [13], and $EPSDE$ [5]) have been compared experimentally with two variants of $CoDE$ (composite trial vector generation strategies and control parameters) [11] and with $b6e6rl$ variant of $competitive\ DE$ [10] recently[1]. Considering the overall performance, $JADE$ appeared the most efficient, $competitive\ DE$, the most reliable among the algorithms in the comparison. $EPSDE$ [5] was efficient in some problems but its reliability was considerable less compared to $competitive\ DE$, in spite of the fact that their adaptive mechanisms are similar in some features.

3.1   Competitive Differential Evolution

Adaptive approach based on competition of different DE strategies and parameter settings was introduced in [9] and is denoted by abbreviation of CDE. Any of H such strategies in the pool can be chosen to generate a new trial

---

[1] Tvrdík, J., Poláková, R., Veselský, J., Bujok, P.: Adaptive Variants of Differential Evolution: Towards Control-Parameter-Free Optimizers, submitted to Handbook of Optimization, I. Zelinka, V. Snasel, and A. Abraham (eds.), Springer, to appear in 2012.

point y for each element x_i. A strategy is selected randomly with probability q_h, $h = 1, 2, \ldots, H$. At the start the values of probability are set uniformly, $q_h = 1/H$, and they are modified according to the success rate in the preceding steps of the search process. The hth setting is considered successful if it generates a trial point y satisfying $f(y) \le f(x_i)$. Probability q_h is evaluated as the relative frequency according to

$$q_h = \frac{n_h + n_0}{\sum_{j=1}^{H}(n_j + n_0)} , \tag{1}$$

where n_h is the current count of the hth strategy successes, and $n_0 > 0$ is an input parameter. The setting of $n_0 > 1$ prevents from a dramatic change in q_h by one random successful use of the hth strategy at beginning. To avoid degeneration of the search process, the current values of q_h are reset to their starting values if any probability q_h decreases below given limit δ, $\delta > 0$.

Several variants of *competitive DE* were tested [10]. The variant of *competitive DE*, denoted *b6e6rl* there, appeared well-performing and robust in different benchmark tests. The *CDE* is used as the label of this *competitive DE* variant hereafter. In this variant, twelve strategies are in competition ($H = 12$), six of them use the binomial crossover, the others use the exponential crossover. The *randrl/1* mutation is applied in all the strategies, two different values of control parameter F are used, $F = 0.5$ and $F = 0.8$. The binomial crossover uses three different values of CR, $CR \in \{0, 0.5, 1\}$. The exponential crossover uses three values of $CR \in \{CR1, CR2, CR3\}$. Values $CR1$, $CR2$, and $CR3$ are evaluated as roots of polynomial equation derived by Zaharie [12] describing the relation between mutation probability p_m and CR for three values of p_m that are set up equidistantly in the interval $(1/D, 1)$. The values of parameters controlling competition are set up to $n_0 = 2$ and $\delta = 1/(5 \times H)$, as it was used in previous applications of this algorithm.

3.2   Ensemble of Mutation Strategies and Parameter Values

The adaptive variant of *DE* called ensemble of mutation strategies and parameter values (*EPSDE*) was proposed in [5]. The mutation strategies and the values of control parameters F and CR are stored in pools. The combinations of the strategies and the parameters in the pools have diverse characteristics, so that they can exhibit distinct performance during different stages of evolution. A triplet of *strategy, F, CR* is stored together with each point of population. The triplets are set randomly for initial generation and then they develop during evolution. If the triplet (*strategy, F, CR*) of target vector x_i produces a successful trial vector y, the triplet survives and it becomes the triplet of parameters of the trial vector y which is now (in next generation) the member of population instead of x_i. Each successful triplet of parameters is also stored in auxiliary memory of length of L, usually $L = NP$. If the stored triplet (*strategy, F, CR*) is not successful, it is re-initialized by a triplet whose items are randomly chosen from respective pools or by a randomly chosen one from the memory of successful triplets. The pool of strategies is {*best/2/bin, rand/1/bin, current-to-rand/1*}, the pool of F values is {$0.4, 0.5, 0.6, 0.7, 0.8, 0.9$} and the pool of CR values is {$0.1, 0.2, 0.3, 0.4, 0.5, 0.6, 0.7, 0.8, 0.9$} in *EPSDE* algorithm described in [5].

There are 54 different pairs of (F, CR) in *EPSDE*, each of them can be joined with *best/2/bin* and *rand/1/bin*. The *current-to-rand/1* mutation can be used with each of 6 different values from pool of F. We obtain together 114 different strategies and control parameter settings applied in *EPSDE*.

3.3 Algorithms in Experimental Comparison

Common features of *CDE* and *EPSDE* are adaptation and usage of the pool of *DE* strategies and the values of control parameters. However, the algorithms differ in the contents of the pools and in the implementation of adaptive mechanisms. In order to evaluate the influence of these approaches on the performance of the algorithms, we compare experimentally the algorithms combining the adaptive mechanisms and the pools used in *CDE* and *EPSDE*. If we denote the adaptive mechanisms and the pools used in these algorithms by the first letter of an algorithm's label, we obtain four possibilities how adaptive mechanisms and the pools can be combined, namely *C-C*, *E-E*, *C-E*, *E-C*, where the first letter stands for the adaptive mechanism and the second for the pool.

Note, that *C-C* and *E-E* symbols denote the original *CDE* described in 3.1 and *EPSDE* described in 3.2, respectively. In the *C-E* algorithm, the pool of strategies and parameter settings of *EPSDE* is used with competitive adaptation, the value of $H = 114$. Vice versa, the adaptive mechanism coming from *EPSDE* is applied to the *CDE* pool of strategies and parameter settings in the *E-C* algorithm. The length of memory of successful triplets is set up to $L = 9$ for this algorithm, because of the fact that the L should be less than the count of all possible strategies, which are only twelve here.

4   Benchmark Functions and Experiments

Six well-known test functions [1,5,8] are used as benchmark in this study. Rosenbrock and Schwefel functions were used in their standard form. Ackley, Dejong1, Griewank, and Rastrigin were used in their shifted version. The shifted version of function was evaluated at the point $z = x - o$, $o \in S$, $o \neq (0, 0, \ldots, 0)$. The shift o was generated randomly from uniform D-dimensional distribution before each run.

Four algorithms (*C-C*, *E-E*, *E-C*, and *C-E*) were compared in six benchmark problems at two levels of dimension, $D = 30$ and $D = 100$. The same size of population ($NP = 60$) was set for every tested algorithms. The stopping condition was defined the same for all tested adaptive variants of DE as follows:

$$f_{max} - f_{min} < \varepsilon_f \quad \text{OR} \quad nfe > D \times maxevals, \tag{2}$$

where $f_{max} - f_{min}$ is the difference between the function values of the worst and the best individual in the population, *nfe* is the current number of function evaluations, ε_f and *maxevals* are input parameters set up to $\varepsilon_f = 1 \times 10^{-6}$ and *maxevals* $= 2 \times 10^4$, respectively.

One hundred of independent runs for each test problem and each tested algorithm were carried out. The number of the function evaluations (nfe) and the minimum function value (f_{min}) were recorded at the end of each run. The solution found in a run is considered acceptable if the minimum function value in the final generation does not differ from the known correct solution of the test problem by more than 1×10^{-4}. The reliability rate (R) of an algorithm in the solved problem is the percentage of runs finding an acceptable solution.

5 Results

The basic characteristics of algorithms' performance, i.e. the mean value of function evaluations and the values of reliability rate, are shown in Tables 1 and 2 for all the algorithms in comparison and each problem in columns labeled by nfe and R, respectively. The least values of nfe for each problem are printed in bold.

Table 1. Characteristics of performance, $D = 30$

	Ackley		Dejong1		Griewank		Rastrigin		Rosenbrock		Schwefel	
	nfe	R	nfe	R	nfe	R	nfe	R	nfe	R	nfe	R
C-C	71297	100	37472	100	51934	100	**73402**	100	**147185**	100	64243	100
E-E	**44899**	100	**23818**	100	**32438**	100	251678	100	163082	100	74555	99
E-C	72894	100	40142	100	56475	94	112639	100	153244	99	76888	100
C-E	54967	100	28793	100	40669	97	111616	100	155491	99	**62018**	100

Table 2. Characteristics of performance, $D = 100$

	Ackley		Dejong1		Griewank		Rastrigin		Rosenbrock		Schwefel	
	nfe	R	nfe	R	nfe	R	nfe	R	nfe	R	nfe	R
C-C	258244	100	145163	100	178750	99	**271464**	100	910790	97	248053	98
E-E	**102604**	89	**61112**	100	**76005**	82	2000040	0	1548091	82	612686	98
E-C	225699	100	128734	100	159421	95	410656	100	**852464**	91	293149	98
C-E	115202	100	67567	100	83472	93	1996477	6	1286119	76	**232939**	100

Relevant pairs of the algorithms were compared statistically. The agreement of the computational costs measured by the number of function evaluations was tested by the Wilcoxon two-sample test, the agreement in reliability rates was tested by Fisher exact test. In the tables with the results of statistical tests, the symbol "+" denotes a significant difference in the case if the first algorithm in a pair is better, the symbol "−" is used for a significant difference if the first algorithm in comparison is worse, and the symbol "=" means no significant difference between the algorithms at the level of 0.05.

Original algorithms C-$C(CDE)$ and E-$E(EPSDE)$ are compared in Table 3. While the computational costs of the algorithms can be considered similar (the counts of significant differences in both directions are equal), the reliability of CDE is substantially better in the problems of $D = 100$.

Table 3. Comparison of C-C vs. E-E algorithms

		Ackley	Dejong1	Griewank	Rastrigin	Rosenbr.	Schwefel
$D = 30$	Fisher R	=	=	=	=	=	=
	Wilcoxon nfe	−	−	−	+	+	+
$D = 100$	Fisher R	+	=	+	+	+	=
	Wilcoxon nfe	−	−	−	+	+	+

Table 4. Comparison of different adaptive approaches with the same pool of strategies

		Ackley	Dejong1	Griewank	Rastrigin	Rosenbr.	Schwefel
C-C vs. E-C							
$D = 30$	Fisher R	=	=	+	=	=	=
	Wilcoxon nfe	+	+	+	+	+	+
$D = 100$	Fisher R	=	=	=	=	=	=
	Wilcoxon nfe	−	−	−	+	−	+
E-E vs. C-E							
$D = 30$	Fisher R	=	=	=	=	=	=
	Wilcoxon nfe	+	+	+	−	−	−
$D = 100$	Fisher R	−	=	−	−	=	=
	Wilcoxon nfe	+	+	+	−	−	−

Comparison of different adaptive approaches with the same pool of strategies is shown in Table 4. The use of $EPSDE$ adaptive mechanism with CDE pool of strategies does not bring any benefit in the problems of $D = 30$, while the efficiency of such combination is significantly higher in four problems of $D = 100$. Replacing of $EPSDE$ adaptive mechanism by the competitive adaptation leads to higher reliability in three problems of $D = 100$ and the influence of this change on efficiency is significant but its direction is problem-depending (three increases, three decreases).

Table 5. Comparison of different pools of strategies in the same adaptive approach

		Ackley	Dejong1	Griewank	Rastrigin	Rosenbr.	Schwefel
C-C vs. C-E							
$D = 30$	Fisher R	=	=	=	=	=	=
	Wilcoxon nfe	−	−	−	+	+	−
$D = 100$	Fisher R	=	=	=	+	+	=
	Wilcoxon nfe	−	−	−	+	+	−
E-E vs. E-C							
$D = 30$	Fisher R	=	=	+	=	=	=
	Wilcoxon nfe	+	+	+	−	−	+
$D = 100$	Fisher R	−	=	−	−	=	=
	Wilcoxon nfe	+	+	+	−	−	−

Comparison of different collections of strategies in the same adaptive approach is presented in Table 5. When we compare two strategy pools applied within the competitive adaptation mechanism, the *EPSDE* pool increases the efficiency of the algorithm in most problems (8 out of 12). However, it is not helpful in Rastrigin and Rosenbrock problems. *C-E* combination is significantly worse for these two problems both in the reliability and efficiency at $D = 100$. Using the *CDE* pool of strategies in *EPSDE* adaptive mechanism increases significantly the reliability in three problems of $D = 100$ but its influence on the efficiency is problem-dependent.

6 Conclusion

Adaptive *DE* variants combining the adaptive mechanisms and strategy pools of *competitive DE* and *EPSDE* were compared experimentally in six benchmark problems at two levels of dimension. The influence of the mechanism and the pool combinations on the performance of the algorithms is problem dependent. However, the algorithms using *EPSDE* pool of strategies need frequently a smaller number of function evaluations to reach the stopping condition, while the algorithms with *CDE* pool of strategies are more reliable. The higher reliability of these variants is probably caused by the presence of exponential crossover in the pool of strategies, which is considered helpful in optimizing the non-separable functions.

Acknowledgments. This paper has been elaborated in the framework of the IT4Innovations Centre of Excellence project, reg. no. CZ.1.05/1.1.00/02.0070 supported by Operational Programme 'Research and Development for Innovations' funded by Structural Funds of the European Union and state budget of the Czech Republic. This work was partially supported by University of Ostrava from the SGS 22/2011 project.

References

1. Ali, M.M., Törn, A.: Population set based global optimization algorithms: Some modifications and numerical studies. Computers and Operations Research 31, 1703–1725 (2004)
2. Brest, J., Greiner, S., Boškovič, B., Mernik, M., Žumer, V.: Self-adapting control parameters in differential evolution: A comparative study on numerical benchmark problems. IEEE Transactions on Evolutionary Computation 10, 646–657 (2006)
3. Das, S., Suganthan, P.N.: Differential evolution: A survey of the state-of-the-art. IEEE Transactions on Evolutionary Computation 15, 27–54 (2011)
4. Kaelo, P., Ali, M.M.: A numerical study of some modified differential evolution algorithms. European J. Operational Research 169, 1176–1184 (2006)
5. Mallipeddi, R., Suganthan, P.N., Pan, Q.K., Tasgetiren, M.F.: Differential evolution algorithm with ensemble of parameters and mutation strategies. Applied Soft Computing 11, 1679–1696 (2011)
6. Neri, F., Tirronen, V.: Recent advances in differential evolution: a survey and experimental analysis. Artificial Intelligence Review 33, 61–106 (2010)
7. Qin, A.K., Huang, V.L., Suganthan, P.N.: Differential evolution algorithm with strategy adaptation for global numerical optimization. IEEE Transactions on Evolutionary Computation 13(2), 398–417 (2009)
8. Storn, R., Price, K.V.: Differential evolution - a simple and efficient heuristic for global optimization over continuous spaces. J. Global Optimization 11, 341–359 (1997)
9. Tvrdík, J.: Competitive differential evolution. In: Matoušek, R., Ošmera, P. (eds.) MENDEL 2006: 12th International Conference on Soft Computing, pp. 7–12. University of Technology, Brno (2006)
10. Tvrdík, J.: Self-adaptive variants of differential evolution with exponential crossover. Mathematics-Informatics, vol. 47, pp. 151–168. Analele of West University Timisoara (2009), http://www1.osu.cz/~tvrdik/
11. Wang, Y., Cai, Z., Zhang, Q.: Differential evolution with composite trial vector generation strategies and control parameters. IEEE Transactions on Evolutionary Computation 15, 55–66 (2011)
12. Zaharie, D.: Influence of crossover on the behavior of differential evolution algorithms. Applied Soft Computing 9, 1126–1138 (2009)
13. Zhang, J., Sanderson, A.C.: JADE: Adaptive Differential Evolution With Optional External Archive. IEEE Transactions on Evolutionary Computation 13, 945–958 (2009)

The Fuzzy-Genetic System
for Multiobjective Optimization

Krzysztof Pytel[1] and Tadeusz Nawarycz[2]

[1] Department of Theoretical Physics and Computer Science
University of Lodz, Poland
[2] Department of Biophysics, Medical University in Lodz, Poland
kpytel@uni.lodz.pl, tadeusz.nawarycz@umed.lodz.pl

Abstract. The article presents the idea of the intelligent system for the multiobjective optimization. The system consists of the genetic algorithm (GA) and the fuzzy logic controller (FLC). In experiments we investigated the maintenance of genetic algorithms with the variable length of genes. The genes of individuals are encoded and represented by real numbers. The FLC controls the length of individuals' genotypes in the genetic algorithm. The variable length of the genotype of individuals allows for the limitation of the computational effort, when the length of the genotype of an individual grows smaller. We chose the problem of the distribution of Access Points in a given area in a wireless network as the test-function for our experiments. In the article we presented the results obtained during the optimization of the test-function. The experiments show, that the proposed system is an efficient tool for solving the multiobjective optimization problems. The proposed system can be used to solve similar problems of multiobjective optimization.

Keywords: fuzzy logic, genetic algorithms, multiobjective optimization.

1 Introduction

Wireless local area networks (WLAN) are one of the most rapidly growing methods of communication and data transfers. A wireless network can use Access Points. In this type of network the Access Point acts like a hub, providing connectivity for the wireless computers. It can connect the wireless LAN to a wired LAN, allowing wireless computers access to LAN resources, such as file servers or Internet. The goal of the network design is to provide the maximum customer service with minimum cost (using minimum Access Points). How to efficiently place Access Points on a given area is a very important issue. The problem, called wireless Access Points placement problem, can be treated by two approaches. The first approach, wireless Access Point selection, is to find the number of Access Points to cover the given area. The second approach is to find the positions of Access Points. Wireless Access Points placement problem is an NP-hard optimization problem so a few heuristic approaches have been proposed. Existing heuristic methods can find approximate positions of Access Points if the number

L. Rutkowski et al. (Eds.): SIDE 2012 and EC 2012, LNCS 7269, pp. 325–332, 2012.

of Access Points is known. The system for solving this problem should find both the number and the positions of Access Points.

Genetic algorithms stand for a class of stochastic optimization methods that simulate the process of natural evolution [2][5]. In a genetic algorithm, a population of strings (called individuals or chromosomes), which encode candidate solutions (called individuals) to an optimization problem, evolves toward better solutions. Individuals can be represented by strings of zeros and ones (the binary representation) or by a set of real numbers (the real representation). They usually search for approximate solutions for composite optimization problems. A characteristic feature of genetic algorithms is that in the process of evolution they do not use the specific knowledge for a given problem, except for the fitness function assigned to all individuals. The genetic algorithms can be used for solving multiobjective optimization problems too [1][6].

The genetic algorithm consists of the following steps:

1. the choice of the first generation,
2. the estimation of each individual's fitness,
3. the check of the stop conditions,
4. the selection of individuals to the parents' pool,
5. the creation of a new generation with the use of operators of crossing and mutation,
6. the printing of the best solution.

Fuzzy Logic (FL) is able to process incomplete and subjective data. The reasoning in FL is similar to human reasoning. FL incorporates a simple, rule-based IF ... THEN ... approach to a solving control problem. FL can provide approximate solutions to problems, where there are no mathematic formula to compute solution.

The fuzzy genetic systems [3][4] is an effective tool for solving difficult optimization problems. The system proposed in this article consists of Genetic Algorithm (GA) and Fuzzy Logic Controller (FLC). The FLC controls the evolution process realized by genetic algorithm. The system allows for simultaneous maximization of the coverage of the network's area and the minimization of the number of Access Points.

2   Problem Formulation

Let us consider a fixed geographic area, on which some Access Points serve as a wireless access to network.

$$A = \{(x_{min}, y_{min}), (x_{max}, y_{max})\} \tag{1}$$

The problem of finding the Access Points' location is to place the minimum number of Access Points in such a way that they can cover all the network area. Each Access Point has a fixed range and cost of installation. To minimize the cost of the installation we have to minimize the number of Access Points.

The formal definition of Wireless Access Points Placement (WAPP) can be stated as follows: Given a network area and the Access Points' features, the problem WAPP is to find the minimum number of Access Points n, and their location (x, y), subject to the cost and area cover constraints.

$$\begin{cases} max & f_1(x) = (x_1, y_1, x_2, y_2, ..., x_n, y_n) \\ min & f_2(n) \\ \text{subject to:} & cost\ and\ area\ constraints \end{cases} \qquad (2)$$

where:

- f_1 - is a function representing the area, wherein the access to the network is possible,
- f_2 - is a function representing the number of Access Points,
- $(x_1, y_1), ..., (x_n, y_n) \in A$ - is a position of the point in the geographic area of the network,
- $1 \le n \le n_{max}$ - is the number of Access Points used in the network.

Mobile devices, like PDAs or laptops, may move around all the network area. Each point in the network area $(x_n, y_n) \in A$ can be covered from zero to n of Access Points. The signal strength from at least one Access Point should be greater than a threshold to maintain quality of service requirement. Each point in the network area is covered by Access Point with the highest signal strength.

3 Proposed Fuzzy-Genetic System

The proposed system consists of two modules: the Genetic Algorithm (GA) and the Fuzzy Logic Controller (FLC). The GA seeks for the optimal placement of Access Points and delivers information concerning the current state of optimization to the FLC. FLC looks for the optimal number of Access Points. The FLC is engaged between generations of GA in fixed intervals. The FLC modifies the number of Access Points in the dependence on information delivered from the GA.

In the proposed GA the individuals' genes are encoded by means of real numbers. The individuals' genes represent the position of Access Points in geographical coordinates. Each individual is represented by a set of coordinates, with length equal to the number of Access Points. Because the number of Access Points is also an object of optimization, the length of the individuals' genotype will be variable.

In our experiment different types of crossing of chromosomes is used. The standard one-point crossing is used when the number of Access Points does not change. We introduce two new crossing operators, used when the number of Access Points changes:

- CR1 - is used when the length of the genotype of the descendant is greater than the length of the genotype of the parents. The genotype of the descendant is obtained by copying all genes from the first parent and lacking genes from the end of the second parent.

- CR2 - is used when the length of the genotype of the descendant is smaller than the length of the genotype of the parents. The number of genes copied from every parent is diminished in proportion to the length of the genotype, to obtain the required length of the genotype of the descendant.

To calculate individuals' fitness function, we cover the network area with grid with fixed step. For each point of the grid the maximum value of the signal strength from all Access Points is calculated. Each point of the grid is associated with the Access Point with the maximum value of the signal strength. The fitness function is calculated as the sum of maximum values of the signal strength in all points of the grid.

The FLC uses the knowledge of experts and the knowledge collected by the GA. A basic task of the FLC in the proposed system is the evaluation of the solutions found till now. The FLC makes a decisions about the diminution or the enlargement of the number of Access Points. These decisions are made with fixed intervals between generations of the GA. The FLC modifies the number of Access Points using the following rules:

- enlarge the number of Access Points if the network coverage ratio is small and the average number of points of the grid covered by Access Points is large,
- do not change the number of Access Points if the network coverage ratio is suitable and the average number of points of the grid covered by Access Points is suitable,
- diminish the number of Access Points if the network coverage ratio is large and the average number of points of the grid covered by Access Point is small.

The FLC calculates the change of the number of Access Points based on two parameters:

- network coverage ratio

$$cov = \frac{\sum_{i=1}^{k} p_{cov}}{p} \tag{3}$$

where:
$\sum_{i=1}^{k} p_{cov}$ - the number of points of the grid covered by the signal,
p - the number of all points in the grid.
- the average number of points of the grid covered by Access Points

$$\overline{cov} = \frac{\sum_{i=1}^{k} p_{cov}}{n} \tag{4}$$

where:
n - the number of Access Points.

As the result from the FLC we accepted:

- w_{AP} - the ratio of the change of the Access Points' number.

Table 1. The rule base for the FLC

		cov			
		VS	S	OK	G
$\overline{cov}$	S	LD	LE	LE	SE
	OK	LD	LD	LE	LE
	G	SD	LD	LD	LE

The modified number of Access Points obeys the formula:

$$n' = w_{AP} * n \tag{5}$$

where:

- n' - the modified number of Access Points,
- n - the number of Access Points,
- w_{AP} - the ratio of the change of the Access Points' number.

The knowledge base (rule base) of FLC is shown in Table 1 (fuzzy values of the ratio of the change of the Access Points' number).

Values in the Table1 are:

- VS - very small,
- S - small,
- OK - suitable,
- G - good,
- SD - strongly diminished,
- LD - lightly diminished,
- LE - lightly enlarged,
- SE - strongly enlarged.

Figures 1 - 3 show the membership functions of the network coverage ratio, the average number of points of the grid covered by Access Points and the ratio of the change of the Access Points' number.

The FLC uses the center of gravity [5] defuzzyfication method.

4   Computational Experiments

The goal of the experiment is the verification of the idea of controlling the process of multiobjective optimization realized by the genetic algorithm. In the modified algorithm we introduce an additional FLC, which controls the value of one objective function. The FLC keeps this value in near-optimal section. We chose the problem of the distribution of Access Points on the given area in a wireless network as the test-function for our experiments. We defined two mutually contradictory objective functions: the coverage of the network area

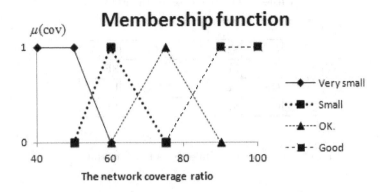

Fig. 1. The membership functions of the network coverage ratio

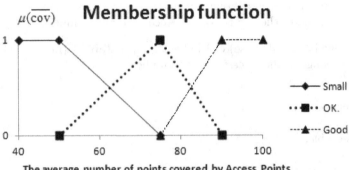

Fig. 2. The membership functions of the average number of points of the grid covered by Access Points

and the number of Access Points (the cost of installation). If the number of Access Points grows, the coverage of the network area grows too, however the cost of installation grows as well. In the considered tasks, the FLC manages the number of Access Points and modifies the length of the individuals' genotype. Access Points are located on the area 30x30 units. We chose a few different ranges of Access Points to check the coverage of the area and the distribution of Access Points. The algorithms' parameters used in the experiment:

- the genes of individuals are represented by real numbers,
- the probability of crossover = 0,8,
- the probability of mutation = 0,15,
- the number of individuals in the population = 25,
- the algorithms were stopped after predefined number of generations.

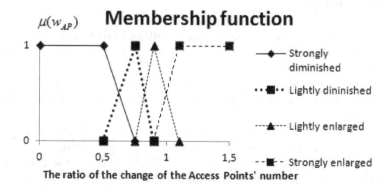

Fig. 3. The membership functions of the ratio of the change of the Access Points' number

Table 2. Average values of the Access Points' number and the coverage of the network area

	The range of Access Points		
	7,5	5	3,75
The optimal number of Access Points	4	9	16
The number of Access Points found by algorithm	4	9	16
The coverage of the network area	93,44	91,77	97,22

Each algorithm was executed 10 times. In Table 2 there are average values of the Access Points' number and the coverage of the network area obtained by the algorithm.

Figure 4. shows the distribution of Access Points in the network area.

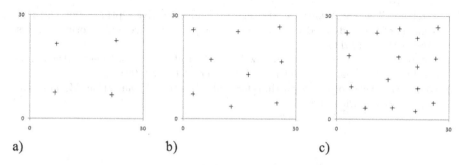

a)   b)   c)

Fig. 4. The distribution of Access Points found by the algorithm at the range of Access Points a) 7.5, b) 5, c) 3.75

5   Conclusions

The proposed fuzzy-genetic system can solve multiobjective optimization problems. The basic advantage of the system is that it can simultaneously optimize many objective functions.

In the considered task the objective functions were mutually contradictory. The total optimum was located in the place, where no objective functions accept the extremum.

The FLC is able to manage the evolution in the genetic algorithm. The FLC found an optimal number of Access Points in all investigated tasks.

The genetic algorithm can find solutions with higher value of the fitness function, but the number of Access Points (and the cost of installation) is greater than optimal in this case. The FLC held the number of Access Points close to the optimum value.

The parameters of the system, eg. the number of generations after the FLC is engaged, can be modified. Experiments show that large number of generations between the FLC engagements, can increase the accuracy of solutions. The diminution of the number of generations between the FLC engagements, causes quicker changes of the value of the objective function controlled by the FLC.

The proposed system can be used to solve similar problems of multiobjective optimization.

References

[1] Sakawa, M.: Genetic Algorithms and fuzzy Multiobjective optimization. Kluwer Academic Publications, Boston (2002)

[2] Michalewicz, Z.: Genetic Algorithms + Data Structures = Evolution Programs. Springer, Berlin (1992)

[3] Pytel, K., Nawarycz, T.: Analysis of the Distribution of Individuals in Modified Genetic Algorithms. In: Rutkowski, L., Scherer, R., Tadeusiewicz, R., Zadeh, L.A., Zurada, J.M. (eds.) ICAISC 2010. LNCS, vol. 6114, pp. 197–204. Springer, Heidelberg (2010)

[4] Pytel, K.: The Fuzzy Genetic Strategy for Multiobjective Optimization. In: Proceedings of the Federated Conference on Computer Science and Information Systems, Szczecin (2011)

[5] Rutkowska, D., Pilinski, M., Rutkowski, L.: Neural Networks, Genetic Algorithms and Fuzzy Systems. PWN Scientific Publisher, Warsaw (1997)

[6] Zitzler, E.: Evolutionary Algorithms for Multiobjective Optimization: Methods and Applications, Zurich (1999)

Fletcher's Filter Methodology as a Soft Selector in Evolutionary Algorithms for Constrained Optimization

Ewaryst Rafajłowicz and Wojciech Rafajłowicz

Ewaryst Rafajłowicz and Wojciech Rafajłowicz are with the Institute of Computer Engineering, Control and Robotics, Wrocław University of Technology, Wybrzeże Wyspiańskiego 27, 50 370 Wrocław, Poland
ewaryst.rafajlowicz@pwr.wroc.pl

Abstract. Our aim is to propose a new approach to soft selection in evolutionary algorithms for optimization problems with constraints. It is based on the notion of a filter as introduced by Fletcher and his co-workers. The proposed approach occurred to be quite efficient.

1 Introduction and Problem Statement

Fletcher and his co-workers introduced the idea of a filter ([4], [5] and earlier papers cited therein) as an ingredient of sequential linear programming (SLP) and sequential quadratic programming, whose aim is to avoid the necessity of adding penalties to a goal function when solving nonlinear optimization problems with constraints. We are convinced that the methodology of applying the filter is much wider and it can be useful in developing new algorithms for many optimization problems with constraints. Our aim in this paper is to propose a new approach that incorporates the filter into evolutionary search algorithms with constraints. The filter plays the role of a soft selector as it takes into account both fitness of an individual and the degree of constraints violation.

The proposed approach occurred to be fruitful in designing a relatively efficient and easy to implement algorithm. However, the proposed algorithm is rather an exemplification of the above idea, which can be further developed in various directions. Furthermore, this approach can be useful in modeling the evolution of natural populations, in the spirit of the seminal papers [6], [7], when resources are constrained.

Earlier Efforts in Developing Evolutionary Algorithms with Constraints. Evolutionary algorithms, by their construction, are not well suited to incorporate constraints. The first attempts to take constraints into account can be traced back to the eighties (see [12] for survey paper and [14]). The number of papers on constraints handling is still growing (see, e.g., [8], [9], [10], [14], [15] and the monograph [3]), indicating that the problem is still difficult.

The idea of using a multi-objective programming approach has also a long history [2], [11], [1], but the approaches proposed in these and related papers do not use the multi-criteria approach with the filter directly as the soft selector.

L. Rutkowski et al. (Eds.): SIDE 2012 and EC 2012, LNCS 7269, pp. 333–341, 2012.
© Springer-Verlag Berlin Heidelberg 2012

The Optimization Problem. Denote by $f(\mathbf{x})$ a real valued function of vector $\mathbf{x} \in R^d$. f is our objective function, which is continuous in X.

We impose inequality constraints of the form: $\mathbf{c}(\mathbf{x}) \leq 0$, where $\mathbf{c}(\mathbf{x})$ is m-dimensional vector of functions, $\mathbf{c} : R^d \to R^m$, which define the following set

$$\mathcal{C} \stackrel{def}{=} \{\mathbf{x} : c^{(1)}(\mathbf{x}) \leq 0, \, c^{(2)}(\mathbf{x}) \leq 0, \ldots c^{(m)}(\mathbf{x}) \leq 0\},$$

where $c^{(j)}(\mathbf{x})$ is j-th component of vector $\mathbf{c}(\mathbf{x})$. The continuity of $c^{(j)}(\mathbf{x})$'s is assumed, which implies that $\mathcal{C}$ is a closed set. We also assume that $\mathcal{C} \subset R^d$ is nonempty and bounded.

Consider the following optimization problem

$$\min_{\mathbf{x}} f(\mathbf{x}) \quad \text{subject to} \quad \mathbf{c}(\mathbf{x}) \leq 0. \tag{1}$$

The continuity of f and the compactness of $\mathcal{C}$ imply existence of its solution.

Our aim is to discuss evolutionary algorithms in which the filter plays the role of a soft selector. Sequences $\mathbf{x}_k \in X$, $k = 1, 2, \ldots$, generated by them are expected to be convergent to (hopefully global) minimizer $\mathbf{x}^*$ of f over $\mathcal{C}$.

Define a penalty function, denoted further h,

$$h(\mathbf{c}(\mathbf{x})) = \sum_{j=1}^{m} \max\left(0, \, c^{(j)}(\mathbf{x})\right). \tag{2}$$

Note that $h(\mathbf{c}(\mathbf{x})) = 0$ iff $\mathbf{x} \in \mathcal{C}$. Observe that $h(\mathbf{c}(\mathbf{x}))$ is not differentiable.

2   How Does the Filter Work ?

The notion of a filter, was introduced as a tool for solving constrained optimization problems by generating sequences that are solutions of quadratic or linear approximations to $f(x)$ and linear approximations to $\mathbf{c}(x)$.

Following Fletcher's idea with minor changes, we define the filter as follows.

Definition 1. *In k-th generation a filter $\mathcal{F}_k$ is a list of pairs (h_k, f_k), which were generated according to the rules described below, where for given $\mathbf{x}_k$ we denote by (h_k, f_k) a pair of the form: $(h(\mathbf{c}(\mathbf{x}_k)), f(\mathbf{x}_k))$. The list of $\mathbf{x}_k$'s, which correspond to $(h_k, f_k) \in \mathcal{F}_k$ is also attached to the filter, but it is not displayed.*

In our case it is necessary to store x_k's together with the corresponding (h_k, f_k)'s. This is not as memory consuming as one can expect, because we do not allow the filter content to grow above a certain level.

We say that a pair (h_k, f_k) dominates (h_l, f_l) if and only if

$$f_k \leq f_l \quad \text{AND} \quad h_k \leq h_l \tag{3}$$

and at least one of these inequalities is strict.

We shall need a somewhat more demanding notion of a dominance between such pairs as discussed later. At k-th generation the following rules govern the behavior of filter $\mathcal{F}_k$.

Rule 1). Filter $\mathcal{F}_k$ contains only pairs (h_l, f_l), which were generated up to k-th generation and the corresponding $\mathbf{x}_l$'s. No pair in $\mathcal{F}_k$ dominates any other in the sense (3).

Rule 2). A new pair (h_j, f_j) it is allowed to be included to $\mathcal{F}_k$, if it is not dominated by any point already contained in $\mathcal{F}_k$.

Rule 3). If for a pair (h_l, f_l) R2) holds, then is acceptable for inclusion in the filter $\mathcal{F}_k$ and all entries dominated by this pair must be removed from $\mathcal{F}_k$ so as to ensure R1).

An example of a filters contents is shown in Fig. 1 by dots. Note that:

- points are pairs (h_l, f_l) included in $\mathcal{F}_k$,
- the horizontal and vertical lines and the shaded area indicate regions where no new points can be entered, because they are dominated by the points already in $\mathcal{F}_k$,
- desirable points for inclusion to $\mathcal{F}_k$ are as closely as possible to $(0, f_{min})$, where $f_{min} = f(x^*)$,
- additional, horizontal and vertical, fat lines are artificially added in order to prevent an undesirable behavior of (f_k, h_k)'s that is described later.

Filter as a Soft Selector in Evolutionary Algorithms. In the above cited papers of Fletcher and his co-workers the role of the filter was to consider a new point, generated by the sequential quadratic programming, as a candidate to the filter. Our idea is to apply the filter to the whole off-spring of a new generation as a soft selector.

Selection. The role of the filter is to decide whether new points, generated by an evolutionary algorithm, should be accepted for further generations or not.

Softness. $\mathcal{F}_k$ provides a soft selection mechanism, because rules R1)-R3) allow a new point to be included into a filter, even if the corresponding value of the objective function is worse than already found. This may happen only if the penalty for constraints violation decreases.

The idea of using a filter as a soft selector has the additional advantage, which seems not to be shared by any other evolutionary algorithm that takes constraints into account. Namely, after stopping our search the filter content provides valuable information on the trade off between attainable values of the objective function and the degree of constraints violation. It is illustrated in Fig. 1 by the point with the smallest value of $f(\mathbf{x})$. This point attains the value of the goal function, which is below f_{min}. This can happen only when the constraints are slightly violated ($h(\mathbf{x}) > 0$). However, if the constraints are not hard, we may decide to pay an additional cost for the constraint violation (e.g., to cover the costs of additional resources), if the decrease of the goal function $f(\mathbf{x})$ is sufficiently large. Below, we discuss additional requirements imposed on the rules governing the filter in order to make it workable in practice.

Rule 2a). A pair (h, f) is allowed to be included to $\mathcal{F}_k$ if for every h_l, f_l from $\mathcal{F}_k$ and selected constants $\beta, \gamma \in (0, 1)$ the following conditions holds

$$h \leq \beta h_l \quad OR \quad f \leq f_l - \gamma h_l. \tag{4}$$

Conditions (4) extend a taboo region determined by $\mathcal{F}_k$ by adding thin strips toward lower values of $f(\mathbf{x})$ and $h(\mathbf{x})$, respectively (see Fig. 1). We refer the reader to [4], [5] for many details concerning more technical aspects of filter handling. Here, we only mention two of them, because it may happen that the filter contains subsequences such that **NW escape:** $f_k \to \infty$ and simultaneously $h_k \to 0$, **SE escape:** $f_k \to -\infty$ and simultaneously $h_k \to \infty$.

It suffices to include the artificial point $(-\infty, h_{max})$ into the filter in order to prevent SE escape, where h_{max} is the largest constraints violation that is allowed, e.g., one can take the largest constraints violation by individuals of the first generation (see the fat vertical line Fig. 1). The problem of preventing NW escapes is more complicated, because we have to predict attainable large values of $f(\mathbf{x})$, e.g., by a linear predictor. For the purposes of this paper we propose a rough bound, obtained by including the point $(f_{ub}, 0)$ into the filter, where f_{ub} is a crude upper bound for $f(\mathbf{x})$. The bottom edge of this bound is sketched out as the fat horizontal line in Fig. 1. The bounds f_{ub} and h_{max} can be updated.

3   Outline of the Evolutionary Algorithm with Filter

We provide an outline of the evolutionary search algorithm with filter for constrained optimization problems, stressing that it is a skeletal algorithm that can be modified in a number of ways.

Definition 2. *Let* $\mathbf{x}'_k \in R^d$, $\mathbf{x}''_k \in R^d$, ... *denote features of individuals in k-th generation. An extended filter* $\bar{\mathcal{F}}_k$ *in k-th generation contains the triples* $(\mathbf{x}'_k, f(\mathbf{x}'_k), h(\mathbf{x}'_k))$, $(\mathbf{x}''_k, f(\mathbf{x}''_k), h(\mathbf{x}''_k))$, ..., *such that for all the corresponding tuples* $(f(\mathbf{x}'_k), h(\mathbf{x}'_k))$, $(f(\mathbf{x}''_k), h(\mathbf{x}''_k))$, ... *the requirements imposed by Rule 1), Rule 2a) and Rule 3) hold. Later on, we shall use the term "filter" also for the extended filter.*

Evolutionary Algorithm with the Filter

Preparations Filter Initialization. Select N_{max} – the largest admissible population size and N_{min} – the smallest reasonable population size. Choose h_{max} and f_{ub} in the way discussed in Section 2.

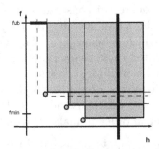

Fig. 1. Example of a filter content: dots indicate points included in the filter, shaded areas are taboo regions, fat horizontal and vertical lines prevent escaping to regions where $f_k \to \infty$ and $h_k \to 0$ as well as $f_k \to -\infty$ and $h_k \to \infty$

Step 0. Set the generations counter $k = 0$.
- Allocate an empty filter (list) $\bar{\mathcal{F}}_0$ and enter the triples $(dummy, -\infty, h_{max})$ and $(dummy, f_{ub}, 0)$ to $\bar{\mathcal{F}}_0$, where $dummy$ is an arbitrary vector.
- If it is possible, select $\mathbf{x}_0 \in \mathcal{C}$, set $h_0 = 0$, $f_0 = f(\mathbf{x}_0)$. If $f_0 < f_{ub}$, enter $(\mathbf{x}_0, f_0, 0)$ into $\bar{\mathcal{F}}_0$, set $k = 1$ and go to Step 2. Otherwise, repeat the selection of $\mathbf{x}_0 \in \mathcal{C}$.
- If it is not possible to select $\mathbf{x}_0 \in \mathcal{C}$, go to Step 1.

Step 1. Initial population. Choose $\gamma > 0$ as a tolerance of the constraints violation.

1. Select at random an initial population of points, admitting non feasible points, i.e., those outside $\mathcal{C}$.
2. Run "a standard evolutionary algorithm" that does not take constraints into account, but minimizes $h(\mathbf{x})$ only as the goal function.
3. Stop this algorithm, if at least one point, $\mathbf{x}_0$ say, with $h(\mathbf{x}_0) \leq \gamma$ is found.
4. Set $h_0 = h(\mathbf{x}_0)$, $f_0 = f(\mathbf{x}_0)$ (or h_0', f_0', h_0'', f_0'' etc., if there is more than one point with the penalty not exceeding γ).
5. Enter $(\mathbf{x}_0, f_0, h_0)$ into $\bar{\mathcal{F}}_0$ (or h_0', f_0', h_0'', f_0'' etc., according to Rules 1-3). Set $k = 1$.

Step 2. Trimming the filter. Denote by $card[\bar{\mathcal{F}}_k]$ the cardinality of filter $\bar{\mathcal{F}}_K$, which is simultaneously the size of a current population.

1. If $N_{min} \leq card[\bar{\mathcal{F}}_k] \leq N_{max}$, go to Step 3
2. If $card[\bar{\mathcal{F}}_k] < N_{min}$, apply random mutations of a moderate size to $\mathbf{x}_k'$, $\mathbf{x}_k''$, ... that are already in $\bar{\mathcal{F}}_k$. Denote the results of mutations as $mut(\mathbf{x}_k')$, $mut(\mathbf{x}_k'')$, ...
3. Calculate $(f(mut(\mathbf{x}_k')), h(mut(\mathbf{x}_k')))$, $(f(mut(\mathbf{x}_k'')), h(mut(\mathbf{x}_k'')))$, ... and confront them with the current filters' content, according to Rules 1, 2a, 3. Repeat these steps unless $card[\bar{\mathcal{F}}_k] \geq N_{min}$, then go to Step 3.
4. If $card[\bar{\mathcal{F}}_k] > N_{max}$, sort the entries of $\bar{\mathcal{F}}_k$ according to increasing penalties h_k's and leave in $\bar{\mathcal{F}}_k$ only the first N_{max} entries. Go to Step 3.

Step 3. The next generation. To each $\mathbf{x}_k'$, $\mathbf{x}_k''$, ... that are already in $\bar{\mathcal{F}}_k$ apply the following operations:

offspring: replicate each individual $\mathbf{x}_k'$, $\mathbf{x}_k''$, ... to $n + Round[n/(1 + h_k')]$, $n + Round[n/(1 + h_k'')]$, ... number of descendants, respectively,

mutations: to each replica add a random vector and calculate the corresponding value of f and h.

soft selection: Confront the results (f, h) of the replications and mutations with the current filter contents and enter (reject) those, which are (not) in agreement with Rules 1, 2a, 3.

Check the stopping condition. If k does not exceed the admissible number of generations, set $k = k + 1$ and go to Step 2.

Remark 1. *In Step 1.2 we propose minimizing the penalty $h(\mathbf{x})$ using any reasonable evolutionary algorithm for unconstraint minimization, expecting that we obtain points, which are in $\mathcal{C}$ or close to it in the sense that their penalties are not larger than $\gamma > 0$. In our simulations reported below we have used the* Mathematica ver. 7 *function* NMinimize *with the option* RandomSearch*. The*

Table 1. Best values of the goal function in subsequent epochs, but only those for which $h(\mathbf{x}_k) \leq 0.005$ (left panel). Basic statistics from 30 simulation runs from f values, but only those with $h < 0.005$ (right panel).

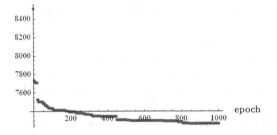

Epochs	1000	3000
Min f	7161.1	7161.2
Max f	7385.9	7266.1
Median f	7264.0	7226.0
Mean f	7265.5	7224.7
Dispersion f	50.0	31.0

idea of using $n + Round[n/(1 + h'_k)]$ as the number of descendants is that $\mathbf{x}'_k$ has more of them, if $h(\mathbf{x}'_k)$ is smaller. At the mutation stage d-dimensional random vectors are added to $\mathbf{x}'_k$, $\mathbf{x}''_k$ and to their replicas. In our experiments independent samples from either $N(0, \sigma)$ or from the uniform distribution on $[-a, a]$ were used, where $\sigma > 0$ and $a > 0$ were selected from $[1, 10]$ interval.

A crossing-over operation is not mentioned in the above algorithm, because it reduces exploration possibilities. However, the following version: $\alpha\, \mathbf{x}'_k + (1 - \alpha)\, \mathbf{x}''_k$, $\alpha \in (0, 1)$ can be useful when the volume of $\mathcal{C}$ is small.

As is known (see [4]), the filter algorithm with SQP has the proof of convergence. One may hope that it is also possible to prove the convergence of the above evolutionary method with a filter, but it is outside the scope of this paper.

4   Simulations

By the lack of space, we report the results of simulations for one of the most difficult benchmark problems, which is the well known G10 problem (see [12]).

Tuning Parameters. The following tuning parameters were used during simulations: $\gamma = 0.01$ and $\beta = 0.99$ in R 2a), $N_{min} = 22$ as the smallest population

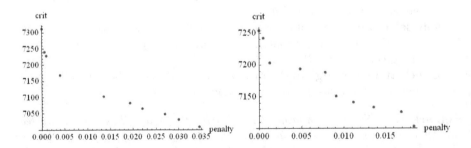

Fig. 2. Example of the filter contents after 1000 epochs (left panel) and after 3000 epochs (right panel)

size and $N_{max} = 100$ as the upper bound for the population size before entering into a new epoch. Note, however, that in Step 3, when the offspring is generated, we allow much larger population of individuals to be confronted with the filter.

A Barrier for SE Escape. $h_{max} = 100$ was used at Step 0, but after performing Step 1 (with $\gamma = 0.3$) h_{max} was updated as follows: $h_{max} = Max[2.5, h_{mc}]$, where h_{mc} is the largest penalty of individuals that were rejected from the filter in Step 2. f_{ub} was set to a very large number and it was not updated later, because we did not observe tendencies to an NW escape.

Mutations. Two kind of mutations were used:
in Step 2.3 $mut(\mathbf{x}'_k)$, $mut(\mathbf{x}'_k)$, ... were mutated as follows:

$$mut(\mathbf{x}'_k) = \mathbf{x}'_k + vec[unif(-(12 + 2/k), 12 + 2/k)], \tag{5}$$

where $unif(-\zeta, \zeta)$ is a random number uniformly distributed in $[-\zeta, \zeta]$, $\zeta > 0$, while $vec[.]$ denotes d-dimensional vector of such numbers and in Step 3:

$$mut(\mathbf{x}'_k) = \mathbf{x}'_k + vec[unif(-(5 + 12/\sqrt{k}), (5 + 12/\sqrt{k}))], \tag{6}$$

The Methodology of Simulations and Their Results

Starting Point. We do not have a point from $\mathcal{C}$ at our disposal and a random random search minimizing $h(\mathbf{x})$ was run with $\gamma = 0.3$. As a result, the following point was found:

$$\mathbf{x}_0 = [1387.42, 2161.53, 4962.31, 142.415, 381.521, 217.502, 280.688, 441.817]$$

with $h(\mathbf{x}_0) = 0.299$ and $f(\mathbf{x}_0) = 8511.26$. Then, 21 additional points acceptable by growing filter were generated, according to Steps 2.2 and 2.3. γ was reduced to 0.005.

1000 epochs. 1000 generations were simulated by circulating between Step 2 and Step 3. The resulting content of the filter is shown in Fig. 2 (left panel), while in Table 1 (left panel) the best value of $f(\mathbf{x}_k)$, among those in the filter, is displayed. Then, the above simulations were repeated 30 times (statistics are reported in Table 1 (right panel, middle column)).

3000 epochs. The filter contents is shown in Fig. 2 (right panel). The statistics (30 repetitions) are summarized in Table 1 (right panel, last column).

Filter. The most valuable result of the algorithm is not the best point, but the final contents of the filter. A quick look at Fig.. 2 (left panel) indicates that
- the best value of $f(\mathbf{x})$ found in this run is 7300, if we insist that the constraints exactly hold,
- however, if we allow that the constraints are only slightly violated, at the level $h(\mathbf{x})$ between 0.0275 and 0.035, then we have found three points with $f(\mathbf{x})$, which is below $f^* = 7049.330923$ that is known to be the exact optimum of the G10 problem.

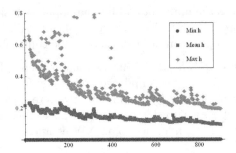

Fig. 3. The maximum, the minimum and the mean of penalties of individuals that are contained in the filter in subsequent epochs

Records. Taking the above discussion into account, the best values found are not so important. We provide them for completeness. From Table 1 (right panel) it follows that our record is $f = 7161.1$, allowing $h < 0.005$. Thus, it is in the middle between f^* and the record 7286.650 that is reported in the well known survey paper [12], where it was also found in 1000 epochs. However, if we allow $h < 0.01$ (instead of $h < 0.005$), then the record found during 3000 epochs is 7121.8.

Filter as a soft selector. In addition to Fig. 2 also Fig. 3 illustrates how the filter works as a soft selector. The largest penalties of individuals that are currently in the filter exhibits large variation, which allows for exploration. Simultaneously, individuals with small penalties are permanently present in the filter, providing guarantees that good solutions that are in C or close to it can be found.

Acknowledgements. The authors acknowledge the support of the computing equipment of the Wroclaw Center for Supercomputing and Computer Networks.

References

1. Aguirre, A.H., et al.: Handling constraints using multiobjective optimization concepts. Int. J. Numer. Meth. Engng. 59, 1989–2017 (2004)
2. Camponogara, E., Talukdar, S.N.: A genetic algorithm for constrained and multiobjective optimization. In: Alander, J.T. (ed.) 3rd Nordic Workshop on Genetic Algorithms and Their Applications (3NWGA), pp. 49–62. University of Vaasa, Vaasa (1997)
3. Coello Coello, C.A., Van Veldhuizen, D.A., Lamont, G.B.: Evolutionary Algorithms for Solving Multi-Objective Problems. Kluwer Academic Publishers, New York (2002); Fletcher, R,. Leyffer, S.: Nonlinear programming without a penalty function. Math. Program. 91, 239-269 (2002)
4. Fletcher, R., Leyffer, S., Toint, P.L.: On the global convergence of a filter-SQP algorithm. SIAM J. Optim. 13, 44–59 (2002)

5. Fletcher, R., Gould, N.I.M., Leyffer, S., Toint, P.L., Wachter, A.: Global convergence of trust-region SQP-filter algorithms for general nonlinear programming. SIAM J. Optimization 13, 635–659 (2002)
6. Galar, R.: Handicapped Individua in Evolutionary Processes. Biol. Cybern. 53, 1–9 (1985)
7. Galar, R.: Evolutionary Search with Soft Selection. Biol. Cybern. 60, 357–364 (1989)
8. Huang, V.L., Qin, A.K., Suganthan, P.N.: Self-adaptive Differential Evolution Algorithm for Constrained Real-Parameter Optimization. In: 2006 IEEE Congress on Evolutionary Computation Sheraton Vancouver Wall Centre Hotel, Vancouver, BC, Canada, July 16-21, pp. 324–331 (2006)
9. Liang, J.J., Suganthan, P.N.: Dynamic Multi-Swarm Particle Swarm Optimizer with a Novel Constraint-Handling Mechanism. In: 2006 IEEE Congress on Evolutionary Computation Sheraton Vancouver Wall Centre Hotel, Vancouver, BC, Canada, July 16-21, pp. 316–323 (2006)
10. Mezura-Montes, E., Velazquez-Reyes, J., Coello Coello, C.A.: Modified Differential Evolution for Constrained Optimization. In: 2006 IEEE Congress on Evolutionary Computation Sheraton Vancouver Wall Centre Hotel, Vancouver, BC, Canada, July 16-21, pp. 332–339 (2006)
11. Mezura-Montes, E., Coello Coello, C.A.: A Simple Multimembered Evolution Strategy to Solve Constrained Optimization Problems. IEEE Transactions On Evolutionary Computation 9(1), 1–17 (2005)
12. Michalewicz, Z., Schoenauer, M.: Evolutionary algorithms for constrained parameter optimization problems. Evolutionary Computation 4(1), 1–32 (1996)
13. Rafajłowicz, E., Styczeń, K., Rafajłowicz, W.: A Modified Filter SQP Method As A Tool For Optimal Control of Nonlinear Systems With Spatio-Temporal Dynamics. Int. J. Applied Mathematics and Computer Science (to appear)
14. Richardson, J.T., Palmer, M.R., Liepins, G., Hilliard, M.: Some guidelines for genetic algorithms with penalty functions. In: Schaffer, J.D. (ed.) Proceedings of the Third International Conference on Genetic Algorithms (ICGA 1989), San Mateo, CA, pp. 191–197. George Mason University, Morgan Kaufmann, Los Altos, CA (1989)
15. Takahama, T., Setsuko Sakai, S.: Constrained Optimization by the Constrained Differential Evolution with Gradient-Based Mutation and Feasible Elites. In: 2006 IEEE Congress on Evolutionary Computation Sheraton Vancouver Wall Centre Hotel, Vancouver, BC, Canada, July 16-21, pp. 308–315 (2006)

Pointwise Convergence
of Discrete Ant System Algorithm

Paweł Rembelski* and Witold Kosiński

Faculty of Computer Science, Polish-Japanese Institute of Information Technology,
02-008 Warsaw, Koszykowa 86, Poland
{rembelski,wkos}@pjwstk.edu.pl

Abstract. Discrete Ant System (DAS) algorithm, a modification of classical Ant System algorithm formulated by M. Dorigo, is presented. Definition of optimization problem and a detailed description of component rules of DAS method are given. Then a probabilistic algebraic model of DAS heuristic describing its evolution in terms of Markov chains is presented. The final result in the form of a pointwise convergence of Discrete Ant System algorithm is established.

1 Introduction

This article is a summary of research work on Discrete Ant System [10], a subclass of probabilistic algorithms inspired by nature. Our aim is to present a new theoretical result on the convergence of DAS method, which has no analogues in the literature [6,7]. For this purpose we refer to the theoretical results on the asymptotic of a simple genetic algorithm given in [9,13], which in turn benefit from the approach used for stochastic dynamic systems [8,12]. Article consists of two integral parts. In the first one (Chapters 2-4) we remind the necessary assumptions and properties related to an optimization problem as well as to a scheme of discrete ant algorithm. Finally a theoretical model of considered heuristic is given. In the second part (Chapter 5) the latest research result aimed at demonstrating a pointwise convergence of DAS method is established. The result obtained is set out in the form of a theorem. At the end, we indicate directions for our future research activities: both theoretical and practical, in the field.

2 Optimization Problem

An *optimization problem* is a five

$$(\Sigma, \mathcal{R}, \Delta, \|\cdot\|, [\searrow | \nearrow]),\tag{1}$$

where:

---

* The authors acconwledges support from Minisrty of Science and Higher Education under Polish-Japanses Institute of Information Technology (grant N N519 5788038).

L. Rutkowski et al. (Eds.): SIDE 2012 and EC 2012, LNCS 7269, pp. 342–349, 2012.

- $\Sigma = \{x_1, x_2, \ldots, x_n\}$ – is a finite set of n indexed **objects** (**symbols**),
- $\mathcal{R} \subset \Sigma^*$ – is a finite set of $\mathfrak{r}$ indexed **solutions** (**words**), where as usual Σ^* denotes the space of all words over Σ,
- $\Delta : \Sigma^* \to \{0, 1\}$ – is a solution **acceptance function** such, that

$$\Delta(\omega) = \begin{cases} 1, \text{ if } \exists \left(\omega' \in \Sigma^*, \omega'' \in \mathcal{R} \right) \left(\omega \circ \omega' = \omega'' \right) \\ 0, \qquad\qquad \text{in other case} \end{cases} \tag{2}$$

- $\|\cdot\| : \mathcal{R} \to \mathbb{R}_+ \cup \{0\}$ – is a solution **quality function**,
- $[\searrow | \nearrow]$ – is an optimization direction, $\searrow$ for minimization, $\nearrow$ for maximization.

Without loss of the generality of considerations later in this work we shall assume to minimize evaluation function in the set of positive real numbers $\mathbb{R}_+$.

Now let ω^* be a *optimal solution*, i.e. such a solution to given optimization problem that the following condition is true

$$\forall (1 \leq i \leq \mathfrak{r}) \left(\|\omega_i\| \geq \|\omega^*\| \right). \tag{3}$$

Then the set of all solutions $\mathcal{R}$ includes subset $\mathcal{R}^* \subseteq \mathcal{R}$ of optimal solutions. The *optimization task* in discrete space Σ^* is to find **any** word $\omega^* \in \mathcal{R}^*$.

It is worth noting that the assumed interpretation of the optimization problem based on the set of indexed symbols Σ and the set of indexed word-solution $\mathcal{R}$ meets most practical computing tasks, including the NP-complete problems. For example, in the Traveling Salesman Problem Σ is the set of vertices of analyzed graph, and $\mathcal{R}$ is the set of all permutations of elements over set Σ. In the case of Discrete Knapsack Problem Σ is the collection of objects of assumed type, while $\mathcal{R}$ is the set of words (representing a way of packing a backpack) of any length with an accuracy to combinations with repetitions and constrained by the cardinality of objects.

3   Discrete Ant System

Discrete Ant System (abbreviated as DAS) is an extension of **Ant System** introduced and modified by M. Dorigo in [1,2,5] mainly for solving the Traveling Salesman Problem instances [3,4]. Considered heuristics assumes a collective work and gathering information by entities (individuals), called **ants**. Construction of customized solutions is based on using global knowledge of the indexed collection of $\mathfrak{m}$ ants $\{a_1, a_2, \ldots, a_m\}$, hereinafter called the **anthill**. DAS algorithm is an iterative method, consisting the sequential repetition of the three main rules of evolution:

- Neighbor Choosing Rule (NCR),
- Solution Construction Rule (SCR),
- Pheromone Update Rule (PUR).

Algorithm 1. DAS schema.

```
while (stop condition is false) do
  for every ant a_i do
    construct solution with SCR (NCR inside)
    update pheromone trails with PUR
```

The general scheme of Discrete Ant System is given in Algorithm 1.

DAS method is based on the concept of a *saturation factor of pheromone trail* $\tau \in \mathbb{N}_+$, which is the carrier of global knowledge of ants about a searched work space $\mathcal{S}$. The value of coefficient τ characterizes the quality of solution (measured by values of a quality function $\|\cdot\|$) connected with symbols from the set Σ in a specific order.

Furthermore, let τ_{max} be the maximum value of the saturation factor of pheromone trail and

$$\mathbb{H} = \{1, 2, \ldots, \tau_{max}\} \tag{4}$$

be the set of all possible values of the saturation factor of pheromone trail. We introduce two sets $\mathcal{F}$ and $\mathcal{H}$ of states of **pheromone structures** which carrying out the process of exchanging information between ants:

- $\mathcal{F} = \{F_1, F_2, \ldots, F_{\mathfrak{f}}\}$ – a finite set of all possible *indexed column vectors* of size $\mathfrak{n}$ of *saturation factor level* such, that $F_i \in \mathbb{H}^{\mathfrak{n}}$, for $1 \leq i \leq \mathfrak{f}$, and $F[j]$ is a value connected with an ant possibility of choosing an object x_j while a solution ω is constructed,
- $\mathcal{H} = \{H_1, H_2, \ldots, H_{\mathfrak{h}}\}$ – a finite set of all possible *indexed matrices* of size $\mathfrak{n} \times \mathfrak{n}$ of *saturation factor level* such, that $H_i \in \mathbb{H}^{\mathfrak{n} \times \mathfrak{n}}$, for $1 \leq i \leq \mathfrak{h}$, and $H[j, k]$ is a value connected with an ant possibility of choosing an object x_k just after x_j while a solution ω is constructed.

Now using introduced sets of pheromone structures we present the principle of three rules of Discrete Ant System, i.e. NCR, SCR, and PUR rule. The first one, Neighbor Choosing Rule, realize the **non-deterministic** selection of symbols $x \in \Sigma$ by a single ant in the order to construct a new solution ω. Thus

$$NCR : \mathcal{F} \times \Sigma^* \to \Sigma, \tag{5}$$

is such, that $NCR(F, \omega) = x_i$ with the probability equals to

$$\begin{cases} \dfrac{F[i]}{\displaystyle\sum_{\{j:\Delta(\omega x_j)=1\}} F[j]} & \text{if } \Delta(\omega x_i) = 1, \\ 0 & \text{in other case.} \end{cases} \tag{6}$$

According to Equation 6 we may present the following claim.

Corollary 1. *For any* $F \in \mathcal{F}$, $\omega \in \Sigma^*$ *and* $x \in \Sigma$, *if* $\Delta(\omega x_j) = 1$, *then* $Pr(NCR(F, \omega) = x) \in (0, 1]$ *else* $Pr(NCR(F, \omega) = x) = 0$.

Neighborhood selection mechanism discussed in the NCR rule stands a basis for the next and consequently also a **non-deterministic** rule, that is Solution Construction Rule. This evolution rule is described by the probabilistic function

$$SCR : \mathcal{F} \times \mathcal{H} \to \mathcal{R}, \tag{7}$$

such, that $SCR\,(F, H) = \omega$, where

- x_{l_1} is a first element of constructed solution ω with the probability equals to

$$Pr\,(NCR\,(F, \epsilon) = x_{l_1}), \tag{8}$$

- repeat until a stop condition is false: let $\omega = x_{l_1} x_{l_2} \ldots x_{l_{r-1}}$ be an actual part of constructed solution, then $\omega \leftarrow \omega x_{l_r}$ with probability equal to

$$Pr\left(NCR\left(H\,[l_r, \cdot], x_{l_1} x_{l_2} \ldots x_{l_{r-1}}\right) = x_{l_r}\right). \tag{9}$$

Corollary 2. *For any $F \in \mathcal{F}$, $H \in \mathcal{H}$ and $\omega \in \mathcal{R}$ such, that $\omega = x_{l_1} x_{l_2} \ldots x_{l_r}$, we have*

$$Pr\,(SCR\,(F, H) = \omega) = Pr\,(NCR\,(F, \epsilon) = x_{l_1}) \cdot$$
$$\prod_{i=1}^{r-1} Pr\left(NCR\,(H\,[l_r, \cdot], x_{l_1} x_{l_2} \ldots x_{l_i}) = x_{l_{i+1}}\right), \tag{10}$$

thus with respect to corollary follows that 1 $Pr\,(SCR\,(F, H) = \omega) \in (0, 1]$.

Corollary 2 has significant probabilistic implications. According to its content any word-solution $\omega \in \mathcal{R}$, and thus also an optimal solution ω^* from the set of optimal solutions $\mathcal{R}^* \subseteq \mathcal{R}$, may (with positive probability) be a result of application of SCR rule in any state of pheromone structures F and H.

Presented so far NCR mechanisms, and the SAR rule are **static** due to the exchange of information inside the nest, and their action depends only on the current state of the heuristic information, stored in a vector F and matrix H. The last PUR rule, which updates pheromone trails, is **dynamic** one in this context. This refers to an earlier direction of evolution of anthill, especially to the direction of changes on pheromone structures H and F.

PUR operator can be divided into two key steps. The firs one is sequentially updating elements of the vector F while the second one refers to updating elements of the matrix H. In both cases, the application of the pheromone update mechanism requires knowledge of two solutions: ω^{-1}, a word constructed by an ant in iteration immediately preceding the currently analyzed, and ω, a word constructed by an ant in the current iteration. Relation of quality function $\|\cdot\|$ value for these two elements gives strictly **local** (short term) characteristic for direction of evolution process.

For the purpose of this article we assume that study of these two values dependency is sufficient. It should be noted, that in practice we consider also **global** (long term) properties of evolution of ants set. This compilation of short and long-term properties gives a more complete picture of behavior of anthill, and thus allows for a more accurate and more deliberate modification of the structures within PUR rule.

Therefore pheromone update rule PUR is a **deterministic** function

$$PUR : \mathcal{F} \times \mathcal{H} \times \mathcal{R}^2 \to \mathcal{F} \times \mathcal{H}, \tag{11}$$

which describes how the pheromone trail is changing after a new solution $\omega = x_{l_1} x_{l_2} \ldots x_{l_r}$ is constructed. Let $\omega' = x_{k_1} x_{k_2} \ldots x_{k_p}$ be a previously built solution (i.e. a solution constructed in a previous algorithm iteration step), then if $\|\omega\| \leq \|\omega'\|$

$$F[l_1] \leftarrow \min\left(\tau_{max}, F[l_1] + 1\right), \ F[k_1] \leftarrow \max\left(1, F[k_1] - 1\right),$$
$$H[l_i, l_{i+1}] \leftarrow \min\left(\tau_{max}, H[l_i, l_{i+1}] + 1\right), \ H[k_j, k_{j+1}] \leftarrow \max\left(1, H[k_j, k_{j+1}] - 1\right),$$

else

$$F[l_1] \leftarrow \max\left(1, F[l_1] - 1\right), \ F[k_1] \leftarrow \min\left(\tau_{max}, F[k_1] + 1\right),$$
$$H[l_i, l_{i+1}] \leftarrow \max\left(1, H[l_i, l_{i+1}] - 1\right), \ H[k_j, k_{j+1}] \leftarrow \min\left(\tau_{max}, H[k_j, k_{j+1}] + 1\right),$$

for every $1 \leq i < r$ or $1 \leq j < p$.

The considerations in this chapter will end with the proposal which describes probabilistic of changes in pheromone structures F and H. Referring directly to the DAS algorithm construction given earlier (see page 344) and SCR rule properties presented in Corollary 2 we get

Corollary 3. *For any pairs of pheromone structures* $(F, H) \in \mathcal{F} \times \mathcal{H}$ *and* $\left(F', H'\right) \in \mathcal{F} \times \mathcal{H}$, *if pair* (F, H) *is reachable form pair* $\left(F', H'\right)$ *with iteration of DAS pheromone update schema, then the probability of transition from structure state* $\left(F', H'\right)$ *to* (F, H) *is positive.*

4   Theoretic Model of DAS Algorithm

For the simplicity of presentation in this chapter we discuss results of a theoretical model of the DAS algorithm with respect to evolution of a **single ant**. This is a purely technical task to extend these results for an anthill consisting of $m > 1$ ants due to their sequential work in an inner iteration loop (for every ant a_i do ...).

Next *state of ant* $s_{(t)}$ in a moment t is a quadruple $\left\langle F_{(t)}, H_{(t)}, \omega_{(t)}, \omega_{(t)}^* \right\rangle$ where:

- $F_{(t)} \in \mathcal{F}$ – is a vector which determines the value of saturation level related with an action of choosing a first object to solution ω, by an ant while changing a state from moment t up to $t + 1$,
- $H_{(t)} \in \mathcal{H}$ – is a matrix which determines the value of saturation level related with an action of choosing every next object to solution ω, by an ant while changing a state from moment t up to $t + 1$,

– $\omega_{(t)} \in \mathcal{R}$ – is a solution which is constructed in moment t,
– $\omega^*_{(t)} \in \mathcal{R}$ – is a best solution which was constructed up to moment t.

Directly from given in the previous section schema of DAS algorithm (see page344) and justly introduced definition of ant state, we may give the following conclusion.

Corollary 4. *State* $s_{(t)}$ *of an individual ant in moment* $t+1$ *is determined only by state* $s_{(t)}$ *of an individual ant in moment* t.

Finally $\mathcal{S} = \mathcal{F} \times \mathcal{H} \times \mathcal{R}^2$ is a set of all possible indexed states of an ant $\{s_1, s_2, \ldots, s_\mathfrak{s}\}$, therefore

$$\mathfrak{s} = \mathfrak{f} \cdot \mathfrak{h} \cdot \mathfrak{r}^2 = (\tau_{max})^{n^2+n} \cdot \mathfrak{r}^2 \tag{12}$$

This leads to the next corollary.

Corollary 5. *Set* $\mathcal{S}$ *of all possible ant states is a finite state.*

Using the notion of individual ant state, now let us move on to discuss how to build an algebraic model for an evolution process of DAS heuristic. As mentioned in the first section, results presented in this paper are based on a probabilistic approach used in [9,13] to analyze the convergence of a simple genetic algorithm with tools adapted form stochastic dynamic systems [8,12].

Therefore, let $\widehat{U}_{(t)} \in [0,1]^\mathfrak{s}$ be a column stochastic vector of size $\mathfrak{s}$ such, that $\widehat{U}_{(t)}[i]$ determines a value of probability of a chance that an ant state in moment t is s_i, Then we define a column stochastic matrix $\widehat{T} \in [0,1]^{\mathfrak{s} \times \mathfrak{s}}$ which determines transitions between an ant states, so that $\widehat{T}[i,j]$ denotes the probability of transition of ant from state s_j to state s_i. Thus, a single iteration of our heuristic under consideration is reduced to the implementation of the algebraic transformation

$$\widehat{U}_{(t)}\widehat{T} = \widehat{U}_{(t+1)}. \tag{13}$$

In general, if $\widehat{U}_{(0)}$ is an initial distribution of probability of an ant initial state, then

$$\widehat{U}_{(t)} = \widehat{U}_{(0)}\widehat{T}^t \tag{14}$$

describes ant state in moment $t = 1, 2, 3, \ldots$.

Therefore by referring to Corollaries 4 and 5 we express the evolution of Discrete Ant Algorithm within the theory of Markov chains on the finite state space $\mathcal{S}$. Thus we meat a key found.

Corollary 6. *DAS algorithm evolution for a single ant is a Markov Process.*

Notice, that this result can be easily expended for $\mathfrak{m} > 1$ ant case (i.e. an anthill case) with the restriction, that an anthill state $s^\mathfrak{m}$ is an element of space $\left(\mathcal{F} \times \mathcal{H} \times \mathcal{R}^2\right)^\mathfrak{m}$.

Importance of Corollary 6 can be extended with practical applications, by indicating the procedure of the filling up the transition matrix $\widehat{T}$ for a particular instance of the optimization problem. The question therefore arises, whether for a given five $(\Sigma, \mathcal{R}, \Delta, \|\cdot\|, \searrow)$ we can determine the value of any element $\widehat{T}[i,j]$. The answer is **yes**. In order to achieve this goal we just go back to previously presented DAS algorithm schema (see page 344) as well as to the property of evolution rules and finally the definition of ant state. Detailed information on this subject the reader can find in [10,11].

These considerations are interesting also for the qualitative aspect. They show that if the vector $\widehat{U}_{(0)}$ is known and we determined a complete form of transition matrix $\widehat{T}$, then designation of the t-th power of matrix $\widehat{T}$ allows us to accurately estimate a probability distribution of state vector $\widehat{U}_{(t)}$ at time $t > 1$. Thus, we are able to give well quality prediction of considered heuristic evolution process. Using these results in the next chapter we formulate the main theorem on a pointwise convergence property for the Discrete Ant Algorithm.

5 Pointwise Convergence of DAS Method

The pointwise convergence of DAS heuristic means an existence of **exactly one** vector $\widehat{U} \in [0,1]^{\mathfrak{s}}$ such, that

$$\forall \widehat{U}_{(0)} \in [0,1]^{\mathfrak{s}} : \lim_{t \to \infty} \widehat{U}_{(0)} \widehat{T}^t = \widehat{U}, \qquad (15)$$

where $\widehat{U}[i] = 1$ if and only if s_i is desired ant state, and $\widehat{U}[j \neq i] = 0$ for all $j = 1, 2, \ldots, \mathfrak{s}$. Next vector $\widehat{U}$ and the state s_i respectively are called a *point of convergence* and a *state of convergence*.

Introduced definition of pointwise convergence assumes a strong criterion on direction of evolution of a single ant. According to its wording irrespective of an initial ant state $\widehat{U}_{(0)}$, properly long iterating of DAS method should always lead to the same fixed final state s, with specific forms of pheromone structures F and H as well as words ω and ω^*. From a practical point of view, this condition is too strong. Returning to the optimization problem definition given in section 2, all states $s \in \mathcal{S}$, for $s = \left\langle F_{(t)}, H_{(t)}, \omega_{(t)}, \omega^*_{(t)} \right\rangle$, where $\omega^* \in \mathcal{R}^*$ are optimal solutions, are indistinguishable relative to the optimization task (we are interested in finding any optimal solution, not a group of all possible optimal solutions).

Based on the above observations all ant states s distributed in the work space $\mathcal{S}$, in which the element ω^*, i.e. best solution so far, is actually one of the optimal solutions, we group now in a super-state s^* such that

$$s^* = \{s \in \mathcal{S} : s \text{ includes optimal solution } \omega^*\}. \qquad (16)$$

Next

$$\mathcal{S}^* = (\mathcal{S} \setminus s^*) \cup \{s^*\} \qquad (17)$$

is a set of all possible indexed states of an ant with the super-state s^*. The reduction of the original state space $\mathcal{S}$ into the space $\mathcal{S}^*$ maintains all previously derived theoretical properties and results of probabilistic model under consideration. In addition, it allows us to formulate the main result of this research article in the form of a theorem about pointwise convergence of DAS method.

Theorem 1. *Discrete Ant System algorithm is point-wise convergent over ant state space S^* with the convergence pointed at super-state s^*.*

Proof can be found in [11].

6 Conclusions

Presented in the previous section result on pointwise convergence of DAS method gives a basis for further work pointed at theoretical analysis of asymptotic properties of Discrete Ant System. Considered algorithm meets convergence property, which other popular heuristic do not have, such as simple genetic algorithm [9,13]. Closely to the above-mentioned theoretical work we also conducts a research focused on self-adaptation mechanisms of a single ant behavior as well as on an effective implementation of DAS scheme on a strongly concurrent computing environment given by NVIDIA GPU cards.

References

1. Dorigo, M.: Optimization, learning and natural algorithms, Ph. D. dissertation (1992)
2. Dorigo, M., Birattari, M., Stutzle, T.: Ant Colony Optimization. IEEE Computional Intelligence Magazine, XI (2006)
3. Dorgio, M., Gambardella, L.M.: Ant Colony System: A cooperative learning approach to the TSP problem. IEEE Transaction on Evolutionary Computation 1 (1997)
4. Dorigo, M., Gambardella, L.M.: Solving symmetric and asymmetric TSPs by ant colonies. In: IEEE International Conference on Evolutionary Computation (1996)
5. Dorigo, M., Maniezzo, V., Colorni, A.: Ant System: optimization by colony of cooperating agents. IEEE Transactions on Systems, Man and Cybernetics 26 (1996)
6. Dorigo, M., Stutzle, T.: A short convergence proof for a class of ACO algorithms. IEEE Transactions on Evolutionary Computation 6 (2002)
7. Gutjahr, W.J.: ACO algorithms with guaranteed convergence proof to the optimal solution. Information Processing Letters 82 (2002)
8. Lasota, A.: Asymptotic properties of Markov semigroups of operators. Applied Mathematics 3(45), 39–51 (2002)
9. Kosiński, W., Kotowski, S.: Limit Properties of Evolutionary Algorithms. In: Kosiński, W. (ed.) Advances in Evolutionary Algorithms, IN-TECH 2008, ch. 1, pp. 1–28 (2008); ISBN 978-953-7619-11-4
10. Rembelski, P.: Theoretical Model of SAS Ant Algorithm. In: Proceedings of the XII International Ph.D. Workshop, OWD 2010, pp. 37–42 (2010)
11. Rembelski, P.: The Markovian Model of Discrete Ant Algorithm. Applied Mathematics 13(54) (2011)
12. Rudnicki, R.: On asymptotic stability and sweeping for Markov operators. Bull. Polish Acad. Sci. Math. 43, 245–262 (1995)
13. Socała, J., Kosiński, W., Kotowski, S.: The asymptotic behavior of a simple genetic algorithm. Applied Mathematics 6(47), 70–86 (2005)

Evolutionary and Meta-evolutionary Approach for the Optimization of Chaos Control

Roman Senkerik[1,*], Zuzana Oplatkova[1], Donald Davendra[2], and Ivan Zelinka[2]

[1] Tomas Bata University in Zlin, Faculty of Applied Informatics,
Nam T.G. Masaryka 5555, 760 01 Zlin, Czech Republic
{senkerik,oplatkova}@fai.utb.cz
[2] Technical University of Ostrava, Faculty of Electrical Engineering and Computer
Science, 17. listopadu 15, 708 33 Ostrava-Poruba, Czech Republic
{donald.davendra,ivan.zelinka}@vsb.cz

Abstract. This paper deals with the optimization of control of Hénon Map, which is a discrete chaotic system. This paper introduces and compares evolutionary approach representing tuning of parameters for an existing control method, as well as meta-evolutionary approach representing synthesis of whole control law by means of Analytic Programming (AP). These two approaches are used for the purpose of stabilization of the stable state and higher periodic orbits, which stand for oscillations between several values of chaotic system. For experimentation, Self-Organizing Migrating Algorithm (SOMA) and Differential Evolution (DE) were used.

1 Introduction

There is a growing interest about the interconnection between evolutionary techniques and control of chaotic systems. The first steps were done in [1] - [3], where the control law was based on the Pyraga's method, which is Extended delay feedback control (ETDAS) [4]. These papers were concerned with tuning several parameters inside the control technique for chaotic system. Compared to this, presented research also shows a possibility for generating the whole control law (not only to optimize several parameters) for the purpose of stabilization of a chaotic systems. The synthesis of control law is inspired by the Pyragas's delayed feedback control TDAS and ETDAS [5], [6].

Analytic programming (AP) is used in this research. AP is a superstructure of EAs and is used for synthesis of analytic solution according to the required behavior. Control law from the proposed system can be viewed as a symbolic structure, which can be synthesized according to the requirements for the stabilization of the chaotic system. The advantage is that it is not necessary to have some "preliminary" control law and to estimate its parameters only. This system will generate the whole structure of the law even with suitable parameter values.

* This work was supported by the grant NO. MSM 7088352101 of the Ministry of Education of the Czech Republic and by grants of Grant Agency of Czech Republic GACR 102/09/1680 and by European Regional Development Fund under the project CEBIA-Tech No. CZ.1.05/2.1.00/03.0089.

L. Rutkowski et al. (Eds.): SIDE 2012 and EC 2012, LNCS 7269, pp. 350–358, 2012.
© Springer-Verlag Berlin Heidelberg 2012

This paper is an extension and cumulation of previous work [2,7] focused either on tuning of parameters for an existing control method [2] or synthesis of whole control laws [7].

2 Analytic Programming

Basic principles of the AP were developed in 2001 [8]. The core of AP is based on a special set of mathematical objects and operations. The set of mathematical objects is a set of functions, operators and so-called terminals, which are usually constants or independent variables. This set of variables is usually mixed together and consists of functions with different number of arguments. Because of a variability of the content of this set, it is termed the "general functional set" (GFS). The structure of GFS is created by subsets of functions according to the number of their arguments.

The second part of the AP core is a sequence of mathematical operations, which are used for the program synthesis. These operations are used to transform an individual of a population into a suitable program. Mathematically stated, it is a mapping from an individual domain into a program domain. This mapping consists of two main parts. The first part is called Discrete Set Handling (DSH) and the second one stands for security procedures, which do not allow synthesizing pathological programs. The method of DSH, when used, allows handling arbitrary objects including nonnumeric objects like linguistic terms {hot, cold, dark...}, logic terms (True, False) or other user-defined functions.

3 Problem Design

3.1 Selected Chaotic System

The chosen example of chaotic system was the two dimensional Hénon map in form (1):

$$x_{n+1} = a - x_n^2 + by_n$$
$$y_{n+1} = x_n$$

(1)

The map depends on two parameters, a and b, which for the canonical Hénon map have values of $a = 1.4$ and $b = 0.3$. For these canonical values the Hénon map is chaotic.

3.2 ETDAS Control Method

This work is focused on explanation of application of AP for synthesis of a whole control law (meta-evolutionary approach) as well as tuning of parameters for EDTAS method control laws (evolutionary approach) to stabilize desired Unstable Periodic Orbits (UPO). In this research desired UPOs were p-1 (stable state) and p-2 (higher periodic orbit – oscillation between two values).

Within the research concentrated on synthesis of control law, an inspiration for preparation of sets of basic functions and operators for AP was also ETDAS control method in its discrete form suitable for two-dimensional Hénon Map given in (2):

$$x_{n+1} = a - x_n^2 + by_n + F_n,$$
$$F_n = K\left[(1-R)\,S_{n-m} - x_n\right], \tag{2}$$
$$S_n = x_n + RS_{n-m}$$

where: K and R are adjustable constants, F is the perturbation; S is given by a delay equation utilizing previous states of the system and m is the period of m-periodic orbit to be stabilized. Due to the recursive attributes of delay equation S utilizing previous states of the system in discrete ETDAS method (2), the data set for AP had to be expanded to cover a longer system output history $(x_n \text{ to } x_{n-9})$, thus to imitate inspiring control method for the successful synthesis of control law securing the stabilization of higher periodic orbits.

3.3   Cost Functions

The used Cost functions are in general based on searching for the desired stabilized periodic orbit and thereafter calculation of the difference between desired and found actual periodic orbit on the short time interval - τ_s (20 iterations – p-1 orbit and 40 iterations – p-2 orbit) from the point, where the first min. value of difference between desired and actual system output is found. Such a design of CF should secure the successful stabilization of either p-1 orbit (stable state) or higher periodic orbit anywise phase shifted. The CF_{Basic} used for meta-evolutionary approach, which is very time demanding, has the form (3).

$$CF_{Basic} = pen_1 + \sum_{t=\tau 1}^{\tau 2} |TS_t - AS_t| \tag{3}$$

where: TS - target state, AS - actual state, τ_1 - the first min value of difference between TS and AS, τ_2 - the end of optimization interval $(\tau_1 + \tau_s)$,

$pen_1 = 0$ if τ_i - τ_2 ? τ_s; $pen_1 = 10*(\tau_i - \tau_2)$ if τ_i - $\tau_2 < \tau_s$ (i.e. late stabilization).

Within the evolutionary approach, which is less time demanding, advanced CF securing the very fast stabilization was used. It was necessary to modify the definition of CF in order to decrease the average number of iteration required for the successful stabilization and avoidance of any associated problem. The easiest but the most problematic way is that the whole CF value is multiplied by the number of iterations (NI) of the first found minimal value of difference between desired and actual system output (i.e. the beginning of fully stabilized UPO). To avoid errors associated with CF returning value 0 and other problems, the small constant (SC) is added to CF value before penalization (multiplying by NI). The SC value (5) is computed with the aid of power of non-penalized basic part of CF (4), thus it is always secured that the penalization is at similar level as the non-penalized CF value.

$$ExpCF = \log_{10}\left(\sum_{t=\tau 1}^{\tau 2} |TS_t - AS_t| + 10^{-15}\right) \tag{4}$$

$$SC = 10^{ExpCF} \tag{5}$$

The CF used for evolutionary approach is given in (6):

$$CF_{Adv} = \sum_{1}^{n} \left((NI \cdot SC) + penalization1 + \sum_{t=\tau 1}^{\tau 2} |TS_t - AS_t| \right), \tag{6}$$

where $x_{initial}$ is from the range $0.05 - 0.95$ and uses step 0.1 (i.e. $n = 10$).

Here the number of steps for stabilization (NI) multiplies only the small constant (SC). Finally, to avoid the problems with fast stabilization only for limited range of initial conditions, the final CF value is computed as a sum of n repeated simulations for different initial conditions. Consequently, the EA should find the robust solutions securing the fast targeting into desired behavior of system for almost any initial conditions.

4   Used Evolutionary Algorithms

This research used two evolutionary algorithms: Self-Organizing Migrating Algorithm (SOMA) [9] and Differential Evolution (DE) [11]. SOMA is a stochastic optimization algorithm that is modeled on the social behavior of cooperating individuals. DE is a population-based optimization method that works on real-number-coded individuals. Both algorithms were chosen because it has been proven that they have the ability to converge towards the global optimum.

4.1   Self Organizing Migration Algorithm – SOMA

SOMA works with groups of individuals (population) whose behavior can be described as a competitive – cooperative strategy. The construction of a new population of individuals is not based on evolutionary principles (two parents produce offspring) but on the behavior of social group, e.g. a herd of animals looking for food. This algorithm can be classified as an algorithm of a social environment. To the same group of algorithms, Particle Swarm Optimization (PSO) algorithm can also be classified sometimes called swarm intelligence. In the case of SOMA, there is no velocity vector as in PSO, only the position of individuals in the search space is changed during one generation, referred to as 'migration loop'. The detailed principle is described in [9]. For the source codes in Mathematica, Matlab and C++ together with detailed description please refer to [10].

4.2   Differential Evolution

DE is quite robust, fast, and effective, with global optimization ability. It does not require the objective function to be differentiable, and it works well even with noisy and time-dependent objective functions. Please refer to [11] and [12] for the description of used DERand1Bin strategy and all other DE strategies.

5   Simulation Results

In this work AP_{meta} version was used. Meta means usage of one evolutionary algorithm for main AP process and the second algorithm for coefficient estimation. SOMA algorithm was used for the main AP process and DE was used in the second evolutionary process. For the tuning of parameters for ETDAS method, only SOMA algorithm was used. Settings of EA parameters for both approaches were based on performed numerous experiments with chaotic systems and evolutionary algorithms (see Tables 1 - 3).

The results shown in Table 4 represent the best founded solution of parameters set up for ETDAS control method for both case studies (p-1 and p-2 orbit stabilization) together with the cost function value comprising 10 runs of chaotic system with initial conditions in the range $0.05 - 0.95$ with step 0.1, and average CF value per 1 run.

The simulation results in Table 5 represent the best examples of synthesized control laws for the p-1 orbit stabilization as well as for p-2 orbit stabilization. Description of the selected simulation results covers output from AP representing the synthesized control law with simplification after estimation of constants by means of second algorithm DE and corresponding CF value.

Evolutionary Approach Experiment Set Up
The ranges of all estimated parameters within evolutionary approach were these:

$$-2 \leq K \leq 2, 0 \leq F_{\max} \leq 0.5 \text{and} 0 \leq R \leq 0.99$$

where $F_{\max}$ is a limitation of feedback perturbation, securing the avoidance of diverging of the chaotic system outside the interval $\{-1.0, 1.5\}$

Table 1. Parameter set up for SOMA algorithm used in evolutionary approach

Parameter	Value
PathLength	3
Step	0.33
PRT	0.1
PopSize	25
Migrations	25
Max. CF Evaluations (CFE)	5400

Meta-Evolutionary Approach Experiment Set Up
Basic set of elementary functions for AP:
$GFS_{2arg} = +, -, /, *, \hat{\ }$
$GFS_{0arg} = \text{data}_{n-1}$ to data_n, K (for p-1 orbit)
$GFS_{0arg} = \text{data}_{n-9}$ to data_n, K (for p-2 orbit).

Table 2. Parameter set up for SOMA used as the main algorithm in meta-evolutionary approach

Parameter	Value
PathLength	3
Step	0.11
PRT	0.1
PopSize	50
Migrations	4
Max. CF Evaluations (CFE)	5345

Table 3. Parameter set up for DE used as the second algorithm in meta-evolutionary approach

Parameter	Value
PopSize	40
F	0.8
CR	0.8
Generations	150
Max. CF Evaluations (CFE)	6000

5.1 Optimization with Evolutionary Approach

From Figure 1 (left) and Figure 1 (right), it follows, that ETDAS control method with optimized parameters set up by means of SOMA algorithm is able to secure robust, fast and precise stabilization of chaotic system on desired behavior.

Table 4. Simulation results for control of Hénon map with evolutionary approach

UPO	K	Fmax	R	CF Value	CF Value per 1 run
p-1	-0.7513	0.4154	0.1280	$3.86 \ 10^{-14}$	$3.86 \ 10^{-15}$
p-2	0.4208	0.1767	0.3451	$5.81 \ 10^{-9}$	$5.81 \ 10^{-10}$

5.2 Optimization with Meta-evolutionary Approach

Simulations depicted in Figure 2 (left) lend weight to the argument, that AP is able to synthesize a new control laws securing very quick and very precise stabilization. Simulation results depicted in Figure 2 (right) shows the ability of AP to synthesize a new control laws securing quick and also precise stabilization for hardly controllable p-2 orbit.

5.3 Comparison of Both Approaches

Following Tables 6 and 7 contain brief statistical comparison of both approaches for 50 runs.

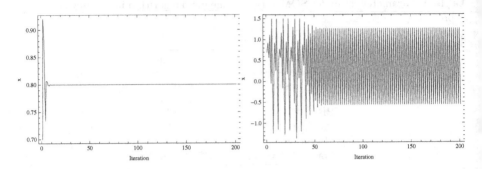

Fig. 1. Simulation results for the optimized ETDAS method settings: p-1 orbit (left) and p-2 orbit (right)

Table 5. Simulation results for control of Hénon map with meta-evolutionary approach

UPO	Synthesized control law	CF Value
p-1	$F_n = (x_n - 1.46956 x_{n-1}) \left(x_{n-1} - x_n - \frac{x_n - x_{n-1}}{x_{n-1}} \right)$	$1.3323.10^{-15}$
p-2	$F_n = 0.342699 x_{n-1} (0.7 - x_{n-3} - x_n)$	$3.8495.10^{-12}$

Table 6. Statistical comparison for both approaches – p-1 orbit

	Evolutionary Approach	Meta-evolutionary approach
Min. CF Value	$3.86.10^{-15}$	$1.33.10^{-15}$
Max. CF Value	$4.89.10^{-15}$	$4.66.10^{-15}$
Avg. CF Value	$4.26.10^{-15}$	$1.71.10^{-15}$
CF Value Median	$4.28.10^{-15}$	$1.67.10^{-15}$
Max CFE	5400	32 070 000

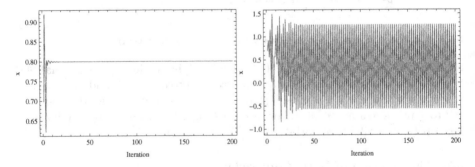

Fig. 2. Simulation results for the best new synthesized control laws: p-1 orbit (left) and p-2 orbit (right)

Table 7. Statistical comparison for both approaches – p-2 orbit

	Evolutionary Approach	Meta-evolutionary approach
Min. CF Value	$5.81.10^{-10}$	$3.85.10^{-12}$
Max. CF Value	5.2332	1.2359
Avg. CF Value	1.8988	0.3358
CF Value Median	1.7475	0.1219
Max CFE	5400	32 070 000

6 Conclusion

This paper introduces two possible approaches for the optimization of stabilization of Hénon Map, which was selected as an example of discrete chaotic system. The first evolutionary approach represented tuning of parameters for an existing control method, and the second meta-evolutionary approach represented synthesis of whole control law by means of Analytic Programming (AP). The control method used within the first approach was an inspiration for the creation of set of rules for AP.

Obtained results show that synthesized control laws have given better results than the original control method, which served as an inspiration. This fact reinforce the argument that AP is able to solve this difficult problems and to produce a new synthesized control law in a symbolic way securing desired behavior of chaotic system. Precise and fast stabilization lends weight to the argument, that AP is a powerful symbolic regression tool, which is able to strictly and precisely follow the rules given by cost function and synthesize any symbolic formula, in the case of this research, to synthesize the feedback controller for chaotic system.

Presented data and statistical comparison can be summarized as follows: Evolutionary approach is easy to implement, very fast and gives satisfactory results. But the quality of results are restricted by the limitations of the mathematical formulas, control laws, models etc., for which the parameters are tuned by EA. Meta-evolutionary approach brings the disadvantage of high time-costs, but it is able to synthesize new symbolic formula, (control law in this case), which gives even better results than the best ones obtained by evolutionary approach.

To obtain a one solution for evolutionary approach, 5400 CF evaluations were required, whereas for meta-evolutionary approach, more than 32 millions CF evaluations were required.

References

1. Senkerik, R., Zelinka, I., Davendra, D., Oplatkova, Z.: Evolutionary Design of Chaos Control in 1D. In: Zelinka, I., Celikovsky, S., Richter, H., Chen, G. (eds.) Evolutionary Algorithms and Chaotic Systems. SCI, vol. 267, pp. 165–190. Springer, Heidelberg (2010)
2. Senkerik, R., Zelinka, I., Davendra, D., Oplatkova, Z.: Utilization of SOMA and differential evolution for robust stabilization of chaotic Logistic equation. Computers & Mathematics with Applications 60, 1026–1037 (2010)

3. Zelinka, I., Senkerik, R., Navratil, E.: Investigation on evolutionary optimization of chaos control. Chaos, Solitons & Fractals 40, 111–129 (2009)
4. Pyragas, K.: Control of chaos via extended delay feedback. Physics Letters A 206, 323–330 (1995)
5. Pyragas, K.: Continuous control of chaos by self-controlling feedback. Physics Letters A 170, 421–428 (1992)
6. Just, W.: Principles of Time Delayed Feedback Control. In: Schuster, H.G. (ed.) Handbook of Chaos Control. Wiley-Vch (1999)
7. Senkerik, R., Oplatkova, Z., Zelinka, I., Davendra, D.: Synthesis of feedback controller for three selected chaotic systems by means of evolutionary techniques: Analytic programming. Mathematical and Computer Modelling (2011), doi:10.1016/j.mcm.2011.05.030
8. Zelinka, I., Oplatkova, Z., Nolle, L.: Boolean Symmetry Function Synthesis by Means of Arbitrary Evolutionary Algorithms-Comparative Study. International Journal of Simulation Systems, Science and Technology 6, 44–56 (2005)
9. Zelinka, I.: SOMA – Self Organizing Migrating Algorithm. In: Babu, B., Onwubolu, G. (eds.) New Optimization Techniques in Engineering, ch. 7, p. 33. Springer, Heidelberg (2004)
10. Zelinka I.: SOMA homepage, http://www.fai.utb.cz/people/zelinka/soma/ (accessed September 22, 2011)
11. Price, K., Storn, R., Lampinen, J.: Differential Evolution: A Practical Approach to Global Optimization. Natural Computing Series. Springer, Heidelberg (1995)
12. Price K, Storn R.: Differential evolution homepage, http://www.icsi.berkeley.edu/~storn/code.html (accessed September 22, 2011)

Evolutionary Multi-objective Optimization of Personal Computer Hardware Configurations*

Adam Slowik

Department of Electronics and Computer Science, Koszalin University of Technology,
Sniadeckich 2 Street, 75-453 Koszalin, Poland
aslowik@ie.tu.koszalin.pl

Abstract. In this paper, we propose an intelligent system developed
for personal computer (PC) hardware configuration. The PC hardware
configuration is a hard decision problem, because nowadays in the computer market we have very large number of PC hardware components.
Therefore, a choice process of personal computer having maximal efficiency and minimal price is a very hard task. Proposed in this paper, the
PC hardware configuration system is based on multi-objective evolutionary algorithm. All detailed information about PC particular components
are stored in database. Using proposed system, personal computer can
be easily configured without any knowledge about PC hardware components. As a test of the proposed system, in this paper we have configured
personal computers for game players and for office work.

1 Introduction

Nowadays, the problem of personal computer (PC) hardware configuration is
more and more complicated especially for users with low knowledge about PC
hardware components [4]. On the market we have very large number of different
graphics cards, processors, RAM memory cards and so on. During the personal
computer purchasing process, the main decision problems concerns the configuration of particular hardware components that can assure a required efficiency
together with acceptable price. In short, we want to obtain maximal efficiency
of PC configuration and minimal price. Moreover, one PC configuration which
ideally works with office software applications, will be probably not efficient for
multimedia applications. In this paper to solve this multi-objective optimization
problem, the PC hardware configuration (PCHC) system is proposed. In presented system we use a database server to store the detailed specifications of
PC hardware components which are currently available at the computer market. Also, the results of hardware components efficiency taken from benchmark
tests and actual price are stored in the database too. The main part of proposed system is an evolutionary multi-objective optimization algorithm. This
algorithm is based on SPEA2 (*Improving the Strength Pareto Evolutionary Algorithm*) algorithm [1, 2]. The evolutionary algorithms [5, 6] are widely used to

---

* This paper, I would like dedicate to my Wife Justyna and my Son Michal – October
2011.

L. Rutkowski et al. (Eds.): SIDE 2012 and EC 2012, LNCS 7269, pp. 359–367, 2012.
© Springer-Verlag Berlin Heidelberg 2012

solve engineering problems like: digital filter design [7], neural network training
[8]. Also, in engineering the evolutionary multi-objective optimization is useful and applied to solve such problems as: medium voltage network design [9],
mechatronic design [10]. However, the problem of evolutionary multi-objective
optimization of PC hardware components configuration is not explored widely
in literature. We can find the papers [4, 11, 12] where intelligent techniques are
used to PC configuration problem. However, in these papers users can not define
the PC preferences in detail. In the proposed PCHC system, each PC component possesses weight of its importance, therefore user can easily define different
variants of PC hardware configuration. We believe that PCHC system proposed
in this paper, can be easily implemented and used in any computer store to
help workers in configuration of personal computers. Also, the proposed PCHC
system can be used by potential customers in order to help in making decision
in purchasing suitable personal computer.

2   Architecture of PC Hardware Configuration System

The proposed PCHC system is developed as a client-server system and composed
of two parts: Windows GUI application (client) with evolutionary multi-objective
optimization algorithm and MySQL database (server) with detailed information
about particular PC hardware components. The PC hardware components can
be added, modified and deleted from the database using Windows GUI application. Also, in this application we have possibility to define our preferences
about personal computer. We can determine which PC hardware components
are important to us. Therefore, the search of possible PC configuration (using
multi-objective evolutionary algorithm) will be based on our previously defined
PC hardware preferences.

3   General Idea of Optimization Algorithm

3.1   Representation of Individuals

In the developed PCHC system individuals represent particular hardware components of the personal computer. The data structure of individual is shown
in Figure 1, and it is composed of 10 genes. Each gene represent one hardware

Processor	Motherboard	Graphics Card	Sound Card	Network Card	RAM Memory	Number of RAM Memory Cards	Hard Disc	Optical Drive	Monitor

Fig. 1. Data structure for each individual in population

component of personal computer. In one gene the identification number (id)
for given hardware component is written down. The identification numbers are
taken from database where each hardware component possess unique id number. In the individual the peripheral components like: printer, scanner, casing,
keyboard and mouse were not included.

3.2   Optimization Algorithm in Detail

The optimization algorithm is a part of developed PCHC system is based on SPEA2 algorithm [1, 2] and is composed of ninth steps.

In the first step, the population P consisting of M individuals (the structure of individual is presented in Figure 1) is created randomly. Also, an empty Pareto front $\overline{P}$ having N places for potential individuals is created.

In the second step, after initialization of population P in optimization algorithm, each individual is checked whether the personal computer hardware configuration stored in is acceptable. If configuration written down in given individual is correct then algorithm jumps to the third step. However, if personal computer hardware configuration is not acceptable then the repair algorithm is started. During repair process it is assumed that the motherboard is the component of the highest priority in the personal computer. Therefore, all other components must fit to the given motherboard. If given components are not compatible with selected motherboard then these components are replaced by other components taken from the database. Also in the repair algorithm, the graphics card possesses higher priority than monitor. It means that in the case when the monitor does not has compatible connections with graphics card, then the monitor is replaced by other model. The repair algorithm is operating until the individual without any hardware conflicts is created.

In the third step, all individuals in population P and in the Pareto front $\overline{P}$ are evaluated. Each individual is evaluated using two criteria. The first is a price (PR) of the given personal computer, and the second is an efficiency (EF) of the configured personal computer. Of course, the price of the personal computer is approximately the sum of the prices of all its elements. The efficiency of personal computer is calculated as the weighted mean of efficiencies of its particular components. The efficiency value for each component is in the range [0; 100]. Both the price and the efficiency values for given personal computer hardware component have been taken from the results of the benchmark tests which can be found in the http://www.chip.pl web site. Due to the efficiency calculation as a weighted mean, we can avoid the overestimate of personal computer efficiency by such components like: monitor or network card. The equations for personal computer price, and personal computer efficiency are as follows:

$$PR_i = \sum_{k=1}^{n} price_k \tag{1}$$

$$EF_i = \frac{\sum_{k=1}^{n} (w_k \cdot efficiency_k)}{n} \tag{2}$$

where: PR_i is a price of the personal computer which components are stored at $i - th$ individual; EF_i is a weighted mean efficiency (in the range [0; 100]) for the personal computer which components are stored at $i - th$ individual; n is a number of personal computer components (in proposed PCHC system we have 10 components); w_k is a weight for a $k - th$ component ($w_k \in [0; 8]$; the "0" is that efficiency of given PC hardware component which is not important for us and the "8" is that efficiency of given PC hardware component which is absolutely important for us), $price_k$ is a price for $k - th$ component; $efficiency_k$ is a efficiency for $k - th$ component; i is a number of individual and it is in the range $[1; M + N]$.

Next, a strength value $S(i)$ is assigned for each individual in the population P and in the Pareto front $\overline{P}$. The strength value $S(i)$ represents the number of solutions dominated by solution $i - th$ both in population P and in the Pareto front $\overline{P}$.

In our case, the personal computer A dominates the personal computer B, if and only if: $(PR_A \leq PR_B \wedge EF_A > EF_B) \vee (PR_A < PR_B \wedge EF_A \geq EF_B)$

After the value of $S(i)$ has been computed for all individuals in the population P and in the Pareto front $\overline{P}$, the raw fitness $R(i)$ for each individual is computed as follows:

$$R(i) = \sum_{j=1, j \succ i}^{P+\overline{P}} S(j) \tag{3}$$

where: $P + \overline{P}$ is a sum of the individuals in population P and Pareto front $\overline{P}$; $\succ$ represents a dominance relation ($j \succ i$ - $j - th$ individual dominates $i - th$ individual).

The value of $R(i)$ is equal to 0 when solution (individual) $i - th$ is non-dominated. Otherwise, when $i - th$ solution is dominated by other solutions, the raw fitness $R(i)$ possesses higher value.

Although the raw fitness assignment provides a sort of niching mechanism based on the concept of Pareto dominance, it may fail when majority of individuals do not dominate each other [2]. Therefore, additional density information is incorporated to discriminate between individuals having identical raw fitness values [2]. The density estimation techniques is based on $k - th$ nearest neighbor method taken from [3].

In order to compute a density $D(i)$ for $i - th$ individual, the distances σ_i^j (in objective domain) between $i - th$ individual and all other $j - th$ individuals from the population P and from Pareto front $\overline{P}$ are computed using Euclidean metric and stored in a list L in the memory of the system.

Next, the results stored in a list L are sorted in increasing order. After sorting process, the $k - th$ value ($k = \sqrt{M + N}$) from the top of the list L is taken as a distance value to $k - th$ nearest neighbor for $i - th$ individual and marked as σ_i^k.

Based on taken distance value σ_i^k, the density $D(i)$ is computed (identical as in paper [2]) for $i - th$ individual as follows:

$$D(i) = \frac{1}{\sigma_i^k + 2} \tag{4}$$

In the denominator of $D(i)$, the number two is added to ensure that its value is greater than zero and that $D(i) < 1$ [2]. Finally, when we add the value of $D(i)$ to the value of raw fitness $R(i)$, we obtain final fitness value $F(i)$ for $i - th$ individual, as follows:

$$F(i) = R(i) + D(i) \tag{5}$$

In the fourth step, all non-dominated solutions (for which $F(i) < 1$) from Pareto front $\overline{P}$ and population P are copied to the new Pareto front $\overline{P}_{new}$. If after copying process, the number of individuals (solutions) in the new Pareto front $\overline{P}_{new}$ is equal to the number of individuals in the old Pareto front $\overline{P}$ then algorithm jumps to the step sixth.

In the fifth step of the algorithm, the individuals are added or removed from the new Pareto front $\overline{P}_{new}$. In the case, when the number of individuals in the new Pareto front $\overline{P}_{new} < N$ then the individuals from the old Pareto front $\overline{P}$ and from population P are stored in a list H. Next, the individuals from the list H are sorted in an increasing order of their fitness value $F(i)$. After sorting process first the best $N - N_{new}$ dominated individuals (where N_{new} is the number of individuals in the new Pareto front $\overline{P}_{new}$) for which fitness value $F(i) \geq 1$ are copied to the new Pareto front $\overline{P}_{new}$. In the case, when number of individuals in the new Pareto front $\overline{P}_{new} > N$ the individuals are iteratively removed from the new Pareto front $\overline{P}_{new}$ until the number of individuals in the new Pareto front $\overline{P}_{new}$ will be equal to the number of individuals in the old Pareto front $\overline{P}$ ($N_{new} = N$). In each iteration the $i - th$ individual from $\overline{P}_{new}$ having the lowest distance to the other individuals from $\overline{P}_{new}$ (the lowest value of σ_i^j) is removed from the new Pareto front $\overline{P}_{new}$. If in the new Pareto front $\overline{P}_{new}$ exist several individuals with the same values of the lowest σ_i^j then the second lowest distance is considered and so forth. And finally, at the end of this step the new Pareto front $\overline{P}_{new}$ is assigned to the old Pareto front $\overline{P}$.

In the sixth step of the algorithm, the termination criterium is checked. In this paper we have assumed maximal number of generation G_{max} as a stopping criterium. If termination criterium is fulfilled then, the result of the algorithm operation are the individuals (solutions) from the actual Pareto front $\overline{P}$. These solutions are returned as a final result and the algorithm operation is stopped. Otherwise, if termination criteria is not fulfilled, the seventh step is executed.

In the seventh step, the selection of individuals to the new population is performed. In proposed algorithm, we have used a tournament selection [5, 6] (with size of tournament group equal to 2 individuals). In tournament selection, the M tournaments are prepared. Two randomly chosen individuals from population P are selected to each tournament. The winner of the tournament becomes the individual having lower value of the fitness function. This winner individual is selected to the new population.

In the eight step, the genetic operators like: crossover and mutation are performed on individuals from population P. In the crossover operation, first we randomly create a crossover pattern CP for each pair of crossed individuals. The crossover pattern CP consist of 10 numbers "0" or "1" taken using pseudo-random generator (we have 10 personal computer hardware components in $PCHC$ system). After CP creating process, we want to have exactly five numbers "1", and five numbers "0" in randomly created crossover pattern CP. Based on CP, the crossover operation is performed as shown in Figure 2.

Next, the mutation operator is performed. In the mutation operation, we have assumed that only one gene can be mutated in the individual which is selected

CP:

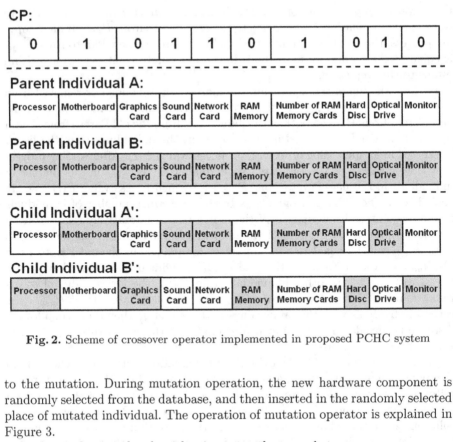

Fig. 2. Scheme of crossover operator implemented in proposed PCHC system

to the mutation. During mutation operation, the new hardware component is randomly selected from the database, and then inserted in the randomly selected place of mutated individual. The operation of mutation operator is explained in Figure 3.

In the ninth step, the algorithm jumps to the second step.

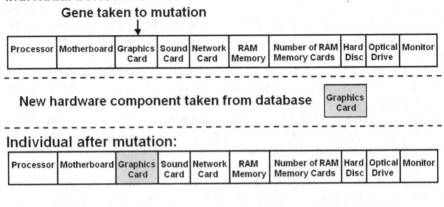

Fig. 3. Scheme of mutation operator implemented in proposed PCHC system

4   Descriptions of Experiments

In the experiment, we have assumed following parameters for the evolutionary algorithm: $M = 100$, $N = 20$, $G_{max} = 1000$, tournament group size equal to 2, probability of mutation equal to 0.01, probability of crossover 0.4. The specifications of PC hardware components (efficiency and price) are taken from http://www.chip.pl.

In the first test, the PC having the highest efficiency is searched. We have assumed, that PC should possess integrated: sound card, and network card. Also, the most important components are processor and graphics card. Such PC is especially required by game players. In the second test, the PC for office work is searched. We have assumed, that PC should possess integrated: sound card, network card, and graphics card. In this PC, the most important components are: processor and RAM memory. Values of the weights w_k for each PC component are presented in Table 1.

In both tests, as results we have obtained 20 PC configurations. In Table 1, we have presented only one solution (which has average price of all prices obtained in given test) obtained for each test.

In the first test, we have obtained the PC configurations with prices in the range between 447 USD and 4475 USD. Also, it is worth to note that 14 PC configurations (on 20 generated) possess efficiency higher than 90 (maximal possible efficiency in PCHC system is equal to 100). The majority of obtained PCs possess Intel processors, because these are more efficient than other processors, but their prices are higher. In the second test, we have obtained the PCs with prices in the range between 418 USD and 2433 USD. The majority of obtained

Table 1. Values of weights w_k and PC configuration obtained using PCHC system

PC hardware components	w_k	Test number one PC for computer games Selected PC components	w_k	Test number two PC for office work Selected PC components
Processor	8	Intel Core i7-870	5	AMD Phenom II X6 1100T Black Edition
Graphics card	8	Sapphire Radeon HD5970 Toxic 4096MB GDDR5	1	Integrated
Motherboard	4	Gigabyte GA-H55-UD3H	3	MSI 890GMX-G65
RAM memory	4	Patriot Viper II Sector 5 4GB (2x2GB) 2400MHz	5	Patriot Viper II Sector 5 4GB (2x2GB) 2400MHz
Hard Disc	4	Western Digital Veloci Raptor WD6000HLHX 600GB	3	Western Digital Veloci Raptor WD1500HLFS 150GB
Sound card	2	Integrated	2	Integrated
Network card	2	Integrated	2	Integrated
Optical drive	1	LG GH22NS50	1	LG GH22NS70
Monitor	1	iiyama ProLite E2200WS	1	Asus VW221D
		Price: 2423 USD Efficiency: 96.93		Price: 993 USD Efficiency: 93.11

PC configurations possess AMD processors which have acceptable prices and efficiencies. Generally, majority of PC configurations are located in the price range from 418 USD to 1254 USD, and are satisfactory for office work. The PC hardware configurations, shown in Table 1 represent a good compromise between their efficiencies and prices.

5 Conclusions

In the paper the intelligent system for PC hardware configuration has been proposed. Using proposed PCHC system personal computers can be configured depending on user preferences. The results of PCHC system is not a single solution, but a whole Pareto front which consists of several (in our experiments with 20 solutions) solutions. Therefore, after optimization process we can finally decide which personal computer hardware configuration is the best for us (cheaper with lower efficiency or more expensive with higher efficiency).

References

1. Amuso, V.J., Enslin, J.: The Strength Pareto Evolutionary Algorithm 2 (SPEA2) applied to simultaneous multi- mission waveform design. In: International Conference on Waveform Diversity and Design, WDDC 2007, June 4-8, pp. 407–417 (2007)
2. Zitzler, E., Laumanns, M., Thiele, L.: SPEA2: Improving the Strength Pareto Evolutionary Algorithm, Technical Report 103, Computer Engineering and Networks Laboratory (TIK), ETH Zürich, Switzerland (2001)
3. Silverman, B.W.: Density estimation for statistics and data analysis. Chapman and Hall, London (1986)
4. Dasgupta, D., Stoliartchouk, A.: Evolving PC system hardware configurations. In: Proceedings of the 2002 World on Congress on Computational Intelligence, WCCI, vol. 1, pp. 517–522 (2002)
5. Michalewicz, Z.: Genetic algorithms + data structures = evolution programs. Springer, Heidelberg (1992)
6. Goldberg, D.E.: Genetic algorithms in search, optimization, and machine learning. Addison-Wesley Publishing Company Inc., New York (1989)
7. Slowik, A.: Application of evolutionary algorithm to design minimal phase digital filters with non-standard amplitude characteristics and finite bit word length. Bulletin of the Polish Academy of Sciences-Technical Sciences 59(2), 125–135 (2011), doi:10.2478/v10175-011-0016-z
8. Slowik, A.: Application of an Adaptive Differential Evolution Algorithm With Multiple Trial Vectors to Artificial Neural Network Training. IEEE Transactions on Industrial Electronics 58(8), 3160–3167 (2011), doi:10.1109/tie.2010.2062474
9. Mendoza, J.E., López, M.E., Coello Coello, C.A., López, E.A.: Microgenetic multiobjective reconfiguration algorithm considering power losses and reliability indices for medium voltage distribution network. IET Generation, Transmission & Distribution 3(9), 825–840 (2009)

10. Portilla-Flores, E.A., Mezura-Montes, E., Gallegos, J.A., Coello-Coello, C.A., Cruz-Villar, C.A., Villareal-Cervantes, M.G.: Parametric Reconfiguration Improvement in Non-Iterative Concurrent Mechatronic Design Using an Evolutionary-Based Approach. Engineering Applications of Artificial Intelligence 24(5), 757–771 (2011)
11. Tam, V., Ma, K.T.: Applying Genetic Algorithms and Other Heuristic Methods to Handle PC Configuration Problems. In: Alexandrov, V.N., Dongarra, J., Juliano, B.A., Renner, R.S., Tan, C.J.K. (eds.) ICCS-ComputSci 2001. LNCS, vol. 2074, pp. 439–446. Springer, Heidelberg (2001)
12. Tam, V., Ma, K.T.: "Optimizing Personal Computer Configurations with Heuristic-Based Search Methods. Artificial Intelligence Review 17(2), 129–140 (2002)

Type-2 Fuzzy Logic Control of Trade-off between Exploration and Exploitation Properties of Genetic Algorithms

Adam Slowik

Department of Electronics and Computer Science, Koszalin University of Technology,
Sniadeckich 2 Street, 75-453 Koszalin, Poland
aslowik@ie.tu.koszalin.pl

Abstract. An optimal trade-off between exploration and exploitation properties of genetic algorithm is very important in optimization process. Due value steering of these two factors we can prevent a premature convergence of the algorithm. Therefore, better results can be obtained during optimization process with the use of genetic algorithm. In this paper the type-2 fuzzy logic control of trade-off between exploration and exploitation properties of genetic algorithm is presented. Our novel selection method (with application of type-2 fuzzy logic to steering of key parameter in this selection method) is based on previously elaborated mix selection method. In proposed method two factors are taken into consideration: the first is a number of generations of genetic algorithm, and second is a population diversity. Due to these two factors, we can control the trade-off between global and local search of solution space; also due to the type-2 fuzzy control the proposed method is more "immune" in falling into the trap of local extremum. The results obtained using proposed method (during optimization of test functions chosen from literature) are compared with the results obtained using other selection methods. Also, a statistically importance of obtained results is checked using statistical t-Student test. In almost all cases, the results obtained using proposed selection method are statistically important and better than the results obtained using other selection techniques.

1 Introduction

In design of effective genetic optimization methods, it is important to assure optimal relation between exploration and exploitation of a solution space. If these two properties are controlled in suitable manner during optimization process, then the optimization process became more effective and better solutions can be obtained at the same time; also the problem of premature convergence is minimized. In 1994 Back has shown that the selection process can control the level of exploration and exploitation of solution space by varying a selection pressure [1]. If in genetic algorithm, the selection pressure is higher then we have larger exploitation property [2], and of course if selection pressure is lower then we have larger exploration property [2]. Therefore, we can see that the value of

L. Rutkowski et al. (Eds.): SIDE 2012 and EC 2012, LNCS 7269, pp. 368–376, 2012.

selection pressure is critical in designing a selection mechanism. The properties of selection pressure have been widely studied in area of genetic algorithms [3, 4] for several decades. However tuning of the selection pressure is still difficult task, and remains an important and open problem in genetic algorithms [5, 6]. Many selection methods have been developed. Among them we can mention: roulette selection [7], elitist selection [8], deterministic selection [9], tournament selection [10], truncation selection [11], fan selection [12], mix selection [13]. The main idea of the mix selection is that at the start of the algorithm operation the whole solution space is searched globally, and together with an increase of the number of algorithm generations the solution space is searched more and more locally [13]. The main advantage of the mix selection is a possibility of defining relations between global and local searches of a potential solution space [13]. However, the problem is how this relations between global and local searches should vary during optimization process. Therefore, in this paper, we propose an application of type-2 fuzzy logic to control the properties of the mix selection. The novel selection method proposed in this paper is called as T2FLM (*Type-2 Fuzzy Logic for Mix selection*). The T2FLM method has been tested using test functions chosen from literature. The results obtained using T2FLM selection are compared with results obtained using other existing selection methods.

2 Type-2 Fuzzy Logic for Mix Selection - T2FLM

The T2FLM selection method is based on elaborated earlier mix selection (more detailed information about mix selection can be found in [13]). In proposed T2FLM method, the α ($\alpha \in$ [-1; 1]) parameter from mix selection is controlled using type-2 fuzzy logic. Described fuzzy logic system with at least one type-2 fuzzy set is called a type-2 fuzzy logic system [14]. Type-1 fuzzy logic systems [15] can not directly handle rule uncertainties, because they use type-1 fuzzy sets that are certain. On the other hand, type-2 fuzzy logic systems, are very useful in circumstances where it is difficult to exactly determine values of parameters [16]. In our case, the population diversity for example is a parameter which is hard to exactly determine. In literature, many different metrics for computation of population diversity in genetic algorithms exist. It is known that type-2 fuzzy sets [17] allow us to model and to minimize the effects of uncertainties in rule-based fuzzy logic system. Unfortunately, type-2 fuzzy sets are more difficult to use and understand than type-1 fuzzy sets; hence, their application is not widespread yet [14]. As we mentioned at the start of this section, the proposed T2FLM selection method is based on mix selection [13]. In the mix selection [13], the values of relative fitness *rfitness* for particular individuals are computed as follows:

- for the best individual (in the case when $\alpha \geq 0$)

$$rfitness'_{max} = rfitness_{max} + (1 - rfitness_{max}) \cdot \alpha \qquad (1)$$

370   A. Slowik

- for others individuals (in the case when $\alpha \geq 0$)

$$rfitness' = rfitness \cdot \left(\frac{rfitness_{max} - rfitness'_{max}}{\sum_{i=1}^{M} rfitness_i - rfitness_{max}} + 1 \right) \qquad (2)$$

- for all individuals (in the case when $\alpha < 0$)

$$rfitness' = rfitness + \left(rfitness - \frac{1}{M} \right) \cdot \alpha \qquad (3)$$

where: $rfitness'_{max}$-new relative fitness of the best individual; $rfitness_{max}$-old relative fitness of the best individual; α-scaling factor $\alpha \in [-1; 1]$; $rfitness'$-new relative fitness of chosen individual; $rfitness$-old relative fitness of chosen individual; M-number of individuals in population.

An interesting question is: how the value of α parameter should be changed in order to assure a good trade-off between exploration and exploitation properties of genetic algorithm. In paper [13] the linear increase of the value of α parameter (during successive algorithm generations) has been proposed. However, this is not a good solution, because the control of exploration and exploitation properties is strongly dependent on the optimization problem being solved.

In this paper, we propose application of type-2 fuzzy logic to control the value of α parameter. We assume two input linguistic variables: population diversity (PD $\in [0; 1]$) which is represented by type-2 fuzzy sets (presented in Figure 1a), and generation percentage (GP $\in [0; 1]$) which is represented by type-1 fuzzy sets (presented in Figure 1b). In the proposed type-2 fuzzy logic system only one output linguistic variable exists. This output variable is the α ($\alpha \in$ [-1; 1]) parameter which is represented by type-1 fuzzy sets (presented in Figure 1c). Each linguistic variable possesses five linguistic values: low (L), medium-low (ML), medium (M), medium-high (MH) and high (H).

A relation between input linguistic variables and output linguistic variable is determined by 25 fuzzy rules. The general idea of these rules is taken from [18]. In short we can say, that at the initial stage of the genetic algorithm operation, the exploitation property should be reduced, and the perturbation factor to

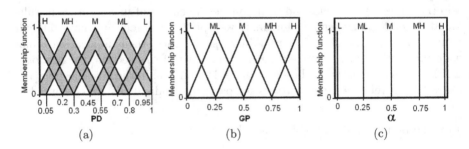

(a)   (b)   (c)

Fig. 1. Graphical representation of fuzzy sets which represent: the input linguistic value PD (a), the input linguistic value GP (b), the output linguistic value α (c)

explore the search space should be increased as much as possible. During successive generations, exploration needs to be reduced gradually (perturbation factor should be lower and lower), and exploitation property should be increased [18]. 25 fuzzy rules $R_k (k \in [1; 25])$ are implemented in the proposed method using following scheme R_k: (PD_k, GP_k, α_k). This scheme for the rule R_k we can read as: IF $(PD$ is $PD_k)$ AND $(GP$ is $GP_k)$ THEN α is α_k

R_1: (L, L, M) R_2: (L, ML, M) R_3: (L, M, MH)
R_4: (L, MH, H) R_5: (L, H, H) R_6: (ML, L, M)
R_7: (ML, ML, M) R_8: (ML, M, M) R_9: (ML, MH, MH)
R_{10}: (ML, H, H) R_{11}: (M, L, ML) R_{12}: (M, ML, M)
R_{13}: (M, M, M) R_{14}: (M, MH, M) R_{15}: (M, H, MH)
R_{16}: (MH, L, L) R_{17}: (MH, ML, ML) R_{18}: (MH, M, M)
R_{19}: (MH, MH, M) R_{20}: (MH, H, M) R_{21}: (H, L, L)
R_{22}: (H, ML, L) R_{23}: (H, M, ML) R_{24}: (H, MH, M)
R_{25}: (H, H, M)

In the type-2 fuzzy controller, we have used MIN-MAX operators, KM algorithm [19] was used to type-reduction, and the defuzzification was performed using center-of-gravity method [16]. The type-2 fuzzy controller was implemented as a table controller. Therefore, the time consumption in proposed T2FLM selection method is not much higher than in other selection methods.

3   The Metrics for GP and PD Factors in T2FLM Method

In the proposed T2FLM method the values of linguistic input variables are computed as follows:

- for GP (generation percentage)

$$GP = \frac{IT}{T_{max}} \tag{4}$$

where: IT - is a current number of iteration of the algorithm, $T_{max}-$ is a maximal number of iterations of the algorithm

- for PD (population diversity)

$$PD = 1 - \sum_{i=1}^{n} \sum_{j=1}^{M} (x_{i,j} - c_i)^2 \, ; c_i = \frac{\sum_{j=1}^{M} x_{i,j}}{M} \tag{5}$$

where: $x_{i,j}$ is a value of i-th decision variable in the j-th individual, M is a number of individuals in population, n is a number of variables in the function being optimized.

Additionally, the value of PD was normalized (in the range $[0; 1]$). The normalization process was performed in order to obtain the full range of variability for this linguistic value. The normalization was dynamically performed after each iteration of the algorithm using formula:

$$PD_{norm,i} = \frac{PD_i - PD_{min}}{PD_{max} - PD_{min}} \qquad (6)$$

where: $PD_{norm,i}$ is a normalized value of linguistic variable PD which is applied to the input of proposed fuzzy controller in i-th iteration of the algorithm, PD_{min} is the lowest value of PD form iteration already performed, PD_{max} is the highest value of PD form iteration already performed, PD_i is the value of PD obtained for i-th iteration of the algorithm.

4 Assumed Test Functions

The test functions were taken from the paper [13] (GM represents the global minimal value, n represents number of variables in the function being optimized, in all functions minimization problem was considered).

- De Jong function F1
$\sum_{i=1}^{n} x_i^2$; $-100 \leq x_i \leq 100$; GM=0 in $(x_1, x_2, ..., x_{30}) = (0, 0, ..., 0)$; $n = 30$
- Ackley function F2
$20 - 20 \cdot \exp\left(-0.2 \cdot \sqrt{\frac{1}{n} \cdot \sum_{i=1}^{n} x_i^2}\right) + \exp(1) - \exp\left(\frac{1}{n} \cdot \sum_{i=1}^{n} \cos(2 \cdot \pi \cdot x_i)\right)$;
$-100 \leq x_i \leq 100$; GM=0 in $(x_1, x_2, ..., x_{30}) = (0, 0, ..., 0)$; $n = 30$
- Griewank function F3
$\frac{1}{4000} \cdot \sum_{i=1}^{n} x_i^2 - \prod_{i=1}^{n} \cos\left(\frac{x_i}{\sqrt{i}}\right) + 1$
$-600 \leq x_i \leq 600$; GM=0 in $(x_1, x_2, ..., x_{30}) = (0, 0, ..., 0)$; $n = 30$
- Rastrigin function F4
$10 \cdot n + \sum_{i=1}^{n} \left(x_i^2 - 10 \cdot \cos(2 \cdot \pi \cdot x_i)\right)$
$-500 \leq x_i \leq 500$; GM=0 in $(x_1, x_2, ..., x_{30}) = (0, 0, ..., 0)$; $n = 20$
- Schwefel function F5
$418.9828872724339 \cdot n - \sum_{i=1}^{n} \left(x_i \cdot \sin\left(\sqrt{|x_i|}\right)\right)$
$-500 \leq x_i \leq 500$;
GM=0 in $(x_1, x_2, ..., x_{30}) = (420.96874636, ..., 420.96874636)$; $n = 30$
- High Conditioned Elliptic function F6
$\sum_{i=1}^{n} \left(10^6\right)^{\frac{i-1}{n-1}} \cdot x_i^2$; $-5 \leq x_i \leq 5$;
GM=0 in $(x_1, x_2, ..., x_{30}) = (0, 0, ..., 0)$; $n = 30$
- Non-Continuous Rastrigin function F7
$\sum_{i=1}^{n} \left(y^2 - 10 \cdot \cos(2 \cdot \pi \cdot y_i) + 10\right)$; $y_i = \begin{cases} x_i, & \text{when } |x_i| < 0.5 \\ round(2 \cdot x_i)/2, & \text{when } |x_i| \geq 0.5 \end{cases}$
$-500 \leq x_i \leq 500$; GM=0 in $(x_1, x_2, ..., x_{30}) = (0, 0, ..., 0)$; $n = 30$
- Non-Continuous Expanded Schaffer function F8
$F(y_1, y_2) + F(y_2, y_3) + ... + F(y_{n-1}, y_n) + F(y_n, y_1)$; $F(x, y) =$
$= 0.5 + \frac{\left(\sin^2\left(\sqrt{x^2 + y^2}\right) - 0.5\right)}{(1 + 0.001 \cdot (x^2 + y^2))^2}$ $y_i = \begin{cases} x_i, & \text{when } |x_i| < 0.5 \\ round(2 \cdot x_i)/2, & \text{when } |x_i| \geq 0.5 \end{cases}$

$-500 \leq x_i \leq 500$; GM=0 in $(x_1, x_2, ..., x_{30}) = (0, 0, ..., 0)$; $n = 30$

• Rotated Expanded Schaffer function F9

$F(x_1, x_2) + F(x_2, x_3) + ... + F(x_{n-1}, x_n) + F(x_n, x_1)$; $F(x, y) =$

$= 0.5 + \dfrac{\left(sin^2 \left(\sqrt{x^2 + y^2} \right) - 0.5 \right)}{(1 + 0.001 \cdot (x^2 + y^2))^2}$ $-500 \leq x_i \leq 500$;

GM=0 in $(x_1, x_2, ..., x_{30}) = (0, 0, ..., 0)$; $n = 30$

• De Jong function F10

$\sum_{i=1}^{n} i \cdot x_i^4$; $-100 \leq x_i \leq 100$;

GM=0 in $(x_1, x_2, ..., x_{30}) = (0, 0, ..., 0)$; $n = 30$

• Bohachevsky function F11

$\sum_{i=1}^{n} \left(x_i^2 + 2 \cdot x_{i+1}^2 - 0.3 \cdot cos(3 \cdot \pi \cdot x_i) - 0.4 \cdot cos(4 \cdot \pi \cdot x_{i+1}) + 0.7 \right)$

$-15 \leq x_i \leq 15$; GM=0 in $(x_1, x_2, ..., x_{30}) = (0, 0, ..., 0)$; $n = 30$

• Rosenbrock function F12

$\sum_{i=1}^{n} \left(100 \cdot \left(x_i^2 - x_{i+1} \right)^2 + (x_i - 1)^2 \right)$

$-5 \leq x_i \leq 5$; GM=0 in $(x_1, x_2, ..., x_{30}) = (0, 0, ..., 0)$; $n = 30$

• Scaled Rastrigin function F13

$10 \cdot n + \sum_{i=1}^{n} \left(\left(10^{\frac{i-1}{n-1}} \cdot x_i \right)^2 - 10 \cdot cos \left(2 \cdot \pi \cdot 10^{\frac{i-1}{n-1}} \cdot x_i \right) \right)$

$-5 \leq x_i \leq 5$; GM=0 in $(x_1, x_2, ..., x_{30}) = (0, 0, ..., 0)$; $n = 30$

• Skew Rastrigin function F14

$10 \cdot n + \sum_{i=1}^{n} \left(y_i^2 - 10 \cdot cos(2 \cdot \pi \cdot y_i) \right)$; $y_i = \begin{cases} 10 \cdot x_i, & \text{when } x_i > 0 \\ x_i, & \text{otherwise} \end{cases}$

$-5 \leq x_i \leq 5$; GM=0 in $(x_1, x_2, ..., x_{30}) = (0, 0, ..., 0)$; $n = 30$

• Schaffer function F15

$\sum_{i=1}^{n-1} \left(x_i^2 + x_{i+1}^2 \right)^{0.25} \cdot \left[sin^2 \left(50 \cdot \left(x_i^2 + x_{i+1}^2 \right)^{0.1} \right) + 1 \right]$

$-100 \leq x_i \leq 100$; GM=0 in $(x_1, x_2, ..., x_{30}) = (0, 0, ..., 0)$; $n = 30$

5 Description of Experiments

The experiments were performed using test functions presented in section four. In genetic algorithm, the following parameters were assumed: individuals were coded as real-number strings (each gene represents one variable in the function being optimized), T_{max}=1000, M=50, probability of crossover = 0.7, probability of mutation = $\frac{1}{n}$. The individuals in population were created randomly. Simple one-point crossover [7] was taken as a crossover operator. The non-uniform mutation [7] was taken as a mutation operator (for mutation operator the level of inhomogeneity was equal to 2). During the operation of the genetic algorithm only selection operator was changed. The parameter a=0.3 was taken for fan selection (identically as in paper [12]). The size of tournament group equal to 2 was assumed for tournament selection. Truncation threshold equal to 0.5 was assumed for truncation selection. In experiments, the evolutionary algorithm was executed 25 times for each test function. In Table 1, the average values of the test functions obtained after 25-fold repetition of genetic algorithm with different kind of selection methods (SM) are presented.

Table 1. Average values of the best results obtained after 25-fold repetition of evolutionary algorithm for each selection method: RO-roulette, EL-elitist, FAN-fan, TOU-tournament, DET-deterministic, TRU-truncation, MIX-mix, T2FLM-type-2 fuzzy mix

SM	F1	F2	F3	F4	F5
RO	351.93±88.10	5.11±0.64	4.58±0.99	3494±825	1201.16±294.79
EL	169.69±55.30	3.69±0.25	2.47±0.37	1493±508	276.06±123.33
FAN	1.15±0.41	0.34±0.09	0.83±0.14	72.33±14.21	2.90±1.42
TOU	78.61±19.25	3.58±0.31	1.72±0.17	811.95±201.71	470.96±187.69
DET	160.63±34.52	3.85±0.32	2.46±0.35	1681±340.73	402.58±161.72
TRU	47.88±13.20	2.94±0.27	1.47±0.11	579.57±123.74	206.08±104.54
MIX	0.42±0.19	0.21±0.06	0.46±0.13	45.63±7.29	67.73±82.63
T2FLM	0.27±0.12	0.16±0.04	0.35±0.09	35.98±5.22	0.94±0.53
SM	F6	F7	F8	F9	F10
RO	50715±22113	9606±2709	9.77±0.73	9.92±0.60	2093696±775961
EL	8059±3493	4056±1024	6.69±0.57	6.83±0.61	430902±168779
FAN	25.40±12.83	112.35±26.15	3.28±0.45	3.40±0.51	2.88±2.53
TOU	578.30±157.29	2612±597	7.66±0.62	7.62±0.56	30555±14153
DET	7042±2895	4710±1275	7.42±0.66	7.39±0.71	451341±163243
TRU	279.63±112.13	1493±360	6.68±0.96	6.91±0.52	11263±6426
MIX	15.23±13.40*	60.25±13.97	2.93±0.43	2.94±0.47*	0.35±0.25
T2FLM	13.30±9.84	45.72±11.20	2.62±0.59	2.65±0.65	0.14±0.21
SM	F11	F12	F13	F14	F15
RO	43.74±6.58	8285±3290	136.12±20.62	117.19±15.18	64.73±7.77
EL	26.87±3.31	2588±942	93.17±14.41	91.96±14.27	51.36±4.93
FAN	1.05±0.37	130.62±27.98	7.89±2.44	4.76±1.90	22.27±2.92
TOU	19.46±2.96	593.36±207.23	67.60±9.27	51.32±9.84	47.63±5.00
DET	26.50±3.31	2412±834.02	86.27±12.48	77.89±11.20	48.74±4.07
TRU	14.04±1.98	480.87±335.83	50.98±5.34	43.43±6.53	41.92±4.22
MIX	0.34±0.10	94.62±37.88*	4.54±2.16	3.90±1.48	17.97±2.41
T2FLM	0.26±0.11	93.85±40.23	2.76±1.12	1.59±0.94	16.48±2.69

In order to check a statistically importance of obtained results for T2FLM method, the t-Student statistical test (with 48 degree of freedom) was performed for all combinations of the results obtained using T2FLM method and results obtained using other selection methods. In Table 1, the symbol "*" represents that given result is not statistically important (with 95% degree of trust). We can see from Table 1, that in all cases results obtained using proposed T2FLM method are better than results obtained using other selection methods. Moreover, the results obtained using T2FLM are in 102 cases (on 105 possible) statistically important with 95% degree of trust.

6   Conclusions

In this paper, the new T2FLM selection method was presented. The T2FLM method is based on mix selection [13] elaborated in 2010. In the T2FLM method the type-2 fuzzy sets were applied to control the values of the α parameter in the mix selection. The computational complexity of T2FLM method is not much higher than in other selection methods (because we have used type-2 fuzzy logic table controller). Unfortunately the results of computation complexity can not be presented in this paper because of space limitation. Based on the results obtained using t-Student statistical test, the results obtained using T2FLM method are statistically important in almost all cases. Compared to the mix selection, the results obtained using T2FLM method are in 12 cases (on 15 possible) statistically important. We believe that proposed method can be used in practical applications of genetic algorithms in order to increase their efficiency.

References

1. Bäck, T.: Selective Pressure in Evolutionary Algorithms: A Characterization of Selection Mechanisms. In: Proc. 1st IEEE Conf. on Evolutionary Computing, pp. 57–62 (1994)
2. Liu, S.-H., Mernik, M., Bryant, B.R.: Entropy-Driven Parameter Control for Evolutionary Algorithms. Informatica 31, 41–50 (2007)
3. Motoki, T.: Calculating the expected loss of diversity of selection schemes. Evolutionary Computation 10(4), 397–422 (2002)
4. Winkler, S., Affenzeller, M., Wagner, S.: Offspring selection and its effects on genetic propagation in genetic programming based system identification. Cybernetics and Systems 2, 549–554 (2008)
5. Xie, H., Zhang, M.: Tuning Selection Pressure in Tournament Selection, Technical Report Series, School of Engineering and Computer Science, Victoria University of Wellington, New Zealand (2009)
6. Jong, K.D.: Parameter setting in eas: a 30 year perspective. In: Parameter Setting in Evolutionary Algorithms, pp. 1–18. Springer, Heidelberg (2007)
7. Michalewicz, Z.: Genetic algorithms + data structures = evolution programs. Springer, Heidelberg (1992)
8. Zen, S., Zhou Yang, C.T.: Comparison of steady state and elitist selection genetic algorithms. In: Proc. of 2004 Int. Conf. on Intelligent Mechatronics and Automation, pp. 495–499 (2004), doi:10.1109/ICIMA.2004.1384245
9. Takaaki, N., Takahiko, K., Keiichiro, Y.: Deterministic Genetic Algorithm. Papers of Technical Meeting on Industrial Instrumentation and Control, IEE Japan, pp. 33–36 (2003)
10. Blickle, T., Thiele, L.: A Comparison of Selection Schemes used in Genetic Algorithms, Computer Engineering and Communication Networks Lab, Swiss Federal Institute of Technology, TIK Report, No. 11, Edition 2 (December 1995)
11. Muhlenbein, H., Schlierkamp-voosen, D.: Predictive Models for the Breeder Genetic Algorithm. Evolutionary Computation 1(1), 25–49 (1993)
12. Słowik, A., Białko, M.: Modified Version of Roulette Selection for Evolution Algorithms – The Fan Selection. In: Rutkowski, L., Siekmann, J.H., Tadeusiewicz, R., Zadeh, L.A. (eds.) ICAISC 2004. LNCS (LNAI), vol. 3070, pp. 474–479. Springer, Heidelberg (2004), doi:10.1007/978-3-540-24844-6_70
13. Słowik, A.: Steering of Balance between Exploration and Exploitation Properties of Evolutionary Algorithms - Mix Selection. In: Rutkowski, L., Scherer, R., Tadeusiewicz, R., Zadeh, L.A., Zurada, J.M. (eds.) ICAISC 2010. LNCS, vol. 6114, pp. 213–220. Springer, Heidelberg (2010), doi:10.1007/978-3-642-13232-2_26

14. Castillo, O., Cazarez, N., Rico, D.: Intelligent Control of Dynamic Systems Using Type-2 Fuzzy Logic and Stability Issues. International Mathematical Forum 1(28), 1371–1382 (2006)
15. Klir, G.J., Yuan, B.: Fuzzy sets and fuzzy logic: theory and applications. Prentice-Hall, Upper Saddle River (1995)
16. Mendel, J.M.: Uncertain Rule-Based Fuzzy Logic: Introduction and new directions. Prentice Hall, USA (2000)
17. Karnik, N.N., Mendel, J.M., Liang, Q.: Type-2 Fuzzy Logic Systems. IEEE Transactions of Fuzzy Systems 7(6), 643–658 (1999), doi:10.1109/91.811231
18. Xue, F., Sanderson, A.C., Bonissone, P., Graves, R.J.: Fuzzy Logic Controlled Multi-Objective Differential Evolution. In: The 14th IEEE International Conference on Fuzzy Systems, pp. 720–725 (2005), doi:10.1109/FUZZY.2005.1452483
19. Karnik, N.N., Mendel, J.M.: Centroid of a type-2 fuzzy set. Information Sciences 132, 195–220 (2001), doi:10.1016/S0020-0255(01)00069-X

A Parallel Genetic Algorithm
for Propensity Modeling in Consumer Finance

Ramasubramanian Sundararajan[1], Tarun Bhaskar[1], and Padmini Rajagopalan[2]

[1] Software Sciences & Analytics, GE Global Research
122 EPIP, Whitefield Road, Bangalore 560066, India
{ramasubramanian.sundararajan,tarun.bhaskar}@ge.com
[2] Department of Computer Science, University of Texas at Autin
1 University Station D9500, Austin, TX 78712, USA
padmini@cs.utexas.edu

Abstract. We consider the problem of propensity modeling in consumer finance. These modeling problems are characterized by the two aspects: the model needs to optimize a business objective which may be nonstandard, and the rate of occurence of the event to be modeled may be very low. Traditional methods such as logistic regression are ill-equipped to deal with nonstandard objectives and low event rates. Methods which deal with the low event rate problem by learning on biased samples face the problem of overlearning. We propose a parallel genetic algorithm method that addresses these challenges. Each parallel process evolves propensity models based on a different biased sample, while a mechanism for validation and cross-pollination between the islands helps address the overlearning issue. We demonstrate the utility of the method on a real-life dataset.

1 Introduction

A financial institution such as a retail bank that offers a portfolio of products (loans, credit cards etc.) to its customers would typically have a database that contains the information pertaining to the history of each customer's relationship with the firm. This information may include socio-demographics, account history and transactional information (disbursements, repayments etc.) pertaining to the various products that the customer has taken with the firm. The prime imperative of Customer Relationship Management (CRM) is to leverage such information to identify and retain customers who are profitable to the bank while limiting the number of unprofitable or risky customers. Given this imperative, the bank may engage in a variety of actions from both a marketing and a risk perspective. These actions could include identifying potential defaulters and initiating risk management actions (such as limiting the credit offered to such customers), identifying potentially profitable borrowers and initiating marketing actions (such as proactively extending credit) etc.

The above actions are often predicated on the existence of predictive models that allow the bank to gauge the propensity of the customer to exhibit a certain type of behaviour (default on a loan, response to a product offer), based on information available about the customer at the time of making the prediction. These models are typically built on the basis of historical data regarding the behaviour of customers in similar

L. Rutkowski et al. (Eds.): SIDE 2012 and EC 2012, LNCS 7269, pp. 377–385, 2012.
© Springer-Verlag Berlin Heidelberg 2012

situations. An example of such a process in the case of response to a product offer is illustrated in figure 1. The model for propensity of a customer to respond to a marketing offer during a campaign is built by linking the customer inputs (labeled 1 in the figure) to the output, namely response (labeled 2). Once this model is built, it is applied on customer-level inputs (labeled 3) in a new campaign, and the predictions are used to pick the customers to target in that campaign. Similar propensity models can be built to predict other aspects of customer behaviour as well, such as default on a loan, attrition on a credit card etc.

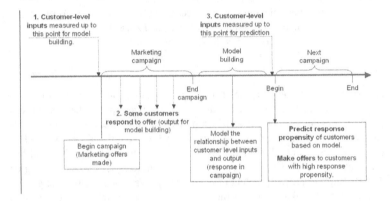

Fig. 1. Propensity Modeling: Example

One problem associated with propensity modeling in consumer finance is that the event in which we are interested in may not occur often. We call the rate of occurrence the *event rate*. In fairly mature consumer finance markets, it is very common to see event rates as low as 1% or less for response to marketing offers. Often, such a problem is also associated with an asymmetric payoff for correct identification of the two classes. For instance, if the rare event to be modeled is that of a customer responding favourably to a marketing offer, then the profit to be gained from the response is usually much higher than the amount saved in marketing costs if that customer is ignored. This means that the performance metrics relevant to such a problem are more likely to focus on the ability to identify the rare event correctly, rather than the number of non-events that are misclassified ([2]).

Owing to the need for easy interpretation of these propensity models and verification of the model coefficients against business insight, they are typically constrained to have a linear functional form. Typically, these models are built using the logistic regression technique. This method models the logarithm of the odds of the event occurring as a linear function of a set of covariates. That is,

$$Pr\left(y|x_1 \ldots x_n\right) \;\; = \;\; \frac{1}{1 + e^{-(\beta_0 + \beta_1 x_1 + \ldots \beta_n x_n)}} \tag{1}$$

where $y \in (0, 1)$ is the desired output (the event to be modeled) and $x_1 \ldots x_n$ are the attributes related to the customer. The logistic regression method essentially finds the model (i.e., the set of values $\beta_0, \beta_1 \ldots \beta_n$) on the basis of a labeled sample.

Logistic regression faces one difficulty, namely that the objective it pursues while finding the various β values is that of maximizing the likelihood function. While this is a well-behaved function, it does not necessarily translate directly to the business objective of interest. For instance, if the business objective in a response modeling problem is to find a model such that most of the potential respondents are captured within the top 10% of the scores, then it is possible that the maximum likelihood estimator does not provide the best model for this purpose. Therefore, we consider the use of a direct search method such as genetic algorithms to build propensity models [1].

Apropos the problem of modeling the propensity of a rare event, it has been shown that better propensity models can be built by "biasing" the training sample in favour of the event in question, such that it has a high proportion of event observations. The use of biased samples for training in rare event problems is quite common in practice [5]. While this allows the learning algorithm to model the separation between events and non-events better, it runs the risk of overlearning (or under-learning), depending on the characteristics of the biased sample.

One option is to introduce several biased samples and develop a method that has the capability of sharing the properties of the models developed on these biased samples, thereby making the models more robust in terms of their performance on an (unbiased) test sample.

In this paper, we present a parallel genetic algorithm-based method that evolves multiple models using a plurality of biased samples. Each of these samples provides a different perspective on the separation between events and non-events in the data. However, in order not to overlearn from any particular sample, we also provide a mechanism for cross-pollination between the models built on these different samples. We address design issues regarding the creation of biased samples, communication between the various model populations evolving in parallel and choice of final model. We illustrate the effectiveness of this approach on a real-life problem from the consumer finance industry.

The organization of this paper is as follows: Section 2 outlines the various issues involved in designing an appropriate GA to solve the rare event problem and then describes the actual algorithm designed. Section 3 illustrates its effectiveness on a real-life problem from the consumer finance industry. Section 4 concludes and suggests directions for further work in this area.

2   Algorithm Design

The problem of learning a rare event can be posed as follows: Find a function f that best approximates the relationship between a set of inputs $x_1 \ldots x_n$ and an output $y \in \{0, 1\}$, wherein the proportion of 1s to 0s in the population is very small.

As discussed in the previous section, there are two challenges which we need to address while developing a propensity model for low event rate data: optimizing objective functions that directly address the business requirements, and building models with good generalization ability from biased samples. This section proposes a Genetic Algorithm based method for propensity modeling which takes care of these requirements.

Genetic algorithms attempt to optimize a given objective, by starting with a population of candidate solutions and evolving to a better set of solutions over a number of generations. The process is stopped when either a prespecified number of generations have passed, or if no performance improvement has been observed over the last few generations. The process can be applied to building propensity models, wherein each model is a candidate solution that attempts to optimize some objective such as, for instance, the area under the receiver operating characteristic (ROC) curve. Figure 2 gives a diagrammatic representation of this process.

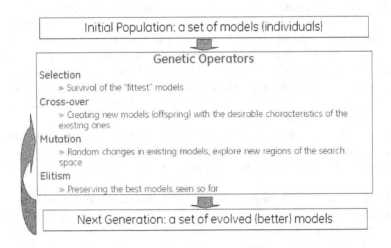

Fig. 2. Genetic algorithm for propensity modeling

In order to use genetic algorithms to model the propensity of occurrence of a rare event, we use a biased sample to calculate the objective function (in this case, the performance of the model on the biased sample). In order to account for the fact that the biased sample may represent only a restricted view of the example space, we use multiple biased samples, and use a GA to train on each of them. This naturally raises a number of questions, which we shall outline below.

1. *How are the various biased samples created? What is the logic behind the method of creation of these samples?* This question is important because it determines the specific perspective of the separating surface between 1s and 0s that each biased sample gets. For instance, if the data is segmented according to some variable (or set of variables) and biased samples are drawn from the various segments, then the relative performance of the models on the various biased samples itself implies a certain hypothesis on how the segmentation method affects the output. This approach might work well if there is some domain knowledge that allows us to decide on the segmentation.

   A random split, on the other hand, might work well if one does not possess this domain knowledge. However, in this case, we might need more biased samples in order to increase the likelihood of capturing the best aspects of the separating surface through some biased sample or the other.

Another aspect of this question is whether or not the various biased samples have an overlap, either in the 1s or the 0s. Usually, due to the low event rate one uses the same (or largely overlapping) set of 1s for all the biased samples and varies the 0s.

2. *Do the various GAs that run on the biased samples work independent of each other, or is there any interaction among them?* In other words, what is the potential benefit of interaction between the various parallel GA processes. As mentioned earlier, the major drawback of using biased samples is that of overlearning. In order to avoid this drawback, one must design a mechanism whereby the progress of the GA is periodically "validated" in terms of the models' performance on an unbiased sample. Since it is possible that the models that work well on an unbiased sample may occur in any of the parallel processes, the mechanism should ideally consider a cross-section of models across these parallel processes.

3. *How do we choose a winning solution, or a set of winning solutions in the end?* The eventual objective is to perform well in a real-world situation, where the model will have to predict the propensity of a rare event. Therefore, we need to choose the model(s) that perform well on an unbiased sample.

One could also consider the possibility of using the predictions from multiple models in a mixture of experts framework. The effectiveness of such an approach depends, to some extent, on the choices made in questions 1 and 2 above. For instance, a mixture of experts framework might work better when each expert has a clearly defined task or perspective. This might occur when the biased samples are taken from distinct segments in the data. Also, there exists an argument that a greater variance among the experts is better from a prediction standpoint. In that case, less cross-pollination among the various parallel GAs might be beneficial.

Apart from these, there are also a number of standard questions regarding the various aspects of genetic algorithms, such as the objective function (that is, the goodness-of-fit metric for the model being built using the GA), population size, method of selection, cross-over and mutation, stopping criterion etc. The above aspects are addressed in the algorithm presented in the following subsection.

2.1 Proposed Method

We now propose a new Genetic Algorithm based method which takes care of the issues discussed earlier. We need to devise an algorithm which can take different biased samples, develop models on them and interact with each other occasionally to make sure that the information about what works well on an unbiased sample is shared well. The proposed method is a parallel implementation of Genetic Algorithm for propensity modeling (for a basic parallel implementation of GA, one can refer to [3]).

Building the propensity model on the biased samples remove the problem of very low event rate for each of these samples and testing it on the validation sample takes care of the over-learning problem. The evaluation of models is done on a fitness function designed to address the desired business objective. We present the algorithm below:

1. Decide on the number of islands (k). Generate biased samples for each islands and one unbiased sample for validation in real-world conditions.
2. Decide on parameters of the genetic algorithm to be run on each island, namely:
   - Cross-over and mutation type and associated probabilities
   - Terminating condition and number of generations
   - Population size
   - Logistic regression models – optional, to initialize solutions on each island
3. Initialize a population of models on each island.
4. Use the genetic operators (selection, cross-over, mutation) to evolve to better models over m generations. Preserve a set of elite solutions based on performance on the biased sample in this island. Each island can be executed as a parallel process.
5. Choose the best n models (based on performance on the biased sample) on each island and send them to the inter-island tournament.
6. In the tournament, select the n models that perform best on the validation sample. Send these n models back to each island.
7. On each island, replace the elite set for validation sample performance with the n models received. In the first iteration of the tournament, there does not exist such an elite set, so replace the worst n models (for that particular biased sample) in that island with the n winners of the tournament.
8. Repeat steps 4 to 7 until the terminating condition is reached.
9. Select the best n models (based on biased sample performance) from each island and send them to a process that picks the final model. This process may operate in a number of ways as explained earlier.

3   Experimental Results

To illustrate the utility of the proposed algorithm, we perform some experiments on a real life data set. To maintain confidentiality, we have used only a subset of the entire data. The problem addressed here is propensity modeling for credit card surfing. The phenomenon of a customer moving from one credit card to another after taking advantage of the activation benefits is called surfing. The bank has a list of its customers and uses some definition to identify who has behaved like a surfer. There are usually very few surfers, but identifying them is useful for the bank. The subset of the database used in this experimentation has around 230000 customers and 7 variables. Only 385 customers (0.16%) in the dataset are classified as surfers. The variables have some demographic and account related information regarding the customers. Some important variables are age of the customer, how often the customer revolves (pays interest) and the number of active accounts.

As discussed in the previous section, we need to form several biased samples to develop the island level models and we need one unbiased sample to validate the models developed on different islands. There can be several ways to extract biased samples. The method we use is to select all the events (385 customers with $y = 1$) for all the islands and randomly distribute the non-events ($y = 0$) to different islands. We use the entire dataset as the validation sample for the inter-island tournament. To observe the effect of number of islands and sharing of models across islands, we change the number of islands from 1 to 10. The case where there is just one island is equivalent to learning from an unbiased sample.

3.1   GA Parameters

In this section, we discuss different GA parameters (such as selection, cross over, mutation) used in the experiment. While designing a GA for a particular problem, there is no prescribed value of these parameters which is bound to work [6]. However, in general the structure of the problem gives us some idea of the parameter space which might be useful to search. Since the problem is difficult because of very low event rate, it would be useful to explore different areas in the search space.

We used a real-coded GA for this problem. We used a population size of 50 in each island. We used three party tournament selection, Blend Crossover (BLX) and Polynomial Mutation operators in this experiment. We varied cross-over probability between $0.5 - 0.8$ and mutation probability between $0.1 - 0.3$, and tried different combinations of the two probabilities in order to consider various possibilities of the exploration-exploitation trade-off. We used 100 generations as the stopping criteria for the algorithm as we observed that the improvement was very small after 80-85 generations in most of the cases. For a description of real-coded GA and the various genetic operators used, see [4].

We use the following objectives as fitness functions for the GA:

Sensitivity at $10\%, 30\%$ ($S10, S30$). This refers to the percentage of actual surfers (responders) captured in the top 10% (or 30%) of customers ranked according to their model scores. This is a useful measure in case the business would like to use the model to eliminate the customers with the top 10% of scores as probable surfers.

Kolmogrov-Smirnov Statistic (KS). This is a statistic which measures the maximum distance between two distributions. In the propensity modeling case, it represents how well the model differentiates between a surfer and a non-surfer.

Area under the ROC curve (AUC). This is another metric to measure the inequality of distributions. In this modeling problem, this metric represents the improvement of performance of the metric over a random model. Both KS and AUC are good general purpose metrics to consider when the business is interested in ranking but does not provide a specific constraint such as performance in the top decile ($S10$).

3.2   Results and Analysis

In this section, we discuss the results obtained by the proposed algorithm and compare them to those obtained by the de-facto method for propensity modeling, namely Logistic Regression (LR). We first discuss the results we obtained by the proposed algorithm (GA) and compare it to the final results obtained by LR on an unbiased validation sample. We observe that the proposed method outperforms Logistic Regression by $4 - 9\%$ on different objective functions. Additionally, it might be instructive to see whether the performance on the biased development samples is better as well (see columns $2 - 3$ of 1). This would give us some idea of whether cross-pollination (sharing the models after few generations) has any effect on the model development process.

We observe that the proposed method also works better in developing models on the biased sample (see columns $2 - 3$ of 1). We observe that the proposed method outperforms the Logistic Regression by $8 - 22\%$. This demonstrates that the use of information regarding performance on the unbiased sample does not adversely affect the performance on the biased sample. If we compare the difference in the performance of the models on the biased training sample and the unbiased validation sample, the difference in the GA is very low (1-2%) whereas the difference in case of Logistic Regression is high (5-14%). This demonstrates that the information sharing due to cross-polination helps the models on the island to learn more about the data and deliver better models.

Table 1. Comparison of Logistic Regression (LR) and our algorithm (GA) on the unbiased (validation) sample and biased (development) samples

Objective	LR (unbiased)	GA (unbiased)	LR (biased)	GA (biased)
S10	30.65%	33.28%	26.8%	32.68%
S30	59.2%	62.9%	56.1%	62.25%
KS	0.31	0.329	0.284	0.327
AUC	0.715	0.724	0.705	0.7215

Now we discuss the effect of islands and information sharing between the islands on the final results. Table 2 represents the performance of the proposed method with changing number of islands. We do this analysis for the first objective function ($S10$). We run the proposed GA with the same cross-over, mutation and other GA parameters with one, two, four and six islands. The results are summarized in Table 2

Table 2. Performance on $S10$ with respect to # of islands

# islands	GA(dev)	GA(full)
1	30.94%	32.20%
2	31.1%	32.20
4	31.64%	32.46%
6	32.68%	33.28%

We observe two main trends in this study. The first trend is that the overall performance of the models on the full validation set increases with increasing number of islands. The second observation is that the difference between performance of the models on the biased and unbiased samples decreases with increasing number of islands. This demonstrates that the islands and the sharing of information between islands help the model to improve in terms of overall performance and reliability.

The above results indicate that the proposed GA method is able to take advantage of the various biased samples while avoiding the trap of overlearning. This points to the effectiveness of the method in meeting the objectives laid out in the beginning of the paper.

4   Conclusions and Future Directions

In this paper we have discussed the problem of propensity modeling in consumer finance, which is characterized by non-standard objectives and very low event rates.

We discussed the challenges associated with these characteristics and proposed a parallel version of Genetic Algorithms to address them. We demonstrated the performance of the proposed method on a real life dataset. The proposed method develops propensity models which optimizes different objectives which are closer to the business objectives. It develops models on several biased samples independently (we refer to them as islands) and every few generations, there is a mechanism for cross-pollination between islands. This helps the models to learn most of the features of the data and enhance the performance.

The work can be extended in a few directions. We have used a particular method to generate biased samples from the dataset. Other methods, such as is suggested in Section 2, can be used. For example, one island might develop models for a particular class of customers (say young, single customers with low income) and others might develop models on different class of customers. One advantage of using this type of sampling method is that one can use the final model in the general case, whereas the best models of a particular island might be used for customers belonging to that particular class.

One can also explore the question of setting the right parameters for the method for a particular class of problems: the number of islands, the sampling method, frequency of inter-island tournaments, method for combining predictions from the best models in various islands etc. Also, most of the GA parameters (which decide the search path) are obtained from past experience rather than any theoretical result. However, some insights on the effectiveness of various parameters can be gained from empirical observation.

References

1. Bhattacharya, S.: Direct marketing performance modeling using genetic algorithms. Informs Journal of Computing 11(3), 248–257 (1999)
2. Biswas, D., Narayanan, B., Sundararajan, R.: Metrics for model selection in consumer finance problems. In: Australian Conference on Artificial Intelligence, pp. 1289–1294 (2005)
3. Cantu-Paz, E.: Designing efficient master-slave parallel genetic algortihms. IlliGAL Report Number 97004, University of Illinois (1997)
4. Deb, K.: Multi-objective optimization using evolutionary algorithms. John Wiley and Sons (2001)
5. King, G., Zeng, L.: Logistic regression in rare events data. Political Analysis 9, 137–163 (2001)
6. Mitchell, M.: An Introduction to Genetic Algorithms. MIT Press (1998)

Hybrid Particle Swarm Optimizer and Its Application in Identification of Room Acoustic Properties

Mirosław Szczepanik[1], Arkadiusz Poteralski[1],
Jacek Ptaszny[1], and Tadeusz Burczyński[1,2]

[1] Silesian University of Technology
Department of Strength of Materials and Computational Mechanics
ul. Konarskiego 18A, 44-100 Gliwice, Poland
{miroslaw.szczepanik,arkadiusz.poteralski,jacek.ptaszny,tb}@polsl.pl
[2] Cracow University of Technology
Institute of Computer Science
ul. Warszawska 24, 31-155 Cracow, Poland
tburczyn@pk.edu.pl

Abstract. The paper deals with an application of an hybrid particle swarm optimizer (HPSO) to identification problems. The HPSO is applied to identify complex impedances of room walls and it is based on the mechanism discovered in the nature during observations of the animals social behaviour and supplemented with some additional gradient information. The numerical example demonstrate that the method based on hybrid swarm optimization is an effective technique for computing in identification problems.

Keywords: particle swarm optimizer, acoustics, identification, method of fundamental solutions, hybrid computational optimization algorithm.

1 Introduction

Identification of parameters in physical systems using the artificial intelligence techniques is a very active field of research. In order to improve the performance of well known global optimization methods inspired by biology processes, the hybrid approaches are proposed. Hybrid methods are based on coupling of the procedures from different optimization methods to improve accuracy and effectiveness of basis optimization methods. the combination of topological sensitivity and genetic algorithms were used for identification inverse problems in anisotropic materials [1]. The gradient-based, genetic and hybrid optimization algorithms for material parameters identification problem was proposed in [2]. Identification of effective elastic constants of composite plates based on a hybrid genetic algorithm was also considered in [3]. Another approach to inverse identification problems, based on hybrid techniques, was developed in [4], where the surrogate-model accelerated random search algorithm for global optimization

L. Rutkowski et al. (Eds.): SIDE 2012 and EC 2012, LNCS 7269, pp. 386–394, 2012.

was applied to inverse material identification. Immune identification of piezo-electric material constants using BEM was shown in [5]. The immune evolution-ary algorithm incorporating chaos optimization was proposed in [6]. In order to improve the PSO performance some hybrid variants have been proposed. The hybrid versions of PSO incorporate the capabilities of other optimization algo-rithms to prevent premature stagnation or to prevent the particles from being trapped in local minima. One can find for example applications of the hybrid of genetic algorithm and PSO in [7,8], evolutionary programming and PSO in [9], and PSO with differential evolution in [10]. Since its origin in1995, the PSO algorithm has been developed to improve its performance and use in different applications [11,12]. This paper concerns the application of the method of fun-damental solutions (MFS) [13] coupled with a hybrid particle swarm optimizer in identification of room acoustic properties. Dutilleux et al. [15] proposed a method for the determination of sound absorption in rooms. They defined a boundary inverse problem which was solved by using the (μ,λ)-ES (evolution strategy). The proposed method consisted in minimization of a cost function dependent on the difference between measured and computed acoustic pressure values. The measurements were simulated by a numerical analysis. The station-ary acoustic pressure field was computed by using the finite difference method (FDM). The proposed method was successfully applied to the solution of low-frequency problems (frequencies up to 240 Hz). This method can be relatively inefficient with respect to the computation time as it requires multiple calcu-lations of the cost function. In order to improve this approach the method of fundamental solutions, which is a boundary collocation method, coupled with hybrid evolutionary algorithm was used in [14]. In the present work an improved swarm optimization algorithm and a hybrid one is applied instead of the evolu-tionary algorithm. Numerical examples are given and good results are obtained. In the authors opinion, no application of the HPSO for solving inverse identi-fication problems in acoustic field modelled by using the MFS can be found in the literature until now.

2   Hybrid Particle Swarm Optimizer

The particle swarm algorithms [16], similarly to other bio-inspired evolutionary [17,18,19] and immune algorithms [20,5], have been developed on the basis of the mechanisms discovered in the nature. The optimization process using PSO is based on finding the better and better locations in the search-space (in the natural environment that are for example hatching or feeding grounds). The position x_{ij} of the i-th particle is changed by stochastic velocity v_{ij}, which is dependent on the particle distance from its earlier best position and position of the swarm leader. This approach is given by the following equations:

$$v_{ij}(k+1) = wv_{ij}(k) + \phi_{1j}(k)\left[q_{ij}(k) - x_{ij}(k)\right] + \phi_{2j}(k)\left[\hat{q}_{ij}(k) - x_{ij}(k)\right], \quad (1)$$

$$x_{ij}(k+1) = x_{ij}(k) + v_{ij}(k+1), \quad i = 1, 2, ..., m; \quad j = 1, 2, ..., n, \quad (2)$$

where:
$\phi_{1j}(k) = c_1 r_{1j}(k); \quad \phi_{2j}(k) = c_2 r_{2j}(k),$
m – number of the particles,
n – number of design variables (problem dimension),
w – inertia weight,
c_1, c_2 – acceleration coefficients,
r_1, r_2 – random numbers with uniform distribution [0,1],
$h_i(k)$ – position of the i-th particle in k-th iteration step,
$v_i(k)$ – velocity of the i-th particle in k-th iteration step,
$q_i(k)$ – the best position of the i-th particle found so far,
$\hat{q}_i(k)$ – the best position found so far by swarm - the position of the swarm leader,
k – iteration step.

It is very important to keep the particles diversification during the optimization process. It guarantees good exploration of the swarm to the end of the optimization process. From the other hand good exploitation involves ability of finding precise value of the global minimum when the area of its neighbourhood is found by the swarm. To achieve the mentioned abilities two additional velocity components are proposed and incorporated. To keep particles diversification during the optimization process the stochastic velocity component (VS) dependent on the maximal $V_{\max}$ and minimal $V_{\min}$ velocity of the particle is applied. To obtain a good local searching the gradient velocity component (VG) is introduced. After modification the improved PSO - VSGPSO has the velocity expression given by the following form:

$$v_{ij}(k+1) = w v_{ij}(k) + \phi_{1j}(k)\left[p_{ij}(k) - x_{ij}(k)\right] + \phi_{2j}(k)\left[\hat{p}_{ij}(k) - x_{ij}(k)\right]$$

$$+\phi_{3j}(k)(V_{\max} - V_{\min}) + \phi_{4j}(k)\left[-b^l \cdot \nabla f\left[x_{ij}(k)\right]\right],$$

$$\tag{3}$$

where: $\phi_{3j}(k)(V_{\max} - V_{\min})$ – the stochastic velocity component (VS),
$\phi_{4j}(k)\left[-b^l \cdot \nabla f\left[x_{ij}(k)\right]\right]$ – the gradient velocity component (VG),
$\phi_{1j}(k) = c_1 r_{1j}(k); \phi_{2j}(k) = c_2 r_{2j}(k); \phi_{3j}(k) = c_3 r_{3j}(k); \phi_{4j}(k) = c_4 r_{4j}(k),$
c_1, c_2, c_3, c_4 - acceleration coefficients,
r_1, r_2, r_3, r_4 - random numbers with uniform distribution [0, 1],
$l = 0, 1, 2, ..., L - 1$, L - number of the trial steps with the minus gradient direction.

According to application of the gradient component the selected particles move with the velocity dependent on the minus gradient of the fitness function. First the gradient for the particular particle is calculated. Next the trial steps of the lengths which create the geometric progression with the first term $-a\nabla f[x_{ij}(k)]$ and the common ratio b are generated ($a > 0$, $b < 1$). The steps are generated to obtain the directional minima. To decrease the risk to get into the local optima, the randomness for the gradient velocity component can be applied. Then the multiplier $\phi_{4j}(k)$ is used instead of a. So the gradient component has the following form: $\phi_{4j}(k)\left[-b^l \cdot \nabla f\left[x_{ij}(k)\right]\right]$. The fitness function values are calculated for the following trial steps. The additional gradient velocity is applied only for the swarm leader because of the computation costs connected with its application for all particles of the swarm. The movement into the fastest decrease direction may cause the convergence to the local optima. In order to minimize this disadvantage the stagnation parameter is introduced. This parameter controls the frequency of gradient applications. When the swarm finds better solution, the application of the gradient is not need. The gradient is used if there is no fitness function improvement or if the improvement is small. The stagnation parameter determine the iteration number without or with small fitness improvement after which the gradient is used.

The efficiency of the proposed modified version of particle swarm optimizer – VSGPSO can be improved by the hybridization with gradient minimization method. Then we obtain hybrid version of the VSGPSO – HVSGPSO. VSGPSO can be stopped after the declared number of iteration or after achievement of the specified fitness function value (close to global optima) and then the limited-memory Broyden-Fletcher-Goldfarb-Shanno procedure (LBFGS) [21], which is a quasi-Newton method, can be executed. The flowchart of the particle swarm optimizer after modifications and hybridization flowchart of HVSGPSO is presented in Fig. 1, which illustrates also the idea of the algorithm. At the beginning

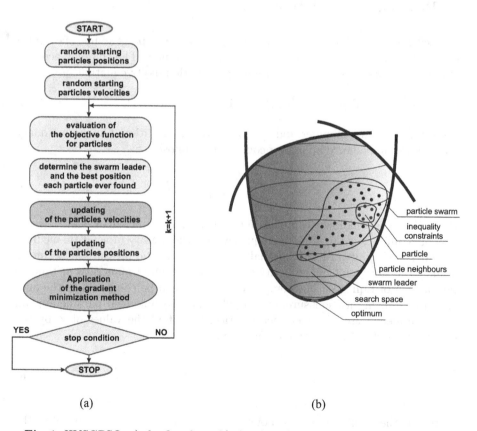

(a)   (b)

Fig. 1. HVSGPSO: a) the flowchart, b) the idea of the particle swarm algorithm

of the algorithm the particle swarm of assumed size is created randomly - starting positions and velocities of the particles are created randomly. The objective function values are evaluated for each particle. In the next step the best positions of the particles are updated and the swarm leader is chosen. Then the particles velocities are modified by means of the Eqn. (3) and particles positions are modified according to the Eqn. (2). The process is iteratively repeated until the stop condition is fulfilled. Then the gradient minimization method can be used to reduce the optimization time.

In the HVSGPSO algorithm two stages can be distinguished and gradient calculations are performed at both the stages. At the first stage, the swarm one, the gradient velocity component improves the convergence of swarm process. This stage can be considered as a concurrent swarm-gradient algorithm VSGPSO. At the second stage the swarm process is terminated and the gradient optimization algorithm is executed. At this stage a rapid convergence to the global optimum is observed. Summarizing, in this work an efficient concurrent-sequential hybrid swarm algorithm HVSGPSO is proposed.

3   Problem Formulation

A closed 2D cavity Ω with a boundary Γ is considered. A point source of complex amplitude A is located within the cavity, at the point s. The complex acoustic pressure field $p(x)$ satisfies the non-homogenous Helmholtz equation:

$$\nabla^2 p\left(x\right) + \kappa^2 p\left(x\right) = -A\delta\left(x - s\right), \quad x, s \in \Omega, \tag{4}$$

where κ is the wave number and δ is the Dirac distribution. On the boundary of cavity the impedance boundary condition is imposed:

$$p\left(x\right) = -\frac{Z}{i\omega\rho}\frac{\partial p\left(x\right)}{\partial n\left(x\right)}, \quad x \in \Gamma, \tag{5}$$

where Z is the unknown complex impedance of room (cavity) wall, i is the imaginary unit, ω is the angular frequency, ρ is the density of acoustic medium and $n(x)$ is the outward unit normal to Γ. The acoustic pressure field can be evaluated at any point of the cavity by the application of numerical method to the solution of Eqn. (4). The computed values p_j can be compared to the ones resulting from in situ measurements p_j^{meas}, and the unknown parameters can be determined. Here, the identification task is to find the values of Z by the minimization of the following cost function:

$$F = \sum_{j=1}^{J} \left|p_j - p_j^{\text{meas}}\right|^2, \tag{6}$$

where J is the number of sensor points. To solve the identification problem the VSGPSO and HVSGPSO are used.

4 The Method of Fundamental Solutions

The solution of Eq. 4 can be expressed by the sum of pressure generated by the source s of amplitude A, and a finite series corresponding to another K sources q_k with unknown coefficients c_k:

$$p(x) = AG(x,s) + \sum_{k=1}^{K} c_k G(x, q_k), \quad x \in \Omega, \ q_k \notin \Omega, \tag{7}$$

where G is the fundamental solution of the Helmholtz equation for 2-D problem:

$$G(x,q) = \frac{i}{4} H_0^{(1)} (\kappa |x - q|). \tag{8}$$

$H_0^{(1)}$ is the Hankel function of the 1st kind, order 0. Applying Eqn. (7) and the boundary condition (5) to the boundary nodes x_l, $l = 1, 2, ..., L$, one obtains the system of equations:

$$\sum_{k=1}^{K} \left[G\left(x_l', q_k\right) + \frac{Z}{i\omega\rho} \frac{\partial G\left(x_l', q_k\right)}{\partial n} \right] c_k = -A \left[G\left(x_l', s\right) + \frac{Z}{i\omega\rho} \frac{\partial G\left(x_l', s\right)}{\partial n} \right] \tag{9}$$

which is solved for the coefficients c_k. Having the values one can evaluate the pressure field at any point of the cavity by using Eqn. (7). More details on the MFS can be found in the literature [13]. In the considered problem the sensitivity analysis can be easily performed by the direct differentiation of Eqn. (9) with respect to the identified parameters.

5 Numerical Example

Complex values of impedances $Z_1 \div Z_4$ of room walls were identified. The geometry and other parameters of the room 2-D model are presented in Fig. 2. The same structure was considered by Dutilleux et al. [15]. The geometric parameters were: $a=3.4$ m and $b=2.5$ m. The acoustic media was air at the temperature $20^\circ C$. The analysis was performed for the frequency equal to 100 Hz. Eight sensors were located at points of coordinates related to the wave length λ and the room dimensions. The number of boundary points and sources was equal to 54. The sources were located at the circle of radius r = 2.5 m centered at the geometric centre of the square (Fig. 2).

The identification problem defined in Section 3 was solved by using the VS-GPSO and HVSGPSO described in Section 2. A single particle was defined by its parameters g_m ($m = 1 \div 8$) related to the real and imaginary parts of the unknown impedances:

$$Z_h = g_{2h-1} - i g_{2h}, \quad h = 1 \div 4. \tag{10}$$

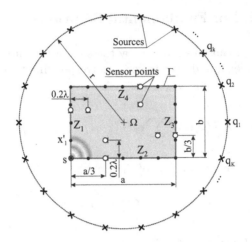

Fig. 2. Scheme of the problem solved by the MFS and the HVSGPSO

Box constrains were imposed on each particle parameter as follows:

$$0 \leq g_m \leq 20000 \ [rayl] \, , \quad m = 1 \div 8. \tag{11}$$

The pressure measurements were simulated by the MFS analysis with the reference impedance values given in Table 1. Also, a comparison of the results with results obtained by other authors [15], by using (λ, μ)-ES, for the same identification problem, are given. The evolution strategy is characterized by the parent and offspring populations of size λ and μ respectively.

The efficiency of proposed method was investigated and compared to the ES case by other authors. The comparison is given in Table 2. The number of cost function calculations in the ES was calculated assuming that the number is equal to the product of iteration number and offspring population size. In the case of VSGPSO and HVSGPSO the swarm size was set to 30. The following parameters of the VSGPSO and HVSGPSO have been introduced: w=0.73, c_1=1.47,

Table 1. Reference values of particle parameters and optimization results

Results	Reference values	(8, 56)-ES [15]	VSGPSO	HVSGPSO
g_1	4920.00	4706	4920.68	4920.00
g_2	1590.00	1591	1590.38	1590.00
g_3	2390.00	2487	2390.12	2390.00
g_4	3720.00	3756	3720.09	3720.00
g_5	3400.00	3400	3400.19	3400.00
g_6	50.00	84	50.14	50.00
g_7	3500.00	3568	3499.52	3500.00
g_8	2200.00	2174	2199.70	2200.00

Table 2. Comparison of the efficiency of the algorithms

No. of	(8, 56)-ES [15]	VSGPSO	HVSGPSO
Iterations	786	1475	98
Cost function calculations	44016	46549	3264
Gradient calculations	-	646	60
LBFGS iterations	-	-	1157

$c_2=1.47$, $c_3=0.002$, $c_4=0.1$, $b=2$, $l=10$. All the VSGPSO and HVSGPSO characteristics are mean values from 5 runs of the algorithm. The gradient calculation time was by an order of magnitude less in relation to the time of the fitness function calculation.

6 Conclusions

The solution of the inverse problem in room acoustics by using the MFS and the VSGPSO and HVSGPSO was presented. The MFS does not require the domain discretization or integration, and is convenient for the sensitivity analysis. The additional gradient velocity component does not influence significantly the overall identification time, as the computing time of gradient calculations is by an order of magnitude smaller in relation to the time of the cost function calculation. The application of the gradient velocity component and the gradient method at the final stage of the identification process by the HVSGPSO causes both the convergence and accuracy improvements. The comparison of presented results with other ones, found in literature, shows that the HVSGPSO can be more efficient than the ES and VSGPSO with respect to the accuracy of the results and the identification time, as the number of the cost function calculations is smaller. It was shown that the proposed coupling of methods provide promising results in the room impedance measurements by the solution of inverse problem. However to confirm the practical importance of the method further investigations should be carried out, involving higher frequencies, measurement errors and 3-D problems.

Acknowledgements. The research is partially financed from the Polish science budget resources as a research project no. N N501 216637.

References

1. Comino, L., Gallego, R., Rus, G.: Combining topological sensitivity and genetic algorithms for identification inverse problems in anisotropic materials. Comput. Mech. 41, 231–242 (2008)
2. Chaparro, B.M., Thullier, S., Menezes, L.F., Manach, P.Y., Fernandes, J.V.: Material parameters identification: Gradient-based, genetic and hybrid optimization. Comp. Materi. Sci. 44, 339–346 (2008)

3. Hwang, S.-F., Wu, J.-C., He, R.S.: Identification of effective elastic constants of composite plates based on a hybrid genetic algorithm. Compos. Struct. 90, 217–224 (2009)
4. Brigham, J.C., Aquino, W.: Surrogate-model accelerated random search algorithm for global optimization with applications to inverse material identification. Comput. Meth. Appl. Mech. Eng. 196, 4561–4576 (2007)
5. Poteralski, A., Szczepanik, M., Dziatkiewicz, G., Ku, W., Burczyński, T.: Immune identification of piezoelectric material constants using BEM. Inverse Probl. Sci. Eng. 19, 103–116 (2010)
6. Zilong, G., Sunan, W., Jian, Z.: A novel immune evolutionary algorithm incorporating chaos optimization. Pattern Recognit. Lett. 27, 2–8 (2006)
7. El-Dib, A., Youssef, H., El-Metwally, M., Osman, Z.: Load flow solution using hybrid particle swarm optimization. In: Proc. Int. Conf. Elect., Electron., Comput. Eng., pp. 742–746 (2004)
8. Naka, S., Genji, T., Yura, T., Fukuyama, Y.: A hybrid particle swarm optimization or distribution state estimation. IEEE Trans. Power Syst., 60–68 (2003)
9. Miranda, V., Fonseca, N.: New evolutionary particle swarm algorithm (EPSO) applied to voltage/VAR control. In: Proc. 14th Power Syst. Comput. Conf. (2002)
10. Zhang, W., Xie, X.: DEPSO: Hybrid particle swarm with differential evolution operator. In: Proc. IEEE Int. Conf. Syst., Man, Cybern., vol. 4, pp. 3816–3821 (2003)
11. Poli, R.: An Analysis of Publications on Particle Swarm Optimisation Applications. Department of Computer Science University of Essex, Technical Report CSM-469 (2007) ISSN: 1744-8050
12. Sedighizadeh, D., Masehian, E.: Particle Swarm Optimization Methods, Taxonomy and Applications. Int. J. Comput. Theory Eng. 1(5), 1793–8201 (2009)
13. Fairweather, G., Karageorghis, A., Martin, P.A.: The method of fundamental solutions for scattering and radiation problems. Eng. Anal. Bound. Elem. 27, 759–769 (2003)
14. Ptaszny, J.: Identification of room acoustic properties by the method of fundamental solutions and a hybrid evolutionary algorithm. In: Burczyński, T., Periaux, J. (eds.) Evolutionary and Deterministic Methods for Design, Optimization and Control. Applications to Industrial and Societal Problems, pp. 122–127. CIMNE, Barcelona (2011)
15. Dutilleux, G., Sgard, F.C., Kristiansen, U.R.: Low-frequency assessment of the in situ acoustic absorption of materials in rooms: an inverse problem approach using evolutionary optimization. Int. J. Numer. Meth. Eng. 53, 2143–2161 (2002)
16. Kennedy, J., Eberhart, R.C.: Swarm Intelligence. Morgamn Kauffman (2001)
17. Burczyński, T., Kuś, W., Długosz, A., Orantek, P.: Optimization and defect identification using distributed evolutionary algorithms. Eng. Appl. Artif. Intell. 17, 337–344 (2004)
18. Burczyński, T., Poteralski, A., Szczepanik, M.: Topological evolutionary computing in the optimal design of 2D and 3D structures. Eng. Optimiz. 39(7), 811–830 (2007)
19. Burczyński, T., Kuś, W., Długosz, A., Poteralski, A., Szczepanik, M.: Sequential and Distributed Evolutionary Computations in Structural Optimization. In: Rutkowski, L., Siekmann, J.H., Tadeusiewicz, R., Zadeh, L.A. (eds.) ICAISC 2004. LNCS (LNAI), vol. 3070, pp. 1069–1074. Springer, Heidelberg (2004)
20. Burczyński, T., Bereta, M., Poteralski, A., Szczepanik, M.: Immune computing: intelligent methodology and its applications in bioengineering and computational mechanics. Adv. Struct. Mater. Comput. Meth. Mech., 165–181 (2010)
21. Liu, D.C., Nocedal, J.: On the limited memory BFGS method for large-scale optimization. Math. Program. 45, 503–528 (1989)

reCORE – A Coevolutionary Algorithm for Rule Extraction

Bogdan Trawiński and Grzegorz Matoga

Wroclaw University of Technology, Instititute of Informatics,
Wybrzeże Wyspiańskiego 27, 50-350 Wrocław, Poland
{bogdan.trawinski,greg.matoga}@pwr.wroc.pl

Abstract. A coevolutionary algorithm called reCORE for rule extraction from databases was proposed in the paper. Knowledge is extracted in the form of simple implication rules IF-THEN-ELSE. There are two populations involved, one for rules and second for rule sets. Each population has a distinct evolution scheme. One individual from rule set population and a number of individuals from rule population contribute to final result. Populations are synchronized to keep the cross-references up to date. The concept of the algorithm and the results of comparative research are presented. A cross-validation is used for examination, and the final conclusions are drawn based upon statistically analyzed results. They state that, the effectiveness of the reCORE algorithm is comparable to other rule classifiers, such as Ridor or JRip.

Keywords: evolutionary algorithm, coevolution, rule learning, cross-validation.

1 Introduction

Rule extraction, from computational complexity point of view, is a NP task. Evolutionary algorithms are well suited for NP tasks in the sense, they explore a vast amount of possible solutions in a short time yielding suboptimal solutions. Moreover, since no strictly optimal solution is to be found, any good solution is valued. Detailed discussion on this topic can be found in publications [9], [3].

Many evolutionary algorithms for classification tasks have been proposed so far. Some, such as XCS [16] and GIL [8] are known and used for more than a decade. Genetic Algorithms, since their first introduction by J. Holland in [6], have been studied and extended widely.

J. Holland was one of the first researchers to use evolution for rule extraction. In the work [7] he proposed an encoding scheme later to be known as the Michigan approach. Every individual in a population represented exactly one rule. The same encoding type was used in Supervised Learning Algorithm [15] and GCCL [4]. Ken De Jong and Steve Smith [12] later popularized another encoding scheme where each individual encoded a whole set of rules. Another example of the approach is the Genetic Inductive Learning by Janikow [8]. GIL is also interesting because of unusually high number of recombination operators: 13 (the classic approach only two: mutation and crossover).

L. Rutkowski et al. (Eds.): SIDE 2012 and EC 2012, LNCS 7269, pp. 395–403, 2012.

Genetic algorithms have been studied and developed in many directions, but the coevolution is far from being completely exploited. One noteworthy work on the topic is [14] by Tan et al. where CORE algorithm was introduced. This work is an attempt to expand on the CORE algorithm. And while conceptual view of the algorithms is the same, they vary much in detail. Also, the rule set population was modelled after the CAREX [11], [10] algorithm. reCORE builds on both of these adding additional evolution enhancing procedures.

The main objective of this work is to present reCORE – a learning algorithm, which extracts knowledge in an easily interpretable, explicit form, and which is driven by a specific type of evolution: coevolution. It was implemented in Java and adapted to WEKA [5] – an environment for knowledge acquisition. This allowed to compare the performance of the coevolutionary algorithm with a few competing algorithms.

2   Description of the Proposed Coevolutionary GA

reCORE is a an algorithm for knowledge acquisition based on cooperative co-evolution. It comprises two chromosome populations involved in evolution. First one consists of individuals representing final result: a rule set. The second population includes individuals representing a single rule. Each rule set individual refers to a number of rule individuals. The two populations are tightly coupled (fig. 1).

Each rule takes a form of:

```
If (Attr1 Op1 Value1) and (Attr2 Op2 Value2) and ... then class1
```

Each conjunction component can be omitted. $Attr_i$ refers to the i-th attribute of source data set. For instance, if source data set has following attributes [wind, sun, rain] than $Attr_1$ is wind, $Attr_2$ is sun and so on. Both Op_j and $Value_j$ depend on the type of source attribute. If it is nominal then $Op_j \in \{'=', '\neq'\}$ and $Value_j$ is an element out of attribute domain. Possible conjunction component interpretation could be: "wind is strong" or "sun does not shine".

If the attribute's domain is numerical then $Op_j \in \{IN, NOT\_IN\}$ and $Value_j$ takes a form of a closed range. In the case, possible conjunction component interpretation could be "temperature is between 5 and 10 degrees Celsius" or "temperature is lower than 0 or higher than 20 degrees Celsius" (temp NOT_IN [0, 20]).

This rule form allows expressing the example fact:

```
If sun shines and temperature is between 15 and 25 degrees
Celsius then play.
```

The result is undefined if the premises are not met. By combining rules in an ordered manner and by defining the default class a much more expressive form is obtained. Example:

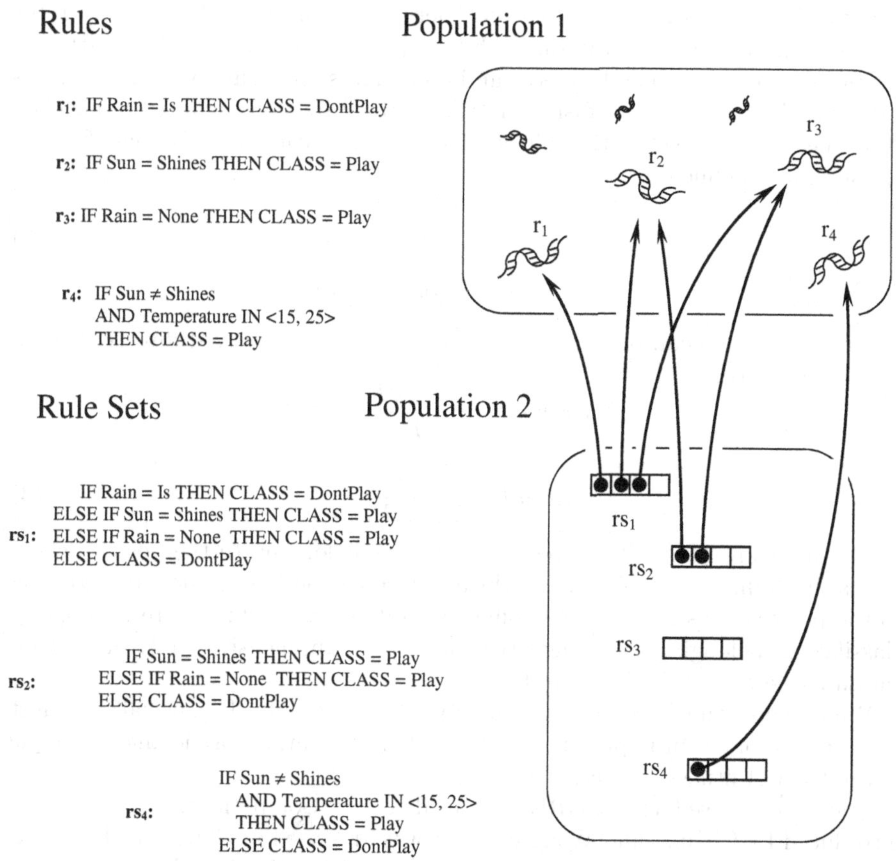

Rules   Population 1

r₁: IF Rain = Is THEN CLASS = DontPlay

r₂: IF Sun = Shines THEN CLASS = Play

r₃: IF Rain = None THEN CLASS = Play

r₄: IF Sun ≠ Shines
    AND Temperature IN <15, 25>
    THEN CLASS = Play

Rule Sets   Population 2

rs₁: IF Rain = Is THEN CLASS = DontPlay
       ELSE IF Sun = Shines THEN CLASS = Play
       ELSE IF Rain = None THEN CLASS = Play
       ELSE CLASS = DontPlay

rs₂: IF Sun = Shines THEN CLASS = Play
       ELSE IF Rain = None THEN CLASS = Play
       ELSE CLASS = DontPlay

rs₄: IF Sun ≠ Shines
       AND Temperature IN <15, 25>
       THEN CLASS = Play
       ELSE CLASS = DontPlay

Fig. 1. Cooperative evolution implemented in reCORE – a conceptual representation and mapping

```
If sun shines then play.
If it does not rain then play.
Do not play.
```

This is the rule set, which is represented by the second population. It is interpreted sequentially. From the implementation point of view, all rule sets (formally *lists*, but the term set is more commonly used) are represented as a list of pointers to rules and the default class type.

Rule sets in reCORE are encoded using decimal, variable-length gene representation. Rules, quite contrary, use binary, fixed-length code. To summarize, reCORE uses a hybrid of Pittsburgh and Michigan coding approaches for first and second population, respectively. Also, two different encoding types are used. It is due to a synchronization procedure, which operates on the rule set population and updates pointers after any possibly destructive operation on the rule population.

Let us focus now on rule population. There is only one recombination operator in place: simple binary mutation. Each gene (bit) can be mutated (flipped) with the probability p_{mut}. The fitness of an individual is an accuracy measure calculated based on a binary confusion matrix obtained by focusing at only one class at a time – the same class the rule is referring to. *F-score* is used a classification measure, it is defined as:

$$F_{score} = \frac{1}{\dfrac{1}{precision} + \dfrac{1}{recall}}. \tag{1}$$

It is a harmonic mean of two terms, both of which are derived directly from a confusion matrix:

$$Precision = \frac{TP}{TP + FP}, \tag{2}$$

$$Recall = \frac{TP}{TP + FN}. \tag{3}$$

TP is the count of results correctly labelled as belonging to the positive class. FP is the count of negative cases which were improperly classified as belonging to the positive class. FN is the count of positive cases which were improperly classified as belonging to the negative class. A comprehensive study on classification measures can be found in [13].

While there is no direct interaction between the rules itself, a special care must be taken to maintain population diversity. For the purpose a niching technique in the form of fitness correction is used.

The scheme used in reCORE is named Token Competition, and was first introduced by Cheung and Wong in [2]. It was also used in CORE by Tan et al. [14] The rules from one generation are being selected to the other by the means of tournament selection. Technically, it is implemented by adjusting the individual's fitness:

$$f' = f \times \frac{T_C}{T_T}. \tag{4}$$

The term T_C is a number of tokens captured by the individual, which fitness f is being modified. T_T is a total number of tokens to capture, within a given class.

The rule population resembles many other Michigan-type schemes. Its purpose is to maintain a pool of the best (by the means of fitness) and the most diverse rules possible. The rule set population is responsible for taking them and combine in a best possible way to form a final classifier. Much care is taken in the synchronization of the populations. This is why the crossover operator was neglected – much of the pointers would have been invalidated otherwise. Mutation does not introduce the threat. Any rule after mutation still much resembles the rule before so no pointer adjustment is needed because of that. It is only selection that can disrupt the best solution at the rule set level. In practice however, it is possible to update some pointers accordingly. Nothing can be done if the rule was dropped from one generation to the other – pointer also must be dropped. In the other case, a simple pointer update can restore the rule set to its primary state. And it is necessary for the evolution to function properly in the second population.

The elitist strategy, in the rule set population, has some impact on the rule population. In order to maintain an individual unchanged during the generation change each rule referred must be kept safe from mutation and must be selected in tournament.

3 Plan of Evaluation Experiment

All experiments were conducted in the Waikato Environment for Knowledge Acquisition – WEKA. reCORE can be plugged into WEKA to see it as a classifier plugin. This allowed for a comparison with a broad selection of easily available competitive algorithms.

Algorithms were assessed using benchmark datasets – taken from the UCI Machine Learning Repository [1]. Basic parameters of the datasets are provided in 1. For the performance comparison 12 datasets are used. They cover a wide range of possible problems encountered in real world machine learning schemes. We opted for the most diverse set of characteristics.

Table 1. Details of data sets used for comparative study

dataset	no. of examples	class distribution	class total	attribute numeric	nominal	total
diabetes	768	500/268	2	8	-	8
ecoli	336	143/77/52/35/20/5/2/2	8	7	-	7
haberman	306	225/81	2	2	1	3
hayes roth	132	51/51/30/0	4	4	-	4
iris	150	50/50/50	3	4	-	4
lymphography	148	2/81/61/4	4	2	16	18
monks1	124	62/62	2	-	5	5
monks2	169	105/64	2	-	5	5
monks3	122	62/60	2	-	5	5
tae	151	49/50/52	3	3	2	2
wine	178	59/71/48	3	13	-	13
zoo	101	41/20/5/13/4/8/10	7	-	17	17

The maximum number of generations was determined by preliminary test runs. Maximum number of rules was set as a compromise between the size of the search space, and the representation scheme's ability to express the most diverse rule possible.

The rule mutation probability was set according the guidance provided in the GA literature. The value of where the value of approximately 1% is considered to be the most optimal.

Table 2. Parameter listing for each tested algorithm

Algorithm	Parameters
reCORE coevolutionary rule extractor	elite selection size = 1, generations = 10000, max rules count = 12, rule mutation probability = 0.02, rule population size = 200, rule set mutation probability = 0.02, rule set population size = 200, selection type = tournament of size 2, token competition enabled = true
DTable decision tables	cross validation = leave one out, evaluation measure = accuracy, search = best first search, search direction = forward, search termination = 5
DTNB Decision Table with Naive Bayes	cross validation = leave one out, evaluation measure = accuracy, search = backwards with delete, use IBk = false
JRip Repeated Incremental Pruning	check error rate = true, folds = 3, min total weight = 2, optimizations = 2, use pruning = true
PART decision list	binary splits = false, confidence factor = 0.25, minimum instances per rule = 2, number of folds = 3, reduced error pruning = false, pruning = false
Ridor RIpple-DOwn Rule learner	number of folds = 3, majority class = false, minimum weight = 2, shuffle = 1, whole data error = false

Population size was set to a number, which allowed most of the runs to last no longer than few minute.

As the tournament size was chosen value 2. Value 0 effectively means a random (blind) selection, which is not very useful. Value 1 is equivalent to a roulette-type selection which has been proven to be inferior to tournament.

One of the most important parameter is the size of an elite selection. If the elitist selection was not applied then the high selective pressure would destroy most of the good solutions. A value 1 was set. It's the value that has the least intrusive impact on other evolutionary operations.

As a fitness function, the F-score was selected. It provides the best characteristics needed in an evolutionary setting.

A summary or run parameters, for every algorithm in comparison, is presented in table 2. Each of the algorithms approach classification task in many ways, e.g. using a divide & conquer strategy, heuristics, Naive Bayes theorem or tree pruning. All of the approaches share common classifier representation, i.e. rule list.

4   Experimental Results

Averaged results of each cross validation run are presented in table 3. In each cell there is a F-score value. Values in parentheses indicate the ranking of an algorithm with respect to a particular dataset. Last row contains averages over all datasets.

Table 3. Mean averages obtained from 5-fold cross-validation repeated 10 times. Number in parenthesis denotes the rank for a given dataset.

Dataset	reCORE	DTable	DTNB	JRip	PART	Ridor	ZeroR
ecoli	0.786 (5)	0.748 (6)	0.806 (2)	0.797 (4)	0.822 (1)	0.799 (3)	0.254 (7)
haberman	0.693 (2)	0.657 (6)	0.665 (5)	0.700 (1)	0.674 (4)	0.677 (3)	0.623 (7)
hayes-roth	0.560 (3)	0.359 (5.5)	0.359 (5.5)	0.515 (4)	0.595 (1)	0.581 (2)	0.208 (7)
iris	0.933 (6)	0.935 (5)	0.941 (2.5)	0.937 (4)	0.941 (2.5)	0.943 (1)	0.167 (7)
lymph	0.761 (3)	0.735 (6)	0.750 (5)	0.756 (4)	0.769 (2)	0.776 (1)	0.387 (7)
monks1	0.409 (3)	0.418 (2)	0.434 (1)	0.407 (5)	0.408 (4)	0.397 (6)	0.389 (7)
monks2	0.584 (1)	0.491 (4)	0.497 (3)	0.459 (5)	0.518 (2)	0.429 (6)	0.330 (7)
monks3	0.392 (6)	0.460 (2)	0.487 (1)	0.439 (3)	0.416 (4)	0.398 (5)	0.352 (7)
diabetes	0.736 (3.5)	0.739 (2)	0.743 (1)	0.736 (3.5)	0.735 (5)	0.713 (6)	0.513 (7)
tae	0.552 (1)	0.364 (6)	0.381 (5)	0.410 (4)	0.526 (2)	0.465 (3)	0.177 (7)
wine	0.891 (5)	0.873 (6)	0.960 (1)	0.920 (3)	0.921 (2)	0.919 (4)	0.228 (7)
zoo	0.899 (4)	0.851 (5)	0.909 (3)	0.822 (6)	0.927 (1)	0.912 (2)	0.235 (7)
mean rank	**3.542**	**4.625**	**2.917**	**3.875**	**2.542**	**3.500**	**7.000**

Table 4. Final algorithm Friedman ranking

	PART	DTNB	Ridor	reCORE	JRip	DTable	ZeroR	Score
PART		#	#	#	#	#	+	1
DTNB	#		#	#	#	#	+	1
Ridor	#	#		#	#	#	+	1
reCORE	#	#	#		#	#	+	1
JRip	#	#	#	#		#	+	1
DTable	#	#	#	#	#		#	0
ZeroR	-	-	-	-	-	#		0

The averages over all sets was used to perform a Friedman statistical test. Statistics according to Friedman's chi-square for 6 degrees of freedom: 33.86 (limit value: 14.45). Iman and Davenport statistics according to the F statistic at 6 and 66 degrees of freedom: 9.76 (threshold value: 2.24). Statistics are greater than the limit, so the hypothesis of equal average was rejected. Thus, pairwise comparison can take place. Results of pairwise comparison are presented in table 4.

For a given cell, an algorithm in the same row is better than the algorithm in the same column when there is a + character. If it is worse than the - character is used. Ties are denoted with a hash mark. In the last column a score for an algorithm in respective row is presented. The higher the score the better the algorithm.

As can be seen in the table 4, there is no single best solution. Most of the algorithms perform with a similar performance, with an exception of ZeroR and DTable.

5   Conclusion

The aim of this study was to verify the applicability of evolutionary algorithms to classification tasks. There are many approaches to the use of evolutionary mechanisms for classification tasks; this work however, was focused on coevolution. reCORE's strongest point is the ability to maintain synchronization of two concurrently evolving populations in the face of rapid and possibly destructive changes.

reCORE was implemented in the Knowledge Acquisition Environment – WEKA in order to compare its performance with other rule extracting algorithms. A set of the most effective parameters was determined in a preliminary study. Once the best set was known a comparative assessment was conducted. A classification score achieved by reCORE and 6 other rule extracting algorithms over 12 datasets was collected. The results were subject to a statistical analysis: Friedman rank was calculated and non-parametric post hoc procedures adequate for multiple comparisons were conducted.

No statistically significant difference was shown between most of the algorithms. Only ZeroR was proven to give substantially worse results from every other rule extraction algorithm in WEKA and reCORE as well. It comes without a surprise since ZeroR is a benchmarking algorithm. If any other algorithm were giving worse results than ZeroR then most probably it would be broken.

The performance difference between algorithms is negligible. It might be because of the nature of datasets. They were chosen to be diverse in their characteristics. If only one type of domain were to be chosen, then the results could differ in favour of a one particular algorithm. It also might be the case that all of them pushed the boundaries of what is possible with rule classifier representation.

reCORE is one of many possible extensions of a evolutionary algorithm. It shows how two different species can cooperate and provide good overall solution. The specialisation allows the use of rule representation specific operators. It presents a framework, on top of which any representation with nested relations may be subject to evolutionary optimisation.

Acknowledgments. This work was funded partially by the Polish National Science Centre under the grant no. N N516 483840.

References

1. Frank, A., Asuncion, A.: UCI machine learning repository (2010)
2. Freitas, A.A.: Book review: Data mining using grammar-based genetic programming and applications. Genetic Programming and Evolvable Machines 2, 197–199 (2001), doi:10.1023/A:1011564616547
3. Giordana, A., Saitta, L., Zini, F.: Learning disjunctive concepts with distributed genetic algorithms. In: International Conference on Evolutionary Computation 1994, pp. 115–119 (1994)
4. Greene, D.P., Smith, S.F.: Competition-based induction of decision models from examples. Mach. Learn. 13, 229–257 (1993)

5. Hall, M., Frank, E., Holmes, G., Pfahringer, B., Reutemann, P., Witten, I.H.: The weka data mining software: an update. SIGKDD Explor. Newsl. 11, 10–18 (2009)
6. Holland, J.H.: Outline for a logical theory of adaptive systems. J. ACM 9, 297–314 (1962)
7. Holland, J.H.: Adaptation in Natural and Artificial Systems: An Introductory Analysis with Applications to Biology, Control, and Artificial Intelligence. A Bradford Book (April 1992)
8. Janikow, C.Z.: A knowledge-intensive genetic algorithm for supervised learning. Mach. Learn. 13, 189–228 (1993)
9. Jourdan, L., Basseur, M., Talbi, E.-G.: Hybridizing exact methods and metaheuristics: A taxonomy. European Journal of Operational Research 199(3), 620–629 (2009)
10. Myszkowski, P.B.: Coevolutionary algorithm for rule induction. In: IMCSIT, pp. 73–79 (2010)
11. Myszkowski, P.B.: Rule Induction Based-On Coevolutionary Algorithms for Image Annotation. In: Nguyen, N.T., Kim, C.-G., Janiak, A. (eds.) ACIIDS 2011, Part II. LNCS, vol. 6592, pp. 232–241. Springer, Heidelberg (2011)
12. Smith, S.F.: Flexible learning of problem solving heuristics through adaptive search. In: Proceedings of the Eighth International Joint Conference on Artificial Intelligence, vol. 1, pp. 422–425. Morgan Kaufmann Publishers Inc., San Francisco (1983)
13. Sokolova, M., Lapalme, G.: A systematic analysis of performance measures for classification tasks. Information Processing & Management 45(4), 427–437 (2009)
14. Tan, K.C., Yu, Q., Ang, J.H.: A coevolutionary algorithm for rules discovery in data mining. International Journal of Systems Science 37(12), 835–864 (2006)
15. Venturini, G.: SIA: A supervised inductive algorithm with genetic search for learning attributes based concepts, pp. 280–296 (1993)
16. Wilson, S.W.: Classifier fitness based on accuracy. Evol. Comput. 3, 149–175 (1995)

MGPSO – The Managed Evolutionary Optimization

Radosław Z. Ziembiński

Institute of Computing Science, Poznan University of Technology,
ul. Piotrowo 2, 60–965 Poznań, Poland
radoslaw.ziembinski@cs.put.poznan.pl

Abstract. This paper introduces a new modular algorithm MGPSO. It merges random probing, new particle swarm optimization and local search algorithms. The proposed algorithm was implemented according to a new proposal of modular architecture. It allows for flexible mixing different techniques of the optimization in a single optimization. The architecture allows to macro–manage the search process by modifiable set of rules. Thus, a selection of suitable tools for different phases of the optimization depending on current requirements is possible. As a consequence, the modular algorithm achieves good performance acknowledged in performed experiments. The proposed architecture can help in application of machine learning methods for the selection of efficient sequence of tools during the optimization.

Keywords: Particle Swarm Optimization, Local Search, Managed Optimization.

1 Introduction

The "no–free lunch" metaphor is frequently cited along new proposals of optimization algorithms. It describes a sort of trade–off between the global and the local search that is differently respected by different algorithms. Therefore, these algorithms show various performance for groups of problems defined according to specific requirements for the search process. Beside that, the "no–free lunch" metaphor teaches also about another important matter. Any optimization algorithm has to carefully select and evaluate new solutions from the search space. Hence, it should avoid a para–random flurry in the solutions generation which is possibly the most robust method in avoidance of local optima. But it also has intrinsically low convergence of the search process. Additionally, careless solutions generation is particularly inefficient for highly dimensional problems because the search space is growing geometrically to the number of dimensions. Thus, the probing intensity should grow similarly to balance the space growth. Finally, the solution evaluation is often the most costly process from the computational perspective in practical applications. Therefore, the evolutionary algorithm has to use the evaluation method advisedly.

Hence, macro–management on the level of the algorithms' selection for special purpose exploration of the search space and the micro–management of the search

L. Rutkowski et al. (Eds.): SIDE 2012 and EC 2012, LNCS 7269, pp. 404–412, 2012.

process on the level of particular algorithm operations are studied together in this paper. This paper describes a new MGPSO (Macro–manaGed PSO) algorithm having following features:

- A modular architecture relying on tasks queue and modules realizing particular algorithms. The queue based processing allows for flexible implementation of the breadth–first and depth–first search paradigms in the optimization. Moreover, particular optimization modules may dynamically modify the task queue content according to requirements.
- Modular integration of exploration methods e.g., particle swarm optimization, local search and random probing. They are executed like plug–ins according to rules.
- New proposals of the particle swarm optimization and the local search algorithms.

This paper begins from a short introduction to related works. Then the MGPSO architecture is presented. Afterward the particle swarm optimization algorithm is described along a brief description of the proposed local search method. Finally, some results from experiments are introduced and concluded at the end.

2 Related Works

The particle swarm optimization method is general purpose optimization method introduced in [1]. This method uses a population of particles exchanging knowledge about the search space. The particles interact by forces exchange in a similar manner like electric charges exchange photons in the plasma. Therefore, main components in the information exchange are force strength and direction. The advantage of this method lies in good global convergence. It can find a region with better fitness values than the neighborhood quite fast. Unfortunately, it also has quite a low performance in exploring fine and strongly diversified landscapes in the neighborhood of the global optimum. This happens partially because particles in the basic version of the algorithm converge quickly to the same location in the search space.

Dozens of extensions have been developed to overcome the basic algorithm limitations. They can be divided into two categories. The first studies have proposed different extensions to the basic algorithm equations by introduction of the swarm center of "gravity" [2] springs [4], dampers [8] mechanics and many others. These techniques prevent from the premature convergence by application of improved equations defining particles interactions. Meanwhile, some other studies have proposed hybrids with other evolutionary optimization methods e.g., genetic algorithms [3], differential evolution [5], tabu search [7], harmony search [6]. These hybrid algorithms have inherited many advantages from constituents. Hence, they are have good performance in the local neighborhood search and inherit good global performance from the original PSO algorithm.

The solution proposed in this paper belongs to the second group. However, it implements modular rule–based architecture instead of melting different solutions into a single algorithm. It tries to select an appropriate tool in a particular search context. Thus, it prefers to choose among masters in particular disciplines instead of using a single algorithm aspirating to be the master in all disciplines at once.

3 Algorithm Description

The MGPSO algorithm uses queue to schedule four different optimization methods. They are the random probing of the whole search space, the particle swarm optimization (PSOMethod), the random local neighborhood search and local search by a gradient walking (LocalSearch). The random probing (GlobalRProb) probes wholes search space with a tries number proportional to the number of dimensions. The local random probing (LocalRProb) is done around a selected point within limited effective range with an intensity dependent on the number of dimensions.

In the main loop (iterateMain), the managing algorithm fetches from the queue a scheduled task. Then, it launches its optimization procedure iteratively until the task implementing module decides that it has finished the processing. Each module is programmed as a state machine that should perform at most one solution evaluation per iteration. If the active task finishes then a following task is fetched from the queues head and the processing continues. During the processing the queue may become empty. Then, the initial task would be inserted again and the processing repeats to use left iterations. The active task may modify the queue by creating and scheduling new tasks or removing some existing ones. Thus, the breadth–fist and the depth–first strategies are realized by inserting new tasks to the head or tail of the queue. The scheduled tasks are interconnected by three–like structure defining the search context (e.g., a center of the processing, bounds, an intensity of the exploration). The structure helps children tasks in the accessing parents data or methods.

```
procedure iterateMain:
P1: if not T.isActive() then
        fetch T from queue // fetch task T
        if T is null
            queue.add(new GlobalRProb); goto P1
    else
        T.iterate()
```

The dependencies between modules that are scheduled during the search in experimental evaluation are following:

```
GlobalRProb   -> for the best k results schedule LocalSearch
                for the best result globally schedule LocalSearchSens
                for the best k results schedule PSOMethod
PSOMethod     -> for the best result locally schedule LocalRProb
                if found for the best globally schedule LocalSearchSens
LocalRProb    -> for the best result locally schedule LocalSearch
```

The rules scheduling tasks are fixed in the experimental example. However, different dynamic conditional mechanisms were studied along some other modules used in the processing. The LocalSearchSens method differs from LocalSearch in the processing way. It does more aggressively the local search delivering a more precise result for a close neighborhood. According to these example rules, MGPSO begins from the random probing and then executes the local search for the optimum. Thus, in case of flat and simple search spaces it finds the best solution quickly. But, if it fails then it uses PSO to locate "promising" regions in fitness landscape according to the space gradients. Afterwards, the local random probing and the following local search are executed for localized regions. During this exploration, if a better solution was found globally by PSO method then the more sensitive local search is dynamically scheduled to explore for better solutions at this location. All tasks are scheduled in the breadth–first manner to better explore the search space.

4 PSO Algorithm Pseudo–code

The implemented new particle swarm optimization algorithm uses following procedure to induce the motion of particles:

```
Fitness normalization:
```
$$N_{\text{fit}}(E) = \left(\frac{s_1 \cdot (E - E_{\text{best}})}{\epsilon + E_{\text{best}}} \right)^{s_2}$$
```
    where: E ∈ [0;∞) - evaluation, E_best - globally the best evaluation,
```
$s_1 > 0$, $s_2 \in [0;1]$
```
Force calculation:
```
$$F(\text{p1, p2, } \rho, \ \delta, \ \lambda) = \ \rho \cdot (\text{p1.mass} + \text{p2.mass}) \cdot \delta \cdot e^{-|\lambda|}$$
```
Damping radius:
```
$$D_R(\text{p, } r) = \frac{radius}{s_3} \cdot \left(1 - \frac{size_{\max} - \text{p.vaporization}}{size_{\max}} \right)$$
```
    where: s₃ > 0
```
where: $s_3 > 0$

```
procedure iteratePSO:
    // stop conditions if no improvement of threshold crossed
    if (swarm.noNewSolution() and swarm.ls.noNewSolution()) or
        r < s₁₀ · rₘₐₓ or swarm.noMovement() then state=finished; return
    // resume local search if no recent swarm center update
    if swarm.isQuiet() then swarm.ls.iterate(); return
    if swarm.isDead() then swarm.reinitializeSwarm(maxsize, r); return
    // calculations are done once per cycle
    if p == 0 then swarm.calculateForces()
    swarm.moveParticle(p++) // one evaluation per iteration
    if p>swarm.maxParticles then p = 0
    r = s₇ · r // search radius reduction

procedure calculateForces:
    inF = 0; outF = 0 // compressing and repulsive forces
    for each p from swarm.Particles do
        p.size-=1; p.markDeadIfVaporizedOrOutOfBounds();
    for each alive p in swarm.Particles do
        // force from swarm center (locally the best solution)
        direction=normalizedVector(p, swarm.center)
```

```
f = r_min/s8 // constant force to swarm center
p.force.addScaledVector(direction, f)
// process other particles
d_r = D_R(p, r)
for each alive q in swarm.Particles.copy() different from p
    direction=normalizedVector(p, q) // begin, end
    δ=euclideanDistance(p, q)
    λ=N_fit(p.sum)  - N_fit(q.sum)
    f = F(p, q, ρ, δ, λ) // calculate force
    if λ < 0 then
        if δ < d_r then f = -f; out_F+ = f else in_F+ = -f
    else f = s4 · f; out_F+ = f
    p.force.addScaledVector(direction, f) // accumulates forces
// calibrate new ρ value to balance total swarm's energy
p.force.scale(s9 - (1 - s9) · (1 - e^{-dimensionality}))) // friction
if in_F > 0 then
    if out_F/in_F > (s4 + s5) then
        ρ = ρ/s6; ρ = limit(ρ, ρ_max, ρ_min)
    else if out_F/in_F < (s4 - s5) then
        ρ = ρ · s6; ρ = limit(ρ, ρ_max, ρ_min)
l_max=max(l_max, p.force.length())
// gluing involves the mass transfer and forces integration
swarm.Particles.glueCloseParticles(r_glue);

procedure moveParticle(p):
    oldsum = p.sum // p.sum is to amortize rapid changes of the fitness
    s=limit(v_max/l_max, v_max, v_min)
    // randomly probe path around particle path direction
    q=p.produceRandomNeighbourInHypercone(α, p.force, s)
    evaluate(q)
    p.position.move(p.force, s)
    evaluate(p) // evaluate() also updates swarm center
                // and globally the best solution if it was found
    if q.E<p.E then p=q // replace p if q is better
                // and adjust the new particle force vector
    p.sum = s11 · oldsum + (1 - s11) · p.E
```

Constants calibration from experiments:

$s_1 = 10$, $s_2 = 0.1$, $s_3 = 10$, $s_4 = 0.2$, $s_5 = 0.1$, $s_6 = 1.2$, $s_7 = 0.9995$, $s_8 = 0.5$, $s_9 = 0.99$, $s_{10} = 0.75$, $s_{11} = 0.8$, $\alpha = 0.26°$, $r_{glue} = 0.0005$, $\rho_{max} = 10000$, $\rho_{min} = 0.0001$, $r_{min} = 0.01$, $r_{max} = 0.5$, $size_{max} = 80$, $v_{max} = 0.08$, $v_{min} = 0.00125$

It is easy to notice that proposed equations do not have strong analogy to the nature. Certainly, the strict resemblance is not necessary in the abstract world where rules of interaction are not constrained by many physical phenomena and limitations. However, it is important to determine to what extend these rules address requirements of the optimization. The proposed algorithm has a lot of constants that allows for the tuning of the properties of forces interacting between particles. But the high number of parameters is not a disadvantage if they do not have to be notoriously modified for each problem separately. Hence, this configuration was unchanged for all described experiments. The algorithm finds minimum of the goal function and it operates on the normalized $0-1$ search space. It helped to avoid some problems related to differently sized dimensions in particles movement equations.

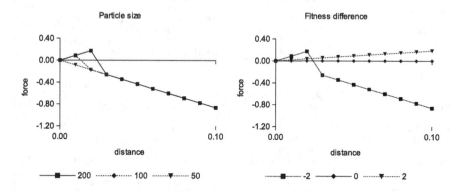

Fig. 1. Force's responses for particle's different size and difference of fitness values (for $size = 150$) - positive values mean repulsion

In the proposed solution, particles interact by exchanging forces between them. They are also pulled by the swarm center being constantly updated by the swarm if locally better solutions were found. This PSO algorithm has a low sensitive local search method implemented for the optimization of the center of the swarm. In the proposed solution the particles have sizes that reduce during the swarm life–cycle due to "vaporization". Their sizes have impact on repulsive forces between particles. Additionally, the forces also depend on the mass of particles. Two closely located particles may glue together to form a single one what involves momentums integration. During the swarm lifetime, the particles become more active and close together but the forces are increasing. Thus, the growing swarm mobility must be dynamically regulated by the ρ variable. The forces between particles are illustrated in Fig. 1.

In the course of the optimization the particle may die if it has vaporized or it was glued to any other particle. The swarm is randomly reinitialized if only a single particle has left or the whole swarm died. However, the reinitialization radius is reducing during the search process. Thus, a new swarm explores the search space more locally.

The local search algorithm finds the most slanted direction by the neighborhood probing. Afterwards, it walks along this path with growing steps until further improvement of the fitness is not possible. Then, the slope finding and the following walking are repeated but with a smaller radius until the radius sensitivity threshold is exceeded. Some flexibility was added to walking down the slope because the algorithm randomly probes the neighborhood along the

Table 1. Results from experiments

Function	Algorithm	Evaluations Max.	Performed (avg.)	Error Average	Std. dev.	Best	Success rate
Griewank:	SPSO'11	4000	4000	4.72E-03	4.32E-03	9.93E-10	0
d=2, b=[-600;600]	DEPSO		4060	7.62E-03	4.59E-03	1.16E-04	0
	MGPSO		3943	3.53E-02	3.11E-02	0.00E+00	4.5
Tripod:	SPSO'11	20000	8831.2	1.36E-01	3.39E-01	8.68E-06	82
d=2; b=[-100;100]	DEPSO		12600	6.00E-01	6.71E-01	4.91E-06	50.5
	MGPSO		1719.7	6.65E-05	2.37E-05	3.15E-06	100
Rastrigin:	SPSO'11	4000	4000	2.27E-05	2.11E-04	1.96E-11	0
d=2; b=[-5.12;5.12]	DEPSO		4060	8.00E-04	1.22E-03	2.87E-07	0
	MGPSO		3571.1	2.14E-01	4.09E-01	0.00E+00	33.5
Neumaier:	SPSO'11	80000	80000	2.60E+02	3.24E+02	2.19E+01	0
d=40; b=[-d², d²]	DEPSO		80010	3.31E+03	3.11E+03	9.30E+01	0
	MGPSO		80016.5	3.59E+02	4.47E+02	2.26E+01	0
G3:	SPSO'11	680000	309365.4	9.09E-07	8.89E-08	5.70E-07	100
d=10; b=[0;1]	DEPSO		27875.4	8.47E-07	1.34E-07	2.56E-07	100
	MGPSO		679926.9	7.42E-06	4.70E-06	9.10E-07	0.5
Schwefel:	SPSO'11	120000	120000	5.06E+03	7.69E+02	2.80E+03	0
d=30; b=[-500, 500]	DEPSO		120050	2.59E+03	6.85E+02	1.01E+03	0
	MGPSO		120014.1	4.00E+03	3.72E+02	2.77E+03	0
Schaffer:	SPSO'11	60000	5570.2	6.06E-05	2.93E-05	2.35E-07	100
d=2; b=[-100;100]	DEPSO		12902.1	4.90E-04	2.00E-03	9.65E-07	95.5
	MGPSO		50249.9	6.43E-03	4.58E-03	1.96E-08	34
Step:	SPSO'11	5000	2198.4	0.00E+00	0.00E+00	0.00E+00	100
d=10; b=[-100; 100]	DEPSO		5039.3	4.65E+00	3.62E+00	0.00E+00	2
	MGPSO		2299.9	5.00E-02	2.40E-01	0.00E+00	95.5
Gear train:	SPSO'11	40000	22407.4	1.13E-11	4.84E-11	8.57E-16	66.5
d=4; b=[12; 60]	DEPSO		18567.1	5.40E-14	5.31E-14	4.31E-16	97
	MGPSO		783.4	4.77E-14	2.85E-14	6.63E-16	100
Perm:	SPSO'11	20000	13692.1	2.46E+02	3.03E+02	0.00E+00	52
d=5; b=[-d; d]	DEPSO		20020	6.00E+01	1.52E+02	5.90E-05	0
	MGPSO		20002.5	3.06E+01	9.48E+01	2.82E-02	0
Shifted Sphere	SPSO'11	2000	2000	7.02E+02	3.39E+00	1.68E+00	0
(CEC2005 F1):	DEPSO		2030	6.96E+02	2.57E+02	1.71E+02	0
d=10; b=[-100;100]	MGPSO		2001.3	2.75E-03	4.64E-03	3.47E-05	0
Shifted Rosenbrock	SPSO'11	200000	134384.7	4.12E+01	1.18E+02	9.91E-03	65
(CEC2005 F6):	DEPSO		41925.1	3.07E-01	1.05E+00	3.90E-03	92.5
d=10; b=[-100;100]	MGPSO		105007.5	1.08E-02	7.73E-03	7.43E-03	98.5
Shifted Rastrigin	SPSO'11	200000	200000	5.09E+00	1.98E+00	9.95E-01	0
(CEC2005 F9):	DEPSO		200060	5.34E+00	2.60E+00	9.95E-01	0
d=10; b=[-5.12; 5.12]	MGPSO		200001.9	6.49E+00	2.21E+00	1.99E+00	0
Schwefel:	SPSO'11	200000	10240.2	8.90E-05	9.70E-06	5.25E-05	100
(CEC2005 F2)	DEPSO		20606.6	7.83E-05	1.66E-05	2.88E-05	100
d=10; b=[-100;100]	MGPSO		3466.3	9.07E-05	8.09E-06	5.79E-05	100
Shifted non–rotated	SPSO'11	200000	135025.6	2.16E-02	1.38E-02	5.01E-03	35.5
Griewank (CEC2005 F7):	DEPSO		200060	8.09E-02	3.55E-02	1.23E-02	0
d=10; b=[-600;600]	MGPSO		199063.2	5.24E-02	2.03E-02	9.98E-03	0.5
Shifted non-rotated	SPSO'11	600000	386939.2	9.02E-01	7.38E-01	8.18E-05	36.5
Ackley (CEC2005 F8):	DEPSO		109360.3	1.29E-01	4.09E-01	8.29E-05	90.5
d=30; b=[-32;32]	MGPSO		471402.5	3.38E-01	5.76E-01	7.00E-05	70

path. As a consequence, it can update to some degree the moving direction dynamically according to the probing result.

Iteration cost of the proposed MGPSO grows linearly to a number of used particles.

5   Experimental Evaluation

The conducted experiment was a comparative study of three algorithms: Standard PSO 2011 (SPSO'11 package was retrieved from [9]), DEPSO described in [5] and proposed MGPSO. Performed tests configurations for SPSO'11 algorithm were taken from SPSO'11 package. The particles populations sizes for MGPSO and SPSO'11 were 100 and 40. The DEPSO configuration was $cr = 0.9$, $w = 0.729$ and 70 agents. Finally, results of MGPSO processing were retrieved for the fixed set of parameters. The optimization duration was constrained by a maximum number of possible goal function evaluations. Obtained results are presented as statistics calculated from 200 subsequent executions with a different pseudo–random generator initialization.

Table 1 contains results of the optimization. In all cases it is a minimization of goal functions. It was set a tiny error threshold above the optimal value for each function. If the threshold was exceeded during the algorithm's execution then the ratio of success was increased and this execution was stopped. Hence, the performed number of evaluations in Table 1 is the average number of evaluations after which the error became smaller than the threshold. However, if the number of evaluations exceeded the maximum allowed and the error threshold was not exceeded then the algorithm could not find an acceptable solution.

6   Conclusions

Particular optimization methods used in MGPSO have alone worse efficiency than DEPSO or SPSO'11. The experiments have shown that appropriately managed algorithms for special purpose exploration of the search space may deliver comparable results to algorithm merging different concepts into single procedure. In contradiction to the monolithic algorithm, the proposed approach is flexible. It allows to tune on–line the processing pipeline according to requirements of the particular optimization problem. Moreover, the rules for modules selection may undergo a simultaneous process of the optimization. Thus, the algorithm may adapt the optimization process according to performance and responses from particular modules. As a consequence, it can determine a sequence of tools solving the particular optimization problem efficiently.

References

1. Kennedy, J., Eberhart, R.C.: Particle swarm optimization. In: Proceedings of the IEEE International Conference on Neural Networks, pp. 1942–1948. IEEE Computer Society (1995)
2. Clerc, M.: The swarm and the queen: towards a deterministic and adaptive particle swarm optimization. In: IEEE Congress on Evolutionary Computation, pp. 1951–1957. IEEE Computer Society (1999)
3. Løvbjerg, M., Rasmussen, T.K., Krink, T.: Hybrid Particle Swarm Optimiser with Breeding and Subpopulations. In: Proceedings of the Genetic and Evolutionary Computation Conference (GECCO 2001), pp. 469–476. Morgan Kaufmann (2001)

4. Brandstatter, B., Baumgartner, U.: Particle swarm optimization - mass-spring system analogon. IEEE Transactions on Magnetics, 997–1000 (2002)
5. Zhang, W.-J., Xie, X.-F.: DEPSO: Hybrid Particle Swarm with Differential Evolution Operator. In: IEEE International Conference on Systems, Man and Cybernetics, pp. 3816–382. IEEE Computer Society (2003)
6. Li, H.-Q., Li, L.: A Novel Hybrid Particle Swarm Optimization Algorithm Combined with Harmony Search for High Dimensional Optimization Problems. In: Proceedings of the The 2007 International Conference on Intelligent Pervasive Computing, pp. 94–97. IEEE Computer Society (2007)
7. Nakano, S., Ishigame, A., Yasuda, K.: Particle swarm optimization based on the concept of tabu search. In: IEEE Congress on Evolutionary Computation 2007, pp. 3258–3263. IEEE Computer Society (2007)
8. Lee, K.-B., Kim, J.-H.: Mass-spring-damper motion dynamics-based particle swarm optimization. In: IEEE Congress on Evolutionary Computation 2008, pp. 2348–2353. IEEE Computer Society (2008)
9. Particle Swarm Central, http://www.particleswarm.info

Author Index